LOEB CLASSICAL LIBRARY

FOUNDED BY JAMES LOEB 1911

EDITED BY

JEFFREY HENDERSON

JULIAN

III

LCL 157

THE WORKS OF THE EMPEROR JULIAN

VOLUME III

WITH AN ENGLISH TRANSLATION BY

WILMER CAVE WRIGHT

HARVARD UNIVERSITY PRESS
CAMBRIDGE, MASSACHUSETTS
LONDON, ENGLAND

First published 1923

ISBN 978-0-674-99173-6

Printed on acid-free paper and bound by The Maple-Vail Book Manufacturing Group

CONTENTS

INTRODUCTION

The more important letters and edicts in this volume are hardly intelligible to a reader unfamiliar with the historical background. The following brief summary of Julian's career is intended to explain the allusions in the text and to supplement the Introduction in Vol. 1. In his more formal works, especially the manifesto *To the Athenians* written in 361 as an apologia for his rebellion against the Emperor Constantius, and the *Misopogon* written in 362, a satire on his own austere habits addressed to the citizens of Antioch, Julian himself relates the main incidents of his childhood and youth. For the last ten years of his life, 353–363, the best authority is Ammianus Marcellinus, the Latin historian, an eye-witness.

Flavius Claudius Julianus was born at Constantinople in 331, the only son of Julius Constantius, half-brother of Constantine the Great, and Basilina, a highly educated woman and devout Christian, who died when Julian was a few months old. From his father's earlier marriage there survived a son, Gallus, a daughter, probably named Galla, who married her cousin the Emperor Constantius II, and another son whose name is unknown. Soon after the death of the Emperor Constantine in 337, the Emperor Constantius removed possible rivals by the murder of certain relatives, among whom were Julian's father and half-brother. Gallus and Julian survived. The latter was sent to Nicomedia in charge of a relative, the Bishop Eusebius, and his education was entrusted to the Christian eunuch Mardonius, who had taught Basilina Greek literature. In *Misopogon* 353 B, Julian says that Mardonius was "of all men most responsible" for his literary tastes and austere morals.[1] Julian also studied at Constantinople with the Christian sophist Hecebolius.[2] During this period he used to visit his grandmother's estate in Bithynia, which is described in *Letter* 25. In 345, when Julian was fourteen, Constantius, who in the twenty-four years of his reign that followed the murder of Julius Constantius lived in apprehension of the vengeance of his sons, interned Gallus and Julian in the lonely castle of Macellum (Fundus Macelli) in Cappadocia. In his manifesto *To the Athenians* 271 C, D, Julian speaks of their six years of solitary imprisonment at Macellum, and says that the cruelty and harshness of Gallus, who proved to be a sort of Christian Caligula, were increased by his life there, while his own love of philosophy saved him from being equally brutalised. From *Letter* 23 we learn that he was able to borrow books from George of Cappadocia, who later became Bishop of Alexandria and was murdered by the Alexandrian mob in 361. Julian at once wrote *Letter* 23 to demand his library.

[1] For the influence of Mardonius see Vol. 2 *Oration* 8, 241 C; *To the Athenians* 274 D; *Misopogon* 352–353. Julian's knowledge of Latin was probably slight, though Ammianus, 16. 5. 7, describes it as "sufficiens."

[2] For Hecebolius see *Letter* 63, and below, p. xlvii.

In 351 Constantius, who had once visited the brothers at Macellum, released them, raised Gallus to the rank of Caesar and gave him his sister Constantia in marriage. Constantius had married as his first wife Galla, the sister of Gallus; she had lately died. Gallus was sent to Antioch to govern the provinces of the East. There he and Constantia, whose cruel and suspicious temper matched his own, embarked on a four years' reign of terror which is described by Ammianus.[1] Constantius meanwhile, at Arles, where he spent the winter of 353, and later at Milan, was just as suspicious and ruthless, but in Gallus Caesar tyrannical conduct seemed to his cousin the prelude to usurpation. He was therefore recalled to Milan in 354. Constantia died of a fever on the journey, and Gallus, escorted by the Emperor's agents as a virtual prisoner, was taken by way of Constantinople to Pola (where in 326 Crispus, the son of Constantine, had been put to death by his father), and was there beheaded, towards the end of 354. Julian later avenged himself on those whom he believed to have been accessory to the death of his brother.

Meanwhile he had devoted four years to study, first at Pergamon with Aedesius and Chrysanthius, the disciples of Iamblichus; but on hearing from Aedesius of the marvels wrought by his pupil Maximus of Ephesus the theurgist, he hastened to Ephesus.[2] Julian had been under Christian influences from his childhood, but he was an ardent admirer of Greek literature and philosophy and

[1] Book XIV.

[2] See the account of his studies at Pergamon and Ephesus in Eunapius, *Lives*, pp. 429–435, Wright.

naturally inclined to superstition. With Maximus he studied the teachings of Iamblichus the Neoplatonist, and though he did not openly profess paganism until 361, he says in *Letter* 47, written in 362, that for twelve years he has ceased to be a Christian.

The Syrian Neoplatonism of the fourth Christian century which followed the teachings of Iamblichus was a religion rather than a philosophy, and was well suited to his love of the mystical and marvellous; for the rest of his life he was the devoted disciple of Maximus. But his apostasy from Christianity was carefully concealed, and his first panegyric on Constantius, *Oration* 1, written in 355, is entirely non-committal, refers vaguely to "the deity" and "providence," and might have been composed by a Christian.

In the second panegyric, *Oration* 2, written in Gaul at a safe distance, he frequently invokes Zeus, and assumes the reality of the gods of Homer in language that goes beyond what was allowed by literary etiquette in rhetorical works of this sort. It could not have been written by a Christian. His brother Gallus, some time between 351 and 354, heard rumours of his devotion to Maximus, and sent his own spiritual adviser Aetius to remonstrate with Julian. *Letter* 82 (Gallus to Julian), the earliest letter in this volume that can be dated, expresses the relief of Gallus at the reassuring report of Aetius as to Julian's adherence to the Christian faith.

On the death of Gallus in 354 Julian was summoned to the court at Milan, and on the way thither visited Troy and had the interview with Pegasius which is described in *Letter* 19. Ammianus says[1] that Julian's life was in danger at Milan from the plots of enemies, who accused him to Constantius of having met Gallus at Constantinople in 354, and of having left Macellum without permission. Julian denies the first of these charges in *Oration* 3. 121 A, and in *To the Athenians* 273 A. He was saved by the intercession of the second wife of Constantius, the Empress Eusebia, who, after seven months of suspense, obtained for him his single audience with the Emperor and permission to go to Athens to study. We know little of his brief stay of about two months in Athens in 355, but he was almost certainly initiated into the Mysteries at Eleusis,[2] and probably attended the lectures of the aged Christian sophist Prohaeresius, to whom in 361 or early in 362 he wrote *Letter* 14. Among his fellow-students were two Cappadocians, Gregory Nazianzen, who after Julian's death wrote bitter invectives against the apostate and an unflattering description of his appearance and manners, and Basil the Great, to whom Julian addressed *Letter* 26. From Athens the Emperor recalled Julian[3] in September to Milan, where after some delay he was raised to the rank of Caesar on November 6, 355, given the task of pacifying the Gallic provinces, and married to Helena, the sister of Constantius. She was much older than he, had little influence on his life, and died in Gaul, without issue, not long after Julian

[1] 15. 2. 7.

[2] The evidence for this is Eunapius, *Lives*, p. 437, Wright.

[3] For his grief at leaving Athens see Vol. 2, *To the Athenians*, 275 A.

had been proclaimed Augustus by the army. The motives of Constantius in making Julian Caesar are not clear. Eunapius says that he hoped his cousin would be killed in Gaul. Eusebia may have persuaded the Emperor that their childlessness was a punishment for his treatment of his relatives. The Gallic provinces were overrun by barbarians, and Constantius could not go there himself because he was occupied on the Danube with the Sarmatians and the Quadi, and by the threat of the Persians in Mesopotamia. Julian set out for Gaul on December 1, 355, with a small troop of 360 men who "only knew how to pray," as he says in *frag.* 5. Eusebia gave him a library of books which he took with him. His task was to expel the hordes of Germans who, having been invited by Constantius to assist in suppressing the usurper Magnentius, had remained to overrun and devastate the country, and had destroyed the Roman forts on the Rhine. In his five years of campaigning in Gaul,[1] though he was continually thwarted by the officers whom Constantius had sent to watch his movements, Julian pacified the provinces and restored their prosperity, recovered 20,000 Gallic prisoners from Germany, expelled the Germans, defeated the Franks and Chamavi, restored the Roman forts, and crossed the Rhine four times. In August 357 he won the famous battle of Argentoratum (Strasbourg), which was fought somewhere between Saverne and Strasbourg, and sent Chnodomar, the king of the Alemanni, captive to Constantius. He spent the winter of 358–359 at Paris, whence he wrote to his

[1] For the condition of Gaul and his achievements there see Vol. 2, *To the Athenians*, 278–280.

friend the physician Oribasius, at Vienne, *Letter* 4, of which the first part, with its dream,[1] is highly sophistic but expresses vague fears that he and Constantius may be involved in ruin together; the second part describes his opposition to the pretorian prefect Florentius, his persistent enemy, whom he forbade to recommend to Constantius increased taxes on the Gallic provincials. In this letter Julian wishes that he may not be deprived of the society of Sallust, his pagan friend and adviser, but Sallust was recalled by the suspicious Constantius in 358.

While he was in Gaul, Julian continued his studies, corresponded with sophists and philosophers such as Maximus, Libanius and Priscus, wrote *Oration* 2, a panegyric of Constantius; *Oration* 3, a panegyric of Eusebia; *Oration* 8, to console himself for the loss of Sallust; an account of the battle of Strasbourg which has perished; and perhaps the treatise on logic which we know only from the reference to it in Suidas.[2] To some of these works he refers at the end of *Letter* 2, *To Priscus*. That he wrote commentaries on his Gallic campaigns has been maintained by some scholars but cannot be proved.

Constantius, who had already suppressed four usurpers, either full-blown or suspected of ambition, Magnentius, Vetranio, Silvanus and Gallus Caesar, was alarmed at the military successes of his cousin, who had left Milan an awkward student, ridiculed by the court, and had transformed himself into a skilful general and administrator, adored by the Gallic

[1] Julian's dream may be, as Asmus thinks, an echo of Herodotus, 1. 108, but the parallel is not close.

[2] *s.v.* Ἰουλιανός.

army and the provincials. The Emperor was on the eve of a campaign against Sapor, the Persian king, and needed reinforcements. It was an opportune moment for weakening Julian's influence by withdrawing the flower of his troops for service in the East. Accordingly, in the winter of 359–360, Julian received peremptory orders, brought by the tribune Decentius, to send to the Emperor, under the command of Julian's officers Lupicinus and Sintula, the finest of his troops, in fact more than half his army of 23,000 men. Many of these were barbarian auxiliaries who had taken service with Julian on condition that they should not serve outside Gaul, and the Celtic troops, when the order became known, were dismayed at the prospect of leaving their lands and families at the mercy of renewed invasions of barbarians. Florentius was at Vienne, and refused to join Julian in Paris and discuss the question of the safety of Gaul if the troops should be withdrawn. Meanwhile two of the legions requisitioned by Constantius were in Britain fighting the Picts and Scots. But when the others reached Paris from their winter quarters in February 360, on their march eastwards, their discontent resulted in open mutiny, and Julian, whose loyalty towards Constantius up to this point is unquestioned, failed to pacify them. They surrounded the palace[1] at night, calling on Julian with the title of Augustus, and when, after receiving a divine sign,[2] he came out

[1] Julian was lodged in what is now the Musée des Thermes.

[2] See *To the Athenians*, 284 C, and cf. *Letter* 2, p. 5. Ammianus 20. 4 gives a full account of the mutiny and of Julian's speeches to the army and letter to Constantius.

at dawn, he was raised on a shield and crowned with a standard-bearer's chain in default of a diadem. Julian sent by Pentadius and the loyal eunuch Eutherius a full account of these events to Constantius, who replied that he must be content with the title of Caesar. Constantius had already gone to Caesarea to prepare for his Persian campaign, and decided to meet the more pressing danger from the East before he reckoned with Julian. The prefect Florentius fled to the Emperor and was made consul for 361. Constantius sent Nebridius the quaestor to succeed Florentius in Gaul, and Julian accepted him as prefect. Julian left Paris for Vienne by way of Besançon, which town he describes in *Letter* 8. Thence he led his troops to another victory, this time over the Attuarii, who were raiding Gaul, and on November 6, 360, he celebrated his quinquennalia or fifth year as Caesar. He had not yet declared his change of religion, and in January 361 at Vienne, where he spent the winter, he took part in the feast of the Epiphany. In July he set out for the East, determined to win from Constantius recognition of his rank as Augustus, either by persuasion or by force. His troops were divided so as to march by three different routes, and he led the strongest division through the Black Forest (see *frag*. 2) and along the Danube. Sirmium (Mitrovitz) welcomed him with acclamation in October, and he went into winter quarters at Naissa (Nish). Thence he addressed to the Roman Senate, the Spartans, Corinthians and Athenians manifestos justifying his conduct towards Constantius and proclaiming his design to restore the Hellenic religion. Of these documents only the letter to the Athenians survives, and a brief fragment of the letter to the Corinthians (*frag.* 3). Meanwhile, as he informs Maximus in *Letter* 8, he and his soldiers openly sacrificed to the gods. He now regarded himself as conducting a war in the name of Hellenism. Some time in 361 he wrote the *Kronia* (*Saturnalia*), and says in *Oration* 4. 157 c that he sent it to his friend Sallust. Of this work Suidas has preserved a few lines (*frag.* 4).[1]

Meanwhile Constantius, who had achieved nothing conclusive against the Persians, had married, at Antioch, his third wife Faustina. Their only child, a daughter, was married later to the Emperor Gratian, but died young. Constantius had now no choice but to lead his army to defend Constantinople against Julian. But at Tarsus he fell ill, and on November 3, 361, died of a fever at Mopsucrene in Cilicia. When Julian heard the news he wrote *Letters* 8 and 13, in which he thanks the gods for his escape from civil war. He entered Constantinople in triumph as Emperor on December 11, 361.

The greater number of the letters in this volume that can be dated were written after Julian's accession, in 362, from Constantinople and Antioch. He lost no time in inviting to his court his friends Maximus from Ephesus (*Letter* 8), Chrysanthius from Sardis,[2] Eutherius the eunuch, his trusted court chamberlain (*Letter* 10), Eustathius (*Letter* 43), Priscus,[3] and Basil (*Letter* 26). Chrysanthius and Basil did not accept this invitation, and Julian, when

[1] Suidas, *s.v.* Empedotimus.
[2] See Eunapius, *Lives*, p. 441, Wright.
[3] *Ibid.*, p. 445.

he had failed to persuade Chrysanthius to follow the example of Maximus and disregard the omens which were unfavourable to their journey, appointed him high priest of Lydia.

In contrast with the wholesale butchery with which Constantius had begun his reign, Julian appointed a commission, partly composed of former officers of Constantius, to sit at Chalcedon across the Bosporus and try his enemies, especially those who had abetted the cruelties of Constantius or were accessory to the death of Gallus. Ammianus, 22. 3, describes the work of this commission, on which were Sallust, Mamertinus and Nevitta the Goth. Among those condemned to death were the notorious informer and agent of Constantius, Paul, nicknamed "the Chain,"[1] the eunuch Eusebius, chamberlain of Constantius (see *Letter* 4, p. 11), and the ex-prefect, the consul Florentius, whose oppression of the Gallic provincials is described in the same letter. Florentius managed to conceal himself till after Julian's death.

On February 4, 362, Julian proclaimed religious freedom in the Empire, and ordered the restoration of the temples. All who had used them as quarries or bought portions of them for building houses were to restore the stone and marble.[2] This often caused great hardship to individuals, and even Libanius, a devout pagan, more than once in his letters[3] intercedes with local officials on behalf of those affected by Julian's edict. The Emperor recalled the ecclesiastics who had been exiled by the Arian Constantius,

[1] See *Letter* 53; Ammianus 14. 5. 6; 19. 12.

[2] See *Letter* 29, to Count Julian, p. 99.

[3] *e.g. Letter* 724, Foerster.

among them Aetius, to whom he wrote *Letter* 15, and the famous orthodox prelate Athanasius, for whom see *Letters* 24, 46, 47.[1] It was perhaps easier to restore the temples than the half-forgotten ritual of the gods, but Julian enlisted the aid of a learned pagan, the Roman antiquarian and senator, Vettius Agorius Praetextatus, whom in 362 he appointed Proconsul of Achaia, while for the rites appropriate to the oriental cults he certainly consulted Maximus of Ephesus, who initiated him into the Mysteries of Mithras.

Constantius, fully occupied with the persecution of non-Arian Christians, had not persecuted pagan intellectuals such as Libanius and Themistius the philosopher, while even pagan officials such as Sallust had been promoted in his reign. But Julian gave instructions that pagans should be preferred to Christians for public offices (*Letter* 37), and, as the progress of "Hellenism" proved slower than he had hoped, he grew more intolerant. For evidence of definite persecution of the Christians in his brief reign we depend on Gregory Nazianzen, Socrates, Sozomen and other historians of the Church. But certain administrative measures referred to in the letters were aimed at the Christians. As a part of Julian's general policy of exacting service in their local senates from all well-to-do citizens, he deprived Christian clerics of their immunity from such service;[2] funerals were no longer allowed to

[1] Cf. the account of the life of Athanasius, p. xxxix

[2] See *Letter* 39, *To the Byzacians*. Libanius, *Oration* 18. 148, praises this reform. For Julian's increase of the Senate at Antioch cf. *Misopogon* 367 D. *Codex Theodosianus* 12. 1. 50–56.

take place in the daytime according to the Christian custom [1]; and one of his earliest reforms in connection with the use of the public post, the *cursus publicus*, directly affected Christian ecclesiastics. The privilege of free transport and the use of inns, horses and mules at the expense of the State had been granted to ecclesiastics by Constantine in 314; and in the reign of Constantius, when the bishops were summoned from all parts of the Empire to one synod after another, the system of public transport broke down under the burden.[2] In an edict preserved in *Codex Theodosianus* 8. 5. 12, dated February 22, 362, Julian reserves to himself, except in certain cases, the right of granting *evectio*, or free transport. In *Letters* 8, 15, and 26 he authorises his correspondents to use State carriages and horses. Libanius says that this reform was so thoroughly carried out that often the animals and their drivers had nothing to do.

But such withdrawals of privileges were pinpricks compared with the famous edict [3] in which Julian reserved to himself the control of the appointments of teachers, and the rescript, *Letter* 36, in which he forbade Christians to read the pagan authors with their pupils. This meant that they must cease to teach, since all education was based on the reading of the poets, historians and philosophers. The Christian sophist Victorinus, who was then lecturing at Rome, and Prohaeresius at Athens, must resign their chairs. Julian offered a special exemption to

[1] See *Letter* 56, the edict on funerals.

[2] See Libanius, *Oration*, 18. 143; Ammianus 21. 16. 18.

[3] The Latin edict, dated June 17, 362, survives in *Codex Theodosianus* 13. 3. 5.

Prohaeresius, but the sophist, says Eunapius,[1] refused the privilege. He could afford to wait in patience, for, like many another distinguished Christian, he consulted the omens through the pagan hierophant of Greece, and learned indirectly, but to his own reassurance, that Julian's power would be short-lived. Even Ammianus the pagan historian deplored the bigotry and malice of Julian's attempt to suppress Christian educators. "It was," he says, "a harsh measure, aud had better be buried in eternal silence."[2] The Christians interpreted it as excluding their children from education; Theodoret, 3. 4. 2, says as much, and quotes a saying of Julian's (*frag.* 7), whose context is lost, to the effect that the Christians arm their intellects to oppose Hellenism by means of the Hellenic masterpieces. Socrates, 3. 12. 7, quotes another saying of the same sort (*frag.* 6). These two quotations perhaps belong to lost rescripts aimed at Christian teachers, which followed the extant edict and rescript. Well-educated Christians can hardly have been consoled by the enterprise of a father and son named Apollinarius, who "within a very brief space of time," says Sozomen, 5. 18, converted the Bible into epics, tragedies, comedies, odes and dialogues for the education of Christian youths. But Christian teachers did not suffer much inconvenience, for Julian's prohibition can hardly have been enforced in the few months that preceded his

[1] *Lives*, p. 513, Wright.

[2] 22. 10. 7: illud inclemens . . . obruendum perenni silentio. He repeats this criticism in 25. 4. 20. Libanius, however, was delighted, and taunted Basil and Gregory as "barbarians."

death. The edict was rescinded by the Emperor Valentinian.

In his dealings with the Jews, Julian reversed the policy of Constantius and Gallus Caesar, who had treated them with extreme harshness.[1] He freed them from the taxes levied on them as Jews, and invited them to renew their ancient sacrifices. When they replied that this could be done only in the Temple at Jerusalem he promised to rebuild the Temple, and restore Jerusalem to the Jews. He may almost be called a Zionist. The historians of the Church say that Julian desired to nullify the prophecy of Christ, that not one stone of the Temple should remain on another, and exult in the fact that his project had to be abandoned, owing to the earthquakes that were experienced in the East in the winter of 362–363. Julian himself speaks of his plan of rebuilding the Temple,[2] and Ammianus says that the work was entrusted to Alypius, the ex-Governor of Britain, to whom Julian when in Gaul wrote *Letters* 6 and 7, and that it was abandoned owing to mysterious "balls of flame" which burned the workmen. Almost the same account is given by Philostorgius 7. 9, Theodoret 3. 15, and other historians of the Church. Nevertheless, Lardner in *Jewish and Heathen Testimony* 4. p. 47, and Adler in the *Jewish Quarterly Review*, 1893, deny that the work was ever undertaken, and assert that Ammianus derived his account from Gregory Nazianzen's

[1] Sozomen 4. 7. 5.

[2] Vol. 2, *Fragment of a Letter* 295 C; *Letter* 51. 398 A; and Lydus, *de Mensibus* 4. 53, quotes Julian as saying ἀνεγείρω . . . . τὸν ναὸν τοῦ ὑψίστου θεοῦ, "I am rebuilding the Temple of the Most High God."

spiteful *Invective against Julian*, and that the Christian historians were taken in by Gregory's invention. But Ammianus was with Julian at Antioch that winter and on the march to Persia in 363, and must have known the facts. He did not need to depend on Gregory for information;—Gregory does not, in fact, mention the appointment of Alypius—nor would Gregory have been likely to write his detailed account of the zealous cooperation of the Jews in the building if he could have been refuted by any resident of Jerusalem. We may therefore believe that the enterprise was begun but was given up because of earthquakes, and possibly also because Julian had withdrawn to Persia. The rescript *To the Community of the Jews* (*Letter* 51), though it is cited by Sozomen 5. 22 and Socrates 3. 20 as Julian's, has been condemned as a forgery by Schwarz, Klimek and Geffcken, was considered "très suspect" by Bidez and Cumont in 1898 (*Recherches*) and is rejected outright by them in their edition of 1922. Their arguments are based on the general tone of the document, and the strange reference to "my brother" the Jewish patriarch, but while the rescript may have been rewritten or edited in a bureau, it probably represents the sentiments of Julian and is consistent with his attitude to the Jews as expressed in the treatise *Against the Galilaeans*. It has therefore been placed with the genuine letters in this volume.

The appeal *On behalf of the Argives* (*Letter* 28), was accepted as genuine by all editors before Bidez and Cumont, and by Schwarz, Geffcken and Asmus, and was formerly assigned by Cumont to the year 355, when Julian was a student at Athens. Bidez and Cumont (1922) now accept the theory of Keil[1] that it is not by Julian, but was composed in the first century A.D. as a letter of recommendation (ἐπιστολὴ συστατική). Maas, however, maintains that it was written by the high-priest Theodorus in Julian's reign, and that the proconsul's rejection of its appeal is referred to in Julian's letter to Theodorus, p. 37. But there is nothing in it that could not have been written by Julian, and it would be natural for him to defend ancient Argos, which had probably remained Hellenic, and her sacred festivals against Romanised and Christianised Corinth, the provincial metropolis. Julian disliked beast shows[2] as much as Constantius had loved them, and the tribute exacted from Argos was used to pay for such shows (see p. 89). He asks a favour rather than gives orders as an Emperor, but this was consistent with his custom of referring such appeals as that of the Argives to the governors of the provinces.[3] We do not know from other sources when the Argives began to pay tribute to Corinth, though there is abundant evidence that under the Empire the minor cities of Greece did pay tribute to Corinth instead of to Rome. On the whole I see no reason for suspecting the authenticity of this document, or for assigning it to Julian's student days at Athens.

In May or June 362 Julian left Constantinople for Antioch, the capital of the provinces of the East,

[1] In *Nachrichten Ges. d. Wiss. zu Göttingen*, 1913.

[2] *i. e.* public exhibitions of combats of wild beasts, such as were regularly given at the expense of the municipalities at this period.

[3] For this policy see Ammianus 16. 5. 13. Heyler's comment on *Letter* 28 is—cogit rogando.

and about this time he wrote *Letter* 35 to Aristoxenus, asking him to meet him at Tyana, and *Letter* 29 to his uncle at Antioch, whom he had appointed Count of the East (Comes Orientis); he refers to their approaching meeting at Antioch (p. 105). On the way he visited and wept over Nicomedia, which had been destroyed by an earthquake in 358,[1] and Pessinus, where he sacrificed to Cybele the Mother of the Gods at her ancient shrine. From *Letter* 42 to Callixeine it appears that as a consequence of his visit he appointed her priestess of Cybele at Pessinus. That the citizens of Pessinus had displeased him by a lack of enthusiasm for the restoration of their famous cult may be gathered from *Letter* 22, p. 73. Julian also visited Tarsus, in whose suburb near the river Cydnus he was destined to be buried in the following year. He arrived at Antioch towards the end of July, and wrote *Letter* 41, the rescript to the citizens of Bostra, on August 1.[2] In January 363 he entered on the consulship (see *Letter* 54).

In the *Misopogon* (Loeb Library, Vol. 2), Julian has himself described his nine months' stay at Antioch. The city was predominantly Christian and opposed to his restoration of paganism, so that when the celebrated temple of Apollo in the beautiful suburb of Daphne was burned in 362, he ascribed it to the malice of the Christians. The citizens, who were notoriously pleasure-loving and luxurious, openly ridiculed his austere way of life and disliked his reforms. During the winter he wrote the

[1] Ammianus 22. 9. 3–5.

[2] Julian's first edict from Antioch in *Codex Theodosianus* 1. 16. 8 is dated July 28, 362.

treatise *Against the Galilaeans.* When he left Antioch on March 5, 363, for his Persian campaign he announced that he would spend the coming winter, not at Antioch, but at Tarsus. This showed that he expected a short campaign. In the extant letters he does not mention his disappointment with his reception at Antioch, though in *Letter* 58, 399 c, written on March 10 or 11 at Hierapolis, he alludes to his interview with the delegates from the senate of Antioch who had followed him as far as Litarbae in the attempt to conciliate his displeasure.[1] This is his last extant letter.

For his brief and fatal campaign against Sapor in 363 we depend on Ammianus and Eutropius who accompanied him, and on Zosimus. On the march Julian avoided Edessa, which was stubbornly Christian (see *Letter* 40). At Carrhae, notorious for the defeat of the Romans under Crassus, he assembled his troops. Procopius was sent towards Nisibis with 18,000 men in order to distract the attention of Sapor, and was ordered to meet the Armenian auxiliaries whom Julian had requisitioned in *Letter* 57, and later rejoin Julian. Meanwhile the Emperor with 65,000 men proceeded to the Euphrates. His fleet of a thousand boats of all kinds he transferred by means of a canal from the Euphrates to the Tigris, and arrived under the walls of Ctesiphon, devastating the country and burning towns and villages as he went. The omens from first to last were unfavourable, his officers were inefficient, and the troops whom he had brought from Gaul began

[1] Cf. Libanius, *Oration* 16. 1, and his *Letter* 824, Foerster, for his attempt to persuade Julian to forgive Antioch.

to suffer from the heat.[1] Though before Ctesiphon he won an important victory over the Persians, he reluctantly decided not to besiege this stronghold, but to try to effect a junction with the forces of Procopius by marching northwards. He burnt his ships rather than take them up the Tigris. But Procopius and the Armenians failed to arrive, and Sapor with his main army was at hand and began to harass Julian's forces from June 16. The Persians were repulsed, but, after about ten days of almost incessant fighting and marching, Julian was mortally wounded in a rear attack on June 26, and died at midnight. On his death-bed he is said to have discussed the immortality of the soul with Maximus and Priscus.[2] The exact name of the place where he fell is not known, but Ammianus 25. 3. 9, says that when Julian learned that the locality was called Phrygia he gave up hope of recovery, because an oracle had said that he would die in Phrygia. His body was carried with the army on its retreat and was later sent to Tarsus for burial in charge of Procopius. The Christian general Jovian was elected Emperor by the troops.

[1] On the lack of discipline among the Gallic troops, both at Antioch and on the march, see Ammianus 22. 12; 25. 7.

[2] The numerous and varying accounts of Julian's death from Ammianus to the Byzantine chroniclers of the thirteenth and fourteenth centuries have been collected by Reinhardt *Der Tod des Kaiser Julian*, 1891. The legend that the dying Emperor threw a handful of his own blood in the air and cried νενίκηκας, Γαλιλαῖε, "Thou hast conquered, O Galilaean!" is found in Theodoret 3. 20, Sozomen 6. 2. Others said he was reproaching the Sun, who had betrayed him, and that his words were misunderstood; cf. Philostorgius 7. 15.

The letters of Julian must have been collected and published before the end of the fourth century, since Eunapius (A.D. 346–414) used them as a source for his *History*, and in his *Lives* mentions several that are not extant. Libanius, not long after Julian's death, wrote to Aristophanes of Corinth that some of Julian's letters were safe to publish, others not, and consoled himself for the Emperor's loss with "these his immortal children." Zosimus the pagan historian, who wrote 450–501, says that from Julian's letters one may best comprehend his activities, "which extended over the whole world." The historians of the Church, notably Socrates of Constantinople, who completed his *History* about A.D. 440, seem to have quoted from a mixed collection of letters and edicts such as has come down to us. Sozomen, a contemporary of Socrates, quotes nine of the extant letters and mentions fourteen that have not survived. Such a collection would be entitled *Letters* because any Imperial edict was called a letter. Julian was an indefatigable letter-writer, and we have only a fraction of his vast correspondence. Many letters must have been suppressed by their owners as dangerous to themselves after his death, or by the Christians because of their disrespectful allusions to Christianity; of those that survive some were mutilated by the Christians for the same reason, while others, such as *Letter* 81, *To Basil*, are suspected of being Christian forgeries designed to display Julian in an unpleasant light. On the other hand, documents which could be used as evidence that Julian persecuted the Christians (*e.g.* *Letter* 37), or pastoral letters written in his character of *pontifex maximus* to admonish pagan priests to imitate the Christian virtues of asceticism and charity to the poor (*e. g. Letter* 20 and the *Fragment of a Letter*, Vol. 2), would not be allowed to perish. Many letters survived in hand-books as models of epistolary style, a fact which, as Cumont pointed out, adds greatly to the difficulties of correct ascription, because the compilers of such hand-books were often careless about the authorship, form of address, or completeness of such extracts.

The "Letters" in this collection are (1) edicts or rescripts, the majority of which are concerned with the Christians; these were certainly worked over by the Imperial secretaries and are only indirectly Julian's; (2) pastoral or encyclical letters to priests; and (3) private correspondence. As a rule Julian dictated to secretaries, and so fast that Libanius says the "tachygraphers" were unable to keep pace with him, but certain postscripts are marked "with his own hand." After his accession in 361 the plea of lack of time or a shortage of secretaries is frequent, and some scholars have rejected certain purely conventional and sophistic letters, such as 59 and 60, or assigned them to his student days, on the ground that Julian after 355 would not write in that strain, and that his undoubtedly genuine letters always have some definite content. They never reject a letter in which pressure of business is mentioned, though one may see from the correspondence of Libanius that the plea of lack of time owing to affairs is a regular sophistic excuse. The purely sophistic letters have been placed last in the present volume in order that they may not interrupt the sequence of those that can be dated with more or less certainty. But I am not convinced that at any time in Julian's career he had renounced writing like a sophist and bandying quotations with his friends. Nothing could be more sophistic than part of his unquestionably genuine letter to Libanius, in which he expresses his admiration for his friend's speech on behalf of Aristophanes.[1] There seems to be only one safe criterion for rejecting letters ascribed in the MS. tradition to Julian: when the historical facts of his life cannot be reconciled with the contents of a letter, or if he cannot have known the person addressed, as is the case with the six letters addressed to Iamblichus, or when the contents are too foolish even for Julian in his sophistic vein,[2] it has seemed better not to confuse the reader by including them, as Hertlein did, with the genuine letters. They are therefore grouped together as apocryphal. After the publication of Hertlein's edition, six letters, ascribed to Julian, were discovered by Papadopoulos-Kerameus in a convent, used as a school for Greek merchants, on the island Chalce (Halki) near Constantinople; they are included in this edition. The text used in this volume is, for the rest of the letters, that of Hertlein (Leipzig, 1876), revised and rearranged in chronological order as far as possible. The marginal numbers correspond to the pages of Spanheim, 1696. The edition of Bidez and Cumont (1922) appeared too late to be used in constructing the present text, but is referred to in this Introduction. All references to Bidez or Cumont in the critical notes refer to their publications before 1922. Their edition includes the Latin edicts of Julian preserved in the *Codex*

[1] See *Letter* 53, 382 D, p. 185.
[2] Cf. *Letter* 80, *To Sarapion*.

Theodosianus and the Imperial edict in Greek, *De auro coronario*, published by Grenfell, Hunt and Hogarth in *Fayûm towns and their Papyri*, p. 116 foll., and assigned by those editors and by Wilcken to Alexander Severus. Bidez and Cumont support Dessau [1] in regarding this edict as by Julian, who, as we know from an edict in *Codex Theodosianus* 12. 13. 1, remitted the *aurum coronarium* on April 29, 362. Ammianus [2] mentions this as an instance of Julian's generosity.

The following biographical notices of Julian's more important correspondents or of persons mentioned in the text, are in alphabetical order and are designed to supplement the notes.

Aetius of Antioch, nicknamed "Atheist" by his Christian opponents, rose from extreme poverty and obscurity to the position of leader of the faction of the Arian sect called Anomoean because its members held that "the substance of the Son is *unlike* the substance of the Father." The less radical of the unorthodox, semi-Arians, like the Emperor Constantius, persecuted the Anomoeans. But Gallus Caesar, Julian's half-brother, soon after his promotion in 351 and his appointment to govern the East, came under the influence of Aetius, who, for the next three years while he resided at Antioch, was his spiritual adviser. When Gallus heard that Julian, then studying at Ephesus with Maximus the theurgist, was inclined to "Hellenism," he more than once sent

[1] In *Revue de Philologie*, 1901. [2] 25. 4. 15.

Aetius to admonish his younger brother, who contrived to reassure them both.[1] After the disgrace and execution of Gallus by Constantius at the end of 354, Aetius was exiled to Phrygia by the Emperor, partly because of his alarming influence and extreme Arianism, partly because of his intimacy with Gallus. Expelled from his office of deacon and repudiated by the Arians, he was still in exile on Julian's accession, when he was recalled to Constantinople and treated with peculiar favour. In spite of the title of Julian's letter of recall,[2] Aetius was not made a bishop until the reign of Valens. After Julian's death he retired to an estate in Lesbos which had been given him by Julian, but later he went to Constantinople, and in spite of his heresy was made a bishop, though probably without a see. In the histories of the fourth-century Church, such as those of Socrates, Sozomen and Theodoret, he is the most important of all the heretics and apparently the most dangerous to the unity of the Church. Philostorgius gives a detailed and fairly tolerant account of his varied life and great influence, and praises his eloquence and learning, whereas the others ridicule as superficial his study of Aristotle, with whose logic this ex-goldsmith of Antioch professed to have fitted himself to found a heresy, and Newman, who intensely disliked his heresy, calls him a mountebank.[3]

[1] See Philostorgius 3. 27 and the letter of Gallus to Julian, p. 288. Sozomen 5. 5 mentions Julian's letter recalling Aetius.

[2] See *Letter* 15 in which Julian refers to their friendship of long standing, and *Against the Galilaeans*, 333 D, p. 413, where the reference may be to the Anomoean Aetius.

[3] *The Arians of the Fourth Century*, 1833.

Alypius, to whom Julian wrote *Letters* 6 and 7, was, according to Ammianus 23. 1. 2, a native of Antioch. In 358 Libanius in an extant letter (324 Foerster), congratulates him on his success as governor of Britain—his title was *Vicarius Britanniarum*, an office subordinate to the prefect of the Gallic provinces—and reports favourably of his young son Hierocles, who had been left at Antioch in the sophist's charge. Seeck and Cumont think that Julian's *Letter* 6 should be dated 355 or 356, and that his summons to Alypius preceded the latter's appointment to Britain; but I agree with Geffcken that Julian's language implies that he had been for some time in Gaul, and that he needed the assistance of Alypius for his expedition against Constantius, so that the letter should be dated 360. As there is nothing in *Letter* 7 to indicate whether Alypius was in Britain or what was the map which he had sent to Julian, I have not altered the traditional order of the two letters to Alypius. If, however, Alypius was still in Britain, *Letter* 7 will naturally antedate *Letter* 6 and will fall between 356 and 360. In that case the illness from which Julian had lately recovered may be the semi-asphyxiation which he himself describes in *Misopogon* 341 D as having occurred when he was at Paris in the winter of 358–9. We know that Alypius was appointed by Julian in 362–3 to superintend the rebuilding of the Temple at Jerusalem (Ammianus 23. 1. 2). The project failed, and Alypius returned to Antioch, where he is mentioned in a letter from Libanius to Basil (1583 Wolf) as a person of distinction. In 372, when the Emperor Valens, in his panic terror of assassination, was persecuting right and left, Alypius was exiled on a false charge of poisoning and his property confiscated (Ammianus 29. 1. 44). Like Priscus and Libanius he is addressed by Julian as "brother," possibly, as Asmus thinks, because they were fellow-initiates in the Mysteries of Mithras.[1] In the MSS. of Julian's *Letters* Alypius is entitled "brother of Caesarius" to distinguish him from the dwarf Alypius of Alexandria, whose *Life* was written first by his friend Iamblichus the philosopher and later by Eunapius. Caesarius held several high offices in the fourth century, and in the reign of Valens, when city prefect of Constantinople, was imprisoned by the usurper Procopius (Ammianus 26. 7. 4). Several letters from Libanius to Caesarius are extant.

Aristophanes of Corinth, about whose reinstatement Julian wrote to Libanius when they were at Antioch towards the end of 362 (*Letter* 53), was an official of no great importance, but the detailed account of his life which Libanius addressed to Julian at that time (*Oration* 14, Vol. 2, Foerster) is a curious record of the vicissitudes of official life in the fourth century. Aristophanes was the son of a rich senator of Corinth and was educated in rhetoric at Athens. He was involved in a ruinous lawsuit and robbed of part of his patrimony by his brother-in-law Eugenius, a favourite of the Emperor Constans, and since, while Constans ruled Greece, it was useless to oppose Eugenius, Aristophanes retired to Syria, some time before 350. There he was appointed an *Agens in rebus,* and, as a sort of Imperial courier, travelled all over the Empire. In 357 he was sent to Egypt with the newly-appointed prefect

[1] See Dieterich, *Mithras-Liturgie*, p. 149.

Parnassius. There they incautiously consulted an astrologer. How dangerous was this proceeding under the Empire, since it aroused suspicion of treasonable interest in the length of the Emperor's life or reign, may be seen from the accounts in Ammianus of the reigns of Constantius and Valens and their wholesale persecution of alleged conspirators. After a trial at Scythopolis (Ammianus 19. 12. 10), conducted by the cruel agent of Constantius, Paul, nicknamed "the Chain," Parnassius was exiled in 359 or 360, while Aristophanes was tortured and barely escaped with his life. He was condemned to travel throughout Egypt under the escort of a soldier and a herald, who proclaimed wherever they went that any Egyptian whom Aristophanes had defrauded might come forward and denounce him. Libanius, who, like all fourth-century writers, gives the Egyptians a very bad character, argues that, if even the Egyptians could not trump up a charge against Aristophanes, he was at least innocent of the charges of peculation that had been brought against him at Scythopolis. He was released by the death of Constantius in 361. No doubt the strongest argument that Libanius used in favour of Aristophanes was the fact that he was a devout pagan who at his trial had openly sworn by the gods. Libanius asked for his protégé some office that would rehabilitate him in the eyes of the Corinthians, and in *Letter* 53 Julian says that he will confer with Libanius as to what this shall be, but we know only that Aristophanes did receive some office and returned to Corinth. Julian was more interested in the eloquence of Libanius than in the fortunes of Aristophanes. Seeck, however, in *Die Briefe des Libanius* states that Julian appointed

Aristophanes to the highest office in Greece, the proconsulship of Achaea, and places him in the lists of proconsuls for 362-3. But already in 362 Julian had given that honour to a man of the highest character, whom he greatly admired, Vettius Agorius Praetextatus, and since we know from Zosimus 4. 3. 3 that Praetextatus still held the office in September 364, when he was able to persuade the Emperor Valentinian not to enforce against the Greeks the edict forbidding the nocturnal celebration of religious rites, there is no room for Aristophanes as proconsul of Achaea; nor is it likely that so strict a moralist as Julian would have conceded so great a distinction to a man for whose loose morals even Libanius felt bound to apologise in his oration.[1] Libanius in a letter (758) expresses his delight at Julian's praise of his speech and says that it shall be published with the Emperor's letter; they do occur together in some MSS. In 364, after Julian's death, Aristophanes wrote to Libanius asking that he might see the correspondence of Julian and Libanius. The sophist replied (1350 Wolf) by reproaching him with having soon forgotten "the divine Julian," and says that he can send only such letters as it would be safe to publish. It was, in fact, a dangerous time for the friends of Julian, who were regarded with suspicion by the Christian Emperors Valens and Valentinian, and, for the most part, lost their offices.

Arsaces, or Arsacius, to whom is addressed *Letter* 57, was king of Armenia in the reigns of Constantius and Julian, and, since Armenia was the buffer state

[1] Cumont in his edition, and Geffcken, *Julianus*, are silent on this point.

between Rome and Persia, he was courted by Romans and Persians alike, whenever they were at war. In his *Oration* 1. 20 D, Julian describes how in the Eastern campaign of Constantius in 337 the Armenians for a time went over to the Persians. When in 361 Constantius was about to march against Julian, leaving his Eastern frontier insecure, he summoned Arsaces to Caesarea in Cappadocia and strengthened the old alliance of Rome and Armenia by giving him in marriage Olympias, the daughter of the prefect Ablabius, who had been betrothed when very young to the Emperor's deceased brother Constans (Ammianus 20. 11). Athanasius reckoned it among the impieties of the Arian Constantius that he had "given over to the barbarians" one who had been all but a Roman Empress. Constantius immediately on his accession had put to death the prefect Ablabius, the low-born favourite of Constantine whose ambitious career and violent end are related in the *Lives* of Eunapius; he now disposed of Ablabius' daughter as he had disposed of his own two sisters, giving one to Gallus and the other to Julian in order to secure their loyalty when they were promoted to the Caesarship. Arsaces remained faithful to Rome and so lost his kingdom and his life to the Persians (Ammianus 27. 12), but his failure to arrive with his auxiliaries to aid Julian at Ctesiphon contributed to the breakdown of the campaign (Ammianus 24. 7). *Letter* 57 is bracketed by Hertlein as spurious and rejected by all modern editors on account of its bombastic style, and its authenticity is dubious. But it was cited by Sozomen 6. 2, in the fifth century, and, if a forgery, was forged early enough to take him in. He criticises its "unbounded arrogance" and speaks of its "blasphemies against Christ"; since these are not in *Letter* 57 he may have seen a somewhat different version. As for the style, since Arsaces was a Christian and a barbarian, Julian may have thought that threats would serve him better than cajoleries, and in any case we cannot tell in what language he or his secretaries might see fit to address a ruler who owed his throne to the Romans and might be suspected of intending treachery in the coming campaign. Accordingly, though its authorship is doubtful, I have not placed this letter with the apocrypha.

Artemius, military governor of Egypt (*Dux Aegypti*) in 361, is mentioned, though not named, by Julian in *Letter* 21, *To the Alexandrians*. He was in high favour with the Emperor Constantius and an ardent Christian. In Alexandria he was hated by the pagans because he despoiled the temples, especially the famous Serapeum, the shrine of Serapis, and not less by the orthodox Christians for his support of the Arian Bishop George. In 362 Julian summoned him to Antioch, deprived him of his office, and had him beheaded on October 20, 362, a day that was consecrated by the Church to his memory as a saint and martyr. There were several reasons why Julian detested Artemius. He was a friend of Constantius, had been foremost in suppressing the pagan cults, and was supposed to have been accessory to the murder of Gallus Caesar, though this last charge Artemius denied. The fullest account of his defiance of Julian at Antioch, his religious controversy with the Emperor, his tortures and death, was preserved by the late fourth-century historian of the Church, Philostorgius (pp. 151–176, Bidez). Ammianus is strangely in error when he says (22. 11. 3) that the news of the death of Artemius was the signal at Alexandria for the outbreak of the populace which resulted in the murder of Bishop George, whose oppression of the citizens Artemius had supported with his troops (Sozomen 4. 30). Ammianus was at Antioch and must have known the date of the death of Artemius; he should also have known that George was murdered nearly a year earlier, in December 361, when the death of Constantius was announced. Artemius, according to Philostorgius, was one of those who resisted Julian's *blanda persecutio* of bribes and eloquent arguments to which so many succumbed, and this accounts for the fact that he was not punished till some time after Julian's accession.

Atarbius[1] to whom the Emperor Julian wrote *Letter* 37 telling him not to persecute the Galilaeans, but to prefer the god-fearing, *i.e.* the pagans, was a native of Ancyra and himself a pagan. At that time, 362, he was governing the province of the Euphrates with the title *Praeses Euphratensis.* The letter as we have it is abrupt and is probably a fragment of a longer letter or edict, often quoted no doubt by the Christians as evidence of their persecution and exclusion from office in Julian's reign. On the general question of Julian's treat-

[1] Hertlein prefers Artabius; both forms occur in the MSS., and in *Codex Justinianus* 11. 70. 1, an edict of Julian on buildings erected on state lands, is addressed to Atarbinus, possibly the same official.

ment of Christian officials or candidates for office the historians of the Church give divergent accounts, but Socrates 3. 13. 2 and Sozomen 5. 18 say that he would not appoint them to govern provinces, on the ground that their law forbade them to inflict capital punishment. Gregory Nazianzen, *Oration* 7, says that Julian bribed the Christians to sacrifice to the gods by promising them appointments, and Jerome says that many could not resist this *blanda persecutio.* In 362–363 Libanius wrote several letters, which are extant, to Atarbius, and especially in *Letter* 741, Foerster, praised his mild administration of the Euphratensis. In 364, when Libanius wrote to him *Letter* 1221 Wolf, Atarbius was *Consularis Macedoniae.*

Athanasius, the saint and orthodox bishop of Alexandria about whom Julian wrote *Letters* 24, 46 and 47, is the most notable Christian with whom on his accession Julian had to deal. He became bishop of Alexandria in 326 and died in 373. But of that time he spent about twenty years away from his see, and went into exile or hiding five times, once under Constantine, twice under Constantius, who supported the Arian heresy of which Athanasius was the determined opponent, once under Julian, and finally for four months under the Arian Emperor Valens in 367. With the death of Valens the Arians lost practically all their influence and the orthodox prelate had won in the end. When, in 362, Julian proclaimed an amnesty for the non-Arian ecclesiastics who had been persecuted by Constantius, Athanasius returned in February to his see at Alexandria. His enemy, the Arian Bishop George of Cappadocia, who then held the bishopric, had been murdered on December 24, 361, when the news of the death of Constantius became known at Alexandria. George was obnoxious to pagans and Athanasians alike, but though Philostorgius 7. 2 says that Athanasius incited the people to murder George, the silence of Julian on this point and the testimony of Socrates 3. 31 and Sozomen 3. 7 that Athanasius was innocent, indicate that the charge was due to the malice of the Arians. Tumults similar to that which resulted in the lynching of George occurred elsewhere in the Empire, and the Christian writers in their invectives against Julian accuse him of having recalled the exiles in order to foment the strife of the Christian sects, whose quarrels were so bitter and unremitting that the story of the reigns of Constantine, Constantius and Valens is mainly that of a heated theological controversy. Julian in *Letter* 21 rebuked the Alexandrians, though not as severely as they deserved, for the murder of George, and with indecent haste demanded for himself in *Letter* 23 the books of the dead bishop, whose library he had used in the past, perhaps in his years of retirement at Macellum in Cappadocia; he may have wished to use them again for his tract *Against the Galilaeans*, which he composed at Antioch in the following winter. When Athanasius after his return proceeded to exercise his functions, Julian in an edict addressed to the Alexandrians, *Letter* 24, banished him from Alexandria, and wrote a sharp rebuke to the prefect of Egypt, Ecdicius Olympus, ordering Athanasius to be expelled from Egypt before December 1. Accordingly, on October 23, 361, Athanasius left Alexandria, saying, "It is but a little cloud and it will pass" (Sozomen 5. 15). In the late autumn of 362 the Alexandrians sent to Julian at Antioch a petition for the recall of Athanasius, but he refused their request in a document (*Letter* 47) which is partly an edict, partly a theological argument for paganism, and contains the statement, useful for his biographers, that he had finally renounced Christianity twelve years earlier, *i.e.* in 350. Athanasius remained in hiding near Alexandria and at Memphis until Julian's death in 363, when he resumed his bishopric.

Basil the Great, commonly called St. Basil, was a native of Cappadocia. He and Julian were about the same age and were fellow-students in Athens in 355. Basil returned to Cappadocia in 356 and was probably in retreat in a monastery near Caesarea, the metropolis of Cappadocia, when Julian addressed to him *Letter* 26 inviting him to the court at Constantinople. The invitation was certainly not accepted, but there is no proof that they did not remain on good terms. Basil had other pagan friends, especially the sophist Libanius, with whom he corresponded and to whom he sent pupils from Cappadocia. Basil became bishop of Caesarea in 370 and died in his fiftieth year in 379. There is no good reason for doubting the genuineness of *Letter* 26, or for supposing that it was addressed to some other Basil than the famous bishop. But *Letter* 81, in which Julian demands from Basil a large sum of money as a fine on Caesarea, and threatens to punish the citizens still more severely if he is not obeyed, is generally regarded as spurious, and equally spurious is Basil's defiant answer, which is extant among the saint's correspondence as *Letter* 41. Even in Byzantine times both letters were regarded as unskilful forgeries, alien to the character of the writers to whom they were ascribed. The main argument against the authenticity of *Letter* 81 is the peculiar language, which is like nothing that we know to be Julianic. A minor point is that he regularly calls the Danube by the name Ister, whereas the writer of the letter does not. Further, the silence of Gregory Nazianzen as to the demand of money from Basil is strange in one who had been a fellow-student of the two men at Athens, and in his invectives against Julian would hardly have omitted this outrage if Basil had been involved. Moreover, the last words of *Letter* 81 are said by Sozomen 5. 18 to have been addressed by Julian "to the bishops," and he says that the bishops made the retort which appears at the end of Basil's alleged reply: ἀνέγνως ἀλλ' οὐκ ἔγνως· εἰ γὰρ ἔγνως, οὐκ ἂν κατέγνως. "What you read you did not understand. For if you had understood you would not have condemned." But Julian's hostility to Caesarea was a fact. Cappadocia as a whole was Christian, and its capital was, as Sozomen 5. 4 says, "Christian to a man." Under Constantius the citizens had pulled down the temples of Zeus and Apollo, and in Julian's reign they invited martyrdom by destroying the temple of Fortune, the only one that remained. Sozomen relates their punishment by Julian, which probably occurred while he was at Antioch in 362–363. The city lost its complimentary name of Caesarea, and was obliged to resume its old name Mazaca; it was expunged from the catalogue of cities, and its church treasures were confiscated.

Libanius, *Oration* 16, describes its fate as a warning to the recalcitrant. That Julian was displeased with the Cappadocians in general may be seen from the tone of *Letter* 35, *To Aristoxenus*, whom he asked to meet him at Tyana on his way to Antioch; nor did he visit Caesarea the metropolis, or Macellum, where he had spent so much of his youth. His death probably prevented the punishment of Caesarea from being fully carried out.

Ecdicius, probably called also Olympus, to whom Julian wrote *Letters* 23, 45, 46, 49, was prefect of Egypt 362–363. The letters all refer to the affairs of Egypt. Julian commissions Ecdicius to secure for him the library of Bishop George; scolds him for not having taken instant action against Athanasius; tells him the height of the Nile flood; and orders him to encourage the study of music at Alexandria. Ammianus 22. 14 says that in 362 Julian received from the prefect of Egypt a report on the sacred bull Apis, but does not give his name. In *Codex Theodosianus* 15. 1. 8, Ecdicius appears by name and receives rescripts from Julian. As the name of the prefect at this time appears also as Olympus, Seeck is probably right in assuming that he had, as was not unusual, two names, and that either could be used. This may be the Ecdicius who studied in Athens with Libanius in 336–340, later corresponded with him, and sent him pupils. On August 20, 363, Ecdicius announced to the Alexandrians the death of Julian in Persia. In informing Ecdicius about the height of the Nile flood Julian, who was at Antioch, wrote what Ecdicius must have known. Julian took a special interest in the Nile flood because he had, on his accession, ordered that the Nilometer, the measure used to gauge its height, should be restored to the temple of Serapis, whence it had been removed by Constantine to a Christian church; Socrates 1. 18, Sozomen 5. 3.

Elpidius "the philosopher," to whom is addressed *Letter* 65, is not otherwise known, and the letter, which is a purely formal type of excuse for the brevity of the writer, was probably preserved on that account in epistolary hand-books. It is placed by Cumont with the spurious letters, though there is nothing against it but its lack of content. Two men named Elpidius attained to high office in the fourth century, and one of them was a favourite with Julian because he had renounced Christianity and become a zealous pagan. He was with Julian at Antioch in the winter of 362 as *Comes rerum privatarum*, and Libanius, in *Letter* 33, written when Julian was in Gaul in 358, says that Julian, though younger than Elpidius, has exercised a good influence on him, and that in his conversation Elpidius echoes Julian's ideas and is as anxious as Libanius himself regarding Julian's future. This probably alludes to the renunciation of Christianity by Elpidius which was to follow Julian's accession (see, too, Libanius, *Oration* 14. 35). It was to him that Libanius applied when he grew anxious as to the fate of Aristophanes (see *Letter* 758, Foerster). The other Elpidius, a Christian, was prefect of the East in 360, and was also at Antioch with Julian in 362. He is often mentioned by Ammianus and Libanius. Neither of these men could correctly be called a philosopher, but it is possible that Julian might so address the former, who was among his intimates.

Eustathius, to whom Julian addressed *Letters* 43 and 44, was a Neo-Platonic philosopher but apparently not a miracle-worker of the type of Maximus. He was a distinguished orator, and in 358 was sent by Constantius on an embassy to the Persian king Sapor, having been chosen for this mission, says Ammanius 17. 5, *ut opifex suadendi.* His extraordinary, though short-lived, influence over Sapor is described by Eunapius (pp. 393–399, Wright). He married Sosipatra the clairvoyant, whose miraculous childhood under the tutelage of Chaldaean thaumaturgists is related by Eunapius. Eustathius had poor health and died soon after Julian had given him permission to return to his native Cappadocia. His widow continued her teaching, and their son Antoninus had a distinguished career as a priest and teacher in Egypt, where his prediction of the destruction of the temples came to rank as an oracle (Eunapius, *Lives*, pp. 415–425). The letter of Eustathius, p. 291, in which he describes his comfortable journey, appeared in the editions of Martin, Estienne and Hertlein with the wrong title, *To Libanius.* Cumont restored the correct title from *Parisinus* 963. It has accordingly been placed in this volume with the apocryphal letters. Eustathius was a kinsman of the philosopher Aedesius, and when the latter migrated to Pergamon he left his interests in Cappadocia in charge of Eustathius. Libanius and Basil corresponded with Eustathius, and in *Letter* 123, written in 359, Libanius calls him "the most renowned of philosophers."

Eutherius, to whom Julian wrote *Letter* 10 announcing his safety and his desire that the other should join him in Constantinople, is otherwise known from the account of his life in Ammianus 16. 7. He was an Armenian, a eunuch of unusual virtue and intellectual attainments, who had been kidnapped and sold to some Roman merchants, rose to a position at Court, became adviser to Constans, and later high chamberlain to Julian when the latter was made Caesar. Eutherius went with Julian to Gaul as his trusted adviser, and had the courage to reprove his master for that un-Roman levity of character which Ammianus says he had acquired by his residence in Asia. Eutherius was sent by Julian to the Court at Milan in 356 to counteract the plots of Marcellus, his late master of horse, and he successfully defended the loyalty of Julian before Constantius; again in 360 Julian sent him to Constantius with the letters in which he sought to justify his action in accepting the title of Augustus from the army in Gaul. After Julian's death, Eutherius, who was a pagan, retired to Rome, where he spent his old age respected by all. Ammianus says that though he has ransacked history he can find no eunuch who in wisdom and accomplishments can be compared with Eutherius. He must have possessed extraordinary tact to have been loved by Constantius, though he was a pagan, and by Julian, though he was the favourite of Constantius.

Evagrius, the rhetorician to whom Julian wrote *Letter* 25, making him the present of a small estate in Bithynia, is otherwise unknown, though he is possibly to be identified with the man of that name who joined Julian at Nish in the autumn of 361 (*Letter* 8, *To Maximus*). Neither the *Comes rerum privatarum* under Constantius, whom Julian banished on his accession (Ammianus 22. 3. 7), nor the friend of Libanius who appears in his correspondence and in that of St. Basil, is likely to have received this gift from Julian, but we know nothing definite on this point. Julian tells us in his *Letter to the Athenians*, Vol. 2, 273 B, that Constantius had kept all his father's property, so that he had the use only of his mother's estate before he was made Caesar. On the other hand we have the statement of Eunapius (*Lives*, p. 428, Wright), that there was at the disposal of Julian when a student, "ample and abundant wealth from every source." In his fragmentary *Letter to a Priest* (Vol. 2, 290 D), Julian says that his grandmother's estate was taken from him for a time only, and boasts of his own generosity in giving when he had little to spare. The date when he gave the small country-place to Evagrius cannot be precisely determined. In the absence of direct evidence I have dated it shortly after his accession; so, too, Schwarz. Cumont places it first in his edition and thinks that it was written from Gaul before 358. In favour of his view is Libanius, *Letter* 369 (Foerster), written to Julian in Gaul, in which he praises his generosity in having given to his friends houses, slaves, lands and money. On the other hand, it is equally likely that the estate which Julian's uncle, Count Julian, asked for too late in the summer of 362, was this very estate in Bithynia, and that it had been recently given to Evagrius.

HECEBOLIUS was a time-serving sophist who taught

Julian rhetoric when he was at Constantinople as a boy in 342. In all editions earlier than Bidez and Cumont, two letters are entitled *To Hecebolius*, namely those numbered 40 and 63 in this volume. The first of these is almost certainly not addressed to Julian's old teacher, who had now changed from Christianity to Hellenism, but to some official at Edessa. Cumont entitles it *To the people of Edessa*. *Letter* 63, rejected by Schwarz, Cumont and Geffcken because of its flowery style and lack of serious content, contains Julianic phrases and is just such a letter as one would expect an Imperial sophist to write to a sophist. Socrates 3. 1 says that Hecebolius taught Julian, and in 3. 13 describes his shamelessness in changing his religion three times in order to win Imperial favour Libanius, *Oration* 18, calls Hecebolius a rascally sophist, but does not mention his name, perhaps because he was writing after Julian's death, when it was not safe to attack openly one who had just become reconverted to Christianity.

Himerius, to whom is addressed *Letter* 69, cannot be identified with certainty; but at any rate we may be sure that he is not the famous Bithynian sophist whom Julian invited to join him at Antioch in 362, since the reference to the family of the widower with whom the writer of *Letter* 69 condoles does not suit what we know of the sophist's private life from his own extant works. Since two MSS. give Julian's correspondent the title "Prefect of Egypt," Cumont identifies him with the Himerius whom we know, from the letters of Libanius, as the father of Iamblichus II; he was the son (or son-in-law ?) of the more famous Iamblichus, the philosopher. From Libanius we learn (*Letter* 573) that this Himerius was an official of some sort, and we know that he died before 357. In that case Julian, if he wrote this letter to him, did so in his student days or from Gaul, after he became Caesar. Cumont suspects its genuineness. The difficulty about this identification of Himerius, son of Iamblichus, with the prefect of the MS. tradition is that we know of no prefect of Egypt of that name, and it does not occur in the list of prefects from 328 A.D. Schenkl therefore suggests (in *Rhein. Mus.* 72) that the real title may be *To Hierius*, since there was an Egyptian prefect of that name in 364, who succeeded Ecdicius Olympus. Hierius was not appointed until after Julian's death, but the title may have been added to the letter after he had received the office. The letter is in Julian's manner, and there are no good grounds for rejecting it. The name of Julian's correspondent appears in the MSS. in various forms, as Amerius (retained by Hertlein), Hemerius, and Himerius. (See under Sopater.)

Iamblichus of Chalcis in Coele-Syria, a pupil of Porphyry, was the chief exponent of the Syrian school of Neo-Platonism in the first half of the fourth century. His *Life* was written by Eunapius (pp. 363-373, Wright), who shows him performing feats of magic, but reluctantly, at the instance of his disciples. The six letters to him which were ascribed to Julian in the MSS. tradition, namely 74-79 of this edition, cannot have been written by the Emperor, who was a mere child when Iamblichus died in the latter part of the reign of Constantine and was succeeded in his school by Aedesius. The letters are therefore either forgeries or were written by some other admirer of Iamblichus whose name may have been Julian. Their writer seems to have marched with the Emperor from Pannonia to the Dardanelles in 323 when the Emperor was proceeding to Nicomedia in pursuit of Licinius, and he dwells on the hardships he had endured in war, sieges, and other dangers. Cumont in his edition (1922), as in 1889 (*Sur l'authenticité de quelques lettres de Julien*), though less confidently, ascribes these letters to the sophist Julian of Caesarea, who taught rhetoric at Athens down to 340 A.D., when he was succeeded by Prohaeresius; but he fails to account for the silence of Eunapius in his *Life* of Julian of Caesarea (pp. 467–477, Wright) as to any such experiences as are alluded to in these letters. Nor does Eunapius indicate that Julian of Caesarea, who left no writings, was interested in philosophy as well as rhetoric; rather he shows us a typical teacher of rhetoric at Athens whose glory was that he had trained the famous Christian sophist Prohaeresius, and had triumphed over the jealousies of his rivals, the other Athenian sophists. The theory that this group of letters was addressed by the Emperor Julian to the younger Iamblichus, the famous philosopher's grandson, who with his father Himerius and his uncle Sopater are known to us chiefly from the correspondence of Libanius, is untenable. Iamblichus II, though he was a philosopher and is mentioned with admiration by the Emperor Julian in *Letter* 2, was not distinguished enough to account for the servile flattery expressed in these letters; and the writer, if he had been addressing the grandson, would hardly have failed to mention his famous grandfather. Moreover, the events alluded to are irreconcilable with what we know of Julian's life. There are in these six letters certain parallels of thought and language which favour the theory that they are by one man; but there are also similarities with the genuine works of Julian, and such parallels cannot be safely counted as evidence either of forgery or of Julianic authorship; they are more probably the common epistolary mannerisms of the fourth century.

Julian, the Emperor Julian's uncle, brother of his mother Basilina, and son of Julius Julianus, to whom are addressed *Letters* 9 and 29, was persuaded by his nephew, after the death of Constantius, to renounce Christianity and to devote himself to the restoration of the Hellenic religion. This he did with such zeal that he became peculiarly odious to the Christians, especially in the East, where he resided at Antioch as *Comes Orientis* (Count of the East). There he died of a painful illness during Julian's visit to Antioch in 362–363. Sozomen 5. 8, Theodoret 3. 12, and Philostorgius 7. 10 recount his persecutions of the Christians and his terrible end. In *Letter* 29 the Emperor Julian directs his uncle, who had preceded him to Antioch, to restore the columns of the famous temple of Apollo in the suburb of Daphne; that this was done, and that the sight of the colonnade irritated the Christians, may be gathered from Ammianus 22. 13. The temple was burned down on October 22, 362, while the Emperor was in residence at Antioch, and the Emperor suspected that this was Christian vengeance, partly for the removal of the bones of St. Babylas from Daphne, partly for the rebuilding of the colonnade. Count Julian's nephew mentions his death in Vol. 2, *Misopogon* 365 c, and praises his administration. He was a correspondent of Libanius, and we have the letter of congratulation, 701, Foerster, sent to him by the sophist when the Emperor appointed him Count of the East in 362.

Libanius of Antioch, the famous teacher whose speeches Julian studied at Nicomedia in 344–345, and to whom he wrote many letters (of which only three, 52, 53 and 58, survive), has left more works, chiefly rhetorical, than any other sophist of his time. His *Life* by Eunapius is in some respects disparaging (see Eunapius, *Lives*, Wright, pp. 333–336), and we can best judge of his career from his own letters, more than 1600 of which are extant, and his numerous orations. He was born in 314, and may have survived as late as 395. From his works may be gathered many details about the officials of the fourth century and the conditions of education. He corresponded with Christians and pagans alike, but the death of Julian was a severe blow to his hopes for the future of Hellenic studies, which he lived to see on the decline, giving place to Latin and Roman law. He himself knew no Latin, and was chagrined when a school of Latin was founded at Antioch in order that students might not have to go to Rome to learn the language. Libanius was with Julian at Antioch in the winter of 362–363, and two of the extant letters to him from Julian were written at that time; the third, 58, is Julian's last extant letter and was written when the Emperor was at Hierapolis on his way to Persia, in March 363. Hertlein, like all earlier editors, published four letters to Libanius, but Cumont (*Recherches*) has shown that Hertlein 74 and 14 are one letter, and they are so arranged in this volume as *Letter* 53. We have the answer of Libanius (760, Foerster) to *Letter* 52, and his answer (758, Foerster) to *Letter* 53. Libanius' *Monody* on the temple of Apollo at Daphne, after it had been destroyed in 362 by fire, and his *Orations*, namely 12, *To Julian*, delivered in January 363; 13, *To Julian*, welcoming him to Antioch in 362; 14, *For Aristophanes*; 15, *To Julian*, on behalf of Antioch, after the Emperor had left the city in 363 declaring that he would not return; 17, the *Monody on Julian*, which was published almost two years after Julian's death; 18, the *Epitaph on Julian*, published probably in 364; and 24, *On Avenging Julian*, addressed to the Emperor Theodosius, are invaluable documents for the attitude of a cultured pagan to Julian's restoration of Hellenism, and for his life and reign. We depend the more on these orations and the letters of Libanius, because the *History* of Eunapius, which was in great part devoted to Julian, exists only in a few fragments. To the enthusiasm of Libanius the Christian fathers, such as Socrates, Sozomen, Philostorgius, Theodoret and, most embittered of all, Julian's fellow-student, Gregory Nazianzen, opposed their accounts of his persecution of the Church and their criticisms of his character and motives. Both estimates of Julian may be corrected by the moderate and impartial account of one who was no sophist, and who, though a pagan, was apparently little influenced by desire for a Hellenic restoration, the Latin historian Ammianus Marcellinus. Socrates 3. 1 is the authority for the statement that Constantius, when he sent Julian, then a boy, to Nicomedia, expressly forbade him to attend the lectures of the pagan Libanius.

Maximus of Ephesus, whose *Life* was written by Eunapius (*Lives*, pp. 431–461, 543–545, Wright), had obtained great influence over Julian in the latter's student days, when he first, as Eunapius relates, studied with Aedesius at Pergamon, but on hearing of the miraculous communications with the unseen powers of the theurgist Maximus, the pupil of Aedesius, proceeded to join him at Ephesus. In *Letter* 8, written soon after the death of Constantius, Julian invited Maximus to his Court, and in spite of the unfavourable omens described by Eunapius in his *Life of Maximus*, pp. 441–445, omens which prevented the more cautious Chrysanthius from obeying Julian's summons, Maximus joined him at Constantinople early in 362. This pseudo-philosopher remained with Julian, and was present at his deathbed. On his return from Persia, Maximus, who had many enemies, paid the penalty of the arrogance and display in which Julian had allowed him to indulge, and after various ups and downs of fortune was executed at Ephesus under the Emperor Valens in 371 on the charge of having been concerned in a conspiracy against the Emperor (Ammianus 29. 1; Zosimus 4. 15). Maximus seems to have initiated Julian into the Mysteries of Mithras, and Julian was wholly in sympathy with the theurgy of this clever charlatan. Of the three extant letters entitled *To Maximus*, *Letters* 12 and 59 are rejected by Geffcken for their sophistic style, and Cumont in his edition places them with the "spurious or doubtful" letters. But there is nothing in them that Julian might not have written, and one rather uncommon illustration in 59, the Celtic test of the legitimacy of children, was used by Julian in *Oration* 2, 81 D, and is probably reflected from his experience in Gaul. There is no evidence for the date of *Letter* 59, but it is not unlikely that Julian was writing to his teacher from Gaul, and therefore used this illustration while it was fresh in his mind.

NILUS DIONYSIUS, to whom Julian addressed *Letter* 50, is not otherwise known, unless he is to be identified with the Roman senator of whom Libanius says in *Oration* 18. 198 that Julian punished his impudence by a letter, when he might have confiscated his property. There is also a possible reference to Nilus in Libanius, *Letter* 758, Foerster, *To Julian*, where Libanius says that while he and Aristophanes were waiting for Julian's decision (see under Aristophanes), they feared that Julian might inflict on Aristophanes τὸ Νείλου κακόν, "the punishment of Nilus" (?). Both these references are uncertain, though Asmus, Geffcken and Cumont relate them to Julian's letter *To Nilus*. We know only what can be gathered from Julian, namely, that Nilus was a senator (446 A) of dubious morals, who had been recommended to the Emperor by one Symmachus; Julian, in a lost letter, had invited him to Court with the intention of giving him an office, but Nilus, who was perhaps a Christian, though Julian does not say so, held back until he received a second and more peremptory summons, which is also lost. Nilus certainly came to Antioch and was snubbed by the Emperor (446 B), and later wrote to him to excuse himself for his silence (443 C) and to say that he would come if again invited. In his answer to this communication Julian descends to personal invective of the sort that he used in his *Oration* 7, *Against the Cynic Heraclius*, but there is nothing to prove that Nilus himself was, as Asmus thinks, a Cynic. Nilus had irritated Julian by praising Alexander (a favourite commonplace of Julian's own, though in this case he found something disparaging to himself), had praised Constans and Magnentius (446 A), and had asked for a reply (446 B). Erudition is always in place in a Greek or Roman invective, and so Julian's innuendoes against the character and career of Nilus are interwoven with allusions to the historians of Alexander, to Phaedo of Elis (for whose *Simon* see Wilamowitz in *Hermes* 14), Demosthenes, Philostratus, Babrius and other authors. Asmus in *Philologus* 71 maintains that in *Letter* 50 we have a contamination of two letters, and that one was written in December 361, the other at the end of 362. But though the arrangement of the letter is strange (for example, five paragraphs begin with the word ἀλλά), we cannot, in our ignorance of the circumstances, and of Julian's real grievance, attempt to rewrite it. We are not even sure as to the man's name. Julian calls him "Dionysius" (444 D, 445 B), and in some MSS. alludes to him as "Nilus" (444 D); *Laurentianus* 58 has the title *Against Nilus*, while the earliest editor Rigalt and all others before Cumont entitled the letter *To Dionysius* because of Julian's use of the name in the letter.

Oribasius, the physician to whom is addressed *Letter* 4, was, next to Galen, the most important medical writer of the Graeco-Roman period. He is the faithful friend of whom Julian speaks in his *Letter to the Athenians* 277c, and he was with Julian in Gaul and at Antioch. According to Eunapius, who wrote his *Life* (pp. 533 537, Wright), he was suspected of having been Julian's accomplice in his rebellion against Constantius. Julian sent him to Delphi to revive the oracle of Apollo there, and received the famous response, preserved by Cedrenus:

"Tell the king, on earth has fallen the glorious
    dwelling,
 And the water-springs that spake are quenched
    and dead.
 Not a cell is left the god, no roof, no cover,
 In his hand the prophet laurel flowers no more."[1]

Eunapius in his *History, frag.* 24, says that Oribasius admonished Julian to use more self-control when he was angry, to which Julian replied that the advice was good and would not be needed a second time. When they were in Gaul Julian requested him to compile an epitome of the works of Galen, and later he expanded the work into an Encyclopaedia of Medicine in 70 Books. This also, as Oribasius says in his Introduction, was done at

[1] Swinburne's translation, in *The Last Oracle*, of the Greek text:

Εἴπατε τῷ βασιλῆι χαμαὶ πέσε δαίδαλος αὐλά.
οὐκέτι Φοῖβος ἔχει καλύβαν, οὐ μάντιδα δάφνην,
οὐ παγὰν λαλέουσαν· ἀπέσβετο καὶ λάλον ὕδωρ.

Julian's wish. This work, entitled Ἰατρικαὶ συναγωγαί, of which only about half survives, was published in 1808 by Matthaei (Moscow) with considerable omissions, and, complete as far as it survives, by Bussemaker-Daremberg, Paris, 1851, with a French translation. Oribasius was a pagan, but his son Eustathius, to whom he bequeathed his medical writings, was a Christian and a friend and correspondent of St. Basil. Eunapius relates that after Julian's death Oribasius was exiled "among the most savage barbarians" by the Christian Emperors. At the courts of "the barbarians" he rose to great renown and was worshipped like a god because of his wonderful cures. He was therefore permitted to return, and recovered his fortune and position. Suidas says that he was born at Sardis, but probably Eunapius, who gives his birthplace as Pergamon, was better informed. He was, however, practising at Sardis, no doubt after his exile, when Eunapius wrote his *Life* and described his skilful treatment of the aged Chrysanthius.

Priscus, whom Eunapius calls "the Thesprotian or Molossian," was born about 305 and died in 395 when Alaric invaded Greece. His *Life* was written by Eunapius (*Lives*, pp. 461–465, Wright). Julian made his acquaintance when he studied at Pergamon, and on his accession summoned him to his Court, and he accompanied the Emperor to Persia. On his return to Antioch in 363, Priscus, like other friends of Julian, fell under the suspicion of Valens and Valentinian, but was acquitted and dismissed with honour to Greece, where he continued to teach for another thirty years. He was evidently not considered as dangerous as Maximus by the Christian Emperors, was probably not a theurgist, and was therefore free from the charge of practising magic. He was a correspondent of Libanius. Julian wrote to him *Letters* 1, 2, and 5, all from Gaul, encouraging Priscus to visit him there, but there is no evidence that the visit was paid. Libanius, *Oration* 14, 32, implies that towards the end of 362 Priscus was with Julian and Maximus at Antioch, though in *Letter* 52 Julian complains to Libanius that Priscus has not yet arrived. As all three men were living at Antioch at the time, we cannot lay any stress on this remark, which may refer to a temporary absence of Priscus. Priscus had a wife Hippia, and children. Eunapius says that his bearing was "deliberate and lofty," and that he had secretive manners and sneered at human weakness, in contrast with his teacher, the expansive and democratic Aedesius.

Prohaeresius, to whom is addressed *Letter* 14, was an Armenian sophist who succeeded Julian of Caesarea in the chair of rhetoric at Athens and taught there for many years. Probably the Emperor Julian studied with him at Athens in 355. When Eunapius went to study at Athens in 362, Prohaeresius was already eighty-seven and had overcome his rivals, whose persecutions of this too successful teacher Eunapius describes. Earlier in his career he had been sent by the Emperor Constans to Rome to display his eloquence and was there honoured with a bronze statue. When Julian issued his notorious decree forbidding Christians to teach the classics, he made a special exception in favour of Prohaeresius, who, however, refused to benefit by the exemption. Eunapius tells a curious story to the effect that this Christian sophist consulted the pagan hierophant of Greece in order to find out indirectly whether Julian's reign would last much longer, and when the hierophant's answer implied that it would not, "Prohaeresius took courage." This was the sort of conduct that later under Valens cost Maximus of Ephesus his head, but apparently under Julian one could forecast the future with impunity. According to Eunapius, Prohaeresius died in 367, at the age of ninety-two, and he seems to have taught to the last, for the edict of Julian can hardly have "shut him out from the field of education" (Eunapius, p. 513, Wright) for more than a few months, if at all.

Sopater (or Sosipater),[1] to whom is addressed *Letter* 61, cannot be identified with certainty, but, if the letter is Julian's, he is not the famous Sopater, the disciple of Iamblichus I, whose violent death in the reign of Constantine is related by Eunapius in his *Lives.* If Schwarz, Geffcken and Cumont are right in rejecting *Letter* 61, chiefly because of the reference to the writer's children (Julian was childless), it may belong to the same period as the six letters to Iamblichus and have been written to Sopater I before 337; but this is impossible to decide. Sopater II, who is mentioned by Julian as his host at Hierapolis in March 363 (*Letter* 58, 401 c, a corrupt passage), and as having resisted the efforts of Gallus and Constantius to convert him to Christianity, is

[1] For the variation in the spelling of the name see *Acts* 20. 4; Sopater of Beroea, Paul's kinsman, who accompanied him to Asia, is called, in some MSS., Sosipater; cf. *Romans*, 16. 21.

perhaps the son (or son-in-law?) of Sopater I, who is mentioned by the writer of *Letter* 78, 418 A. Julian, however, calls him a κηδεστής of Sopater I, a vague word which may mean "son-in-law" or even "relative"; the passage is mutilated.[1]

Theodorus, to whom Julian wrote *Letter* 16 rejoicing in his safety, and 20 appointing him high-priest "of all the temples in Asia," was not necessarily a priest, as the office of high-priest was often given to rich laymen; the high-priest presided *ex officio* over the public games and the provincial assemblies. We know of Theodorus only from these letters of Julian. In *Letter* 20 he speaks of the teacher they had had in common, probably Maximus of Ephesus, and the word used, καθηγεμών, may indicate that Maximus had initiated Theodorus as well as Julian into the Mysteries of Mithras. Theodorus was certainly a philosopher, and as Neo-Platonism was, under Julian, the religion of the State, he was doubtless a Neo-Platonist of the Syrian school. Julian writes to him with great deference, though he never forgets in a pastoral letter that as Emperor he is *Pontifex Maximus* in-

[1] The Sopater who is mentioned in the six spurious *Letters* to Iamblichus is almost certainly Sopater I. Wilhelm, in *Rhein. Mus.* 72, assigns to Sopater I the letter, partly preserved by Stobaeus 4, p. 212, to Hemerius (or Himerius) from his brother Sopater, a typical sophistic sermon on the ideal ruler to one in high office, a λόγος παραινετικός. Others assign this work to Sopater II of Apamea, who, as we know from the correspondence of Libanius, died about 364, and is not known to have left any writings. In *Letter* 1448 Libanius tells Sopater II that he has shown the latter's letter to a friend, whose comment was that Sopater was imitating his distinguished father.

structing a trusted subordinate in the duties of priests. *Letter* 16 is one of the six letters discovered on Chalce (Halki) in 1885 by Papadopoulos. It has been rejected by Schwarz and Geffcken on account of the difficulty found by all commentators in explaining the allusion in it to a quarrel between Julian (reading ἡμᾶς with the MSS.) or Theodorus (reading ὑμᾶς with Maas) and the proconsul of Achaea, for which incident there is no other evidence. We do not expect to find Theodorus concerned with the affairs of Greece, as his interests were evidently in Asia; nor do we know of any trouble between Julian and the proconsul. Asmus, by altering the text to read "ruler of the Hellespont" (Ἑλλησπόντου for Ἑλλάδος), tries to localise in Asia the quarrel referred to. The letter is decidedly Julianic in manner, and its genuineness is defended by Asmus in *Philologus* 72. *Letter* 20, together with the fragment of a letter *To a Priest* (Vol. 2, pp. 297–339), is important as evidence of Julian's desire, at which the Christian fathers scoffed, to introduce among the pagans certain reforms in the lives of the priests and in the treatment of the poor and of strangers, based on his experience of the charities and the aceticism of the Christian Church. Cumont, following Asmus, regards *Letter* 20 (89 in his edition) as an integral part of the fragment *To a Priest* (Vol. 2, Wright), and accordingly includes that fragment in his edition as 89 b. But the similarities between *Letter* 20 and the fragment in Vol. 2 amount to unnecessary repetition if they occur in one letter, and it is certainly implied in *Letter* 20 that Julian and Theodorus have not yet met, whereas the fragment *To a Priest*, which mentions Julian's design to rebuild the temple at Jerusalem, probably, though not certainly, should be dated later, while the Emperor was in residence at Antioch. That that fragment is addressed to Theodorus, rather than to some other priest whose aid Julian had enlisted in his reforms, cannot be proved, and on the whole seems to me unlikely in view of their very similar contents and the tone of 298 B, where καθηγεμὼν is apparently used of a superior official or priest—perhaps Theodorus, who had reported favourably to Julian about the person addressed. On the other hand, the reference may be to Maximus, as in *Letter* 20.

ZENO, the physician and professor of medicine at Alexandria, to whom Julian wrote *Letter* 17, was driven from Alexandria by Bishop George in 360 for reasons unknown, and at the request of the Alexandrians was recalled to his previous dignity of chief physician or head of the medical faculty, ἀρχίατρος, by Julian on his accession. He was famous as a teacher. Libanius in *Letter* 171, written 359–360, condoles with him on his exile and hints at a coming change for the better, by which he must have meant the rise of Julian to power. Libanius says that though they have never met he owes much to the skill of Zeno's pupils, some of whom had evidently tried to cure his chronic headache. Cumont, following Boissonade, identifies Zeno of Alexandria with another famous teacher of medicine, Zeno of Cyprus, the "healing sophist," whose *Life* by Eunapius is extant.[1] But Eunapius

[1] See Eunapius, *Lives of the Sophists*, Wright, pp. 336, 529–531.

does not say that this Zeno practised at Alexandria. He had been the teacher of Julian's friend the physician Oribasius, and Eunapius says that he lived "down to the time of Julian the sophist," *i. e.* Julian of Caesarea, who died at Athens in 340. It appears, therefore, that Zeno of Cyprus can hardly have been alive in 361. Moreover, Julian would not have failed to mention Zeno's oratorical talent if he had been addressing the teacher of Oribasius. The Alexandrian is, therefore, almost certainly another and a younger man.

BIBLIOGRAPHY

Prepared by Professor A. F. Norman, Hull, 1969.

MANUSCRIPTS:

The *Letters*.—Of the 60 or more MSS. which contain Letters of Julian either as collections or as florilegia, *Vossianus* 77 (V), Leiden, s. xiii, supplemented by its copy, *Parisinus* 2964 (U), s. xv, is most important, despite damage and mutilation. *Harleianus* 5610 (H), London, B.M., s. xiv, *Baroccianus* 219 (B), Oxford, s. xiv, and *Varsaviensis* (Δ), Warsaw, s. xv, represent this same tradition. The oldest MS., *Ambrosianus* B 4 (A), Milan, s. x, exhibits a variant tradition with which *Monacensis* 490 (M), Munich, s. xv, and *Harleianus* 5635 (O), B.M., s. xv, are connected with varying degrees of affinity. *Laurentianus* 58 (L), Florence, s. xv, a sylloge of Greek epistolographers, contains the largest selection of Julian's letters as part of its contents. Two fragmentary MSS., *Chalceni* (X and Y), s. xv, discovered in the monastery of Chalke, near Constantinople, produced six letters unknown to Hertlein or his predecessors (*Nos.* 2, 16, 29, 32, 34, 73). These, originally published in 1885 in Constantinople (reviewed by Weil, *Rev. de Philol.* 10, 1886), were republished by their finder, Papadopoulos-Kerameus, more conveniently in *Rhein. Mus.* 42, 1887, with Buecheler's notes. The fundamental study of the MSS. by Bidez and Cumont, *Recherches sur la tradition manuscrite des lettres de l'empereur Julien,* Brussels, 1898, is condensed, with minor amendments, in their critical edition, *Epistulae Leges Fragmenta,* Paris and London, 1922. For a Byzantine florilegium containing some letters of Julian (*Patmius* 706 (*Π*), s. xii), cf. Darrouzès in *REByz.* 14, 1956.

Excluding the critical editions of Hertlein and Bidez and Cumont, textual studies are: Horkel, *Emendationes Julianae,* Berlin, 1841; Sintenis and Henning in *Hermes,* 1866 and 1875 respectively; Klimek, *Coniectanea in Julianum,* Breslau, 1883, and in *Hermes,* 1886; Asmus in *Philologus* 61, 71, 72, in *Archiv f. Gesch. d. Philos.,* 1902, in *Zeitsch. f. Kirchengesch.* 16, 23, 31, and in *Rhein. Mus.* 1908; Thomas in *Rev. d'instruction publique en Belgique,* 1889, and *Rev. Belge de philol. et d'hist.,* 1922; Eitrem in *Rhein. Mus.* 1957 (*Epp.* 21, 48) and *Symbolae Osloenses* 1957; van Groningen in *Vigiliae Christianae* 1960.

Authenticity is discussed by Cumont, *Sur l'authenticité de quelques lettres de Julien,* Gand, 1889; by Bidez in *R.E.G.* 1919 and Wilamowitz in *Hermes* (the Iamblichan corpus); by den Boer in *Vig. Christ.* 1962 (*Ep.* 51 and Gallus' letter, *E.L.F.*, Appendix, p. 287). Content is treated by Schemmel in *Ph.W.* 1926 (*Epp.* 43, 44, 83), Seel in Klio 1939 (*Epp.* 24, 46, 47), and K. Weis in *Hermes* 1964 (*Ep.* 48).

EDITIONS:

The *editio princeps*, Aldine, by Musurus, Venice, 1499, had 48 letters, a number expanded by Martinius, Rigalt, Petau (Paris, 1583, 1601, 1630) to 63. These, with Cyril of Alexandria's '*Contra Iulianum*', were included in Spanheim's edition of Julian's works (Latin translation), Leipzig, 1696, the pagination of which forms the conventional standard of reference. Further additions by Muratorius, *Anecdota Graeca*, Padua, 1709, Fabricius, *Salutaris lux Evangelii*, Hamburg, 1731, and others, were included in the editions of the *Letters* by Heyler, Mainz, 1828, Hercher, *Epistolographi Graeci*, Paris, 1873, and Bidez and Cumont, *E.L.F.*, Paris and London, 1922, this last appearing too late to be used for the present text. Standard editions of Julian's complete works are those of Hertlein (Teubner), Leipzig, 1876 (the text upon which the present edition is based), and Bidez, Rochefort and Lacombrade (Budé), Paris, 1924–64 (2 vols. in 4, the *Letters* forming vol. 1, ii). *Iuliani Imp. epistulae selectae*, ed. van Groningen, appeared in 1960 (*Textus Minores* No. 37, Leiden), containing 20 letters.

Against the Galilaeans.—Spanheim's pagination

of the text of Cyril's *Contra Iulianum* was used by Neumann as his standard of reference in his reconstruction of Julian's diatribe, *Juliani Imp. librorum contra Christianos quae supersunt*, Leipzig, 1880, textual criticism appearing in the *Prolegomena.* For later textual criticism cf. Gollwitzer, *Observationes criticae in Juliani Imp. contra Christianos libros*, Erlangen, 1886, and Asmus, *Julians Galiläerschrift*, Freiburg, 1904, which also contains a concordance of Julian's works with this polemic.

Translations:

Spanheim, Latin. Talbot, Paris, 1863—the complete works as then known—French. Neumann, German translation of his text, Leipzig, 1880. Asmus, *Kaiser Julians philosophische Werke*, Leipzig, 1908: with notes, no letters. Bidez, *L' Empereur Julien, Oeuvres Complètes*, Vol. 1, ii (Budé), Paris, 1924: without *Contra Galilaeos.*

Sources:

Ammianus Marcellinus, Loeb Library, 3 vols., 1935–9. Libanius, *The Julianic Orations* (Vol. 1, Loeb, 1969) and *Letters* (Libanii Opera, Vols. 10–11, ed. Foerster (Teubner), Leipzig, 1921–2). Themistius, *Orationes* Vol. 1, ed. Downey (Teubner), Leipzig, 1965. Mamertinus, *Gratiarum Actio* (Panégyriques Latins iii, ed. Galletier (Budé), Paris, 1955). Eunapius, *Lives of the Sophists*, ed. Wright, Loeb, 1922. Zosimus, ed.

Mendelssohn, Leipzig, 1887. Socrates, *Historia Ecclesiastica*, Migne, Patrologia Graeca, Vol. 67. Sozomen, *Historia Ecclesiastica*, Migne, Patrologia Graeca, Vol. 67. *Codex Theodosianus*, ed. Mommsen and Meyer, Berlin 1954 (reprint); translated Pharr, Princeton, 1952. Suidas, ed. Adler, Leipzig, 1928–38.

LITERATURE:

The *Letters*. This material is integral to biographical studies of Julian, e.g., Allard, *Julien l'Apostat*, Paris, 1906–10 (3 vols.); Geffcken, *Kaiser Julianus*, Leipzig, 1914; Rostagni, *Giuliano l'Apostata*, Turin, 1920; Simpson, *Julian the Apostate*, Aberdeen, 1930; Bidez, *La vie de l'empereur Julien*, Paris, 1930: also to general studies of the period, e.g., Seeck, *Geschichte des Untergangs der Antiken Welt* (vol. 4), Berlin, 1911; Stein, *Gesch. des spätröm. Reiches*, Vienna, 1928; Piganiol, *L'Empire Chrétien*, Paris, 1947; Jones, *Social and economic history of the later Roman Empire* (Blackwell), Oxford, 1964. A fundamental study of Julian's legislation is Ensslin, Kaiser Julians Gesetzgebungswerk, *Klio* 18, 1923; also, Andreotti in *N. Riv. Stor.* 14, 1930, and Weis, *Das Restitutions-Edikt Kaiser Julians*, Heidelberg, 1933. For religious policy, cf. Vollert, *Kaiser Julians religiose u. philos. Ueberzeugung*, Gütersloh, 1899; Mau, *Die Religionsphilosophie K. Julians*, Leipzig, 1907; Farney, *La religion de l'empereur Julien et le mysticisme de son temps*, Paris, 1934; and articles by de Labriolle,

Rev. Quest. Hist. 58, 1930, and Kock, *Rev. Belge de philol. et d'hist.*, 6, 1927–8. Aspects of Julian's relations with Antioch are treated by Thompson, *Historical work of Ammianus Marcellinus*, Cambridge, 1947; Petit, *Libanius et la vie municipale à Antioche*, Paris, 1955; Festugière, *Antioche paienne et chrétienne*, Paris, 1959; Downey, *History of Antioch in Syria from Seleucus to the Arab conquest*, Princeton, 1961. The Persian campaign is treated by Cumont in Études Syriennes, 1917 (La marche de l'empereur Julien), and by Brok, *De Perzische Expeditie van Kaiser Julianus*, Leiden, 1959. Prosopography of the *Letters* is treated by Seeck, *Die Briefe des Libanius zeitlich geordnet*, Leipzig, 1906, and Jones, *Prosopography of the later Roman Empire*, 1969.

Against the Galilaeans.—Relevant literature is: Geffcken, *Zwei Griechische Apologeten*, Leipzig, 1907; Bidez, *Vie de Porphyre*, Gand, 1913; Harnack, *Porphyrius gegen die Christen*, Berlin, 1916; de Labriolle, cited above; Regazzoni, Il 'Contra Galilaeos' dell' Imp.[e] Giuliano e il 'Contra Julianum' di San Cirillo Alessandrino, *Didaskaleion*, 6, 1928. Cf. also Leipoldt, Der Römische Kaiser Julian in der Religionsgeschichte, *S.B. Sachs. Akad. d. Wiss.*, cx, 1, 1964.

THE WORKS OF THE EMPEROR JULIAN

III

1

Πρίσκῳ[1]

Ἐγὼ δεξάμενός σου τὰ γράμματα παραχρῆμα τὸν Ἀρχέλαον ἀπέστειλα, δοὺς αὐτῷ φέρειν ἐπιστολὰς πρὸς σέ, καὶ τὸ σύνθημα, καθάπερ ἐκέλευσας, εἰς πλείονα χρόνον. ἱστορῆσαι δέ σοι τὸν ὠκεανὸν ἐθέλοντι ὑπάρξει σὺν θεῷ πάντα κατὰ γνώμην, εἰ μὴ τὴν τῶν Γαλατῶν ἀμουσίαν καὶ τὸν χειμῶνα διευλαβηθείης. ἀλλὰ τοῦτο μὲν ὅπως ἂν ᾖ τῷ θεῷ φίλον γενήσεται, ἐγὼ δὲ ὄμνυμί σοι τὸν πάντων ἀγαθῶν ἐμοὶ αἴτιον καὶ σωτῆρα, ὅτι διὰ τοῦτο ζῆν εὔχομαι, ἵν' ὑμῖν τι χρήσιμος γένωμαι. τὸ δὲ ὑμῖν ὅταν εἴπω, τοὺς ἀληθινούς φημι φιλοσόφους, ὧν εἶναί σε πεισθεὶς οἶσθα πῶς ἐφίλησα καὶ φιλῶ καὶ ὁρᾶν εὔχομαι. ἐρρωμένον σε ἡ θεία πρόνοια διαφυλάξειε πολλοῖς χρόνοις, ἀδελφὲ ποθεινότατε καὶ φιλικώτατε. τὴν ἱερὰν Ἱππίαν καὶ τὰ παιδία ὑμῶν προσαγορεύω.

2

Πρίσκῳ[2]

Περὶ τοῦ τὴν σὴν ἀγαθότητα πρός με ἥκειν, εἴπερ διανοῇ, νῦν σὺν τοῖς θεοῖς βούλευσαι καὶ

[1] Hertlein 71
[2] Papadopoulos 4*; not in Hertlein.

---

[1] For another letter to Priscus, see p. 15.

[2] Literally "token," a synonym of τὸ σύμβολον. This, like the Latin tessera, could be of various kinds, but here Julian probably refers to a document, the equivalent of the

1

To Priscus[1]

On receiving your letter I at once despatched Archelaus, and gave him letters to carry to you, and the passport,[2] as you wished, for a longer time. If you are inclined to explore the ocean, everything, with the god's help, will be provided for you as you would wish, unless you dread the boorishness of the Gauls and the winter climate. This, however, will turn out as the god sees fit; but I swear to you by him who is the giver and preserver of all my good fortune that I desire to live only that I may in some degree be of use to you. When I say "you," I mean the true philosophers, and convinced as I am that you are one of these, how much I have loved and love you you well know, and how I desire to see you. May Divine Providence preserve you in health for many a year, my dearest and best beloved brother! I salute the admirable Hippia and your children.[3] 359 A.D? From Gaul

2

To the Same

As regards a visit to me from your good self,[4] if you have it in mind, make your plans now, with the 358-359 From Gaul

modern passport, which he had visaed for Priscus in order that he might proceed to Gaul.

[3] For the life of Priscus, cf. Eunapius, *Lives of the Sophists and Philosophers*. He visited Julian in Gaul, was summoned to Constantinople not long after Julian's accession, and went with him to Persia. See Introduction, under Priscus.

[4] Lit. "your goodness." For Julian's use of this and similar abstract words, see p. 109.

προθυμήθητι· τυχὸν γὰρ ὀλίγον ὕστερον οὐδὲ ἐγὼ σχολὴν ἄξω.[1] τὰ Ἰαμβλίχου πάντα μοι τὰ εἰς τὸν ὁμώνυμον ζήτει· δύνασαι δὲ μόνος· ἔχει γὰρ ὁ τῆς σῆς ἀδελφῆς γαμβρὸς εὐδιόρθωτα. εἰ δὲ μὴ σφάλλομαι, καὶ σημεῖόν τί μοι, ἡνίκα τοῦτο τὸ μέρος ἔγραφον, ἐγένετο θαυμάσιον. ἱκετεύω σε, μὴ διαθρυλείτωσαν οἱ Θεοδώρειοι καὶ τὰς σὰς ἀκοάς, ὅτι ἄρα φιλότιμος ὁ θεῖος ἀληθῶς καὶ μετὰ Πυθαγόραν καὶ Πλάτωνα τρίτος Ἰάμβλιχος· εἰ δὲ τολμηρὸν πρὸς σὲ τὴν αὐτοῦ διάνοιαν φανερὰν ποιεῖν, ὡς ἕπεται τοῖς ἐνθουσιῶσιν, οὐ παράλογος ἡ συγγνώμη· καὶ αὐτὸς δὲ περὶ μὲν Ἰάμβλιχον ἐν φιλοσοφίᾳ, περὶ δὲ τὸν ὁμώνυμον[2] ἐν θεοσοφίᾳ μέμηνας.[3] καὶ νομίζω τοὺς ἄλλους, κατὰ τὸν Ἀπολλόδωρον, μηθὲν εἶναι πρὸς τούτους. ὑπὲρ δὲ τῶν Ἀριστοτέλους συναγωγῶν ἃς ἐποιήσω, τοσοῦτόν σοι λέγω· πεποίηκάς με ψευδεπίγραφον εἶναί σου μαθητήν· ὁ μὲν γὰρ Τύριος Μάξιμος ἒξ[4] βιβλίοις με τῆς Πλατωνικῆς λογικῆς ὀλίγα μυεῖν εἶχε, σὺ δέ με δι' ἑνὸς βιβλίου τῆς Ἀριστοτελικῆς φιλοσοφίας ἐποίησας ἴσως δὴ καὶ βάκχον, ἀλλ' οὖν γε[5] ναρθηκοφόρον. εἰ δὲ ἀληθῆ λέγω, παραγενομένῳ σοι

[1] ἄξω Wright, ἄγω MSS.

[2] Bidez ὁμώνυμόν μου to support his theory that Julian refers to Julian the theurgist.

[3] μέμηνας Weil, μενοινῶ Bidez, μενοινᾷ MS. μενοινᾷς Papadopoulos.

[4] ἓξ—εἶχε Cumont; εἰς βιβλία μοι δυεῖν πλείονα τῆς λογικῆς ὀλίγα εἶπε Papadopoulos; εἰς βιβλία μὲν πλείονα τῆς λογικῆς ὀλίγα δυεῖν εἶπε MS. I accept Cumont's bold and ingenious version of this corrupt passage. Buecheler first suggested that Plato's name should be restored out of πλείονα τῆς.

[5] Weil supplies γε; Cumont ἀλλ' οὖν; MS. ἀλλ' οὔτι.

help of the gods, and exert yourself; for perhaps a little later I too shall have no time to spare. Hunt up for me all the writings of Iamblichus to his[1] namesake. Only you can do this, for your sister's son-in-law owns a thoroughly revised version. And, if I am not mistaken, while I was writing this sentence, a marvellous sign[2] was vouchsafed me. I entreat you not to let Theodorus[3] and his followers deafen you too by their assertions that Iamblichus, that truly godlike man, who ranks next to Pythagoras and Plato, was worldly and self-seeking. But if it be rash to declare my own opinion to you, I may reasonably expect you to excuse me, as one excuses those who are carried away by a divine frenzy. You are yourself an ardent admirer of Iamblichus for his philosophy and of his namesake for his theosophy. And I too think, like Apollodorus, that the rest are not worth mentioning compared with those two. As for your collection of the works of Aristotle, so much I will say, you have made me style myself your pupil, though I have no right to the title. For while Maximus of Tyre in six books was able to initiate me to some little extent into Plato's logic, you, with one book, have made me, perhaps I may even say, a complete initiate in the philosophy of Aristotle, but at any rate a thyrsus-bearer.[4] When you join me I

[1] Bidez prefers "my namesake," and makes the writer refer to Julian the theurgist or Chaldean, whom we know from Suidas. More probably the younger Iamblichus is meant.

[2] Cf. Vol. 2, 284c, for a similar sign of approval given to Julian by Zeus.

[3] Theodorus of Asine was a disciple of the great Iamblichus; we know of no such polemics as are indicated here.

[4] Plato, *Phaedo* 69c, says that "many carry the thyrsus of Dionysus, but few are really inspired."

πολλὰ πάνυ τοῦ πέρυσιν χειμῶνος ἐξελέγξει πάρεργα.

3

Εὐμενίῳ καὶ Φαριανῷ[1]

441 Εἴ τις ὑμᾶς πέπεικεν, ὅτι τοῦ φιλοσοφεῖν ἐπὶ σχολῆς ἀπραγμόνως ἐστὶν ἥδιον ἢ λυσιτελέστερόν
B τι τοῖς ἀνθρώποις, ἠπατημένος ἐξαπατᾷ· εἰ δὲ μένει παρ' ὑμῖν ἡ πάλαι προθυμία καὶ μὴ καθάπερ φλὸξ λαμπρὰ ταχέως ἀπέσβη, μακαρίους ἔγωγε ὑμᾶς ὑπολαμβάνω. τέταρτος ἐνιαυτὸς ἤδη παρελήλυθε καὶ μὴν οὑτοσὶ τρίτος ἐπ' αὐτῷ σχεδόν, ἐξότε κεχωρίσμεθα ἡμεῖς ἀλλήλων. ἡδέως δ' ἂν σκεψαίμην,[2] ἐν τούτῳ πόσον τι προεληλύθατε. τὰ δὲ ἐμά, εἰ καὶ φθεγγοίμην Ἑλληνιστί, θαυμά-
C ζειν ἄξιον· οὕτως ἐσμὲν ἐκβεβαρβαρωμένοι διὰ τὰ χωρία. μὴ καταφρονεῖτε τῶν λογιδίων, μηδὲ ἀμελεῖτε ῥητορικῆς μηδὲ τοῦ ποιήμασιν ὁμιλεῖν. ἔστω δὲ τῶν μαθημάτων ἐπιμέλεια πλείων, ὁ δὲ πᾶς πόνος τῶν Ἀριστοτέλους καὶ Πλάτωνος δογμάτων ἐπιστήμη. τοῦτο ἔργον ἔστω, τοῦτο
D κρηπίς, θεμέλιος, οἰκοδομία, στέγη· τἆλλα δὲ πάρεργα, μετὰ μείζονος σπουδῆς παρ' ὑμῶν ἐπιτελούμενα ἢ παρά τισι τὰ ἀληθῶς ἔργα. ἐγὼ νὴ τὴν θείαν Δίκην ὑμᾶς ὡς ἀδελφοὺς φιλῶν ταῦτα

[1] Hertlein 55.
[2] Hertlein suggests; ἐσκεψάμην MSS.

---

[1] Julian went to Gaul in 355; he probably knew these students in Athens, earlier in the same year.

can prove the truth of my words by the great number of works that I wrote in my spare time, during last winter.

3

To Eumenius and Pharianus [1]

359 From Gaul

If anyone has persuaded you that there is anything more delightful or more profitable for the human race than to pursue philosophy at one's leisure without interruptions, he is a deluded man trying to delude you. But if your old-time zeal still abides in you and has not been swiftly quenched like a brilliant flame, then I regard you as peculiarly blest. Four years have already passed, yes and almost three months besides, since we parted from one another. It would give me pleasure to observe how far you have progressed in this period. As for my own progress, if I can still so much as speak Greek it is surprising, such a barbarian have I become because of the places I have lived in.[2] Do not despise the study of mere words or be careless of rhetoric or fail to read poetry. But you must devote still more attention to serious studies, and let your whole effort be to acquire understanding of the teachings of Aristotle and Plato. Let this be your task, the base, the foundation, the edifice, the roof. For all other studies are by the way, though they are completed by you with greater zeal than some bestow on really important tasks. I call sacred Justice to witness that I give you this advice because

[2] Like all the sophists Julian recognises only Greek culture, and for him Latin literature or the culture of Gaul did not exist.

ὑμῖν συμβουλεύω· γεγόνατε γάρ μοι συμφοιτηταὶ καὶ πάνυ φίλοι. εἰ μὲν οὖν πεισθείητε, πλέον στέρξω, ἀπειθοῦντας δὲ ὁρῶν λυπήσομαι. λύπη δὲ συνεχὴς εἰς ὅ ποτε τελευτᾶν εἴωθεν, εἰπεῖν παραιτοῦμαι οἰωνοῦ κρείττονος ἕνεκα.

4

Ὀριβασίῳ[1]

384 Τῶν ὀνειράτων δύο πύλας εἶναί φησιν ὁ θεῖος Ὅμηρος, καὶ διάφορον εἶναι αὐτοῖς καὶ τὴν ὑπὲρ
B τῶν ἀποβησομένων πίστιν. ἐγὼ δὲ νομίζω σε νῦν, εἴπερ ποτὲ καὶ ἄλλοτε, σαφῶς ἑορακέναι περὶ τῶν μελλόντων· ἐθεασάμην γὰρ καὶ αὐτὸς τοιοῦτον σήμερον. δένδρον γὰρ ᾤμην ὑψηλὸν ἔν τινι τρικλίνῳ σφόδρα μεγάλῳ πεφυτευμένον εἰς ἔδαφος ῥέπειν, τῇ ῥίζῃ παραπεφυκότος ἑτέρου μικροῦ καὶ νεογενοῦς, ἀνθηροῦ λίαν. ἐγὼ δὲ περὶ τοῦ μικροῦ σφόδρα ἠγωνίων, μή τις αὐτὸ μετὰ τοῦ
C μεγάλου συναποσπάσῃ. καὶ τοίνυν ἐπειδὴ πλησίον ἐγενόμην, ὁρῶ τὸ μέγα μὲν ἐπὶ τῆς γῆς ἐκτεταμένον, τὸ μικρὸν δὲ ὀρθὸν μέν, μετέωρον δὲ ἀπὸ γῆς. ὡς οὖν εἶδον, ἀγωνιάσας ἔφην· "Οἵου δένδρου! κίνδυνός ἐστι μηδὲ τὴν παραφυάδα σωθῆναι." καί τις ἀγνὼς ἐμοὶ παντελῶς

[1] Hertlein 17. This letter exists in only one MS. of importance, the *Vossianus*.

---

[1] Oribasius was the physician, friend, and perhaps accomplice of Julian in his ambitions: cf. *Letter to the Athenians* Vol. 2, p. 265; and for his career, Eunapius, *Lives of the Sophists and Philosophers*. He was at Vienne when Julian wrote this letter.

I love you like brothers. For you were my fellow-students and my very good friends. If therefore you follow my advice I shall love you the more, but if I see that you disregard it I shall grieve. And grief, if it lasts, usually results in something that, for the sake of a happier augury, I forbear to mention.

4

To Oribasius[1]

THE divinely inspired Homer says[2] that there are two gates of dreams, and that with regard to future events we cannot trust them both equally. But I think that this time, if ever before, you have seen clearly into the future; for I too this very day saw a vision of the same sort. I thought that in a certain very spacious room a tall tree had been planted, and that it was leaning down to the ground, while at its root had sprouted another, small and young and very flourishing. Now I was very anxious on behalf of the small tree, lest someone in pulling up the large one should pull it up as well. And in fact, when I came close I saw that the tall tree was lying at full length on the ground, while the small one was still erect, but hung suspended away from the earth. Now when I saw this I said, in great anxiety, "Alas for this tall tree! There is danger that not even its offspring will be preserved." Then one[3] 358-9 From Paris

[2] *Odyssey* 19. 562. Oribasius had evidently reported to Julian some dream of his which augured well for their hopes. In the dream that follows the tall tree is Constantius, the sapling is Julian.

[3] Hermes, who was Julian's guide in the myth in *Oration* 7. 230c.

"Ὅρα, ἔφησεν, ἀκριβῶς καὶ θάρρει· τῆς ῥίζης γὰρ ἐν τῇ γῇ μενούσης τὸ μικρότερον ἀβλαβὲς διαμενεῖ
D καὶ βεβαιότερον ἱδρυνθήσεται." τὰ μὲν δὴ τῶν ὀνειράτων τοιαῦτα, θεὸς δὲ οἶδεν εἰς ὅτι φέρει.

περὶ δὲ τοῦ μιαροῦ ἀνδρογύνου μάθοιμ' ἂν ἡδέως ἐκεῖνο, πότε διελέχθη περὶ ἐμοῦ ταῦτα, πότερον πρὶν ἢ συντυχεῖν ἐμοὶ ἢ μετὰ τοῦτο. δήλωσον οὖν ἡμῖν ὅ,τι ἂν οἷός τε ᾖς.

ὑπὲρ δὲ τῶν πρὸς αὐτὸν ἴσασιν οἱ θεοὶ[1] ὅτι πολλάκις, αὐτοῦ τοὺς ἐπαρχιώτας ἀδικήσαντος, ἐσιώπησα παρὰ τὸ πρέπον ἐμαυτῷ, τὰ μὲν οὐκ ἀκούων, τὰ δὲ οὐ προσιέμενος, ἄλλοις δὲ ἀπιστῶν,
385 ἔνια δὲ εἰς τοὺς συνόντας αὐτῷ τρέπων. ὅτι δέ μοι μεταδοῦναι τῆς τοιαύτης ἠξίωσεν αἰσχύνης, ἀποστείλας τὰ μιαρὰ καὶ πάσης αἰσχύνης ἄξια ὑπομνήματα, τί με πράττειν ἐχρῆν; ἆρα σιωπᾶν ἢ μάχεσθαι; τὸ μὲν οὖν πρῶτον ἦν ἠλίθιον καὶ δουλοπρεπὲς καὶ θεομίσητον, τὸ δεύτερον δὲ δίκαιον μὲν καὶ ἀνδρεῖον καὶ ἐλευθέριον, ὑπὸ δὲ τῶν κατεχόντων[2] ἡμᾶς πραγμάτων οὐ συγχωρού-
B μενον. τί τοίνυν ἐποίησα; πολλῶν παρόντων, οὓς ᾔδειν ἀναγγελοῦντας αὐτῷ "Πάντη καὶ πάντως, εἶπον, διορθώσει τὰ ὑπομνήματα οὗτος[3]

[1] Hercher supplies οἱ θεοί. [2] Cobet; MS. ἐχόντων.
[3] Hertlein brackets, Asmus defends.

---

[1] Probably Eusebius the chamberlain of Constantius whose intrigues against Julian are mentioned in *Letter to the Athenians* 274A. The epithet is unsuitable to Florentius, though some editors refer it to him.

[2] In spite of the abruptness of the transition, I follow Asmus in supposing that Julian here, partly for prudence and partly because of his sophistic habit of avoiding names, refers to Florentius, prefect of Gaul 357–360 and consul

who was altogether a stranger to me said: "Look carefully and take courage. For since the root still remains in the earth, the smaller tree will be uninjured and will be established even more securely than before." So much then for my dreams. God knows what they portend.

As for that abominable eunuch,[1] I should be glad to learn when he said these things about me, whether it was before he met me, or since. So tell me whatever you can about this.

But with regard to my behaviour towards him,[2] the gods know that often, when he wronged the provincials, I kept silence, at the expense of my own honour; to some charges I would not listen, others I would not admit, others again I did not believe, while in some cases I imputed the blame to his associates. But when he thought fit to make me share in such infamy by sending to me to sign those shameful and wholly abominable reports,[3] what was the right thing for me to do? Was I to remain silent, or to oppose him? The former course was foolish, servile and odious to the gods, the latter was just, manly and liberal, but was not open to me on account of the affairs that engaged me. What then did I do? In the presence of many persons who I knew would report it to him I said: "Such-a-one will certainly and by all means revise his reports, for they pass

361 A.D., who was at Vienne at this time. For his oppression of the province, see Ammianus 17. 3. 2; Julian, *Letter to the Athenians* 282C. When Julian was proclaimed Augustus, he fled to Constantius, and later, though condemned to death by Julian, remained in hiding till the latter's death, Ammianus 22. 3. 6.

[3] For Julian's refusal to sign or even read the prefect's orders for fresh taxes, see Ammianus 17. 3. 5.

ὁ δεῖνα, ἐπεὶ δεινῶς ἀσχημονεῖ." τοῦτο ἐκεῖνος ἀκούσας τοσοῦτον ἐδέησε σωφρόνως τι πρᾶξαι, ὥστε πεποίηκεν οἷα μὰ τὸν θεὸν οὐδ' ἂν εἷς μέτριος τύραννος, οὕτω μου πλησίον ὄντος. ἐνταῦθα τί πράττειν ἐχρῆν ἄνδρα τῶν Πλάτωνος καὶ Ἀριστοτέλους ζηλωτὴν δογμάτων; ἆρα περιορᾶν ἀνθρώπους ἀθλίους τοῖς κλέπταις ἐκδι-
C δομένους, ἢ κατὰ δύναμιν αὐτοῖς ἀμύνειν, ὡς[1] ἤδη τὸ κύκνειον ἐξᾴδουσι διὰ τὸ θεομισὲς ἐργαστήριον τῶν τοιούτων; ἐμοὶ μὲν οὖν αἰσχρὸν εἶναι δοκεῖ τοὺς μὲν χιλιάρχους, ὅταν λείπωσι τὴν τάξιν, καταδικάζειν· καίτοι χρῆν ἐκείνους[2] τεθνάναι παραχρῆμα καὶ μηδὲ ταφῆς ἀξιοῦσθαι· τὴν δὲ ὑπὲρ τῶν ἀθλίων ἀνθρώπων ἀπολείπειν τάξιν, ὅταν δέῃ πρὸς κλέπτας ἀγωνίζεσθαι τοιούτους, καὶ ταῦτα τοῦ θεοῦ συμμαχοῦντος ἡμῖν, ὅσπερ
D οὖν ἔταξεν. εἰ δὲ καὶ παθεῖν τι συμβαίη, μετὰ καλοῦ τοῦ συνειδότος οὐ μικρὰ παραμυθία πορευθῆναι. τὸν δὲ χρηστὸν Σαλούστιον θεοὶ μέν μοι χαρίσαιντο. κἂν συμβαίνῃ δὲ διὰ τοῦτο τυγχάνειν διαδόχου, λυπήσει τυχὸν οὐδέν· ἄμεινον γὰρ ὀλίγον ὀρθῶς ἢ πολὺν κακῶς πρᾶξαι χρόνον. οὐκ ἔστιν, ὥς λέγουσί τινες, τὰ Περιπατητικὰ δόγματα τῶν Στωικῶν ἀγεννέστερα, τοσούτῳ δὲ μόνον ἀλλήλων, ὡς ἐγὼ κρίνω, διαφέρει· τὰ μὲν γάρ ἐστιν ἀεὶ θερμότερα καὶ ἀβουλότερα, τὰ δὲ

[1] Before ὡς Hercher deletes, Hertlein brackets, οἶμαι.
[2] Boissonade, MS. ἱκανά.

---

[1] Sallust, who accompanied Julian as civil adviser, was recalled by Constantius in 358. Julian, *Oration* 8; *Oration* 4 is dedicated to him.

the bounds of decency." When he heard this, he was so far from behaving with discretion that he did things which, by heaven, no tyrant with any moderation would have done, and that too though I was so near where he was. In such a case what was the proper conduct for a man who is a zealous student of the teachings of Plato and Aristotle? Ought I to have looked on while the wretched people were being betrayed to thieves, or to have aided them as far as I could, for they were already singing their swan-song because of the criminal artifices of men of that sort? To me, at least, it seems a disgraceful thing that, while I punish my military tribunes when they desert their post—and indeed they ought to be put to death at once, and not even granted burial—I should myself desert my post which is for the defence of such wretched people; whereas it is my duty to fight against thieves of his sort, especially when God is fighting on my side, for it was indeed he who posted me here. And if any harm to myself should result, it is no small consolation to have proceeded with a good conscience. But I pray that the gods may let me keep the excellent Sallust![1] If, however, it turns out that because of this affair I receive his successor,[2] perhaps it will not grieve me. For it is better to do one's duty for a brief time honestly than for a long time dishonestly. The Peripatetic teachings are not, as some say, less noble than the Stoic In my judgement, there is only this difference between them; the former are always more sanguine and not so much the result of deliberate thought, while the latter have a greater

[2] This strains the construction but seems more probable than the rendering "If I should be superseded."

φρονήσεως ἀξιώτερα καὶ τοῖς ἐγνωσμένοις μᾶλλον ἐμμένει.[1]

5

Πρίσκῳ[2]

425 Ἄρτι μοι παυσαμένῳ τῆς χαλεπῆς πάνυ καὶ
B τραχείας νόσου τῇ τοῦ πάντα ἐφορῶντος προνοίᾳ
γράμματα εἰς χεῖρας ἦλθεν ὑμέτερα, καθ' ἣν ἡμέ-
ραν πρῶτον ἐλουσάμην. δείλης ἤδη ταῦτα ἀνα-
C γνοὺς οὐκ ἂν εἴποις ῥᾳδίως ὅπως ἐρρωννύμην,
αἰσθανόμενος τῆς σῆς ἀκραιφνοῦς καὶ καθαρᾶς
εὐνοίας, ἧς εἴθε γενοίμην ἄξιος, ὡς ἂν μὴ καται-
σχύναιμι τὴν σὴν φιλίαν. τὰς μὲν οὖν ὑμετέρας
ἐπιστολὰς εὐθὺς ἀνέγνων, καίπερ οὐ σφόδρα τοῦτο
ποιεῖν δυνάμενος, τὰς δὲ τοῦ Ἀντωνίου πρὸς τὸν
Ἀλέξανδρον εἰς τὴν ὑστεραίαν ἐταμιευσάμην.
ἐκεῖθεν ἑβδόμῃ σοι ταῦτα ἔγραφον ἡμέρᾳ,[3] κατὰ
λόγον μοι τῆς ῥώσεως προχωρούσης διὰ τὴν τοῦ
θεοῦ προμήθειαν. σώζοιό μοι, ποθεινότατε καὶ
φιλικώτατε ἀδελφέ, ὑπὸ τοῦ τὰ πάντα ἐφορῶντος
D θεοῦ· ἴδοιμί σε, ἐμὸν ἀγαθόν. καὶ ἰδίᾳ χειρί· νὴ
τὴν σὴν σωτηρίαν καὶ τὴν ἐμήν, νὴ τὸν πάντα
ἐφορῶντα θεόν, ὡς φρονῶ γέγραφα. ἀγαθώτατε,

[1] ἀξιώτερα καὶ τ. ε. μᾶλλον Asmus ; ἄξια τ. ε. ἐμμένει Hertlein.
[2] Hertlein 44. Λιβανίῳ Hertlein, *Parisinus* and all editions ; Πρίσκῳ *Baroccianus*, *Laurentianus* lviii, Cumont.
[3] Naber suggests ὥρᾳ.

---

[1] I translate the suggested reading of Asmus, but the sense remains unsatisfactory.

claim to practical wisdom, and are more rigidly consistent with the rules of conduct that they have laid down.[1]

5

To Priscus[2]

I HAD only just recovered by the providence of the All-Seeing One[3] from a very severe and sharp attack of sickness, when your letters reached my hands, on the very day when I took my first bath. It was already evening when I read them, and it would be hard for you to tell how my strength began to return when I realised your pure and sincere affection. May I become worthy of it, that I may not shame your love for me! Your letters I read at once, though I was not very well able to do so, but those of Antonius to Alexander I stored up for the next day. On the seventh day from their receipt I began to write this to you, since my strength is improving reasonably well, thanks to Divine Providence. May the All-Seeing god preserve you, my dearest and best beloved brother. May I see you, my treasure! *Added with his own hand.* I swear by your well-being and my own, by the All-Seeing god, that I really feel as I have written. Best of men, when can I see you

358-359 Winter From Paris

[2] So Cumont, following the ascription of MS. *Baroccianus.* Hertlein with hesitation addressed it to Libanius. So, too, Schwarz, who accordingly gives the date as 362 A.D. But as assigned to Priscus, it should be connected with the foregoing invitation to that sophist to come to Gaul, and the illness to which Julian refers is almost certainly his semi-asphyxiation in Paris described in *Misopogon* 340–342A.

[3] *i.e.* Helios-Mithras.

πότε σε ἴδω καὶ περιλάβωμαι; νῦν γάρ σου καὶ τοὔνομα καθάπερ οἱ δυσέρωτες φιλῶ.[1]

6

Ἀλυπίῳ ἀδελφῷ Καισαρίου[2]

402 D Ὁ Συλοσῶν ἀνῆλθε, φασί, παρὰ τὸν Δαρεῖον, καὶ ὑπέμνησεν αὐτὸν τῆς χλανίδος, καὶ ᾔτησεν ἀντ' ἐκείνης παρ' αὐτοῦ τὴν Σάμον. εἶτα ἐπὶ τούτῳ Δαρεῖος μὲν ἐμεγαλοφρονεῖτο, μεγάλα ἀντὶ μικρῶν νομίζων ἀποδεδωκέναι· Συλοσῶν δὲ λυπη-
403 ρὰν ἐλάμβανε χάριν. σκόπει δὴ τὰ ἡμέτερα νῦν πρὸς ἐκεῖνα. ἑνὶ μὲν δὴ τὸ πρῶτον οἶμαι κρεῖσσον ἔργον ἡμέτερον· οὐδὲ γὰρ ὑπεμείναμεν ὑπομνησθῆναι παρ' ἄλλου· τοσούτῳ δὲ χρόνῳ τὴν μνήμην τῆς σῆς φιλίας διαφυλάξαντες ἀκέραιον, ἐπειδὴ πρῶτον ἡμῖν ἔδωκεν ὁ θεός, οὐκ ἐν δευτέροις, ἀλλ' ἐν τοῖς πρώτοις σε μετεκαλέσαμεν. τὰ μὲν οὖν πρῶτα τοιαῦτα· περὶ δὲ τῶν μελλόντων ἆρά μοι δώσεις τι· καὶ γάρ εἰμι μαντικός· προαγο-
B ρεῦσαι; μακρῷ νομίζω κρείττονα ἐκείνων, Ἀδράστεια δ' εὐμενὴς εἴη. σύ τε γὰρ οὐδὲν δέῃ συγκαταστρεφομένου πόλιν βασιλέως, ἐγώ τε πολλῶν δέομαι τῶν συνεπανορθούντων μοι τὰ πεπτωκότα

[1] ὑπὸ (six lines above) to φιλῶ in *Baroccianus* only, bracketed by Spanheim and Hertlein, Hercher rejects.
[2] Hertlein 29.

---

[1] For Alypius see Introduction.
[2] The story of Syloson from Herodotus 3. 139, is told by Julian, Vol. 1. *Oration* 3. 117B. The "cloak of Syloson" became a proverb for the overpayment of a benefit.
[3] *i. e.* to Susa.

and embrace you? For already, like doting lovers, I adore your very name.

6

To Alypius, brother of Caesarius[1]

SYLOSON,[2] it is said, went up[3] to Darius, reminded him of his cloak and asked him for Samos in return for it. Then Darius prided himself greatly on this, because he considered that he had given much for little; though after all it proved a grievous gift for Syloson.[4] Now consider my conduct compared with that of Darius. In the first place I think that I have behaved better than he in one point at any rate, I mean that I did not wait to be reminded by another. But after preserving the memory of your friendship so long undimmed, the first moment that the god granted me power I summoned you, not among the second but among the very first. So much for the past. Now with reference to the future, will you allow me—for I am a prophet[5]—to foretell something? I think that it will be far more prosperous than in the case I spoke of, only let not Adrasteia[6] take offence when I say so! For you need no king to help you to conquer a city,[7] while I on the other hand need many to help me to raise up again what has fallen on evil days. Thus does

361 Before July From Gaul

[4] The Persians devastated Samos before Syloson could benefit by the gift.

[5] An echo of Plato, *Phaedrus* 343B.

[6] Another name for Nemesis, cf. Vol. 2. *Misopogon* 370B.

[7] If the date assigned to the letter is correct this must be Constantinople which Julian was preparing to occupy in his march against Constantius.

κακῶς. ταῦτά σοι Γαλλικὴ καὶ βάρβαρος Μοῦσα
προσπαίζει, σὺ δὲ ὑπὸ τῇ τῶν θεῶν πομπῇ χαίρων
ἀφίκοιο. καὶ τῇ αὐτοῦ χειρί· λῆις ἐρίφων καὶ
τῆς ἐν τοῖς χειμαδίοις θήρας[1] τῶν προβατίων.[2]
C ἧκε πρὸς τὸν φίλον, ὅς σε τότε, καίπερ οὔπω
γινώσκειν οἷος[3] εἶ δυνάμενος, ὅμως περιεῖπον.[1]

7

Τῷ αὐτῷ[4]

Ἤδη μὲν ἐτύγχανον ἀνειμένος τῆς νόσου,[5] τὴν
γεωγραφίαν ὅτε ἀπέστειλας· οὐ μὴν ἔλαττον διὰ
τοῦτο ἡδέως ἐδεξάμην τὸ παρὰ σοῦ πινάκιον ἀπο-
D σταλέν. ἔχει γὰρ καὶ τὰ διαγράμματα τῶν
πρόσθεν βελτίω, καὶ κατεμούσωσας αὐτὸ προσ-
θεὶς τοὺς ἰάμβους, οὐ μάχην ἀείδοντας τὴν Βου-
πάλειον κατὰ τὸν Κυρηναῖον ποιητήν, ἀλλ' οἵους
ἡ καλὴ Σαπφὼ βούλεται τοῖς νόμοις ἁρμόττειν.
καὶ τὸ μὲν δῶρον τοιοῦτόν ἐστιν, ὁποῖον ἴσως σοί
τε ἔπρεπε δοῦναι, ἐμοί τε ἥδιστον δέξασθαι. περὶ
δὲ τὴν διοίκησιν τῶν πραγμάτων ὅτι δραστηρίως
ἅμα καὶ πρᾴως ἅπαντα περαίνειν προθυμῇ, συνη-
δόμεθα· μῖξαι γὰρ πρᾳότητα καὶ σωφροσύνην
404 ἀνδρείᾳ καὶ ῥώμῃ, καὶ τῇ μὲν χρήσασθαι πρὸς

[1] καί τις—θήρα Capps suggests.
[2] Obscure and perhaps corrupt. Hertlein suggests προβάτων τῶν ἀγρίων, "wild sheep."
[3] Klimek; ὅσος Hertlein.
[4] Hertlein 30.
[5] Hertlein suggests παρειμένος τῇ νόσῳ or ὑπὸ τῆς νόσου.

---

[1] This is perhaps a veiled allusion to Julian's plot to defeat the adherents of Constantius.

my Gallic and barbarian Muse jest for your benefit. But be of good cheer and come, and may the gods attend you.

Added with his own hand. There is good spoil of deer and hunting of small sheep in the winter quarters.[1] Come to your friend who valued you even when he could not yet know your merit.

7

To the Same

It happened that when you sent me your map I had just recovered from my illness, but I was none the less glad on that account to receive the chart that you sent. For not only does it contain diagrams better than any hitherto made; but you have embellished it by adding those iambic verses, not such as "Sing the War of Bupalus," [2] as the poet of Cyrene [3] expresses it, but such as beautiful Sappho is wont to fashion for her songs.[4] In fact the gift is such as no doubt it well became you to give, while to me it is most agreeable to receive.[5] With regard to your administration of affairs, inasmuch as you study to act in all cases both energetically and humanely, I am well pleased with it. For to blend mildness and moderation with courage and force, and to exercise the former towards the most virtuous,

[2] For Bupalus cf. Horace, *Epodes* 6. 14; Lucian, *Pseudologist* 2.

[3] Callimachus, *frag.* 90, Ernesti.

[4] Literally "nomes," though Julian may only have meant "poetry"; in any case he refers to lyric iambics.

[5] An echo of Isocrates, *Nicocles* 29B.

τοὺς ἐπιεικεστάτους, τῇ δὲ ἐπὶ τῶν πονηρῶν ἀπαραιτήτως πρὸς ἐπανόρθωσιν οὐ μικρᾶς ἐστὶ φύσεως οὐδ᾽ ἀρετῆς ἔργον, ὡς ἐμαυτὸν πείθω. τούτων εὐχόμεθά σε τῶν σκοπῶν ἐχόμενον ἄμφω πρὸς ἓν τὸ καλὸν αὐτοὺς συναρμόσαι· τοῦτο γὰρ ἁπάσαις προκεῖσθαι ταῖς ἀρεταῖς τέλος οὐκ εἰκῇ τῶν παλαιῶν
B ἐπίστευον οἱ λογιώτατοι. ἐρρωμένος καὶ εὐδαιμονῶν διατελοίης ἐπὶ μήκιστον, ἀδελφὲ ποθεινότατε καὶ φιλικώτατε.

8

Μαξίμῳ φιλοσόφῳ [1]

414 Πάντα ἀθρόα ἔπεισί μοι καὶ ἀποκλείει τὴν φωνὴν ἄλλο ἄλλῳ προελθεῖν οὐ συγχωροῦν τῶν ἐμῶν διανοημάτων, εἴτε τῶν ψυχικῶν [2] παθῶν εἴτε ὅπως φίλον κατονομάζειν τὰ τοιαῦτα. ἀλλ᾽ ἀποδῶμεν αὐτοῖς ἣν ὁ χρόνος ἀπέδωκε τάξιν,
B εὐχαριστήσαντες τοῖς πάντα ἀγαθοῖς θεοῖς, οἳ τέως μὲν γράφειν ἐμοὶ συνεχώρησαν, ἴσως δὲ ἡμῖν καὶ ἀλλήλους ἰδεῖν συγχωρήσουσιν. ὡς πρῶτον αὐτοκράτωρ ἐγενόμην ἄκων,[3] ὡς ἴσασιν οἱ θεοί, καὶ τοῦτο αὐτόθι [4] καταφανὲς ὃν ἐνεδέχετο τρόπον ἐποίησα· στρατεύσας ἐπὶ τοὺς βαρβάρους, ἐκείνης μοι γενομένης τριμήνου τῆς στρατείας,

[1] Hertlein 38.
[2] τῶν Bidez adds, ψυχρὸν τῶν MSS., Hertlein, who suspects corruption; ψυχικῶν παθῶν Papadopoulos MSS. XY.
[3] ἄκων ἐγενόμην Hertlein, from *Parisinus* 2755.
[4] αὐτοῖς εἰ MSS; αὐτοῖς Hertlein; αὐτόθι Capps.

---

[1] Cf. *Oration* I. 3D, Vol. 1.

and the latter implacably in the case of the wicked for their regeneration, is, as I am convinced, a task that calls for no slight natural endowment and virtue. I pray that you may ever hold fast to these ambitions and may adapt them both solely to what is fair and honourable.[1] Not without reason did the most eloquent of the ancient writers believe that this is the end and aim set for all the virtues. May you continue in health and happiness as long as possible, my well-beloved and most dear brother!

8

To Maximus, the philosopher[2]

EVERYTHING crowds into my mind at once and chokes my utterance, as one thought refuses to let another precede it, whether you please to class such symptoms among psychic troubles, or to give them some other name. But let me arrange what I have to tell in chronological order, though not till I have first offered thanks to the all-merciful gods, who at this present have permitted me to write and will also perhaps permit us to see one another. Directly after I had been made Emperor—against my will, as the gods know; and this I made evident then and there in every way possible,—I led the army against the barbarians.[3] That expedition lasted for three

361 November From Naissa (Nish)

[2] The theurgist. His life was written by Eunapius, *Lives of the Sophists and Philosophers*. Maximus was at Ephesus; Julian's headquarters were at Naissa, where he had received news of the death of Constantius, November 3rd, 361. Schwarz dates this letter October or November.

[3] *i.e.* when he recrossed the Rhine in 360. For this campaign, see Ammianus 20. 10.

C ἐπανιὼν εἰς τοὺς Γαλατικοὺς αἰγιαλοὺς[1] ἐπεσκόπουν καὶ τῶν ἐκεῖθεν ἡκόντων ἀνεπυνθανόμην, μή τις φιλόσοφος, μή τις σχολαστικὸς ἢ τριβώνιον ἢ χλανίδιον φορῶν κατῆρεν. ἐπεὶ δὲ περὶ τὸν Βισεντίωνα[2] ἦν· πολίχνη[3] δὲ νῦν ἐστιν[4] ἀνειλημμένη, πάλαι δὲ μεγάλη τε ἦν καὶ πολυτελέσιν ἱεροῖς ἐκεκόσμητο, καὶ τείχει καρτερῷ καὶ προσέτι τῇ φύσει τοῦ χωρίου· περιθεῖ γὰρ αὐτὸ ὁ Δοῦβις ποταμός· ἡ δὲ ὥσπερ ἐν θαλάττῃ πετρώδης ἄκρα ἀνέστηκεν, ἄβατος ὀλίγου δέω φάναι καὶ αὐτοῖς
D ὄρνισι, πλὴν ὅσα ὁ ποταμὸς αὐτὴν περιρρέων ὥσπερ τινὰς αἰγιαλοὺς ἔχει προκειμένους· ταύτης πλησίον τῆς πόλεως ἀπήντησε κυνικός τις ἀνήρ, ἔχων τρίβωνα καὶ βακτηρίαν. τοῦτον πόρρωθεν θεασάμενος οὐδὲν ἄλλο[5] ὑπέλαβον ἢ σέ, πλησίον δὲ ἤδη προσιὼν παρὰ σοῦ πάντως ἥκειν αὐτὸν ἐνόμιζον. οὗτος[6] δ' ἀνὴρ φίλος μέν, ἥττων[7] δὲ τῆς προσδοκωμένης ἐλπίδος. ἓν μὲν δὴ τοιοῦτον ὄναρ ἐγένετό μοι. μετὰ τοῦτο δὲ πάντως[8] ᾤμην
415 σε πολυπραγμονήσαντα τὰ κατ' ἐμὲ τῆς Ἑλλάδος ἐκτὸς οὐδαμῶς εὑρήσειν.[9] ἴστω Ζεύς, ἴστω μέγας Ἥλιος, ἴστω Ἀθηνᾶς κράτος καὶ πάντες θεοὶ καὶ πᾶσαι, πῶς κατιὼν ἐπὶ τοὺς Ἰλλυριοὺς ἀπὸ τῶν Κελτῶν ἔτρεμον ὑπὲρ σοῦ. καὶ ἐπυνθανόμην τῶν

[1] Schwarz suggests σταθμοὺς because of the strange use of αἰγιαλός, "beach," for the bank of a river.
[2] Βισεντίωνα X, Βικεντίωνα *Parisinus*, Hertlein. ἦν Schwarz adds.
[3] πολίχνη Cobet, πολίχνιον MSS., Hertlein.
[4] δέ ἐστι νῦν X. [5] οὐδένα ἄλλον XY. [6] ὤφθη δὲ XY.
[7] ἥττων XY, ἧττον *Parisinus*, Hertlein.
[8] πάντως *Parisinus* omits, followed by Hertlein.
[9] εὑρεθῆναι Hertlein.

months, and when I returned to the shores of Gaul, I was ever on the watch and kept enquiring from all who came from that quarter whether any philosopher or any scholar wearing a philosopher's cloak or a soldier's tunic had arrived there. Then I approached Besontio.[1] It is a little town that has lately been restored, but in ancient times it was a large city adorned with costly temples, and was fortified by a strong wall and further by the nature of the place; for it is encircled by the river Doubis.[2] It rises up like a rocky cliff in the sea, inaccessible, I might almost say, to the very birds, except in those places where the river as it flows round it throws out what one may call beaches, that lie in front of it. Near this city there came to meet me a certain man who looked like a Cynic with his long cloak and staff. When I first caught sight of him in the distance, I imagined that he was none other than yourself. And when I came nearer to him I thought that he had surely come from you. The man was in fact a friend of mine though he fell short of what I hoped and expected. This then was one vain dream I had! And afterwards I thought that, because you were busied with my affairs, I should certainly find you nowhere outside of Greece. Zeus be my witness and great Helios, mighty Athene and all the gods and goddesses, how on my way down to Illyricum from Gaul[3] I trembled for your safety! Also I kept

[1] Cf. Ammianus 20. 10, per Besontionem Viennam hiematurus abscessit. Besontio or Vesontio (Besançon), the capital of the Sequani, is described in much the same language by Caesar, *Gallic War* 1. 38.

[2] Doubs.

[3] Ammianus 21. 7, Zosimus 3. 10 describe this march.

θεῶν (αὐτὸς μὲν οὐ τολμῶν· οὐ γὰρ ὑπέμενον οὔτε ἰδεῖν τοιοῦτον οὔτε ἀκοῦσαι οὐδέν, οἷον ἄν τις ὑπέ-
B λαβε δύνασθαι τηνικαῦτα περὶ σὲ γίγνεσθαι, ἐπέτρεπον δὲ ἄλλοις), οἱ θεοὶ δὲ ταραχὰς μέν τινας ἔσεσθαι περὶ σὲ περιφανῶς[1] ἐδήλουν, οὐδὲν μέντοι δεινὸν οὐδὲ εἰς ἔργον τῶν ἀθέων[2] βουλευμάτων.

Ἀλλ' ὁρᾷς ὅτι μεγάλα καὶ πολλὰ παρέδραμον. μάλιστά σε πυθέσθαι ἄξιον, πῶς μὲν ἀθρόως τῆς ἐπιφανείας ᾐσθόμεθα τῶν θεῶν, τίνα δὲ τρόπον τὸ τοσοῦτον τῶν ἐπιβούλων πλῆθος διαπεφεύγαμεν, κτείναντες οὐδένα, χρήματα οὐδενὸς ἀφελόμενοι,
C φυλαξάμενοι δὲ μόνον οὓς ἐλαμβάνομεν ἐπ' αὐτοφώρῳ. ταῦτα μὲν οὖν ἴσως οὐ γράφειν, ἀλλὰ φράζειν χρή, οἶμαι δέ σε καὶ μάλα ἡδέως πεύσεσθαι. θρησκεύομεν τοὺς θεοὺς ἀναφανδόν, καὶ τὸ πλῆθος τοῦ συγκατελθόντος μοι στρατοπέδου θεοσεβές ἐστιν. ἡμεῖς φανερῶς βουθυτοῦμεν. ἀπεδώκαμεν τοῖς θεοῖς χαριστήρια[3] ἑκατόμβας πολ-
D λάς. ἐμὲ κελεύουσιν οἱ θεοὶ τὰ πάντα ἁγνεύειν εἰς δύναμιν, καὶ πείθομαί γε καὶ προθύμως αὐτοῖς· μεγάλους γὰρ καρποὺς τῶν πόνων ἀποδώσειν φασίν, ἢν μὴ ῥᾳθυμῶμεν. ἦλθε πρὸς ἡμᾶς Εὐάγριος.[4] . . . . τοῦ παρ' ἡμῖν τιμωμένου θεοῦ.[5] . . . .

Πολλὰ γοῦν ἐπέρχεταί μοι πρὸς τούτοις, ἀλλὰ χρὴ ταμιεύσασθαί τινα καὶ τῇ παρουσίᾳ τῇ σῇ.

[1] φανερῶς XY. [2] ἀθέων Asmus, ἀθέσμων MSS., Hertlein.
[3] After χαριστήρια XY have περὶ ἡμῶν.
[4] In Hertlein the letter ends at Εὐάγριος. In XY (Papadopoulos) a lacuna of about 82 letters follows.
[5] A lacuna follows in XY.

enquiring of the gods—not that I ventured to do this myself, for I could not endure to see or hear anything so terrible as one might have supposed would be happening to you at that time, but I entrusted the task to others; and the gods did indeed show clearly that certain troubles would befal you, nothing terrible however, nor to indicate that impious counsels would be carried out.[1]

But you see that I have passed over many important events. Above all, it is right that you should learn how I became all at once conscious of the very presence of the gods, and in what manner I escaped the multitude of those who plotted against me, though I put no man to death, deprived no man of his property, and only imprisoned those whom I caught red-handed. All this, however, I ought perhaps to tell you rather than write it, but I think you will be very glad to be informed of it. I worship the gods openly, and the whole mass of the troops who are returning with me worship the gods.[2] I sacrifice oxen in public. I have offered to the gods many hecatombs as thank-offerings. The gods command me to restore their worship in its utmost purity, and I obey them, yes, and with a good will. For they promise me great rewards for my labours, if only I am not remiss. Evagrius[3] has joined me. . . . of the god whom we honour. . . .

Many things occur to my mind, besides what I have written, but I must store up certain matters to tell you when you are with me. Come here,

[1] Julian's friends in the East were in danger after his quarrel with Constantius.

[2] Cf. Libanius, *Oration* 18. 114.

[3] Cf. *Letter* 25, *To Evagrius.*

δεῦρο οὖν, τοὺς θεούς σοι, τὴν ταχίστην, εἴτε δύο εἴτε πλείοσι χρησάμενος ὀχήμασιν. ἀπέστειλα δὲ καὶ δύο τῶν πιστοτάτων ὑπηρετῶν, ὧν ὁ μὲν εἷς ἄχρι τοῦ στρατοπέδου παραπέμψει σε· ἕτερος δὲ ἐξεληλυθέναι σε καὶ ἥκειν ἤδη μηνύσει· πότερον δὲ ὑπὸ ποτέρου γενέσθαι θέλεις αὐτὸς τοῖς νεανίσκοις σήμηνον.[1]

9

Ἰουλιανῷ θείῳ[2]

382 Τρίτης ὥρας νυκτὸς ἀρχομένης, οὐκ ἔχων οὐδὲ
B τὸν ὑπογράψοντα[3] διὰ τὸ πάντας ἀσχόλους εἶναι, μόλις ἴσχυσα πρὸς σὲ ταῦτα γράψαι. ζῶμεν διὰ τοὺς θεοὺς ἐλευθερωθέντες τοῦ παθεῖν ἢ δρᾶσαι τὰ ἀνήκεστα· μάρτυς δὲ ὁ Ἥλιος, ὃν μάλιστα πάντων ἱκέτευσα συνάρασθαί μοι, καὶ ὁ βασιλεὺς Ζεύς, ὡς οὐπώποτε ηὐξάμην ἀποκτεῖναι Κωνστάντιον, μᾶλλον δὲ ἀπηυξάμην. τί οὖν ἦλθον; ἐπειδή μοι οἱ θεοὶ διαρρήδην ἐκέλευσαν, σωτηρίαν μὲν ἐπαγγελλόμενοι πειθομένῳ, μένοντι
C δὲ ὃ μηδεὶς θεῶν ποιήσειεν· ἄλλως τε ὅτι καὶ

[1] πολλὰ . . . . . σήμηνον restored from XY, not in Hertlein.
[2] Hertlein 13; after θείῳ X adds αὐτοῦ.
[3] Hertlein suggests, MSS. ὑπογράφοντα.

---

[1] Maximus did not join Julian at Naissa, but, as Eunapius relates in his *Life of Chrysanthius*, p. 554 (Wright), he lingered at Ephesus in the vain attempt to secure favourable omens for the journey, and finally joined Julian at Constanti-

then, in the name of the gods, as quickly as you can, and use two or more public carriages. Moreover, I have sent two of my most trusted servants, one of whom will escort you as far as my headquarters; the other will inform me that you have set out and will forthwith arrive. Do you yourself tell the youths which of them you wish to undertake which of these tasks.[1]

9

To his Uncle Julian [2]

THE third hour of the night has just begun, and as I have no secretary to dictate to because they are all occupied, I have with difficulty made the effort to write this to you myself. I am alive, by the grace of the gods, and have been freed from the necessity of either suffering or inflicting irreparable ill.[3] But the Sun, whom of all the gods I besought most earnestly to assist me, and sovereign Zeus also, bear me witness that never for a moment did I wish to slay Constantius, but rather I wished the contrary. Why then did I come? Because the gods expressly ordered me,[4] and promised me safety if I obeyed them, but if I stayed, what I pray no god may do to me! Furthermore I came because, having been de-

361 Late November or early December From Naissa (Nish)

nople early in 362; cf. Eunapius, *Life of Aedesius*, pp. 440 foll.

[2] For Count Julian, see Introduction.

[3] A proverbial phrase; cf. *Letter to Nilus*, p. 159. The sudden death of Constantius had simplified Julian's course.

[4] Cf. Vol. 3, *Letter to the Athenians* 284B–285D, for Julian's own account of the mutiny against Constantius and the sign given by the gods.

πολέμιος ἀποδειχθεὶς ᾤμην φοβῆσαι μόνον καὶ εἰς ὁμιλίας ἥξειν ἐπιεικεστέρας τὰ πράγματα· εἰ δὲ μάχῃ κριθείη, τῇ τύχῃ τὰ πάντα καὶ τοῖς θεοῖς ἐπιτρέψας περιμένειν ὅπερ ἂν αὐτῶν τῇ φιλανθρωπίᾳ δόξῃ.

10

Ἰουλιανὸς Εὐθηρίῳ [1]

Ζῶμεν ὑπὸ τῶν θεῶν σωθέντες· ὑπὲρ ἐμοῦ δὲ αὐτοῖς θῦε τὰ χαριστήρια. θύσεις δὲ οὐχ ὑπὲρ ἑνὸς ἀνδρός, ἀλλ' ὑπὲρ τοῦ κοινοῦ τῶν Ἑλλήνων. εἰ δέ σοι σχολὴ καὶ μέχρι τῆς Κωνσταντίνου πόλεως διαβῆναι, τιμησαίμην ἂν οὐκ ὀλίγου τὴν σὴν ἐντυχίαν.

11

Ἰουλιανὸς Λεοντίῳ [2]

389 Ὁ λογοποιὸς ὁ Θούριος ὦτα εἶπεν ἀνθρώποις
B ὀφθαλμῶν ἀπιστότερα. τούτῳ δ' ἐπὶ σοῦ τὴν ἐναντίαν ἔχω γνώμην ἐγώ· πιστότερα γάρ ἐστί μοι τὰ ὦτα τῶν ὀφθαλμῶν. οὐ γάρ, εἴποτε εἶδόν σε δεκάκις, οὕτως ἂν ἐπίστευσα τοῖς ὀφθαλμοῖς,

[1] Hertlein 69. [2] Hertlein 22.

[1] An Armenian eunuch, a pagan who had been kidnapped, sold into slavery, and finally attained to the office of court chamberlain and confidential adviser to Constans and Julian; see Ammianus 16. 7. 4. He was employed by Julian in Gaul as a trusted messenger to Constantius at Milan; Ammianus 20. 8. 19.

clared a public enemy, I meant to frighten him merely, and that our quarrel should result in intercourse on more friendly terms; but if we should have to decide the issue by battle, I meant to entrust the whole to Fortune and to the gods, and so await whatever their clemency might decide.

10

To Eutherius[1]

I AM alive, and have been saved by the gods. Therefore offer sacrifices to them on my behalf, as thank-offerings. Your sacrifice will be not for one man only, but for the whole body of Hellenes.[2] If you have time to travel as far as Constantinople I shall feel myself highly honoured by your presence. 361 About December 1st From Naissa (Nish)

11

To Leontius

THE Thurian historian[3] said that men's ears are less to be trusted than their eyes.[4] But in your case I hold the opposite opinion from this, since here my ears are more trustworthy than my eyes. For not if I had seen you ten times would I have trusted my eyes as I now trust my ears, instructed 361 From Naissa (Nish) or Constantinople

[2] In the fourth century this word has lost some of its national meaning, and is used of pagans as opposed to Christians, especially by Julian. The sophists of that period called themselves and all students of rhetoric "Hellenes."

[3] Herodotus

[4] Herodotus 1. 8; cf. Julian *Oration* 1. 37C, and 4. 145D.

ὡς νῦν ταῖς ἀκοαῖς πιστεύω ταῖς ἐμαυτοῦ, παρ' ἀνδρὸς οὐδαμῶς οἵου τε ψεύδεσθαι δεδιδαγμένος, ὅτι πάντα ἀνὴρ ὢν αὐτὸς σεαυτοῦ κρείττων εἶ περὶ τὸ ῥέξαι, φησὶν Ὅμηρος, χερσί τε καὶ ποσίν. ἐπιτρέψαντες οὖν σοι τὴν τῶν ὅπλων χρῆσιν ἀπεστείλαμέν τε πανοπλίαν, ἥτις[1] τοῖς πεζοῖς ἁρμόττει·[2] ἐγκατελέξαμέν τέ σε τῷ τῶν οἰκείων συντάγματι.[3]

12

Μαξίμῳ φιλοσόφῳ[4]

383 Ἀλέξανδρον μὲν τὸν Μακεδόνα τοῖς Ὁμήρου ποιήμασιν ἐφυπνώττειν λόγος, ἵνα δὴ καὶ νύκτωρ καὶ μεθ' ἡμέραν αὐτοῦ τοῖς πολεμικοῖς ὁμιλῇ συνθήμασιν· ἡμεῖς δέ σου ταῖς ἐπιστολαῖς ὥσπερ παιωνίοις τισὶ φαρμάκοις συγκαθεύδομεν, καὶ οὐ
B διαλείπομεν ἐντυγχάνοντες ἀεὶ καθάπερ νεαραῖς ἔτι καὶ πρῶτον εἰς χεῖρας ἡκούσαις. εἴπερ οὖν ἐθέλεις ἡμῖν εἰκόνα τῆς σῆς παρουσίας τὴν ἐν τοῖς γράμμασιν ὁμιλίαν προξενεῖν, γράφε καὶ μὴ λῆγε συνεχῶς τοῦτο πράττων· μᾶλλον δὲ ἧκε σὺν θεοῖς, ἐνθυμούμενος ὡς ἡμῖν γ' ἕως ἂν ἀπῇς

[1] Hertlein suggests, MSS. ἡ τέως.

[2] MSS. add κουφοτέρα δέ ἐστιν αὕτη τῆς τῶν ἱππέων deleted by Wyttenbach, Hertlein brackets.

[3] MSS. add γίνονται δὲ ἀπὸ τῶν ὁπλοφορησάντων οὗτοι καὶ στρατευσαμένων deleted by Wyttenbach, Hertlein brackets.

[4] Hertlein 15.

[1] An echo of Demosthenes, *Olynthiac* 2. 17.

as I have been by a man who is in no wise capable of speaking falsely,[1] that, while in all respects you show yourself a man, you surpass yourself[2] in your achievements "with hand and foot," as Homer says.[3] I therefore entrust you with the employment of arms, and have despatched to you a complete suit of armour such as is adapted for the infantry. Moreover I have enrolled you in my household corps.[4]

12

To the philosopher Maxims

End of 361 or early in 362 From Constantinople

THERE is a tradition[5] that Alexander of Macedon used to sleep with Homer's poems under his pillow, in order that by night as well as by day he might busy himself with his martial writings. But I sleep with your letters as though they were healing drugs of some sort, and I do not cease to read them constantly as though they were newly written and had only just come into my hands. Therefore if you are willing to furnish me with intercourse by means of letters, as a semblance of your own society, write, and do not cease to do so continually. Or rather come,[6] with heaven's help, and consider that while

[2] Cf. Julian, *Oration* 7. 235B, *Letter to Themistius* 264D, *Caesars* 309D, 327C.

[3] *Odyssey* 8. 148; the phrase is there used of the athletic sports of the Phaeacians.

[4] *i. e.* the *protectores domestici*; cf. Symmachus, *Letter* 67. In C.I.L. III 5670A (Dessau 774), a Leontius is mentioned as praepositus militum auxiliarium in 370 A.D.

[5] Plutarch, *Alexander* 12.

[6] Ammianus 22. 7. 3 describes Julian's effusive greeting of Maximus, for which he interrupted a meeting of the Senate.

οὐδ' ὅτι ζῶμεν εἰπεῖν ἔστιν, εἰ μὴ ὅσον τοῖς παρὰ σοῦ γραφομένοις ἐντυχεῖν ἔξεστιν.

13

Ἑρμογένει ἀποϋπάρχῳ Αἰγύπτου[1]

389 Δός μοί τι κατὰ τοὺς μελικτὰς[2] εἰπεῖν ῥήτορας,
D Ὦ παρ' ἐλπίδα σεσωσμένος ἐγώ, ὦ παρ' ἐλπίδας[3]
ἀκηκοώς, ὅτι διαπέφευγας τὴν τρικέφαλον ὕδραν,
οὔτι μὰ Δία τὸν ἀδελφόν φημι Κωνστάντιον·
ἀλλ' ἐκεῖνος μὲν ἦν οἷος ἦν· ἀλλὰ τὰ περὶ αὐτὸν
θηρία πᾶσιν ἐποφθαλμιῶντα, ἃ κἀκεῖνον ἐποίει
χαλεπώτερον, οὐδὲ τὸ καθ' ἑαυτὸν παντάπασι
390 πρᾷον, εἰ καὶ ἐδόκει πολλοῖς τοιοῦτος. ἐκείνῳ
μὲν οὖν, ἐπειδὴ μακαρίτης ἐγένετο, κούφη γῆ,
καθάπερ λέγεται· τούτους δὲ ἀδίκως μέν τι παθεῖν
οὐκ ἂν ἐθέλοιμι, ἴστω Ζεύς· ἐπειδὴ δὲ αὐτοῖς
ἐπανίστανται πολλοὶ κατήγοροι, δικαστήριον
ἀποκεκλήρωται. σὺ δέ, ὦ φίλε, πάρει, καὶ παρὰ
B δύναμιν ἐπείχθητι· θεάσασθαι γάρ σε πάλαι τε
εὔχομαι νὴ τοὺς θεούς, καὶ νῦν εὐμενέστατα ὅτι
διεσώθης ἀκηκοώς, ἥκειν παρακελεύομαι.

[1] Hertlein 23.
[2] μειλιχίους ? Cumont suggests.
[3] Asmus suggests ἐλπίδα σέ.

---

[1] Hermogenes had been Prefect of Egypt before 328, since his name does not occur in the list of prefects after that year, which is extant complete.

you are away I cannot be said to be alive, except in so far as I am able to read what you have written.

13

To Hermogenes, formerly Prefect of Egypt[1]

361 December? From Constantinople

Suffer me to say, in the language of the poetical rhetoricians, O how little hope had I of safety! O how little hope had I of hearing that you had escaped the three-headed hydra! Zeus be my witness that I do not mean my brother Constantius[2]—nay, he was what he was—but the wild beasts who surrounded him and cast their baleful eyes on all men; for they made him even harsher than he was by nature, though on his own account he was by no means of a mild disposition, although he seemed so to many. But since he is now one of the blessed dead, may the earth lie lightly on him, as the saying is! Nor should I wish, Zeus be my witness, that these others should be punished unjustly; but since many accusers are rising up against them, I have appointed a court[3] to judge them. Do you, my friend, come hither, and hasten, even if it task your strength. For, by the gods, I have long desired to see you, and, now that I have learned to my great joy that you are safe and sound, I bid you come.

[2] Cf. for Julian's attitude to Constantius, *Misopogon* 357B.

[3] The special commission appointed by Julian to try his enemies sat at Chalcedon in Dec 361. Its work is described by Ammianus 22. 3; Libanius, *Oration* 18. 152. Among the judges were Mamertinus the rhetorician and Nevitta the Goth, who were the Consuls designate for 362, and Sallust.

14

Προαιρεσίῳ[1]

373 Τί δὲ οὐκ ἔμελλον ἐγὼ Προαιρέσιον τὸν καλὸν
D προσαγορεύειν, ἄνδρα ἐπαφιέντα τοῖς νέοις λόγους, ὥσπερ οἱ ποταμοὶ τοῖς πεδίοις ἐπαφιᾶσι τὰ ῥεύματα, καὶ ζηλοῦντα τὸν Περικλέα κατὰ τοὺς
374 λόγους ἔξω τοῦ συνταράττειν καὶ ξυγκυκᾶν τὴν Ἑλλάδα; θαυμάζειν δ' οὐ χρὴ τὴν Λακωνικὴν εἰ πρὸς σὲ βραχυλογίαν ἐμιμησάμην. ὑμῖν γὰρ πρέπει τοῖς σοφοῖς μακροὺς πάνυ καὶ μεγάλους ποιεῖσθαι λόγους, ἡμῖν δὲ ἀρκεῖ καὶ τὰ βραχέα πρὸς ὑμᾶς. ἴσθι δῆτά μοι πολλὰ πανταχόθεν κύκλῳ πράγματα ἐπιρρεῖν. τῆς καθόδου τὰς αἰτίας, εἰ μὲν ἱστορίαν γράψεις,[2] ἀκριβέστατα
B ἀπαγγελῶ σοι, δοὺς τὰς ἐπιστολὰς ἀποδείξεις ἐγγράφους· εἰ δ' ἔγνωκας ταῖς μελέταις καὶ τοῖς γυμνάσμασιν εἰς τέλος ἄχρι γήρως προσκαρτερεῖν, οὐδὲν ἴσως μου τὴν σιωπὴν μέμψῃ.

15

Ἀετίῳ ἐπισκόπῳ[3]

404
B Κοινῶς μὲν ἅπασι τοῖς ὁπωσοῦν ὑπὸ τοῦ μακαρίτου Κωνσταντίου πεφυγαδευμένοις ἕνεκεν τῆς

[1] Hertlein 2. [2] Cobet, γράφεις MSS. Hertlein. [3] Hertlein 31.

---

[1] The Armenian sophist, a Christian, who taught at Athens. For his *Life* see Eunapius, *Lives of the Sophists and Philosophers*, pp. 477–515 (Wright). See Introduction.

[2] Aristophanes, *Acharnians* 531, ξυνεκύκα τὴν Ἑλλάδα.

14

To Prohaeresius[1]

WHY should I not address the excellent Prohaeresius, a man who has poured forth his eloquence on the young as rivers pour their floods over the plain; who rivals Pericles in his discourses, except that he does not agitate and embroil Greece?[2] But you must not be surprised that I have imitated Spartan brevity in writing to you. For though it becomes sages like you to compose very long and impressive discourses, from me to you even a few words are enough. Moreover you must know that from all quarters at once I am inundated by affairs. As for the causes of my return,[3] if you are going to write an historical account I will make a very precise report for you, and will hand over to you the letters,[4] as written evidence. But if you have resolved to devote your energies to the last, till old age,[5] to your rhetorical studies and exercises, you will perhaps not reproach me for my silence. End of 361 (or early in 362) From Constantinople

15

To Bishop Aetius[6]

I HAVE remitted their sentence of exile for all in common who were banished in whatever fashion by Constantius of blessed memory, on account of the 362 Jan. From Constantinople

[3] *i.e.* from Gaul, when he marched against the Emperor Constantius, in 361. This letter was probably written after his triumphal entry into Constantinople on December 11th.

[4] For the correspondence between Julian and Constantius cf. Ammianus Marcellinus 20. 8. 5.

[5] Prohaeresius was already in the late eighties.

[6] See Introduction under Aetius.

C τῶν Γαλιλαίων ἀπονοίας ἀνῆκα τὴν φυγήν, σοὶ[1] δὲ οὐκ ἀνίημι μόνον, ἀλλὰ γὰρ καὶ παλαιᾶς γνώσεώς τε καὶ συνηθείας μεμνημένος ἀφικέσθαι προτρέπω μέχρις ἡμῶν. χρήσῃ δὲ ὀχήματι δημοσίῳ μέχρι τοῦ στρατοπέδου τοῦ ἐμοῦ καὶ ἑνὶ παρίππῳ.

16

Θεοδώρῳ ἀρχιερεῖ.[2]

Δεξάμενός σου τὴν ἐπιστολὴν ἥσθην μέν, ὡς εἰκός· τί γὰρ οὐκ ἔμελλον ἄνδρα ἑταῖρον ἐμοὶ καὶ φίλων φίλτατον σῶν εἶναι πυνθανόμενος; ὡς δὲ καὶ ἀφελὼν τὸν ἐπικείμενον δεσμὸν ἐπῄειν πολλάκις, οὐκ ἂν ἐγὼ παραστῆσαι τῷ λόγῳ δυναίμην, τίς καὶ ὁποῖος ἐγενόμην· γαλήνης ἐμπιπλάμενος καὶ θυμηδίας, ὥσπερ εἰκόνα τινὰ τοῦ γενναίου σου καθορῶν τρόπου τὴν ἐπιστολὴν ἠσπαζόμην· ὑπὲρ ἧς τὰ μὲν καθέκαστα γράφειν μακρὸν ἂν εἴη καὶ περιττῆς ἴσως ἀδολεσχίας οὐκ ἔξω. ἃ δ᾿ οὖν ἐπῄνεσα διαφερόντως, ταῦτα εἰπεῖν οὐκ ἂν ὀκνήσαιμι· πρῶτον μέν, ὅτι τὴν[3] παροινίαν ἣν εἰς ὑμᾶς[4] ὁ τῆς Ἑλλάδος[5] ἡγεμὼν πεπαρῴνηκεν, εἴ γε τὸν τοιοῦτον ἡγεμόνα χρὴ καλεῖν ἀλλὰ μὴ τύραννον, οὔπω βαρέως[6] ἤνεγκας, οὐδὲν ἡγού-

[1] σοὶ Hertlein suggests, σὲ MSS.

[2] Papadopoulos 3* in *Rheinisches Museum* 42. 1887; not in Hertlein.

[3] τὴν παροινίαν—Νέρων is quoted by Suidas, *Musonius*; he omits εἴ γε—τύραννον. Hertlein, who gives this extract as *frag.* 3, follows Suidas.

[4] ἡμᾶς MS., ὑμᾶς Maas, see Introduction under Theodorus.

[5] Asmus suggests Ἑλλησπόντου, but this is too violent a change.

folly of the Galilaeans.[1] But in your case, I not only remit your exile, but also, since I am mindful of our old acquaintance and intercourse, I invite you to come to me. You will use a public conveyance [2] as far as my headquarters, and one extra horse.

16

To the High-priest Theodorus [3]

WHEN I received your letter I was delighted, of course. How could I feel otherwise on learning that my comrade and dearest friend is safe? And when I had removed the fastening from it and perused it many times, I cannot convey to you in words my feelings and state of mind. I was filled with serenity and felicity and welcomed the letter as though I beheld in it an image, so to speak, of your noble disposition. To try to answer it point by point would take too long and perhaps I could not avoid excessive garrulity; but at any rate I shall not hesitate to say what it was that I especially approved. In the first place, the fact that the insolent behaviour to you of the Governor of Greece, if indeed a man of that sort can be called a Governor and not a tyrant, did not provoke your resentment,

362 Jan. (or end of 361) From Constantinople.

[1] Julian always scoffed at the disputes of the Arians with the various other sects of the Church.

[2] *i.e.* he was given the privilege of using an official carriage, provided by the state.

[3] For the question of the authenticity of this letter see Introduction, on Theodorus.

[6] MS. *οὔτω βαθέως*, Weil *οὔτω σταθερῶς*, Hercher, Hertlein *οὔτοι βαρέως*, Papadopoulos *οὔπω βαρέως*.

μενος τούτων εἰς σὲ γεγονέναι. τό γε μὴν τῇ πόλει βοηθεῖν ἐκείνῃ βούλεσθαι καὶ προθυμεῖσθαι, περὶ ἣν ἐποιήσω τὰς διατριβάς, ἐναργές[1] ἐστι φιλοσόφου γνώμης[2] τεκμήριον· ὥστε μοι δοκεῖ τὸ μὲν πρότερον Σωκράτει προσήκειν, τὸ δεύτερον δέ, οἶμαι, Μουσωνίῳ· ἐκεῖνος μὲν γὰρ ἔφη, ὅτι μὴ θεμιτὸν ἄνδρα σπουδαῖον πρός του τῶν χειρόνων καὶ φαύλων βλαβῆναι, ὁ δὲ ἐπεμέλετο Γυάρων[3] ἡνίκα[4] φεύγειν αὐτὸν ἐπέταττε Νέρων. ταῦτα ἐγὼ τῆς ἐπιστολῆς τῆς σῆς ἐπαινέσας, τὸ τρίτον οὐκ οἶδα ὅντινα τρόπον ἀποδέξομαι· γράφεις γὰρ κελεύων σημαίνειν ὅ τι ἄν μοι παρὰ μέλος πράττειν αὐτὸς ἢ λέγειν δοκῇς· ἐγὼ δέ, ὅτι μὲν πλέον ἐμαυτῷ νῦν ἢ σοὶ τῶν τοιούτων δεῖν ὑπολαμβάνω παραινέσεων, πολλὰ ἔχων εἰπεῖν, ἐς αὖθις ἀναβαλοῦμαι. τὸ μὲν οὖν αἴτημα τυχὸν οὐδὲ σοὶ προσήκει· περίεστι[5] γάρ σοι καὶ σχολή, καὶ φύσεως ἔχεις εὖ, καὶ φιλοσοφίας ἐρᾷς, εἴπερ τις ἄλλος τῶν πώποτε. τρία δὲ ἅμα ταῦτα ξυνελθόντα ἤρκεσεν ἀποφῆναι τὸν Ἀμφίονα τῆς παλαιᾶς μουσικῆς εὑρετήν, χρόνος,

[1] ἐναργὲς is omitted by Suidas in his quotation of the passage.

[2] ψυχῆς Suidas.

[3] βαρῶν Suidas, quoting from a faulty MS.

[4] ἡνίκα Suidas; MS. ὁπηνίκα, not Julianic.

[5] περίεστι—δεόμενοι quoted from a more complete text by Suidas, *Amphion*; given by Hertlein as *frag.* 1; τὸ μὲν—προσήκει omitted by Papadopoulos Y.

because you considered that none of these things had to do with you. Then again, that you are willing and eager to aid that city[1] in which you had spent your time is a clear proof of the philosophic mind; so that in my opinion the former course is worthy of Socrates, the latter, I should say, of Musonius. For Socrates declared[2] that heaven would not permit a righteous man to be harmed by anyone inferior to him and worthless, while Musonius concerned himself with the welfare of Gyara[3] when Nero decreed his exile. These two points in your letter I approve, but I am at a loss how to take the third. For you write to urge me to warn you whenever I think that you yourself do or say anything out of tune. For my part I could give you many proofs that I believe myself to be more in need than you are of such advice at the present time, but I will put that off till later. However the request is perhaps not even suitable for you to make; for you have abundant leisure, excellent natural gifts, and you love philosophy as much as any man who ever lived. And these three things combined sufficed to make Amphion known as the inventor of ancient music, namely, leisure, divine inspiration

[1] We cannot identify this city. Theodorus may have improved its water supply, which would give point to the allusion to Musonius at Gyara below.

[2] Plato, *Apology* 30D, Julian, *Oration* 2. 69B.

[3] The Emperors banished offenders to this barren island, one of the Cyclades. For the discovery of water there by Musonius see Philostratus, *Life of Apollonius* 7. 16. The *Nero* of Philostratus is an imaginary dialogue with Musonius at Corinth, where he is supposed to have been set by Nero to dig the Corinthian canal; Julian praises Musonius in Vol. 2, *To Themistius* 265C, D.

θεοῦ πνεῦμα,[1] ἔρως τε [2] ὑμνῳδίας· οὐδὲ [3] γὰρ ἡ τῶν ὀργάνων ἔνδεια πρὸς ταῦτα πέφυκεν ἀντιτάττεσθαι, ἀλλὰ καὶ ταῦτα ῥᾳδίως ἂν ὁ τῶν τριῶν τούτων μέτοχος ἐξεύροι. ἦ γὰρ οὐχὶ τοῦτον αὐτὸν ἀκοῇ παραδεδέγμεθα οὐ τὰς ἁρμονίας μόνον, αὐτὴν δὲ ἐπ' αὐταῖς ἐξευρεῖν τὴν λύραν, εἴτε δαιμονιωτέρᾳ χρησάμενον ἐπινοίᾳ, εἴτε τινὶ θείᾳ δόσει διά τινα συμμαχίαν ἀμήχανον; καὶ τῶν παλαιῶν οἱ πλεῖστοι τοῖς τρισὶ τούτοις ἐοίκασι μάλιστα προσσχόντες οὔτι πλαστῶς φιλοσοφῆσαι, οὐδενὸς ἄλλου δεόμενοι. χρὴ οὖν σε παρίστασθαι καὶ διὰ τῶν ἐπιστολῶν τὰ πρακτέα καὶ τὰ μὴ παραινεῖν ἡμῖν[4] προθύμως. ὁρῶμεν γὰρ καὶ τῶν στρατευομένων οὐ τοὺς εἰρηνεύοντας συμμαχίας δεομένους, τοὺς πονουμένους δέ, οἶμαι, τῷ πολέμῳ, καὶ τῶν κυβερνητῶν οὐχ οἱ μὴ πλέοντες τοὺς πλέοντας παρακαλοῦσιν, οἱ ναυτιλλόμενοι δὲ τοὺς σχολὴν ἄγοντας. οὕτως ἐξ ἀρχῆς δίκαιον ἐφάνη τοὺς σχολὴν ἄγοντας τοῖς ἐπὶ τῶν ἔργων ἀμύνειν καὶ παρεστάναι καὶ τὸ πρακτέον ὑφηγεῖσθαι, ἐπειδάν, οἶμαι, τὰ αὐτὰ πρεσβεύωσι. ταῦτα διανοούμενόν σε προσήκει τοῦθ' ὅπερ ἀξιοῖς παρ' ἡμῶν εἰς σὲ γίνεσθαι, δρᾶν, καὶ εἴ σοι φίλον, ταυτὶ ξυνθώμεθα, ἵν' ἐγὼ μέν, ὅ τι ἄν μοι φαίνηται περὶ τῶν σῶν ἁπάντων,

[1] θεοῦ πνεῦμα Suidas Hertlein; πνεῦμα θεῶν MSS. The former is more Julianic.

[2] τε Suidas omits. After ὑμνῳδίας Suidas gives eight verses not found in the MSS.

[3] οὐδὲ—δεόμενοι Suidas quotes; omitted by Papadopoulos MSS.

[4] ἡμῖν Buecheler adds.

and a love of minstrelsy.[1] For not even the lack of instruments avails to offset these gifts, but one who had these three for his portion could easily invent instruments also. Indeed, have we not received the tradition by hearsay that this very Amphion invented not only harmonies, but besides these the lyre itself, by employing either an almost godlike intelligence or some gift[2] of the gods in a sort of extraordinary co-operation with them? And most of the great ones of old seem to have attained to genuine philosophy[3] by setting their hearts on these three things above all, and not to have needed anything else. Therefore it is you who ought to stand by me and in your letters show your willingness to advise me what I ought to do and what not. For we observe in the case of soldiers that it is not those of them who are at peace who need allies, but, I should say, those who are hard pressed in war, and in the case of pilots those who are not at sea do not call to their aid those who are at sea, but those who are navigating call on those who are at leisure. Thus it has from the very first seemed right that men who are at leisure should help and stand by those who are occupied with tasks, and should suggest the right course of action, that is whenever they represent the same interests. It is well, then, that you should bear this in mind and act towards me as you think I should act towards you, and, if you like, let us make

[1] Possibly an echo of the lost play of Euripides, *Amphion frag.* 192 Nauck; cf. Philostratus, *Life of Apollonius* 7. 34, for a similar passage.

[2] Apollo son of Zeus is said to have given the lyre to Amphion.

[3] An echo of Plato, *Sophist* 216C and *Laws* 642C; cf. Julian, Vol. 1, *Oration* 2. 82B, 92B.

πρὸς σὲ σημαίνω,[1] σὺ δὲ αὖθις πρὸς ἐμέ περὶ τῶν ἐμῶν λόγων καὶ πράξεων· ταύτης γάρ, οἶμαι, τῆς ἀμοιβῆς οὐδὲν ἂν ἡμῖν γένοιτο κάλλιον. ἐρρωμένον σε ἡ θεία πρόνοια διαφυλάξαι πολλοῖς χρόνοις ἀδελφὲ ποθεινότατε. ἴδοιμί σε διὰ ταχέων, ὡς εὔχομαι.

17

Ζήνωνι.[2]

426 Πολλὰ μὲν καὶ ἄλλα σοι μαρτυρεῖ καὶ τῆς ἰατρικῆς τέχνης εἰς τὰ πρῶτα ἀνήκειν, καὶ ἤθους καὶ ἐπιεικείας καὶ βίου σωφροσύνης συμφώνως πρὸς τὴν τέχνην ἔχειν, νῦν δὲ προσῆλθε τὸ
B κεφάλαιον τῆς μαρτυρίας· τὴν τῶν Ἀλεξανδρέων πόλιν ἀπὼν ἐπιστρέφεις εἰς σεαυτόν· τοσοῦτον αὐτῇ κέντρον ὥσπερ μέλιττα ἐγκαταλέλοιπας.[3] εἰκότως· καλῶς γὰρ εἰρῆσθαι καὶ Ὁμήρῳ δοκεῖ τὸ

Εἷς ἰητρὸς ἀνὴρ πολλῶν ἀντάξιος ἄλλων.

σὺ δὲ οὐκ ἰατρὸς ἁπλῶς, ἀλλὰ καὶ διδάσκαλος τοῖς βουλομένοις τῆς τέχνης, ὥστε σχεδὸν ὃ πρὸς τοὺς πολλούς εἰσιν οἱ ἰατροί, τοῦτο ἐκείνοις σύ.
C λύει δέ σοι τὴν φυγὴν καὶ ἡ πρόφασις αὐτή, καὶ μάλα λαμπρῶς. εἰ γὰρ διὰ Γεώργιον μετέστης

[1] Weil; MS. ἐμμένω.
[2] Hertlein 45; ἀρχιητρῷ is added to the title in χ.
[3] Wyttenbach, καταλέλοιπας MSS. Hertlein.

[1] Zeno had been exiled by George, the Arian bishop of Alexandria, in 360. He was a friend and correspondent of

this compact, that I am to point out to you what are my views concerning all your affairs, and you in return are to do the same for me concerning my sayings and doings. Nothing, in my opinion, could be more valuable for us than this reciprocity. May divine Providence keep you in good health for long to come, my well-beloved brother! May I see you soon, as I pray to do!

17

To Zeno[1]

THERE is indeed abundant evidence of other kinds that you have attained to the first rank in the art of medicine and that your morals, uprightness and temperate life are in harmony with your professional skill. But now has been added the crowning evidence. Though absent, you are winning to your cause the whole city of Alexandria. So keen a sting, like a bee's, have you left in her.[2] This is natural; for I think that Homer was right when he said "One physician is worth many other men."[3] And you are not simply a physician, but also a teacher of that art for those who desire to learn, so that I might almost say that what physicians are as compared with the mass of men, you are, compared with other physicians. This is the reason for putting an end to your exile, and with very great distinction for yourself. For if it was owing to George that you were removed

362 early From Constantinople

Libanius. George had been murdered by the mob on December 24th, 361.

[2] For this echo of Eupolis, a sophistic commonplace, cf. Vol. I. *Oration* I. 33A.

[3] *Iliad* 11. 514; in our texts the line begins ἰητρὸς γάρ.

τῆς Ἀλεξανδρείας, οὐ δικαίως μετέστης, καὶ δικαιότατα ἂν ὀπίσω κατέλθοις. κάτιθι τοίνυν ἐπίτιμος καὶ τὸ πρότερον ἔχων ἀξίωμα, καὶ ἡμῖν κοινὴ παρ' ἀμφοτέροις χάρις ἀποκείσθω, Ἀλεξανδρεῦσι μὲν Ζήνωνα, σοὶ δὲ ἀποδοῦσα τὴν Ἀλεξάνδρειαν.

18[1]

450 . . . . τοῦθ' ὅπερ ὑπάρχει τοῖς ξύλοις, οὐκ ἄξιόν
B ἐστι νέμειν ἀνθρώποις; ὑποκείσθω γὰρ ἄνθρωπον ἱερωσύνης ἀντειλῆφθαι τυχὸν οὐκ ἄξιον· οὐ χρὴ φείδεσθαι μέχρι τοσούτου, μέχρις ἂν ἐπιγνόντες ὡς πονηρός ἐστι καὶ τῆς λειτουργίας αὐτὸν εἴρξαντες τὸ προπετῶς ἴσως προστεθὲν ὄνομα τοῦ ἱερέως ὑπεύθυνον ἀποδείξωμεν ὕβρει καὶ κολάσει καὶ ζημίᾳ; ταῦτα εἰ μὲν ἀγνοεῖς, οὐδὲ
C τῶν ἄλλων ἔοικας εἰδέναι τι τῶν μετρίων. ἐπεὶ σοὶ ποῦ μέτεστιν ἐμπειρίας ὅλως τῶν δικαίων, ὃς οὐκ οἶσθα τί μὲν ἱερεύς, τί δὲ ἰδιώτης; ποῦ δέ σοι μέτεστι σωφροσύνης, ὅσπερ[2] ἠκίσω τοῦτον, ᾧ καὶ θώκων ἐχρῆν ἐξανίστασθαι; ὃ αἴσχιστον[3]

[1] Hertlein 62. The title is lost.
[2] ὅσπερ for εἴπερ Reiske, Hertlein.
[3] ὃ αἴσχιστον Hertlein suggests; MSS., Hertlein τὸ αἰσχρόν.

---

[1] Julian writes as supreme pontiff, to whom a high-priest, perhaps Theodorus, had appealed for protection for a priest who had been assaulted. There is no evidence that this priest was the Pegasius of *Letter* 19, as Asmus thinks.
[2] The first part of the letter with the title is lost.

from Alexandria, you were removed unjustly, and it would be most just that you should return from exile. Do you, therefore, return in all honour, and in possession of your former dignity. And let the favour that I bestow be credited to me by both parties in common, since it restores Zeno to the Alexandrians and Alexandria to you.

18

To an Official[1]

. . .[2] is it not right to pay to human beings this respect that we feel for things made of wood?[3] For let us suppose that a man who has obtained the office of priest is perhaps unworthy of it. Ought we not to show forbearance until we have actually decided that he is wicked, and only then by excluding him from his official functions show that it was the overhasty bestowal of the title of "priest" that was subject to punishment by obloquy and chastisement and a fine? If you do not know this you are not likely to have any proper sense at all of what is fitting. What experience can you have of the rights of men in general if you do not know the difference between a priest and a layman? And what sort of self-control can you have when you maltreated one at whose approach you ought to have risen from your seat? For this is the most

362 Before May 12th From Constantinople

[3] *i.e.* images of the gods. In Vol. 2, *Fragment of a Letter* 297A, Julian says that we must respect priests no less than the stones of which altars are made. There are several close resemblances between these two pastoral letters. Reiske translated ξύλοις "trees," *i.e.* we allow them time to recover before cutting them down.

ἁπάντων καί σοι μάλιστα μήτε πρὸς θεοὺς μήτε πρὸς ἀνθρώπους ἔχον καλῶς. οἱ μὲν τῶν Γαλιλαίων ἴσως ἐπίσκοποι καὶ πρεσβύτεροι συγκαθίζουσί σοι, καὶ εἰ μὴ δημοσίᾳ[1] δι' ἐμέ,
D λάθρᾳ καὶ ἐν τῷ οἴκῳ· διὰ σὲ δὲ τέτυπται ὁ ἱερεύς· οὐ γὰρ ἂν ἦλθεν ἐπὶ ταύτην ὁ παρ' ὑμῖν ἀρχιερεὺς μὰ Δία τὴν δέησιν. ἀλλ' ἐπειδή σοι πέφηνε μυθώδη τὰ παρ' Ὁμήρῳ, τῶν τοῦ Διδυμαίου δεσπότου χρησμῶν ἐπάκουσον, εἴ σοι φανείη πάλαι μὲν ἔργῳ νουθετήσας καλῶς τοὺς Ἕλληνας, ὕστερον δὲ τοὺς οὐ[2] σωφρονοῦντας διδάσκων τοῖς λόγοις·

451 Ὅσσοι ἐς ἀρητῆρας ἀτασθαλίῃσι νόοιο
Ἀθανάτων ῥέζουσ' ἀποφώλια, καὶ γεράεσσιν
Ἀντία βουλεύουσιν ἀδεισιθέοισι λογισμοῖς,
Οὐκέθ' ὅλην βιότοιο διεκπερόωσιν ἀταρπόν,
Ὅσσοι περ μακάρεσσιν ἐλωβήσαντο θεοῖσιν
B Ὧν κεῖνοι θεόσεπτον ἕλον θεραπηΐδα τιμήν.

ὁ μὲν οὖν θεὸς οὐ τοὺς τύπτοντας οὐδὲ τοὺς ὑβρίζοντας, ἀλλὰ τοὺς ἀποστεροῦντας τῶν τιμῶν εἶναι φησί[3] θεοῖς ἐχθρούς· ὁ δὲ τυπτήσας ἱερόσυλος ἂν εἴη. ἐγὼ τοίνυν, ἐπειδήπερ εἰμὶ κατὰ μὲν τὰ πάτρια μέγας ἀρχιερεύς, ἔλαχον δὲ νῦν καὶ τοῦ Διδυμαίου
C προφητεύειν, ἀπαγορεύω σοι τρεῖς περιόδους σε-

[1] δημοσίᾳ Cobet, δημοσίως Hertlein, MSS.
[2] οὐ Cobet adds.
[3] For the lacuna after εἶναι Spanheim suggests φησί.

disgraceful thing of all, and for it in the eyes of gods and men alike you are peculiarly to blame. Perhaps the bishops and elders of the Galilaeans sit with you, though not in public because of me, yet secretly and in the house; and the priest has actually been beaten by your order, for otherwise your high-priest would not, by Zeus, have come to make this appeal. But since what happened in Homer[1] seems to you merely mythical, listen to the oracular words of the Lord of Didymus,[2] that you may see clearly that, even as in bygone days he nobly exhorted the Hellenes in very deed, so too in later times he admonished the intemperate in these words: "Whosoever with reckless mind works wickedness against the priests of the deathless gods and plots against their honours with plans that fear not the gods, never shall he travel life's path to the end, seeing that he has sinned against the blessed gods whose honour and holy service those priests have in charge." Thus, then, the god declares that those who even deprive priests of their honours are detested by the gods, not to mention those who beat and insult them! But a man who strikes a priest has committed sacrilege. Wherefore, since by the laws of our fathers I am supreme pontiff, and moreover have but now received the function of prophecy from the god of Didymus,[3] I forbid you for three revolutions

[1] Probably Julian refers to the wrong done to the priest Chryses which was avenged by Apollo in *Iliad* 1.

[2] Apollo. For this oracle cf. Vol. 2, *Fragment of a Letter* 297CD, where it is also quoted.

[3] The oracle of the Didymaean Apollo was at Didyma, Miletus, where an inscription on a column in honour of Julian has been discovered; cf. *Bulletin de correspondance hellénique*, 1877.

λήνης μή τοι τῶν εἰς ἱερέα μηδὲν ἐνοχλεῖν· εἰ δὲ ἐν τούτῳ τῷ χρόνῳ φανείης ἄξιος, ἐπιστείλαντός μοι τοῦ τῆς πόλεως ἀρχιερέως, εἰ παραδεκτὸς εἴης ἡμῖν, ἐσαῦθις μετὰ τῶν θεῶν βουλεύσομαι. ταύτην ἐγώ σοι τῆς προπετείας ἐπιτίθημι ζημίαν. τὰς δὲ ἐκ τῶν θεῶν ἀρὰς πάλαι μὲν εἰώθεσαν οἱ παλαιοὶ λέγειν καὶ γράφειν, οὐ μὴν ἔμοιγε φαί-
D νεται καλῶς ἔχειν· οὐδαμοῦ γὰρ αὐτοὶ πεποιηκότες οἱ θεοὶ φαίνονται. καὶ ἄλλως εὐχῶν εἶναι δεῖ διακόνους ἡμᾶς. ὅθεν οἶμαι καὶ συνεύχομαί σοι πολλὰ λιπαρήσαντι τοὺς θεοὺς ἀδείας τυχεῖν ὧν ἐπλημμέλησας.

19[1]

Πηγάσιον ἡμεῖς οὔποτ᾽ ἂν προσήκαμεν ῥᾳδίως, εἰ μὴ σαφῶς ἐπεπείσμεθα, ὅτι καὶ πρότερον εἶναι δοκῶν τῶν Γαλιλαίων ἐπίσκοπος ἠπίστατο σέβεσθαι καὶ τιμᾶν τοὺς θεούς. οὐκ ἀκοὴν ἐγώ σοι ταῦτα ἀπαγγέλλω τῶν πρὸς ἔχθραν καὶ φιλίαν λέγειν εἰωθότων, ἐπεὶ καὶ ἐμοὶ πάνυ διετεθρύλητο τὰ τοιαῦτα περὶ αὐτοῦ, καὶ ναὶ μὰ τοὺς θεοὺς ᾤμην οὕτω χρῆναι μισεῖν αὐτὸν ὡς οὐδένα τῶν πονηροτάτων. ἐπεὶ δὲ κληθεὶς εἰς τὸ στρατόπεδον

[1] Hertlein 78; first published from *Harleianus* 5610 by Henning in *Hermes*, 1875. The title is lost.

---

[1] We do not know the name of this city and cannot identify the official who is in disgrace.

of the moon to meddle in anything that concerns a priest. But if during this period you appear to be worthy, and the high-priest of the city[1] so writes to me, I will thereupon take counsel with the gods whether you may be received by us once more. This is the penalty that I award for your rash conduct. As for curses from the gods, men of old in days of old used to utter them and write them, but I do not think that this was well done; for there is no evidence at all that the gods themselves devised those curses. And besides, we ought to be the ministers of prayers, not curses. Therefore I believe and join my prayers to yours that after earnest supplication to the gods you may obtain pardon for your errors.

19

To a Priest[2]

I SHOULD never have favoured Pegasius unhesitatingly if I had not had clear proofs that even in 362 or early in 363
former days, when he had the title of Bishop of the Galilaeans, he was wise enough to revere and honour the gods. This I do not report to you on hearsay from men whose words are always adapted to their personal dislikes and friendships, for much current gossip of this sort about him has reached me, and the gods know that I once thought I ought to detest him above all other depraved persons.[3] But when I

[2] Asmus is positive that this is the high-priest Theodorus, but there is no evidence for this. He dates the letter from Constantinople early in 362. Pegasius is otherwise unknown.

[3] *i. e.* Christians, whom Julian often calls πονηροί, "depraved."

ὑπὸ τοῦ μακαρίτου Κωνσταντίου ταύτην ἐπορευόμην τὴν ὁδόν, ἀπὸ τῆς Τρῳάδος ὄρθρου βαθέος διαναστὰς ἦλθον εἰς τὸ Ἴλιον περὶ πλήθουσαν ἀγοράν. ὁ δὲ ὑπήντησέ μοι[1] καὶ βουλομένῳ τὴν πόλιν ἱστορεῖν—ἦν γάρ μοι τοῦτο πρόσχημα τοῦ φοιτᾶν εἰς τὰ ἱερά—περιηγητής τε ἐγένετο καὶ ἐξενάγησέ με πανταχοῦ. ἄκουε τοίνυν ἔργα καὶ λόγους, ἀφ' ὧν ἄν τις εἰκάσειεν οὐκ ἀγνώμονα τὰ πρὸς τοὺς θεοὺς αὐτόν.

Ἡρῷόν ἐστιν Ἕκτορος, ὅπου χαλκοῦς ἕστηκεν ἀνδριὰς ἐν ναΐσκῳ βραχεῖ. τούτῳ τὸν μέγαν ἀντέστησαν Ἀχιλλέα κατὰ τὸ ὕπαιθρον. εἰ τὸν τόπον ἐθεάσω, γνωρίζεις δήπουθεν ὃ λέγω. τὴν μὲν οὖν ἱστορίαν, δι' ἣν ὁ μέγας Ἀχιλλεὺς ἀντιτεταγμένος αὐτῷ πᾶν τὸ ὕπαιθρον κατείληφεν, ἔξεστί σοι τῶν περιηγητῶν ἀκούειν. ἐγὼ δὲ καταλαβὼν ἐμπύρους ἔτι, μικροῦ δέω φάναι λαμπροὺς ἔτι τοὺς βωμοὺς καὶ λιπαρῶς ἀληλιμμένην τὴν τοῦ Ἕκτορος εἰκόνα, πρὸς Πηγάσιον ἀπιδὼν "Τί ταῦτα"; εἶπον, "Ἰλιεῖς θύουσιν"; ἀποπειρώμενος ἠρέμα, πῶς ἔχει γνώμης· ὁ δὲ "Καὶ τί τοῦτο ἄτοπον, ἄνδρα ἀγαθὸν ἑαυτῶν πολίτην, ὥσπερ ἡμεῖς," ἔφη, "τοὺς μάρτυρας, εἰ θεραπεύουσιν"; ἡ μὲν οὖν εἰκὼν οὐχ ὑγιής· ἡ δε προαίρεσις ἐν ἐκείνοις ἐξεταζομένη τοῖς καιροῖς ἀστεία. τί δὴ τὸ μετὰ τοῦτο; "Βαδίσωμεν," ἔφην, "ἐπὶ τὸ τῆς Ἰλιάδος Ἀθηνᾶς τέμενος."

[1] μοι Hertlein would add.

was summoned[1] to his headquarters by Constantius of blessed memory I was travelling by this route, and after rising at early dawn I came from Troas to Ilios about the middle of the morning. Pegasius came to meet me, as I wished to explore the city,—this was my excuse for visiting the temples,—and he was my guide and showed me all the sights. So now let me tell you what he did and said, and from it one may guess that he was not lacking in right sentiments towards the gods.

Hector has a hero's shrine there and his bronze statue stands in a tiny little temple. Opposite this they have set up a figure of the great Achilles in the unroofed court. If you have seen the spot you will certainly recognise my description of it. You can learn from the guides the story that accounts for the fact that great Achilles was set up opposite to him and takes up the whole of the unroofed court. Now I found that the altars were still alight, I might almost say still blazing, and that the statue of Hector had been anointed till it shone. So I looked at Pegasius and said: "What does this mean? Do the people of Ilios offer sacrifices?" This was to test him cautiously to find out his own views. He replied: "Is it not natural that they should worship a brave man who was their own citizen, just as we worship the martyrs?" Now the analogy was far from sound; but his point of view and intentions were those of a man of culture, if you consider the times in which we then lived. Observe what followed. "Let us go," said he, "to the shrine of Athene of

[1] In the winter of 354, when he was on his way from Nicomedia to the court at Milan, after the death of Gallus; first he came to Alexandria Troas, and then to New Ilios.

ὁ δὲ καὶ μάλα προθύμως ἀπήγαγέ με καὶ ἀνέῳξε τὸν νεών, καὶ ὥσπερ μαρτυρόμενος ἐπέδειξέ μοι πάντα ἀκριβῶς σῶα τὰ ἀγάλματα, καὶ ἔπραξεν οὐδὲν ὧν εἰώθασιν οἱ δυσσεβεῖς ἐκεῖνοι πράττειν, ἐπὶ τοῦ μετώπου τοῦ δυσσεβοῦς τὸ ὑπόμνημα σκιαγραφοῦντες, οὐδὲ ἐσύριττεν, ὥσπερ ἐκεῖνοι, αὐτὸς καθ' ἑαυτόν· ἡ γὰρ ἄκρα θεολογία παρ' αὐτοῖς ἐστι δύο ταῦτα, συρίττειν τε πρὸς τοὺς δαίμονας καὶ σκιαγραφεῖν ἐπὶ τοῦ μετώπου τὸν σταυρόν.

Δύο ταῦτα ἐπηγγειλάμην εἰπεῖν σοι· τρίτον δὲ ἐλθὸν ἐπὶ νοῦν οὐκ οἶμαι χρῆναι σιωπᾶν. ἠκολούθησέ μοι καὶ πρὸς τὸ Ἀχίλλειον ὁ αὐτός, καὶ ἀπέδειξε τὸν τάφον σῶον· ἐπεπύσμην δὲ καὶ τοῦτον ὑπ' αὐτοῦ διεσκάφθαι. ὁ δὲ καὶ μάλα σεβόμενος αὐτῷ προσῄει. ταῦτα εἶδον αὐτός. ἀκήκοα δὲ παρὰ τῶν νῦν ἐχθρῶς ἐχόντων πρὸς αὐτόν, ὅτι καὶ προσεύχοιτο λάθρᾳ καὶ προσκυνοίη τὸν Ἥλιον. ἆρα οὐκ ἂν ἐδέξω με καὶ ἰδιώτην μαρτυροῦντα; τῆς περὶ τοὺς θεοὺς διαθέσεως ἑκάστου τίνες ἂν εἶεν ἀξιοπιστότεροι μάρτυρες αὐτῶν τῶν θεῶν; ἡμεῖς ἂν ἱερέα Πηγάσιον ἐποιοῦμεν, εἰ συνεγνώκειμεν αὐτῷ τι περὶ τοὺς θεοὺς δυσσεβές; εἰ δὲ ἐν ἐκείνοις τοῖς χρόνοις εἴτε δυναστείας ὀρεγόμενος, εἴθ', ὅπερ πρὸς ἡμᾶς ἔφη πολλάκις, ὑπὲρ τοῦ σῶσαι τῶν θεῶν τὰ ἕδη τὰ ῥάκια ταῦτα περιαμπέσχετο[1] καὶ τὴν ἀσέβειαν

[1] περιημπίσχετο? Hertlein.

Ilios." Thereupon with the greatest eagerness he led me there and opened the temple, and as though he were producing evidence he showed me all the statues in perfect preservation, nor did he behave at all as those impious men do usually, I mean when they make the sign on their impious foreheads, nor did he hiss[1] to himself as they do. For these two things are the quintessence of their theology, to hiss at demons and make the sign of the cross on their foreheads.

These are the two things that I promised to tell you. But a third occurs to me which I think I must not fail to mention. This same Pegasius went with me to the temple of Achilles as well and showed me the tomb in good repair; yet I had been informed that this also had been pulled to pieces by him. But he approached it with great reverence; I saw this with my own eyes. And I have heard from those who are now his enemies that he also used to offer prayers to Helios and worship him in secret. Would you not have accepted me as a witness even if I had been merely a private citizen? Of each man's attitude towards the gods who could be more trustworthy witnesses than the gods themselves? Should I have appointed Pegasius a priest if I had any evidence of impiety towards the gods on his part? And if in those past days, whether because he was ambitious for power, or, as he has often asserted to me, he clad himself in those rags in order to save the temples of the gods, and only pretended to be irreligious so far as the name

[1] Dieterich, *Mithrasliturgie*, pp. 40, 221, discusses the practice in magic, and especially in the ritual of Mithras, of hissing and whistling.

μέχρις ὀνόματος ὑπεκρίνατο· πέφηνε γὰρ οὐδὲν οὐδαμοῦ τῶν ἱερῶν ἠδικηκὼς πλὴν ὀλίγων παντάπασι λίθων ἐκ καλύμματος,[1] ἵνα αὐτῷ σώζειν ἐξῇ τὰ λοιπά· τοῦτο ἐν λόγῳ ποιούμεθα καὶ οὐκ αἰσχυνόμεθα ταῦτα περὶ αὐτὸν πράττοντες ὅσαπερ Ἀφόβιος ἐποίει καὶ οἱ Γαλιλαῖοι πάντες προσεύχονται πάσχοντα ἰδεῖν αὐτόν; εἴ τί μοι προσέχεις, οὐ τοῦτον μόνον, ἀλλὰ καὶ τοὺς ἄλλους, οἳ μετατέθεινται, τιμήσεις, ἵν' οἱ μὲν ῥᾷον ὑπακούσωσιν ἡμῖν ἐπὶ τὰ καλὰ προκαλουμένοις, οἱ δ' ἧττον χαίρωσιν. εἰ δὲ τοὺς αὐτομάτους ἰόντας ἀπελαύνοιμεν, οὐδεὶς ὑπακούσεται ῥᾳδίως παρακαλοῦσιν.

20

Ἰουλιανὸς Θεοδώρῳ ἀρχιερεῖ.[2]

452 Ἐμοὶ πρὸς σὲ πεποίηται παρὰ τοὺς ἄλλους ἰδιαίτερον ἐπιστολῆς εἶδος, ὅτι σοι καὶ πλέον μέτεστι τῆς πρὸς ἐμὲ φιλίας ἤπερ οἶμαι τοῖς ἄλλοις· ἔστι γὰρ ἡμῖν ὁ κοινὸς καθηγεμὼν οὐ μικρά, καὶ μέμνησαι δήπου. χρόνος δὲ οὐ βραχὺς ὅτε
B διατρίβων ἔτι κατὰ τὴν ἑσπέραν, ἐπειδή σε λίαν ἀρέσκειν ἐπυθόμην αὐτῷ, φίλον ἐνόμισα· καίτοι δοκεῖν[3] ἔχον ἐκεῖνο καλῶς εἴωθεν ἐμοὶ διὰ περιττὴν εὐλάβειαν τὸ οὐ γὰρ ἔγωγε ἤντησ' οὐδὲ ἴδον, καὶ

[1] For καταλύματος MSS. Hertlein suggests καλύμματος.
[2] Hertlein 63. Before Θεοδώρῳ Hertlein, following Heyler, brackets Καῖσαρ the reading of *Vossianus*.
[3] δοκεῖν so Capps for a lacuna here; Spanheim συμβαίνειν.

---

[1] See Introduction. Those who date this letter early in 363, following Reiske, regard it as part of the *Letter to a Priest*, Vol. 2, written after the burning of the temple of

of the thing went—indeed it is clear that he never injured any temple anywhere except for what amounted to a few stones, and that was as a blind, that he might be able to save the rest—well then we are taking this into account and are we not ashamed to behave to him as Aphobius did, and as the Galilaeans all pray to see him treated? If you care at all for my wishes you will honour not him only but any others who are converted, in order that they may the more readily heed me when I summon them to good works, and those others may have less cause to rejoice. But if we drive away those who come to us of their own free will, no one will be ready to heed when we summon.

20

To the High-priest Theodorus[1]

I HAVE written you a more familiar sort of letter than to the others, because you, I believe, have more friendly feelings than others towards me. For it means much that we had the same guide,[2] and I am sure you remember him. A long time ago, when I was still living in the west,[3] I learned that he had the highest regard for you, and for that reason I counted you my friend, and yet because of their excessive caution, I have usually thought these words well said,

362 Before May 12th From Constantinople

"For I never met or saw him";[4]

Apollo at Daphne in October 362. It seems more likely that that fragment contains the general instructions for priests promised by Julian in this letter.

[2] Maximus of Ephesus, who had initiated Julian and perhaps Theodorus also into the Mysteries of Mithras.

[3] *i.e.* in Gaul. [4] *Iliad* 4. 374; *Odyssey* 4. 200.

καλῶς[1] ἡγεῖσθαι χρὴ φιλίας μὲν γνῶσιν, γνώσεως δὲ πεῖραν. ἀλλ' ἦν τις, ὡς ἔοικεν, οὐκ ἐλάχιστος
C παρ' ἐμοὶ λόγος καὶ τοῦ Αὐτὸς ἔφα. διόπερ ἐγὼ καὶ τότε σε τοῖς γνωρίμοις ᾤμην δεῖν ἐγκαταλέγειν, καὶ νῦν ἐπιτρέπω πρᾶγμα ἐμοὶ μὲν φίλον, ἀνθρώποις δὲ πᾶσι πανταχοῦ λυσιτελέστατον. σὺ δὲ εἰ καλῶς, ὥσπερ οὖν ἄξιον ἐλπίζειν, αὐτὸ μεταχειρίσαιο, ἴσθι πολλὴν μὲν εὐφροσύνην ἐνταῦθα παρέξων, ἐλπίδα δὲ ἀγαθὴν μείζονα τὴν εἰς τὸ μέλλον. οὐ γὰρ δὴ καὶ ἡμεῖς ἐσμεν τῶν πεπει-
D σμένων τὰς ψυχὰς ἤτοι προαπόλλυσθαι τῶν σωμάτων ἢ συναπόλλυσθαι, πειθόμεθα δὲ τῶν μὲν ἀνθρώπων οὐδενί, τοῖς θεοῖς δὲ μόνον, οὓς δὴ καὶ μάλιστα ταῦτα εἰκὸς εἰδέναι μόνους, εἴ γε χρὴ καλεῖν εἰκὸς τὸ ἀναγκαῖον· ὡς τοῖς μὲν ἀνθρώποις ἁρμόζει περὶ τῶν τοιούτων εἰκάζειν, ἐπίστασθαι δὲ αὐτὰ τοὺς θεοὺς ἀνάγκη.

Τί τοῦτο οὖν ἐστιν ὅ φημί σοι νῦν ἐπιτρέπειν; ἄρχειν τῶν περὶ τὴν Ἀσίαν ἱερῶν ἁπάντων αἱρου-
453 μένῳ[2] τοὺς καθ' ἑκάστην πόλιν ἱερέας καὶ ἀπονέμοντι τὸ πρέπον ἑκάστῳ. πρέπει δὲ ἐπιείκεια μὲν πρῶτον ἄρχοντι χρηστότης τε ἐπ' αὐτῇ καὶ φιλανθρωπία πρὸς τοὺς ἀξίους αὐτῶν τυγχάνειν. ὡς ὅστις γε ἀδικεῖ μὲν ἀνθρώπους, ἀνόσιος δ' ἐστὶ πρὸς θεούς, θρασὺς δὲ πρὸς πάντας, ἢ διδακτέος μετὰ παρρησίας ἐστὶν ἢ μετ' ἐμβριθείας κολαστέος. ὅσα μὲν οὖν χρὴ κοινῇ συντάξαι περὶ τῶν ἱερέων[3]

[1] καὶ καλῶς Capps; ὡς MSS., Hertlein.
[2] . . . ουμενω Vossianus; ἐπισκοπουμένῳ Hertlein; αἱρουμένῳ Cobet.
[3] Hertlein, MSS. ἱερῶν.

and well said is "Before we love we must know, and before we can know we must test by experience." But it seems that after all a certain other saying has most weight with me, namely, "The Master has spoken."[1] That is why I thought even then that I ought to count you among my friends, and now I entrust to you a task that is dear to my heart, while to all men everywhere it is of the greatest benefit. And if, as I have the right to expect, you administer the office well, be assured that you will rejoice me greatly now and give me still greater good hope for the future life. For I certainly am not one of those who believe that the soul perishes before the body or along with it, nor do I believe any human being but only the gods; since it is likely that they alone have the most perfect knowledge of these matters, if indeed we ought to use the word "likely" of what is inevitably true; since it is fitting for men to conjecture about such matters, but the gods must have complete knowledge.

What then is this office which I say I now entrust to you? It is the government of all the temples in Asia, with power to appoint the priests in every city and to assign to each what is fitting. Now the qualities that befit one in this high office are, in the first place, fairness, and next, goodness and benevolence towards those who deserve to be treated thus. For any priest who behaves unjustly to his fellow men and impiously towards the gods, or is overbearing to all, must either be admonished with plain speaking or chastised with great severity. As for the regulations which I must make more complete for the guidance of priests in general, you

[1] This Pythagorean phrase is the original of *Ipse dixit.*

ἁπάντων ἐντελέστερον, αὐτίκα μάλα σὺν τοῖς ἄλ-
λοις εἴσει, μικρὰ δὲ τέως ὑποθέσθαι σοι βούλομαι.
B δίκαιος δὲ εἶ πείθεσθαί μοι τὰ τοιαῦτα. καὶ γὰρ
οὐδὲ ἀποσχεδιάζω τὰ πολλὰ τῶν τοιούτων, ὡς
ἴσασιν οἱ θεοὶ πάντες, ἀλλά, εἴπερ τις ἄλλος,
εὐλαβής εἰμι καὶ φεύγω τὴν καινοτομίαν ἐν ἅπασι
μέν, ὡς ἔπος εἰπεῖν, ἰδίᾳ δὲ ἐν τοῖς πρὸς τοὺς
θεούς, οἰόμενος χρῆναι τοὺς πατρίους ἐξ ἀρχῆς
φυλάττεσθαι νόμους, οὓς ὅτι μὲν ἔδοσαν οἱ θεοί,
φανερόν· οὐ γὰρ ἂν ἦσαν οὕτω καλοὶ παρὰ ἀνθρώ-
C πων ἁπλῶς γενόμενοι. συμβὰν δὲ αὐτοὺς ἀμε-
ληθῆναι καὶ διαφθαρῆναι πλούτου καὶ τρυφῆς
ἐπικρατησάντων, οἶμαι δεῖν ὥσπερ ἀφ᾽ ἑστίας ἐπι-
μεληθῆναι τῶν τοιούτων. ὁρῶν οὖν πολλὴν μὲν
ὀλιγωρίαν οὖσαν ἡμῖν πρὸς τοὺς θεούς, ἅπασαν
δὲ εὐλάβειαν τὴν εἰς τοὺς κρείττονας ἀπεληλα-
μένην ὑπὸ τῆς ἀκαθάρτου καὶ χυδαίας [1] τρυφῆς, ἀεὶ
μὲν ὠδυράμην ἐγὼ κατ᾽ ἐμαυτὸν τὰ τοιαῦτα, τοὺς
μὲν τῇ Ἰουδαίων [2] εὐσεβείας σχολῇ προσέχοντας
D οὕτω διαπύρους, ὡς αἱρεῖσθαι μὲν ὑπὲρ αὐτῆς
θάνατον, ἀνέχεσθαι δὲ πᾶσαν ἔνδειαν καὶ λιμόν,
ὑείων ὅπως μὴ γεύσαιντο μηδὲ πνικτοῦ [3] μηδ᾽ ἄρα
τοῦ ἀποθλιβέντος· ἡμᾶς δὲ οὕτω ῥᾳθύμως τὰ
πρὸς τοὺς θεοὺς διακειμένους, ὥστε ἐπιλελῆσθαι
μὲν τῶν πατρίων, ἀγνοεῖν δὲ λοιπόν, εἰ καὶ ἐτάχθη

[1] καὶ χυδαίας Hertlein suggests for lacuna; ταύτης Cobet.
[2] τῇ Ἰουδαίων Hertlein suggests for lacuna μὲν . . . ων.
[3] . . . τοῦ MS. πνικτοῦ Spanheim.

---

[1] Literally "from the hearth," *i.e.* from their origin, a proverb.
[2] For Julian's tolerant attitude to the Jewish religion, cf. *To the Jews*, p. 177.

as well as the others will soon learn them from me, but meanwhile I wish to make a few suggestions to you. You have good reason to obey me in such matters. Indeed in such a case I very seldom act offhand, as all the gods know, and no one could be more circumspect; and I avoid innovations in all things, so to speak, but more peculiarly in what concerns the gods. For I hold that we ought to observe the laws that we have inherited from our forefathers, since it is evident that the gods gave them to us. For they would not be as perfect as they are if they had been derived from mere men. Now since it has come to pass that they have been neglected and corrupted, and wealth and luxury have become supreme, I think that I ought to consider them carefully as though from their cradle.[1] Therefore, when I saw that there is among us great indifference about the gods and that all reverence for the heavenly powers has been driven out by impure and vulgar luxury, I always secretly lamented this state of things. For I saw that those whose minds were turned to the doctrines of the Jewish religion [2] are so ardent in their belief that they would choose to die for it, and to endure utter want and starvation rather than taste pork or any animal that has been strangled [3] or had the life squeezed out of it; whereas we are in such a state of apathy about religious matters that we have forgotten the customs of our forefathers, and therefore we actually do not know whether any such rule has

[3] This is not directly prohibited in the Old Testament, but cf. *Deuteronomy* 12. 23, where it is implied; and, for the New Testament, *Acts* 15. 29 "That ye abstain from things strangled."

πώποτέ τι τοιοῦτον. ἀλλ' οὗτοι μὲν ἐν μέρει θεοσεβεῖς ὄντες, ἐπείπερ θεὸν[1] τιμῶσι τὸν ὡς[2]
454 ἀληθῶς ὄντα δυνατώτατον καὶ ἀγαθώτατον, ὃς ἐπιτροπεύει τὸν αἰσθητὸν κόσμον, ὃν εὖ οἶδ' ὅτι καὶ ἡμεῖς ἄλλοις θεραπεύομεν ὀνόμασιν, εἰκότα μοι δοκοῦσι ποιεῖν, τοὺς νόμους μὴ παραβαίνοντες, ἐκεῖνο δὲ[3] μόνον ἁμαρτάνειν, ὅτι μὴ καὶ τοὺς ἄλλους θεούς, ἀρέσκοντες τούτῳ μάλιστα τῷ θεῷ, θεραπεύουσιν, ἀλλ' ἡμῖν οἴονται τοῖς ἔθνεσιν ἀπο-
B κεκληρῶσθαι μόνοις αὐτούς, ἀλαζονείᾳ βαρβαρικῇ πρὸς ταυτηνὶ τὴν ἀπόνοιαν ἐπαρθέντες· οἱ δὲ ἐκ τῆς Γαλιλαίας[4] δυσσεβείας ὥσπερ τι νόσημα τῷ βίῳ τὴν ἑαυτῶν . . .

21

Αὐτοκράτωρ Καῖσαρ Ἰουλιανὸς Μέγιστος Σεβαστὸς Ἀλεξανδρέων τῷ δήμῳ[5]

378 Εἰ μὴ τὸν Ἀλέξανδρον τὸν οἰκιστὴν ὑμῶν καὶ πρό γε τούτου τὸν θεὸν τὸν μέγαν τὸν ἁγιώτατον
D Σάραπιν αἰδεῖσθε, τοῦ κοινοῦ γοῦν ὑμᾶς καὶ ἀνθρωπίνου καὶ πρέποντος πῶς οὐκ εἰσῆλθε λόγος οὐδείς; προσθήσω δὲ ὅτι[6] καὶ ἡμῶν, οὓς οἱ θεοὶ πάντες, ἐν

[1] θεὸν Cobet suggests, ὃν MSS.
[2] τὸν ὡς Cobet suggests τιμῶσι . . . ἀλλ' MSS. οὐ νεκρὸν ἀλλ' Heyler suggests.
[3] δὲ Reiske adds. [4] Γαλιλαίων Hercher.
[5] Hertlein 10. Asmus thinks that before Μέγιστος the word Ἀρχιερεύς, "high priest," has fallen out; cf. Vol. 2, *Fragment of a Letter*, 298 D. The phrase would then mean "Pontifex Maximus."
[6] Hertlein suggests ἔτι.

ever been prescribed. But these Jews are in part god-fearing, seeing that they revere a god who is truly most powerful and most good and governs this world of sense, and, as I well know, is worshipped by us also under other names.[1] They act as is right and seemly, in my opinion, if they do not transgress the laws; but in this one thing they err in that, while reserving their deepest devotion for their own god, they do not conciliate the other gods also; but the other gods they think have been allotted to us Gentiles only, to such a pitch of folly have they been brought by their barbaric conceit. But those who belong to the impious sect of the Galilaeans, as if some disease . . .[2]

21

The Emperor Julian Caesar, most Mighty Augustus, to the People of Alexandria[3]

If you do not revere the memory of Alexander, your founder, and yet more than him the great god, the most holy Serapis, how is it that you took no thought at least for the welfare of your community, for humanity, for decency? Furthermore, I will add that you took no thought for me either, though all 362 January From Constantinople

[1] Cf. *Against the Galilaeans* 354B, where Julian says that he always worships the God of Abraham, who is gracious to those that do him reverence μέγας τε ὢν πάνυ καὶ δυνατός, "for he is very great and powerful."

[2] The conclusion of the sentence is lost, and was probably deleted by a Christian because of some disrespectful reference to Christ.

[3] Quoted entire by Socrates, *History of the Church* 3. 3; cited by Sozomen, 5. 7. 9; for the murder of Bishop George to which it refers, see Introduction, under Athanasius.

πρώτοις δὲ ὁ μέγας Σάραπις ἄρχειν ἐδικαίωσαν τῆς οἰκουμένης· οἷς πρέπον ἦν τὴν ὑπὲρ τῶν ἠδικηκότων ὑμᾶς φυλάξαι διάγνωσιν. ἀλλ' ὀργὴ τυχὸν ἴσως ὑμᾶς ἐξηπάτησε καὶ θυμός, ὅσπερ οὖν εἴωθε "τὰ δεινὰ πράττειν, τὰς φρένας μετοικίσας," οἳ τὰ[1] τῆς ὁρμῆς ἀναστείλαντες τοῖς παραχρῆμα
379 βεβουλευμένοις καλῶς ὕστερον ἐπηγάγετε τὴν παρανομίαν, οὐδὲ ᾐσχύνθητε δῆμος ὄντες τολμῆσαι ταὐτά, ἐφ' οἷς ἐκείνους ἐμισήσατε δικαίως. εἴπατε γάρ μοι πρὸς τοῦ Σαράπιδος, ὑπὲρ ποίων ἀδικημάτων ἐχαλεπήνατε Γεωργίῳ; τὸν μακαρίτην[2] Κωνστάντιον, ἐρεῖτε δήπουθεν, ὅτι καθ' ὑμῶν παρώξυνεν, εἶτα εἰσήγαγεν εἰς τὴν ἱερὰν πόλιν στρατόπεδον, καὶ κατέλαβεν ὁ στρατηγὸς τῆς
B Αἰγύπτου τὸ ἁγιώτατον τοῦ θεοῦ τέμενος, ἀποσυλήσας ἐκεῖθεν εἰκόνας καὶ ἀναθήματα καὶ τὸν ἐν τοῖς ἱεροῖς κόσμον. ὑμῶν δὲ ἀγανακτούντων εἰκότως καὶ πειρωμένων ἀμύνειν τῷ θεῷ, μᾶλλον δὲ τοῖς τοῦ θεοῦ κτήμασιν, ὁ δὲ ἐτόλμησεν ὑμῖν ἐπιπέμψαι τοὺς ὁπλίτας ἀδίκως καὶ παρανόμως καὶ ἀσεβῶς, ἴσως Γεώργιον μᾶλλον ἢ τὸν Κωνστάντιον δεδοικώς, ὃς αὐτὸν παρεφύλαττεν, εἰ μετριώτερον ὑμῖν καὶ πολιτικώτερον, ἀλλὰ μὴ τυραννι-
C κώτερον πόρρωθεν προσφέροιτο. τούτων οὖν ἕνεκεν ὀργιζόμενοι τῷ θεοῖς ἐχθρῷ Γεωργίῳ τὴν

[1] οἳ τὰ Hertlein suggests; εἰ τὰ Heyler; εἶτα MSS.
[2] Cobet; μακαριώτατον MSS., Hertlein.

---

[1] Plutarch, *On the Restraint of Anger* 453; quoted from Melanthius the tragic poet; *frag.* 1, Nauck. This is the only extant fragment of Melanthius and is often quoted.
[2] Artemius, military prefect of Egypt; he was executed

the gods, and, above all, the great Serapis, judged it right that I should rule over the world. The proper course was for you to reserve for me the decision concerning the offenders. But perhaps your anger and rage led you astray, since it often "turns reason out of doors and then does terrible things"[1]; for after you had restrained your original impulse, you later introduced lawlessness to mar the wise resolutions which you had at the first adopted, and were not ashamed, as a community, to commit the same rash acts as those for which you rightly detested your adversaries. For tell me, in the name of Serapis, what were the crimes for which you were incensed against George? You will doubtless answer: He exasperated against you Constantius of blessed memory; then he brought an army into the holy city, and the general[2] in command of Egypt seized the most sacred shrine of the god and stripped it of its statues and offerings and of all the ornaments in the temples. And when you were justly provoked and tried to succour the god, or rather the treasures of the god,[3] Artemius dared to send his soldiers against you, unjustly, illegally and impiously, perhaps because he was more afraid of George than of Constantius; for the former was keeping a close watch on him to prevent his behaving to you too moderately and constitutionally, but not to prevent his acting far more like a tyrant. Accordingly you will say it was because you were angered for these reasons against George, the enemy of the

by Julian at the request of the Alexandrians, in the summer of 362; Ammianus 22. 11.

[3] Serapis; the Serapeum according to Ammianus 22. 16, was, next to the Capitol at Rome, the most splendid temple in the world. For this incident see Sozomen 4. 30. 2.

ἱερὰν αὖθις ἐμιάνατε πόλιν, ἐξὸν ὑποβάλλειν αὐτὸν ταῖς τῶν δικαστῶν ψήφοις· οὕτω γὰρ ἐγένετο ἂν οὐ φόνος οὐδὲ παρανομία τὸ πρᾶγμα, δίκη δὲ ἐμμελής, ὑμᾶς μὲν ἀθῴους πάντῃ φυλάττουσα, τιμωρουμένη μεῦ[1] τὸν ἀνίατα δυσσεβήσαντα, σω-
D φρονίζουσά δὲ[2] τοὺς ἄλλους πάντας ὅσοι τῶν θεῶν ὀλιγωροῦσι καὶ προσέτι τὰς τοιαύτας πόλεις καὶ τοὺς ἀνθοῦντας δήμους ἐν οὐδενὶ τίθενται, τῆς ἑαυτῶν δὲ ποιοῦνται πάρεργον δυναστείας τὴν κατ᾽ ἐκείνων ὠμότητα.

Παραβάλλετε τοίνυν ταύτην μου τὴν ἐπιστολὴν ᾗ μικρῷ πρῴην ἐπέστειλα, καὶ τὸ διάφορον κατανοήσατε. πόσους μὲν ὑμῶν ἐπαίνους ἔγραφον τότε; νυνὶ δὲ μὰ τοὺς θεοὺς ἐθέλων ὑμᾶς ἐπαινεῖν οὐ δύναμαι διὰ τὴν παρανομίαν. τολμᾷ
380 δῆμος ὥσπερ οἱ κύνες λύκον[3] ἄνθρωπον σπαράττειν, εἶτα οὐκ αἰσχύνεται τὰς χεῖρας προσάγειν τοῖς θεοῖς αἵματι ῥεούσας. ἀλλὰ Γεώργιος ἄξιος ἦν τοῦ τοιαῦτα παθεῖν. καὶ τούτων ἴσως ἐγὼ φαίην ἂν χείρονα καὶ πικρότερα. καὶ δι᾽ ὑμᾶς, ἐρεῖτε. σύμφημι καὶ αὐτός· παρ᾽ ὑμῶν δὲ εἰ λέγοιτε, τοῦτο οὐκέτι συγχωρῶ. νόμοι γὰρ ὑμῖν εἰσίν, οὓς χρὴ τιμᾶσθαι μάλιστα μὲν ὑπὸ πάντων
B ἰδίᾳ καὶ στέργεσθαι. πλὴν ἐπειδὴ συμβαίνει τῶν καθ᾽ ἕκαστόν τινας παρανομεῖν, ἀλλὰ τὰ κοινὰ γοῦν εὐνομεῖσθαι χρὴ καὶ πειθαρχεῖν τοῖς νόμοις

[1] Hertlein suggests δὲ from correction in margin.
[2] Hertlein suggests τε.
[3] Asmus supplies; cf. Vol. 1, *Oration* 1. 48c.

---

[1] On the turbulence of the Alexandrians cf. Ammianus 22. 11. 4.

gods, that you once more[1] desecrated the holy city, when you might have subjected him to the votes of the judges. For in that case the affair would not have resulted in murder[2] and lawlessness but in a lawsuit in due form, which would have kept you wholly free from guilt, while it would have punished that impious man for his inexpiable crimes, and would have checked all others who neglect the gods, and who moreover lightly esteem cities like yours and flourishing communities, since they think that cruel behaviour towards these is a perquisite of their own power.

Now compare this letter of mine with the one[3] that I wrote to you a short time ago, and mark the difference well. What words of praise for you did I write then! But now, by the gods, though I wish to praise you, I cannot, because you have broken the law. Your citizens dare to tear a human being in pieces as dogs tear a wolf, and then are not ashamed to lift to the gods those hands still dripping with blood! But, you will say, George deserved to be treated in this fashion. Granted, and I might even admit that he deserved even worse and more cruel treatment. Yes, you will say, and on your account. To this I too agree; but if you say by your hands, I no longer agree. For you have laws which ought by all means to be honoured and cherished by you all, individually. Sometimes, no doubt, it happens that certain persons break one or other of these laws; but nevertheless the state as a whole ought to be well governed and you ought to obey the laws

[2] Ammianus 22. 11. 8 describes the murder by the mob of Bishop George and two officials of the Emperor Constantius on December 24th, 361.

[3] This letter is not extant.

ὑμᾶς, καὶ μὴ παραβαίνειν ὅσαπερ ἐξ ἀρχῆς ἐνομίσθη καλῶς. Εὐτύχημα γέγονεν ὑμῖν, ἄνδρες Ἀλεξανδρεῖς, ἐπ' ἐμοῦ πλημμελῆσαι τοιοῦτό τι ὑμᾶς, ὃς αἰδοῖ τῇ πρὸς τὸν θεὸν καὶ διὰ τὸν θεῖον
C τὸν ἐμὸν καὶ ὁμώνυμον, ὃς ἦρξεν αὐτῆς τε Αἰγύπτου καὶ τῆς ὑμετέρας πόλεως, ἀδελφικὴν εὔνοιαν ὑμῖν ἀποσώζω. τὸ γὰρ τῆς ἐξουσίας ἀκαταφρόνητον καὶ τὸ ἀπηνέστερον καὶ καθαρὸν τῆς ἀρχῆς οὔποτε ἂν δήμου περιίδοι τόλμημα μὴ οὐ καθάπερ νόσημα χαλεπὸν πικροτέρῳ διακαθῆραι φαρμάκῳ. προσφέρω δ' ἐγὼ ὑμῖν δι' ἅσπερ ἔναγχος ἔφην αἰτίας τὸ προσηνέστατον, παραίνεσιν καὶ λόγους,
D ὑφ' ὧν εὖ οἶδ' ὅτι πείσεσθε μᾶλλον, εἴπερ ἐστέ, καθάπερ ἀκούω, τό τε ἀρχαῖον Ἕλληνες καὶ τὰ νῦν ἔτι τῆς εὐγενείας ἐκείνης ὕπεστιν ὑμῖν ἀξιόλογος καὶ γενναῖος ἐν τῇ διανοίᾳ καὶ τοῖς ἐπιτηδεύμασιν ὁ χαρακτήρ.

Προτεθήτω τοῖς ἐμοῖς πολίταις Ἀλεξανδρεῦσιν.

22

429 Ἀρσακίῳ ἀρχιερεῖ Γαλατίας.[1]

C Ὁ Ἑλληνισμὸς οὔπω πράττει κατὰ λόγον ἡμῶν ἕνεκα τῶν μετιόντων αὐτόν· τὰ γὰρ τῶν θεῶν λαμπρὰ καὶ μεγάλα, κρείττονα πάσης μὲν εὐχῆς, πάσης δὲ ἐλπίδος. ἵλεως δὲ ἔστω τοῖς
D λόγοις ἡμῶν Ἀδράστεια· τὴν γὰρ ἐν ὀλίγῳ τοιαύ-

[1] Hertlein 49. This letter is quoted in full by Sozomen 5. 16, and is not extant in any MS. of Julian.

and not transgress those that from the beginning were wisely established.

It is a fortunate thing for you, men of Alexandria, that this transgression of yours occurred in my reign, since by reason of my reverence for the god and out of regard for my uncle[1] and namesake, who governed the whole of Egypt and your city also, I preserve for you the affection of a brother. For power that would be respected and a really strict and unswerving government would never overlook an outrageous action of a people, but would rather purge it away by bitter medicine, like a serious disease. But, for the reasons I have just mentioned, I administer to you the very mildest remedy, namely admonition and arguments, by which I am very sure that you will be the more convinced if you really are, as I am told, originally Greeks, and even to this day there remains in your dispositions and habits a notable and honourable impress of that illustrious descent.

Let this be publicly proclaimed to my citizens of Alexandria.

22

To Arsacius, High-priest of Galatia

THE Hellenic religion does not yet prosper as I desire, and it is the fault of those who profess it; for the worship of the gods is on a splendid and magnificent scale, surpassing every prayer and every hope. May Adrasteia[2] pardon my words, for indeed 362 On his way to Antioch in June?

[1] Julian, Count of the East; cf. *Misopogon* 365c; he had held some high office in Egypt, under Constantius.

[2] The goddess "whom none may escape" is a variant of Nemesis, often invoked in a saving clause, cf. *To Alypius*, p. 17.

τὴν καὶ τηλικαύτην μεταβολὴν οὐδ' ἂν εὔξασθαί
τις ὀλίγῳ πρότερον ἐτόλμα. τί οὖν ἡμεῖς οἰόμεθα
ταῦτα ἀρκεῖν, οὐδὲ ἀποβλέπομεν, ὡς μάλιστα τὴν
ἀθεότητα συνηύξησεν ἡ περὶ τοὺς ξένους φιλαν
θρωπία καὶ ἡ περὶ τὰς ταφὰς τῶν νεκρῶν προ-
μήθεια καὶ ἡ πεπλασμένη σεμνότης κατὰ τὸν
430 βίον; ὧν ἕκαστον οἴομαι χρῆναι παρ' ἡμῶν ἀλη-
θῶς ἐπιτηδεύεσθαι. καὶ οὐκ ἀπόχρη τὸ σὲ μόνον
εἶναι τοιοῦτον, ἀλλὰ πάντας ἁπαξαπλῶς ὅσοι
περὶ τὴν Γαλατίαν εἰσὶν ἱερεῖς· οὓς ἢ δυσώπησον
ἢ πεῖσον εἶναι σπουδαίους, ἢ τῆς ἱερατικῆς λει-
τουργίας ἀποστῆσον, εἰ μὴ προσέρχοιντο μετὰ γυ-
ναικῶν καὶ παίδων καὶ θεραπόντων τοῖς θεοῖς,
B ἀλλὰ ἀνέχοιντο τῶν οἰκετῶν ἢ υἱέων ἢ τῶν γαμε-
τῶν ἀσεβούντων μὲν εἰς τοὺς θεούς, ἀθεότητα δὲ
θεοσεβείας προτιμώντων. ἔπειτα παραίνεσον ἱερέα
μήτε θεάτρῳ παραβάλλειν μήτε ἐν καπηλείῳ πί-
νειν ἢ τέχνης τινὸς καὶ ἐργασίας αἰσχρᾶς καὶ
ἐπονειδίστου προΐστασθαι· καὶ τοὺς μὲν πειθομέ-
νους τίμα, τοὺς δὲ ἀπειθοῦντας ἐξώθει. ξενοδο-
κεῖα καθ' ἑκάστην πόλιν κατάστησον πυκνά, ἵν'
C ἀπολαύσωσιν οἱ ξένοι τῆς παρ' ἡμῶν φιλανθρω-
πίας, οὐ τῶν ἡμετέρων μόνον, ἀλλὰ καὶ ἄλλων
ὅστις ἂν δεηθῇ[1] χρημάτων. ὅθεν δὲ εὐπορήσεις,
ἐπινενόηταί μοι τέως. ἑκάστου γὰρ ἐνιαυτοῦ τρισ-
μυρίους μοδίους κατὰ πᾶσαν τὴν Γαλατίαν ἐκέ-
λευσα δοθῆναι σίτου καὶ ἑξακισμυρίους οἴνου

[1] ἐνδεηθῇ Hertlein, not necessary.

---

[1] Julian often calls Christianity "atheism."

[2] In the *Fragment of a Letter*, Vol. 2, Julian admonishes priests to imitate Christian virtues, cf. especially 289–290; it is the favourite theme of his pastoral letters; for a fuller

no one, a little while ago, would have ventured even to pray for a change of such a sort or so complete within so short a time. Why, then, do we think that this is enough, why do we not observe that it is their benevolence to strangers, their care for the graves of the dead and the pretended holiness of their lives that have done most to increase atheism?[1] I believe that we ought really and truly to practise every one of these virtues.[2] And it is not enough for you alone to practise them, but so must all the priests in Galatia, without exception. Either shame or persuade them into righteousness or else remove them from their priestly office, if they do not, together with their wives, children and servants, attend the worship of the gods but allow their servants or sons or wives to show impiety towards the gods and honour atheism more than piety. In the second place, admonish them that no priest may enter a theatre or drink in a tavern or control any craft or trade that is base and not respectable. Honour those who obey you, but those who disobey, expel from office. In every city establish frequent hostels in order that strangers may profit by our benevolence; I do not mean for our own people only, but for others also who are in need of money. I have but now made a plan by which you may be well provided for this; for I have given directions that 30,000 modii of corn shall be assigned every year for the whole of Galatia, and 60,000 pints[3] of

account of his attempt to graft Christian discipline on paganism, see Gregory Nazianzen, *Against Julian*, *Oration* 3, and Sozomen 5. 16.

[3] *Modius*, "peck," and *sextarius*, "pint," are Latin words; cf. use in the *Letters* of *πριβάτοις*, *privatis*, *βρέβια*, *brevia*, *σκρινίοις*, *scriniis*.

ξέστας· ὧν τὸ μὲν πέμπτον εἰς τοὺς πένητας τοὺς τοῖς ἱερεῦσιν ὑπηρετουμένους ἀναλίσκεσθαί φημι χρῆναι, τὰ δὲ ἄλλα τοῖς ξένοις καὶ τοῖς μεταιτοῦ-
D σιν ἐπινέμεσθαι παρ' ἡμῶν. αἰσχρὸν γάρ, εἰ τῶν μὲν Ἰουδαίων οὐδεὶς μεταιτεῖ, τρέφουσι δὲ οἱ δυσσεβεῖς Γαλιλαῖοι πρὸς τοῖς ἑαυτῶν καὶ τοὺς ἡμετέρους, οἱ δὲ ἡμέτεροι τῆς παρ' ἡμῶν ἐπικουρίας ἐνδεεῖς φαίνονται. δίδασκε δὲ καὶ συνεισφέρειν τοὺς Ἑλληνιστὰς εἰς τὰς τοιαύτας λειτουργίας
431 καὶ τὰς Ἑλληνικὰς κώμας ἀπάρχεσθαι τοῖς θεοῖς τῶν καρπῶν, καὶ τοὺς Ἑλληνικοὺς ταῖς τοιαύταις εὐποιίαις προσέθιζε, διδάσκων αὐτούς, ὡς τοῦτο πάλαι ἦν ἡμέτερον ἔργον. Ὅμηρος γοῦν τοῦτο[1] πεποίηκεν Εὔμαιον λέγοντα·

> ξεῖν', οὔ μοι θέμις ἔστ', οὐδ' εἰ κακίων σέθεν ἔλθοι,
> B ξεῖνον ἀτιμῆσαι· πρὸς γὰρ Διός εἰσιν ἅπαντες
> ξεῖνοί τε πτωχοί τε. δόσις δ' ὀλίγη τε φίλη τε.

μὴ δὴ τὰ παρ' ἡμῖν ἀγαθὰ παραζηλοῦν ἄλλοις συγχωροῦντες αὐτοὶ τῇ ῥᾳθυμίᾳ καταισχύνωμεν, μᾶλλον δὲ καταπροώμεθα τὴν εἰς τοὺς θεοὺς εὐλάβειαν. εἰ ταῦτα πυθοίμην ἐγώ σε πράττοντα, μεστὸς εὐφροσύνης ἔσομαι.

C Τοὺς ἡγεμόνας ὀλιγάκις ἐπὶ τῆς οἰκίας ὅρα, τὰ πλεῖστα δὲ αὐτοῖς ἐπίστελλε. εἰσιοῦσι δὲ εἰς τὴν πόλιν ὑπαντάτω μηδεὶς αὐτοῖς ἱερέων, ἀλλ', ὅταν εἰς τὰ ἱερὰ φοιτῶσι τῶν θεῶν, εἴσω τῶν προθύρων. ἡγείσθω δὲ μηδεὶς αὐτῶν εἴσω στρατιώτης, ἑπέσθω δὲ ὁ βουλόμενος· ἅμα γὰρ εἰς τὸν οὐδὸν ἦλθε τοῦ

[1] Klimek; αὐτὸ MSS., Hertlein.

wine. I order that one-fifth of this be used for the poor who serve the priests, and the remainder be distributed by us to strangers and beggars. For it is disgraceful that, when no Jew ever has to beg, and the impious Galilaeans support not only their own poor but ours as well, all men see that our people lack aid from us.[1] Teach those of the Hellenic faith to contribute to public service of this sort, and the Hellenic villages to offer their first fruits to the gods; and accustom those who love the Hellenic religion to these good works by teaching them that this was our practice of old. At any rate Homer makes Eumaeus say: "Stranger, it is not lawful for me, not even though a baser man than you should come, to dishonour a stranger. For from Zeus come all strangers and beggars. And a gift, though small, is precious."[2] Then let us not, by allowing others to outdo us in good works, disgrace by such remissness, or rather, utterly abandon, the reverence due to the gods. If I hear that you are carrying out these orders I shall be filled with joy.

As for the government officials, do not interview them often at their homes, but write to them frequently. And when they enter the city no priest must go to meet them, but only meet them within the vestibule when they visit the temples of the gods. Let no soldier march before them into the temple, but any who will may follow them; for the moment that one of them passes over the threshold of the sacred

[1] For a comparison of the charity of the Galilaeans with Pagan illiberality, cf. Vol. 2, *Misopogon* 363A, B.

[2] *Odyssey* 14. 56; cf. *Fragment of a Letter* 291B, where it is quoted in a similar context.

D τεμένους καὶ γέγονεν ἰδιώτης. ἄρχεις γὰρ αὐτός, ὡς οἶσθα, τῶν ἔνδον, ἐπεὶ καὶ ὁ θεῖος ταῦτα ἀπαιτεῖ θεσμός. καὶ οἱ μὲν πειθόμενοι κατὰ ἀλήθειάν εἰσι θεοσεβεῖς, οἱ δὲ ἀντεχόμενοι τοῦ τύφου δοξοκόποι καὶ κενόδοξοι.

Τῇ Πεσσινοῦντι βοηθεῖν ἕτοιμός εἰμι, εἰ τὴν μητέρα τῶν θεῶν ἵλεων καταστήσουσιν ἑαυτοῖς· ἀμελοῦντες δὲ αὐτῆς οὐκ ἄμεμπτοι μόνον, ἀλλά, μὴ πικρὸν εἰπεῖν, μὴ καὶ τῆς παρ' ἡμῶν ἀπολαύσωσι δυσμενείας.

432 οὐ γάρ μοι θέμις ἐστὶ κομιζέμεν οὐδ' ἐλεαίρειν
ἀνέρας, οἵ κε θεοῖσιν ἀπέχθωντ' ἀθανάτοισιν.

πεῖθε τοίνυν αὐτούς, εἰ τῆς παρ' ἐμοῦ κηδεμονίας ἀντέχονται, πανδημεὶ τῆς μητρὸς τῶν θεῶν ἱκέτας γενέσθαι.

23

377 Ἐκδικίῳ ἐπάρχῳ Αἰγύπτου [1]

D Ἄλλοι μὲν ἵππων, ἄλλοι δὲ ὀρνέων, ἄλλοι δὲ [2]
378 θηρίων ἐρῶσιν· ἐμοὶ δὲ βιβλίων κτήσεως ἐκ παιδαρίου δεινὸς ἐντέτηκε πόθος. ἄτοπον οὖν, εἰ ταῦτα περιίδοιμι σφετερισαμένους ἀνθρώπους, οἷς οὐκ ἀρκεῖ τὸ χρυσίον μόνον ἀποπλῆσαι τὸν πολὺν ἔρωτα τοῦ πλούτου, πρὸς δὲ καὶ ταῦτα ὑφαι-

[1] Hertlein 9.
[2] Doehner suggests; Hertlein suggests ἄλλων.

[1] This letter was probably written after Julian's visit to Pessinus on his way to Antioch. The probable date for his arrival at Antioch is the first half of July.

precinct he becomes a private citizen. For you yourself, as you are aware, have authority over what is within, since this is the bidding of the divine ordinance. Those who obey it are in very truth god-fearing, while those who oppose it with arrogance are vainglorious and empty-headed.

I am ready to assist Pessinus[1] if her people succeed in winning the favour of the Mother of the Gods. But, if they neglect her, they are not only not free from blame, but, not to speak harshly, let them beware of reaping my enmity also. "For it is not lawful for me to cherish or to pity men who are the enemies of the immortal gods."[2] Therefore persuade them, if they claim my patronage, that the whole community must become suppliants of the Mother of the Gods.

23

To Ecdicius, Prefect of Egypt[3]

Some men have a passion for horses, others for birds, others, again, for wild beasts; but I, from childhood, have been penetrated by a passionate longing[4] to acquire books. It would therefore be absurd if I should suffer these to be appropriated by men whose inordinate desire for wealth gold alone

362 End of January From Constantinople

[2] *Odyssey* 10. 73; Julian alters the original which is said by Aeolus to Odysseus:

> οὐ γάρ μοι θέμις ἐστὶ κομιζέμεν οὐδ' ἀποπέμπειν
> ἄνδρα τὸν ὅς κε θεοῖσιν ἀπέχθηται μακάρεσσιν.

[3] See Introduction, under Ecdicius.

[4] A proverbial phrase; cf. Vol. 1, *Oration* 4. 130c, Vol. 2, *Oration* 8. 251D; Plato, *Menexenus* 245D. For Julian's love of books, Vol. 1, *Oration* 3. 123D. foll.

ρεῖσθαι ῥᾳδίως διανοουμένους. ταύτην οὖν ἰδιωτι-
κήν μοι δὸς τὴν χάριν, ὅπως ἀνευρεθῇ πάντα τὰ
B Γεωργίου βιβλία. πολλὰ μὲν γὰρ ἦν φιλόσοφα
παρ' αὐτῷ, πολλὰ δὲ ῥητορικά, πολλὰ δὲ ἦν καὶ
τῆς τῶν δυσσεβῶν Γαλιλαίων διδασκαλίας· ἃ
βουλοίμην μὲν ἠφανίσθαι πάντῃ, τοῦ δὲ μὴ σὺν
τούτοις ὑφαιρεθῆναι τὰ χρησιμώτερα, ζητείσθω
κἀκεῖνα μετ' ἀκριβείας ἅπαντα. ἡγεμὼν δὲ τῆς
ζητήσεως ἔστω σοι ταύτης ὁ νοτάριος Γεωργίου,
ὃς μετὰ πίστεως μὲν ἀνιχνεύσας αὐτὰ γέρως ἴστω
τευξόμενος ἐλευθερίας, εἰ δ' ἀμωσγέπως γένοιτο
C κακοῦργος περὶ τὸ πρᾶγμα, βασάνων εἰς πεῖραν
ἥξων. ἐπίσταμαι δὲ ἐγὼ τὰ Γεωργίου βιβλία,
καὶ εἰ μὴ πάντα, πολλὰ μέντοι· μετέδωκε γάρ μοι
περὶ τὴν Καππαδοκίαν ὄντι πρὸς μεταγραφήν
τινα, καὶ ταῦτα ἔλαβε πάλιν.

24

398 Ἀλεξανδρεῦσι διάταγμα[1]

C Ἐχρῆν τὸν ἐξελαθέντα βασιλικοῖς πολλοῖς
πάνυ καὶ πολλῶν αὐτοκρατόρων προστάγμασιν
D ἓν γοῦν ἐπίταγμα περιμεῖναι βασιλικόν, εἶθ' οὕτως
εἰς τὴν ἑαυτοῦ κατιέναι, ἀλλὰ μὴ τόλμῃ μηδ' ἀπο-
νοίᾳ χρησάμενον ὡς οὐκ οὖσιν ἐνυβρίζειν τοῖς
νόμοις, ἐπεί τοι καὶ τὸ νῦν τοῖς Γαλιλαίοις τοῖς

[1] Hertlein 26.

---

[1] Perhaps to be identified with Porphyrius, to whom Julian wrote the threatening *Letter* 38, p. 123.

[2] *i.e.* when he was interned for six years by Constantius at

cannot satiate, and who unscrupulously design to steal these also. Do you therefore grant me this personal favour, that all the books which belonged to George be sought out. For there were in his house many on philosophy, and many on rhetoric; many also on the teachings of the impious Galilaeans. These latter I should wish to be utterly annihilated, but for fear that along with them more useful works may be destroyed by mistake, let all these also be sought for with the greatest care. Let George's secretary[1] take charge of this search for you, and if he hunts for them faithfully let him know that he will obtain his freedom as a reward, but that if he prove in any way whatever dishonest in the business he will be put to the test of torture. And I know what books George had, many of them, at any rate, if not all; for he lent me some of them to copy, when I was in Cappadocia,[2] and these he received back

24

To the Alexandrians, an Edict[3]

One who had been banished by so many imperial decrees issued by many Emperors ought to have waited for at least one imperial edict, and then on the strength of that returned to his own country, and not displayed rashness and folly, and insulted the laws as though they did not exist. For we have not, even now, granted to the Galilaeans who

362 From Constantinople

Macellum in Cappadocia. George was then at Caesarea near Macellum.

[3] See Introduction, under Athanasius.

φυγαδευθεῖσιν ὑπὸ τοῦ μακαρίτου Κωνσταντίου
οὐ κάθοδον εἰς τὰς ἐκκλησίας αὐτῶν, ἀλλὰ τὴν
εἰς τὰς πατρίδας συνεχωρήσαμεν. Ἀθανάσιον δὲ
πυνθάνομαι τὸν τολμηρότατον ὑπὸ τοῦ συνήθους
ἐπαρθέντα θράσους ἀντιλαβέσθαι τοῦ λεγομένου
παρ' αὐτοῖς ἐπισκοπῆς θρόνου, τοῦτο δὲ εἶναι καὶ
τῷ θεοσεβεῖ τῶν Ἀλεξανδρέων δήμῳ οὐ μετρίως
399 ἀηδές. ὅθεν αὐτῷ προαγορεύομεν ἀπιέναι τῆς πό-
λεως, ἐξ ἧς ἂν ἡμέρας τὰ τῆς ἡμετέρας ἡμερότη-
τος γράμματα δέξηται παραχρῆμα· μένοντι δ'
αὐτῷ τῆς πόλεως εἴσω μείζους πολὺ καὶ χαλεπω-
τέρας προαγορεύομεν τιμωρίας.

25

426 Εὐαγρίῳ[1]

D Συγκτησειδιον μικρὸν ἀγρῶν τεττάρων δοθέν-
των μοι παρὰ τῆς τήθης ἐν τῇ Βιθυνίᾳ τῇ σῇ
διαθέσει δῶρον δίδωμι, ἔλαττον μὲν ἢ ὥστε ἄνδρα
εἰς περιουσίαν ὀνῆσαί τι μέγα καὶ ἀποφῆναι ὄλ-
427 βιον, ἔχον δὲ οὐδὲ ὡς παντάπασιν ἀτερπῆ τὴν
δόσιν, εἴ σοι τὰ καθ' ἕκαστα περὶ αὐτοῦ διέλθοι-
μι. παίζειν δὲ οὐδὲν κωλύει πρὸς σὲ χαρίτων
γέμοντα καὶ εὐμουσίας. ἀπῴκισται μὲν τῆς θα-

[1] Hertlein 46. In the codex found at Chalke, ῥήτορι is added to the title.

---

[1] Constantius was an Arian and had appointed Bishop George of Cappadocia to the see of Alexandria. Athanasius was then in exile by the decree of Constantius.

[2] Athanasius had installed himself in his church on February 21st, 362.

were exiled by Constantius[1] of blessed memory to return to their churches, but only to their own countries. Yet I learn that the most audacious Athanasius, elated by his accustomed insolence, has again seized what is called among them the episcopal throne,[2] and that this is not a little displeasing to the God-fearing citizens[3] of Alexandria. Wherefore we publicly warn him to depart from the city forthwith, on the very day that he shall receive this letter of our clemency. But if he remain within the city, we publicly warn him that he will receive a much greater and more severe punishment.[4]

25

To Evagrius[5]

A small estate of four fields, in Bithynia, was given to me by my grandmother,[6] and this I give as an offering to your affection for me. It is too small to bring a man any great benefit on the score of wealth or to make him appear opulent, but even so it is a gift that cannot wholly fail to please you, as you will see if I describe its features to you one by one. And there is no reason why I should not write in a light vein to you who are so full of the graces and amenities of culture. It is situated not more

362 From Constantinople

[3] *i.e.* the Pagans.

[4] Athanasius withdrew from Alexandria, but not from Egypt, in consequence of this edict. For a second edict banishing him from Egypt, see p. 151.

[5] For Evagrius see above, p. 25.

[6] Cf. Vol. 2. 290D; and 251D for his childhood's associations with this coast.

λάττης σταδίους οὐ πλέον εἴκοσι, καὶ οὔτε ἔμπορος
οὔτε ναύτης ἐνοχλεῖ λάλος καὶ ὑβριστὴς τῷ χωρίῳ.
B οὐ μὴν ἀφῄρηται τὰς παρὰ τοῦ Νηρέως χάριτας
παντελῶς, ἔχει δὲ ἰχθὺν πρόσφατον ἀεὶ καὶ ἀσπαί-
ροντα, καὶ ἐπί τινος ἀπὸ τῶν δωμάτων προελθὼν
γηλόφου ὄψει τὴν θάλατταν τὴν Προποντίδα καὶ
τὰς νήσους τήν τε ἐπώνυμον πόλιν τοῦ γενναίου
βασιλέως, οὐ φυκίοις ἐφεστὼς καὶ βρύοις, οὐδὲ ἐνο-
χλούμενος ὑπὸ τῶν ἐκβαλλομένων εἰς τοὺς αἰγια-
λοὺς καὶ τὰς ψάμμους ἀτερπῶν πάνυ καὶ οὐδὲ
ὀνομάζειν ἐπιτηδείων λυμάτων, ἀλλ᾽ ἐπὶ σμίλακος
C καὶ θύμου καὶ πόας εὐώδους. ἡσυχία δὲ πολλὴ
κατακλινομένῳ καὶ εἴς τι[1] βιβλίον ἀφορῶντι, εἶτα
διαναπαύοντι τὴν ὄψιν ἥδιστον ἀπιδεῖν εἰς τὰς
ναῦς καὶ τὴν θάλατταν. τοῦτο ἐμοὶ μειρακίῳ
κομιδῇ νέῳ θερίδιον ἐδόκει φίλτατον· ἔχει γὰρ καὶ
πηγὰς οὐ φαύλας καὶ λουτρὸν οὐκ ἀναφρόδιτον
καὶ κῆπον καὶ δένδρα. ἀνὴρ δ᾽ ὢν ἤδη τὴν πα-
λαιὰν ἐκείνην ἐπόθουν δίαιταν, καὶ ἦλθον πολλά-
κις, καὶ γέγονεν ἡμῖν οὐκ ἔξω λόγων ἡ σύνοδος.
D ἔστι δ᾽ ἐνταῦθα καὶ γεωργίας ἐμῆς μικρὸν ὑπό-
μνημα, φυταλία βραχεῖα, φέρουσα οἶνον εὐώδη τε
καὶ ἡδύν, οὐκ ἀναμένοντά τι παρὰ τοῦ χρόνου
προσλαβεῖν. τὸν Διόνυσον ὄψει καὶ τὰς Χάριτας.
ὁ βότρυς δὲ ἐπὶ τῆς ἀμπέλου καὶ ἐπὶ τῆς ληνοῦ
θλιβόμενος ἀπόζει τῶν ῥόδων, τὸ γλεῦκος δὲ ἐν
τοῖς πίθοις ἤδη νέκταρός ἐστιν ἀπορρὼξ Ὁμήρῳ
428 πιστεύοντι. τί δῆτα οὐ πολλὴ[2] γέγονεν οὐδ᾽ ἐπὶ
πλέθρα πάνυ πολλὰ ἡ τοιαύτη ἄμπελος;[3] τυχὸν

[1] Hertlein suggests; MSS. εἰς τό.
[2] Hercher suggests; πολὺ MSS, Hertlein.
[3] Hercher suggests; τοιούτων ἀμπέλων MSS., Hertlein.

than twenty stades from the sea, so that no trader or sailor with his chatter and insolence disturbs the place. Yet it is not wholly deprived of the favours of Nereus, for it has a constant supply of fish, fresh and still gasping; and if you walk up on to a sort of hill away from the house, you will see the sea, the Propontis and the islands, and the city that bears the name of the noble Emperor;[1] nor will you have to stand meanwhile on seaweed and brambles, or be annoyed by the filth that is always thrown out on to seabeaches and sands, which is so very unpleasant and even unmentionable; but you will stand on smilax and thyme and fragrant herbage. Very peace ful it is to lie down there and glance into some book, and then, while resting one's eyes, it is very agreeable to gaze at the ships and the sea. When I was still hardly more than a boy I thought that this was the most delightful summer place, for it has, moreover, excellent springs and a charming bath and garden and trees. When I had grown to manhood I used to long for my old manner of life there and visited it often, and our meetings there did not lack talks about literature. Moreover there is there, as a humble monument of my husbandry, a small vineyard that produces a fragrant, sweet wine, which does not have to wait for time to improve its flavour. You will have a vision of Dionysus and the Graces. The grapes on the vine, and when they are being crushed in the press, smell of roses, and the new-made wine in the jars is a "rill of nectar," if one may trust Homer.[2] Then why is not such a vine as this abundant and growing over very many acres?

[1] Constantinople, named after Constantine.

[2] *Odyssey* 9. 359 νέκταρός ἐστιν ἀπορρώξ.

μὲν οὐδὲ ἐγὼ γεωργὸς γέγονα πρόθυμος· ἀλλὰ
ἐπεὶ ἐμοὶ νηφάλιος ὁ τοῦ Διονύσου κρατὴρ καὶ
ἐπὶ πολὺ τῶν νυμφῶν δεῖται, ὅσον εἰς ἐμαυτὸν καὶ
τοὺς φίλους· ὀλίγον δέ ἐστι τὸ χρῆμα τῶν ἀνδρῶν·
παρεσκευασάμην. νῦν δή σοι δῶρον, ὦ φίλη
B κεφαλή, δίδωμι μικρὸν μὲν ὅπερ ἐστί, χαρίεν δὲ
φίλῳ παρὰ φίλου, οἴκοθεν οἴκαδε, κατὰ τὸν σοφὸν
ποιητὴν Πίνδαρον. τὴν ἐπιστολὴν ἐπισύρων πρὸς
λύχνον γέγραφα, ὥστε, εἴ τι ἡμάρτηται, μὴ
πικρῶς ἐξέταζε μηδ' ὡς ῥήτωρ ῥήτορα.

26

Βασιλείῳ[1]

381 Ἡ μὲν παροιμία φησὶν Οὐ πόλεμον ἀγγέλλεις,
ἐγὼ δὲ προσθείην ἐκ τῆς κωμῳδίας Ὦ χρυσὸν
ἀγγείλας ἐπῶν. ἴθι οὖν ἔργοις αὐτὸ δεῖξον, καὶ
B σπεῦδε παρ' ἡμᾶς· ἀφίξῃ γὰρ φίλος παρὰ φίλον.
ἡ δὲ περὶ τὰ πράγματα κοινὴ καὶ συνεχὴς ἀσχολία
δοκεῖ μὲν εἶναί πως τοῖς μὴ πάρεργον αὐτὰ ποιοῦ-
σιν ἐπαχθής, οἱ δὲ τῆς ἐπιμελείας κοινωνοῦντές
εἰσιν ἐπιεικεῖς, ὡς ἐμαυτὸν πείθω, καὶ συνετοὶ καὶ
πάντως ἱκανοὶ πρὸς πάντα. διδοῦσιν οὖν μοι
ῥᾳστώνην, ὥστε ἐξεῖναι μηδὲν ὀλιγωροῦντι καὶ
ἀναπαύεσθαι· σύνεσμεν γὰρ ἀλλήλοις οὐ μετὰ
τῆς αὐλικῆς ὑποκρίσεως, ἧς μόνης οἶμαί σε μέχρι

[1] Hertlein 12.

---

[1] *i.e.* of water.
[2] *Olympian Ode* 6. 99; 7. 5.
[3] For Basil, see Introduction.

Perhaps I was not a very industrious gardener. But since my mixing bowl of Dionysus is inclined to soberness and calls for a large proportion of the nymphs,[1] I only provided enough for myself and my friends—and they are very few. Well then, I now give this to you as a present, dear heart, and though it be small, as indeed it is, yet it is precious as coming from a friend to a friend, "from home, homeward bound," in the words of the wise poet Pindar.[2] I have written this letter in haste, by lamplight, so that, if I have made any mistakes, do not criticise them severely or as one rhetorician would another.

26

To Basil [3]

"Not of war is thy report,"[4] says the proverb, but I would add, from comedy, "O thou whose words bring tidings of gold!"[5] Come then, show it by your deeds and hasten to me, for you will come as friend to friend.[6] It is true that continuous attention to public business is thought to be a heavy burden on men who pursue it with all their energy; but those who share the task of administration with me are, I am convinced, honest and reasonable men, intelligent and entirely capable for all they have to do. So they give me leisure and the opportunity of resting without neglecting anything. For our intercourse with one another is free from that hypocrisy of courts of which alone you have

Early in 362 From Constantinople

[4] Plato, *Phaedrus* 242B, *Laws* 102D, cf. *paroles de paix*.
[5] Aristophanes, *Plutus* 268. [6] Plato, *Menexenus* 247B.

C τοῦ δεῦρο πεπειρᾶσθαι, καθ' ἣν ἐπαινοῦντες μισοῦσι τηλικοῦτον μῖσος ἡλίκον οὐδὲ τοὺς πολεμιωτάτους, ἀλλὰ μετὰ τῆς προσηκούσης ἀλλήλοις ἐλευθερίας ἐξελέγχοντές τε ὅταν δέῃ καὶ ἐπιτιμῶντες οὐκ ἔλαττον φιλοῦμεν ἀλλήλους τῶν σφόδρα ἑταίρων· ἔνθεν ἔξεστιν ἡμῖν· ἀπείη δὲ φθόνος· ἀνειμένοις τε σπουδάζειν καὶ σπουδάζουσι μὴ ταλαιπωρεῖσθαι, καθεύδειν δὲ ἀδεῶς. ἐπεὶ καὶ ἐγρηγορὼς οὐχ ὑπὲρ ἐμαυτοῦ μᾶλλον
D ἢ καὶ ὑπὲρ τῶν ἄλλων ἁπάντων, ὡς εἰκός, ἐγρήγορα.

Ταῦτα ἴσως κατηδολέσχησά σου καὶ κατελήρησα, παθών τι βλακῶδες· ἐπῄνεσα γὰρ ἐμαυτὸν ὥσπερ Ἀστυδάμας. ἀλλ' ἵνα σε πείσω προὔργου τι μᾶλλον ἡμῖν τὴν σὴν παρουσίαν ἅτε ἀνδρὸς ἔμφρονος ποιήσειν ἢ παραιρήσεσθαί τι τοῦ καιροῦ,
382 ταῦτα ἐπέστειλα. σπεῦδε οὖν, ὅπερ ἔφην, δημοσίῳ χρησάμενος δρόμῳ· συνδιατρίψας δὲ ἡμῖν ἐφ' ὅσον σοι φίλον, οἷπερ ἂν θέλῃς ὑφ' ἡμῶν πεμπόμενος, ὡς προσῆκόν ἐστι, βαδιεῖ.

27

Θρᾳξίν[1]

428 Βασιλεῖ μὲν πρὸς κέρδος ὁρῶντι χαλεπὸν ἂν
C ὑμῶν ἐφάνη τὸ αἴτημα, καὶ οὐκ ἂν ᾠήθη δεῖν τὴν δημοσίαν εὐπορίαν βλάπτειν τῇ πρός τινας ἰδίᾳ

[1] Hertlein 47.

[1] A proverb derived from Philemon, *frag.* 190; for the whole verse, see below, p. 159.

[2] *i.e.* the *cursus publicus*; cf. *To Eustathius*, p. 139.

hitherto, I think, had experience, that hypocrisy which leads men to praise one another even while they hate with a hatred more deadly than they feel for their worst enemies in war. But we, though we refute and criticise one another with appropriate frankness, whenever it is necessary, love one another as much as the most devoted friends. Hence it is that I am able—if I may say so without odium—to work and yet enjoy relaxation, and when at work to be free from strain and sleep securely. For when I have kept vigil it was less on my own behalf probably than on behalf of all my subjects.

But perhaps I have been wearying you with my chatter and nonsense, displaying stupid conceit, for I have praised myself, like Astydamas.[1] However, I have despatched this letter to you to convince you that your presence, wise man that you are, will be serviceable to me rather than any waste of my time. Make haste then, as I said, and use the state post.[2] And when you have stayed with me as long as you desire you shall go your way whithersoever you please, with an escort furnished by me, as is proper.

27

To the Thracians[3]

To an Emperor who had an eye solely to gain, your request would have appeared hard to grant, and he would not have thought that he ought to injure the public prosperity by granting a particular 362 Before May From Constantinople

[3] An answer to a petition. For Julian's remission of arrears, ἐλλείματα, Latin *reliqua*, of taxes at Antioch, cf. *Misopogon*, 365B. For his popularity with the provincials due to this liberality, cf. Ammianus 25. 4. 15.

χάριτι· ἐπεὶ δὲ ἡμεῖς οὐχ ὅ, τι πλεῖστα παρὰ τῶν ὑπηκόων ἀθροίζειν πεποιήμεθα σκοπόν, ἀλλ' ὅτι πλείστων ἀγαθῶν αὐτοῖς αἴτιοι γίγνεσθαι, τοῦτο καὶ ὑμῖν ἀπολύσει τὰ ὀφλήματα. ἀπολύσει δὲ
D οὐχ ἁπλῶς ἅπαντα, ἀλλὰ μερισθήσεται τὸ πρᾶγμα, τὸ μὲν εἰς ὑμᾶς, τὸ δὲ εἰς τὴν τῶν στρατιωτῶν χρείαν, ἐξ ἧς οὐκ ἐλάχιστα καὶ αὐτοὶ δήπου φέρεσθε, τὴν εἰρήνην καὶ τὴν ἀσφάλειαν. τοιγαροῦν μέχρι μὲν τῆς τρίτης ἐπινεμήσεως ἀφίεμεν ὑμῖν πάντα, ὅσα ἐκ τοῦ φθάνοντος ἐλλείπει χρόνου· μετὰ ταῦτα δὲ εἰσοίσετε κατὰ τὸ ἔθος. ὑμῖν τε γὰρ τὰ ἀφιέμενα χάρις ἱκανή, καὶ ἡμῖν τῶν
429 κοινῶν οὐκ ἀμελητέον. περὶ τούτου καὶ τοῖς ἐπάρχοις ἐπέσταλκα, ἵν' ἡ χάρις ὑμῖν εἰς ἔργον προχωρήσῃ. ἐρρωμένους ὑμᾶς οἱ θεοὶ σώζοιεν τὸν ἅπαντα χρόνον.

28

407 Ἀνεπίγραφος ὑπὲρ Ἀργείων[1]

B Ὑπὲρ τῆς Ἀργείων πόλεως πολλὰ μὲν ἄν τις εἰπεῖν ἔχοι, σεμνύνειν αὐτὴν ἐθέλων, παλαιὰ καὶ νέα πράγματα. τοῦ τε γὰρ Τρωικοῦ, καθάπερ

[1] Hertlein 35.

---

[1] Apparently he means that the arrears are remitted down to the year 359, but they must pay what is due from that date.

[2] If the date is correct, this was probably a private communication to the newly-appointed Proconsul of Achaia, Praetextatus. Under the Roman dominion, Greek cities to settle their disputes had recourse to lawsuits which were often long and tedious. Seven years before Julian's accession, Corinth had successfully claimed the right to tax Argos.

indulgence to any. But since I have not made it my aim to collect the greatest possible sums from my subjects, but rather to be the source of the greatest possible blessings to them, this fact shall for you too cancel your debts. Nevertheless it will not cancel the whole sum absolutely, but there shall be a division of the amount, and part shall be remitted to you, part shall be used for the needs of the army; since from it you yourselves assuredly gain no slight advantages, namely, peace and security. Accordingly I remit for you, down to the third assessment,[1] the whole sum that is in arrears for the period preceding. But thereafter you will contribute as usual. For the amount remitted is sufficient indulgence for you, while for my part I must not neglect the public interest. Concerning this I have sent orders to the prefects also, in order that your indulgence may be carried into effect. May the gods keep you prosperous for all time!

28

On behalf of the Argives; unaddressed [2]

On behalf of the city of Argos, if one wished to recount her honours, many are the glorious deeds both old and new that one might relate. For instance, in the achievements of the Trojan War 362 From Constantinople

The money was spent on wild beast shows and similar entertainments at Corinth. The Argives appealed to Julian for a revision of the case, and he now writes to the Proconsul of Achaia, leaving the decision to him, but strongly supporting the claim of Argos. As this letter is the only evidence for the Corinthian exaction or the Argive appeal, we do not know the result. Nor can we determine whether Julian is writing in 362 or 363. It seems unlikely that the Argives appealed to him when he was a student at Athens in 355, as some scholars have maintained. See Introduction.

C ὕστερον Ἀθηναίοις καὶ Λακεδαιμονίοις τοῦ Περσι-
κοῦ,[1] προσήκει τὸ πλέον ἐκείνοις ἔργου. δοκεῖ μὲν
γὰρ ἄμφω κοινῇ πραχθῆναι παρὰ τῆς Ἑλλάδος·
ἄξιον δὲ ὥσπερ τῶν ἔργων καὶ τῆς φροντίδος,
οὕτω καὶ τῶν ἐπαίνων τοὺς ἡγεμόνας τὸ πλέον
μετέχειν. ἀλλὰ ταῦτα μὲν ἀρχαῖά πως εἶναι δο-
κεῖ, τὰ δὲ ἐπὶ τούτοις, ἥ τε Ἡρακλειδῶν κάθοδος
καὶ ὡς τῷ πρεσβυτάτῳ γέρας ἐξῃρέθη, ἥ τε εἰς
D Μακεδόνας ἐκεῖθεν ἀποικία, καὶ τὸ Λακεδαιμο-
νίοις οὕτω πλησίον παροικοῦντας ἀδούλωτον ἀεὶ
καὶ ἐλευθέραν φυλάξαι τὴν πόλιν, οὐ μικρᾶς οὐδὲ
τῆς τυχούσης ἀνδρείας ἦν. ἀλλὰ δὴ καὶ τὰ το-
σαῦτα περὶ τοὺς Πέρσας ὑπὸ τῶν Μακεδόνων
γενόμενα ταύτῃ προσήκειν τῇ πόλει δικαίως ἂν
τις ὑπολάβοι· Φιλίππου τε γὰρ καὶ Ἀλεξάνδρου
408 τῶν πάνυ τῶν προγόνων πατρὶς ἦν αὕτη. Ῥω-
μαίοις δὲ ὕστερον οὐχ ἁλοῦσα μᾶλλον ἢ κατὰ
ξυμμαχίαν ὑπήκουσε, καὶ ὥσπερ οἶμαι μετεῖχε
καὶ αὐτὴ καθάπερ αἱ λοιπαὶ τῆς ἐλευθερίας καὶ
τῶν ἄλλων δικαίων, ὁπόσα νέμουσι ταῖς περὶ τὴν
Ἑλλάδα πόλεσιν οἱ κρατοῦντες ἀεί.

Κορίνθιοι δὲ νῦν αὐτὴν προσνεμομένην[2] αὐτοῖς·
οὕτω γὰρ εἰπεῖν εὐπρεπέστερον· ὑπὸ[3] τῆς βασι-

[1] Duebner suggests; lacuna Hertlein, MSS.
[2] Hertlein suggests; MSS προσγενομένην.
[3] Hertlein suggests; ἀπὸ MSS.

---

[1] Temenus the Heraclid received Argos as his share; his descendants were expelled and colonised Macedonia; cf. Julian, *Oration* 3. 106D; Herodotus 8. 137.

they may claim to have played the chief part even as did the Athenians and Lacedaemonians, in later times, in the Persian War. For though both wars are held to have been waged by all Greece in common, yet it is fitting that the leaders, just as they had the larger share of toils and anxiety, should have also a larger share of the praise. These events, however, may seem somewhat antiquated. But those that followed, I mean the return of the Heracleidae, the taking of his birthright from the eldest,[1] the sending from Argos of the colony to Macedonia, and the fact that, though they were such near neighbours to the Lacedaemonians, they always preserved their city unenslaved and free, are proofs of no slight or common fortitude. But, furthermore, all those great deeds accomplished by the Macedonians against the Persians might with justice be considered to belong to this city; for this was the native land of the ancestors of Philip and Alexander,[2] those illustrious men. And in later days Argos obeyed the Romans, not so much because she was conquered as in the character of an ally, and, as I think, she too, like the other states, shared in the independence and the other rights which our rulers always bestow on the cities of Greece.

But now the Corinthians, since Argos has been assigned to their territory—for this is the less invidious way of expressing it—by the sovereign city,[3]

[2] Alexander claimed to be an Argive. For the colonisation of Macedonia cf. Herodotus 5. 22.

[3] Rome, cf. *Oration* 4. 131D. Corinth had been made a Roman colony by Augustus, and claimed authority over certain other cities that were not colonies; the Roman Proconsul regularly resided at Corinth.

λευούσης πόλεως εἰς κακίαν ἐπαρθέντες συντελεῖν
B αὐτοῖς ἀναγκάζουσι, καὶ ταύτης ἦρξαν, ὥς φασι,
τῆς καινοτομίας ἕβδομος οὗτος ἐνιαυτός, οὔτε τὴν
Δελφῶν οὔτε τὴν Ἠλείων ἀτέλειαν, ἧς ἠξιώθησαν
ἐπὶ τῷ διατιθέναι τοὺς παρὰ σφίσιν ἱεροὺς ἀγῶνας,
αἰδεσθέντες. τεττάρων γὰρ ὄντων, ὡς ἴσμεν, τῶν
μεγίστων καὶ λαμπροτάτων ἀγώνων περὶ τὴν Ἑλ-
λάδα, Ἠλεῖοι μὲν Ὀλύμπια, Δελφοὶ δὲ Πύθια,
καὶ τὰ ἐν Ἰσθμῷ Κορίνθιοι, Ἀργεῖοι δὲ τὴν τῶν
C Νεμέων συγκροτοῦσι πανήγυριν. πῶς οὖν εὔλο-
γον ἐκείνοις μὲν ὑπάρχειν τὴν ἀτέλειαν τὴν πάλαι
δοθεῖσαν, τοὺς δὲ ἐπὶ τοῖς ὁμοίοις δαπανήμασιν
ἀφεθέντας πάλαι, τυχὸν δὲ οὐδὲ τὴν ἀρχὴν ὑπα-
χθέντας νῦν ἀφῃρῆσθαι τὴν προνομίαν ἧς ἠξιώ-
θησαν; πρὸς δὲ τούτοις Ἠλεῖοι μὲν καὶ Δελφοὶ
διὰ τῆς πολυθρυλήτου πενταετηρίδος ἅπαξ ἐπι-
τελεῖν εἰώθασι, διττὰ δ' ἐστὶ Νέμεα παρὰ τοῖς
Ἀργείοις, καθάπερ Ἴσθμια παρὰ Κορινθίοις. ἐν
μέντοι τούτῳ τῷ χρόνῳ καὶ δύο πρόκεινται παρὰ
τοῖς Ἀργείοις ἀγῶνες ἕτεροι τοιοίδε, ὥστε εἶναι
D τέσσαρας τοὺς πάντας ἐν ἐνιαυτοῖς τέσσαρσι. πῶς
οὖν εἰκὸς ἐκείνους μὲν ἀπράγμονας εἶναι λειτουρ-
γοῦντας ἅπαξ, τούτους δὲ ὑπάγεσθαι καὶ πρὸς ἑτέ-
ρων συντέλειαν ἐπὶ τετραπλασίοις τοῖς οἴκοι λει-
τουργήμασιν, ἄλλως τε οὐδὲ πρὸς Ἑλληνικὴν οὐδὲ
παλαιὰν πανήγυριν; οὐ γὰρ ἐς χορηγίαν ἀγώνων
γυμνικῶν ἢ μουσικῶν οἱ Κορίνθιοι τῶν πολλῶν
409 δέονται χρημάτων, ἐπὶ δὲ τὰ κυνηγέσια τὰ πολ-

---

[1] *i. e.* the Corinthians ought to have allowed similar immunity to Argos.

[2] One of these festivals was the Heraean games.

have grown insolent in ill-doing and are compelling the Argives to pay them tribute; it is seven years, as I am told, since they began this innovation, and they were not abashed by the immunity of Delphi or of the Eleans,[1] which was granted to them so that they might administer their sacred games. For there are, as we know, four very important and splendid games in Greece; the Eleans celebrate the Olympian games, the Delphians the Pythian, the Corinthians those at the Isthmus, and the Argives the Nemean festival. How then can it be reasonable that those others should retain the immunity that was granted to them in the past, whereas the Argives, who, in consideration of a similar outlay, had their tribute remitted in the past, or perhaps were not even subject to tribute originally, should now be deprived of the privilege of which they were deemed worthy? Moreover, Elis and Delphi are accustomed to contribute only once in the course of their far-famed four-year cycles, but in that period there are two celebrations of the Nemean games among the Argives, and likewise of the Isthmian among the Corinthians. And besides, in these days two other games[2] of this sort have been established among the Argives, so that there are in all in four years four games. How then is it reasonable that those others who bear the burden of this function only once should be left free from the tax, whereas the Argives are obliged to contribute to yet other games in addition to their fourfold expenditure at home; especially as the contribution is for a festival that is neither Hellenic nor of ancient date? For it is not to furnish gymnastic or musical contests that the Corinthians need so much money, but they

λακις ἐν τοῖς θεάτροις ἐπιτελούμενα ἄρκτους καὶ παρδάλεις ὠνοῦνται. ἀτὰρ αὐτοὶ μὲν εἰκότως φέρουσι διὰ τὸν πλοῦτον τῶν ἀναλωμάτων τὸ μέγεθος, ἄλλως τε καὶ πολλῶν πόλεων, ὡς εἰκός, αὐτοῖς εἰς τοῦτο συναιρομένων, ὥστε ὠνοῦνται τὴν τέρψιν τοῦ φρονήματος.[1] Ἀργεῖοι δὲ χρημάτων τε ἔχοντες ἐνδεέστερον καὶ ξενικῇ θέᾳ καὶ παρ' ἄλλοις
B ἐπιδουλεύειν ἀναγκαζόμενοι πῶς οὐκ ἄδικα μὲν καὶ παράνομα, τῆς δὲ περὶ τὴν πόλιν ἀρχαίας δυνάμεώς τε καὶ δόξης ἀνάξια πείσονται, ὄντες γ' αὐτοῖς ἀστυγείτονες, οὓς προσῆκον ἦν ἀγαπᾶσθαι μᾶλλον, εἴπερ ὀρθῶς ἔχει τὸ "οὐδ' ἂν βοῦς ἀπόλοιτο, εἰ μὴ διὰ κακίαν γειτόνων"· Ἀργεῖοι δὲ ἐοίκασιν οὐχ ὑπὲρ ἑνὸς πολυπραγμονούμενοι βοιδίου ταῦτα τοὺς Κορινθίους αἰτιᾶσθαι, ἀλλ' ὑπὲρ πολλῶν καὶ μεγάλων ἀναλωμάτων, οἷς οὐ δικαίως εἰσὶν ὑπεύθυνοι.

C Καίτοι πρὸς τοὺς Κορινθίους εἰκότως ἄν τις καὶ τοῦτο προσθείη, πότερον αὐτοῖς δοκεῖ καλῶς ἔχειν τοῖς τῆς παλαιᾶς Ἑλλάδος ἕπεσθαι νομίμοις ἢ μᾶλλον οἷς ἔναγχος δοκοῦσι παρὰ τῆς βασιλευούσης προσειληφέναι πόλεως; εἰ μὲν γὰρ τὴν τῶν παλαιῶν νομίμων ἀγαπῶσι σεμνότητα, οὐκ Ἀργείοις μᾶλλον εἰς Κόρινθον ἢ Κορινθίοις εἰς Ἄργος συντελεῖν προσήκει· εἰ δὲ τοῖς νῦν ὑπάρ-

[1] ὥστε Bidez suggests; ὧν Reiske; ὠνοῦνται—φρόνηματος Hertlein, following Horkel, would delete; ὠνοῦνται οὖν Capps suggests; ὠνουμένων Keil.

I follow Heyler in interpreting φρόνημα as the pleasure-

buy bears and panthers for the hunting shows which they often exhibit in their theatres. And they themselves by reason of their wealth are naturally able to support these great expenses,—especially as many other cities, as is to be expected, help by contributing for this purpose,—so that they purchase the pleasure of indulging their temperaments.[1] But the Argives are not so well off for money, and compelled as they are to slave for a foreign spectacle held in the country of others, will they not be suffering unjust and illegal treatment and moreover unworthy of the ancient power and renown of their city being, as they are, near neighbours of Corinth, who therefore ought to be the more kindly treated, if indeed the saying is true, "Not so much as an ox would perish[2] except through the wrongdoing of one's neighbours"? But it appears that when the Argives bring these charges against the Corinthians they are not raising a dispute about a single paltry ox, but about many heavy expenses to which they are not fairly liable.

And yet one might put this question also to the Corinthians, whether they think it right to abide by the laws and customs of ancient Greece, or rather by those which it seems they recently took over from the sovereign city? For if they respect the high authority of ancient laws and customs, it is no more fitting for the Argives to pay tribute to Corinth than for the Corinthians to pay it to Argos. If, on

loving "temperament," *genius*, of the Corinthians. Others translate "pride."

[2] A paraphrase of Hesiod, *Works and Days* 348, οὐδ' ἂν βοῦς ἀπόλοιτ, εἰ μὴ γείτων κακὸς εἴη; cf. Plautus, *Mercator* 4. 4. 31.

D ξασι τῇ πόλει,[1] ἐπειδὴ τὴν Ῥωμαϊκὴν ἀποικίαν ἐδέξαντο, ἰσχυριζόμενοι πλέον ἔχειν ἀξιοῦσι, παραιτησόμεθα μετρίως αὐτοὺς μὴ τῶν πατέρων φρονεῖν μεῖζον, μηδὲ ὅσα καλῶς ἐκεῖνοι κρίναντες ταῖς περὶ τὴν Ἑλλάδα διεφύλαξαν πόλεσιν ἔθιμα, ταῦτα καταλύειν καὶ καινοτομεῖν ἐπὶ βλάβῃ καὶ λύμῃ τῶν ἀστυγειτόνων, ἄλλως τε καὶ νεωτέρᾳ χρωμένους τῇ ψήφῳ καὶ τὴν ἀπραγμοσύνην τοῦ λαχόντος ὑπὲρ τῆς Ἀργείων πόλεως τὴν δίκην εἰσελθεῖν ἕρμαιον ἔχοντας τῆς πλεονεξίας. εἰ γὰρ ἐφῆκεν ἔξω τῆς Ἑλλάδος ἀπάγων τὴν δίκην, οἱ
410 Κορίνθιοι ἔλαττόν τε ἰσχύειν ἔμελλον καὶ τὸ δίκαιον ἐξεταζόμενον κακῶς φαίνεσθαι πρὸς τῶν πολλῶν καὶ γενναίων τούτων συνηγόρων, ὑφ᾿ ὧν εἰκός ἐστι τὸν δικαστήν, προστιθεμένου καὶ τοῦ κατὰ τὴν πόλιν ἀξιώματος, δυσωπούμενον ταύτην τὴν ψῆφον ἐξενεγκεῖν.

Ἀλλὰ τὰ μὲν ὑπὲρ τῆς πόλεως δίκαια καὶ τῶν
B ῥητόρων, εἰ μόνον ἀκούειν ἐθέλοις καὶ λέγειν αὐτοῖς ἐπιτραπείη τὴν δίκην, ἐξ ὑπαρχῆς πεύσῃ, καὶ τὸ παραστὰν ἐκ τῶν λεγομένων ὀρθῶς κριθήσεται. ὅτι δὲ χρὴ καὶ τοῖς τὴν πρεσβείαν ταύτην προσάγουσι δι᾿ ἡμῶν πεισθῆναι, μικρὰ προσθεῖναι χρὴ περὶ αὐτῶν. Διογένης μέν τοι καὶ Λαμπρίας φιλοσοφοῦσι μέν, εἴπερ τις ἄλλος τῶν καθ᾿ ἡμᾶς,

[1] Hertlein suggests ; εἰς τὴν πόλιν Reiske ; τὴν πόλιν MSS.

---

[1] *i.e.* the present embassy led by Diogenes and Lamprias ; see below, 410B.

[2] Julian now addresses the Proconsul directly. If 355 is the

the other hand, in reliance on the laws they now have, they claim that their city has gained advantages since they received the colony from Rome, then we will exhort them in moderate language not to be more arrogant than their fathers and not to break up the customs which their fathers with sound judgment maintained for the cities of Greece, or remodel them to the injury and detriment of their neighbours; especially since they are relying on a recent decision, and, in their avarice, regard as a piece of luck the inefficiency of the man who was appointed to represent the case of the city of Argos. For if he had appealed and taken the suit outside of the jurisdiction of Greece, the Corinthians would have had less influence; their rights, would have been shown to be weak, when investigated by these numerous and upright advocates,[1] and, swayed by these, it is likely that the judge would have been awed into giving the proper decision, especially as the renown of Argos would also have had weight.

But as for the rights of the case with respect to the city you[2] will learn them from the beginning from the orators if only you will consent to hear them and they are permitted to present their case, and then the situation will be correctly judged from their arguments. But in order to show that we ought to place confidence in those who have come on this embassy, I must add a few words concerning them. Diogenes and Lamprias[3] are indeed philosophers equal to any in our time, and they have

correct date the Proconsul may be the insolent person referred to in *To Theodorus*, p. 37, as having slighted Julian's wishes.

[3] These men are otherwise unknown.

τῆς πολιτείας δὲ τὰ μὲν ἔντιμα[1] καὶ κερδαλέα διαπεφεύγασι· τῇ πατρίδι δὲ ἐπαρκεῖν ἀεὶ κατὰ δύναμιν προθυμούμενοι, ὅταν ἡ πόλις ἐν χρείᾳ
C μεγάλῃ γένηται, τότε ῥητορεύουσι καὶ πολιτεύονται καὶ πρεσβεύουσι καὶ δαπανῶσιν ἐκ τῶν ὑπαρχόντων προθύμως, ἔργοις ἀπολογούμενοι τὰ φιλοσοφίας ὀνείδη καὶ τὸ δοκεῖν ἀχρήστους εἶναι ταῖς πόλεσι τοὺς μετιόντας φιλοσοφίαν ψεῦδος ἐλέγχοντες· χρῆται γὰρ αὐτοῖς ἥ τε πατρὶς εἰς ταῦτα, καὶ πειρῶνται βοηθεῖν αὐτῇ τὸ δίκαιον δι' ἡμῶν, ἡμεῖς δ' αὖθις διὰ σοῦ. τοῦτο γὰρ καὶ μόνον λείπεται τοῖς ἀδικουμένοις εἰς τὸ σωθῆναι,
D τὸ τυχεῖν δικαστοῦ κρίνειν τε ἐθέλοντος καὶ δυναμένου καλῶς· ὁπότερον[2] γὰρ ἂν ἀπῇ τούτων, ἐξαπατηθέντος ἢ καταπροδόντος αὐτοῦ τὸ δίκαιον οἴχεσθαι πάντως ἀνάγκη. ἀλλ' ἐπειδὴ νῦν ἡμῖν τὰ μὲν τῶν δικαστῶν ὑπάρχει κατ' εὐχάς, λέγειν δ' οὐκ ἔνι μὴ τότε ἐφέντας, ἀξιοῦσι τοῦτο πρῶτον αὐτοῖς ἀνεθῆναι, καὶ μὴ τὴν ἀπραγμοσύνην τοῦ τότε συνειπόντος τῇ πόλει καὶ τὴν δίκην ἐπιτροπεύσαντος αἰτίαν αὐτῇ γενέσθαι εἰς τὸν ἔπειτα αἰῶνα βλάβης τοσαύτης.

411 Ἄτοπον δὲ οὐ χρὴ νομίζειν τὸ τὴν δίκην αὖθις ἀνάδικον ποιεῖν· τοῖς μὲν γὰρ ἰδιώταις ξυμφέρει τὸ κρεῖττον καὶ λυσιτελέστερον ὀλίγον παριδεῖν, τὴν εἰς τὸν ἔπειτα χρόνον ἀσφάλειαν ὠνουμένοις· ὄντος γὰρ αὐτοῖς ὀλίγου βίου, ἡδὺ μὲν καὶ τὸ ἐπ' ὀλίγον ἡσυχίας ἀπολαῦσαι, φοβερὸν δὲ καὶ τὸ

[1] Hertlein suggests; MSS., Hertlein ἔννομα.
[2] ὅ τι Hertlein suggests for lacuna, cf. τίς for πότερος *Caesars* 320 C; ὁπότερον Aldine.

avoided the honours and lucrative offices of the state; but they are ever zealous to serve their country to the best of their ability, and whenever the city is in any great emergency, then they plead causes, assist in the government, go on embassies, and spend generously from their own resources. Thus by their actions they refute the reproaches brought against philosophy,[1] and disprove the common opinion that those who pursue philosophy are useless to the state. For their country employs them for these tasks and they are now endeavouring to aid her to obtain justice by my assistance, as I in turn by yours. For this is indeed the only hope of safety left for the oppressed, that they may obtain a judge who has both the will and ability to give a fair decision. For if either of these qualities be lacking, so that he is either imposed on or faithless to his trust, then there is no help for it—the right must perish. But now, since we have judges who are all that we could wish, and yet are not able to plead because they did not appeal at the time, they beg that this disability may first of all be removed for them, and that the lack of energy of the man who at that time was the city's advocate and had the suit in charge may not be the cause of so great detriment to her for all time to come.

And we ought not to think it irregular that the case should again be brought to trial. For, though in the affairs of private persons it is expedient to forego a little one's advantage and the more profitable course, and thereby purchase security for the future—since in their little life it is pleasant, even for a little, to enjoy peace and quiet; moreover it

[1] Cf. Plato, *Republic* 489A.

πρὸς τῶν δικαστηρίων ἀπολέσθαι κρινόμενον, καὶ
B παισὶ παραπέμψαι τὴν δίκην ἀτελῆ· ὥστε κινδυνεύει κρεῖσσον εἶναι τὸ καὶ ὁπωσοῦν προσλαβεῖν ἥμισυ ἢ περὶ τοῦ παντὸς ἀγωνιζόμενον ἀποθανεῖν· τὰς πόλεις δὲ ἀθανάτους οὔσας εἰ μή τις δικαίως κρίνας τῆς πρὸς ἀλλήλας φιλονεικίας ἀπαλλάξει, ἀθάνατον ἔχειν τὴν δύσνοιαν πάντως ἀναγκαῖον, καὶ τὸ μῖσος δὲ ἰσχυρὸν τῷ χρόνῳ κρατυνόμενον. εἴρηται, φασὶν οἱ ῥήτορες, ὅ γ' ἐμὸς λόγος, κρίνοις δ' ἂν αὐτὸς τὰ δέοντα.

29

Ἰουλιανῷ θείῳ[1]

Εἰ τὰς σὰς ἐπιστολὰς ἐγὼ παρὰ φαῦλον ποιοῦμαι,

ἐξ ἄρα δή μοι ἔπειτα θεοὶ φρένας ὤλεσαν αὐτοί.

τί γὰρ οὐκ ἔνεστιν ἐν τοῖς σοῖς καλόν; εὔνοια, πίστις, ἀλήθεια, καὶ τὸ πρὸ τούτων, οὗ χωρὶς οὐδέν ἐστι τἆλλα, φρόνησις ἅπασι τοῖς ἑαυτῆς μέρεσιν, ἀγχινοίᾳ, συνέσει, εὐβουλίᾳ διαδεικνυμένη. ὅτι δὲ οὐκ ἀντιγράφω, τοῦτο γὰρ καὶ κατεμέμψω, σχολὴν οὐκ ἄγω, μὰ τοὺς θεούς, καὶ μὴ νομίσῃς ἀκκισμὸν εἶναι μηδὲ παιδιὰν τὸ πρᾶγμα. μαρτύρομαι τοὺς λογίους θεούς, ὅτι πλὴν Ὁμήρου καὶ Πλάτωνος οὐκ ἀκολουθεῖ μοι πυκτίον οὔτε φιλόσοφον οὔτε ῥητορικὸν οὔτε γραμματικὸν οὔθ' ἱστορία τις τῶν ἐν κοινῇ χρείᾳ·

[1] Papadopoulos 1 *; not in Hertlein.

is a terrible thought that one may die while one's case is on trial before the courts and hand down the lawsuit to one's heirs unsettled, so that it seems better to secure the half by any possible means than to die while struggling to gain the whole,—cities on the other hand do not die, and unless there be found someone to give a just decision that will free them from their quarrels with one another, they must inevitably maintain undying ill-will, and their hatred moreover is deep-rooted and gains strength with time.

I have said my say, as the orators express it. You must yourselves determine what is proper to do.

29

To his Uncle Julian

If I set small store by your letters, "Then the gods themselves have destroyed my wits."[1] For all the virtues are displayed in them: goodwill, loyalty, truth, and what is more than all these, since without it the rest are nought, wisdom, displayed by you in all her several kinds, shrewdness, intelligence and good judgement. You reproached me for not answering them, but I have no time, heaven knows, and pray do not suppose that this is affectation or a jest. The gods of eloquence bear me witness that, except for Homer and Plato, I have with me not so much as a pamphlet[2] on philosophy, rhetoric, or grammar, or any historical work of the sort that is in general use. And even these that I have are

362 April From Constantinople

[1] *Iliad* 7. 360.

[2] Lit. "folding tablet;" the more usual form is πτυκτίον.

καὶ ταῦτα δὲ αὐτὰ τοῖς περιάπτοις ἔοικε καὶ φυλακτηρίοις· δέδεται γὰρ ἀεί. ὀλίγα λοιπὸν καὶ εὔχομαι καίτοι δεόμενος, ὡς εἰκός, εἴ πέρ ποτε ἄλλοτε καὶ νῦν εὐχῶν πολλῶν πάνυ, καὶ μεγάλων. ἀλλ' ἄγχει πάντοθεν[1] περιεχόμενα τὰ πράγματα, ὄψει δὲ ἴσως καὶ αὐτός, ὅταν εἰς τὴν Συρίαν γένωμαι.

Περὶ δὲ ὧν ἐπέστειλάς μοι, πάντα ἐπαινῶ, πάντα θαυμάζω ἃ ἐννοεῖς,[2] οὐδέν ἐστιν ἀπόβλητον ἐξ ἐκείνων.[3] ἴσθι οὖν ὅτι καὶ πάντα πράξω σὺν θεοῖς.

τοὺς κίονας τοὺς Δαφναίους θοῦ πρὸ τῶν ἄλλων· τοὺς ἐκ βασιλείων τῶν πανταχοῦ λαβὼν ἀποκόμισον, ὑπόστησον δὲ εἰς τὰς ἐκείνων χώρας τοὺς ἐκ τῶν ἔναγχος κατειλημμένων οἰκιῶν· εἰ δὲ κἀκεῖθεν ἐπιλείποιεν, ὀπτῆς πλίνθου καὶ κόνεως τέως[4] ἔξωθεν μαρμαρώσαντες εὐτελεστέροις χρησώμεθα· τὸ δὲ ὅσιον[5] ὅτι πολυτελείας ἐστὶ κρεῖττον καὶ τοῖς εὖ φρονοῦσιν ἡδονὴν ἐν βίῳ καὶ τῇ χρήσει ἔχον πολλήν, αὐτὸς οἶδας.

1 Weil, πάντοτε MS.
2 MS. ἐν οἷς; ἃ ἐννοεῖς Weil.
3 πάντα ἐπαινῶ—ἐκείνων Weil regards as quotation from the elder Julian's letter.
4 Capps; MS. ἕως, Bücheler deletes.
5 Asmus, cf. Vol. 2, 213D; MS. αἴσιον.

---

1 For the use of such amulets in the Mithraic ritual to which Asmus here sees an allusion, see *Mithrasliturgie*, p. 20, Dieterich.

2 Julian left Constantinople soon after May 12th for Antioch, where his uncle then was.

3 The temple of Apollo at Daphne, the suburb of Antioch, which was burned on October 22nd during Julian's visit,

like personal ornaments or amulets,[1] for they are always tied fast to me. For the rest I do not even offer up many prayers, though naturally I need now more than ever to pray very often and very long. But I am hemmed in and choked by public business, as you will perhaps see for yourself when I arrive in Syria.[2]

As for the business mentioned in your letter, I approve of everything and admire everything you propose, nothing of that must be rejected. Be assured, then, that with the aid of the gods I shall leave nothing undone.

First of all set up the pillars of the temple of Daphne;[3] take those that are in any palace anywhere, and convey them thence; then set up in their places others taken from the recently occupied houses.[4] And if there are not enough even from that source, let us use cheaper ones meanwhile, of baked brick and plaster, casing them with marble,[5] for you are well aware that piety is to be preferred to splendour, and, when put in practice, secures much pleasure for the righteous in this life. Concerning the affair

had fallen into disrepair in the reign of Constantius, and columns had been removed by the Christians; cf. Zonaras 13. 12, who relates that at Tarsus, on his way to Persia, Julian learned that the Christians had robbed the temple of Asclepius at Aegae, on the coast, of its columns and used them to build a church. Julian ordered the columns to be restored to the temple at the expense of the Christians.

[4] Perhaps he means the Christian church dedicated to St. Babylas, which his half-brother Gallus had erected opposite the temple.

[5] *i.e.* a coat of stucco made with marble dust.

Περὶ δὲ τῶν πρὸς Λαυρίκιον[1] οὐθὲν οἶμαι δεῖν ἐπιστέλλειν σοι, πλὴν τοσοῦτον παραινῶ, πᾶσαν ὀργὴν ἄφες, ἐπίτρεψον ἅπαντα τῇ δίκῃ, τὰς ἀκοὰς ὑφέξων αὐτοῦ τοῖς λόγοις μετὰ πάσης πίστεως τῆς πρὸς τὸ δίκαιον. καὶ οὔ φημι τοῦτο, ὡς οὐκ ἐπαχθῆ τὰ πρὸς σὲ γραφέντα καὶ πλήρη πάσης ὕβρεως καὶ ὑπεροψίας, ἀλλὰ χρὴ φέρειν· ἀνδρὸς γάρ ἐστιν ἀγαθοῦ καὶ μεγαλοψύχου ἀκούειν μὲν κακῶς, λέγειν δὲ μὴ κακῶς. ὥσπερ γὰρ τὰ βαλλόμενα πρὸς τοὺς στερεοὺς καὶ γενναίους τοίχους ἐκείνοις μὲν οὐ προσιζάνει, οὐδὲ πλήττει, οὐδὲ ἐγκάθηται, σφοδρότερον δὲ ἐπὶ τοὺς βάλλοντας ἀνακλᾶται, οὕτω πᾶσα λοιδορία καὶ βλασφημία καὶ ὕβρις ἄδικος ἀνδρὸς ἀγαθοῦ καταχυθεῖσα θιγγάνει μὲν οὐδαμῶς ἐκείνου, τρέπεται δὲ ἐπὶ τὸν καταχέοντα. ταῦτά σοι παραινῶ, τὰ δὲ ἑξῆς ἔσται τῆς κρίσεως. ὑπὲρ δὲ τῶν ἐμῶν ἐπιστολῶν ἅς φησί σε λαβόντα παρ' ἐμοῦ δημοσιεῦσαι, γελοῖον εἶναί μοι φαίνεται φέρειν εἰς κρίσιν· οὐθὲν γὰρ ἐγώ, μὰ τοὺς θεούς, πρός σε πώποτε γέγραφα οὔτε πρὸς ἄλλον ἄνθρωπον οὐδένα, ὃ μὴ δημοσίᾳ τοῖς πᾶσι προκεῖσθαι βούλομαι· τίς γὰρ ἀσέλγεια, τίς ὕβρις, τίς προπηλακισμός, τίς λοιδορία, τίς αἰσχρορρημοσύνη ταῖς ἐμαῖς ἐπιστολαῖς ἐνεγράφη ποτέ; ὅς γε, καὶ εἰ πρός τινα τραχύτερον εἶχον,[2] διδούσης μοι τῆς ὑποθέσεως ὥσπερ ἐξ ἁμάξης

[1] Λαυράκιον MS., Λαυρίκιον Geffcken, to identify him with the correspondent of Libanius.

[2] Bücheler; MS. εἰ καὶ—ἔχων; καίπερ—ἔχων Papadopoulos suggests.

---

[1] Possibly to be identified with Bassidius Lauricius, governor of the province of Isauria in 359, a Christian

of Lauricius,[1] I do not think I need write you any instructions; but I give you just this word of advice: renounce all feeling of anger, trust all to justice, submitting your ears to his words with complete confidence in the right. Yet I do not deny that what he wrote to you was annoying and full of every kind of insolence and arrogance; but you must put up with it. For it becomes a good and great-souled man to make no counter charge when he is maligned. For, just as missiles that are hurled against hard, well-built walls, do not settle on them, or penetrate them, or stay where they strike, but rebound with increased force against the hand that throws them, just so every aspersion directed against an upright man, slander, calumny, or unmerited insolence, touches him not at all, but recoils on the head of him who made the aspersion. This is my advice to you, but the sequel will be for the law to decide. With regard, however, to the letters which he asserts you made public after receiving them from me, it seems to me ridiculous to bring them into court. For I call the gods to witness, I have never written to you or any other man a word that I am not willing to publish for all to see. Have I ever in my letters employed brutality or insolence, or abuse or slander, or said anything for which I need to blush? On the contrary, even when I have felt resentment against someone and my subject gave me a chance to use ribald language like a woman from a cart,[2] the sort

correspondent of Libanius; Ammianus 19. 13. 2; Libanius, *Letter* 585, Foerster. The little that we know about Lauricius gives no clue to what follows.

[2] A proverbial reference to the scurrilous language permitted to the women who rode in wagons in the Eleusinian processions; cf. Aristophanes, *Plutus* 1014.

εἰπεῖν, οἷα ψευδῶς ἐπὶ τοῦ Λυκάμβου[1] Ἀρχίλοχος, σεμνότερον αὐτὰ[2] καὶ σωφρονέστερον ἐφθεγξάμην ἤ τις[3] ἱερὰν ὑπόθεσιν μετῄει. εἰ δὲ τῆς ὑπαρχούσης ἡμῖν πρὸς ἀλλήλους εὐνοίας ἔμφασιν εἶχε τὰ γράμματα, τοῦτο ἐγὼ λανθάνειν ἠβουλόμην ἢ ἀποκρύπτεσθαι;[4] διὰ τί; μάρτυρας ἔχω τοὺς θεοὺς πάντας τε καὶ πάσας, ὅτι, καὶ ὅσα μοι πρὸς τὴν γαμετήν, οὐκ ἂν ἠχθέσθην, εἴ τις ἐδημοσίευσεν· οὕτως ἦν πάντα σωφροσύνης πλήρη. εἰ δέ, ἃ πρὸς τὸν ἐμαυτοῦ θεῖον ἐπέστειλα, ταῦτα καὶ ἄλλος τις ἀνέγνω καὶ δεύτερος, ὁ πικρῶς οὕτως ἀνιχνεύσας αὐτὰ δικαιοτέραν ἂν ὑπόσχοι μέμψιν ἢ ὁ γράψας ἐγὼ ἢ σὺ ἢ καὶ ἄλλος ἀναγνούς. πλὴν ἀλλὰ τοῦτο συγχώρει καὶ μὴ ταραττέτω σε, σκόπει δὲ ἐκεῖνο μόνον· πονηρός ἐστι Λαυρίκιος, ὑπέξελθε γενναίως αὐτόν. εἰ δὲ ἐπιεικὴς καὶ μέτριός ἐστι, καὶ ἥμαρτε περὶ σέ, δὸς αὐτῷ συγγνώμην· τοὺς γὰρ ἀγαθοὺς δημοσίᾳ, κἂν ἰδίᾳ περὶ ἡμᾶς οὐ καθήκοντες γένωνται, φιλεῖν χρή. τοὺς πονηροὺς δὲ ἐν τοῖς κοινοῖς, κἂν ἡμῖν κεχαρισμένοι διὰ χειρὸς ἔχειν, οὐ μισεῖν οὐδὲ ἐκτρέπεσθαί φημι, φυλακὴν δὲ προβεβλῆσθαί[5] τινα, ὅπως μὴ λήσωσι κακουργοῦντες, εἰ δὲ δυσφύλακτοι λίαν εἶεν, χρῆσθαι πρὸς μηδὲν αὐτοῖς. ὑπὲρ οὗ γέγραφας καὶ αὐτός, ὅτι θρυλούμενος ἐπὶ πονηρίᾳ τὴν ἰατρικὴν ὑποκρίνεται, ἐκλήθη μὲν παρ' ἡμῶν ὡς σπουδαῖος, πρὶν δὲ εἰς ὄψιν ἐλθεῖν

[1] Weil, MS. Λαυδακίδου.
[2] Bidez, MS. αὐτόν.
[3] Bidez, ἤ τις Weil, ὡς εἴτις Papadopoulos. . . εἴτις MS.
[4] ; Weil adds ; Papadopoulos inserts μὴ before λανθάνειν.
[5] Bücheler ; MS. προβέβλησό.

of libels that Archilochus launched against Lycambes,[1] I have always expressed myself with more dignity and reserve than one observes even on a sacred subject. And if my letters did give emphatic proof of the kindly feeling that you and I have towards one another, did I wish this to be unknown or concealed? For what purpose? I call all the gods and goddesses to witness that I should not have resented it, even if someone had published abroad all that I ever wrote to my wife, so temperate was it in every respect. And if this or that person has read what I wrote to my own uncle, it would be fairer to blame the man who ferreted it out with such malevolence, rather than me, the writer, or you, or any other who read it. Nevertheless, concede this to me, do not let it disturb your peace of mind, only look at the matter thus—if Lauricius is really dishonest get rid of him in a dignified way. But if he is a well-meaning person of average honesty, and has treated you badly, forgive him. For when men are honest in public life we must be on good terms with them, even though they do not behave properly to us in their private capacity. On the other hand, when men are dishonest in public affairs, even though they have won our favour, we must keep them under control; I do not mean that we must hate or avoid them, but keep careful watch on them, so that we may not fail to detect them when they misbehave, though if they are too hard to control in this way, we must not employ them at all. As for what you, as well as others, have written, that though notorious for bad conduct he masquerades as a physician, I did send for him, thinking that he was trustworthy, but before he had an interview with me

[1] Cf. Horace, *Epode* 6. 13.

φωραθεὶς ὅστις ἦν, μᾶλλον δὲ καταμηνυθείς· τὸ δὲ ὑπὸ τίνος αὐτὸς ἐντυχὼν φράσω σοι· κατεφρονήθη· σοὶ δὲ καὶ ὑπὲρ τούτου χάριν οἶδα.

Τῶν αἰτηθέντων ἀγρῶν ἐπειδήπερ ἔφθην ἐκείνους δεδωκώς· εἰσί δέ μοι μάρτυρες ὁμόγνιοι καὶ φίλιοι[1] θεοί· δώσω μακρῷ λυσιτελεστέρους, αἰσθήσῃ δὲ καὶ αὐτός.

30

Ἰουλιανὸς Φιλίππῳ[2]

Ἐγὼ νὴ τοὺς θεοὺς ἔτι καῖσαρ ὢν ἐπέστειλά σοι, καὶ νομίζω πλέον ἢ ἅπαξ. ὥρμησα μέντοι πολλάκις, ἀλλ' ἐκώλυσαν ἄλλοτε ἄλλαι προφάσεις, εἶτα ἡ γενομένη διὰ τὴν ἀνάρρησιν ἐμοί τε καὶ τῷ μακαρίτῃ Κωνσταντίῳ λυκοφιλία· παντάπασι γὰρ ἐφυλαττόμην ὑπὲρ τὰς Ἄλπεις ἐπιστεῖλαί τινι, μὴ πραγμάτων αὐτῷ χαλεπῶν αἴτιος γένωμαι. τεκμήριον δέ μοι[3] ποιοῦ τῆς εὐνοίας τὸ μὴ γράφειν· οὐ γὰρ ἐθέλει πολλάκις ὁμολογεῖν ἡ γλῶττα τῇ διανοίᾳ. καὶ ἴσως ἔχει μέν τι πρὸς τὸ γαυριᾶν καὶ ἀλαζονεύεσθαι τοῖς ἰδιώταις ἡ τῶν βασιλικῶν ἐπιστολῶν ἐπίδειξις, ὅταν πρὸς τοὺς ἀσυνήθεις, ὥσπερ δακτύλιοί τινες ὑπὸ τῶν ἀπειροκάλων φερόμενοι, κομίζωνται. φιλία δὲ

[1] φίλοι MS., φίλιοι Weil. [2] Hertlein 68.
[3] μοι ποιοῦ τοῦτο—γράφειν MSS.; μὴ—γράφειν Reiske, Hertlein; μοι—μὴ γράφειν Cobet.

---

[1] Schwarz wrongly suspects this letter on stylistic grounds. Philip was perhaps the Cappadocian to whom Libanius wrote several extant letters, *e.g.* *Letter* 1190. For his zeal in aiding

his true character was detected, or rather he was denounced to me—when I meet you I will tell you by whom—and he was treated with contempt. For this too I have to thank you.

Instead of the estates that you asked for, since I have already given those away—I call to witness the gods of our family and of friendship—I will give you some that pay far better, as you shall yourself discover.

30

To Philip[1]

I CALL the gods to witness that, when I was still Caesar I wrote to you, and I think it was more than once. However, I started to do so many times, but there were reasons that prevented me, now of one kind, now another, and then followed that wolf's friendship that arose between myself and Constantius of blessed memory, in consequence of the proclamation.[2] I was exceedingly careful not to write to anyone beyond the Alps for fear of getting him into serious trouble. So consider the fact that I did not write a proof of my goodwill. For it is often impracticable to make one's language harmonise with one's real sentiments. Then, too, letters from the Emperor to private persons might well lead to their display for bragging and making false pretences when they come into the hands of persons with no sense of propriety, who carry them about like seal-rings and show them to the inexperienced. Nay, genuine

362 Spring From Constantinople

Julian to restore paganism he suffered persecution after the Emperor's death.

[2] *i.e.* of himself as Augustus by the army in Gaul, early in 360; cf. Vol. 2, *Letter to the Athenians* 283–286; he was Caesar 355–360.

ἀληθινὴ γίνεται μάλιστα μὲν δι' ὁμοιότητος, ἡ δευτέρα δέ, ὅταν τις ἀληθῶς, ἀλλὰ μὴ πλαστῶς θαυμάζῃ, καὶ παρὰ τοῦ τύχῃ καὶ συνέσει κρείττονος ὁ πρᾷος καὶ μέτριος καὶ σώφρων ἀγαπηθῇ. τὰ γραμματεῖα δὲ ταῦτα πολλοῦ τύφου καὶ πολλῆς φλυαρίας ἐστὶ μεστά, καὶ ἔγωγε πολλάκις ἐμαυτῷ μέμφομαι μακρότερα ποιούμενος αὐτὰ καὶ λαλίστερος ὤν, ἐξὸν Πυθαγόρειον διδάσκειν τὴν γλῶτταν.

Ὑπεδεξάμην μέντοι τὰ σύμβολα, φιάλην ἀργυρᾶν, ἕλκουσαν μίαν μνᾶν, καὶ χρυσοῦ νόμισμα. καλέσαι δέ σε πρὸς ἐμαυτόν, ὥσπερ ἐπέστειλας, ἐβουλόμην. ἤδη δὲ ἔαρ ὑποφαίνει καὶ τὰ δένδρα βλαστάνει, χελιδόνες δὲ ὅσον οὔπω προσδοκώμεναι τοὺς συστρατευομένους ἡμᾶς, ὅταν ἐπεισέλθωσιν, ἐξελαύνουσι τῶν οἰκιῶν, καί φασι δεῖν ὑπερορίους εἶναι. πορευσόμεθα δὲ δι' ὑμῶν, ὥστε μοι βέλτιον ἂν ἐντύχοις, ἐθελόντων θεῶν, ἐν τοῖς σαυτοῦ. τοῦτο δὲ οἶμαι ταχέως ἔσεσθαι, πλὴν εἰ μή τι δαιμόνιον γένοιτο κώλυμα. καὶ τοῦτο δὲ αὐτὸ τοῖς θεοῖς εὐχόμεθα.

31

Ἰουλιανοῦ νόμος περὶ τῶν ἰατρῶν.[1]

398 Τὴν ἰατρικὴν ἐπιστήμην σωτηριώδη τοῖς
B ἀνθρώποις τυγχάνειν τὸ ἐναργὲς τῆς χρείας

[1] Hertlein 25 *b*. In the MSS. this document has no title; it was placed by Hertlein after *Letter* 25 in his edition.

---

[1] Such tokens were often sent to friends; cf. *To Hecebolius*, p. 219.

friendship is produced first and foremost by similarity of disposition, but a second kind is, when one feels true and not pretended admiration, and a humane, moderate and virtuous man is cherished by one who is his superior in fortune and intelligence. Moreover letters of this sort are full of conceit and nonsense, and, for my part, I often blame myself for making mine too long, and for being too loquacious when I might discipline my tongue to Pythagorean silence.

Yes, I received the tokens, namely, a silver bowl weighing one mina and a gold coin.[1] I should be very glad to invite you to visit me as you suggest in your letter. But the first signs of spring are here already, the trees are in bud, and the swallows, which are expected almost immediately, as soon as they come drive our band of campaigners out of doors, and remind us that we ought to be over the border. We shall travel through your part of the country,[2] so that you would have a better chance of seeing me, if the gods so will it, in your own home. This will, I think, be soon, unless some sign from heaven should forbid it. For this same meeting I am praying to the gods.

31

A decree concerning Physicians[3]

THAT the science of medicine is salutary for mankind is plainly testified by experience. Hence the 362 May 12th From Constantinople

[2] Julian set out for Antioch about May 12th, 362, and expected to see Philip in Cappadocia.

[3] This edict, preserved more briefly in *Codex Theodosianus* 13. 3. 4, was Julian's last known legislative act before he left Constantinople. It confirmed the immunity granted to physicians by Constantine, and was probably meant to apply only to the heads of the medical faculties, *archiatri*, since the Latin edict is addressed to them.

μαρτυρεῖ. διὸ καὶ ταύτην ἐξ οὐρανοῦ πεφοιτηκέναι δικαίως φιλοσόφων παῖδες κηρύττουσι. τὸ γὰρ ἀσθενὲς τῆς ἡμετέρας φύσεως καὶ τὰ τῶν ἐπισυμβαινόντων ἀρρωστημάτων ἐπανορθοῦται διὰ ταύτης. ὅθεν κατὰ τὸν τοῦ δικαίου λογισμὸν συνῳδὰ τοῖς ἄνωθεν βασιλεῦσι θεσπίζοντες ἡμετέρᾳ φιλανθρωπίᾳ κελεύομεν τῶν βουλευτικῶν λειτουργημάτων ἀνενοχλήτους ὑμᾶς τοὺς λοιποὺς χρόνους διάγειν.

32

Θεοδώρᾳ.[1]

Τὸ βιβλίον, ὅπερ ἀπέστειλας διὰ Μυγδονίου, δεδέγμεθα, καὶ προσέτι πάντα ὅσα σύμβολα διὰ τῆς ἑορτῆς ἡμῖν ἐπέμπετο. ἔστι μὲν οὖν μοι καὶ τούτων ἕκαστον ἡδὺ,[2] παντὸς δὲ ἥδιον, εὖ ἴσθι, τὸ πεπύσθαι με περὶ τῆς σῆς ἀγαθότητος, ὅτι σὺν θεοῖς ἔρρωταί σοι τὸ σῶμα, καὶ τὰ περὶ τοὺς θεοὺς ἐπιμελέστερον ἅμα καὶ συντονώτερον σπουδάζεται παρὰ σοῦ. περὶ δὲ ὧν πρὸς τὸν φιλόσοφον Μάξιμον ἔγραψας, ὡς τοῦ φίλου μου Σελεύκου διαφόρως ἔχοντος πρὸς σέ, πέπεισο μηθὲν αὐτὸν παρ' ἐμοὶ τοιοῦτον πράττειν ἢ λέγειν, ἐξ ὧν ἄν σε

[1] Papadopoulos 2* ; not in Hertlein.
[2] Weil ; MS. ἰδεῖν.

---

[1] For Mygdonius cf. *Letter* 33, and Libanius, *Letters* 471, 518 written in 357.

[2] Literally "tokens," *tesserae*, probably the same as the συνθήματα mentioned by Sozomen 5. 16 ; they were letters of recommendation for the use of Christian travellers ; Sozomen says that Julian wished to establish this custom among the pagans.

sons of the philosophers are right in proclaiming that this science also is descended from heaven. For by its means the infirmity of our nature and the disorders that attack us are corrected. Therefore, in accordance with reason and justice, we decree what is in harmony with the acts of former Emperors, and of our benevolence ordain that for the future ye may live free from the burdens attaching to senators.

32

To the priestess Theodora

362 Jan–May? From Constantinople or from Antioch in the Autumn

I HAVE received through Mygdonius[1] the books that you sent me, and besides, all the letters of recommendation[2] that you forwarded to me throughout the festival. Every one of these gives me pleasure, but you may be sure that more pleasant than anything else is the news about your excellent self,[3] that by the grace of the gods you are in good physical health, and are devoting yourself to the service of the gods more earnestly and energetically. As regards what you wrote to the philosopher Maximus, that my friend Seleucus[4] is ill-disposed towards you, believe me that he neither does nor says in my presence anything that he could possibly intend as

[3] Literally "your Goodness"; with this use of ἀγαθότης cf. Oribasius, Introduction to his ἰατρικαὶ συναγωγαὶ 1. παρὰ τῆς σῆς θειότητος, αὐτόκρατορ Ἰουλιανὲ = "by your god-like self," literally "your Divinity"; see above, p. 3.

[4] Of Cilicia. He was an old friend of the Emperor's and accompanied him on the Persian campaign. From the letters of Libanius it seems that Julian had appointed Seleucus to some high priestly office in 362.

μάλιστα διαβάλλοι· τοὐναντίον δὲ πάντα εὔφημα διεξέρχεται περὶ σοῦ, καὶ οὔπω λέγω τοῦθ' ὅτι καὶ διάκειται περὶ σὲ καλῶς· ἐκεῖνο μὲν γὰρ αὐτὸς ἂν εἰδείη καὶ οἱ πάντα ὁρῶντες θεοί· τὸ δὲ ὅτι πάντων ἀπέχεται τῶν τοιούτων ἐπ' ἐμοῦ, λίαν ἀληθεύων φημί. γελοῖον οὖν εἶναί μοι φαίνεται, μὴ τὰ πραττόμενα παρ' αὐτοῦ σκοπεῖν ἀλλὰ τὰ κρυπτόμενα, καὶ ὧν οὐδέν ἐστί μοι φανερὸν τεκμήριον ἐξετάζειν. ἐπεὶ δὲ κατέδραμες αὐτοῦ πολλὰ πάνυ, καὶ περὶ αὐτῆς ἐδήλωσάς τινα, τὴν αἰτίαν μοι τῆς πρὸς αὐτὸν ἀπεχθείας φανερὰν ποιοῦσα, τοσοῦτον ἐγώ φημι πρός σε διαρρήδην, ὡς, εἴ τινα ἀνδρῶν ἢ γυναικῶν ἢ ἐλευθέρων ἢ δούλων ἀγαπᾷς οὔτε νῦν σέβοντα θεοὺς οὔτε ἐν ἐλπίδι τοῦ πείσειν αὐτὸν ἔχουσα, ἁμαρτάνεις. ἐννόησον γὰρ ὡς ἐπὶ σαυτῆς πρῶτον, εἴ τις οἰκετῶν τῶν φιλουμένων ὑπὸ σοῦ τοῖς λοιδορουμένοις καὶ βλασφημοῦσί σε συμπράττοι καὶ θεραπεύοι πλέον ἐκείνους, ἀποστρέφοιτο δὲ καὶ βδελύττοιτο τοὺς σοὺς φίλους ἡμᾶς, ἆρ' οὐ τοῦτον αὐτίκα ἂν ἀπολέσθαι ἐθέλοις,[1] μᾶλλον δὲ καὶ αὐτὴ τιμωρήσαιο; τί οὖν; οἱ θεοὶ τῶν φίλων εἰσὶν ἀτιμότεροι; λόγισαι καὶ ἐπ' αὐτῶν τοῦτο, δεσπότας μὲν ἐκείνους ὑπολαβοῦσα, δούλους δὲ ἡμᾶς. εἴ τις οὖν ἡμῶν, οἵ φαμεν εἶναι θεράποντες θεῶν, οἰκέτην στέργοι τὸν βδελυττόμενον αὐτοὺς καὶ ἀποστρεφόμενον αὐτῶν τὴν θρησκείαν, ἆρ' οὐ δίκαιον ἢ πείθειν αὐτὸν καὶ σῴζειν, ἢ τῆς οἰκίας ἀποπέμπεσθαι καὶ πιπράσκειν, εἴ τῳ μὴ

[1] Weil; MS. ἐθέλεις.

slandering. On the contrary, all that he tells me about you is favourable; and while I do not go so far as to say that he actually feels friendly to you—only he himself and the all-seeing gods can know the truth as to that—still I can say with perfect sincerity that he does refrain from any such calumny in my presence. Therefore it seems absurd to scrutinise what is thus concealed rather than what he actually does, and to search for proof of actions of which I have no shred of evidence. But since you have made so many accusations against him, and have plainly revealed to me a definite cause for your own hostility towards him, I do say this much to you frankly; if you are showing favour to any person, man or woman, slave or free, who neither worships the gods as yet, nor inspires in you any hope that you may persuade him to do so, you are wrong. For do but consider first how you would feel about your own household. Suppose that some slave for whom you feel affection should conspire with those who slandered and spoke ill of you, and showed deference to them, but abhorred and detested us who are your friends, would you not wish for his speedy destruction, or rather would you not punish him yourself?[1] Well then, are the gods to be less honoured than our friends? You must use the same argument with reference to them, you must consider that they are our masters and we their slaves. It follows, does it not, that if one of us who call ourselves servants of the gods has a favourite slave who abominates the gods and turns from their worship, we must in justice either convert him and keep him, or dismiss him from the house and sell him, in case some one does not

[1] An echo of Plato, *Euthyphro* 13D; cf. Vol. 2, 289B.

ῥᾴδιον ὑπερορᾶν οἰκέτου κτήσεως; ἐγὼ δὲ οὐκ ἂν δεξαίμην ὑπὸ τῶν μὴ φιλούντων θεοὺς ἀγαπᾶσθαι· ὃ δὴ καὶ σὲ καὶ πάντας φημὶ δεῖν τοὺς ἱερατικῶν[1] ἀντιποιουμένους ἐντεῦθεν ἤδη διανοηθέντας ἅψασθαι συντονώτερον τῆς εἰς τοὺς θεοὺς ἁγιστείας· ἀπὸ τῆς οἰκίας δὲ σεβασμὸν[2] εὔλογον παρέχεσθαι τῆς ἑαυτοῦ τὸν ἱερέα, καὶ πρώτην αὐτὴν ὅλην δι' ὅλης ἀποφῆναι καθαρὰν τῶν τηλικούτων νοσημάτων.

33

Θεοδώρᾳ τῇ αἰδεσιμωτάτῃ.[3]

375 D Τὰ πεμφθέντα παρὰ σοῦ βιβλία πάντα ὑπεδεξάμην καὶ τὰς ἐπιστολὰς ἄσμενος διὰ τοῦ βελτίστου Μυγδονίου. καὶ μόγις ἄγων σχολήν, ὡς ἴσασιν οἱ θεοί, οὐκ ἀκκιζόμενος λέγω,[4] ταῦτα ἀντέγραψα πρός σε. σὺ δὲ εὖ πράττοις καὶ γράφοις ἀεὶ τοιαῦτα.

34

Ἐδεξάμην[5] ὅσα ἐπέστειλεν ἡ σὴ φρόνησις ἀγαθὰ καὶ καλὰ παρὰ τῶν θεῶν ἡμῖν ἐπαγγέλματα καὶ δῶρα· καὶ πολλὴν ὁμολογήσας

[1] Bücheler, Weil; Papadopoulos ἱερατικῆς (λειτουργίας); MS. ἱερατικῶς.

[2] Weil; MS. ἕκαστον.

[3] Hertlein 5.

[4] Cobet; οὐ κακιζομένην λόγῳ MSS, Hertlein; οὐκ ἀκκιζομένην Reiske.

[5] Papadopoulos 6*. Not in Hertlein.

find it easy to dispense with owning a slave? For my part I would not consent to be loved by those who do not love the gods; wherefore I now say plainly that you and all who aspire to priestly offices must bear this in mind, and engage with greater energy in the temple worship of the gods. And it is reasonable to expect that a priest should begin with his own household in showing reverence, and first of all prove that it is wholly and throughout pure of such grave distempers.

33

To the most reverend Theodora [1]

I WAS glad to receive all the books that you sent me, and your letters through the excellent Mygdonius.[2] And since I have hardly any leisure,—as the gods know, I speak without affectation,—I have written you these few lines. And now farewell, and may you always write me letters of the same sort! 362 About the same date as Letter 32

34

To Theodora? [3]

I HAVE received from you who are wisdom itself your letter telling me of the fair and blessed promises and gifts of the gods to us. First I 362

[1] The epithet as well as the preceding letter show that she was a priestess.

[2] Mygdonius protected Libanius in Constantinople in 343. There is nothing to show whether Julian was at Antioch or Constantinople when he wrote these letters to Theodora.

[3] This unaddressed letter must have been written to a priestess, who was almost certainly Theodora.

χάριν τοῖς οὐρανίοις θεοῖς ἐν δευτέρῳ τῇ σῇ μεγαλοψυχίᾳ χάριν ἔσχον, ὅτι καὶ προσλιπαρεῖν ὑπὲρ ἡμῶν τοὺς θεοὺς ἐν τοῖς μάλιστα προθυμῇ καὶ τὰ φανέντα παρ' αὐτῇ ἀγαθὰ διὰ ταχέων ἡμῖν καταμηνύειν σπουδάζεις.

35

Ἀριστοξένῳ φιλοσόφῳ.[1]

375 Ἆρά γε χρὴ περιμένειν κλῆσιν, καὶ τὸ ἀκλητὶ προτιμᾶν μηδαμοῦ; ἀλλ' ὅρα μὴ χαλεπὴν ταύτην εἰσαγάγωμεν νομοθεσίαν, εἰ ταὐτὰ χρὴ παρὰ τῶν φίλων περιμένειν, ὅσα καὶ παρὰ τῶν ἁπλῶς καὶ
B ὡς ἔτυχε γνωρίμων. ἀπορήσει τις ἐνταῦθα, πῶς οὐκ ἰδόντες[2] ἀλλήλους ἐσμὲν φίλοι; πῶς δὲ τοῖς πρὸ χιλίων ἐτῶν γεγονόσι καὶ ναὶ μὰ Δία δισχιλίων; ὅτι σπουδαῖοι πάντες ἦσαν καὶ τὸν τρόπον καλοί τε κἀγαθοί. ἐπιθυμοῦμεν δὲ καὶ ἡμεῖς εἶναι τοιοῦτοι, εἰ καὶ τοῦ εἶναι, τό γε εἰς ἐμέ, πάμπληθες ἀπολειπόμεθα. πλὴν ἀλλ' ἥ γε ἐπιθυμία τάττει πως ἡμᾶς εἰς τὴν αὐτὴν ἐκείνοις μερίδα. καὶ τί ταῦτα ἐγὼ ληρῶ μακρότερον;
C εἴτε γὰρ ἄκλητον ἰέναι χρή, ἥξεις δήπουθεν· εἴτε καὶ κλῆσιν περιμένεις, ἰδού σοι καὶ παράκλησις ἥκει παρ' ἡμῶν. ἔντυχε οὖν ἡμῖν περὶ τὰ Τύανα πρὸς Διὸς φιλίου, καὶ δεῖξον ἡμῖν ἄνδρα ἐν Καπ-

[1] Hertlein 4.
[2] Wyttenbach, Cobet from *Parisinus*; εἰδότες MSS., Hertlein.

acknowledged the great gratitude that I owed to the heavenly gods, and in the second place I rendered thanks to your generosity of soul, in that you are zealous, no one more so, in entreating the gods on my behalf, and moreover you lose no time but inform me without delay of the blessings that have been revealed where you are.

35

To Aristoxenus, a Philosopher[1]

MUST you then really wait for an invitation and never prefer to come uninvited? Nay, see to it that you and I do not introduce this tiresome convention of expecting the same ceremony from our friends as from mere chance acquaintances. At this point will somebody or other raise the question how we come to be friends when we have never seen one another? I answer: How are we the friends of those who lived a thousand, or, by Zeus, even two thousand years ago? It is because they were all virtuous, of upright and noble character. And we, likewise, desire to be such as they, even though, to speak for myself, we completely fail in that aspiration. But, at any rate, this ambition does in some degree rank us in the same category as those persons. But why do I talk at length about these trifles? For if it is right that you should come without an invitation you will certainly come; if, on the other hand, you are really waiting for an invitation, herewith you have from me an urgent summons. Therefore meet me at Tyana, in the name of Zeus the god of friendship, and show me

362 June On the way to Antioch

[1] This Hellenised Cappadocian is otherwise unknown.

παδόκαις καθαρῶς Ἕλληνα. τέως γὰρ τοὺς μὲν οὐ βουλομένους, ὀλίγους δέ τινας ἐθέλοντας μέν, οὐκ εἰδότας δὲ θύειν ὁρῶ.

36

422 Παιδείαν[1] ὀρθὴν εἶναι νομίζομεν οὐ τὴν ἐν
τοῖς ῥήμασι καὶ τῇ γλώττῃ πραγματευομένην[2]
εὐρυθμίαν, ἀλλὰ διάθεσιν ὑγιῆ νοῦν ἐχούσης
διανοίας καὶ ἀληθεῖς δόξας ὑπέρ τε ἀγαθῶν καὶ
κακῶν, ἐσθλῶν τε καὶ αἰσχρῶν. ὅστις οὖν ἕτερα
B μὲν φρονεῖ, διδάσκει δὲ ἕτερα τοὺς πλησιάζοντας,
οὗτος ἀπολελεῖφθαι τοσούτῳ δοκεῖ τῆς παιδείας,
ὅσῳ καὶ τοῦ χρηστὸς ἀνὴρ εἶναι. καὶ εἰ μὲν ἐπὶ
σμικροῖς εἴη τὸ διάφορον τῆς γνώμης πρὸς τὴν
γλῶτταν, κακὸν μὲν οἰστὸν δὲ ὅμως ὁπωσοῦν
γίνεται· εἰ δὲ ἐν τοῖς μεγίστοις ἄλλα μὲν φρονοίη
τις, ἐπ' ἐναντίον δὲ ὧν φρονεῖ διδάσκοι, πῶς οὐ
τοῦτο ἐκεῖνο καπήλων ἐστίν, οὔτι χρηστῶν, ἀλλὰ
C παμπονήρων ἀνθρώπων, οἳ μάλιστα[3] ἐπαινοῦσιν[4]
ὅσα μάλιστα φαῦλα νομίζουσιν, ἐξαπατῶντες καὶ
δελεάζοντες τοῖς ἐπαίνοις εἰς οὓς μετατιθέναι[5] τὰ
σφέτερα ἐθέλουσιν, οἶμαι, κακά. πάντας μὲν οὖν
χρὴ τοὺς καὶ ὁτιοῦν διδάσκειν ἐπαγγελλομένους
εἶναι τὸν τρόπον ἐπιεικεῖς καὶ μὴ μαχόμενα οἷς

[1] Hertlein 42. Suidas quotes the first three sentences.

[2] πραγματευομένην Asmus; πολιτευομένην Suidas, Hertlein; πολυτελῆ MSS. ("expensive") may be defended.

[3] μάλιστα Klimek would delete.

[4] ἐπαινοῦσιν Naber because of ἐπαίνοις below; παιδεύουσιν Hertlein, MSS.

[5] διατίθεσθαι? Hertlein.

a genuine Hellene among the Cappadocians.[1] For I observe that, as yet, some refuse to sacrifice, and that, though some few are zealous, they lack knowledge.

36

Rescript on Christian Teachers[2]

I HOLD that a proper education results, not in laboriously acquired symmetry of phrases and language, but in a healthy condition of mind, I mean a mind that has understanding and true opinions about things good and evil, honourable and base. Therefore, when a man thinks one thing and teaches his pupils another, in my opinion he fails to educate exactly in proportion as he fails to be an honest man. And if the divergence between a man's convictions and his utterances is merely in trivial matters, that can be tolerated somehow, though it is wrong. But if in matters of the greatest importance a man has certain opinions and teaches the contrary, what is that but the conduct of hucksters, and not honest but thoroughly dissolute men in that they praise most highly the things that they believe to be most worthless, thus cheating and enticing by their praises those to whom they desire to transfer their worthless wares. Now all who profess to teach anything whatever ought to be men of upright character, and ought

362 After June 17th From Antioch

[1] The Cappadocians were, for the most part, Christians; Julian visited Tyana in June on his way to Antioch.

[2] For this law see Introduction; Zonaras 13. 12; Sozomen 5. 18; Socrates 3. 16. 1; Theodoret 3. 8. This version is, no doubt, incomplete.

δημοσίᾳ μεταχειρίζονται[1] τὰ ἐν τῇ ψυχῇ φέρειν
δοξάσματα, πολὺ δὲ πλέον ἁπάντων οἶμαι δεῖν
εἶναι τοιούτους ὅσοι ἐπὶ λόγοις τοῖς νέοις συγ-
γίγνονται, τῶν παλαιῶν ἐξηγηταὶ γιγνόμενοι
D συγγραμμάτων, εἴτε ῥήτορες εἴτε γραμματικοί,
καὶ ἔτι πλέον οἱ σοφισταί. βούλονται γὰρ πρὸς
τοῖς ἄλλοις οὐ λέξεων μόνον, ἠθῶν δὲ εἶναι διδά-
σκαλοι, καὶ[2] κατὰ σφᾶς εἶναί φασι τὴν πολιτικὴν
φιλοσοφίαν. εἰ μὲν οὖν ἀληθὲς ἢ μή, τοῦτο
ἀφείσθω τὰ[3] νῦν. ἐπαινῶν δὲ αὐτοὺς οὕτως
ἐπαγγελμάτων καλῶν ὀρεγομένους ἐπαινέσαιμ'
ἂν ἔτι πλέον, εἰ μὴ ψεύδοιντο μηδ' ἐξελέγχοιεν
αὑτοὺς ἕτερα μὲν φρονοῦντας, διδάσκοντας δὲ
τοὺς πλησιάζοντας ἕτερα. τί οὖν; Ὁμήρῳ
423 μέντοι καὶ Ἡσιόδῳ καὶ Δημοσθένει καὶ Ἡροδότῳ
καὶ Θουκυδίδῃ καὶ Ἰσοκράτει καὶ Λυσίᾳ θεοὶ
πάσης ἡγοῦνται παιδείας. οὐχ οἱ μὲν Ἑρμοῦ
σφᾶς ἱερούς, οἱ δὲ Μουσῶν ἐνόμιζον; ἄτοπον μὲν
οὖν[4] οἶμαι τοὺς ἐξηγουμένους τὰ τούτων ἀτιμάζειν
τοὺς ὑπ' αὐτῶν τιμηθέντας θεούς. οὐ μὴν ἐπειδὴ
τοῦτο ἄτοπον οἶμαι, φημὶ δεῖν αὐτοὺς μετα-
θεμένους τοῖς νέοις συνεῖναι· δίδωμι δὲ αἵρεσιν
μὴ διδάσκειν ἃ μὴ νομίζουσι σπουδαῖα, βουλο-
B μένους δὲ διδάσκειν ἔργῳ πρῶτον[5] πείθειν τοὺς
μαθητὰς ὡς οὔτε Ὅμηρος οὔτε Ἡσίοδος οὔτε
τούτων τις, οὓς ἐξηγοῦνται καὶ ὧν κατεγνωκότες

[1] οἷς—μεταχειρίζονται Bidez; τοῖς δημοσίᾳ [μεταχαρακτηρίζοντας] Hertlein.
[2] καὶ τὸ κατὰ Hertlein MSS; τὸ Asmus deletes.
[3] τὰ Asmus adds.
[4] μὲν MSS., Hertlein; μέντοι Reiske; μὲν οὖν Hertlein suggests.
[5] καὶ after πρῶτον MSS.; Hertlein would delete.

not to harbour in their souls opinions irreconcilable with what they publicly profess; and, above all, I believe it is necessary that those who associate with the young and teach them rhetoric should be of that upright character; for they expound the writings of the ancients, whether they be rhetoricians or grammarians, and still more if they are sophists. For these claim to teach, in addition to other things, not only the use of words, but morals also, and they assert that political philosophy is their peculiar field. Let us leave aside, for the moment, the question whether this is true or not. But while I applaud them for aspiring to such high pretensions, I should applaud them still more if they did not utter falsehoods and convict themselves of thinking one thing and teaching their pupils another. What! Was it not the gods who revealed all their learning to Homer, Hesiod, Demosthenes, Herodotus, Thucydides, Isocrates and Lysias?[1] Did not these men think that they were consecrated, some to Hermes,[2] others to the Muses? I think it is absurd that men who expound the works of these writers should dishonour the gods whom they used to honour. Yet, though I think this absurd, I do not say that they ought to change their opinions and then instruct the young. But I give them this choice; either not to teach what they do not think admirable, or, if they wish to teach, let them first really persuade their pupils that neither Homer nor Hesiod nor any of these writers whom they expound and have

[1] So too in *Oration* 7. 236–237C. Julian compares the impiety of the Cynics, who in his opinion had much in common with the Christians, with Plato's and Aristotle's reverence for religion.

[2] Hermes was the god of eloquence.

εἰσὶν ἀσέβειαν ἄνοιάν τε καὶ πλάνην εἰς τοὺς θεούς, τοιοῦτός ἐστιν. ἐπεὶ δ' ἐξ ὧν ἐκεῖνοι γεγράφασι παρατρέφονται μισθαρνοῦντες, εἶναι ὁμολογοῦσιν αἰσχροκερδέστατοι καὶ δραχμῶν ὀλίγων ἕνεκα πάντα ὑπομένειν. ἕως μὲν οὖν τούτου πολλὰ ἦν τὰ αἴτια τοῦ μὴ φοιτᾶν εἰς τὰ
C ἱερά, καὶ ὁ πανταχόθεν ἐπικρεμάμενος φόβος ἐδίδου συγγνώμην ἀποκρύπτεσθαι τὰς ἀληθεστάτας ὑπὲρ τῶν θεῶν δόξας· ἐπειδὴ δὲ ἡμῖν οἱ θεοὶ τὴν ἐλευθερίαν ἔδοσαν, ἄτοπον εἶναί μοι φαίνεται διδάσκειν ἐκεῖνα τοὺς ἀνθρώπους, ὅσα μὴ νομίζουσιν εὖ ἔχειν. ἀλλ' εἰ μὲν οἴονται σοφοὺς ὧν εἰσιν ἐξηγηταὶ καὶ ὧν ὥσπερ προφῆται
D κάθηνται, ζηλούντων αὐτῶν πρῶτοι[1] τὴν εἰς τοὺς θεοὺς εὐσέβειαν· εἰ δε εἰς τοὺς τιμιωτάτους ὑπολαμβάνουσι πεπλανῆσθαι, βαδιζόντων εἰς τὰς τῶν Γαλιλαίων ἐκκλησίας ἐξηγησόμενοι Ματθαῖον καὶ Λουκᾶν, οἷς πεισθέντες ἱερείων ὑμεῖς ἀπέχεσθαι νομοθετεῖτε. βούλομαι ὑμῶν ἐγὼ καὶ τὰς ἀκοὰς ἐξαναγεννηθῆναι,[2] ὡς ἂν ὑμεῖς εἴποιτε, καὶ τὴν γλῶτταν τούτων, ὧν ἔμοιγε εἴη μετέχειν ἀεὶ καὶ ὅστις ἐμοὶ φίλα νοεῖ τε καὶ πράττει. τοῖς μὲν καθηγεμόσι καὶ διδασκάλοις
424 οὑτωσὶ κοινὸς κεῖται νόμος· ὁ βουλόμενος δὲ τῶν νέων φοιτᾶν οὐκ ἀποκέκλεισται. οὐδὲ γὰρ οὐδὲ εὔλογον ἀγνοοῦντας ἔτι τοὺς παῖδας, ἐφ' ὅ

[1] πρῶτοι Hertlein suggests for πρῶτον MSS.
[2] ἐξαναγεννηθῆναι follows γλῶτταν in MSS. Hertlein; transposed by Cobet as a peculiarly Christian word.

---

[1] *i. e.* under the Christian Emperors Constantine and Constantius it was dangerous to worship the gods openly.
[2] *i. e.* the beliefs of the poets about the gods.

declared to be guilty of impiety, folly and error in regard to the gods, is such as they declare. For since they make a livelihood and receive pay from the works of those writers, they thereby confess that they are most shamefully greedy of gain, and that, for the sake of a few drachmae, they would put up with anything. It is true that, until now, there were many excuses for not attending the temples, and the terror that threatened on all sides absolved men for concealing the truest beliefs about the gods.[1] But since the gods have granted us liberty, it seems to me absurd that men should teach what they do not believe to be sound. But if they believe that those whose interpreters they are and for whom they sit, so to speak, in the seat of the prophets, were wise men, let them be the first to emulate their piety towards the gods. If, however, they think that those writers were in error with respect to the most honoured gods, then let them betake themselves to the churches of the Galilaeans to expound Matthew and Luke, since you Galilaeans are obeying them when you ordain that men shall refrain from temple-worship. For my part, I wish that your ears and your tongues might be "born anew," as you would say, as regards these things[2] in which may I ever have part, and all who think and act as is pleasing to me.

For religious[3] and secular teachers let there be a general ordinance to this effect: Any youth who wishes to attend the schools is not excluded; nor indeed would it be reasonable to shut out from the best way[4] boys who are still too ignorant to know

[3] Καθηγεμὼν in Julian has this implication; cf. *To Theodorus*, p. 55.
[4] Cf. *To the Alexandrians*, p. 149.

τι τρέπωνται, τῆς βελτίστης ἀποκλείειν ὁδοῦ, φόβῳ δὲ καὶ ἄκοντας ἄγειν ἐπὶ τὰ πάτρια. καίτοι δίκαιον ἦν, ὥσπερ τοὺς φρενιτίζοντας, οὕτω καὶ τούτους ἄκοντας ἰᾶσθαι, πλὴν ἀλλὰ συγγνώμην ὑπάρχειν ἅπασι τῆς τοιαύτης νόσου. καὶ γάρ, οἶμαι, διδάσκειν, ἀλλ' οὐχὶ κολάζειν χρὴ τοὺς ἀνοήτους.

37

Ἀταρβίῳ[1]

376 C Ἐγὼ μὰ τοὺς θεοὺς οὔτε κτείνεσθαι τοὺς Γαλιλαίους οὔτε τύπτεσθαι παρὰ τὸ δίκαιον οὔτε ἄλλο τι πάσχειν κακὸν βούλομαι. προτιμᾶσθαι μέντοι τοὺς θεοσεβεῖς καὶ πάνυ φημὶ δεῖν· διὰ μὲν γὰρ τὴν Γαλιλαίων μωρίαν ὀλίγου δεῖν ἅπαντα ἀνε-
D τράπη, διὰ δὲ τὴν τῶν θεῶν εὐμένειαν σωζόμεθα πάντες. ὅθεν χρὴ τιμᾶν τοὺς θεοὺς καὶ τοὺς θεοσεβεῖς ἄνδρας τε καὶ πόλεις.

38

Ἰουλιανοῦ τοῦ παραβάτου πρὸς Πορφύριον[2]

411 C Πολλή τις ἦν πάνυ καὶ μεγάλη βιβλιοθήκη Γεωργίου παντοδαπῶν μὲν φιλοσόφων, πολλῶν

[1] Hertlein 7. According to Cumont, ἰδιόγραφον should be added to the title, and this was one of the few letters that Julian wrote with his own hand.

[2] Hertlein 36. This is the title in Suidas, from whose Lexicon the letter was copied into the MSS. καθολικόν, "revenue official" is added in Suidas, but is almost certainly an error. Hertlein's title Ἰουλιανὸς αὐτοκράτωρ Πορφυρίῳ χαίρειν is derived from *Parisinus* 2131; Hertlein deleted Γεωργίῳ before Πορφυρίῳ.

---

[1] For Christianity a disease cf. *To Libanius*, p. 207; for

which way to turn, and to overawe them into being led against their will to the beliefs of their ancestors. Though indeed it might be proper to cure these, even against their will, as one cures the insane, except that we concede indulgence to all for this sort of disease.[1] For we ought, I think, to teach, but not punish, the demented.

37

To Atarbius [2]

I AFFIRM by the gods that I do not wish the Galilaeans to be either put to death or unjustly beaten, or to suffer any other injury; but nevertheless I do assert absolutely that the god-fearing must be preferred to them. For through the folly of the Galilaeans almost everything has been overturned, whereas through the grace of the gods are we all preserved. Wherefore we ought to honour the gods and the god-fearing, both men and cities.[3]

362 From Constantinople or Antioch

38

Julian the Apostate to Porphyrius [4]

THE library of George was very large and complete and contained philosophers of every school and many

362 After the middle of July From Antioch

indulgence to be shown to persons so afflicted, cf. *To the Citizens of Bostra* 438B, p. 135.

[2] This is probably Atarbius (so spelled in the *Letters* of Libanius) a native of Ancyra and at this time administrator of the district of the Euphrates. In 364 he held high office in Macedonia.

[3] For other letters on the same subject cf. *To the Citizens of Byzacium*, p. 125, and *To Hecebolius*, p. 127.

[4] Perhaps this is George's secretary mentioned in the *Letter to Ecdicius*, p. 73. Geffcken thinks this letter was a Christian forgery because it seems to ignore the earlier order to Ecdicius. Probably the books had not arrived, and Julian became impatient.

δὲ ὑπομνηματογράφων, οὐκ ἐλάχιστα δ' ἐν αὐτοῖς
D καὶ τὰ τῶν Γαλιλαίων πολλὰ καὶ παντοδαπὰ
βιβλία. πᾶσαν οὖν ἀθρόως ταύτην τὴν βιβλιοθήκην ἀναζητήσας φρόντισον εἰς Ἀντιόχειαν ἀποστεῖλαι, γινώσκων ὅτι μεγίστῃ δὴ καὶ αὐτὸς περιβληθήσῃ ζημίᾳ, εἰ μὴ μετὰ πάσης ἐπιμελείας ἀνιχνεύσειας, καὶ τοὺς ὁπωσοῦν ὑπονοίας ἔχοντας ὑφῃρῆσθαι τῶν βιβλίων πᾶσι μὲν ἐλέγχοις, παντοδαποῖς δὲ ὅρκοις, πλείονι δὲ τῶν οἰκετῶν βασάνῳ, πείθειν εἰ μὴ δύναιο, καταναγκάσειας εἰς μέσον πάντα προκομίσαι. ἔρρωσο.

39

380 D
Βυζακίοις[1]

Τοὺς βουλευτὰς πάντας ὑμῖν ἀποδεδώκαμεν καὶ τοὺς πατροβούλους,[2] εἴτε τῇ τῶν Γαλιλαίων ἑαυ-
381 τοὺς ἔδοσαν δεισιδαιμονίᾳ, εἴτε πως ἄλλως πραγματεύσαιντο διαδρᾶναι τὸ βουλευτήριον, ἔξω τῶν ἐν τῇ μητροπόλει λελειτουργηκότων.

[1] Hertlein 11. Βυζαντίνοις MSS., Hertlein; Βισανθηνοῖς Gibbon. For the Byzacians see *Codex Theodosianus* 12. 1. 59.
[2] πατροβόλους *Parisinus*; πατροβούλους X, Ducange; πατροκόλους edd.; προβούλους Cobet. See Cumont, *Revue de Philologie*, 1902.

---

[1] Cumont thinks that a scribe added this inappropriate greeting.
[2] Byzacium was in the district of Tunis. This is Cumont's conjecture for MS. title Τοῖς Βυζαντίνοις, *To the Byzantines.* Julian never calls Constantinople Byzantium. Gibbon suspected the title and conjectured that it was addressed to the town Bisanthe (Rodosto) in Thrace.
[3] The meaning of this word is not clear; Cumont translates

historians, especially, among these, numerous books of all kinds by the Galilaeans. Do you therefore make a thorough search for the whole library without exception and take care to send it to Antioch. You may be sure that you will yourself incur the severest penalty if you do not trace it with all diligence, and do not by every kind of enquiry, by every kind of sworn testimony and, further, by torture of the slaves, compel, if you cannot persuade, those who are in any way suspected of having stolen any of the books to bring them all forth. Farewell.[1]

39

To the citizens of Byzacium [2]

362 Probably from Antioch

I HAVE restored to you all your senators and councillors[3] whether they have abandoned themselves to the superstition of the Galilaeans or have devised some other method of escaping from the senate,[4] and have excepted only those who have filled public offices in the capital.

"patroni" *i.e.* protectors, but we cannot be certain as to the functions of these local dignitaries in Africa.

[4] On the burden of being a Senator cf. Libanius, *Oration* 2; Ammianus 21. 12. 23; Julian, *Misopogon* 367D. It was one of Julian's most widespread reforms to enrol all wealthy men in the senates of their cities. By an edict of March 362 he deprived the Christian clerics of their immunities from such public offices which had been conferred on them by Constantine (cf. Sozomen 5. 5) and in the present case his edict is directed mainly against those who had become clerics in order to escape municipal service. Philostorgius 7. 4 says that this was part of Julian's malignant policy. The Emperor Valentinian restored their privileges to the clerics in 364.

40

Ἐκηβολίῳ [1]

424 C Ἐγὼ μὲν κέχρημαι τοῖς Γαλιλαίοις ἅπασιν οὕτω πρᾴως καὶ φιλανθρώπως, ὥστε μηδένα μηδαμοῦ βίαν ὑπομένειν μηδὲ εἰς ἱερὸν ἕλκεσθαι μηδ' εἰς ἄλλο τι τοιοῦτον ἐπηρεάζεσθαι παρὰ τὴν οἰκείαν πρόθεσιν. οἱ δὲ τῆς Ἀρειανικῆς ἐκκλησίας ὑπὸ τοῦ πλούτου τρυφῶντες ἐπεχείρησαν τοῖς ἀπὸ τοῦ Οὐαλεντίνου καὶ τετολμήκασι τοιαῦτα κατὰ τὴν Ἔδεσσαν, οἷα οὐδέποτε ἐν εὐνομουμένῃ πόλει γένοιτ' ἄν. οὐκοῦν ἐπειδὴ αὐτοῖς ὑπὸ τοῦ θαυμα-
D σιωτάτου νόμου προείρηται πωλῆσαι τὰ ὑπάρχοντα καὶ δοῦναι πτωχοῖς [2] ἵν' εἰς τὴν βασιλείαν τῶν οὐρανῶν εὐκοπώτερον [3] πορευθῶσι, πρὸς τοῦτο συναγωνιζόμενοι τοῖς ἀνθρώποις αὐτῶν τὰ χρήματα τῆς Ἐδεσσηνῶν ἐκκλησίας ἅπαντα ἐκελεύσαμεν ἀναληφθῆναι δοθησόμενα τοῖς στρατιώταις, καὶ τὰ κτήματα τοῖς ἡμετέροις προστεθῆναι πριβάτοις, ἵνα πενόμενοι σωφρονῶσι καὶ μὴ στερη-
425 θῶσιν ἧς ἔτι ἐλπίζουσιν οὐρανίου βασιλείας. τοῖς

[1] Hertlein 43.

[2] πωλῆσαι—πτωχοῖς Asmus supplies from *Luke* 12. 33 for lacuna in MSS.; Thomas suggests τὰ ὑπάρχοντα ἀφιέναι *Matthew* 19. 27. Hertlein suggests πένεσθαι "to embrace poverty."

[3] Asmus suggests, from *Matthew* 19. 24; εὐοδώτερον Hertlein, MSS.

---

[1] This can hardly be the sophist to whom Julian addressed one of his most flowery and sophistic letters, for which see p. 217. Probably he was some leading official of Edessa, the capital of Osroene in Northern Mesopotamia. Constantius had favoured the Arians there and encouraged their fanatical sectarianism by handing over to them the great

40

To Hecebolius[1]

I HAVE behaved to all the Galilaeans with such kindness and benevolence that none of them has suffered violence anywhere or been dragged into a temple or threatened into anything else of the sort against his own will. But the followers of the Arian church, in the insolence bred by their wealth, have attacked the followers of Valentine[2] and have committed in Edessa such rash acts as could never occur in a well-ordered city. Therefore, since by their most admirable law they are bidden to sell all they have and give to the poor that so they may attain more easily to the kingdom of the skies, in order to aid those persons in that effort, I have ordered that all their funds, namely, that belong to the church of the people of Edessa, are to be taken over that they may be given to the soldiers, and that its property[3] be confiscated to my private purse.[4] This is in order that poverty may teach them to behave properly and that they may not be deprived of that heavenly kingdom for which they still hope. And I publicly

End of 362 or early in 363 From Antioch

basilica of St. Thomas. Sozomen 6. 1, says that on his way to Persia Julian hurried past Edessa because the city remained obstinately Christian; later he relates, 6. 18, that the Emperor Valens visited Edessa and persecuted the non-Arian Christians; cf. Socrates 4. 18.

[2] Valentine founded one of the sects of the Gnostics in the first century A.D.: by the fourth century the Valentinian heresy had very few adherents.

[3] Probably Julian means the valuables such as Church plate belonging to the various churches in Edessa; for his spoliation of the churches cf. Gregory Nazianzen, *Against Julian* 3. 86 D, and Sozomen 5. 5.

[4] πριβάτοις=*privatis*; or "to lay uses."

οἰκοῦσι δὲ τὴν Ἔδεσσαν προαγορεύομεν ἀπέχεσθαι πάσης στάσεως καὶ φιλονεικίας, ἵνα μή, τὴν ἡμετέραν φιλανθρωπίαν κινήσαντες, καθ' ὑμῶν αὐτῶν ὑπὲρ τῆς τῶν κοινῶν ἀταξίας[1] δίκην τίσητε, ξίφει καὶ φυγῇ καὶ πυρὶ ζημιωθέντες.

41

Βοστρηνοῖς[2]

Ὤιμην ἐγὼ τοὺς τῶν Γαλιλαίων προστάτας
436 ἕξειν μοι μείζονα χάριν ἢ τῷ φθάσαντι πρὸ ἐμοῦ τὴν ἀρχὴν ἐπιτροπεῦσαι. συνέβη γὰρ ἐπὶ μὲν ἐκείνου τοὺς πολλοὺς αὐτῶν καὶ φυγαδευθῆναι καὶ διωχθῆναι καὶ δεσμευθῆναι, πολλὰ δὲ ἤδη καὶ σφαγῆναι πλήθη τῶν λεγομένων αἱρετικῶν, ὡς ἐν Σαμοσάτοις καὶ Κυζίκῳ καὶ Παφλαγονίᾳ καὶ Βιθυνίᾳ καὶ Γαλατίᾳ, καὶ ἐν[3] πολλοῖς ἄλλοις
B ἔθνεσιν ἄρδην ἀνατραπῆναι πορθηθείσας κώμας,[4] ἐπ' ἐμοῦ δὲ τοὐναντίον. οἵ τε γὰρ ἐξορισθέντες ἀφείθησαν, καὶ οἱ δημευθέντες ἀπολαμβάνειν[5] τὰ σφέτερα ἅπαντα νόμῳ παρ' ἡμῶν ἔλαβον. οἱ δ' εἰς τοσοῦτον λυσσομανίας ἥκουσι καὶ ἀπονοίας, ὥστε, ὅτι μὴ τυραννεῖν ἔξεστιν αὐτοῖς μηδὲ ἃ ποτε ἔπραττον κατ' ἀλλήλων, ἔπειτα καὶ ἡμᾶς τοὺς θεοσεβεῖς εἰργάζοντο, διατιθέναι, παροξυνό-

[1] Hertlein suggests εὐταξίας or ὑπὲρ τῶν κοινῶν τῆς ἀταξίας.

[2] Hertlein 52. The only MS. that contains this edict is *Parisinus* 2964.

[3] Hertlein adds.

[4] For κώμας Cobet suggests ἐκκλησίας.

[5] Hertlein would delete ἀπολαμβάνειν and read ἀπέλαβον for ἔλαβον.

command you citizens of Edessa to abstain from all feuds and rivalries, else will you provoke even my benevolence against yourselves, and being sentenced to the sword and to exile and to fire pay the penalty for disturbing the good order of the commonwealth.

41

To the citizens of Bostra [1]

I THOUGHT that the leaders of the Galilaeans would be more grateful to me than to my predecessor in the administration of the Empire. For in his reign it happened to the majority of them to be sent into exile, prosecuted, and cast into prison, and moreover, many whole communities of those who are called "heretics" [2] were actually butchered, as at Samosata and Cyzicus, in Paphlagonia, Bithynia, and Galatia, and among many other tribes also villages were sacked and completely devastated; whereas, during my reign, the contrary has happened. For those who had been exiled have had their exile remitted, and those whose property was confiscated have, by a law of mine received permission to recover all their possessions.[3] Yet they have reached such a pitch of raving madness and folly that they are exasperated because they are not allowed to behave like tyrants or to persist in the conduct in which they at one time indulged against one another, and afterwards carried on towards us who revered

362 August 1st From Antioch

[1] This edict is cited by Sozomen 5. 15. Bostra, or Bosra, was one of the largest fortified cities in Arabia and is described by Ammianus 14. 8. 13 as murorum firmitate cautissima.

[2] Constantius persecuted Christians who did not belong to the Arian sect.

[3] For this see Sozomen 5. 5.

μενοι πάντα κινοῦσι λίθον καὶ συνταράττειν τολμῶσι τὰ πλήθη καὶ στασιάζειν, ἀσεβοῦντες μὲν εἰς τοὺς θεούς, ἀπειθοῦντες δὲ τοῖς ἡμετέροις
C προστάγμασι, καίπερ οὕτως οὖσι φιλανθρώποις. οὐδένα γοῦν αὐτῶν ἄκοντα πρὸς βωμοὺς ἐῶμεν ἕλκεσθαι, διαρρήδην δὲ αὐτοῖς προαγορεύομεν, εἴ τις ἑκὼν χερνίβων καὶ σπονδῶν ἡμῖν ἐθέλει κοινωνεῖν, καθάρσια προσφέρεσθαι πρῶτον καὶ τοὺς ἀποτροπαίους ἱκετεύειν θεούς. οὕτω πόρρω τυγχάνομεν τοῦ τινα[1] τῶν δυσσεβῶν ἐθελῆσαί ποτε
D ἢ διανοηθῆναι τῶν παρ' ἡμῖν εὐαγῶν μετασχεῖν θυσιῶν, πρὶν τὴν μὲν ψυχὴν ταῖς λιτανείαις πρὸς τοὺς θεούς, τὸ δὲ σῶμα τοῖς νομίμοις καθαρσίοις καθήρασθαι.

Τὰ γοῦν πλήθη τὰ παρὰ τῶν λεγομένων κληρικῶν ἐξηπατημένα πρόδηλον ὅτι ταύτης ἀφαιρεθείσης στασιάζει τῆς ἀδείας. οἱ γὰρ εἰς τοῦτο
437 τετυραννηκότες οὐκ ἀγαπῶσιν ὅτι μὴ τίνουσι δίκην ὑπὲρ ὧν ἔπραξαν κακῶν, ποθοῦντες δὲ τὴν προτέραν δυναστείαν, ὅτι μὴ δικάζειν ἔξεστιν αὐτοῖς καὶ γράφειν διαθήκας καὶ ἀλλοτρίους σφετερίζεσθαι κλήρους καὶ τὰ πάντα ἑαυτοῖς προσνέμειν, πάντα κινοῦσιν ἀκοσμίας κάλων καί, τὸ λεγόμενον, πῦρ ἐπὶ πῦρ ὀχετεύουσι καὶ τοῖς προτέροις κακοῖς μείζονα ἐπιθεῖναι τολμῶσιν, εἰς διάστασιν ἄγοντες τὰ πλήθη. ἔδοξεν οὖν μοι

[1] So Reiske for MS. τοῦ διά τινα; Hertlein suggests νὴ Δία τοῦ τινα; βίᾳ Heyler suggests.

---

[1] *i. e.* for others. Julian no longer allowed legacies to be left to churches; cf. *Codex Theodos.* 3. 1. 3. The clergy and especially the bishops had exercised certain civil functions of

the gods. They therefore leave no stone unturned, and have the audacity to incite the populace to disorder and revolt, whereby they both act with impiety towards the gods and disobey my edicts, humane though these are. At least I do not allow a single one of them to be dragged against his will to worship at the altars; nay, I proclaim in so many words that, if any man of his own free will choose to take part in our lustral rites and libations, he ought first of all to offer sacrifices of purification and supplicate the gods that avert evil. So far am I from ever having wished or intended that anyone of those sacrilegious men should partake in the sacrifices that we most revere, until he has purified his soul by supplications to the gods, and his body by the purifications that are customary.

It is, at any rate, evident that the populace who have been led into error by those who are called "clerics," are in revolt because this license has been taken from them. For those who have till now behaved like tyrants are not content that they are not punished for their former crimes, but, longing for the power they had before, because they are no longer allowed to sit as judges and draw up wills [1] and appropriate the inheritances of other men and assign everything to themselves, they pull every string [2] of disorder, and, as the proverb says, lead fire through a pipe to fire,[3] and dare to add even greater crimes to their former wickedness by leading on the populace to disunion. Therefore I have

which Julian deprived them, and they lost the immunity from taxation that had been granted by Christian emperors. For this cf. Sozomen 5. 5.

[2] Literally "cable," a proverb. [3] Cf. "add fuel to fire."

B πᾶσι τοῖς δήμοις προαγορεῦσαι διὰ τοῦδε τοῦ δια-
τάγματος καὶ φανερὸν καταστῆσαι, μὴ συστα-
σιάζειν τοῖς κληρικοῖς μηδὲ ἀναπείθεσθαι παρ'
αὐτῶν λίθους αἴρειν μηδὲ ἀπιστεῖν τοῖς ἄρχουσιν,
ἀλλὰ συνιέναι μὲν ἕως ἂν ἐθέλωσιν, εὔχεσθαι δὲ
ἃς νομίζουσιν εὐχὰς ὑπὲρ ἑαυτῶν· εἰ δὲ ἀναπεί-
θοιεν ὑπὲρ ἑαυτῶν στασιάζειν, μηκέτι συνᾴδειν,
ἵνα μὴ δίκην δῶσι.

C Ταῦτα δέ μοι παρέστη τῇ Βοστρηνῶν ἰδίᾳ προ-
αγορεῦσαι πόλει διὰ τὸ τὸν ἐπίσκοπον Τίτον καὶ
τοὺς κληρικοὺς ἐξ ὧν ἐπέδοσαν βιβλίων τοῦ μετὰ
σφῶν πλήθους κατηγορηκέναι, ὡς αὐτῶν μὲν
παραινούντων τῷ πλήθει μὴ στασιάζειν, ὁρμω-
μένου δὲ τοῦ πλήθους πρὸς ἀταξίαν. ἐν γοῦν
τοῖς βιβλίοις καὶ αὐτὴν ἣν ἐτόλμησεν ἐγγράψαι
τὴν φωνὴν ὑπέταξά μου τῷδε τῷ διατάγματι.
D "Καίτοι Χριστιανῶν ὄντων ἐφαμίλλων τῷ πλήθει
τῶν Ἑλλήνων, κατεχομένων δὲ τῇ ἡμετέρᾳ παρ-
αινέσει μηδένα μηδαμοῦ ἀτακτεῖν." ταῦτα γάρ
ἐστιν ὑπὲρ ὑμῶν τοῦ ἐπισκόπου τὰ ῥήματα. ὁρᾶτε
ὅπως τὴν ὑμετέραν εὐταξίαν οὐκ ἀπὸ τῆς ὑμε-
τέρας εἶναί φησι γνώμης, οἵ γε ἄκοντες, ὥς γε
438 εἶπε, κατέχεσθε διὰ τὰς αὐτοῦ παραινέσεις. ὡς
οὖν κατήγορον ὑμῶν ἑκόντες [1] τῆς πόλεως διώξατε,
τὰ πλήθη δὲ ὁμονοεῖτε πρὸς ἀλλήλους, καὶ μηδεὶς
ἐναντιούσθω μηδὲ ἀδικείτω· μήθ' οἱ πεπλανημένοι

[1] Klimek suggests ἑλόντες.

---

[1] So far the edict has a general character and may have been sent out broadcast. The last paragraph is apparently added as a special instruction to the citizens of Bostra, and especially to the Christians, whom he incites against their bishop.

decided to proclaim to all communities of citizens, by means of this edict, and to make known to all, that they must not join in the feuds of the clerics or be induced by them to take stones in their hands or disobey those in authority; but they may hold meetings for as long as they please and may offer on their own behalf the prayers to which they are accustomed; that, on the other hand, if the clerics try to induce them to take sides on their behalf in quarrels, they must no longer consent to do so, if they would escape punishment.[1]

I have been led to make this proclamation to the city of Bostra in particular, because their bishop Titus and the clerics, in the reports that they have issued, have made accusations against their own adherents, giving the impression that, when the populace were on the point of breaking the peace, they themselves admonished them not to cause sedition. Indeed, I have subjoined to this my decree the very words which he dared to write in his report: "Although the Christians are a match for the Hellenes in numbers, they are restrained by our admonition that no one disturb the peace in any place." For these are the very words of the bishop about you. You see how he says that your good behaviour was not of your own choice, since, as he at any rate alleged, you were restrained against your will by his admonitions! Therefore, of your own free will, seize your accuser and expel him from the city,[2] but do you, the populace, live in agreement with one another, and let no man be quarrelsome or act unjustly. Neither

[2] Julian's advice was not followed, since Socrates, *History of the Church* 3. 25, mentions Titus as bishop of Bostra under the Emperor Jovian in 363.

τοῖς ὀρθῶς καὶ δικαίως τοὺς θεοὺς θεραπεύουσι κατὰ τὰ ἐξ αἰῶνος ἡμῖν παραδεδομένα, μήθ᾽ οἱ θεραπευταὶ τῶν θεῶν λυμαίνεσθε ταῖς οἰκίαις ἢ
B διαρπάζετε τῶν ἀγνοίᾳ μᾶλλον ἢ γνώμῃ πεπλανημένων. λόγῳ δὲ πείθεσθαι χρὴ καὶ διδάσκεσθαι τοὺς ἀνθρώπους, οὐ πληγαῖς οὐδὲ ὕβρεσιν οὐδὲ αἰκισμῷ τοῦ σώματος. αὖθις δὲ καὶ πολλάκις παραινῶ τοῖς ἐπὶ τὴν ἀληθῆ θεοσέβειαν ὁρμωμένοις μηδὲν ἀδικεῖν τῶν Γαλιλαίων τὰ πλήθη, μηδὲ ἐπιτίθεσθαι μηδὲ ὑβρίζειν εἰς αὐτούς. ἐλεεῖν δὲ χρὴ μᾶλλον ἢ μισεῖν τοὺς ἐν[1] τοῖς μεγίστοις
C πράττοντας κακῶς· μέγιστον γὰρ τῶν καλῶν ὡς ἀληθῶς ἡ θεοσέβεια, καὶ τοὐναντίον τῶν κακῶν ἡ δυσσέβεια. συμβαίνει δὲ τοὺς ἀπὸ θεῶν ἐπὶ τοὺς νεκροὺς καὶ τὰ λείψανα μετατετραμμένους ταύτην ἀποτῖσαι τὴν ζημίαν·[2] ὡς τοῖς μὲν ἐνεχομένοις νόσῳ[3] τινὶ συναλγοῦμεν, τοῖς δὲ ἀπολυομένοις καὶ ἀφιεμένοις ὑπὸ τῶν θεῶν συνηδόμεθα.

Ἐδόθη τῇ τῶν Καλανδῶν Αὐγούστων ἐν Ἀντιοχείᾳ.

42

Καλλιξείνῃ[4]

388 Χρόνος δίκαιον ἄνδρα δείκνυσιν μόνος,
C ὡς παρὰ τῶν ἔμπροσθεν ἔγνωμεν· ἐγὼ δ᾽ ἂν φαίην

[1] ἐπὶ MSS. ἐν Hertlein suggests.
[2] After ζημίαν Hertlein thinks some words are lost.
[3] νόσῳ Hertlein would add; Heyler κακῷ understood.
[4] Hertlein 21.

---

[1] Sozomen 5, 5 and 15 seems to be an echo of Julian.

let those of you who have strayed from the truth outrage those who worship the gods duly and justly, according to the beliefs that have been handed down to us from time immemorial; nor let those of you who worship the gods outrage or plunder the houses of those who have strayed rather from ignorance than of set purpose. It is by reason that we ought to persuade and instruct men, not by blows, or insults, or bodily violence. Wherefore, again and often I admonish those who are zealous for the true religion not to injure the communities of the Galilaeans or attack or insult them.[1] Nay, we ought to pity rather than hate men who in matters of the greatest importance are in such evil case. (For in very truth the greatest of all blessings is reverence for the gods, as, on the other hand, irreverence is the greatest of all evils. It follows that those who have turned aside from the gods to corpses[2] and relics pay this as their penalty.)[3] Since we suffer in sympathy with those who are afflicted by disease,[4] but rejoice with those who are being released and set free by the aid of the gods. Given at Antioch on the First of August.

42

To Callixeine[5]

"TIME alone proves the just man,"[6] as we learn from men of old; but I would add the god-fearing 362 From Antioch

[2] So Julian styles Christ and the martyrs; cf. *Against the Galilaeans* 335B; Vol. 2, *Misopogon* 361B.

[3] *i. e.* that they are in evil case.

[4] For Christianity a disease cf. Vol. 2, 229D, and below, p. 207.

[5] Otherwise unknown. Julian visited Pessinus in Phrygia on his way to Antioch. See Introduction.

[6] Sophocles, *Oedipus Rex* 614.

ὅτι καὶ τὸν εὐσεβῆ καὶ τὸν φιλόθεον. ἀλλ' ἐμαρτυρήθη, φής, καὶ ἡ Πηνελόπη φίλανδρος. εἶτα μετὰ τὸ φίλανδρον[1] τὸ φιλόθεον τίς ἐν γυναικὶ δεύτερον τίθησι, καὶ οὐ φαίνεται[2] πολὺν πάνυ τὸν μανδραγόραν ἐκπεπωκώς; εἰ δὲ καὶ τοὺς
D καιρούς τις ἐν νῷ λάβοι καὶ τὴν μὲν Πηνελόπην ἐπαινουμένην σχεδὸν ὑπὸ πάντων ἐπὶ τῇ φιλανδρίᾳ, κινδυνευούσας δὲ τὰς εὐσεβεῖς ὀλίγῳ πρότερον γυναῖκας, καὶ προσθήκην δὲ τῶν κακῶν, ὅτι καὶ διπλάσιος ὁ χρόνος, ἆρ' ἔστι σοὶ τὴν Πηνελόπην ἀξίως παραβάλλειν; ἀλλὰ μὴ μικροὺς ποιοῦ τοὺς ἐπαίνους· ἀνθ' ὧν ἀμείψονται μέν σε
389 πάντες οἱ θεοί, τὸ παρ' ἡμῶν δὲ διπλῇ σε τιμήσομεν τῇ ἱερωσύνῃ. πρὸς ᾗ γὰρ πρότερον εἶχες τῆς ἁγιωτάτης θεοῦ Δήμητρος, καὶ τῆς μεγίστης Μητρὸς θεῶν τῆς Φρυγίας ἐν τῇ θεοφιλεῖ Πεσσινοῦντι τὴν ἱερωσύνην ἐπιτρέπομέν σοι.

43

Εὐσταθίῳ φιλοσόφῳ[3]

Μὴ λίαν ᾖ κοινὸν τὸ προοίμιον Τὸν ἐσθλὸν ἄνδρα. τὰ δὲ ἐφεξῆς οἶσθα δήπουθεν. ἀλλὰ καὶ

[1] Reiske suggests; Hertlein, MSS. τοῦ φιλάνδρου.
[2] Klimek; φανεῖται Hertlein, MSS.
[3] Hertlein 76. This letter is preserved in *Vaticanus* 1353 only.

---

[1] To drink mandragora (mandrake), is a proverb for sluggish wits; but mandrake was used also as a stimulus to love.

and pious man also. However, you say, the love of Penelope for her husband was also witnessed to by time. Now who would rank a woman's piety second to her love for her husband without appearing to have drunk a very deep draught of mandragora?[1] And if one takes into account the conditions of the times and compares Penelope, who is almost universally praised for loving her husband, with pious women who not long ago hazarded their lives; and if one considers also that the period was twice as long, which was an aggravation of their sufferings; then, I ask, is it possible to make any fair comparison between you and Penelope? Nay, do not belittle my praises. All the gods will requite you for your sufferings and for my part I shall honour you with a double priesthood. For besides that which you held before of priestess to the most venerable goddess Demeter, I entrust to you the office of priestess to the most mighty Mother of the gods in Phrygia at Pessinus, beloved of the gods.

43

To Eustathius the Philosopher[2]

Perhaps the proverb "An honest man"[3]—is too 362
hackneyed. I am sure you know the rest. More From Antioch

[2] See Introduction under Eustathius. He evidently accepted this invitation; see the next letter. He was a pagan and a friend of Libanius; cf. Ammianus 17. 5. 15; Eunapius, *Lives*, pp. 392 foll. (Wright).

[3] Euripides *frag.* 902, Nauck:

Τὸν ἐσθλὸν ἄνδρα, κἂν ἑκὰς ναίῃ χθονός,
Κἂν μήποτ' ὄσσοις εἰσίδω, κρίνω φίλον.

"An honest man, though he dwell far away and I never see him with my eyes, him I count a friend."

ἔχεις. οἶσθα μὲν γὰρ ἅτε λόγιος ὢν καὶ φιλόσοφος τὸ ἑπόμενον αὐτῷ, ἐμὲ δὲ ἔχεις φίλον, εἴπερ γοῦν[1] ἄμφω ἐσθλοί ἐσμεν. ὑπὲρ γὰρ σοῦ τοῦτο κἂν διατειναίμην, ὅτι τοιοῦτος εἶ, περὶ δὲ ἐμαυτοῦ σιωπῶ· γένοιτο δὲ τοὺς ἄλλους αἰσθέσθαι καὶ ἐμοῦ τοιούτου. τί οὖν ὥσπερ ἄτοπόν τι λέξων[2] κύκλῳ περίειμι δέον[3] εἰπεῖν; ἧκε καὶ σπεῦδε καί, τὸ λεγόμενον, ἵπτασο. πορεύσει δέ σε θεὸς εὐμενὴς μετὰ τῆς Ἐνοδίας παρθένου, καὶ ὑπουργήσει δρόμος δημόσιος ὀχήματι βουλομένῳ χρήσασθαι, καὶ παρίπποις δυσίν.

44

Εὐσταθίῳ φιλοσόφῳ[4]

Χρὴ ξεῖνον παρεόντα φιλεῖν, ἐθέλοντα δὲ πέμπειν

416 Ὅμηρος ὁ σοφὸς ἐνομοθέτησεν· ἡμῖν δὲ ὑπάρχει πρὸς ἀλλήλους ξενικῆς φιλίας ἀμείνων ἥ τε διὰ τῆς ἐνδεχομένης παιδείας καὶ τῆς περὶ τοὺς θεοὺς εὐσεβείας, ὥστ' οὐκ ἄν μέ τις ἐγράψατο δικαίως ὡς τὸν Ὁμήρου παραβαίνοντα νόμον, εἰ

[1] γοῦν Hertlein suggests; οὖν MSS., Hertlein.
[2] λέξων Hertlein suggests; λέγων MSS., Hertlein.
[3] After δέον Thomas would add ἁπλῶς.
[4] Hertlein 39. Cumont restores Εὐσταθίῳ from X (Papadopoulos); Hertlein, following Martin, τῷ αὐτῷ *i.e.* Maximus, to whom the preceding letter in Hertlein's edition is addressed; Estienne Μαξίμῳ φιλοσόφῳ. The Aldine has no title.

than this, you possess it; for, rhetorician and philosopher as you are, you know the words that come next, and you possess me for a friend, at least if we are both honest men. On your behalf I would strenuously maintain that you are in that category, but about myself I say nothing. I only pray that others may find by experience that I also am honest! You ask why I go round in a circle as though I were going to say something extraordinary when I ought to speak out? Come, then, lose no time; fly hither, as we say. A kindly god will speed you on your way with the aid of the Maiden of the Cross Roads and the state post[1] will be at your disposal if you wish to use a carriage; and two extra horses.

44

To Eustathius[2]

"Entreat kindly the guest in your house, but speed him when he would be gone."[3] 362 From Antioch

Thus did wise Homer decree. But the friendship that exists between us two is stronger than that between guest and host, because it is inspired by the best education attainable and by our pious devotion to the gods. So that no one could have fairly indicted me for transgressing the law of Homer if

[1] The *cursus publicus* was the system of posting stations where horses were kept ready for the use of the Emperor or his friends; cf. above, p. 83 *To Basil*, end.

[2] Hertlein, following an error in the editions of Martin and Estienne, makes Julian address this letter to Maximus. For the answer of Eustathius see p. 291.

[3] *Odyssey* 15. 74; this had become a proverb, cf. Libanius, *Letter* 130.

καὶ ἐπὶ πλεῖόν σε μένειν παρ' ἡμῖν ἠξίωσα. ἀλλά
σοι τὸ σωμάτιον ἰδὼν ἐπιμελείας πλείονος δεόμενον
B ἐπέτρεψα βαδίζειν εἰς τὴν πατρίδα, καὶ ῥᾳστώνης
ἐπεμελήθην τῆς πορείας. ὀχήματι γοῦν ἔξεστί σοι δημοσίῳ χρήσασθαι, πορεύοιεν δέ σε σὺν Ἀσκληπιῷ πάντες οἱ θεοί, καὶ πάλιν ἡμῖν συντυχεῖν δοῖεν.

45

Ἐκδικίῳ ἐπάρχῳ Αἰγύπτου [1]

432 Ἡ μὲν παροιμία φησίν "ἐμοὶ διηγοῦ σὺ [2] τοὐ-
B μὸν ὄναρ," ἐγὼ δ' ἔοικα σοὶ τὸ σὸν ὕπαρ ἀφηγεῖσθαι. πολύς, φασίν, ὁ Νεῖλος ἀρθεὶς μετέωρος τοῖς πήχεσιν ἐπλήρωσε πᾶσαν τὴν Αἴγυπτον· εἰ δὲ καὶ τὸν ἀριθμὸν ἀκοῦσαι ποθεῖς, εἰς τὴν εἰκάδα τοῦ Σεπτεμβρίου τρὶς πέντε. μηνύει δὲ ταῦτα Θεόφιλος ὁ στρατοπεδάρχης. εἰ τοίνυν ἠγνόησας αὐτό, παρ' ἡμῶν ἀκούων εὐφραίνου.

46

Ἐκδικίῳ ἐπάρχῳ Αἰγύπτου [3]

376 Εἰ καὶ τῶν ἄλλων ἕνεκα μὴ γράφεις ἡμῖν, ἀλλ' ὑπέρ γε τοῦ θεοῖς ἐχθροῦ χρῆν σε γράφειν Ἀθανα-

[1] Hertlein 50.
[2] This is the reading of Suidas, who quotes ἐμοὶ—ἀφηγεῖσθαι; *Ambrosianus* σὺ διηγοῦ; Hertlein, following *Vossianus*, διηγεῖ.
[3] Hertlein 6.

---

[1] Cappadocia.
[2] The premature death of Julian prevented the fulfilment of this wish.

I had insisted that you should remain still longer with us. But I see that your feeble frame needs more care, and I have therefore given you permission to go to your own country,[1] and have provided for your comfort on the journey. That is to say, you are allowed to use a state carriage, and may Asclepius and all the gods escort you on your way and grant that we may see you again![2]

45

To Ecdicius, Prefect of Egypt[3]

As the proverb says, "You told me my own dream."[4] And I fancy that I am relating to you your own waking vision. The Nile, they tell me, had risen in full flood, cubits high, and has inundated the whole of Egypt. If you want to hear the figures, it had risen fifteen cubits[5] on the twentieth of September. Theophilus, the military prefect, informs me of this. So, if you did not know it, hear it from me, and let it rejoice your heart.

362 October From Antioch

46

To Ecdicius, Prefect of Egypt

Even though you do not write to me[6] on other matters, you ought at least to have written about

362 About October From Antioch

[3] For Ecdicius see p. 155.

[4] Cf. "Queen Anne is dead." Ecdicius presumably knew what Julian tells him.

[5] Pliny, *Natural History* 5. 9, says that a rise of 15 cubits gives Egypt security, 16 is luxury; Ammianus 22. 15 says that cultivators fear a rise of more than 16 cubits. The Egyptian cubit was about 22 inches.

[6] Egypt was the peculiar property of the Roman Emperors and reports were made by the prefect to them.

σίου, καὶ ταῦτα πρὸ πλείονος ἤδη χρόνου τὰ καλῶς ἡμῖν ἐγνωσμένα πεπυσμένον. ὄμνυμι δὲ τὸν μέγαν Σάραπιν, ὡς εἰ μὴ πρὸ τῶν Δεκεμβρίων Καλανδῶν ὁ θεοῖς ἐχθρὸς Ἀθανάσιος ἐξέλθοι ἐκείνης τῆς πό-
B λεως,[1] μᾶλλον δὲ καὶ πάσης τῆς Αἰγύπτου, τῇ ὑπακουούσῃ σοι τάξει προστιμήσομαι χρυσοῦ λίτρας ἑκατόν. οἶσθα δὲ ὅπως εἰμὶ βραδὺς μὲν εἰς τὸ καταγνῶναι, πολλῷ δὲ ἔτι βραδύτερος εἰς τὸ ἅπαξ καταγνοὺς ἀνεῖναι. καὶ τῇ αὐτοῦ χειρί· πάνυ με λυπεῖ τὸ καταφρονεῖσθαι. μὰ τοὺς θεοὺς πάντας οὐδὲν οὕτως ἂν ἴδοιμι, μᾶλλον δὲ ἀκούσαιμι ἡδέως παρὰ σοῦ πραχθέν, ὡς Ἀθανάσιον ἐξελη-
C λαμένον τῶν τῆς Αἰγύπτου ὅρων,[2] τὸν μιαρόν, ὃς ἐτόλμησεν Ἑλληνίδας ἐπ' ἐμοῦ γυναῖκας τῶν ἐπισήμων βαπτίσαι. διωκέσθω.

47

Ἀλεξανδρεῦσιν[3]

432 Εἰ μέν τις τῶν Γαλιλαίων[4] ἦν ὑμῶν οἰκιστής,
D οἳ τὸν ἑαυτῶν παραβάντες νόμον ἀπέτισαν ὁποίας ἦν εἰκὸς δίκας, ἑλόμενοι μὲν ζῆν παρανόμως, εἰσαγαγόντες δὲ κήρυγμα καινὸν[5] καὶ διδασκαλίαν

[1] τῆς πόλεως Hertlein suggests.
[2] ὅρων Asmus, τόπων Hertlein, MSS.
[3] Hertlein 51. [4] Asmus; ἄλλων Hertlein, MSS.
[5] καινὸν Asmus adds; see below 433B.

---

[1] Athanasius had disregarded the order to leave Alexandria, but he now, on October 24th, went into exile in Upper Egypt; Socrates 3. 14; Sozomen 5. 15; see p. 75.

that enemy of the gods, Athanasius,[1] especially since, for a long time past, you have known my just decrees. I swear by mighty Serapis that, if Athanasius the enemy of the gods does not depart from that city, or rather from all Egypt, before the December Kalends, I shall fine the cohort which you command a hundred pounds[2] of gold. And you know that, though I am slow to condemn, I am even much slower to remit when I have once condemned. *Added with his own hand.*[3] It vexes me greatly that my orders are neglected. By all the gods there is nothing I should be so glad to see, or rather hear reported as achieved by you, as that Athanasius has been expelled beyond the frontiers of Egypt. Infamous man! He has had the audacity to baptise Greek women of rank[4] during my reign! Let him be driven forth![5]

47

To the Alexandrians

If your founder had been one of the Galilaeans, men who have transgressed their own law[6] and have paid the penalties they deserved, since they elected to live in defiance of the law and have introduced a new doctrine and newfangled teaching, even then

362 Nov. or Dec. From Antioch

[2] The Greek word used is the equivalent of the Latin *libra* = 12 ounces.

[3] For similar postscripts see pp. 15, 19.

[4] Or "wives of distinguished men."

[5] In the *Neapolitanus* MS. the following has been added by a Christian: μακάριος οὗτος, κυὼν μιαρὲ καὶ τρισκατάρατε παράβατα καὶ τρισάθλιε.—"This man is a blessed saint, O vile dog of an apostate, thrice accursed and thrice miserable!"

[6] *i.e.* the Hebraic law; cf. *Against the Galilaeans*, 238B, foll., 305E, foll.

νεαράν, λόγον ἂν εἶχεν οὐδ' ὣς Ἀθανάσιον ὑφ' ὑμῶν ἐπιζητεῖσθαι· νυνὶ δὲ κτίστου μὲν ὄντος Ἀλεξάνδρου τῆς πόλεως, ὑπάρχοντος δὲ ὑμῖν πολιούχου θεοῦ τοῦ βασιλέως Σαράπιδος ἅμα τῇ
433 παρέδρῳ κόρῃ καὶ τῇ βασιλίδι τῆς Αἰγύπτου πάσης Ἴσιδι[1] . . . . τὴν ὑγιαίνουσαν οὐ ζηλοῦντες πόλιν· ἀλλὰ τὸ νοσοῦν μέρος ἐπιφημίζειν ἑαυτῷ τολμᾷ τὸ τῆς πόλεως ὄνομα.

Λίαν αἰσχύνομαι νὴ τοὺς θεούς, ἄνδρες Ἀλεξανδρεῖς, εἴ τις ὅλως Ἀλεξανδρέων ὁμολογεῖ Γαλιλαῖος εἶναι. τῶν ὡς ἀληθῶς Ἑβραίων οἱ πατέρες
B Αἰγυπτίοις ἐδούλευον πάλαι, νυνὶ δὲ ὑμεῖς, ἄνδρες Ἀλεξανδρεῖς, Αἰγυπτίων κρατήσαντες· ἐκράτησε γὰρ ὁ κτίστης ὑμῶν τῆς Αἰγύπτου· τοῖς κατωλιγωρηκόσι τῶν πατρίων δογμάτων δουλείαν ἐθελούσιον ἄντικρυς τῶν παλαιῶν θεσμῶν ὑφίστασθε. καὶ οὐκ εἰσέρχεται μνήμη τῆς παλαιᾶς ὑμᾶς ἐκείνης εὐδαιμονίας, ἡνίκα ἦν κοινωνία μὲν πρὸς τοὺς[2] θεοὺς Αἰγύπτῳ τῇ πάσῃ, πολλῶν δὲ ἀπελαύομεν ἀγαθῶν. ἀλλ' οἱ νῦν εἰσαγαγόντες ὑμῖν τὸ καινὸν
C τοῦτο κήρυγμα τίνος αἴτιοι γεγόνασιν ἀγαθοῦ τῇ πόλει, φράσατέ μοι. κτίστης ὑμῖν ἦν ἀνὴρ θεοσεβὴς Ἀλέξανδρος ὁ Μακεδών, οὔτι μὰ Δία κατά τινα τούτων ὧν οὐδὲ κατὰ πάντας Ἑβραίους μακρῷ γεγονότας αὐτῶν κρείττονας. ἐκείνων μὲν οὖν καὶ ὁ τοῦ Λάγου Πτολεμαῖος ἦν ἀμείνων,

[1] Some words, *e. g.* οὐχ ὑγιαίνετε (Capps) have dropped out; lacuna Hertlein, following Petavius.
[2] τοὺς Asmus adds.

---

[1] Athanasius had left Alexandria on October 24th, 362, and, not long after, the Alexandrians petitioned Julian for

it would have been unreasonable for you to demand back Athanasius.[1] But as it is, though Alexander founded your city and the lord Serapis is the city's patron god, together with his consort the Maiden, the Queen of all Egypt, Isis . . .[2] not emulating the healthy part of the city; but the part that is diseased has the audacity to arrogate to itself the name of the whole.

I am overwhelmed with shame, I affirm it by the gods, O men of Alexandria, to think that even a single Alexandrian can admit that he is a Galilaean. The forefathers of the genuine Hebrews were the slaves of the Egyptians long ago, but in these days, men of Alexandria, you who conquered the Egyptians —for your founder was the conqueror of Egypt— submit yourselves, despite your sacred traditions, in willing slavery to men who have set at naught the teachings of their ancestors. You have then no recollection of those happy days of old when all Egypt held communion with the gods and we enjoyed many benefits therefrom. But those who have but yesterday introduced among you this new doctrine, tell me of what benefit have they been to the city? Your founder was a god-fearing man, Alexander of Macedon, in no way, by Zeus, like any of these persons, nor again did he resemble any Hebrews, though the latter have shown themselves far superior to the Galilaeans. Nay, Ptolemy[3] son of Lagus

his return. This is his answer to them. After this edict Athanasius remained in hiding in Egypt and the Sudan till Julian's death in 363, when he recovered his see.

[2] After "Isis" some words are missing.

[3] Ptolemy the First took Jerusalem and led many Jews captive into Egypt, Josephus 1. 12. 1.

Ἀλέξανδρος δὲ κἂν Ῥωμαίοις εἰς ἅμιλλαν ἰὼν ἀγῶνα παρεῖχε. τί οὖν μετὰ τὸν κτίστην οἱ
D Πτολεμαῖοι, τὴν πόλιν ὑμῶν ὥσπερ γνησίαν θυγατέρα παιδοτροφήσαντες; οὔτι τοῖς Ἰησοῦ λόγοις ηὔξησαν αὐτήν, οὐδὲ τῇ τῶν θεοῖς[1] ἐχθίστων Γαλιλαίων διδασκαλίᾳ τὴν οἰκονομίαν αὐτῇ ταύτην, ὑφ' ἧς νῦν ἐστιν εὐδαίμων, ἐξειργάσαντο. τρίτον, ἐπειδὴ Ῥωμαῖοι κύριοι γεγόναμεν αὐτῆς, ἀφελόμενοι τοὺς Πτολεμαίους οὐ καλῶς ἄρχοντας, ὁ Σεβαστὸς ἐπιδημήσας ὑμῶν τῇ πόλει καὶ πρὸς τοὺς ὑμετέρους πολίτας διαλεχθείς, "Ἄνδρες,
434 εἶπεν, Ἀλεξανδρεῖς, ἀφίημι τὴν πόλιν αἰτίας πάσης αἰδοῖ τοῦ μεγάλου θεοῦ Σαράπιδος αὐτοῦ τε ἕνεκα τοῦ δήμου καὶ τοῦ μεγέθους τῆς πόλεως· αἰτία δέ μοι τρίτη τῆς εἰς ὑμᾶς εὐνοίας ἐστὶ καὶ ὁ ἑταῖρος Ἄρειος." ἦν δὲ ὁ Ἄρειος οὗτος πολίτης μὲν ὑμέτερος, Καίσαρος δὲ τοῦ Σεβαστοῦ συμβιωτής, ἀνὴρ φιλόσοφος.

B Τὰ μὲν οὖν ἰδίᾳ περὶ τὴν πόλιν ὑμῶν ὑπάρξαντα παρὰ τῶν Ὀλυμπίων θεῶν, ὡς ἐν βραχεῖ φράσαι, τοιαῦτα, σιωπῶ δὲ διὰ τὸ μῆκος τὰ πολλά· τὰ δὲ κοινῇ καθ' ἡμέραν οὐκ ἀνθρώποις ὀλίγοις οὐδὲ ἑνὶ γένει οὐδὲ μιᾷ πόλει, παντὶ δὲ ὁμοῦ τῷ κόσμῳ παρὰ τῶν ἐμφανῶν[2] θεῶν διδόμενα πῶς ὑμεῖς οὐκ

[1] θεοῖς Asmus adds.
[2] ἐμφανῶν Asmus; ἐπιφανῶν Hertlein, MSS.

[1] For the Alexandrine Stoic, Areius, cf. Julian, *Caesars*, Vol. 2, 326B; *Letter to Themistius*, Vol. 2, 265C, where Areius is said to have refused the prefecture of Egypt; and Philo-

proved stronger than the Jews, while Alexander, if he had had to match himself with the Romans, would have made even them fight hard for supremacy. And what about the Ptolemies who succeeded your founder and nurtured your city from her earliest years as though she were their own daughter? It was certainly not by the preachings of Jesus that they increased her renown, nor by the teaching of the Galilaeans, detested of the gods, did they perfect this administration which she enjoys and to which she owes her present good fortune. Thirdly, when we Romans became her masters and took her out of the hands of the Ptolemies who misgoverned her, Augustus visited your city and made the following speech to your citizens: "Men of Alexandria, I absolve the city of all blame, because of my reverence for the mighty god Serapis, and further for the sake of the people themselves and the great renown of the city. But there is a third reason for my goodwill towards you, and that is my comrade Areius."[1] Now this Areius was a fellow-citizen of yours and a familiar friend of Caesar Augustus, by profession a philosopher.

These, then, to sum them up briefly, are the blessings bestowed by the Olympian gods on your city in peculiar, though I pass over very many because they would take too long to describe. But the blessings that are vouchsafed by the visible gods to all in common, every day, not merely to a few persons or a single race, or to one city, but to the whole world at the same time, how can you fail to

stratus, *Lives of the Sophists*, Introduction, p. xxiii (Loeb Library Edition). See Seneca, *Dialogues* **6. 4**, where Areius consoles and exhorts the Empress Livia.

ἴστε; μόνοι τῆς ἐξ Ἡλίου κατιούσης αὐγῆς ἀναισθήτως ἔχετε; μόνοι θέρος οὐκ ἴστε καὶ χειμῶνα
C παρ' αὐτοῦ γινόμενον; μόνοι ζῳογονούμενα καὶ φυόμενα παρ' αὐτοῦ τὰ πάντα; τὴν δὲ ἐξ αὐτοῦ καὶ παρ' αὐτοῦ δημιουργὸν τῶν ὅλων Σελήνην οὖσαν[1] οὐκ αἰσθάνεσθε πόσων ἀγαθῶν αἰτία τῇ πόλει γίνεται; καὶ τούτων μὲν τῶν θεῶν οὐδένα προσκυνεῖν τολμᾶτε· ὃν δὲ οὔτε ὑμεῖς οὔτε οἱ πατέρες ὑμῶν ἑοράκασιν Ἰησοῦν οἴεσθε χρῆναι θεὸν λόγον[1] ὑπάρχειν. ὃν δὲ ἐξ αἰῶνος ἅπαν ὁρᾷ τὸ τῶν ἀνθρώπων γένος καὶ βλέπει καὶ
D σέβεται καὶ σεβόμενον εὖ πράττει, τὸν μέγαν Ἥλιον λέγω, τὸ ζῶν ἄγαλμα καὶ ἔμψυχον καὶ ἔννουν καὶ ἀγαθοεργὸν τοῦ νοητοῦ πατρός,[2] . . . εἴ τι μοι πείθεσθε παραινοῦντι, καὶ μικρὰ ὑμᾶς αὐτοὺς ἐπαναγάγετε πρὸς τὴν ἀλήθειαν. οὐχ ἁμαρτήσεσθε γὰρ τῆς ὀρθῆς ὁδοῦ πειθόμενοι τῷ πορευθέντι κἀκείνην τὴν ὁδὸν ἄχρις ἐτῶν εἴκοσι καὶ ταύτην ἤδη σὺν θεοῖς πορευομένῳ δωδέκατον ἔτος.

435 Εἰ μὲν οὖν φίλον ὑμῖν πείθεσθαι, μειζόνως

[1] Cobet omits λόγον as a theologian's gloss, but Julian is thinking of the beginning of S. John's Gospel; cf. *Against the Galilaeans*, 327B, 333B, C for his attack on the doctrine of Christ the Word.

[2] Here some words are lost, probably omitted by Christian copyists as blasphemous. Asmus rightly restores πατρός; Hertlein, following Osann, παντός.

---

[1] For Selene as the artificer of the visible world cf. Vol. 1, *Oration* 4, 150A.

know what they are? Are you alone insensible to the beams that descend from Helios? Are you alone ignorant that summer and winter are from him? Or that all kinds of animal and plant life proceed from him? And do you not perceive what great blessings the city derives from her who is generated from and by him, even Selene who is the creator of the whole universe?[1] Yet you have the audacity not to adore any one of these gods; and you think that one whom neither you nor your fathers have ever seen, even Jesus, ought to rank as God the Word. But the god whom from time immemorial the whole race of mankind has beheld and looked up to and worshipped, and from that worship prospered, I mean mighty Helios, his intelligible father's living image,[2] endowed with soul and intelligence, cause of all good . . . if you heed my admonition, do ye lead yourselves even a little towards the truth. For you will not stray from the right road[3] if you heed one who till his twentieth year walked in that road of yours, but for twelve years now has walked in this road I speak of, by the grace of the gods.[4]

Therefore, if it please you to obey me, you will

[2] Cf. *Fragment of a Letter to a Priest*, Vol. 2, 295A, where the stars are called "living images." Julian here refers not to the visible sun, but to the "intellectual" (νοερὸς) Helios who is in the likeness of his "intelligible" (νοητὸς) father, the transcendental Helios, for whom cf. *Oration* 4, Vol. 1, 133C, note.

[3] For Julian's reproach against the Christians that they had taken "their own road" and abandoned the teaching of Moses, cf. *Against the Galilaeans* 43A.

[4] Cf. Vol. 1, *Oration* 4, 131A where he also refers to the time when he was a Christian and desires that it may be forgotten.

εὐφρανεῖτε· τῇ δεισιδαιμονίᾳ δὲ καὶ κατηχήσει τῶν πανούργων ἀνθρώπων ἐμμένειν εἴπερ ἐθέλοιτε, τὰ πρὸς ἀλλήλους ὁμονοεῖτε καὶ τὸν Ἀθανάσιον μὴ ποθεῖτε. πολλοὶ πάντως εἰσὶ τῶν αὐτοῦ μαθητῶν δυνάμενοι τὰς ἀκοὰς ὑμῶν κνησιώσας καὶ
B δεομένας ἀσεβῶν ῥημάτων ἱκανῶς παραμυθήσασθαι. ὤφελε γὰρ Ἀθανασίῳ ὁμοῦ[1] ἡ τοῦ δυσσεβοῦς αὐτοῦ διδασκαλείου κατακεκλεῖσθαι μοχθηρία. νῦν δέ ἐστι πλῆθος ὑμῖν οὐκ ἀγεννές, καὶ πρᾶγμά δὲ[2] οὐδέν. ὃν γὰρ ἂν ἕλησθε τοῦ πλήθους, ὅσα γε εἰς τὴν τῶν γραφῶν διδασκαλίαν ἥκει, χείρων οὐδὲν ἔσται τοῦ παρ' ὑμῶν ποθουμένου. εἰ δὲ τῆς ἄλλης ἐντρεχείας ἐρῶντες Ἀθα-
C νασίου· πανοῦργον γὰρ εἶναι τὸν ἄνδρα πυνθάνομαι· ταύτας ἐποιήσασθε τὰς δεήσεις, ἴστε δι' αὐτὸ τοῦτο[3] αὐτὸν ἀπεληλαμένον τῆς πόλεως· ἀνεπιτήδειος γὰρ φύσει προστατεύειν δήμου πολυπράγμων ἀνήρ. εἰ δὲ μηδὲ ἀνήρ, ἀλλ' ἀνθρωπίσκος εὐτελής, καθάπερ οὗτος ὁ μέγας οἰόμενος περὶ τῆς κεφαλῆς κινδυνεύειν, τοῦτο δὲ[4] δίδωσιν ἀταξίας ἀρχήν. ὅθεν, ἵνα μὴ γένηται τοιοῦτο περὶ ὑμᾶς μηδέν, ἀπελθεῖν αὐτῷ προηγορεύσαμεν τῆς πόλεως
D πάλαι, νυνὶ δὲ καὶ Αἰγύπτου πάσης.

Προτεθήτω τοῖς ἡμετέροις πολίταις Ἀλεξανδρεῦσιν.

[1] Asmus ὁμοῦ or ἅμα; Sintenis μόνον; Hertlein, MSS. μόνῳ; Hertlein suggests μόνῳ γε.
[2] τε Hertlein, MSS.; δὲ Hertlein suggests; Hercher would delete τε.
[3] MSS. διὰ τοῦτο; Reiske διὰ τοῦτο αὐτό; Hertlein suggests δι' αὐτὸ τοῦτο.
[4] Sintenis deletes δέ; Hercher lacuna after ἀρχήν; Capps suggests δή.

rejoice me the more. But if you choose to persevere in the superstition and instruction of wicked men, at least agree among yourselves and do not crave for Athanasius. In any case there are many of his pupils who can comfort well enough those itching ears of yours that yearn to hear impious words. I only wish that, along with Athanasius, the wickedness of his impious school had been suppressed. But as it is you have a fine crowd of them and need have no trouble. For any man whom you elect from the crowd will be in no way inferior to him for whom you crave, at any rate for the teaching of the scriptures. But if you have made these requests because you are so fond of the general subtlety of Athanasius—for I am informed that the man is a clever rascal—then you must know that for this very reason he has been banished from the city. For a meddlesome man is unfit by nature to be leader of the people. But if this leader is not even a man but only a contemptible puppet, like this great personage who thinks he is risking his head, this surely gives the signal for disorder. Wherefore, that nothing of the sort may occur in your case, as I long ago gave orders[1] that he depart from the city, I now say, let him depart from the whole of Egypt.

Let this be publicly proclaimed to my citizens of Alexandria.

[1] See above, *To the Alexandrians*, p. 75.

48

Ἀλεξανδρεῦσιν[1]

443 Ὀβελὸν εἶναι παρ' ὑμῖν ἀκούω λίθινον εἰς ὕψος
B ἱκανὸν ἐπηρμένον, ἐπὶ τῆς ᾐόνος ὥσπερ ἄλλο τι
τῶν ἀτιμοτάτων ἐρριμμένον. ἐπὶ τοῦτον ἐναυπηγήσατο σκάφος ὁ μακαρίτης Κωνστάντιος, ὡς μετάξων αὐτὸν εἰς τὴν ἐμὴν πατρίδα Κωνσταντίνου πόλιν. ἐπεὶ δε ἐκείνῳ συνέβη θεῶν ἐθελόντων ἐνθένδε ἐκεῖσε πορευθῆναι τὴν εἱμαρμένην πορείαν, ἡ πόλις ἀπαιτεῖ παρ' ἐμοῦ τὸ ἀνάθημα, πατρὶς οὖσά μου[2] καὶ προσήκουσα πλέον ἤπερ ἐκείνῳ. ὁ μὲν γὰρ αὐτὴν ὡς ἀδελφήν, ἐγὼ δὲ ὡς μητέρα φιλῶ· καὶ γὰρ ἐγενόμην παρ' αὐτῇ καὶ ἐτράφην ἐκεῖσε, καὶ οὐ δύναμαι περὶ αὐτὴν ἀγνωμονῆσαι. τί οὖν; ἐπειδὴ καὶ ὑμᾶς οὐδὲν ἔλαττον τῆς πατρίδος φιλῶ, δίδωμι καὶ παρ' ὑμῖν ἀναστῆσαι τὴν χαλκῆν εἰκόνα. πεποίηται δὲ ἔναγχος ἀνδριὰς τῷ μεγέθει κολοσσικός, ὃν ἀναστήσαντες ἕξετε ἀντὶ ἀναθήματος λιθίνου χαλκοῦν, ἀνδρός, οὗ φατε ποθεῖν, εἰκόνα καὶ μορφὴν ἀντὶ τετραγώνου[3] λίθου χαράγματα ἔχοντος Αἰγύπτια. καὶ τὸ λεγόμενον δέ, ὥς τινές εἰσιν οἱ θεραπεύοντες καὶ

[1] Hertlein 58; the first part of this letter was published by Rigaltius, Paris, 1601, the whole letter by Muratorius, Padua, 1709.

[2] Hertlein suggests *μοι*.

[3] *τριγώνου* Hertlein, MSS.; *τετραγώνου* La Bléterie, as the obelisk is four-sided.

---

[1] This granite monolith, which stands in the At Meidán (the hippodrome) in Constantinople, was originally erected by Thothmes III. (about 1515 B.C.), probably at Heliopolis.

48

To the Alexandrians

I AM informed that there is in your neighbourhood a granite obelisk[1] which, when it stood erect, reached a considerable height, but has been thrown down and lies on the beach as though it were something entirely worthless. For this obelisk Constantius of blessed memory had a freight-boat built, because he intended to convey it to my native place, Constantinople. But since by the will of heaven he has departed from this life to the next on that journey to which we are fated,[2] the city claims the monument from me because it is the place of my birth and more closely connected with me than with the late Emperor. For though he loved the place as a sister I love it as my mother. And I was in fact born there and brought up in the place, and I cannot ignore its claims. Well then, since I love you also, no less than my native city, I grant to you also permission to set up the bronze statue[3] in your city. A statue has lately been made of colossal size. If you set this up you will have, instead of a stone monument, a bronze statue of a man whom you say you love and long for, and a human shape instead of a quadrangular block of granite with Egyptian characters on it. Moreover the news has reached me that there are certain

Early 363 From Antioch

The Alexandrians obeyed Julian's orders, but the boat containing the obelisk was driven by a storm to Athens, where it remained till the Emperor Theodosius (379–395 A.D.) conveyed it to Constantinople. There, as an inscription on its base records, it took 32 days to erect; see *Palatine Anthology* 9. 682.

[2] Plato, *Phaedo*, 117C.

[3] Of himself (?) or of Constantius. The Emperor's permission was necessary for the erection of a statue by a city.

προσκαθεύδοντες αὐτοῦ τῇ κορυφῇ, πάνυ με πείθει χρῆναι τῆς δεισιδαιμονίας ἕνεκα ταύτης ἀπάγειν αὐτόν. οἱ γὰρ θεώμενοι τοὺς καθεύδοντας ἐκεῖ, πολλοῦ μὲν ῥύπου, πολλῆς δὲ ἀσελγείας περὶ τὸν τόπον ὡς ἔτυχεν οὔσης, οὔτε πιστεύουσιν αὐτὸν θεῖον εἶναι, καὶ διὰ τὴν τῶν προσεχόντων αὐτῷ δεισιδαιμονίαν ἀπιστότεροι περὶ τοὺς θεοὺς καθίστανται. δι' αὐτὸ δὴ οὖν τοῦτο καὶ μᾶλλον ὑμῖν προσήκει συνεπιλαβέσθαι καὶ πέμψαι τῇ ἐμῇ πατρίδι τῇ ξενοδοκούσῃ καλῶς ὑμᾶς, ὅτε εἰς τὸν Πόντον εἰσπλεῖτε, καὶ ὥσπερ εἰς τὰς τροφὰς καὶ εἰς τὸν ἐκτὸς κόσμον συμβάλλεσθαι. πάντως οὐκ ἄχαρι καὶ παρ' αὐτοῖς ἑστάναι τι τῶν ὑμετέρων, εἰς ὃ προσπλέοντες τῇ πόλει μετ' εὐφροσύνης ἀποβλέψετε.

49

Ἐκδικίῳ[1]

422 Ἄξιόν ἐστιν, εἴπερ ἄλλου τινός, καὶ τῆς ἱερᾶς ἐπιμεληθῆναι μουσικῆς. ἐπιλεξάμενος οὖν ἐκ τοῦ δήμου τῶν Ἀλεξανδρέων εὖ γεγονότας μειρακίσκους ἀρτάβας ἑκάστῳ σίτου[2] κέλευσον δύο τοῦ

[1] Hertlein 56.
[2] σίτου Hertlein adds.

---

[1] Possibly there was a martyr's grave near, at which the Christians worshipped; more probably, Christian or Jewish ascetics who flourished at Alexandria and were called therapeuts," "worshippers," had settled near the obelisk. Sozo-

persons who worship there and sleep[1] at its very apex, and that convinces me beyond doubt that on account of these superstitious practices I ought to take it away. For men who see those persons sleeping there and so much filthy rubbish and careless and licentious behaviour in that place, not only do not believe that it[2] is sacred, but by the influence of the superstition of those who dwell there come to have less faith in the gods. Therefore, for this very reason it is the more proper for you to assist in this business and to send it to my native city, which always receives you hospitably when you sail into the Pontus, and to contribute to its external adornment, even as you contribute to its sustenance. It cannot fail to give you pleasure to have something that has belonged to you standing in their city, and as you sail towards that city you will delight in gazing at it.

49

To Ecdicius, Prefect of Egypt

IF there is anything that deserves our fostering care, it is the sacred art of music. Do you therefore select from the citizens of Alexandria[3] boys of good birth, and give orders that two artabae[4] of corn are 362 or early in 363 From Antioch

men 6. 29 says that about 2000 ascetic monks lived in the neighbourhood of Alexandria. See also Sozomen 1. 12.

[2] *i.e.* the obelisk, which was originally dedicated to the Sun.

[3] For the study of music at Alexandria cf. Ammianus Marcellinus 22. 16. 17, nondumque apud eos penitus exaruit musica, nec harmonia conticuit.

[4] The artaba, an Egyptian dry measure, was equivalent to about nine gallons.

μηνὸς χορηγεῖσθαι, ἔλαιόν τε ἐπ αὐτῷ[1] καὶ οἶνον·
B ἐσθῆτα δὲ παρέξουσιν οἱ τοῦ ταμιείου προεστῶτες. οὗτοι δὲ τέως ἐκ φωνῆς καταλεγέσθωσαν. εἰ δέ τινες δύναιντο καὶ τῆς ἐπιστήμης αὐτῆς εἰς ἄκρον μετασχεῖν, ἴστωσαν[2] ἀποκείμενα πάνυ μεγάλα τοῦ πόνου τὰ ἔπαθλα καὶ παρ' ἡμῖν. ὅτι γὰρ πρὸ ἡμῶν αὐτοὶ τὰς ψυχὰς ὑπὸ τῆς θείας μουσικῆς καθαρθέντες ὀνήσονται, πιστευτέον τοῖς προαποφαινομένοις ὀρθῶς ὑπὲρ τούτων. ὑπὲρ μὲν οὖν
C τῶν παίδων τοσαῦτα. τοὺς δὲ νῦν ἀκροωμένους τοῦ μουσικοῦ Διοσκόρου ποίησον ἀντιλαβέσθαι τῆς τέχνης προθυμότερον, ὡς ἡμῶν ἑτοίμων ἐπὶ ὅπερ ἂν ἐθέλωσιν αὐτοῖς συνάρασθαι.

50

Διονυσίῳ[3]

443 Ἀμείνων ἦσθα σιωπῶν πρότερον ἢ νῦν ἀπολογούμενος· οὐδὲ γὰρ ἐλοιδοροῦ τότε, καίτοι διανοούμενος ἴσως αὐτό· νυνὶ δὲ ὥσπερ ὠδίνων τὴν καθ' ἡμῶν λοιδορίαν ἀθρόαν ἐξέχεας. ἢ γὰρ
D οὐ χρή με καὶ λοιδορίαν αὐτὸ καὶ βλασφημίαν νομίζειν, ὅτι με τοῖς σεαυτοῦ φίλοις ὑπελάμβανες εἶναι προσόμοιον, ὧν ἑκατέρῳ δέδωκας σεαυτὸν

[1] After αὐτῷ Hertlein brackets καὶ σῖτον.
[2] ἴστων Hertlein suggests.
[3] Hertlein 59. In *Laurentianus* LVIII the title is Ἰουλιανὸς κατὰ τοῦ Νείλου; Διονυσίῳ first appears in the Paris edition, 1630.

to be furnished every month to each of them, with olive oil also, and wine. The overseers of the Treasury will provide them with clothing. For the present let these boys be chosen for their voices, but if any of them should prove capable of attaining to the higher study of the science of music, let them be informed that very considerable rewards for their work have been set aside at my court also. For they must believe those who have expressed right opinions on these matters that they themselves rather than we will be purified in soul by divinely inspired[1] music, and benefit thereby. So much, then, for the boys. As for those who are now the pupils of Dioscorus the musician, do you urge them to apply themselves to the art with still more zeal, for I am ready to assist them to whatever they may wish.

50

To Nilus, surnamed Dionysius[2]

YOUR earlier silence was more creditable than your present defence; for then you did not utter abuse, though perhaps it was in your mind. But now, as though you were in travail, you have poured out your abuse of me wholesale. For must I not regard it as abuse and slander that you supposed me to be like your own friends, to each of whom you offered yourself uninvited; or rather, by the first[3] 362-363 Winter From Antioch

[1] Julian does not mean sacred music in particular; cf. Vol. 1, *Oration* 3. 111C, where θεία is used of secular music.

[2] For the name and personality of Nilus see Introduction, under Nilus.

[3] Constans; cf. Vol. 1, *Oration* 1. 9D.

ἄκλητον, μᾶλλον δὲ τῷ μὲν ἄκλητον, τῷ προτέρῳ, τῷ δευτέρῳ δὲ ἐνδειξαμένῳ μόνον, ὅτι σε συνεργὸν ἐθέλει προσλαβεῖν, ὑπήκουσας. ἀλλ' εἰ μὲν ἐγὼ προσόμοιός εἰμι Κώνσταντι καὶ Μαγνεντίῳ, τὸ πρᾶγμα αὐτό, φασί, δείξει· σὺ δ' ὅτι κατὰ τὸν κωμικὸν

σαυτὴν ἐπαινεῖς ὥσπερ Ἀστυδάμας, γύναι,

444 πρόδηλόν ἐστιν ἐξ ὧν ἐπέστειλας. ἡ γὰρ ἀφοβία καὶ τὸ μέγα θάρσος καὶ τὸ εἴθε με γνοίης ὅσος καὶ οἷός εἰμι, καὶ πάντα ἁπλῶς τὰ τοιαῦτα, βαβαί, πηλίκου κτύπου καὶ κόμπου ῥημάτων ἐστίν. ἀλλὰ καὶ πρὸς τῶν Χαρίτων καὶ τῆς Ἀφροδίτης, εἰ τολμηρὸς οὕτως εἶ[1] καὶ γενναῖος, τί καὶ τρίτον ηὐλαβήθης, ἂν δέῃ, προσκρούειν; οἱ γὰρ τοῖς κρατοῦσιν ἀπεχθανόμενοι, τὸ μὲν κουφότατον καί, ὡς ἂν εἴποι τις, ἥδιστον τῷ γε νοῦν ἔχοντι, τοῦ πράγματα ἔχειν ταχέως ἀπαλλάττονται, μικρὰ δὲ εἰ χρὴ προσζημιωθῆναι, περὶ τὰ χρήματα πταίουσι· τὸ δὲ κεφάλαιόν ἐστι τῆς ὀργῆς καὶ τὸ παθεῖν, φασί, τὰ ἀνήκεστα, τὸ ζῆν προέσθαι. τούτων δὴ πάντων ὑπερορῶν, ὅτι καὶ τὸν ἰδίως ἄνδρα[2] ἐπέγνωκας· καὶ τὸν κοινῶς καὶ γενικῶς ἄνθρωπον ὑφ' ἡμῶν τῶν ὀψιμαθῶν ἀγνοούμενον, ἀνθ' ὅτου, πρὸς τῶν θεῶν, εὐλα-

[1] οὕτως εἶ Hertlein suggests; Fabricius οὑτωσί; MSS. οὑτοσί, or εἰ καὶ τ. οὕτω.
[2] Lacuna Hertlein, MSS.; ἄνδρα Asmus.

---

[1] Magnentius; cf. *Oration* 1 for the defeat of this usurper by Constantius. Magnentius had murdered Constans, see *Oration* 1. 26B, 2. 55D. [2] Cf. Vol. 2, *Caesars* 307A.

you were not invited, and you obeyed the second[1] on his merely indicating that he wished to enlist you to help him. However, whether I am like Constans and Magnentius the event itself, as they say, will prove.[2] But as for you, from what you wrote it is very plain that, in the words of the comic poet,[3]

"You are praising yourself, lady, like Astydamas."

For when you write about your "fearlessness" and "great courage," and say "Would that you knew my real value and my true character!" and, in a word, all that sort of thing,—for shame! What an empty noise and display of words is this! Nay, by the Graces and Aphrodite, if you are so brave and noble, why were you "so careful to avoid incurring displeasure," if need be, "for the third time"?[4] For when men fall under the displeasure of princes, the lightest consequence—and, as one might say, the most agreeable to a man of sense—is that they are at once relieved from the cares of business; and if they have to pay a small fine as well, their stumbling block is merely money; while the culmination of the prince's wrath, and the "fate beyond all remedy" as the saying is, is to lose their lives. Disregarding all these dangers, because, as you say, "you had come to know me in my private capacity for the man I am"[5]—and in my common and generic capacity for the human being I am, though unknown to myself, late learner that I am!—why, in heaven's name, did you say that you were careful to avoid

[3] Philemon *frag.* 190; cf. *Letter to Basil*, p. 83; this had become a proverb.

[4] *i.e.* after his experiences with Constans and Magnentius.

[5] A quotation from the other's letter.

βεῖσθαι ἔφης, μὴ τρίτον προσκρούσῃς; οὐ γὰρ δὴ πονηρὸν ἐκ χρηστοῦ σε ποιήσω χαλεπήνας ἐγώ· ζηλωτὸς γὰρ ἂν ἦν ἐν δίκῃ τοῦτο δυνάμενος· ἢ γάρ, ὥς φησι Πλάτων, καὶ τοὐναντίον οἷός τε ἦν ἄν. ἀδεσπότου δὲ τῆς ἀρετῆς οὔσης ἐχρῆν ὑπολογίζεσθαι μηδὲν τῶν τοιούτων. ἀλλ᾽ οἴει μέγα τὸ πάντας μὲν βλασφημεῖν, πᾶσι δὲ ἁπλῶς λοιδορεῖσθαι, καὶ τὸ τῆς εἰρήνης τέμενος ἀποφαίνειν ἐργαστήριον πολέμου. ἦ τοῦτο νομίζεις
B ὑπὲρ τῶν παλαιῶν ἁμαρτημάτων ἀπολογεῖσθαι πρὸς ἅπαντας, καὶ τῆς πάλαι ποτὲ μαλακίας παραπέτασμα τὴν νῦν ἀνδρείαν εἶναί σοι; τὸν μῦθον ἀκήκοας τὸν Βαβρίου "Γαλῆ ποτ᾽ ἀνδρὸς εὐπρεποῦς ἐρασθεῖσα"· τὰ δὲ ἄλλα ἐκ τοῦ βιβλίου μάνθανε. πολλὰ εἰπὼν οὐδένα ἂν πείσειας ἀνθρώπων, ὡς οὐ γέγονας ὅπερ οὖν γέγονας καὶ οἷον πολλοὶ πάλαι σε ἠπίσταντο. τὴν νῦν δὲ ἀμαθίαν καὶ τὸ θάρσος οὐχ ἡ φιλοσοφία μὰ τοὺς θεοὺς ἐνεποίησέ σοι, τοὐναντίον δὲ ἡ διπλῆ
C κατὰ Πλάτωνα ἄγνοια.[1] κινδυνεύων γὰρ εἰδέναι μηδέν, ὡς οὐδὲ ἡμεῖς, οἴει δὴ[2] πάντων εἶναι σοφώτατος, οὐ τῶν νῦν ὄντων μόνον, ἀλλὰ καὶ τῶν γεγονότων, ἴσως δὲ καὶ τῶν ἐσομένων. οὕτω σοι πρὸς ὑπερβολὴν ἀμαθίας τὰ τῆς οἰήσεως ἐπιδέδωκεν.

[1] ἄνοια Schwarz, cf. Plato, *Timaeus* 86B, δύο δ' ἀνοίας γένη.
[2] δὴ Asmus adds.

---

[1] *Crito* 44D. [2] Plato, *Republic* 617E.
[3] The Senate; for the phrase ἐργαστήριον πολέμου cf. Xenophon, *Hellenica* 3. 4. 17.

incurring displeasure for the third time? For surely my anger will not change you from a good man into a bad. I should be enviable indeed, and with justice, if I had the power to do that; for then, as Plato says,[1] I could do the converse as well. But since virtue owns no master,[2] you ought not to have taken into account anything of the sort. However, you think it is a fine thing to speak ill of all men, and to abuse all without exception, and to convert the shrine of peace[3] into a workshop of war. Or do you think in this way to excuse yourself in the sight of all for your past sins, and that your courage now is a screen to hide your cowardice of old? You have heard the fable of Babrius:[4] "Once upon a time a weasel fell in love with a handsome youth." The rest of the fable you may learn from the book. However much you may say, you will never convince any human being that you were not what you were, and such as many knew you to be in the past. As for your ignorance and audacity now, it was not philosophy that implanted them in you, no, by heaven! On the contrary, it was what Plato[5] calls a twofold lack of knowledge. For though you really know nothing, just as I know nothing, you think forsooth that you are the wisest of all men, not only of those who are alive now, but also of those who have ever been, and perhaps of those who ever will be. To such a pitch of ignorance has your self-conceit grown!

[4] *Fable* 32, the weasel or cat, transformed into a woman, could not resist chasing a mouse.

[5] Cf. Proclus on *Cratylus* 65 for this Neo-Platonic phrase; and Plato, *Apology* 21D. In *Sophist* 229B Plato defines the ignorance of those who do not even know that they are ignorant, as τῶν κακῶν αἰτία, καὶ ἡ ἐπονείδιστος ἀμαθία.

Ἀλλὰ σοῦ μὲν ἕνεκα καὶ ταῦτα τῶν ἱκανῶν εἴρηταί μοι πλείω, δεῖ δὲ ἴσως ἀπολογήσασθαι διὰ σὲ καὶ τοῖς ἄλλοις, ὅτι προχείρως ἐπὶ κοινωνίαν
D σε παρεκάλεσα πραγμάτων. τοῦτ' οὐ πρῶτος οὐδὲ μόνος ἔπαθον, ὦ Διονύσιε. ἐξηπάτησε καὶ Πλάτωνα τὸν μέγαν ὁ σὸς ὁμώνυμος, ἀλλὰ καὶ [1] ὁ Ἀθηναῖος Κάλλιπος· εἰδέναι μὲν γὰρ αὐτόν φησι πονηρὸν ὄντα,[2] τηλικαύτην δὲ ἐν αὐτῷ τὸ μέγεθος κακίαν οὐδ' ἂν [3] ἐλπίσαι πώποτε. καὶ τί χρὴ λέγειν ὑπὲρ τούτων, ὅπου καὶ τῶν Ἀσκληπιαδῶν ὁ ἄριστος Ἱπποκράτης ἔφη· Ἔσφηλαν δέ μου τὴν γνώμην αἱ ἐν τῇ κεφαλῇ ῥαφαί; εἶτ' ἐκεῖνοι μὲν ὑπὲρ ὧν ᾔδεσαν ἐξηπατῶντο, καὶ τὸ τεχνικὸν ἐλάνθανε τὸν ἰατρὸν θεώρημα, θαυμαστὸν δέ, εἴπερ Ἰουλιανὸς ἀκούσας ἐξαίφνης ἀνδρίζεσθαι τὸν Νεῖλον [4] Διονύσιον
445 ἐξηπατήθη; ἀκούεις ἐκεῖνον τὸν Ἠλεῖον Φαίδωνα, καὶ τὴν ἱστορίαν ἐπίστασαι· εἰ δὲ ἀγνοεῖς, ἐπιμελέστερον πολυπραγμόνησον, ἐγὼ δ' οὖν [5] ἐρῶ τοῦτο. ἐκεῖνος ἐνόμιζεν οὐδὲν ἀνίατον εἶναι τῇ φιλοσοφίᾳ, πάντας δὲ ἐκ πάντων ὑπ' αὐτῆς καθαίρεσθαι βίων, ἐπιτηδευμάτων, ἐπιθυμιῶν,

[1] Δίωνα Hertlein adds. [2] ὄντα Cobet adds.

[3] οὐδὲ Hertlein, MSS.; οὐδ' ἂν Hertlein suggests.

[4] Hertlein, following Hercher, [τὸν Νειλῷον ἢ]; *Laurentianus* Asmus τὸν Νεῖλον; Wilamowitz τὸν δειλὸν omitting Διονύσιον; Heyler regards ἢ Διονύσιον as a gloss.

[5] δ' οὖν Wright; δὲ οὐκ MSS., Hertlein; μόνον Hertlein suggests; Asmus retains οὐκ.

---

[1] The tyrant of Syracuse.

[2] Callippus, who assassinated Dio in 353 B.C., was himself put to death by the Syracusans after he had usurped the government.

However, as far as you are concerned, this that I have said is more than enough; but perhaps I ought to apologise on your account to the others because I too hastily summoned you to take part in public affairs. I am not the first or the only one, Dionysius, who has had this experience. Your namesake[1] deceived even great Plato; and Callippus[2] the Athenian also deceived Dio. For Plato says[3] that Dio knew he was a bad man but that he would never have expected in him such a degree of baseness. Why need I quote the experience of these men, when even Hippocrates,[4] the most distinguished of the sons of Asclepius, said: "The sutures of the head baffled my judgement." Now if those famous men were deceived about persons whom they knew, and the physician was mistaken in a professional diagnosis, is it surprising that Julian was deceived when he heard that Nilus Dionysius had suddenly become brave? You have heard tell of the famous Phaedo of Elis,[5] and you know his story. However, if you do not know it, study it more carefully, but at any rate I will tell you this part. He thought that there is nothing that cannot be cured by philosophy, and that by her all men can be purified from all their modes of life, their habits, desires, in a word from

[3] Plato, *Epistle* 7. 351D, E.

[4] Hippocrates, 5. 3. 561 Kühn. This candid statement of Hippocrates, who had failed to find a wound in a patient's head, was often cited as a proof of a great mind; cf. Plutarch, *De profectu in virtute*, 82D

[5] For the reformation of Phaedo by philosophy, see Aulus Gellius 2. 18 and Julian, Vol. 2, 264D (Wright). He was a disciple of Socrates and wrote several dialogues; for his *Life* see Diogenes Laertius, 2. 105; cf. Wilamowitz in *Hermes* 14.

πάντων ἁπαξαπλῶς τῶν τοιούτων. εἰ γὰρ τοῖς εὖ πεφυκόσι καὶ καλῶς τεθραμμένοις ἐπήρκει μόνον, οὐδὲν ἂν ἦν θαυμαστὸν τὸ κατ᾿ αὐτήν· εἰ δὲ καὶ τοὺς οὕτω διακειμένους ἀνάγει πρὸς τὸ φῶς, δοκεῖ μοι διαφερόντως εἶναι θαυμάσιον. ἐκ τούτων ἡ περὶ σέ μοι κατ᾿ ὀλίγον γνώμη, ὡς ἴσασιν οἱ θεοὶ πάντες, ἔρρεπεν ἐπὶ τὸ βέλτιον. οὔτοι γοῦν οὔτε ἐν πρώτοις οὔτε ἐν δευτέροις τῶν κρατίστων ἐθέμην ἀνδρῶν τὸ κατὰ σέ. ἐπίστασαι ἴσως αὐτός· εἰ δὲ ἀγνοεῖς, τοῦ καλοῦ
B Συμμάχου πυνθάνου. πέπεισμαι γάρ, ἐκεῖνος ὅτι οὔποτ᾿ ἂν ἑκὼν εἶναι ψεύσαιτο, τὰ πάντα ἀληθίζεσθαι πεφυκώς. εἰ δὲ ἀγανακτεῖς, ὅτι μὴ πάντων σε προυτιμήσαμεν, ἐγὼ μὲν ἐμαυτῷ, ὅτι σε καὶ ἐν ἐσχάτοις ἔταξα, μέμφομαι, καὶ χάριν οἶδα τοῖς θεοῖς πᾶσί τε καὶ πάσαις, οἳ κοινωνῆσαί σε πραγμάτων καὶ φίλους ἡμᾶς γενέσθαι διεκώλυσαν. . . . καὶ γὰρ εἰ πολλὰ περὶ τῆς φήμης οἱ ποιηταί φασιν ὡς ἔστι θεός, ἔστω δέ, εἰ βούλει, δαιμόνιόν γε[1] τὸ τῆς φήμης, οὐ πάνυ τι[2] προσεκτέον αὐτῇ, διότι πέφυκε τὸ δαιμόνιον οὐ πάντα καθαρὸν οὐδὲ ἀγαθὸν τελείως ὡς τὸ τῶν θεῶν εἶναι γένος, ἀλλ᾿ ἐπικοινωνεῖ πως καὶ πρὸς θάτερον. εἰ δὲ ὑπὲρ τῶν ἄλλων δαιμόνων οὐ

[1] δαιμόνιόν γε Asmus; δαιμόνιον, καὶ MSS., Hertlein; τὸ τῆς φήμης Asmus rejects as a gloss. Thomas reads ἔστω—φήμης as a parenthesis; so too Asmus.

[2] πάνυ τι Asmus; πάντῃ MSS., Hertlein.

---

[1] *i. e.* as Phaedo. Wilamowitz thinks that this sentence and the preceding are quoted or paraphrased from Phaedo.

[2] This was probably L. Aurelius Avianius Symmachus the Roman senator, prefect of the city in 364–5, father of the orator Quintus Aurelius Symmachus; Ammianus 21.

everything of the sort. If indeed she only availed those who are well born and well bred there would be nothing marvellous about philosophy; but if she can lead up to the light men so greatly depraved,[1] then I consider her marvellous beyond anything. For these reasons my estimate of you, as all the gods know, inclined little by little to be more favourable; but even so I did not count your sort in the first or the second class of the most virtuous. Perhaps you yourself know this; but if you do not know it, enquire of the worthy Symmachus[2] For I am convinced that he would never willingly tell a lie, since he is naturally disposed to be truthful in all things. And if you are aggrieved that I did not honour you before all others, I for my part reproach myself for having ranked you even among the last in merit, and I thank all the gods and goddesses who hindered us from becoming associated in public affairs and from being intimate . . .[3] And indeed, though the poets have often said of Rumour that she is a goddess,[4] and let us grant, if you will, that she at least has demonic power, yet not very much attention ought to be paid to her, because a demon is not altogether pure or perfectly good, like the race of the gods, but has some share of the opposite quality. And even though it be not permissible to say this

12. 24, describes the meeting of the elder Symmachus and Julian in 361 at Nish.

[3] The lack of connection indicates a lacuna though there is none in the MSS. Probably Julian said that their intimacy existed only as a rumour.

[4] Hesiod, *Works and Days* 763

> φήμη δ' οὔτις πάμπαν ἀπόλλυται, ἥν τινα πολλοὶ
> λαοὶ φημίζωσι· θεός νύ τίς ἐστι καὶ αὐτή.

θέμις τοῦτο φάναι, περὶ τῆς φήμης οἶδ' ὅτι λέγων ὡς πολλὰ μὲν ψευδῶς, πολλὰ δὲ ἀληθῶς ἀγγέλλει, οὔποτ' ἂν αὐτὸς ἁλοίην ψευδομαρτυριῶν.

Ἀλλὰ τὴν παρρησίαν τὴν σὴν οἴει τεττάρων εἶναι ὀβολῶν, τὸ λεγόμενον, ἀξίαν; οὐκ οἶσθ' ὅτι καὶ Θερσίτης ἐν τοῖς Ἕλλησιν ἐπαρρησιάζετο, καὶ Ὀδυσσεὺς μὲν αὐτὸν ὁ συνετώτατος ἔπαιε τῷ σκήπτρῳ, τῷ δὲ Ἀγαμέμνονι τῆς Θερσίτου παροινίας ἔλαττον ἔμελεν ἢ χελώνῃ μυιῶν, τὸ τῆς παροιμίας; πλὴν οὐ μέγα ἔργον ἐστὶν ἐπιτιμᾶν ἄλλοις, ἑαυτὸν δὲ ἀνεπιτίμητον παρασχεῖν. εἰ δέ σοι ταύτης μέτεστι τῆς μερίδος, ἐπίδειξον ἡμῖν. ἆρ' ὅτε νέος ἦσθα, καλὰς ἔδωκας ὑπὲρ σαυτοῦ τοῖς πρεσβυτέροις ὁμιλίας; ἀλλ' ἐγὼ κατὰ τὴν Εὐριπίδειον Ἠλέκτραν τὰς τοιαύτας σιγῶ τύχας. ἐπεὶ δὲ ἀνὴρ γέγονας καὶ στρατοπέδῳ παρέβαλες, ἔπραξας πῶς πρὸς τοῦ Διός; ὑπὲρ τῆς ἀληθείας φῂς προσκρούσας ἀπηλλάχθαι. ἐκ τίνων τοῦτο ἔχων δεῖξαι, ὥσπερ οὐ πολλῶν καὶ πονηροτάτων, ὑφ' ὧνπερ καὶ αὐτὸς ἀπηλάθης, ἐκτοπισθέντων; οὐ τοῦτό ἐστιν, ὦ συνετώτατε Διονύσιε, σπουδαίου καὶ σώφρονος ἀνδρός, ἀπεχθανόμενον ἀπελθεῖν τοῖς κρατοῦσιν. ἦσθα δὲ ἂν βελτίων, εἰ τοὺς ἀνθρώπους ἐκ τῆς πρὸς
C σεαυτὸν συνουσίας ἀπέφηνας ἡμῖν μετριωτέρους. ἀλλὰ τοῦτο μὲν οὐ κατὰ σέ, μὰ τοὺς θεούς, οὐδὲ κατὰ μυρίους ἄλλους, ὅσοι ζηλοῦσι τὸν σὸν τρόπον·

---

[1] Cf. Julian's reverence for φήμη in Vol. 1, pp. 409, 423; Vol. 2, p. 347, Wright.

[2] *Iliad* 2. 265.

[3] *Orestes* 16; τὰς γὰρ ἐν μέσῳ σιγῶ τύχας. Cf. Vol. 2, *To Themistius*, 254B, p. 204, Wright.

concerning the other demons, I know that when I say of Rumour that she reports many things falsely as well as many truthfully, I shall never myself be convicted of bearing false witness.[1]

But as for your "freedom of speech," do you think that it is worth four obols, as the saying is? Do you not know that Thersites also spoke his mind freely among the Greeks, whereupon the most wise Odysseus beat him with his staff,[2] while Agamemnon paid less heed to the drunken brawling of Thersites than a tortoise does to flies, as the proverb goes? For that matter it is no great achievement to criticise others, but rather to place oneself beyond the reach of criticism. Now if you can claim to be in this category, prove it to me. Did you not, when you were young, furnish to your elders fine themes for gossip about you? However, like Electra in Euripides,[3] I keep silence about happenings of this sort. But when you came to man's estate and betook yourself to the camp,[4] how, in the name of Zeus, did you behave? You say that you left it because you gave offence in the cause of truth. From what evidence can you prove this, as though many men[5] and of the basest sort had not been exiled by the very persons by whom you yourself were driven away? O most wise Dionysius, it does not happen to a virtuous and temperate man to go away obnoxious to those in power! You would have done better if you had proved to us that men from their intercourse with you were better behaved. But this was not in your power, no, by the gods, nor is it in the power of tens of thousands who emulate

[4] *i.e.* of Constans.

[5] We do not know to whom Julian refers.

πέτραι γὰρ πέτραις καὶ λίθοι λίθοις προσαρττόμενοι οὐκ ὠφελοῦσι μὲν ἀλλήλους, ὁ δ' ἰσχυρότερος τὸν ἥττονα εὐχερῶς συντρίβει.

Ἆρα μὴ Λακωνικῶς ταῦτα καὶ συντόμως λέγω;
D ἀλλ' ἐγὼ μέν οἶμαι λαλίστερος διὰ σὲ καὶ τῶν
Ἀττικῶν ἀποπεφάνθαι τεττίγων. ὑπὲρ δὲ ὧν
εἰς ἐμὲ πεπαρῴνηκας, ἐπιθήσω σοι δίκην τὴν
πρέπουσαν, ἐθελόντων θεῶν καὶ τῆς δεσποίνης
Ἀδραστείας. τίς οὖν ἡ δίκη καὶ τί μάλιστα τὸ
δυνάμενόν σου τὴν γλῶτταν καὶ τὴν διάνοιαν
ὀδυνῆσαι; ὡς ἐλάχιστα πειράσομαι διά τε τῶν
λόγων καὶ διὰ τῶν ἔργων ἐξαμαρτὼν μὴ παρασχέσθαι
σου τῇ κακηγόρῳ γλώττῃ πολλὴν
φλυαρίαν. καίτοι με οὐ λέληθεν, ὅτι καὶ τῆς
Ἀφροδίτης φασὶν ὑπὸ τοῦ Μώμου ἐσκῶφθαι
446 τὸ σάνδαλον. ἀλλ' ὁρᾷς ὅτι πολλὰ καὶ ὁ Μῶμος
ἐρρήγνυτο, καὶ μόλις ἐλαμβάνετο τοῦ σανδάλου.
εἴη δὲ καὶ σὲ περὶ ταῦτα τριβόμενον καταγηρᾶσαι
καὶ τοῦ Τιθωνοῦ βαθύτερον καὶ τοῦ Κινύρου
πλουσιώτερον καὶ τοῦ Σαρδαναπάλου τρυφηλότερον,
ὅπως τὸ τῆς παροιμίας ἐπὶ σοῦ
πληρωθῇ Δὶς παῖδες οἱ γέροντες.

Ἀλλ' ὁ θεσπέσιος Ἀλέξανδρος ἐκ τίνων ἐφάνη σοι τηλικοῦτος; ἆρ' ὅτι μιμητὴς αὐτοῦ γενόμενος ἐζήλωσας ὅσα ἐκείνῳ τὸ μειράκιον ὁ Ἑρμόλαος ὠνείδισεν; ἢ τοῦτο μὲν οὐδεὶς οὕτως ἐστὶν

---

[1] See the similar passage on p. 101. Asmus thinks that the Lauricius there mentioned and Nilus were both Cynics and therefore obnoxious to Julian.

[2] A reference to the letter of Nilus, who had perhaps asked for a brief answer.

[3] Cf. *Misopogon* 370B, vol. 2, p. 508, Wright.

your way of life. For when rocks grind against rocks and stones against stones they do not benefit one another, and the stronger easily wears down the weaker.[1]

I am not saying this in Laconic fashion[2] and concisely, am I? Nay, I think that on your account I have shown myself even more talkative than Attic grasshoppers. However, in return for your drunken abuse of myself, I will inflict on you the appropriate punishment, by the grace of the gods and our lady Adrasteia.[3] What, then, is this punishment, and what has the greatest power to hurt your tongue and your mind? It is this: I will try, by erring as little as may be in word and deed, not to provide your slanderous tongue with so much foolish talk. And yet I am well aware that it is said that even the sandal of Aphrodite was satirised by Momus. But you observe that though Momus poured forth floods[4] of criticism he could barely find anything to criticise in her sandal.[5] Even so may you grow old fretting yourself over things of this sort, more decrepit than Tithonus, richer than Cinyras, more luxurious than Sardanapalus, so that in you may be fulfilled the proverb, "Old men are twice children."

But why does the divine Alexander seem to you so pre-eminent? Is it because you took to imitating him and aspired to that for which the youth Hermolaus[6] reproached him? Or rather, no one is

[4] Or "burst with the effort," cf. rumpi invidia.

[5] Philostratus, *Epistle* 37; Momus complained that Aphrodite wore a sandal that squeaked.

[6] For the plot of Hermolaus and Callisthenes against Alexander, cf. Quintus Curtius 8. 6; Arrian, *Anabasis* 4. 13. 14; Plutarch, *Alexander* 55.

ἀνόητος ὡς ὑπονοῆσαι περὶ σοῦ· τοὐναντίον δὲ καὶ ὅπερ ἀπωδύρετο παθὼν Ἑρμόλαος, καὶ διόπερ διενοεῖτο τὸν Ἀλέξανδρον, ὥς φασιν, ἀποκτεῖναι, τοῦτο δὲ οὐδεὶς ὅστις πεπεισμένος οὐκ ἔστι περὶ σοῦ; πολλῶν δὲ ἐγὼ νὴ τοὺς θεοὺς καὶ σφόδρα σε φαμένων φιλεῖν ἀκήκοα πολλὰ ὑπὲρ ταύτης ἀπολογουμένων τῆς ἁμαρτίας, ἤδη δέ τινος καὶ ἀπιστοῦντος. ἀλλ' οὗτός ἐστιν ἡ μία χελιδών, οὐ ποιεῖ τὸ ἔαρ. ἀλλ' ἴσως ἐκεῖθεν Ἀλέξανδρος ὤφθη σοι μέγας, ὅτι Καλλισθένη μὲν ἀπέκτεινε πικρῶς, Κλεῖτος δὲ αὐτοῦ τῆς παροινίας ἔργον ἐγένετο, Φιλώτας τε καὶ Παρμενίων καὶ τὸ Παρμενίωνος παιδίον.[1] ἐπεὶ τὰ περὶ τὸν Ἕκτορα τὸν ἐν Αἰγύπτῳ[2] τοῦ Νείλου ταῖς δίναις ἢ ταῖς Εὐφράτου· λέγεται γὰρ ἑκάτερον· ἐναποπνιγέντα καὶ τὰς ἄλλας αὐτοῦ παιδιὰς σιωπῶ, μὴ βλασφημεῖν ἄνδρα δόξω τὸ κατωρθωμένον μὲν οὐδαμῶς ἔχοντα, κράτιστον μέντοι τὰ πολεμικὰ στρατηγόν.[3] ὧν σὺ κατὰ τὴν προαίρεσιν καὶ κατὰ τὴν ἀνδρείαν ἔλαττον μετέχεις ἢ τριχῶν ἰχθύες. ἄκουε δὴ τῆς παραινέσεως μὴ λίαν ὀργίλως,

οὔ τοι, τέκνον ἐμόν, δέδοται πολεμήια ἔργα,

τὸ δὲ ἑξῆς οὐ παραγράφω σοι, αἰσχύνομαι γὰρ

[1] καὶ—παιδίον Heyler and Hertlein would delete as a gloss, Asmus retains and reads ἐπεὶ τὰ for ἔπειτα τά.
[2] ἐν Αἰγύπτῳ Hertlein would delete, Asmus retains, seeing in the phrase some sneer, the point of which is not now clear.
[3] στρατηγὸν Hertlein would delete, Asmus retains.

---

[1] The historian who accompanied Alexander to the East.
[2] Cf. Vol. 2, *Caesars* 331c, p. 403, note, Wright.

so foolish as to suspect you of that. But the very opposite, that which Hermolaus lamented that he had endured, and which was the reason for his plotting, as they say, to kill Alexander—everyone believes this about you also, do they not? I call the gods to witness that I have heard many persons assert that they were very fond of you and who made many excuses for this offence of yours, but I have found just one person who did not believe it. However he is that one swallow who does not make a spring. But perhaps the reason why Alexander seemed in your eyes a great man was that he cruelly murdered Callisthenes,[1] that Cleitus[2] fell a victim to his drunken fury, and Philotas too, and Parmenio[3] and Parmenio's son; for that affair of Hector,[4] who was smothered in the whirlpools of the Nile in Egypt or the Euphrates—the story is told of both rivers—I say nothing about, or of his other follies, lest I should seem to speak ill of a man who by no means maintained the ideal of rectitude but nevertheless excelled as a general in the works of war. Whereas you are less endowed with both these, namely, good principles and courage, than a fish with hair. Now listen to my advice and do not resent it too much.

"Not to thee, my child, have been given the works
of war."[5]

The verse that follows[6] I do not write out for you,

[3] The general Parmenio and his son Philotas were executed for treason; Arrian, *Anabasis* 3. 26.

[4] Cf. Quintus Curtius 5. 8. 7; Hector, a son of Parmenio, was, according to Curtius, accidentally drowned, though Julian ascribes his death to Alexander.

[5] *Iliad* 5. 428, Zeus to Aphrodite.

[6] ἀλλὰ σύ γ' ἱμερόεντα μετέρχεο ἔργα γάμοιο.

νὴ τοὺς θεούς. ἀξιῶ μέντοι σε προσυπακούειν αὐτό· καὶ γὰρ εὔλογον ἕπεσθαι τοῖς ἔργοις τοὺς λόγους, ἀλλὰ μὴ φεύγειν τὰ ῥήματα τὸν μηδαμῶς διαπεφευγότα τὰ ἔργα.

Ἀλλ' ὁ τὴν Μαγνεντίου καὶ Κώνσταντος ὁσίαν αἰσχυνόμενος, ἀνθ' ὅτου τοῖς ζῶσι πολεμεῖς καὶ τοῖς ὁπωσοῦν βελτίστοις λοιδορῇ; πότερον ὅτι μᾶλλον ἐκεῖνοι δύνανται τῶν ζώντων ἀμύνεσθαι τοὺς λυποῦντας; ἀλλὰ σοὶ τοῦτο οὐ προσήκει λεγειν· εἶ γάρ, ὡς γράφεις, θαρραλεώτατος. ἀλλ' εἰ μὴ τοῦτο, τυχὸν ἕτερον· ὡς γὰρ οὐκ αἰσθανομένους ἐπισκώπτειν ἴσως οὐ βούλει. τῶν ζώντων δὲ ἆρά τις οὕτως εὐήθης ἐστὶν ἢ μικρόψυχος, ὃς ἀξιώσειεν ἂν αὑτοῦ παρὰ σοὶ λόγον εἶναί τινα, καὶ οὐ βουλήσεται μάλιστα μὲν ἀγνοεῖσθαι παρὰ σοῦ παντάπασιν, εἰ δ' ἀδύνατον εἴη, λοιδορεῖσθαι παρὰ σοῦ μᾶλλον, καθάπερ ἐγὼ νῦν,[1] ἢ τιμᾶσθαι; μήποτε οὕτω κακῶς φρονήσαιμι, μήποτε τῶν παρὰ σοῦ μᾶλλον ἐπαίνων ἢ ψόγων ἀντιποιησαίμην.

Ἀλλ' αὐτὸ τοῦτο τὸ γράφειν πρός σε δακνομένου τυχὸν ἴσως ἐστίν; οὐ μὰ τοὺς θεοὺς τοὺς σωτῆρας, ἀλλ' ἐπικόπτοντος τὴν ἄγαν αὐθάδειαν καὶ τὴν θρασύτητα καὶ τὴν ἀκολασίαν τὴν τῆς γλώττης καὶ τὸ τῆς ψυχῆς ἄγριον καὶ τὸ μαινόμενον τῶν φρενῶν καὶ τὸ παρακεκινηκὸς ἐν πᾶσιν. ἐξῆν γοῦν, εἴπερ ἐδεδήγμην, ἔργοις ἀλλὰ μὴ λόγοις σε σφόδρα νομίμως κολάσαι. πολίτης γὰρ ὢν καὶ

[1] καθάπερ—νῦν Cobet would delete as a gloss.

---

[1] Julian seems to anticipate the criticism of Nilus that he is not showing himself superior to Alexander.

[2] For Julian's mildness in such cases, see Ammianus. 25.4. 9. Constat eum in apertos aliquos inimicos insidiatores suos

because, by the gods, I am ashamed to do so. However I ask you to understand it as said. For it is only fair that words should follow on deeds, and that he who has never avoided deeds should not avoid the phrases that describe them.

Nay, if you revere the pious memory of Magnentius and Constans, why do you wage war against the living and abuse those who excel in any way? Is it because the dead are better able than the living to avenge themselves on those who vex them? Yet it does not become you to say this. For you are, as your letter says, "Very brave indeed." But if this is not the reason, perhaps there is a different one. Perhaps you do not wish to satirise them because they cannot feel it. But among the living is there anyone so foolish or so cowardly as to demand that you should take any notice of him at all, and who will not prefer if possible to be altogether ignored by you; but if that should be impossible, to be abused by you, as indeed I am now abused rather than honoured? May I never be so ill-advised—may I never aspire to win praise rather than blame from you!

But perhaps you will say that the very fact that I am writing to you is a proof that I am stung?[1] No, I call the Saviour Gods to witness that I am but trying to check your excessive audacity and boldness, the license of your tongue and the ferocity of your soul, the madness of your wits and your perverse fury on all occasions. In any case it was in my power, if I had been stung, to chastise you with deeds and not merely with words,[2] and I should have been entirely within the law. For you are a citizen

ita consurrexisse mitissime, ut poenarum asperitatem genuina lenitudine castigaret.

τῆς γερουσίας μετέχων αὐτοκράτορος ἐπίταγμα παρητήσω· τοῦτο δὲ οὐκ ἐξῆν δήπουθεν τῷ μὴ μεγάλην ἀνάγκην προϊσχομένῳ. οὔκουν ἐξήρκει μοι ὑπὲρ τούτου ζημιῶσαί σε παντοίαν ζημίαν, ἀλλ' ᾠήθην δεῖν γράψαι πρός σε πρῶτον, νομίζων ἰάσιμον ἐπιστολίῳ βραχεῖ. ὡς δέ σ' ἐμμένοντα τοῖς αὐτοῖς, μᾶλλον δὲ τὸ λεληθὸς τέως τῆς μανίας ἐφώρασα, . . .[1] μή τι καὶ νομισθείης ἀνήρ, οὐκ ἀνὴρ ὤν, καὶ παρρησίας μεστός, ἐμβροντησίας ὢν πλήρης, καὶ παιδείας μετεσχηκώς, οὐδὲ γρὺ λόγων ἁψάμενος, ὅσα γε εἰκός ἐστι ταῖς ἐπιστολαῖς σου τεκμήρασθαι. τὸ γὰρ φροῦδον οὐδεὶς εἶπε τῶν ἀρχαίων ἐπὶ τοῦ προ-
B φανοῦς, ὥσπερ σὺ νῦν, ἐπεὶ τὰς ἄλλας σου τῆς ἐπιστολῆς ἁμαρτίας οὐδεὶς ἂν ἐπεξελθεῖν ἐν μακρῷ βιβλίῳ δυνηθείη καὶ τὸ μαστροπὸν ἐκεῖνο καὶ βδελυρὸν ἦθος, ὑφ' οὗ σεαυτὸν προαγωγεύεις. οὐ γὰρ τοὺς ἐξ ἑτοίμου φῂς ἥκοντας οὐδὲ τοὺς ἐφεδρεύοντας ταῖς ἀρχαῖς, ἀλλὰ τοὺς βεβαίᾳ κρίσει χρωμένους καὶ κατὰ τοῦτο τὸ δέον αἱρουμένους τούτους δεῖν, ἀλλ' οὐ τοὺς ἑτοίμως ὑπακούοντας, αἱρεῖσθαι. καλάς γε ἡμῖν ἐλπίδας ὑποφαίνεις οὐδὲν δεομένοις ὡς ὑπείξων, ἤν αὖθίς σε καλῶμεν ἐπὶ κοινωνίαν[2] πραγμάτων. ἐμοὶ δὲ τοσοῦτον μέρος τούτου περίεστιν, ὥστε σε, τῶν

[1] Lacuna. Some reference to the letters written by Nilus is needed here.

[2] κοινωνίαν Asmus cf. 444c; κοινωνίᾳ Hertlein, MSS.

and of senatorial rank and you disobeyed a command of your Emperor; and such behaviour was certainly not permissible to anyone who could not furnish the excuse of real necessity. Therefore I was not satisfied with inflicting on you any sort of penalty for this conduct, but I thought I ought to write to you first, thinking that you might be cured by a short letter. But since I have discovered that you persist in the same errors, or rather how great your frenzy is which I previously did not know . . .[1] lest you should be thought to be a man, when that you are not, or brimful of freedom of speech, when you are only full of insanity, or that you have had the advantage of education when you have not the smallest acquaintance with literature, as far, at any rate, as one may reasonably judge from your letters. For instance, no one of the ancients ever used φροῦδος[2] to mean "manifest" as you do here,—for, as for the other blunders displayed in your letter, no one could describe them even in a long book, or that obscene and abominable character of yours that leads you to prostitute yourself. You tell me indeed that it is not those who arrive offhand or those who are hunting for public office whom we ought to choose, but those who use sound judgement and in accordance with this prefer to do their duty rather than those who are ready and eager to obey. Fair, truly, are the hopes you hold out to me though I made no appeal to you, implying that you will yield if I again summon you to take part in public business. But I am so far from doing that,

[1] Some words have fallen out.
[2] In Attic the word means "vanished."

ἄλλων εἰσιεμένων,[1] οὐδὲ προσείρηκα πώποτε. καίτοι γε πρὸς πολλοὺς ἔγωγε τοῦτο ἐποίησα γνωρίμων τε καὶ ἀγνοουμένων ἐμοὶ κατὰ τὴν θεοφιλῆ Ῥώμην διατρίβοντας. οὕτω σου τῆς φιλίας ἀντεποιούμην, οὕτω σε σπουδῆς ἄξιον ᾠόμην. εἰκὸς οὖν ὅτι καὶ τὰ μέλλοντα πρός σε τοιαῦτα ἔσται. καὶ γὰρ νῦν ἔγραψα ταυτηνὶ τὴν ἐπιστολήν, οὐ σοὶ μόνον ἀνάγνωσμα, ἐπεὶ καὶ ἀναγκαίαν πολλοῖς αὐτὴν ᾔδειν, καὶ δώσω γε πᾶσιν οὐκ ἄκουσιν, ὡς ἐμαυτὸν πείθω, ληψομένοις· σεμνότερον γὰρ ὁρῶντές σε καὶ ὀγκωδέστερον τῶν ἔμπροσθέν σοι βεβιωμένων ἄχθονται.

Τελείαν ἔχεις παρ᾽ ἡμῶν τὴν ἀπόκρισιν, ὥστε σε μηδὲν ἐπιποθεῖν. οὔκουν οὐδὲ ἡμεῖς παρὰ σοῦ τι πλέον ἀπαιτοῦμεν· ἀλλ᾽ ἐντυχών, εἰς ὅ τι[2] βούλει τοῖς γράμμασι χρῆσαι· τὰ γὰρ τῆς ἡμετέρας φιλίας πεπέρανταί[3] σοι. ἔρρωσο τρυφῶν καὶ λοιδορούμενος ἐμοὶ παραπλησίως.

51

396 Ἰουδαίων τῷ κοινῷ[4]

D Πάνυ ὑμῖν φορτικώτατον γεγένηται ἐπὶ τῶν παρῳχηκότων καιρῶν τῶν ζυγῶν τῆς δουλείας τὸ διαγραφαῖς ἀκηρύκτοις ὑποτάττεσθαι ὑμᾶς
397 καὶ χρυσίου πλῆθος ἄφατον εἰσκομίζειν τοῖς τοῦ ταμιείου λόγοις· ὧν πολλὰ μὲν αὐτοψεὶ

[1] Asmus suggests μετ᾽ ἄλλων εἰσιέμενον to improve the sense.
[2] εἰς ὅ τι Asmus; ὅτε Hertlein, MSS.
[3] πεπέρανταί Cobet, πέπραταί Hercher, Hertlein; ἐπέπραται MSS., ἐπείραται A. Asmus suggests ἐκπέπραται = "sold out," "ruined."

that, when the others were admitted, I never even addressed you at any time. And yet I did address many who were known and unknown to me and dwell in Rome, beloved of the gods. Such was my desire for your friendship, so worthy of consideration did I think you! Therefore it is likely that my future conduct towards you will be much the same. And indeed I have written this letter now, not for your perusal alone, since I knew it was needed by many besides yourself, and I will give it to all, since all, I am convinced, will be glad to receive it. For when men see you more haughty and more insolent than befits your past life, they resent it.

You have here a complete answer from me, so that you can desire nothing more. Nor do I ask for any further communication from you. But when you have read my letters use them for whatever purpose you please. For our friendship is at an end. Farewell, and divide your time between luxurious living and abuse of me!

51

To the community of the Jews[1]

In times past, by far the most burdensome thing in the yoke of your slavery has been the fact that you were subjected to unauthorised ordinances and had to contribute an untold amount of money to the accounts of the treasury. Of this I used to Late 362 or early 363 From Antioch

[1] For this rescript see Introduction.

[a] Hertlein 25.

ἐθεώρουν, πλείονα δὲ τούτων ἔμαθον εὑρὼν τὰ βρέβια τὰ καθ' ὑμῶν φυλαττόμενα· ἔτι δὲ καὶ μέλλουσαν πάλιν εἰσφορὰν καθ' ὑμῶν προστάττεσθαι εἶρξα, καὶ τὸ τῆς τοιαύτης δυσφημίας ἀσέβημα ἐνταῦθα ἐβιασάμην στῆσαι, καὶ πυρὶ παρέδωκα τὰ βρέβια τὰ καθ' ὑμῶν ἐν τοῖς ἐμοῖς σκρινίοις ἀποκείμενα, ὡς μηκέτι δύνασθαι καθ' ὑμῶν τινὰ τοιαύτην ἀκοντίζειν ἀσεβείας φήμην.
B καὶ τούτων μὲν ὑμῖν οὐ τοσοῦτον αἴτιος κατέστη ὁ τῆς μνήμης ἄξιος Κωνστάντιος ὁ ἀδελφός, ὅσον οἱ τὴν γνώμην βάρβαροι καὶ τὴν ψυχὴν ἄθεοι, οἱ τὴν τούτου τράπεζαν ἑστιώμενοι, οὓς ἐγὼ μὲν ἐν χερσὶν ἐμαῖς λαβόμενος εἰς βόθρον ὤσας ὤλεσα, ὡς μηδὲ μνήμην ἔτι φέρεσθαι παρ' ἡμῖν τῆς αὐτῶν ἀπωλείας. ἐπὶ πλέον δὲ ὑμᾶς εὐωχεῖσθαι βουλό-
C μενος, τὸν ἀδελφὸν Ἴουλον, τὸν αἰδεσιμώτατον πατριάρχην, παρῄνεσα καὶ τὴν λεγομένην εἶναι παρ' ὑμῖν ἀποστολὴν κωλυθῆναι, καὶ μηκέτι δύνασθαι τὰ πλήθη ὑμῶν τινὰ ἀδικεῖν τοιαύταις φόρων εἰσπράξεσιν, ὡς πανταχόθεν ὑμῖν τὸ ἀμέριμνον ὑπάρχειν ἐπὶ[1] τῆς ἐμῆς βασιλείας, ἵνα ἀπολαύοντες εἰρήνης[2] ἔτι μείζονας εὐχὰς ποιῆσθε ὑπὲρ[3] τῆς ἐμῆς βασιλείας τῷ πάντων κρείττονι καὶ δημιουργῷ θεῷ, τῷ καταξιώσαντι στέψαι με
D τῇ ἀχράντῳ αὐτοῦ δεξιᾷ. πέφυκε γὰρ τοὺς ἔν τινι μερίμνῃ ἐξεταζομένους περιδεῖσθαι τὴν διά-

[1] Reiske ἐπὶ τῆς; τῆς Hertlein, MSS.
[2] εἰρήνης Reiske supplies for lacuna after ἀπολαύοντες, Hertlein lacuna; ἡσυχίας Thomas.
[3] Reiske ὑπὲρ τῆς; Hertlein, MSS. τῆς.

---

[1] Or ἀπωλεία may be active = "their wickedness."

see many instances with my own eyes, and I have learned of more, by finding the records which are preserved against you. Moreover, when a tax was about to be levied on you again I prevented it, and compelled the impiety of such obloquy to cease here; and I threw into the fire the records against you that were stored in my desks; so that it is no longer possible for anyone to aim at you such a reproach of impiety. My brother Constantius of honoured memory was not so much responsible for these wrongs of yours as were the men who used to frequent his table, barbarians in mind, godless in soul. These I seized with my own hands and put them to death by thrusting them into the pit, that not even any memory of their destruction[1] might still linger amongst us. And since I wish that you should prosper yet more, I have admonished my brother Iulus,[2] your most venerable patriarch, that the levy[3] which is said to exist among you should be prohibited, and that no one is any longer to have the power to oppress the masses of your people by such exactions; so that everywhere, during my reign, you may have security of mind, and in the enjoyment of peace may offer more fervid prayers[4] for my reign to the Most High God, the Creator, who has deigned to crown me with his own immaculate right hand. For it is natural that men who are distracted by any anxiety should be hampered

[2] The Patriarch Hillel II. was at this time about seventy.

[3] Literally "the apostole," paid by the Jews to maintain the Patriarchate. It was later suppressed by the Emperor Theodosius II.

[4] Sozomen 5. 22 says that Julian wrote to the community of the Jews asking them to pray for him: *εὔχεσθαι ὑπὲρ αὐτοῦ καὶ τῆς αὐτοῦ βασιλείας.*

νοιαν καὶ μὴ τοσοῦτον εἰς τὴν προσευχὴν τὰς χεῖρας ἀνατείνειν τολμᾶν, τοὺς δὲ πανταχόθεν ἔχοντας τὸ ἀμέριμνον ὁλοκλήρῳ ψυχῇ χαίροντας ὑπὲρ τοῦ βασιλείου ἱκετηρίους λατρείας ποιεῖσθαι τῷ μείζονι, τῷ δυναμένῳ κατευθῦναι τὴν βασιλείαν ἡμῶν ἐπὶ τὰ κάλλιστα, καθάπερ προαιρούμεθα. ὅπερ χρὴ ποιεῖν ὑμᾶς, ἵνα κἀγὼ τὸν τῶν Περσῶν
398 πόλεμον διορθωσάμενος[1] τὴν ἐκ πολλῶν ἐτῶν ἐπιθυμουμένην παρ' ὑμῶν ἰδεῖν οἰκουμένην πόλιν ἁγίαν Ἱερουσαλὴμ ἐμοῖς καμάτοις ἀνοικοδομήσας οἰκίσω καὶ ἐν αὐτῇ δόξαν δῶ μεθ' ὑμῶν τῷ κρείττονι.

52

Λιβανίῳ[2]

374 Ἐπειδὴ τῆς ὑποσχέσεως ἐπελάθου· τρίτη γοῦν
C ἐστὶ σήμερον, καὶ ὁ φιλόσοφος Πρίσκος αὐτὸς μὲν οὐχ ἧκε, γράμματα δ' ἀπέστειλεν ὡς ἔτι χρονίζων·[3] ὑπομιμνήσκω σε τὸ χρέος ἀπαιτῶν. ὄφλημα δέ ἐστιν, ὡς οἶσθα, σοὶ μὲν ἀποδοῦναι ῥᾴδιον, ἐμοὶ δὲ ἥδιστον πάνυ κομίσασθαι. πέμπε δὴ τὸν λόγον καὶ τὴν ἱερὰν συμβουλήν, ἀλλὰ πρὸς Ἑρμοῦ καὶ Μουσῶν ταχέως, ἐπεὶ καὶ τούτων με τῶν τριῶν ἡμερῶν ἴσθι συντρίψας, εἴπερ ἀληθῆ φησιν ὁ Σικελιώτης ποιητής, ἐν ἤματι
D φάσκων τοὺς ποθοῦντας γηράσκειν. εἰ δὲ ταῦτα

[1] Asmus would read κατορθωσάμενος.
[2] Hertlein 3. σοφιστῇ καὶ κοιαίστωρι (quaestor) is added to the title in one MS., X; cf. p. 201. [3] Cobet χρονιῶν.

[1] For Julian's project of rebuilding the Temple, see Introduction.

in spirit, and should not have so much confidence in raising their hands to pray; but that those who are in all respects free from care should rejoice with their whole hearts and offer their suppliant prayers on behalf of my imperial office to Mighty God, even to him who is able to direct my reign to the noblest ends, according to my purpose. This you ought to do, in order that, when I have successfully concluded the war with Persia, I may rebuild by my own efforts the sacred city of Jerusalem,[1] which for so many years you have longed to see inhabited, and may bring settlers there, and, together with you, may glorify the Most High God therein.

52

To Libanius[2]

SINCE you have forgotten your promise—at any rate three days have gone by and the philosopher Priscus[3] has not come himself but has sent a letter to say that he still delays—I remind you of your debt by demanding payment. The thing you owe is, as you know, easy for you to pay and very pleasant for me to receive. So send your discourse and your "divine counsel," and do it promptly, in the name of Hermes and the Muses, for I assure you, in these three days you have worn me out, if indeed the Sicilian poet[4] speaks the truth when he says, "Those who long grow old in a day." And if this be true,

362 Winter At Antioch

[2] Both Libanius and Julian were at this time at Antioch. We have the answer to this letter, Libanius, *Letter* 760 Foerster; Libanius had promised to send Julian his speech, *For Aristophanes*, *Oration* 14, for which see below, p. 183.

[3] For Priscus, see above, pp. 3, 15.

[4] Theocritus, 12. 2 οἱ δὲ ποθεῦντες ἐν ἤματι γηράσκουσιν.

ἔστιν, ὥσπερ οὖν ἔστι, τὸ γῆρας ἡμῖν ἐτριπλασίασας, ὦ γενναῖε. ταῦτα μεταξὺ τοῦ πράττειν ὑπηγόρευσά σοι· γράφειν γὰρ οὐχ οἷός τε ἦν, ἀργοτέραν ἔχων τῆς γλώττης τὴν χεῖρα. καίτοι μοι καὶ τὴν γλῶτταν εἶναι συμβέβηκεν ὑπὸ τῆς ἀνασκησίας ἀργοτέραν καὶ ἀδιάρθρωτον. ἔρρωσό μοι, ἀδελφὲ ποθεινότατε καὶ προσφιλέστατε.

53

Λιβανίῳ[1]

Ἀποδέδωκας Ἀριστοφάνει τὰς ἀμοιβὰς τῆς τε περὶ τοὺς θεοὺς εὐσεβείας καὶ τῆς περὶ σεαυτὸν προθυμίας, ἀμείψας αὐτῷ καὶ μεταθεὶς τὰ πρόσθεν ἐπονείδιστα πρὸς εὔκλειαν, οὐ τὴν νῦν μόνον, ἀλλὰ καὶ εἰς τὸν ἔπειτα χρόνον, ὡς οὐχ ὅμοιόν γε ἡ Παύλου συκοφαντία καὶ ἡ τοῦ δεῖνος κρίσις τοῖς ὑπὸ σοῦ γραφομένοις λόγοις· ἐκεῖνα μὲν γὰρ ἀνθοῦντά τε ἐμισεῖτο καὶ συναπέσβη τοῖς δράσασιν, οἱ δὲ σοὶ λόγοι καὶ νῦν ὑπὸ τῶν ἀληθῶς Ἑλλήνων ἀγαπῶνται, καὶ εἰς τὸν ἔπειτα χρόνον, εἰ μή τι σφάλλομαι κρίσεως ὀρθῆς, ἀγαπήσονται. πεύσῃ δὴ λοιπὸν εἰ πέπεικάς με, μᾶλλον δὲ μεταπέπεικας ὑπὲρ Ἀριστοφάνους. μὴ νομίζειν αὐτὸν ἡδονῶν ἥττονα καὶ χρημάτων ὁμολογῶ. τί δὲ οὐ μέλλω τῷ φιλοσοφωτάτῳ καὶ φιλαληθε-

[1] Hertlein 74 + 14; Cumont, following *Vaticanus* 941 and certain other MSS., restored Hertlein 14 to its proper place as postscript to Hertlein 74.

---

[1] Plato, *Phaedrus* 242E εἰ δ' ἐστίν, ὥσπερ οὖν ἐστί, θεός. . . .
[2] Sophocles, *Philoctetes* 97 γλῶσσαν μὲν ἀργόν, χεῖρα δ' εἶχον ἐργάτιν.

as in fact it is,[1] you have trebled my age, my good friend. I have dictated this to you in the midst of public business. For I was not able to write myself because my hand is lazier than my tongue.[2] Though indeed my tongue also has come to be somewhat lazy and inarticulate from lack of exercise. Farewell, brother, most dear and most beloved!

53

To Libanius

You have requited Aristophanes[3] for his piety towards the gods and his devotion to yourself by changing and transforming what was formerly a reproach against him so that it redounds to his honour, and not for to-day only but for the future also, since the malicious charges of Paul[4] and the verdict of So-and-so[5] have no force compared with words written by you. For their calumnies were detested even while they flourished, and perished along with their perpetrators, whereas your speeches are not only prized by genuine Hellenes to-day but will still be prized in future times, unless I am mistaken in my verdict. For the rest, you shall judge whether you have convinced, or rather converted, me on behalf of Aristophanes. I now agree not to believe that he is too weak to resist pleasure and money. What point would I not yield to the most

362 Winter At Antioch

[3] For Aristophanes of Corinth and for the answer of Libanius, *Letter* 758, Foerster, see Introduction, Aristophanes.

[4] Paul, the notary nicknamed Catena, "the chain," a tool of Constantius, was burned alive on Julian's accession, by order of the Chalcedon Commission; Ammianus 14. 5. 6; 22. 3. 11. He was a Spaniard, malevolent and inquisitorial.

[5] The real name is suppressed, probably by a cautious editor when the letter was first published.

στάτῳ τῶν[1] ῥητόρων εἴκειν; ἕπεται καὶ τὸ ἐπὶ τούτοις παρὰ σοῦ προσανερωτᾶσθαι· τί οὖν οὐ μετατίθεμεν αὐτῷ τὰς συμφορὰς εἰς ἀμείνω τύχην καὶ ἀφανίζομεν τὰ κατασχόντα διὰ τὰς δυσπραγίας ὀνείδη; σύν τε δύ' ἐρχομένω, φασίν, ἐγὼ καὶ σὺ βουλευσώμεθα. δίκαιος δὲ εἶ μὴ συμβουλεύειν μόνον, ὅτι χρὴ βοηθεῖν ἀνδρὶ τοὺς θεοὺς ἀδόλως τετιμηκότι, ἀλλὰ καὶ ὃν χρὴ τρόπον. καίτοι καὶ[2] τοῦτο ᾐνίξω τρόπον τινά. βέλτιον δὲ ἴσως ὑπὲρ τῶν τοιούτων οὐ γράφειν, ἀλλὰ διαλέγεσθαι πρὸς ἀλλήλους. ἔρρωσό μοι, ἀδελφὲ ποθεινότατε καὶ προσφιλέστατε.

382 D Ἀνέγνων δὲ[3] χθὲς τὸν λόγον πρὸ ἀρίστου σχεδόν, ἀριστήσας δέ, πρὶν ἀναπαύσασθαι, τὸ λοιπὸν προσαπέδωκα τῆς ἀναγνώσεως. μακάριος εἶ λέγειν οὕτω, μᾶλλον δὲ φρονεῖν οὕτω δυνάμενος. ὦ λόγος, ὦ φρένες, ὦ σύνεσις,[4] ὦ διαίρεσις, ὦ ἐπιχειρήματα, ὦ τάξις, ὦ ἀφορμαί, ὦ λέξις, ὦ ἁρμονία, ὦ συνθήκη.

54

387 D

Εὐστοχίῳ[5]

388 Ἡσιόδῳ μὲν δοκεῖ τῷ σοφῷ καλεῖν ἐπὶ τὰς ἑορτὰς τοὺς γείτονας ὡς συνησθησομένους, ἐπειδὴ

[1] τῶν Hercher supplies, Cumont omits.

[2] Before τοῦτο Cumont restores καὶ omitted by Hertlein and some MSS.

[3] δὲ Cumont restores, omitted by Hertlein following MSS., which make this section a separate letter. After χθὲς Hercher supplied σοῦ unnecessarily.

[4] σύνεσις Asmus following *Monacensis*, σύνθεσις Hertlein following *Vossianus*, but cf. συνθήκη at end of letter with same meaning. Both readings have good MS. authority.

[5] Hertlein 20.

philosophic and truth-loving of orators? Naturally you will proceed to ask me why, in that case, I do not alter his unhappy lot for the better and blot out the disgrace that attaches to him on account of his ill fortune. "Two walking together,"[1] as the proverb says, namely, you and I, must take counsel. And you have the right, not only to advise that we ought to assist a man who has honoured the gods so straightforwardly, but also as to how it ought to be done. Indeed, you did hint at this in an obscure way. But it is perhaps better not to write about such matters, but to talk it over together. Farewell, brother, most dear and most beloved!

I read yesterday almost all your speech before breakfast, and after breakfast, before resting, I gave myself up to reading the remainder. Happy man to be able to speak so well, or rather to have such ideas! O what a discourse! what wit! what wisdom! what analysis! what logic! what method! what openings! what diction! what symmetry! what structure![2]

54

To Eustochius[3]

THE wise Hesiod[4] thinks that we ought to invite our neighbours to our feasts that they may rejoice Late in 362 From Antioch

[1] *Iliad* 10. 224 *σύν τε δύ' ἐρχομένω, καί τε πρὸ ὁ τοῦ ἐνόησεν*, cf. Plato, *Symposium* 174D.

[2] Julian may have read Marcus Aurelius, *To Fronto*: O ἐπιχειρήματα! O τάξις! O argutiae! O ἄσκησις! O omnia!

[3] This is either Eustochius of Palestine, whose knowledge of law and eloquence is praised by Libanius, *Letter* 699 (789 Foerster), or a sophist of Cappadocia of the same name. We do not know which of these men it was to whom Gregory Nazianzen addressed his *Letters* 189–191.

[4] *τὸν δὲ μάλιστα καλεῖν ὅς τις σεθεν ἐγγύθι ναίει*; *Works and Days* 343, a favourite quotation.

καὶ συναλγοῦσι καὶ συναγωνιῶσιν, ὅταν τις ἀπροσδόκητος ἐμπέσῃ ταραχή. ἐγὼ δέ φημι τοὺς φίλους δεῖν καλεῖν, οὐχὶ τοὺς γείτονας· τὸ αἴτιον δέ, ὅτι γείτονα μὲν ἔνεστιν ἐχθρὸν ἔχειν, φίλον δὲ ἐχθρὸν οὐ μᾶλλον ἢ τὸ λευκὸν μέλαν εἶναι καὶ τὸ θερμὸν ψυχρόν. ὅτι δὲ ἡμῖν οὐ νῦν μόνον, ἀλλὰ καὶ πάλαι φίλος εἶ καὶ διετέλεσας εὐνοϊκῶς ἔχων, εἰ καὶ μηδὲν ὑπῆρχεν ἄλλο τεκ-
B μήριον, ἀλλὰ τό γε ἡμᾶς οὕτω διατεθεῖσθαι καὶ διακεῖσθαι[1] περὶ σὲ μέγα ἂν εἴη τούτου σημεῖον. ἧκε τοίνυν μεθέξων τῆς ὑπατείας αὐτός. ἄξει δέ σε ὁ δημόσιος δρόμος ὀχήματι χρώμενον ἑνὶ καὶ παρίππῳ.[2] εἰ δὲ χρή τι καὶ ἐπεύξασθαι, τὴν Ἐνοδίαν εὐμενῆ σοι καὶ τὸν Ἐνόδιον παρακεκλήκαμεν.

55

Iulianus[3] *etenim Christo perfidus Imperator sic Photino haeresiarchae adversus Diodorum scribit :*

[1] καὶ διακεῖσθαι bracketed by Hertlein, Cobet deletes.

[2] ἑνὶ παρίππῳ Hercher ; some MSS. ἑνὶ καὶ παρίππῳ, others, followed by Hertlein, omit ἑνί.

[3] Hertlein 79. These fragments of a lost letter are preserved only in the Latin version of Facundus Hermianensis, who wrote at Constantinople about 546 A.D. For a partial reconstruction of the original see Neumann, *Contra Christianos*, Leipzig, 1880, p. 5.

---

[1] Julian, with Sallustius as colleague, entered on the consulship January 1st, 363.

[2] Hecate, Latin Trivia. [3] Hermes.

[4] This letter may have been written at any time between

with us, since they sorrow and mourn with us when any unexpected misfortune befals us. But I say that it is our friends that we ought to invite, rather than our neighbours; and for this reason, that it is possible to have a neighbour who is one's enemy, but that a friend should be an enemy is no more possible than for white to be black, or hot cold. And if there were no other proof that you are my friend not now only, but for a long time past, and that you have steadily maintained your regard for me, nevertheless the fact that my feeling for you has been and is what it is, would be strong evidence of that friendship. Come, therefore, that you may in person share my consulship.[1] The state post will bring you, and you may use one carriage and an extra horse. And in case we ought to pray for further aid, I have invoked for you the blessing of the goddess of the Crossroads[2] and the god of the Ways.[3]

55

To Photinus[4]

Moreover the Emperor Julian, faithless to Christ, in his attack on Diodorus[5] writes as follows to Photinus the

Julian's arrival at Antioch in July 362 and his departure thence, in March 363. The Greek original is represented by curious and sometimes untranslatable Latin. Photinus, bishop of Sirmium, where Constantius resided in 351, was tried, deposed and banished by a synod convened there by Constantius. According to Sozomen 4. 6, he wrote many Greek and Latin works in support of his heretical views on the divinity of Christ, which were opposed by both Arians and Nicaeans. He is mentioned by Julian, *Against the Galilaeans* 262c.

[5] Bishop of Tarsus, a celebrated teacher; he was at Antioch in 362.

Tu quidem, o Photine, verisimilis videris, et proximus salvari,[1] benefaciens nequaquam in utero inducere quem credidisti deum. Diodorus autem Nazaraei magus, eius pigmentalibus manganis [2] acuens irrationabilitatem, acutus apparuit sophista religionis agrestis. *Et post paululum:* Quod si nobis opitulati fuerint dii et deae et musae omnes et fortuna, ostendemus infirmum et corruptorem legum et rationum et mysteriorum paganorum et deorum infernorum [3] et illum novum eius deum Galilaeum, quem aeternum fabulose praedicat,[4] indigna morte et sepultura denudatum confictae a Diodoro deitatis. *Sicut autem solent errantes convicti fingere, quod arte magis quam veritate vincantur, sequitur dicens:* Iste enim malo communis utilitatis Athenas navigans et philosophans imprudenter musicarum participatus est rationum, et rhetoricis confictionibus [5] odibilem adarmavit linguam adversus caelestes deos, usque adeo ignorans paganorum mysteria, omnemque miserabiliter imbibens, ut aiunt, degenerum et imperitorum ejus theologorum piscatorum errorem. Propter quod iam diu est quod ab ipsis punitur diis. Iam enim per multos annos in periculum conversus et in corruptionem thoracis incidens, ad

[1] *salvari* Neumann; *salvare* Facundus, Hertlein.
[2] *manganis* Neumann; *manganes* Facundus, Hertlein.
[3] *infernorum,* Hertlein, comma deleted by Neumann.
[4] *praedicat, sepultura* Neumann; *praedicat—sepultura* Facundus, Hertlein. Before *indigna* Asmus supplies *et.*
[5] *rhetoricis confictionibus* Asmus; *rhetoris confectionibus* Facundus, Hertlein.

heresiarch:[1] O Photinus, you at any rate seem to maintain what is probably true, and come nearest to being saved, and do well to believe that he whom one holds to be a god can by no means be brought into the womb. But Diodorus, a charlatan priest of the Nazarene, when he tries to give point to that nonsensical theory about the womb by artifices and juggler's tricks, is clearly a sharp-witted sophist of that creed of the country-folk. *A little further on he says:* But if only the gods and goddesses and all the Muses and Fortune will lend me their aid, I hope to show[2] that he is feeble and a corrupter of laws and customs, of pagan[3] Mysteries and Mysteries of the gods of the underworld, and that that new-fangled Galilaean god of his, whom he by a false myth styles eternal, has been stripped by his humiliating death and burial of the divinity falsely ascribed to him by Diodorus. *Then, just as people who are convicted of error always begin to invent, being the slaves of artifice rather than of truth, he goes on to say:* For the fellow sailed to Athens to the injury of the general welfare, then rashly took to philosophy and engaged in the study of literature, and by the devices of rhetoric armed his hateful tongue against the heavenly gods, and being utterly ignorant of the Mysteries of the pagans he so to speak imbibed most deplorably the whole mistaken folly of the base and ignorant creed-making fishermen. For this conduct he has long ago been punished by the gods themselves. For, for many years past, he has been in danger, having contracted a wasting disease

1 The italicised passages are the words of Facundus.

2 This is a forecast of Julian's treatise *Against the Galilaeans.*

3 Twice in this letter Facundus translates Julian's "Hellenic" as "pagan."

summum pervenit supplicium. Omne eius corpus consumptum est. Nam malae eius conciderunt, rugae vero in altitudinem corporis descenderunt. Quod non est philosophicae conversationis indicio, sicut videri vult a se deceptis, sed iustitiae pro certo deorumque poenae, qua percutitur competenti ratione, usque ad novissimum vitae suae finem asperam et amaram vitam vivens et faciem pallore confectam.

56

Χρῆν [1] μὲν οἴκοθεν διανοηθέντα ὃ δὴ νῦν ἔδοξε κρατῦναι τῷ νόμῳ, τὸ παλαιὸν ἔθος ἀναλαβεῖν, ὃ διανοούμενοι μὲν οἱ πάλαι καλῶς θέμενοι τοὺς νόμους, εἶναι πλεῖστον ὑπέλαβον ἐν μέσῳ ζωῆς τε καὶ θανάτου, ἰδίᾳ δὲ ἑκατέρῳ πρέπειν ἐνόμισαν τὰ ἐπιτηδεύματα τῶν ἔργων. εἶναι μὲν γὰρ τὸν θάνατον ἡσυχίαν διηνεκῆ—καὶ τοῦτο ἄρα ἐστὶν ὁ χαλκοῦς ὕπνος ὁ ὑπὸ τῶν ποιητῶν ὑμνούμενος—, ἀπεναντίας δὲ τὴν ζωὴν ἔχειν πολλὰ μὲν ἀλγεινὰ πολλὰ δὲ ἡδέα, καὶ τὸ πράττειν νῦν μὲν ἑτέρως, αὖθις δὲ ἄμεινον. ὃ δὴ διανοηθέντες ἔταξαν ἰδίᾳ

[1] Hertlein 77. This edict, which has no Greek title, does not appear in any MS. collection of the *Letters* and was first published by Hertlein (from *Marcianus* 366) in *Hermes* 8.

---

[1] Here and in the last sentence I give what seems to be the general meaning.

[2] This is probably the earlier form of the Latin Edict in *Codex Theodosianus* 9. 17. 5 dated February 12th, 363. It is not clear whether it was aimed at the Christians, but of course

of the chest, and he now suffers extreme torture. His whole body has wasted away. For his cheeks have fallen in and his body is deeply lined with wrinkles.[1] But this is no sign of philosophic habits, as he wishes it to seem to those who are deceived by him, but most certainly a sign of justice done and of punishment from the gods which has stricken him down in suitable proportion to his crime, since he must live out to the very end his painful and bitter life, his appearance that of a man pale and wasted.

56

Edict on Funerals[2]

It was my duty, after considering with myself, to restore the ancient custom which I have now decided to confirm by a law. For when they considered the matter, the men of old, who made wise laws, believed that there is the greatest possible difference between life and death and thought that each of these two states has customs and practices peculiarly appropriate to it. For they thought that death is an unbroken rest, —and this is surely that "brazen sleep" of which the poets sing,[3]—but that life, on the contrary, brings many pains and many pleasures, and now adversity, now greater prosperity. Considering thus, they en-

363 About February 12th From Antioch

they had to observe it. They buried their dead by day, and did not share the pagan fear of pollution by a corpse, for which cf. Eunapius, *Life of Iamblichus*, p. 367, Wright. Julian desired to suppress the Christian demonstrations at public funerals such as that of the bones of St. Babylas, at Antioch, for which see Philostorgius 7. 8, Sozomen 5. 19, Julian, *Misopogon* 361B, note, p. 485, Wright.

[3] *Iliad* 11. 241, χάλκεον ὕπνον; Vergil, *Aeneid* 10. 745 ferreus Somnus.

μὲν ἀφοσιοῦσθαι τὰ πρὸς τοὺς κατοιχομένους, ἰδίᾳ δὲ τὰ πρὸς τὸν καθ' ἡμέραν οἰκονομεῖσθαι βίον. ἔτι δὲ πάντων ὑπελάμβανον ἀρχὴν εἶναι καὶ τέλος τοὺς θεούς, ζῶντάς τε ἡμᾶς ἐνόμισαν ὑπὸ θεοῖς εἶναι καὶ ἀπιόντας πάλιν πρὸς τοὺς θεοὺς πορεύεσθαι. τὸ μὲν οὖν ὑπὲρ τούτων λέγειν, εἴτε τοῖς αὐτοῖς ἀμφότερα προσήκει θεοῖς, εἴτε ἕτεροι μὲν ἐπιτροπεύουσι τοὺς ζῶντας, ἕτεροι δὲ τοὺς τεθνεῶτας, οὐδ' ἄξιον ἴσως δημοσιεύειν. εἴ γε μὴν καθάπερ ἡμέρας καὶ νυκτὸς αἴτιος ἥλιος καὶ χειμῶνος καὶ θέρους ἀπιὼν καὶ προσιών, οὕτω δὲ καὶ αὐτῶν τῶν θεῶν ὁ πρεσβύτατος, εἰς ὃν πάντα καὶ ἐξ οὗ πάντα, ζῶσί τε ἔταξεν ἄρχοντας καὶ τελευτήσασιν ἀπεκλήρωσε κυρίους, ἑκατέρῳ τὰ πρέποντα χρὴ νέμειν ἐν μέρει, καὶ μιμεῖσθαι διὰ τοῦ καθ' ἡμέραν βίου τὴν ἐν τοῖς οὖσι τῶν θεῶν διακόσμησιν.

Οὐκοῦν ἡσυχία μὲν ὁ θάνατός ἐστιν, ἡσυχίᾳ δὲ ἡ νὺξ ἁρμόττει. διόπερ οἶμαι πρέπειν ἐν αὐτῇ τὰ περὶ τὰς ταφὰς πραγματεύεσθαι τῶν τελευτησάντων, ἐπεὶ τό γε ἐν ἡμέρᾳ πράττειν τι τοιοῦτο πολλῶν ἕνεκα παραιτητέον. ἄλλος ἐπ' ἄλλῃ πράξει στρέφεται κατὰ τὴν πόλιν, καὶ μεστὰ πάντα ἐστὶ τῶν μὲν εἰς δικαστήρια πορευομένων τῶν δὲ εἰς ἀγορὰν καὶ ἐξ ἀγορᾶς, τῶν δὲ ταῖς τέχναις προσκαθημένων, τῶν δὲ ἐπὶ τὰ ἱερὰ φοιτώντων, ὅπως τὰς ἀγαθὰς ἐλπίδας παρὰ τῶν θεῶν βεβαιώσαιντο· εἶτα οὐκ οἶδα οἵτινες ἀναθέντες ἐν κλίνῃ νεκρὸν διὰ μέσων ὠθοῦνται τῶν ταῦτα σπουδαζόντων. καὶ τὸ πρᾶγμά ἐστι πάντα τρόπον οὐκ ἀνεκτόν. ἀναπίμπλανται γὰρ οἱ

joined that expiations connected with the departed should be conducted apart, and that apart from them the daily business of life should be carried on. Moreover, they held that the gods are the beginning and end of all things, and believed that while we live we are subject to the gods, and when we depart from this life we travel back to the gods. But perhaps it is not right to speak openly about these matters or to divulge whether both are in the hands of the same gods or one set of gods has charge of the living and another set the dead. However, if, as the Sun is the cause of day and night and winter and summer by his departure and arrival, so also the most venerable one of the gods themselves, unto whom are all things and from whom all things proceed, has appointed rulers over the living and allotted lords over the dead, then we ought to assign to both of these classes in turn what is fitting for them, and to imitate in our daily life the orderly arrangement of the gods in things which exist.

As I have said, death is rest; and night harmonises with rest. Therefore I think it is fitting that business connected with the burials of the dead should be performed at night, since for many reasons we ought to forbid anything of the sort to go on by day. Throughout the city men are going to and fro each on his own business, and all the streets are full of men going to the lawcourts, or to or from the market, or sitting at work at their crafts, or visiting the temples to confirm the good hopes that the gods have vouchsafed. And then some persons or other, having laid a corpse on the bier, push their way into the midst of those who are busy about such matters. The thing is in every way intolerable. For those

προστυχόντες πολλάκις ἀηδίας, οἱ μὲν οἰόμενοι πονηρὸν τὸ οἰώνισμα, τοῖς δὲ εἰς ἱερὰ βαδίζουσιν οὐ θέμις προσελθεῖν ἐστι πρὶν ἀπολούσασθαι. τοῖς γὰρ αἰτίοις τοῦ ζῆν θεοῖς καὶ μάλιστα πάντων ἀλλοτριώτατα πρὸς φθορὰν διακειμένοις οὐ θέμις προσελθεῖν ἀπὸ τοιαύτης ὄψεως. καὶ οὔπω τὰ μείζω κατηγόρηκα τοῦ γιγνομένου. τίνα δὲ ταῦτά ἐστιν; ἱεροὶ περίβολοι καὶ θεῶν ναοὶ ἀνεῴγασι· καὶ πολλάκις θύει τις ἔνδον καὶ σπένδει καὶ εὔχεται, οἱ δὲ παρέρχονται παρ' αὐτὸ τὸ ἱερὸν νεκρὸν κομίζοντες, καὶ ἡ τῶν ὀδυρμῶν φωνὴ καὶ δυσφημία ἄχρι τῶν βωμῶν φέρεται.

Οὐκ ἴστε ὅτι πρὸ πάντων τῶν ἄλλων τὰ τῆς ἡμέρας καὶ τὰ τῆς νυκτὸς ἔργα διῄρηται; οὕτως[1] οὖν εἰκότως τῆς μὲν ἀφῃρέθη, τῇ δὲ ἂν[2] ἀνακέοιτο. οὐ γὰρ δὴ τῆς ἐσθῆτος τὴν λευκὴν ἐπὶ τοῖς πένθεσιν ὀρθῶς ἔχον ἐστὶ παραιτεῖσθαι, θάπτειν δὲ τοὺς τελευτήσαντας ἐν ἡμέρᾳ καὶ φωτί. βέλτιον ἦν ἐκεῖνο, εἴ γε εἰς οὐδένα τῶν θεῶν ἐπλημμελεῖτο, τοῦτο δὲ οὐκ ἐκφεύγει τὸ μὴ εἰς ἅπαντας τοὺς θεοὺς εἶναι δυσσέβειαν. τοῖς τε γὰρ Ὀλυμπίοις οὐ δέον αὐτὸ προσνέμουσι, καὶ τῶν χθονίων, ἢ ὁπωσοῦν ἄλλως οἱ τῶν ψυχῶν ἐπίτροποι καὶ κύριοι χαίρουσιν ὀνομαζόμενοι, παρὰ τὸ δέον ἀλλοτριοῦσιν. ἐγὼ δὲ οἶδα καὶ τοὺς περιττοὺς καὶ ἀκριβεῖς τὰ θεῖα θεοῖς τοῖς κάτω νύκτωρ ἢ πάντως μετὰ δεκάτην ἡμέρας ὥραν ἱερὰ δρᾶν ἀξιοῦντας. εἰ δὲ τῆς ἐκείνων θεραπείας οὗτος

[1] οὕτως—τῆς Hertlein suggests for corrupt οὗτος—τοῖς.
[2] ἂν Hertlein suggests; τῇ δὲ ἀνήκει τοῦτο "appertains to," Capps suggests. The sentence remains unsatisfactory.

who meet the funeral are often filled with disgust, some because they regard it as an evil omen, while for others who are on the way to the temples it is not permitted to approach for worship till they have cleansed themselves from the pollution. For after such a sight it is not permitted to approach the gods who are the cause of life and of all things least akin to decay. And I have still to mention what is worse than this. And what is that? The sacred precincts and temples of the gods lie open; and it often happens that in one of them someone is sacrificing or pouring libations or praying, at the moment when men carrying a corpse are passing close by the temple itself, and the voice of lamentations and speech of ill omen is carried even to the altars.

Do you not understand that the functions belonging to the day and the night have been separated more than all other things? With good reason, therefore, has burial been taken out of the day and would be reserved for the night. For it is not right to deprecate the wearing of white for mourning and yet to bury the dead in the daytime and sunlight. The former was better, at least if it was not offensive to any of the gods, but the latter cannot escape being an act of impiety towards all the gods. For thereby men wrongly assign burial to the Olympian gods and wrongly alienate it from the gods of the underworld, or whatever else the guardians and lords of souls prefer to be called. And I know that those who are thoroughly versed and punctilious in sacred rites think it right to perform at night the ritual to the gods below or in any case not till after the tenth hour of the day. But if this is the better time for

ἀμείνων ὁ καιρός, οὐδὲ τῇ θεραπείᾳ πάντως τῶν τεθνεώτων ἕτερον ἀποδώσομεν.

Τοῖς μὲν οὖν ἑκοῦσι πειθομένοις ἐξαρκεῖ ταῦτα. ἃ γὰρ ἡμάρτανον μαθόντες, μετατιθέσθων πρὸς τὸ βέλτιον. εἰ δέ τις τοιοῦτός ἐστιν οἷος ἀπειλῆς καὶ ζημίας δεῖσθαι, ἴστω τὴν μεγίστην ὑφέξων δίκην, εἰ πρὸ δεκάτης ἡμερινῆς ὥρας τολμήσει τε τῶν ἀπογινομένων τινὸς κηδεῦσαι σῶμα καὶ διὰ τῆς πόλεως ἐνεγκεῖν· ἀλλὰ δύντος ἡλίου καὶ αὖ πρὶν ἀνίσχειν ταῦτα γενέσθω. ἡ δὲ ἡμέρα καθαρὰ καθαροῖς τοῖς τε ἔργοις[1] καὶ τοῖς Ὀλυμπίοις ἀνακείσθω θεοῖς.

57

Ἀρσάκῃ Ἀρμενίων σατράπῃ[2]

Ἐπείχθητι πρὸς τὴν τῶν πολεμίων παράταξιν, Ἀρσάκιε, θᾶττον ἢ λόγος, τὴν δεξιὰν κατὰ τῆς Περσικῆς μανίας ὁπλίσας. ἡ γὰρ ἡμετέρα παρασκευή τε καὶ προθυμία δυοῖν θάτερον βεβούλευται, ἢ τὸ χρεὼν ἀποδοῦναι ἐπὶ τῆς Παρθυαίων ἐνορίας[3] τὰ μέγιστα διαπραξαμένους καὶ τὰ δεινότατα διαθεμένους τοὺς ἀντιπάλους, ἢ τούτους χειρωσαμένους, πρυτανευόντων ἡμῖν τῶν θεῶν,

[1] For τοῖς τε ἔργοις Hercher conjectures τοῖς ἱεροῖς. Before τοῖς Ὀλυμπίοις Hertlein suspects the loss of τοῖς λόγοις.

[2] Hertlein 66; he regards the letter as spurious, and brackets the title. Schwarz, Geffcken, and Cumont also reject it.

[3] εὐορίας *Ambrosianus*; ἐνορίας *Monacensis*; εὐοδίας Muratorius; ἐφορίας Reiske.

the worship of these gods, we will certainly not assign another time for the service of the dead.

What I have said suffices for those who are willing to obey. For now that they have learned what errors they used to commit, let them change to the better way. But if there be any man of such a character that he needs threat and penalty, let him know that he will incur the severest punishment if, before the tenth hour of the day, he shall venture to perform the offices for the corpse of any dead person and to carry it through the city. But let these things be done at sunset and before sunrise, and let the pure day be consecrated for pure deeds and the pure gods of Olympus.

57

To Arsaces, Satrap of Armenia [1]

Make haste, Arsacius,[2] to meet the enemy's battle line and quicker than I tell [3] you arm your right hand against the madness of the Persians. For my military preparations and my set purpose are for one of two things; either to pay the debt of nature within the Parthian [4] frontier, after I have won the most glorious victories and inflicted on my foes the most terrible reverses, or to defeat them under the leadership of the gods and return to my native land 363 At Antioch Just before Julian's Persian campaign

[1] See Introduction, under Arsaces.

[2] This form is given also by Sozomen 6. 1. who gives the general contents of the letter. The correct form Arsaces occurs in Ammianus.

[3] Cf. *To Hermogenes*, p. 32, 390 B παρὰ δύναμιν ἐπείχθητι.

[4] The writer seems to confuse the Persians and the Parthians: Julian, however, distinguishes them in *Oration* 2. 63A, Vol. 1, p. 169, Wright; Ammianus sometimes confuses them.

καλλινίκους ἐπανελθεῖν ἐπὶ τὴν ἐνεγκαμένην, τρόπαια κατὰ τῶν πολεμίων ἐγείραντας. πᾶσαν οὖν ῥᾳστώνην καὶ φενακισμὸν ἀποθέμενος, καὶ τὸν μακαρίτην Κωνσταντῖνον[1] καὶ τὰς τῶν εὖ γεγονότων περιουσίας τὰς εἰς σέ τε καὶ τοὺς ὁμοτρόπους σοι βαρβάρους ὑπὸ τοῦ ἀβροτάτου καὶ πολυτελοῦς[2] Κωνσταντίου κενωθείσας, νῦν μοι τὸν Ἰουλιανόν, τὸν ἀρχιερέα, τὸν καίσαρα, τὸν αὔγουστον, τὸν θεῶν τε καὶ Ἄρεως θεραπευτὴν ἐννόησον,[3] τὸν Φραγκῶν[4] τε καὶ βαρβάρων ὀλετῆρα, τὸν Γάλλων τε καὶ Ἰταλῶν ἐλευθερωτήν. εἰ δὲ ἕτερόν τι βουλεύσαιο· πυνθάνομαι γὰρ εἶναί σε πανοῦργον καὶ κακὸν στρατιώτην καὶ ἀλαζόνα, ὡς τὰ παρόντα μοι πράγματα δείκνυσιν· ἐχθρὸν γάρ τινα τῆς κοινῆς λυσιτελείας λανθάνοντα ἀποκρύπτειν παρὰ σοὶ πειρᾶσθαι· τέως μὲν τοῦτο ὑπερτίθεμαι διὰ τὴν τοῦ πολέμου τύχην· ἀρκεῖ γὰρ ἡμῖν ἡ τῶν θεῶν συμμαχία πρὸς τὴν τῶν πολεμίων καθαίρεσιν. εἰ δέ τι τὰ τῆς εἱμαρμένης κρίνειε· θεῶν γὰρ βούλησις ἡ ταύτης ἐξουσία· ἀδεῶς καὶ γενναίως οἴσω τοῦτο. ἴσθι δὲ ὡς σὺ μὲν πάρεργον ἔσῃ τῆς Περσικῆς χειρός, συναφθείσης σοι παγγενεὶ τῆς ἑστίας καὶ τῆς Ἀρμενίων ἀρχῆς· κοινωνήσει δέ σοι τῆς δυστυχίας καὶ ἡ

[1] Wright restores Κωνσταντῖνον from *Laurentianus*; ἐκεῖνον Hertlein following *Monacensis*.

[2] πολυετοῦς MSS. (Constantius died aged about 45); Teuffel ἀσεβοῦς, cf. Sozomen 6. 1, who says that Julian in this letter reviled Constantius ὡς ἀνάνδρῳ καὶ ἀσεβεῖ. Hertlein πολυτελοῦς following Sintenis.

[3] εὐνόησον *Ambrosianus*; εὐνόϊσον Muratorius.

[4] Julian uses the form Φράγγοι in *Oration* 1. 34 D.

as a conquering hero, after I have set up trophies of the enemy's defeat. Accordingly you must discard all sloth and cheating, and the Emperor Constantine of blessed memory, and the wealth of the nobles which was lavished in vain on you and on barbarians of your character by the most luxurious and extravagant Constantius, and now I warn you, take heed of me, Julian, supreme pontiff, Caesar, Augustus, the servant of the gods and of Ares, the destroyer of the Franks and barbarians,[1] the liberator of the Gauls and of Italy. But if you form some other design,—for I learn that you are a rascal[2] and a coward in war and a boaster, as the present condition of affairs proves; indeed I have heard that you are secretly trying to conceal at your court a certain enemy of the public welfare,—for the present I postpone this matter because of the fortune of war; for my alliance with the gods is enough to secure the destruction of the enemy. But if Destiny should also play some part in the decision,—for the purpose of the gods is her opportunity,—I will endure it fearlessly and like a brave man. Be assured that you will be an easy victim[3] of the power of Persia when your hearth and home, your whole race and the kingdom of Armenia all blaze together. And the city of Nisibis[4] also will

[1] Cf. Ammianus 22. 5, of Julian: saepeque dictitabat "audite me quem Alemanni audierunt et Franci."

[2] Arsaces was almost certainly a Christian; cf. Sozomen 6. 1.

[3] For this phrase cf. Vol. 2. *Caesars* 326A πάρεργον . . . τῆς ἐμαυτοῦ στρατηγίας.

[4] After Julian's death Nisibis reverted to the Persians; their king Sapor captured and killed Arsaces; Ammianus 27. 12.

Νισιβίων πόλις, τῶν οὐρανίων θεῶν τοῦτο πάλαι ἡμῖν προαγορευσάντων.

58

Λιβανίῳ σοφιστῇ καὶ κοιαίστωρι[1]

399 Μέχρι τῶν Λιτάρβων ἦλθον· ἔστι δὲ κώμη
B Χαλκίδος· καὶ ἐνέτυχον ὁδῷ λείψανα ἐχούσῃ χειμαδίων Ἀντιοχικῶν. ἦν δὲ αὐτῆς, οἶμαι, τὸ μὲν τέλμα τὸ δὲ ὄρος, τραχεῖα δὲ πᾶσα, καὶ ἐνέκειντο τῷ τέλματι λίθοι ὥσπερ ἐπίτηδες ἐρριμμένοις ἐοικότες, ὑπ᾽ οὐδεμιᾶς τέχνης συγκείμενοι,
C ὃν τρόπον εἰώθασιν ἐν ταῖς ἄλλαις[2] πόλεσι τὰς λεωφόρους οἱ ἐξοικοδομοῦντες ποιεῖν, ἀντὶ μὲν τῆς κονίας πολὺν τὸν χοῦν ἐποικοδομοῦντες,[3] πυκνοὺς δὲ ὥσπερ ἐν τοίχῳ τιθέντες τοὺς λίθους. ἐπεὶ δὲ διαβὰς μόλις ἦλθον εἰς τὸν πρῶτον σταθμόν, ἐννέα που σχεδὸν ἦσαν ὧραι, καὶ ἐδεξάμην εἴσω τῆς αὐλῆς τὸ πλεῖστον τῆς παρ᾽ ὑμῖν βουλῆς. ἃ δὲ διελέχθημεν πρὸς ἀλλήλους, ἴσως ἐπύθου· μάθοις δ᾽ ἂν καὶ ἡμῶν ἀκούσας, εἰ θεοὶ θέλοιεν.

D Ἀπὸ τῶν Λιτάρβων εἰς τὴν Βέρροιαν ἐπορευόμην, καὶ ὁ Ζεὺς αἴσια πάντα ἐσήμηνεν, ἐναργῆ δείξας τὴν διοσημείαν.[4] ἐπιμείνας δὲ ἡμέραν ἐκεῖ

[1] Hertlein 27.
[2] ἄλλαις Hertlein suspects.
[3] ὑποσκεδάννυντες Cumont, as more suitable in connection with χοῦς = loose soil.
[4] διοσημείαν Asmus; διοσημίαν Hertlein, MSS.

---

[1] Julian's march is described by Ammianus 23. 2, to the end of 24; he was a member of the expedition; cf. Zosimus 3. 12–28; Cumont, *Études Syriennes*, Paris, 1917.

share in your misfortune, for this the heavenly gods long since foretold to me.

58

To Libanius, Sophist and Quaestor [1]

I TRAVELLED as far as Litarbae,—it is a village of Chalcis,—and came on a road that still had the remains of a winter camp of Antioch. The road, I may say, was partly swamp, partly hill, but the whole of it was rough, and in the swamp lay stones which looked as though they had been thrown there purposely, as they lay together without any art, after the fashion followed also by those who build public highways in cities and instead of cement make a deep layer of soil and then lay the stones close together as though they were making a boundary-wall. When I had passed over this with some difficulty and arrived at my first halting-place it was about the ninth hour, and then I received at my headquarters the greater part of your senate.[2] You have perhaps learned already what we said to one another, and, if it be the will of heaven, you shall know it from my own lips.

363 March 10th From Hierapolis

From Litarbae I proceeded to Beroea,[3] and there Zeus by showing a manifest sign from heaven declared all things to be auspicious.[4] I stayed there

[2] The Senators of Antioch followed Julian to plead for the city, which had offended him; see Libanius, *Oration* 16. 1.

[3] Aleppo.

[4] Ammianus 23. 2 records certain fatal accidents at Hierapolis and Batnae which were regarded as of ill omen for the campaign.

τὴν ἀκρόπολιν εἶδον, καὶ ἔθυσα τῷ Διὶ βασιλικῶς ταῦρον λευκόν, διελέχθην δὲ ὀλίγα τῇ βουλῇ περὶ θεοσεβείας. ἀλλὰ τοὺς λόγους ἐπῄνουν μὲν ἅπαντες, ἐπείσθησαν δὲ αὐτοῖς ὀλίγοι πάνυ, καὶ οὗτοι οἳ καὶ πρὸ τῶν ἐμῶν λόγων ἐδόκουν ἔχειν
400 ὑγιῶς. εὐλαβοῦντο[1] δὲ ὥσπερ παρρησίας ἀποτρίψασθαι τὴν αἰδῶ καὶ ἀποθέσθαι· περίεστι γάρ, ὦ θεοί, τοῖς ἀνθρώποις ἐπὶ μὲν τοῖς καλοῖς ἐρυθριᾶν, ἀνδρείᾳ ψυχῆς καὶ εὐσεβείᾳ, καλλωπίζεσθαι δὲ ὥσπερ τοῖς χειρίστοις, ἱεροσυλίᾳ καὶ μαλακίᾳ γνώμης καὶ σώματος.

Ἔνθεν ὑποδέχονταί με Βάτναι, χωρίον οἷον παρ' ὑμῖν οὐκ εἶδον ἔξω τῆς Δάφνης, ἣ νῦν ἔοικε
B ταῖς Βάτναις· ὡς τά γε πρὸ μικροῦ, σωζομένου τοῦ νεὼ καὶ τοῦ ἀγάλματος, Ὄσσῃ καὶ Πηλίῳ καὶ ταῖς Ὀλύμπου κορυφαῖς καὶ τοῖς Θετταλικοῖς Τέμπεσιν ἄγων ἐπίσης ἢ καὶ προτιμῶν ἁπάντων ὁμοῦ τὴν Δάφνην οὐκ ἂν αἰσχυνοίμην.[2] ἀλλ' ἐπὶ μὲν τῇ Δάφνῃ γέγραπταί σοι λόγος, ὁποῖον ἄλλος οὐδ' ἂν εἷς τῶν οἳ νῦν βροτοί εἰσι καὶ μάλα ἐπι-
C χειρήσας καμεῖν ἐργάσαιτο, νομίζω δὲ καὶ τῶν ἔμπροσθεν οὐ πολλοὺς πάνυ. τί οὖν ἐγὼ νῦν ἐπιχειρῶ περὶ αὐτῆς γράφειν, οὕτω λαμπρᾶς μονῳδίας[3] ἐπ' αὐτῇ συγγεγραμμένης; ὡς μήποτε

[1] Cobet; Hertlein, MSS. ἐλάβοντο.
[2] ἱερὸν Διὸς Ὀλυμπίου καὶ Ἀπόλλωνος Πυθίου τὸ χωρίον follows in MSS., bracketed by Hertlein as a gloss; Heyler retains.
[3] Lacuna Hercher, Hertlein; μονῳδίας Heyler.

---

[1] The Emperors sacrificed white victims; cf. Ammianus 25. 4. 17.
[2] Julian was at Batnae March 8th; a few days later he halted at another Batnae, in Osroëne, beyond the Euphrates.

for a day and saw the Acropolis and sacrificed to Zeus in imperial fashion a white bull.[1] Also I conversed briefly with the senate about the worship of the gods. But though they all applauded my arguments very few were converted by them, and these few were men who even before I spoke seemed to me to hold sound views. But they were cautious and would not strip off and lay aside their modest reserve, as though afraid of too frank speech. For it is the prevailing habit of mankind, O ye gods, to blush for their noble qualities, manliness of soul and piety, and to plume themselves, as it were, on what is most depraved, sacrilege and weakness of mind and body.

Next, Batnae [2] entertained me, a place like nothing that I have ever seen in your country, except Daphne [3]; but that is now very like Batnae, though not long ago, while the temple and statue were still unharmed,[4] I should not have hesitated to compare Daphne with Ossa and Pelion or the peaks of Olympus, or Thessalian Tempe, or even to have preferred it to all of them put together. But you have composed an oration [5] on Daphne such as no other man "of such sort as mortals now are" [6] could achieve, even though he used his utmost energies on the task, yes, and I think not very many of the ancient writers either. Why then should I try to write about it now, when so brilliant a monody has been composed in its honour? Would

[3] A suburb of Antioch; cf. *Misopogon* 361; Ammianus 19. 12. 19. The temple of Apollo was burned October 22nd, 362.

[4] Cf. *Misopogon* 346B; Vol. 2, Wright.

[5] We have the monody of Libanius, *On the Temple of Apollo at Daphne*, *Oration* 60; cf. his *Oration* 11. 235.

[6] *Iliad* 5. 304; Julian, *Oration* 6. 191A.

ὤφελε τοιοῦτον. αἵ γε μὴν Βάτναι· βαρβαρικὸν ὄνομα τοῦτο· χωρίον ἐστὶν Ἑλληνικόν, πρῶτον μὲν ὅτι διὰ πάσης τῆς πέριξ χώρας ἀτμοὶ λιβανωτοῦ πανταχόθεν ἦσαν, ἱερεῖά τε ἐβλέπομεν εὐτρεπῆ πανταχοῦ. τοῦτο μὲν οὖν εἰ καὶ λίαν ηὔφραινέ με, θερμότερον ὅμως ἐδόκει καὶ τῆς εἰς τοὺς θεοὺς
D εὐσεβείας ἀλλότριον. ἐκτὸς πάτου γὰρ εἶναι χρὴ καὶ δρᾶσθαι καθ' ἡσυχίαν, ἐπ' αὐτὸ τοῦτο πορευομένων, οὐκ ἐπ' ἄλλο τι βαδιζόντων, τὰ πρὸς τοὺς θεοὺς ἱερά τε καὶ ὅσια. τοῦτο μὲν οὖν ἴσως τεύξεται τῆς ἁρμοζούσης ἐπιμελείας αὐτίκα.

Τὰς Βάτνας δὲ ἑώρων πεδίον λάσιον ἄλση κυπαρίττων ἔχον νέων· καὶ ἦν ἐν ταύταις οὐδὲν γεράνδρυον οὐδὲ σαπρόν, ἀλλὰ ἐξ ἴσης ἅπαντα θάλλοντα
401 τῇ κόμῃ· καὶ τὰ βασίλεια πολυτελῆ μὲν ἥκιστα· πηλοῦ γὰρ ἦν μόνον καὶ ξύλων οὐδὲν ποικίλον ἔχοντα· κῆπον δὲ τοῦ μὲν Ἀλκίνου καταδεέστερον, παραπλήσιον δὲ τῷ Λαέρτου, καὶ ἐν αὐτῷ μικρὸν ἄλσος πάνυ, κυπαρίττων μεστόν, καὶ τῷ θριγκίῳ δὲ πολλὰ τοιαῦτα παραπεφυτευμένα δένδρα στίχῳ καὶ ἐφεξῆς. εἶτα τὸ μέσον πρασιαί, καὶ ἐν ταύταις λάχανα καὶ δένδρα παντοίαν ὀπώραν φέροντα.
B τί οὖν ἐνταῦθα; ἔθυσα δείλης, εἶτ' ὄρθρου βαθέος, ὅπερ εἴωθα ποιεῖν ἐπιεικῶς ἑκάστης ἡμέρας. ἐπεὶ δὲ ἦν καλὰ τὰ ἱερά, τῆς Ἱερᾶς πόλεως εἰχόμεθα, καὶ ὑπαντῶσιν ἡμῖν οἱ πολῖται, καὶ ὑποδέχεταί

---

[1] *i.e.* it maintained the pagan cults.

[2] *Odyssey* 7. 112 foll., a favourite commonplace; cf. *Misopogon* 352A.

[3] *Odyssey* 24. 245 foll.

[4] Hierapolis is now Membej; Julian arrived there about March 10th; it was the rendezvous for the Roman troops

that none had been needed! However, to return to Batnae. Its name is barbarous but the place is Hellenic;[1] I say so because through all the country round about the fumes of frankincense arose on all sides, and I saw everywhere victims ready for sacrifice. But though this gave me very great pleasure, nevertheless it looked to me like overheated zeal, and alien to proper reverence for the gods. For things that are sacred to the gods and holy ought to be away from the beaten track and performed in peace and quiet, so that men may resort thither to that end alone and not on the way to some other business. But this matter will perhaps before long receive the attention that is appropriate.

Batnae I saw to be a thickly wooded plain containing groves of young cypresses; and among these there was no old or decaying trunk, but all alike were in vigorous leafage. The imperial lodging was by no means sumptuous, for it was made only of clay and logs and had no decorations; but its garden, though inferior to that of Alcinous,[2] was comparable to the garden of Laertes.[3] In it was a quite small grove full of cypresses and along the wall many trees of this sort have been planted in a row one after the other. Then in the middle were beds, and in these, vegetables and trees bearing fruits of all sorts. What did I do there, you ask? I sacrificed in the evening and again at early dawn, as I am in the habit of doing practically every day. And since the omens were favourable, we kept on to Hierapolis[4] where the inhabitants came to meet

for this campaign; and was about twenty miles west of the Euphrates. Julian stayed there three days; Ammianus 23. 2. 6.

με ξένος, ὀφθεὶς μὲν ἄρτι, φιλούμενος δὲ ὑπ' ἐμοῦ πάλαι. τὴν δὲ αἰτίαν αὐτὸς μὲν εὖ οἶδα ὅτι συνήδεις,[1] ἐμοὶ δὲ ἡδὺ καὶ ἄλλως φράσαι· τὸ γὰρ ἀεὶ περὶ αὐτῶν ἀκούειν καὶ λέγειν ἐστί μοι νέκταρ. Ἰαμβλίχου τοῦ θειοτάτου τὸ θρέμμα Σώπατρος ἐγένετο[2] ὁ τούτου κηδεστής· ἐξίσου ἐμοὶ[3] γὰρ τὸ
C μὴ πάντα ἐκείνων τῶν ἀνδρῶν ἀγαπᾶν ἀδικημάτων οὐδενὸς τῶν φαυλοτάτων ἔλαττον[4] εἶναι δοκεῖ. πρόσεστι ταύτης αἰτία μείζων. ὑποδεξάμενος γὰρ πολλάκις τόν τε ἀνεψιὸν τὸν ἐμὸν καὶ τὸν ὁμοπάτριον ἀδελφὸν καὶ προτραπεὶς ὑπ' αὐτῶν, οἷα εἰκός, πολλάκις ἀποστῆναι τῆς εἰς τοὺς θεοὺς εὐσεβείας, ὃ χαλεπόν ἐστιν, οὐκ ἐλήφθη τῇ νόσῳ.

Ταῦτα εἶχον ἀπὸ τῆς Ἱερᾶς πόλεώς σοι γράφειν
D ὑπὲρ τῶν ἐμαυτοῦ. τὰς δὲ στρατιωτικὰς ἢ πολιτικὰς οἰκονομίας αὐτὸν ἐχρῆν οἶμαι παρόντα ἐφορᾶν καὶ ἐπιμελεῖσθαι· μεῖζον γάρ ἐστιν ἢ κατ' ἐπιστολήν, εὖ ἴσθι, καὶ τοσοῦτον ὅσον οὐ ῥᾴδιον οὐδὲ τριπλασίᾳ ταύτης περιλαβεῖν σκοποῦντι τἀκριβές. ἐπὶ κεφαλαίου[5] δέ σοι καὶ ταῦτα φράσω δι' ὀλίγων. πρὸς τοὺς Σαρακηνοὺς ἔπεμψα

[1] συνήδεις Reiske, συνείδεις MSS. εὖ οἶδ' ὅτι συνείρεις Bidez, cf. αἰτίαν αἰτίᾳ συνείρων = make the connection. Hertlein omits εὖ by an oversight. [2] ἐγένετο Bidez adds.

[3] κηδεστής· ἐξίσου ἐμοὶ Bidez; κηδεστὴς ἐξ ὅσου· MSS., Hertlein; Reiske thinks ἐξ ὅσου conceals a proper name or a lacuna.

[4] οὐδενὸς τῶν φαυλοτάτων ἔλαττον Wright (cf. *Oration* 3. 102 B); οὐδενὸς ἧττον τῶν φαυλοτάτων Reiske; οὐδὲν οὕτω φαυλότατον MSS., Hertlein.

[5] Frederich, MSS. ἐπεὶ καὶ φαίην.

---

[1] This elder Sopater was put to death by Constantine.

us. Here I am being entertained by a friend who, though I have only lately met him for the first time has long been dear to me. I know that you yourself are well aware of the reason, but for all that it gives me pleasure to tell you. For it is like nectar to me to hear and to speak of these things continually. Sopater,[1] the pupil of the god-like Iamblichus, was a relative by marriage of this Sopater.[2] Not to love even as myself all that belonged to those men is in my opinion equivalent to the lowest baseness. But there is another more powerful reason than this. Though he often entertained my cousin and my half-brother[3] and was often urged by them, naturally enough, to abandon his piety towards the gods, and though this is hard to withstand, he was not infected with this disease.[4]

Thus much, then, I was able to write to you from Hierapolis about my own affairs. But as regards the military or political arrangements, you ought, I think, to have been present to observe and pay attention to them yourself. For, as you well know, the matter is too long for a letter, in fact so vast that if one considered it in detail it would not be easy to confine it to a letter even three times as long as this. But I will tell you of these matters also, summarily, and in a very few words. I sent an embassy to the Saracens[5] and suggested that

[2] For the younger Sopater, see Introduction.

[3] Constantius and Gallus; cf. *Misopogon* 340A.

[4] For Christianity a disease, cf. *Oration* 7. 229D and *Against the Galilaeans* 327B.

[5] According to Ammianus 23. 3. 8, the Saracens offered themselves to Julian as allies, but they apparently deserted later to the Persians, cf. Zosimus 3. 27. 3; Ammianus 25. 6. 10.

πρέσβεις, ὑπομιμνήσκων αὐτοὺς ἥκειν, εἰ βού-
402 λοιντο. ἓν μὲν δὴ τοιοῦτον· ἕτερον δέ, λίαν ἐγρηγορότας ὡς ἐνεδέχετο τοὺς παραφυλάξοντας ἐξέπεμψα, μή τις ἐνθένδε πρὸς τοὺς πολεμίους ἐξέλθῃ λαθών, ἐσόμενος αὐτοῖς ὡς κεκινήμεθα μηνυτής. ἐκεῖθεν ἐδίκασα δίκην στρατιωτικήν, ὡς ἐμαυτὸν πείθω, πρᾳότατα καὶ δικαιότατα. ἵππους περιττοὺς καὶ ἡμιόνους παρεσκεύασα, τὸ
B στρατόπεδον εἰς ταὐτὸ συναγαγών. ναῦς πληροῦνται ποτάμιαι πυροῦ, μᾶλλον δὲ ἄρτων ξηρῶν καὶ ὄξους. καὶ τούτων ἕκαστον ὅπως ἐπράχθη καὶ τίνες ἐφ᾽ ἑκάστῳ γεγόνασι λόγοι, πόσου μήκους ἐστὶ συγγράφειν ἐννοεῖς. ἐπιστολαῖς δὲ ὅσαις ὑπέγραψα καὶ βίβλοις· ἑπόμενα γὰρ ὡσπερεὶ σκιά[1] μοι καὶ ταῦτα συμπερινοστεῖ πανταχοῦ· τί δεῖ νῦν πράγματα ἔχειν ἀπαριθμούμενον;[1]

59[2]

Μαξίμῳ φιλοσόφῳ[3]

383 Ὁ μὲν μῦθος ποιεῖ τὸν ἀετόν, ἐπειδὰν τὰ γνήσια
C τῶν κυημάτων βασανίζῃ, φέρειν ἄπτιλα πρὸς τὸν

[1] ὥσπερ σκιά Cobet; ὥσπερ αἴσια MSS.; ὡσπερεὶ σκιά Hertlein.

[2] *Letters* 59–73 cannot be dated, even approximately, from their contents.

[3] Hertlein 16; the preceding letter, Hertlein 15, was addressed to Maximus, hence his title τῷ αὐτῷ.

[1] This is Julian's last extant letter. On leaving Hierapolis he marched to Carrhae, which place he left on March 25th. He crossed the Tigris in May, declined the siege of Ctesiphon,

they could come if they wished. That is one affair of the sort I have mentioned. For another, I despatched men as wide-awake as I could obtain that they might guard against anyone's leaving here secretly to go to the enemy and inform them that we are on the move. After that I held a court martial and, I am convinced, showed in my decision the utmost clemency and justice. I have procured excellent horses and mules and have mustered all my forces together. The boats to be used on the river are laden with corn, or rather with baked bread and sour wine. You can understand at what length I should have to write in order to describe how every detail of this business was worked out and what discussions arose over every one of them. As for the number of letters I have signed, and papers,—for these too follow me everywhere like my shadow,—why should I take the trouble to enumerate them now? [1]

59

To Maximus the Philosopher [2]

We are told in the myth that the eagle,[3] when he would test which of his brood are genuine, carries

the Persian capital, burnt his fleet on the Tigris early in June, and was killed in a skirmish on June 26th, somewhere between Ctesiphon and Samarra on the Tigris. His body was carried back and buried at Tarsus in Cilicia, where he had told the people of Antioch he should spend the winter; Ammianus 25. 10. 5.

[2] Cumont and Geffcken reject, without good grounds, Schwarz defends, the authenticity of this sophistic letter, which was probably written from Gaul.

[3] A rhetorical commonplace; cf. *To Iamblichus*, p. 259, note; Lucian, *The Fisherman* 46.

αἰθέρα καὶ ταῖς ἡλίου προσάγειν ἀκτῖσιν, ὥσπερ ὑπὸ μάρτυρι τῷ θεῷ πατέρα τε ἀληθοῦς νεοττοῦ γινόμενον καὶ νόθου γονῆς ἀλλοτριούμενον· ἡμεῖς δέ σοι καθάπερ Ἑρμῇ λογίῳ τοὺς ἡμετέρους λό-
D γους ἐγχειρίζομεν. κἂν μὲν ὑπομείνωσι τὴν ἀκοὴν τὴν σήν, ἐπὶ σοὶ τὸ κρῖναι περὶ αὐτῶν, εἰ καὶ πρὸς τοὺς ἄλλους εἰσὶ πτήσιμοι· εἰ δὲ μή, ῥῖψον εἰκῇ [1] καθάπερ Μουσῶν ἀλλοτρίους, ἢ ποταμῷ κλύσον ὡς νόθους. πάντως οὐδὲ ὁ Ῥῆνος ἀδικεῖ τοὺς Κελτούς, ὃς τὰ μὲν νόθα τῶν βρεφῶν ὑποβρύχια ταῖς δίναις ποιεῖ, καθάπερ ἀκολάστου λέχους τιμωρὸς πρέπων· ὅσα δ' ἂν ἐπιγνῷ καθαροῦ σπέρματος, ὑπεράνω τοῦ ὕδατος αἰωρεῖ, καὶ τῇ μητρὶ τρεμούσῃ πάλιν εἰς χεῖρας δίδωσιν, ὥσπερ ἀδέκα-
384 στόν τινα μαρτυρίαν αὐτῇ καθαρῶν καὶ ἀμέμπτων γάμων τὴν τοῦ παιδὸς σωτηρίαν ἀντιδωρούμενος.

60

Εὐγενίῳ φιλοσόφῳ [2]

386 Δαίδαλον μὲν Ἰκάρῳ [3] φασὶν ἐκ κηροῦ πτερὰ
B συμπλάσαντα τολμῆσαι τὴν φύσιν βιάσασθαι τῇ τέχνῃ. ἐγὼ δὲ ἐκεῖνον μὲν εἰ καὶ τῆς τέχνης

[1] εἰκῇ *Ambrosianus* L 73, ἐκεῖ *Vossianus*, Hertlein; Hercher regards as dittography of εἰ καὶ above.
[2] Hertlein 18.
[3] Ἰκάρῳ Hertlein suggests, Ἰκαρίῳ MSS.

---

[1] The allusion to Julian's writings is too vague to be used to date this letter.
[2] A commonplace of rhetoric; cf. Julian, Vol. 1, *Oration* 2. 81D; Claudian, *In Rufinum* 2. 112, et quos nascentes

them still unfledged into the upper air and exposes them to the rays of the sun, to the end that he may become, by the testimony of the god, the sire of a true nursling and disown any spurious offspring. Even so I submit my speeches[1] to you as though to Hermes the god of eloquence; and, if they can bear the test of being heard by you, it rests with you to decide concerning them whether they are fit to take flight to other men also. But if they are not, then fling them away as though disowned by the Muses, or plunge them in a river as bastards. Certainly the Rhine does not mislead the Celts,[2] for it sinks deep in its eddies their bastard infants, like a fitting avenger of an adulterous bed; but all those that it recognises to be of pure descent it supports on the surface of the water and gives them back to the arms of the trembling mother, thus rewarding her with the safety of her child as incorruptible evidence that her marriage is pure and without reproach

60

To Eugenius[3] the Philosopher

We are told that Daedalus dared to do violence to nature by his art, and moulded wings of wax for Icarus. But for my part, though I applaud him

explorat gurgite Rhenus; Galen 6. 51 Kühn, says that the ordeal was to strengthen their bodies as well as to test their legitimacy; cf. Voltaire, *Essai sur les mœurs* 146.

[3] A philosopher named Eugenius was the father of the sophist and philosopher Themistius, an older contemporary of Julian, but this letter with its familiar tone cannot have been addressed to a man of advanced age. Schwarz, Cumont and Geffcken reject it on the ground of its sophistic mannerisms, but see Introduction.

ἐπαινῶ, τῆς γνώμης οὐκ ἄγαμαι· μόνος γὰρ κηρῷ λυσίμῳ τοῦ παιδὸς ὑπέμεινε τὴν σωτηρίαν πιστεῦσαι. εἰ δέ μοι θέμις ἦν κατὰ τὸν Τήιον ἐκεῖνον μελοποιὸν τὴν τῶν ὀρνίθων ἀλλάξασθαι φύσιν, οὐκ ἂν δήπου πρὸς Ὄλυμπον οὐδὲ ὑπὲρ μέμψεως
C ἐρωτικῆς, ἀλλ' εἰς αὐτοὺς ἂν τῶν ὑμετέρων ὀρῶν τοὺς πρόποδας ἔπτην, ἵνα σὲ τὸ μέλημα τοὐμόν, ὥς φησιν ἡ Σαπφώ, περιπτύξωμαι. ἐπεὶ δέ με ἀνθρωπίνου σώματος δεσμῷ κατακλείσασα ἡ φύσις οὐκ ἐθέλει πρὸς τὸ μετέωρον ἁπλῶσαι, τῶν λόγων οἷς ἔχω σε πτεροῖς μετέρχομαι, καὶ γράφω, καὶ σύνειμι τὸν δυνατὸν τρόπον. πάντως που καὶ Ὅμηρος αὐτοὺς οὐκ ἄλλου του χάριν ἢ τούτου πτερόεντας ὀνομάζει, διότι δύνανται πανταχοῦ
D φοιτᾶν, ὥσπερ οἱ τάχυτατοι τῶν ὀρνίθων ᾗ ἂν ἐθέλωσιν ἄττοντες. γράφε δὲ καὶ αὐτός, ὦ φίλος· ἴση γὰρ δήπου σοι τῶν λόγων, εἰ μὴ καὶ μείζων, ὑπάρχει πτέρωσις, ᾗ τοὺς ἑταίρους μεταβῆναι[1] δύνασαι καὶ πανταχόθεν ὡς παρὼν εὐφραίνειν.

61

Σωπάτρῳ[2]

Ἔστι τις ἡδονῆς ἀφορμὴ πλείων, ὅταν ἐξῇ δι' ἀνδρὸς οἰκείου τοὺς φίλους προσφωνεῖν· οὐ γὰρ

[1] μεταβῆναι *Ambrosianus* L 73; μεταθεῖν Wyttenbach, Hertlein; μεταθεῖναι *Vossianus*.

[2] Hertlein 67. Σωσιπάτρῳ Hertlein, but prefers Σωπάτρῳ Fabricius. See Introduction, under Sopater.

---

[1] Anacreon *frag.* 22, Bergk Ἀναπέτομαι δὴ πρὸς Ὄλυμπον πτερύγεσσι κουφαῖς διὰ τὸν Ἔρωτ'. [2] *Frag.* 126, Bergk.

for his art, I cannot admire his judgement. For he is the only man who ever had the courage to entrust the safety of his son to soluble wax. But if it were granted me, in the words of the famous lyric poet of Teos,[1] to change my nature to a bird's, I should certainly not "fly to Olympus for Love,"—no, not even to lodge a complaint against him—but I should fly to the very foothills of your mountains to embrace "thee, my darling," as Sappho[2] says. But since nature has confined me in the prison of a human body[3] and refuses to lighten and raise me aloft, I approach you with such wings as I possess,[4] the wings of words, and I write to you, and am with you in such fashion as I can. Surely for this reason and this only Homer calls words "winged," that they are able to go to and fro in every direction, darting where they will, like the swiftest of birds. But do you for your part write to me too, my friend! For you possess an equal if not a larger share of the plumage of words, with which you are able to travel to your friends and from wherever you may be, just as though you were present, to cheer them.

61

To Sopater[5]

It is an occasion to rejoice the more when one has the chance to address friends through an intimate friend. For then it is not only by what

[3] A Platonic commonplace; cf. Julian, *Oration* 6. 198B; 7. 206B. [4] Cf. *Letter* 76. 449D, p. 244, note.

[5] This letter is rejected by Schwarz, Cumont and Geffcken; Schwarz on the slender evidence of style classes it with the apocryphal letters to Iamblichus; Cumont also places it in that series, and thinks that this Sopater is the friend of the elder Iamblichus executed by Constantine.

μόνον οἷς γράφεις τὸ τῆς σεαυτοῦ ψυχῆς ἴνδαλμα οτῖς ἐντυγχάνουσι ξυναρμόττῃ. ὃ δὴ καὶ αὐτὸς ποιῶ. τὸν γὰρ τροφέα τῶν ἐμαυτοῦ παίδων Ἀντίοχον ὡς ὑμᾶς ἐκπέμπων, ἀπρόσρητόν σε καταλιπεῖν οὐκ ἠνεσχόμην· ὥστε, εἴ τι τῶν καθ᾽ ἡμᾶς ποθεῖς, ἔχοις ἂν οἰκειότερον παρ᾽ αὐτοῦ γνῶναι. εἰ δέ τι καὶ σοὶ μέλει τῶν σῶν ἐραστῶν, ὡς ἔγωγε ὅτι μέλει πιστεύω, δείξεις ἕως[1] ἂν ἐξῇ γράφειν μηδαμῶς ἐλλείπων.

62

Εὐκλείδῃ φιλοσόφῳ[2]

Πότε γὰρ ἡμῶν ἀπελείφθης, ἵνα καὶ γράφωμεν, ἢ πότε οὐχὶ τοῖς τῆς ψυχῆς ὀφθαλμοῖς ὡς παρόντα σε θεωροῦμεν; οἵ γε οὐ μόνον ἀεί σοι συνεῖναι καὶ συνομιλεῖν δοκοῦμεν, ἀλλὰ καὶ τῶν γε νῦν προσηκόντων ὡς ὑπὸ παρουσίᾳ τῇ σῇ τὰ εἰκότα κηδόμεθα. εἰ δὲ καὶ γράφεσθαί σοι παρ᾽ ἡμῶν ὡς ἀπόντι θέλεις, ὅρα μὲν ὅπως μὴ αὐτὸς τὸ δοκεῖν ἡμῶν ἀπεῖναι μᾶλλον αὐτῷ τῷ γράφειν ἐθέλειν ἐκφήνῃς· πλὴν ἀλλ᾽ εἴ γε σοι φίλον ἐστί, καὶ πρὸς τοῦτο ἑκόντες ὑπακούομεν. πάντως γε, τὸ τοῦ

[1] ἕως Hertlein suggests; MSS., Hertlein ἐν οἷς.
[2] Hertlein 73.

[1] No forger would have referred to children of Julian's body; but the phrase may refer to his writings. Libanius, *Epitaphius*, says of Julian's letters παῖδας τούτους ἀθανάτους καταλέλοιπεν. See also *To Iamblichus*, p. 255.

[2] Libanius often mentions a certain Eucleides, a native of Constantinople, to whom this letter may be addressed; the

you write that you unite the image of your own soul with your readers. And this is what I myself am doing. For when I despatched the custodian of my children,[1] Antiochus, to you, I could not bear to leave you without a word of greeting. So that if you want to have news of me, you can have from him information of a more intimate sort. And if you care at all for your admirers, as I believe you do care, you will prove it by never missing an opportunity while you are able to write.

62

To Eucleides the Philosopher[2]

NAY, when did you ever leave me, so that I need to write, or when do I not behold you with the eyes of the soul as though you were here with me? For not only do I seem to be with you continually and to converse with you, but I pay attention to my duties now just as zealously as when you were here to guide me. But if you do wish me to write to you, just as though you were not here, then take care that you do not yourself create the impression of not being with me all the more by your very wish that I should write. However, if you do really find pleasure in it I am willing to obey you in this also. At any rate, by your request, you will, as the proverb

reference to public affairs may imply that Julian was already Emperor, but it cannot be dated with certainty. Schwarz rejects the letter on stylistic grounds, and Cumont for the same reason attributed it to the sophist Julian of Caesarea, for whom see Introduction under Iamblichus; but, though it is conventional and sophistic, there is nothing in it that the Emperor Julian might not have written.

λόγου, θέοντα τῇ παρακελεύσει τὸν ἵππον εἰς πεδίον ἄξεις. ἄγε οὖν ὅπως ἀντιδώσεις[1] τὰ ἴσα, καὶ πρὸς τὴν ἀντίκλησιν ἐν τῇ τῶν ἀμοιβαίων συνεχείᾳ μὴ κατοκνήσεις.[2] καίτοι ἔγωγε εἰς τὴν ὑπὲρ τοῦ κοινοῦ σοι γινομένην σπουδὴν οὐκ ἐθέλω διοχλεῖν, ἀλλ' ὅσῳ[3] σε φυλάττω[4] τῇ θήρᾳ τῶν καλῶν, οὐ μόνον οὐκ ἀδικεῖν, ἀλλὰ καὶ ξύμπαν ὁμοῦ τὸ Ἑλληνικὸν ὠφελεῖν ἂν δοκοίην, ὥσπερ σκύλακα γενναῖον, ἀόχλητον ἀφιεὶς ἐσχολακέναι σε τοῖς περὶ τοὺς λόγους ἴχνεσιν ὁλοκλήρῳ τῷ λήματι· εἰ δέ σοι τοσοῦτον τάχος περίεστιν, ὡς μήτε τῶν φίλων ἀμελεῖν μήτ' ἐκείνοις ἐνδεῖν, ἴθι χρῆσαι παρ'[5] ἄμφω τῷ δρόμῳ.

63

Ἐκηβολίῳ[6]

Πινδάρῳ μὲν ἀργυρέας εἶναι δοκεῖ τὰς Μούσας,
387 οἱονεὶ τὸ ἔκδηλον αὐτῶν καὶ περιφανὲς τῆς τέχνης ἐς τὸ τῆς ὕλης λαμπρότερον ἀπεικάζοντι· Ὅμηρος δὲ ὁ σοφὸς τόν τε ἄργυρον αἰγλήεντα λέγει καὶ τὸ ὕδωρ ἀργύρεον ὀνομάζει, καθάπερ ἡλίου καθαραῖς ἀκτῖσιν αὐτῷ τῷ τῆς εἰκόνος φαιδρῷ μαρμαρύσσον· Σαπφὼ δ' ἡ καλὴ τὴν σελήνην ἀργυρέαν φησὶ καὶ διὰ τοῦτο τῶν ἄλλων ἀστέρων ἀποκρύπτειν τὴν ὄψιν. οὕτω καὶ θεοῖς τὸν ἄργυρον

[1] ἀντιδώσεις Cobet; ἀντιδίδως Hertlein, MSS.
[2] κατοκνήσεις Cobet; κατοκνήσῃς Hertlein, MSS.
[3] ὅλον X.
[4] Hertlein suggests ἀλλὰ τῷ σε φυλάττειν.
[5] Hertlein suggests πρός.
[6] Hertlein 19.

says, lead a galloping horse into the plain. Come then, see that you return like for like, and in answer to my counter-summons do not grow weary of the unbroken series of letters exchanged between us. And yet I have no wish to hinder the zeal that you display on behalf of the public welfare, nevertheless, in proportion as I keep you free for the pursuit of noble studies, I shall be thought, far from injuring it, to benefit the whole body of Hellenes at once, that is to say, if I leave you like a young and well-bred dog without interference, free to give all your time to tracking down, with a mind wholly free from all else, the art of writing discourses; but if you possess such swiftness that you need neither neglect your friends nor slacken in those other pursuits, come, take both courses and run at full speed!

63

To Hecebolius[1]

Pindar[2] thinks that the Muses are "silvery," and it is as though he likened the clearness and splendour of their art to the substance that shines most brilliantly. And the wise Homer[3] calls silver "shining," and gives to water the epithet "silvery" because it gleams with the very brightness of the reflected image of the sun, as though under its direct rays. And Sappho[4] the fair says that the moon is "silvery," and that because of this it dims the radiance of the other stars. Similarly one might

[1] See Introduction, under Hecebolius.
[2] *Frag.* 272, Bergk.; cf. *Pythian* 9. 65, *Isthmian* 2. 13.
[3] These epithets for silver and water are not in our Homer.
[4] *Frag.* 3, Bergk.; cf. Julian, *Oration* 3. 109c, note, Wright.

μᾶλλον ἢ τὸν χρυσὸν εἰκάσειεν ἄν τις πρέπειν·
B ἀνθρώποις γε μὴν ὅτι πρὸς τὴν χρείαν ἐστὶν ὁ ἄργυρος τοῦ χρυσοῦ τιμιώτερος καὶ σύνεστι μᾶλλον αὐτοῖς, οὐχ ὥσπερ ὁ χρυσὸς ὑπὸ γῆς κρυπτόμενος ἢ φεύγων αὐτῶν τὴν ὄψιν, ἀλλὰ καὶ ὀφθῆναι καλὸς καὶ ἐν διαιτήματι κρείττων, οὐκ ἐμὸς ἴδιος, ἀλλὰ παλαιῶν ἀνδρῶν ὁ λόγος ἐστίν. εἰ
C δέ σοι τοῦ πεμφθέντος ὑπὸ σοῦ χρυσοῦ νομίσματος εἰς τὸ ἴσον τῆς τιμῆς ἕτερον ἀργύρεον ἀντιδίδομεν, μὴ κρίνῃς ἥττω τὴν χάριν, μηδὲ ὥσπερ τῷ Γλαύκῳ πρὸς τὸ ἔλαττον οἰηθῇς εἶναι τὴν ἀντίδοσιν, ἐπεὶ μηδὲ ὁ Διομήδης ἴσως ἀργυρᾶ χρυσῶν ἀντέδωκεν ἄν,[1] ἅτε δὴ πολλῷ τῶν ἑτέρων ὄντα χρησιμώτερα καὶ τὰς αἰχμὰς οἱονεὶ[2] μολίβδου δίκην ἐκτρέπειν εἰδότα. ταῦτά σοι προσπαίζομεν, ἀφ᾿ ὧν αὐτὸς γράφεις τὸ ἐνδόσιμον εἰς σὲ τῆς
D παρρησίας λαμβάνοντες. σὺ δὲ εἰ τῷ ὄντι χρυσοῦ τιμιώτερα ἡμῖν δῶρα ἐθέλεις ἐκπέμπειν, γράφε, καὶ μὴ λῆγε συνεχῶς τοῦτο πράττων· ἐμοὶ γὰρ καὶ γράμμα παρὰ σοῦ μικρὸν ὅτου περ ἂν εἴπῃ τις ἀγαθοῦ κάλλιον εἶναι κρίνεται.

64

Λουκιανῷ σοφιστῇ[3]

404 D Καὶ γράφω καὶ ἀντιτυχεῖν ἀξιῶ τῶν ἴσων. εἰ

[1] ἂν Cobet adds.
[2] οἱονεὶ Hercher deletes, Hertlein brackets, but the construction οἱονεὶ–δίκην occurs in letters not certainly Julian's; cf. 393C, p. 274, 440D, p. 222.
[3] Hertlein 32.

---

[1] For this Julianic commonplace cf. *Oration* 6. 197B, note.
[2] A sophistic commonplace; cf. Vol. 2, *Letter to Themistius* 260A, note. He exchanged bronze armour for golden; *Iliad* 6. 236.

imagine silver to be more appropriate to the gods than gold; but that to man, at any rate, silver is more precious than gold and more familiar to them because it is not, like gold, hidden under the earth and does not avoid their eyes, but is both beautiful to the eye and more serviceable in daily life,—this, I say, is not my own theory[1] but was held by men of old. If, therefore, in return for the gold coin sent by you I give you a piece of silver of equal value, think not that the favour is less and do not imagine that, as with Glaucus,[2] the exchange is to your disadvantage; for perhaps not even Diomede would have exchanged silver armour for golden, seeing that the former is far more serviceable than the latter, and like lead well fitted to turn the points of spears.[3] All this I am saying in jest, and I take the cue[4] for my freedom of speech to you from what you write yourself. But if you really wish to send me gifts more precious than gold, write, and keep on writing regularly. For even a short letter from you I hold to be more precious than any other blessing that one could name.

64

To Lucian the Sophist[5]

Not only do I write to you but I demand to receive payment in kind. And if I treat you ill by

[3] *Iliad* 11. 237 ἀργύρῳ ἀντομένη, μόλιβος ὥς, ἐτράπετ' αἰχμή.

[4] Literally "keynote"; cf. *To Iamblichus* 421A, p. 238.

[5] A merely sophistic letter of compliment such as this is a conventional "type" of the sort recommended in the contemporary handbooks on epistolary style. Gesner thinks it was addressed to the Lucian who wrote the dialogue *Philopatris*, preserved with the works of his illustrious namesake, but there is no evidence of this.

δὲ ἀδικῶ συνεχῶς ἐπιστέλλων, ἀνταδικηθῆναι δέομαι τὰ ὅμοια παθών.

65

Ἐλπιδίῳ φιλοσόφῳ[1]

442 Ἔστι καὶ μικροῦ γράμματος ἡδονὴ μείζων, ὅταν
D ἡ τοῦ γράφοντος εὔνοια μὴ τῇ τῆς ἐπιστολῆς σμι-
κρότητι μᾶλλον ἢ τῷ τῆς ψυχῆς μεγέθει μετρῆται·
εἰ δὲ δὴ καὶ νῦν βραχέα τὰ τῆς προσρήσεως ὑφ'
ἡμῶν γεγένηται, μηδ' οὕτω[2] τὸν ἐπ' αὐτοῖς πόθον
τεκμηριώσῃ, ἀλλ' εἰδώς, ἐφ' ὅσον ὁ παρ' ἡμῶν
ἔρως ἐπὶ σοὶ τέταται, τῇ μὲν τοῦ γράμματος βρα-
χύτητι συγγνώμην νέμε, τοῖς ἴσοις δὲ ἡμᾶς ἀμεί-
βεσθαι μὴ κατόκνει. πᾶν γὰρ ὅ τι ἂν διδῷς, κἂν
443 μικρὸν ᾖ, παντὸς ἀγαθοῦ γνώρισμα παρ' ἡμῖν
σώζει.

66

Γεωργίῳ Καθολικῷ[3]

440 Ἡ μὲν ἠχὼ θεὸς ἔστω κατὰ σὲ καὶ λάλος, εἰ δὲ
B βούλει, καὶ Πανὶ σύζυγος· οὐ γὰρ διοίσομαι. κἂν
γὰρ ἐθέλῃ με διδάσκειν ἡ φύσις ὅτι ἐστὶν ἠχὼ
φωνῆς ἐς ἀέρος πλῆξιν ἀντίτυπος ἠχὴ πρὸς τοὔμ-

[1] Hertlein 57.
[2] μὴ τούτῳ Hertlein suggests.
[3] Hertlein 54.

---

[1] We know from Libanius, *Letter* 758 Foerster, *To Julian*, that towards the end of 362 Elpidius was at Antioch and in Julian's confidence. This letter is purely formal and may have been written then, or earlier. There are several letters extant from Libanius to Elpidius. Cumont ascribed this letter to Julian of Caesarea.

writing continually, then I beg you to illtreat me in return and make me suffer in the same way.

65

To Elpidius, a Philosopher[1]

Even a short letter gives more pleasure when the writer's affection can be measured by the greatness of his soul rather than by the meagre proportions of what he writes. So that if I now address you briefly, do not even so conclude that the accompanying affection is equally slight, but since you know the full extent of my love for you, forgive the brevity of my letter and do not hesitate to answer me in one equally short. For whatever you send me, however trifling, keeps alive in my mind a remembrance of all that is good.

66

To George, a Revenue Official[2]

Well, let us grant that Echo is a goddess, as you say she is, and a chatterbox, and, if you like, the wife of Pan[3] also; for I shall not object. And even though nature would fain inform me that Echo is only the sound of the voice answering back when the air is struck, and bent back upon that which is

[2] Otherwise unknown. The title *Catholicus* (cf. our "General") was used of officials in charge of the collection of tribute, especially in Africa; it is equivalent to *procurator fisci*. George was probably a sophist. This and the following letter are rejected by Schwarz, Cumont and Geffcken, because of their sophistic mannerisms.

[3] Moschus, *Idyl* 6.

πάλιν τῆς ἀκοῆς ἀντανακλωμένη, ὅμως, παλαιῶν ἀνδρῶν ἔτι καὶ νέων οὐκ ἔλαττον ἢ τῷ σῷ πειθό-
C μενος λόγῳ, θεὸν εἶναι τὴν ἠχὼ δυσωποῦμαι. τί γοῦν ἂν εἴη τοῦτο πρὸς ἡμᾶς, εἰ πολλῷ τῷ μέτρῳ τοῖς πρὸς σὲ φιλικοῖς τὴν ἠχὼ νικῶμεν; ἡ μὲν γὰρ οὐ πρὸς ἅπαντα, ὅ τι ἂν ἀκούσῃ, μᾶλλον ἢ[1] πρὸς τὰ ἔσχατα τῆς φωνῆς ἀντιφθέγγεται, καθάπερ ἐρωμένη φειδωλὸς ἄκροις ἀντιφιλοῦσα τὸν ἐραστὴν τοῖς χείλεσιν· ἡμεῖς δὲ καὶ τῶν πρὸς σὲ κατάρχομεν ἡδέως, καὶ αὖθις εἰς τὴν παρὰ σοῦ
D πρόκλησιν οἱονεὶ[2] σφαίρας δίκην τὸ ἴσον ἀντιπέμπομεν. ὥστε οὐκ ἂν φθάνοις αὐτὸς ἔνοχος ὢν οἷς γράφεις, καὶ σαυτόν, ἀφ' ὧν πλέον λαμβάνων ἐλάχιστον ἀντιδίδως, οὐχ ἡμᾶς, ἐν οἷς ἐπ' ἄμφω πλεονεκτεῖν σπεύδομεν, ἐς τὸ ὅμοιον τῆς εἰκόνος ἐγκρίνων· πλὴν ἄν τε ἴσῳ τῷ μέτρῳ διδῷς ᾧπερ ἂν λάβῃς, ἄν τε μή, ἡμῖν ὅ τι ἂν ἐξῇ παρὰ σοῦ
441 λαβεῖν ἡδὺ καὶ πρὸς τὸ ὅλον ἀρκεῖν πιστεύεται.

67

Γεωργίῳ Καθολικῷ[3]

Ἦλθες, Τηλέμαχε, φησὶ τὸ ἔπος· ἐγὼ δέ σε καὶ εἶδον ἤδη τοῖς γράμμασι, καὶ τῆς ἱερᾶς σοῦ ψυχῆς

[1] δὲ Hertlein suggests, but cf. *Letter* 71, p. 234.
[2] See note to *Letter* 63, 387c.
[3] Hertlein 8. Following *Vossianus* he omits καθολικῷ, which is preserved in *Ambrosianus* L 73.

---

[1] For this conventional phrase, often used by Julian, cf. *To Hecebolius*, p. 219, and *To Sarapion*, pp. 271, 277.

opposite the ear that hears it, nevertheless, since I put my faith in the account given by men both ancient and modern,[1] and in your own account no less, I am abashed into admitting that Echo is a goddess.[2] What, in any case, would that matter to me, if only, in my expressions of friendship towards you, I excel Echo in a considerable degree? For she does not reply to all the sounds that she hears, but rather to the last syllables uttered by the voice, like a grudging sweetheart who returns her lover's kisses with the merest touch of her lips. I, on the other hand, in my correspondence with you, lead off sweetly, and then again, in reply to your challenge, I return you like for like as though I threw back a ball. Therefore you cannot be too quick in recognising that your letters put you in default, and that it is yourself, since you receive more and give back very little, whom you consign to the similitude of the figure, and not me, since I am eager to score off you in both ways.[3] However, whether you give in just the same degree as you receive, or not, whatever I am permitted to receive from you is a boon, and is credited as sufficient to balance the whole.[4]

67

To George, a Revenue Official[5]

"Thou hast come, Telemachus!"[6] as the verse says, but in your letters I have already seen you and

[2] George had evidently used the figure of Echo, and accused Julian of imitating her.

[3] *i.e.* both in sending and receiving letters.

[4] Perhaps the last two sentences are a playful allusion to George's profession as a financier.

[5] Geffcken and Cumont reject this letter.

[6] *Odyssey* 16. 23.

377 τὴν εἰκόνα καθάπερ ὀλίγῃ σφραγῖδι μεγάλου χα-
ρακτῆρος τύπον ἀνεμαξάμην. ἔστι γὰρ ἐν ὀλίγῳ
πολλὰ δειχθῆναι· ἐπεὶ καὶ Φειδίας ὁ σοφὸς οὐκ
ἐκ τῆς Ὀλυμπίασι μόνον ἢ Ἀθήνησιν εἰκόνος
ἐγνωρίζετο, ἀλλ' ᾔδει καὶ μικρῷ γλύμματι μεγά-
λης τέχνης ἔργον ἐγκλεῖσαι, οἷον δὴ τὸν τέττιγά
B φασιν αὐτοῦ καὶ τὴν μέλιτταν, εἰ δὲ βούλει, καὶ
τὴν μυῖαν εἶναι· ὧν ἕκαστον, εἰ καὶ τῇ φύσει κε-
χάλκωται, τῇ τέχνῃ γ' ἐψύχωται. ἀλλ' ἐν ἐκεί-
νοις μὲν ἴσως αὐτῷ καὶ ἡ σμικρότης τῶν ζῴων εἰς
τὴν κατὰ λόγον τέχνην τὸ εἰκὸς ἐχαρίζετο· σὺ δ'
ἀλλὰ τὸν ἀφ' ἵππου θηρῶντα Ἀλέξανδρον, εἰ
δοκεῖ, σκόπει, οὗ τὸ μέτρον ἐστὶ πᾶν ὄνυχος οὐ
μεῖζον. οὕτω δ' ἐφ' ἑκάστου τὸ θαῦμα τῆς τέχνης
κέχυται, ὥστε ὁ μὲν Ἀλέξανδρος ἤδη τὸ θηρίον
C βάλλει καὶ τὸν θεατὴν φοβεῖ, δι' ὅλου δυσωπῶν
τοῦ σχήματος, ὁ δὲ ἵππος, ἐν ἄκρᾳ τῶν ποδῶν τῇ
βάσει τὴν στάσιν φεύγων, ἐν τῇ τῆς ἐνεργείας
κλοπῇ τῇ τέχνῃ κινεῖται· ὃ δὴ καὶ αὐτὸς ἡμῖν, ὦ
γενναῖε, ποιεῖς. ὥσπερ γὰρ ἐν Ἑρμοῦ λογίου
σταδίοις δι' ὅλου πολλάκις τοῦ δρόμου στεφανω-
θεὶς ἤδη, δι' ὧν ἐν ὀλίγοις γράφεις τῆς ἀρετῆς τὸ
ἄκρον ἐμφαίνεις, καὶ τῷ ὄντι τὸν Ὀδυσσέα τὸν
D Ὁμήρου ζηλοῖς, ὃς καὶ μόνον εἰπὼν ὅστις ἦν ἤρκει

---

[1] The ascription to Pheidias the sculptor of works in the 'microtechnique' described here, is sometimes due to the confusion, in the Roman period, of the fifth century Pheidias with a gem-cutter of the same name who lived in the third century B.C. In the *Jahrbuch d.k.d. Arch. Instituts*, 1889, p. 210, Furtwängler, who does not quote this letter, reproduces a gem from the British Museum collection signed by this later Pheidias; it is an Alexander on foot. The anachronism here makes the letter suspect.

the image of your noble soul, and have received the impression thereof as of an imposing device on a small seal. For it is possible for much to be revealed in little. Nay even Pheidias the wise artist not only became famous for his statue at Olympia or at Athens, but he knew also how to confine a work of great art within the limits of a small piece of sculpture; for instance, they say that his grasshopper and bee, and, if you please, his fly also, were of this sort; for every one of these, though naturally composed of bronze, through his artistic skill became a living thing. In those works, however, the very smallness of the living models perhaps contributed the appearance of reality to his skilful art; and do you, please, look at his Alexander[1] hunting on horseback, for its whole measurement is no larger than a fingernail.[2] Yet the marvellous skill of the workmanship is so lavished on every detail that Alexander at one and the same time strikes his quarry and intimidates the spectator, scaring him by his whole bearing, while the horse, reared on the very tips of his hoofs, is about to take a step and leave the pedestal, and by creating the illusion of vigorous action is endowed with movement by the artist's skill. This is exactly the effect that you have on me, my excellent friend. For after having been crowned often, already, as victor over the whole course, so to speak, in the lists of Hermes, the God of Eloquence, you now display the highest pitch of excellence in a few written words. And in very truth you imitate Homer's Odysseus,[3] who, by merely saying who he

[2] See Vol. 1, *Oration* 3, 112A for a reference to this kind of carving.

[3] *Odyssey* 9. 19.

τοὺς Φαίακας ἐκπλῆξαι. εἰ δέ τι καὶ παρ' ἡμῶν τοῦ κατὰ σὲ φιλικοῦ καπνοῦ δέει,[1] φθόνος οὐδείς. πάντως που καὶ παρὰ τῶν ἡττόνων εἶναί τι χρηστὸν ὁ μῦς τὸν λέοντα ἐν τῷ μύθῳ σώσας ἀρκούντως δείκνυσιν.

68

Δοσιθέῳ[2]

Μικροῦ μοι ἐπῆλθε δακρῦσαι· καίτοι γε ἐχρῆν
405 εὐφημεῖν τοὔνομα τὸ σὸν φθεγξάμενον· ἀνεμνήσθην γὰρ τοῦ γενναίου καὶ πάντα θαυμασίου πατρὸς ἡμῶν,[3] ὃν εἰ μὲν ζηλώσεις, αὐτός τε εὐδαίμων ἔσῃ, καὶ τῷ βίῳ δώσεις, ὥσπερ ἐκεῖνος, ἐφ' ὅτῳ φιλοτιμήσεται· ῥᾳθυμήσας δὲ λυπήσεις ἐμέ, σαυτῷ δὲ ὅτε μηδὲν ὄφελος μέμψῃ.

69

Ἱμερίῳ[4]

412 Οὐκ ἀδακρυτί σου τὴν ἐπιστολὴν ἀνέγνων, ἣν ἐπὶ τῷ τῆς συνοικούσης θανάτῳ πεποίησαι, τοῦ πάθους τὴν ὑπερβολὴν ἀγγείλας. πρὸς γὰρ τῷ

[1] δέῃ, *Parisinus* 2964, Heyler, cf. *Letter* 6, 403B.
[2] Hertlein 33. [3] ὑμῶν Reiske.
[4] Hertlein 37. *Varsaviensis*, Y, Ἱμερίῳ Cumont accepts; *Baroccianus* Ἱμερίῳ ἐπάρχῳ Αἰγύπτου ἐπὶ τῇ γυναικὶ according to Hertlein, Ἡμερίῳ κ.τ.λ. Cumont. *Parisinus*, Hertlein Ἀμερίῳ.

---

[1] George had perhaps in his letter referred to the longing of Odysseus to see even the smoke of his native land, and had compared his friend's letters to that smoke.

was, was able to dazzle the Phaeacians. But if even from me you require some of what you call "friendly smoke,"[1] I shall not begrudge it. Surely the mouse who saved the lion in the fable[2] is proof enough that something useful may come even from one's inferiors.

68

To Dositheus[3]

I AM almost in tears—and yet the very utterance of your name ought to have been an auspicious sound,—for I recall to mind our noble and wholly admirable father.[4] If you make it your aim to imitate him, not only will you yourself be happy but also you will give to human life, as he did, an example of which it will be proud. But if you are indolent you will grieve me, and you will blame yourself when blaming will not avail.

69

To Himerius[5]

I COULD not read without tears the letter which you wrote after your wife's death, in which you told me of your surpassing grief. For not only does the

[2] Babrius, *Fable* 107; Aesop, *Fable* 256.

[3] Otherwise unknown.

[4] If the MS. reading is retained, Julian must be referring to someone who had taught them both. This was a regular usage and the teacher of one's own teacher could be referred to as "grandfather."

[5] Of Hertlein's "Amerius" we know nothing. See Introduction, under Himerius.

*καὶ καθ' ἑαυτὸ λύπης τὸ ξυμβὰν ἄξιον εἶναι,
γυναῖκα νέαν καὶ σώφρονα καὶ θυμήρη τῷ γή-
μαντι, πρὸς δὲ καὶ παίδων ἱερῶν*[1] *μητέρα, πρὸ
B ὥρας ἀναρπασθῆναι καθάπερ δᾷδα λαμπρῶς ἡμ-
μένην, εἶτα ἐν ὀλίγῳ καταβαλοῦσαν τὴν φλόγα,
ἔτι καὶ τὸ τὰ τοῦ πάθους εἰς σὲ τείνειν οὐχ ἧττόν
μοι δοκεῖ λυπηρὸν εἶναι. ἥκιστα γὰρ δὴ πάντων
ἄξιος ἦν ὁ καλὸς ἡμῖν Ἱμέριος*[2] *ἀλγεινοῦ τινὸς εἰς
πεῖραν ἐλθεῖν, ἀνὴρ καὶ λόγῳ χρηστὸς καὶ ἡμῖν
εἰς τὰ μάλιστα τῶν φίλων ὁ ποθεινότατος. οὐ
C μὴν ἀλλ' εἰ μὲν ἕτερος ἦν, ᾧ γράφειν περὶ τούτων
ἐχρῆν, πάντως ἂν ἔδει μοι πλειόνων εἰς τοῦτο
λόγων, τό τε συμβὰν ὡς ἀνθρώπινον καὶ τὸ φέρειν
ὡς ἀναγκαῖον καὶ τὸ μηδὲν ἐκ τοῦ μᾶλλον ἀλγεῖν
ἔχειν πλέον, καὶ πάντα ὅσα ἐδόκει πρὸς τὴν τοῦ
πάθους παραμυθίαν ἁρμόττειν ὡς ἀγνοοῦντα διδά-
σκοντι. ἐπεὶ δὲ αἰσχρὸν ἡγοῦμαι πρὸς ἄνδρα καὶ
τοὺς ἄλλους νουθετεῖν εἰδότα ποιεῖσθαι λόγους,
οἷς χρὴ τοὺς μὴ εἰδότας σωφρονεῖν παιδεύειν, φέρε
D σοι τὰ ἄλλα παρεὶς ἀνδρὸς εἴτ' εἴπω σοφοῦ μῦθον
εἴτε δὴ λόγον ἀληθῆ, σοὶ μὲν ἴσως οὐ ξένον, τοῖς
πλείοσι δέ, ὡς εἰκός, ἄγνωστον, ᾧ δὴ καὶ μόνῳ χρη-
σάμενος ὥσπερ φαρμάκῳ νηπενθεῖ λύσιν ἂν εὕροις
τοῦ πάθους οὐκ ἐλάττω τῆς κύλικος, ἣν ἡ Λάκαινα
τῷ Τηλεμάχῳ πρὸς τὸ ἴσον τῆς χρείας ὀρέξαι πι-*

[1] *νεαρῶν* Thomas suggests, but *ἱερὸς* is Julianic in the sense of "precious." [2] *Ἀμέριος*, *Parisinus* 2755.

event in itself call for sorrow, when a young and virtuous wife, the joy of her husband's heart,[1] and moreover the mother of precious children, is prematurely snatched away like a torch that has been kindled and shines brightly, and in a little while its flame dies down, but over and above this, the fact that it is you to whom this sorrow has come seems to me to make it still more grievous. For least of all men did our good Himerius deserve to experience any affliction, excellent orator that he is, and of all my friends the best beloved. Moreover, if it were any other man to whom I had to write about this, I should certainly have had to use more words in dealing with it; for instance, I should have said that such an event is the common lot, that we must needs submit, that nothing is gained by excessive grief, and I should have uttered all the other commonplaces considered appropriate for the alleviation of suffering, that is if I were exhorting one who did not know them. But since I think it unbecoming to offer to a man who well knows how to instruct others the sort of argument by which one must school those who are too ignorant for self-control, see now, I will forbear all such phrases; but I will relate to you a fable, or it may be a true story, of a certain wise man, which perhaps is not new to you, though it is probably unfamiliar to most people; and if you will use this and this alone, as though it were a drug to relieve pain, you will find release from your sorrow, as surely as from that cup which the Spartan woman[2] is believed to have offered to Telemachus when his need was as

[1] An echo of *Iliad* 9. 336 ἄλοχον θυμαρέα.

[2] Helen, *Odyssey* 4. 220, a rhetorical commonplace; cf. Vol. 2, *Oration* 8. 240B, p. 167, note.

413 στεύεται. φασὶ γὰρ Δημόκριτον τὸν Ἀβδηρίτην,
ἐπειδὴ Δαρείῳ γυναικὸς καλῆς ἀλγοῦντι θάνατον
οὐκ εἶχεν ὅ τι ἂν εἰπὼν εἰς παραμυθίαν ἀρκέσειεν,
ὑποσχέσθαι οἱ τὴν ἀπελθοῦσαν εἰς φῶς ἀνάξειν,
ἢν ἐθελήσῃ τῶν εἰς τὴν χρείαν ἡκόντων ὑποστῆναι
τὴν χορηγίαν. κελεύσαντος δʼ ἐκείνου μηδενὸς
φείσασθαι, ὅ τι δʼ ἂν ἐξῇ λαβόντα τὴν ὑπόσχεσιν
B ἐμπεδῶσαι, μικρὸν ἐπισχόντα χρόνον εἰπεῖν, ὅτι
τὰ μὲν ἄλλα αὐτῷ πρὸς τὴν τοῦ ἔργου πρᾶξιν
συμπορισθείη, μόνου δὲ ἑνὸς προσδέοιτο, ὃ δὴ
αὐτὸν μὲν οὐκ ἔχειν ὅπως ἂν λάβοι, Δαρεῖον δὲ
ὡς βασιλέα ὅλης τῆς Ἀσίας οὐ χαλεπῶς ἂν ἴσως
εὑρεῖν. ἐρομένου δʼ ἐκείνου, τί ἂν εἴη τοσοῦτον ὃ
μόνῳ βασιλεῖ γνωσθῆναι συγχωρεῖται, ὑπολα-
βόντα φασὶ τὸν Δημόκριτον εἰπεῖν, εἰ τριῶν ἀπεν-
θήτων ὀνόματα τῷ τάφῳ τῆς γυναικὸς ἐπιγρά-
C ψειεν, εὐθὺς αὐτὴν ἀναβιώσεσθαι τῷ τῆς τελετῆς
νόμῳ δυσωπουμένην. ἀπορήσαντος δὲ τοῦ Δαρείου
καὶ μηδένα ἄρα δυνηθέντος εὑρεῖν ὅτῳ μὴ καὶ
παθεῖν λυπηρόν τι συνηνέχθη, γελάσαντα συνή-
θως τὸν Δημόκριτον εἰπεῖν "Τί οὖν, ὦ πάντων
ἀτοπώτατε, θρηνεῖς ἀνέδην ὡς μόνος ἀλγεινῷ το-
σούτῳ συμπλακείς, ὁ μηδὲ ἕνα τῶν πώποτε γεγο-
D νότων ἄμοιρον οἰκείου πάθους ἔχων εὑρεῖν." ἀλλὰ
ταῦτα μὲν ἀκούειν ἔδει Δαρεῖον, ἄνδρα βάρβαρον

[1] The Atomistic philosopher, cf. Diels, *Die Fragmente der Vorsokratiker* 2. 16. 41. This is a traditional anecdote, told of Herodes Atticus and Demonax by Lucian, *Demonax* 25, and only here of Darius and Democritus.

great as your own. Now the story is that when Darius was in great grief for the death of a beautiful wife, Democritus[1] of Abdera could not by any argument succeed in consoling him; and so he promised him that he would bring back the departed to life, if Darius were willing to undertake to supply him with everything necessary for the purpose. Darius bade him spare no expense but take whatever he needed and make good his promise. After waiting a little, Democritus said that he was provided with everything else for carrying out his task, but still needed one thing only, which he himself did not know how to obtain; Darius, however, as King of all Asia, would perhaps find it without difficulty. And when the King asked him what it might be, this great thing which it was possible for only a king to know of, they say that Democritus in reply declared that if he would inscribe on his wife's tomb the names of three persons who had never mourned for anyone, she would straightway come to life again, since she could not disobey the authority of this mystic rite Then Darius was in a dilemma, and could not find any man who had not had to bear some great sorrow, whereupon Democritus burst out laughing,[2] as was his wont, and said: "Why, then, O most absurd of men, do you mourn without ceasing, as though you were the only man who had ever been involved in so great a grief, you who cannot discover a single person of all who have ever lived who was without his share of personal sorrow?" But though it was necessary to say these things to Darius, a barbarian and a man of no education, the slave

[2] Democritus was known as "the laughing Philosopher"; cf. *Oration* 6. 186c, Vol. 2, p. 20, Wright.

καὶ ἀπαίδευτον, ἔκδοτον ἡδονῇ καὶ πάθει· σὲ δέ, ἄνδρα Ἕλληνα καὶ παιδείαν ἀληθῆ πρεσβεύοντα, καὶ παρὰ σαυτοῦ τὸ ἄκος ἐχρῆν ἔχειν, ἐπεὶ καὶ ἄλλως αἰσχύνῃ τῷ λογισμῷ γένοιτ' ἄν, εἰ μὴ ταὐτὸν σθένοι τῷ χρόνῳ.

70

Διογένει[1]

Διογένης ὁ σὸς υἱὸς ὀφθείς μοι μετὰ τὴν ἔξοδον τὴν σὴν καὶ φήσας ὠργίσθαι σέ τι πρὸς αὐτόν, οἷον ἂν πατὴρ πρὸς παῖδα χαλεπήνειεν, ἐδεήθη μέσον με τῶν πρὸς αὐτὸν καταλλαγῶν παρὰ σοὶ γενέσθαι. εἰ μὲν οὖν μέτρια καὶ οἷα δύνασθαι φέρειν ἥμαρτεν, εἶξον τῇ φύσει καὶ τὸ πατὴρ εἶναι γνοὺς ἐπάνελθε πρὸς τὸν παῖδα τῇ γνώμῃ· εἰ δέ τι μεῖζον ἔπταικεν ἢ οἷον πρὸς συγγνώμην ἐλθεῖν, αὐτὸς ἂν εἴης δικαιότερος κριτής, εἴτε δεῖ καὶ τοῦτο γενναίως ἐνεγκόντα νικῆσαι τοῦ παιδὸς τὴν βουλὴν γνώμῃ κρείττονι, εἴτε καὶ πλείονος χρόνου σωφρονισμῷ τὴν ἐπὶ τῷ πταισθέντι βάσανον πιστεῦσαι.

71

Γρηγορίῳ ἡγεμόνι[2]

402 Ἐμοὶ καὶ γράμμα παρὰ σοῦ μικρὸν ἀρκεῖ μεγά-
C λης ἡδονῆς πρόφασιν μνηστεῦσαι. καὶ τοίνυν,

[1] Hertlein 70. [2] Hertlein 28.

[1] Diogenes is otherwise unknown. Schwarz places this letter between January and June 362, when Julian was at Constantinople. The tone seems to imply that he was already

both of pleasure and of grief, you, on the other hand, are a Greek, and honour true learning, and you must find your remedy from within; for surely it would be a disgrace to the reasoning faculty if it had not the same potency as time.

70

To Diogenes[1]

Your son Diogenes, whom I saw after you went away, told me that you had been much irritated with him for some reason that would naturally make a father feel vexed with his child, and he implored me to act as mediator in a reconciliation between him and yourself. Now, if he has committed some error of a mild and not intolerable kind, do you yield to nature, recognise that you are a father, and again turn your thoughts to your child. But if his offence is too serious to admit of immediate forgiveness, it is right for you yourself rather than for me to decide whether you ought to bear even that with a generous spirit and overcome your son's purpose by wiser thoughts, or to entrust the offender's probation to a longer period of discipline.

71

To Commander Gregory[2]

Even a short letter from you is enough to provide me with grounds for feeling greatly pleased. Ac-

Emperor, but the note is purely conventional, a "type" of the letter of intervention.

[2] A Gregorius Dux was pretorian prefect in 336, according to *Codex Theodosianus* 3. 1. 2, but this purely formal letter of the type that survived in epistolary handbooks is probably addressed to a younger man.

οἷς ἔγραψας ἄγαν ἡσθείς, ἀντιδίδωμι καὶ αὐτὸς τὴν ἴσην, οὐ τῷ τῶν ἐπιστολῶν μήκει μᾶλλον ἢ τῷ τῆς εὐνοίας μεγέθει τὰς τῶν ἑταίρων φιλίας ἐκτίνεσθαι δεῖν κρίνων.

72

429 B Πλουτάρχῳ[1]

Πάντων μὲν ἕνεκά μοι τὸ σῶμα διάκειται μετρίως, οὐ μὴν ἀλλὰ καὶ τὰ τῆς γνώμης ἔχει καλῶς. οἶμαι δ' ἐγὼ τούτου προοίμιον εἶναι μηδὲν κρεῖττον ἐπιστολῇ φίλῳ παρὰ φίλου πεμπομένῃ. τίνος οὖν ἐστι τὸ προοίμιον; αἰτήσεως, οἶμαι. τίς δὲ ἡ αἴτησις; ἐπιστολῶν ἀμοιβαίων, ἃς εἴη γε καὶ κατὰ διάνοιαν ὁμολογῆσαι ταῖς ἐμαῖς, αἴσια παρὰ σοῦ ταὐτὰ πρὸς ἡμᾶς ἐξαγγελλούσας.

73

Μαξιμίνῳ[2]

Ναῦς ἐπέταξα γενέσθαι περὶ τὰς Κεγχρέας· τὸ μὲν οὖν ὅσας ὁ τῶν Ἑλλήνων ἡγούμενος φράσει, τὸ δὲ ὅπως χρὴ ποιεῖσθαι τὴν ἐπιμέλειαν ἄκουε παρ' ἡμῶν· ἀδωροδοκήτως καὶ ταχέως. ὅπως δὲ μὴ μεταμελήσει σοι τῆς τοιαύτης ὑπουργίας, αὐτὸς σὺν θεοῖς ἐπιμελήσομαι.

[1] Hertlein 48, Ζήνωνι, *To Zeno*; I follow Cumont in rejecting this title, which does not appear in any MS and was introduced by Heyler, who derived it from the Paris edition 1605. Πλουτάρχῳ is the title in the Papadopoulos (Chalce) MSS. [2] Papadopoulos 5*.

---

[1] This may be the obscure Athenian philosopher, a contemporary of Julian; cf. Marinus, *Proclus* 12.

cordingly, since I was exceedingly pleased with what you wrote to me, I in turn send you a letter of the same length, because in my judgement the friendly greetings of comrades ought to be rewarded not by length of letter so much as by magnitude of goodwill.

72

To Plutarch[1]

In all respects my bodily health is fairly good, and indeed my state of mind is no less satisfactory. I fancy there can be no better prelude than this to a letter sent from one friend to another. And to what is this the prelude? To a request, of course! And what is the request? It is for letters in return, and in their sentiments may they harmonise with my own letters and bring me similar news from you, and equally auspicious.

73

To Maximinus[2]

I have given orders that there shall be ships at Cenchreae.[3] The number of these you will learn from the governor of the Hellenes,[4] but as to how you are to discharge your commission you may now hear from me. It must be without bribery and without delay. I will myself, with the help of the gods, see that you do not repent of having done your duty as I have indicated.

[2] Nothing is known of Maximinus or the circumstances; if the letter is genuine, as is probable, it may refer to Julian's preparations for his march against Constantius in 361.
[3] A coast town S.W. of the Isthmus of Corinth.
[4] *i.e.* the proconsul of Achaia who resided at Corinth.

74

Ἰαμβλίχῳ [1]

420 Ἐχρῆν μὲν ἡμᾶς τῷ γράμματι πειθομένους τῷ
B Δελφικῷ γιγνώσκειν ἑαυτοὺς καὶ μὴ τολμᾶν ἀνδρὸς
ἀκοῆς τοσούτου καταθαρρεῖν, ᾧ καὶ ὀφθέντι μόνον
ἀντιβλέψαι δυσχερές, ἤ που τὴν πάνσοφον ἁρμο-
νίαν κινοῦντι πρὸς τὸ ἴσον ἐλθεῖν, ἐπεὶ κἂν Πανὶ
C μέλος λιγυρὸν ἠχοῦντι πᾶς ὅστις ἐκσταίη, κἂν
Ἀρισταῖος ᾖ, καὶ Ἀπόλλωνι πρὸς κιθάραν ψάλ-
λοντι πᾶς ὅστις ἠρεμοίη, κἂν τὴν Ὀρφέως μου-
σικὴν εἰδῇ. τὸ γὰρ ἧττον τῷ κρείττονι, καθ᾽ ὅσον
ἧττόν ἐστιν, εἴκοι ἂν δικαίως, εἰ μέλλοι τό τε
οἰκεῖον καὶ τὸ μὴ τί ἐστι γιγνώσκειν. ὅστις δ᾽
ἐνθέῳ μουσικῇ θνητὸν ἀνθαρμόσαι μέλος ἤλπισεν,
οὐκ ἔμαθέ που τὸ Μαρσύου τοῦ Φρυγὸς πάθος,
οὐδὲ τὸν ὁμώνυμον ἐκείνῳ ποταμόν, ὃς μανέντος
D αὐλητοῦ τιμωρίαν μαρτυρεῖ, ἀλλ᾽ οὐδὲ τὴν Θαμύ-
ριδος τοῦ Θρᾳκὸς τελευτὴν ἤκουσεν, ὃς ταῖς
Μούσαις οὐκ εὐτυχῶς ἀντεφθέγξατο. τί γὰρ δεῖ
τὰς Σειρῆνας λέγειν, ὧν ἔτι τὸ πτερὸν ἐπὶ τοῦ

[1] Hertlein 41, τῷ αὐτῷ, as his *Letter* 40 is to Iamblichus.

---

[1] *Letters* 74–83, with the possible exception of 81, are certainly not by Julian.

THE APOCRYPHAL LETTERS[1]

74

To Iamblichus

I OUGHT indeed to have obeyed the Delphic inscription "Know Thyself," and not have ventured to affront the ears of so great a man as yourself; for only to look you in the face, when one meets your eye, is no easy matter, and it is much less easy to try to rival you when you wake the harmony of your unfailing wisdom, seeing that if Pan roused the echoes with his shrill song everyone would yield him place, yes, even though it were Aristaeus[2] himself, and when Apollo played the lyre everyone would keep silence, even though he knew the music of Orpheus. For it is right that the inferior, in so far as it is inferior, should yield to the superior, that is if it is to know what is appropriate to itself and what is not. But he who has conceived the hope of matching his mortal song with inspired music has surely never heard of the sad fate of Marsyas the Phrygian, or of the river which is named after him and bears witness to the punishment of that insane flute-player, nor has he heard of the end of Thamyris, the Thracian who, in an evil hour, strove in song against the Muses. Need I mention the Sirens, whose feathers the victorious Muses still wear on

[2] For Aristaeus see Vergil, *Georgics* 4; he is a vegetation deity not usually associated with music.

μετώπου φέρουσιν αἱ νικήσασαι; ἀλλ' ἐκείνων
μὲν ἕκαστος ἀμούσου τόλμης ἀρκοῦσαν ἔτι καὶ
νῦν ἐκτίνει τῇ μνήμῃ δίκην, ἡμᾶς δὲ ἔδει μέν, ὡς
ἔφην, εἴσω τῶν οἰκείων ὅρων ἑστάναι καὶ τῆς ὑπὸ
σοῦ μουσικῆς ἐμφορουμένους ἠρεμεῖν, ὥσπερ οἱ
421 τὴν Ἀπόλλωνος μαντείαν ἐξ ἀδύτων ἱερῶν προϊ-
οῦσαν ἡσυχῇ δέχονται· ἐπεὶ δ' αὐτὸς ἡμῖν τοῦ
μέλους τὸ ἐνδόσιμον μνηστεύεις καὶ οἷον Ἑρμοῦ
ῥάβδῳ τῷ παρὰ σαυτοῦ λόγῳ κινεῖς καὶ διεγείρεις
καθεύδοντας, φέρε σοι, καθάπερ οἱ τῷ Διονύσῳ
τὸν θύρσον κρούσαντι πρὸς τὴν χορείαν ἄνετοι
φέρονται, οὕτω καὶ ἡμεῖς ὑπὸ τῷ σῷ πλήκτρῳ τὸ
B εἰκὸς ἀντηχήσωμεν, ὥσπερ οἱ τῷ χοροστάτῃ πρὸς
τὸ ἀνάκλημα τοῦ ῥυθμοῦ συνομαρτοῦντες. καὶ
πρῶτόν σοι τῶν λόγων, οὓς βασιλεῖ κελεύσαντι
πρὸς τὴν ἀοίδιμον τοῦ πορθμοῦ[1] ζεῦξιν ἔναγχος
ἐξειργασάμεθα, ἐπειδὴ τοῦτό ἐστί σοι δοκοῦν,
ἀπαρξώμεθα, μικρὰ μὲν ἀντὶ μεγάλων καὶ τῷ ὄντι
χαλκᾶ χρυσῶν ἀντιδιδόντες, οἷς δὲ ἔχομεν ξενίοις
τὸν Ἑρμῆν τὸν ἡμέτερον ἑστιῶντες. πάντως οὐδὲ
τῆς Ἑκάλης ὁ Θησεὺς τοῦ δείπνου τὸ λιτὸν ἀπη-
C ξίωσεν, ἀλλ' ᾔδει καὶ μικροῖς ἐς τὸ ἀναγκαῖον
ἀρκεῖσθαι. ὁ Πὰν δὲ ὁ νόμιος τοῦ παιδὸς τοῦ
βουκόλου τὴν σύριγγα προσαρμόσαι τοῖς χείλεσιν

[1] Cumont would read ποταμοῦ.

---

[1] The Muses, having defeated the Sirens in a singing competition, tore out their feathers and wore them as a symbol of victory.

[2] Geffcken tries to connect this passage with the order of Constantius to Julian to send his troops across the Bosporus *en route* to Persia. Cumont's reading ποταμοῦ "of the river" supposes that Constantine's bridge over the Danube in 328 is

their brows?[1] But each one of those that I have named is still even now paying in the tradition the fitting penalty for his boorishness and temerity, and I, as I said, ought to have stayed within my own boundaries and held my peace while I enjoyed my fill of the music uttered by you, like those who receive in silence the oracle of Apollo when it issues from the sacred shrine. But since you yourself furnish me with the keynote of my song, and by your words, as though with the wand of Hermes, arouse and wake me from sleep, lo now, even as when Dionysus strikes his thyrsus his followers rush riotous to the dance, so let me too in response to your plectron make answering music, like those who accompany the choirmaster, keeping time to the call of the rhythm. And in the first place let me make a first-offering to you, since this is your pleasure, of the speeches which I recently composed at the Emperor's command in honour of the glorious bridging of the strait,[2] though what I offer you is returning small for great and in very truth bronze for gold[3]; yet I am entertaining our Hermes with such fare as I have. Surely Theseus did not disdain the plain meal that Hecale[4] provided, but knew how to content himself with humble fare when the need arose. Nor was Pan, the god of shepherds, too proud to set to his lips the pipe of the boy neat-herd.[5] Then do you also in your

meant; cf. Aurelius Victor 41. 18, pons per Danubium ductus. In my opinion the sophist who wrote this letter had composed speeches on the stock theme of Xerxes and the Hellespont. [3] See p. 218.

[4] The tale is told in the brief epic of Callimachus, the *Hecale*, of which we have fragments; also in Plutarch, *Theseus*.

[5] Theocritus 1. 128.

οὐκ ἠτίμασε. προσοῦ δὴ καὶ αὐτὸς τὸν λόγον εὐμενεῖ νεύματι, καὶ μὴ ἀποκνήσῃς ὀλίγῳ μέλει μεγάλην ἀκοὴν ἐνδοῦναι. ἀλλ' ἐὰν μὲν ἔχῃ τι δεξιόν, αὐτός τε ὁ λόγος εὐτυχεῖ καὶ ὁ ποιητὴς αὐτοῦ τῆς παρὰ τῆς Ἀθηνᾶς ψήφου τὴν μαρτυρίαν
D προσλαβών. εἰ δ' ἔτι χειρὸς ἐντελοῦς εἰς τὸ τοῦ ὅλου πλήρωμα προσδεῖται, μὴ ἀπαξιώσῃς αὐτὸς τὸ ἐνδέον προσθεῖναι. ἤδη που καὶ ἀνδρὶ τοξότῃ κληθεὶς ὁ θεὸς παρέστη καὶ συνεφήψατο τοῦ βέλους, καὶ κιθαρῳδῷ τὸν ὄρθιον ᾄδοντι πρὸς τὸ ἐλλεῖπον τῆς χορδῆς ὑπὸ τῷ τέττιγι τὸ ἴσον ὁ Πύθιος ἀντεφθέγξατο.

75

438 D

τῷ αὐτῷ [1]

Ὦ Ζεῦ, πῶς ἔχει καλῶς ἡμᾶς μὲν ἐν Θρᾴκῃ διάγειν μέσῃ καὶ τοῖς ἐνταῦθα σιροῖς ἐγχειμάζειν, παρ' Ἰαμβλίχου δὲ τοῦ καλοῦ καθάπερ ἑῴου τινὸς
439 ἔαρος ἡμῖν τὰς ἐπιστολὰς ἀντὶ χελιδόνων πέμπεσθαι, καὶ μήτε ἡμῖν εἶναι μηδέπω παρ' αὐτὸν ἐλθεῖν μήτ' αὐτῷ παρ' ἡμᾶς ἥκειν ἐξεῖναι [2]; τίς ἂν ἑκὼν εἶναι ταῦτα δέξαιτο, ἐὰν μὴ Θρᾴξ τις ᾖ καὶ Τηρέως ἀντάξιος;

Ζεῦ ἄνα, ἀλλὰ σὺ ῥῦσαι ἀπὸ Θρήκηθεν Ἀχαιούς·
ποίησον δ' αἴθρην, δὸς δ' ὀφθαλμοῖσιν ἰδέσθαι

[1] Hertlein 53, entitled Ἰαμβλίχῳ φιλοσόφῳ.
[2] ἥξειν ἐξεῖναι MSS., Horkel would delete; Hertlein ἥκειν or delete.

turn accept my discourse in a gracious spirit and do not refuse to lend your mighty ear to my humble strain. But if it has any cleverness at all, then not only is my discourse itself fortunate but so too is its author, in that he has obtained the testimony of Athene's vote.[1] And if it still needs a finishing touch to complete it as a whole, do not refuse to add to it yourself what it needs. Before now the god in answer to prayer has stood by the side of a bowman and set his hand to the arrow, and again, when a bard was playing the cithara and singing a high and stirring strain, the Pythian god, when the string failed, assumed the guise of a cicada and uttered a note of the same tone.

75

To the Same

O ZEUS, how can it be right that I should spend my time in the middle of Thrace and winter in the grain-pits[2] here, while from charming Iamblichus, as though from a sort of spring in the East, letters come to me like swallows and I cannot yet go to him nor can he come to me? Who would be willing to put up with this unless he were some Thracian and as bad as Tereus?[3]

"Lord Zeus do thou rescue the Achaeans from Thrace and make clear weather and grant us to see

[1] The *suffragium Minervae;* the proverb is derived from Aeschylus, *Eumenides*, where Athene, by breaking a tie vote, saved Orestes.

[2] The phrase is borrowed from Demosthenes, *On the Chersonese* 45.

[3] Tereus was king of Thrace.

B ποτὲ τὸν ἡμέτερον Ἑρμῆν καὶ τά τε ἀνάκτορα αὐτοῦ προσειπεῖν καὶ τοῖς ἕδεσιν ἐμφῦναι, καθάπερ τὸν Ὀδυσσέα φασίν, ὅτε ἐκ τῆς ἄλης τὴν Ἰθάκην εἶδεν. ἀλλ᾽ ἐκεῖνον μὲν οἱ Φαίακες ἔτι καθεύδοντα ὥσπερ τι φορτίον ἐκθέμενοι τῆς νεὼς ᾤχοντο· ἡμᾶς δὲ οὐδὲ ὕπνος αἱρεῖ, μέχρις ἂν σέ, τὸ μέγα τῆς οἰκουμένης ὄφελος, ἰδεῖν ἐγγένηται. καίτοι
C σὺ μὲν τὴν ἑῴαν ὅλην ἐμέ τε καὶ τὸν ἑταῖρον Σώπατρον εἰς τὴν Θρᾴκην μετενηνοχέναι προσπαίζεις· ἡμῖν δέ, εἰ χρὴ τἀληθὲς εἰπεῖν, ἕως ἂν Ἰάμβλιχος μὴ παρῇ, Κιμμερίων ἀχλὺς συνοικεῖ. καὶ σὺ μὲν δυοῖν θάτερον αἰτεῖς, ἢ ἡμᾶς παρὰ σὲ ἥκειν ἢ αὐτόν σε παρ᾽ ἡμᾶς. ἡμῖν δὲ
D τὸ μὲν ἕτερον εὐκταῖόν τε ὁμοῦ καὶ σύμφορον, αὐτοὺς ἐπανελθεῖν ὡς σὲ καὶ τῶν παρὰ σοὶ καλῶν ἀπολαῦσαι· τὸ δὲ ἕτερον εὐχῆς μὲν ἁπάσης κρεῖττον. ἐπεὶ δὲ ἀδύνατόν σοί γε καὶ ἀξύμφορόν ἐστι, σὺ μὲν οἴκοι μένειν καὶ χαίρειν καὶ τὴν ἡσυχίαν ἣν ἔχεις σώζειν, ἡμεῖς δὲ ὅ,τι ἂν θεὸς διδῷ γενναίως οἴσομεν. ἀνδρῶν γὰρ ἀγαθῶν εἶναί φασι
440 τὸ μὲν εὔελπι κεκτῆσθαι καὶ τὰ δέοντα πράττειν, ἕπεσθαι δὲ τοῖς ἀναγκαίοις τοῦ δαίμονος.

76

448 D

Τῷ αὐτῷ[1]

Ἱκανὴν ὁμολογῶ τῆς σῆς ἀπολείψεως ἐκτετικέναι δίκην οὐ μόνον οἷς παρὰ τὴν ἀποδημίαν

[1] Hertlein 61.

---

[1] Julian paraphrases *Iliad* 17. 645.

with our eyes"[1] our own Hermes some day, and salute his shrine and embrace his statue as they tell us Odysseus did when after his wandering he beheld Ithaca.[2] Nay, but he was still asleep when the Phaeacians unloaded him from their ship like a piece of freight and went their way; but as for me sleep can never lay hold on me till it be my lot to see you that are the benefactor of the whole world. And yet you say in jest that I and my friend Sopater have transported the whole East into Thrace. Yet, if I must speak the truth, Cimmerian gloom abides with me so long as Iamblichus is not here. And you demand one of two things, that I should go to you or that you yourself should come to me. To my mind one of these alternatives is both desirable and expedient, I mean that I should go to you and benefit by the blessings that you bestow, while the other surpasses all my prayers. But since this is impossible for you and inexpedient, do you remain at home and prosper and preserve the tranquillity that you enjoy, while I will endure with a brave spirit whatever God may send.[3] For we are told that it is the proof of a good man to keep hoping for the best, to do his duty and follow his fate and the will of God.

76

To the Same

I CONFESS that I had paid a full and sufficient penalty for leaving you, not only in the annoyances

[2] *Odyssey* 13. 354.
[3] Cf. *Oration* 8. 243D for the same phrase, derived from Demosthenes, *On the Crown* 97.

449 συνηνέχθην ἀνιαροῖς, ἀλλὰ γὰρ καὶ αὐτῷ τούτῳ πλέον, ὅτι σου τὸν τοσοῦτον ἀπελείφθην χρόνον, καίτοι πολλαῖς καὶ ποικίλαις πανταχοῦ χρησάμενος τύχαις, ὡς μηδὲν ἀπείρατον καταλιπεῖν. ἀλλὰ καὶ πολέμων θορύβους καὶ πολιορκίας ἀνάγκην καὶ φυγῆς πλάνην καὶ φόβους παντοίους, ἔτι δὲ χειμώνων ὑπερβολὰς καὶ νόσων κινδύνους καὶ τὰς ἐκ Παννονίας τῆς ἄνω μέχρι τοῦ κατὰ τὸν Καλχηδόνιον πορθμὸν διάπλου μυρίας δὴ καὶ πολυ-
B τρόπους συμφορὰς ὑπομείνας οὐδὲν οὕτω λυπηρὸν οὐδὲ δυσχερὲς ἐμαυτῷ συμβεβηκέναι φαίην ἂν ὡς ὅτι σὲ τὸ κοινὸν τῶν Ἑλλήνων ἀγαθὸν ἐπὶ τοσοῦτον χρόνον τὴν ἑῴαν ἀπολιπὼν οὐκ εἶδον· ὥστ᾿ εἴπερ ἀχλύν τινα τοῖς ἐμοῖς ὀφθαλμοῖς καὶ νέφος πολὺ περικεῖσθαι λέγοιμι, μὴ θαυμάσῃς. τότε γὰρ δή με καὶ ἀὴρ εὔδιος καὶ φέγγος ἡλίου λαμπρότατον καὶ οἷον ἔαρ ἀληθῶς τοῦ βίου περιέξει κάλλιστον,
C ὅταν σὲ τὸ μέγα τῆς οἰκουμένης ἄγαλμα περιπτύξωμαι καί, καθάπερ ἀγαθῷ πατρὶ παῖς γνήσιος ἐκ πολέμου τινὸς ἢ διαποντίου κλύδωνος ἀνελπίστως ὀφθείς, εἶτα ὅσα ἔπαθον καὶ δι᾿ ὅσων ἦλθον κινδύνων εἰπὼν καὶ οἷον ἐπ᾿ ἀγκύρας ἱερᾶς ὁρμιζόμενος ἀρκοῦσαν ἤδη παραψυχὴν τῶν ἀλγεινῶν εὕρωμαι. παραμυθεῖται γάρ, ὡς εἰκός, καὶ ἐπικουφίζει τὰς συμφοράς, ὅταν τις ἃ πέπονθεν εἰς τοὺς ἄλλους
D ἔκφορα καθιστὰς διανείμῃ τοῦ πάθους τὴν γνῶσιν ἐν[1] τῇ κοινωνίᾳ τοῦ λόγου. τέως γε μὴν οἷς ἔχω[2]

[1] Hertlein would delete ἐν, but see 449D, p. 246.
[2] Brambs would insert πτέροις after ἔχω; cf. *Letter* 60. 386C.

---

[1] The reference is probably to Constantine's march in 323 from Pannonia to Nicomedia by way of the Dardanelles.

that I encountered on my journey, but far more in the very fact that I have been away from you for so long, though I have indeed endured so many and various fortunes everywhere, that I have left nothing untried. But though I have undergone the alarms of war, the rigour of a siege, the wandering of exile and all sorts of terrors, and moreover the extreme cold of winter, the dangers of disease and countless mischances of many kinds in my journey from Upper Pannonia till I crossed the Chalcedonian straits,[1] I may say that nothing so painful or so distressing has happened to me as the fact that after I left the East I have not, for so long a time, seen you, the universal blessing of the Hellenes. So do not be surprised if I say that a sort of mist and thick cloud overshadows my eyes. For only then will a clear atmosphere and the brilliant light of the sun, and, so to speak, the fairest and truest springtime of my life, encompass me when I can embrace you, the delight and glory of the whole world, and, like the true son of a noble father who when hope is given up is seen returning from war, it may be, or from the stormy billows of the sea,[2] can proceed to recount to you all that I have suffered and what dangers I have been through, and as I, so to speak, ride safely on a sacred anchor,[3] can find at last a sufficient consolation for my misfortunes. For naturally it is a consolation and lightens the weight of sorrow when one unburdens one's experiences to others and shares with them the knowledge of one's sufferings in the intercourse of speech. Meanwhile, however, with what means I have I will,

[2] For a similar idea cf. Julian, *To the Athenians*, Vol. 2, Wright, 285C, p. 285.

[3] Cf. ancoram sacram (or ultimam) solvere, a proverb implying the use of what has been kept in reserve.

σε κατὰ δύναμιν τὴν ἐμὴν μέτειμι· καὶ γὰρ οὐ παύσομαι τὸν ἐν μέσῳ τῆς ἀπολείψεως χρόνον ἐν τῷ τῶν γραμμάτων θεραπεύων συνθήματι. εἰ δὲ δὴ καὶ ἀντιτύχοιμι παρὰ σοῦ τῶν ἴσων, ὑφήσω τί καὶ μικρόν, οἷον ἀντὶ σωτηρίου τινὸς συμβόλου[1] τοῖς σοῖς ὁμιλῶν γράμμασι. σὺ δὲ δέχοιο μὲν εὐμενῶς τὰ παρ' ἡμῶν, παρέχοις δὲ καὶ σεαυτὸν εἰς ἀμοιβὴν εὐμενέστερον, ὡς ὅ τι ἂν σημήνῃς καλὸν ἢ γράψῃς, τοῦτο ἀντὶ τῆς Ἑρμοῦ λογίου φωνῆς ἢ τῆς Ἀσκληπιοῦ χειρὸς παρ' ἡμῶν κρίνεται.

77

446 Τῷ αὐτῷ[2]

C Ἦλθες κάλ' ἐπόησας· ἦλθες γὰρ δὴ καὶ ἀπὼν οἷς γράφεις· "ἐγὼ δέ σε μαόμαν, ἂν δ' ἔφλεξας ἐμὰν φρένα καιομέναν πόθῳ."[3] οὔκουν οὔτε ἀρνοῦμαι τὸ φίλτρον οὔτε ἀπολείπω σε κατ' οὐδέν ἀλλὰ καὶ ὡς παρόντα τῇ ψυχῇ θεωρῶ καὶ ἀπόντι
D σύνειμι, καὶ οὐδὲν ἱκανόν ἐστί μοι πρὸς κόρον ἀρκέσαι. καίτοι σύ γε οὐκ ἀνίης καὶ παρόντας εὖ ποιῶν ἀεὶ καὶ ἀπόντας οὐκ εὐφραίνων μόνον οἷς γράφεις, ἀλλὰ καὶ σῴζων. ὅτε γοῦν ἀπήγ-

[1] Hertlein, following Reiske, συμβούλου but the reading of the MSS., συμβόλου echoes συνθήματι above and should be retained.

[2] Hertlein 60, with title Ἰαμβλίχῳ.

[3] Reiske first recognized this quotation from Sappho not found elsewhere: MSS , Hertlein καὶ ἐποίησας—ἐγὼ· δέ σε μὰ ἐμὰν ἂν δὲ φύλαξας; Reiske ἐγὼ δέ σ' ἐματεύμαν (for ἐματευόμην), τὺ δ' ἐψάλαξας ἐμὰν φρένα; Wesseling ἂν δ' ἔφλεξας; Spanheim ἐμὰν ἂν δ' ἐφύλαξας; Petavius ἔμαν ἂν δὲ

so far as I can approach you; and indeed I shall not cease, for the whole period of our separation, to conciliate you with letters by way of a token. And if I only receive the like from you, I shall be somewhat more submissive and shall hold converse with your letters, regarding them as a sort of symbol that you are safe and well. Do you, then, graciously accept what arrives from me, and show yourself still more gracious in making requital, since every noble utterance of yours, every written word, is reckoned by me as equivalent to the voice of Hermes the god of eloquence, or to the hand of Asclepius.[1]

77

To the Same

"Thou hast come! well hast thou done!" You have indeed come, even though absent, by means of your letter—"And I was yearning for thee, and thou didst set ablaze my heart, already aflame with longing for thee."[2] Nay, I neither refuse the love-philtre nor do I ever leave you at all, but with my soul I behold you as though you were present, and am with you when absent, and nothing is enough to quench my insatiate desire. Moreover, you also never slacken, but without ceasing you benefit those who are present with you and by your letters not only cheer but even heal those who are absent. At

[1] See *Letter* 79. 406D.

[2] The quotations are from an ode of Sappho and perhaps run through the whole letter; see critical note.

φύλαξας. I give the version of Bidez. For ἔφλεξας Wilamowitz ἔφλυξας, cf. Isyllus 120; ἂν δ'ἔψυξας Thomas.

γειλέ μοί τις ἔναγχος, ὡς παρὰ σοῦ γράμματα κομίσας ἑταῖρος ἥκοι, ἐτύγχανον μὲν ἐν ἀηδίᾳ τοῦ στομάχου τριταῖος ἤδη καθεστὼς καί τι καὶ περιαλγῶς ἔχων τοῦ σώματος, ὡς μηδὲ ἔξω
447 πυρετοῦ μεῖναι· σημανθὲν δέ, ὡς ἔφην, ὅτι μοι πρὸς ταῖς θύραις ὁ τὰ γράμματα ἔχων εἴη, ἐγὼ μὲν ὥσπερ τις ἀκρατὴς ἑαυτοῦ καὶ κάτοχος ἀναπηδήσας ᾖξα πρὶν ὅ τι δέοι παρεῖναι. ἐπεὶ δὲ καὶ ἔλαβον εἰς χεῖρας τὴν ἐπιστολὴν μόνον, ὀμνύω τοὺς θεοὺς αὐτοὺς καὶ τὸν ἐπὶ σοί με ἀνάψαντα πόθον, ὡς ἅμα τε ἔφυγον οἱ πόνοι καί με καὶ ὁ πυρετὸς ἀνῆκεν εὐθύς, ὥσπερ τινὶ τοῦ
B σωτῆρος ἐναργεῖ παρουσίᾳ δυσωπούμενος. ὡς δὲ καὶ λύσας ἀνέγνων, τίνα με ἡγῇ ψυχὴν ἐσχηκέναι τότε ἢ πόσης ἡδονῆς ἀνάπλεων γεγενῆσθαι, τὸν φίλτατον, ὡς φής, ἀνέμων, τὸν ἐρωτικὸν ἀληθῶς, τὸν διάκονον τῶν καλῶν ὑπερεπαινοῦντά τε καὶ φιλοῦντα δικαίως, ὅτι μοι τῶν παρὰ σοῦ γραμμάτων ὑπηρέτης γέγονεν, οἱονεὶ[1] πτηνοῦ δίκην ἡμῖν τὴν ἐπιστολὴν διευθύνας οὐρίῳ τε καὶ πομπίμῳ πνεύματι, δι' ἧς οὐ μόνον ὑπῆρξεν
C ἡσθῆναί μοι τὰ εἰκότα περὶ σοῦ γνόντι, ἀλλὰ καὶ αὐτῷ κάμνοντι παρὰ σοῦ σωθῆναι; τά γε μὴν ἄλλα πῶς ἃ πρῶτον[2] πρὸς τὴν ἐπιστολὴν ἔπαθον εἴποιμ' ἄν, ἢ πῶς ἂν ἀρκούντως ἐμαυτοῦ τὸν ἔρωτα καταμηνύσαιμι; ποσάκις ἀνέδραμον εἰς ἀρχὴν ἐκ μέσου; ποσάκις ἔδεισα μὴ πληρώσας λάθω; ποσάκις ὥσπερ ἐν κύκλῳ τινὶ καὶ

[1] Hertlein following Hercher would delete οἱονεί, but it occurs with δίκην too often to be an oversight; see p 218, note.

[2] For ἃ πρῶτον Hertlein suggests ἅπερ, Hercher would delete πρῶτον.

any rate, when someone not long ago gave me the news that a friend had come and brought letters from you, it happened that for three days I had been suffering from a disorder of the stomach, and in fact I was in acute physical pain, so that I was not even free from fever. But, as I said, when I was told that the person who had the letters was at my door I jumped up like one possessed, who has lost control of himself, and rushed out before what I wanted could arrive. And the moment that I merely took the letter in my hands, I swear by the very gods and by the love that burns in me for you, that instant my pains forsook me and at once the fever let me go, as though it were abashed by some manifest saving presence. But when I broke the seal and read the letter, can you imagine what feelings took possession of my soul at that moment or with what delight I was filled, or how I praised to the skies that dearest of winds,[1] to quote your words, the lover's wind in very truth, the messenger of glad tidings—and loved it with good reason, since it had done me this service of bringing a letter from you, and like a winged thing had guided straight to me, with a fair and hurrying blast, that letter which brought me not only the pleasure of hearing good news of you but also salvation at your hands in my own illness? But how could I describe my other sensations when first I read the letter, or how could I find adequate words to betray my own passion? How often did I hark back from the middle to the beginning? How often did I fear that I should finish it before I was aware? How often, as though I

[1] An echo of Sophocles, *Philoctetes* 237 τίς προσήγαγεν; . . . . τίς ἀνέμων ὁ φίλτατος;

στροφῆς περιόδῳ τοῦ συμπεράσματος τὸ πλή-
D ρωμα πρὸς τὴν ἀρχὴν ἀνεῖλκον, οἷον ἐν ᾄσματι μουσικῷ ταὐτὸν τοῦ ῥυθμοῦ τῷ τέλει τὸ πρὸς τὴν ἀρχὴν ἡγούμενον μέλος ἀντιδιδούς· ἢ καὶ νὴ Δία τὰ ἑξῆς τούτων, ὁσάκις μὲν τῷ στόματι τὴν ἐπιστολὴν προσήγαγον, ὥσπερ αἱ μητέρες τὰ παιδία περιπλέκονται,[1] ὁσάκις δὲ ἐνέφυν τῷ στόματι καθάπερ ἐρωμένην ἐμαυτοῦ φιλτάτην ἀσπαζόμενος, ὁσάκις δὲ τὴν ἐπιγραφὴν αὐτήν, ἣ χειρὶ σῇ καθάπερ ἐναργεῖ σφραγῖδι ἐσεσήμαντο, προσειπὼν καὶ φιλήσας, εἶτα ἐπέβαλον τοῖς
448 ὀφθαλμοῖς, οἱονεὶ τοῖς τῆς ἱερᾶς ἐκείνης δεξιᾶς δακτύλοις τῷ τῶν γραμμάτων ἴχνει προσπεφυκώς. χαῖρε δὲ καὶ αὐτὸς ἡμῖν πολλά, καθάπερ ἡ καλὴ Σαπφώ φησι, καὶ οὐκ ἰσάριθμα μόνον τῷ χρόνῳ, ὃν ἀλλήλων ἀπελείφθημεν,[2] ἀλλὰ γὰρ καὶ ἀεὶ χαῖρε, καὶ γράφε καὶ μέμνησο ἡμῶν τὰ εἰκότα. ὡς ἡμᾶς γε οὐκ ἐπιλείψει χρόνος, ἐν ᾧ σε μὴ
B πάντη[3] καὶ ἐν παντὶ καιρῷ καὶ λόγῳ διὰ μνήμης ἕξομεν. ἀλλ' ἡμῖν εἴ[4] ποθι Ζεὺς δοίη ἱκέσθαι ἐς πατρίδα γαῖαν, καί σου τὴν ἱερὰν ἐκείνην ἑστίαν αὖθις ὑπέλθοιμεν, μὴ φείσῃ λοιπὸν ὡς φυγάδος, ἀλλὰ δῆσον, εἰ δοκεῖ, πρὸς τοῖς σεαυτοῦ θώκοις τοῖς φιλτάτοις, ὥσπερ τινὰ Μουσῶν λιποτάκτην ἑλών, εἶτα τοῖς εἰς τιμωρίαν ἀρκοῦσι παιδεύων. πάντως οὐδὲ ἄκων ὑποστήσομαι τὴν δίκην, ἀλλ' ἑκὼν δὴ καὶ χαίρων, ὥσπερ ἀγαθοῦ πατρὸς

[1] περιπλέκονται Hertlein suggests, προσπλέκονται MSS.

[2] Blass in *Cl. Philology* I. p. 253 reconstructs a fragment of Sappho, as follows: χαῖρε πολλά τέ μοι καὶ ἰσάριθμα τῷ χρόνῳ, ὃν σεθεν . . . ἀπελειπόμαν.

were going round in a circle in the evolutions of a strophe,[1] did I try to connect the contents of the last paragraph with the first, just as though in a song set to music I were making the leading note of the beginning the same as the closing bars of the measure? Or how describe what I did next—how often I held the letter to my lips, as mothers embrace their children, how often I kissed it with those lips as though I were embracing my dearest sweetheart, how often I invoked and kissed and held to my eyes even the superscription which had been signed by your own hand as though by a clear cut seal, and how I clung to the imprint of the letters as I should to the fingers of that sacred right hand of yours! I too "wish thee joy in full measure,"[2] as fair Sappho says, and not only "for just so long as we have been parted from one another," but may you rejoice evermore, and write to me and remember me with kindly thoughts. For no time shall ever pass by me in which I shall forget you, in any place, at any hour, in any word I speak. "But if ever Zeus permits me to return to my native land,"[3] and once more I humbly approach that sacred hearth of yours, do not spare me hereafter as you would a runaway, but fetter me, if you will, to your own beloved dwelling, making me captive like a deserter from the Muses, and then discipline me with such penalties as suffice for my punishment. Assuredly I shall submit to your jurisdiction not unwillingly, but with a good will and

[1] *e.g.* in the chorus of the drama.
[2] *Frag.* 85, Bergk. [3] *Odyssey* 4. 475.

---

[3] πάντη Hercher suggests, πάντα Hertlein, MSS.
[4] ἀλλ' ἡμῖν εἴ Hertlein suggests; ἀλλήλων δὲ MSS.

ἐπανόρθωσιν προμηθῆ καὶ σωτήριον. εἰ δὲ δή μοι καὶ κατ' ἐμαυτοῦ τὴν κρίσιν ἐθέλοις πισ-
C τεῦσαι καὶ διδοίης ἐνεγκεῖν ἣν βούλομαι, ἐμαυτόν, ὦ γενναῖε, τῷ σῷ χιτωνίσκῳ προσάψαιμι ἂν ἡδέως, ἵνα σου κατὰ μηδὲν ἀπολειποίμην, ἀλλὰ συνείην ἀεὶ καὶ πανταχῇ προσφεροίμην, ὥσπερ οὓς οἱ μῦθοι διφυεῖς ἀνθρώπους πλάττουσιν. εἰ μὴ κἀκεῖνο οἱ μῦθοι λέγουσι μὲν ὡς παίζοντες, αἰνίττονται δὲ εἰς τὸ τῆς φιλίας ἐξαίρετον, ἐν τῷ τῆς κοινωνίας δεσμῷ τὸ δι' ἑκατέρου τῆς ψυχῆς ὁμογενὲς ἐμφαίνοντες.

78

Τῷ αὐτῷ [1]

416 Αἰσθάνομαί σου τῆς ἐν τῇ μέμψει γλυκύτητος,
C καὶ ὡς ἑκάτερον ἐξ ἴσου πράττεις, καὶ οἷς γράφεις τιμῶν καὶ οἷς ἐγκαλεῖς παιδεύων. ἐγὼ δὲ εἰ μέν τι συνῄδειν ἐμαυτῷ τοῦ πρὸς σὲ γιγνομένου καὶ κατὰ μικρὸν ἐλλιπόντι, πάντως ἢ προφάσεις εὐλόγους εἰπὼν ἐπειρώμην ἂν τὴν μέμψιν ἐκκλίνειν, ἢ συγγνώμην ἁμαρτὼν αἰτεῖν οὐκ ἠρνούμην, ἐπεὶ μηδὲ ἄλλως ἀσύγγνωστον οἶδά σε πρὸς τοὺς σούς, εἴ τι τῶν πρὸς σὲ φιλικῶν
D ἐξήμαρτον ἄκοντες. νῦν δέ· οὐ γὰρ ἦν οὔτε σὲ παροφθῆναι θέμις οὔτε ἡμᾶς ἀμελεῖν, ἵνα τύ-

[1] Hertlein 40, with title Ἰαμβλίχῳ.

gladly, as to a kind father's provident and salutary correction. Moreover, if you would consent to trust me to sentence myself and allow me to suffer the penalty that I prefer, I would gladly fasten myself to your tunic, my noble friend, so that I might never for a moment leave your side but be with you always and closely attached to you wherever you are, like those two-bodied beings invented in the myths. Unless, indeed, in this case also the myths, though they tell us the story in jest, are describing in enigmatical words an extraordinary sort of friendship and by that close tie of a common being express the kinship of soul in both beings.[1]

78

To the Same.

I AM sensible of the sweet-tempered manner in which you reproach me, and that you achieve two things with equal success, for you do me honour by what you write and instruct me by your criticisms. And for my part, if I were conscious of even the least failure in the attention due to you, I should certainly try by making reasonable excuses to parry your criticism, or if I were in fault I should not hesitate to ask your forgiveness, especially as I know that you are not implacable towards your friends when they have involuntarily failed in some friendly office to you. But as it is—since it was not right either for you to be neglected or for me to be careless if we

[1] For Julian's allegorising interpretation of myths see *Oration*, 5. 170; 7. 216c, 222c; and for the illustration here Lucian, *Toxaris* 62.

χοιμεν ὧν ἀεὶ ζητοῦντες ποθοῦμεν· φέρε σοι καθάπερ ἐν ὅρῳ γραφῆς ἀπολογήσωμαι, καὶ δείξω μηδὲν ἐμαυτὸν ὧν ἐχρῆν εἰς σὲ παριδεῖν, ἀλλὰ μηδὲ μελλῆσαι τολμήσαντα.

Ἦλθον ἐκ Παννονίας ἤδη τρίτον ἔτος τουτί,
417 *μόλις ἀφ' ὧν οἶσθα κινδύνων καὶ πόνων σωθείς. ὑπερβὰς δὲ τὸν Καλχηδόνιον πορθμὸν καὶ ἐπιστὰς τῇ Νικομήδους πόλει σοὶ πρώτῳ καθάπερ πατρίῳ θεῷ τὰ πρωτόλεια τῶν ἐμαυτοῦ σώστρων ἀπέδωκα, σύμβολον τῆς ἀφίξεως τῆς ἐμῆς οἷον ἀντ' ἀναθήματος ἱεροῦ τὴν εἰς σὲ πρόσρησιν ἐκπέμπων. καὶ ἦν ὁ κομίζων τὰ γράμματα τῶν βασιλείων ὑπασπιστῶν εἷς, Ἰουλιανὸς ὄνομα, Βακχύλου*
B *παῖς, Ἀπαμεὺς τὸ γένος, ᾧ διὰ τοῦτο μάλιστα τὴν ἐπιστολὴν ἐνεχείριζον, ὅτι καὶ πρὸς ὑμᾶς ἥξειν καί σε ἀκριβῶς εἰδέναι καθυπισχνεῖτο. μετὰ ταῦτά μοι καθάπερ ἐξ Ἀπόλλωνος ἱερὸν ἐφοίτα παρὰ σοῦ γράμμα, τὴν ἄφιξιν τὴν ἡμετέραν ἀσμένως σε ἀκηκοέναι δηλοῦν· ἦν δὲ τοῦτο ἐμοὶ δεξιὸν οἰώνισμα καὶ χρηστῶν ἐλπίδων ἀρχή, Ἰάμβλιχος ὁ σοφὸς καὶ τὰ Ἰαμβλίχου πρὸς ἡμᾶς γράμματα. τί με δεῖ λέγειν ὅπως*
C *ηὐφράνθην ἢ ἃ περὶ τὴν ἐπιστολὴν ἔπαθον σημαίνειν; εἰ γὰρ ἐδέξω τὰ παρ' ἡμῶν ἕνεκα τούτων γραφέντα· ἦν δὲ δι' ἡμεροδρόμου τῶν ἐκεῖθεν ἡκόντων ὡς σὲ πεμφθέντα· πάντως ἂν ὁπόσην ἐπ' αὐτοῖς ἡδονὴν ἔσχον ἀφ' ὧν ἐδήλουν ἐγίνωσκες. πάλιν ἐπανιόντος οἴκαδε τοῦ τροφέως*

[1] Constantine marched from Pannonia to Nicomedia in 323, so perhaps this letter can be dated 326. In Julian's authentic writings we always find Paeonia for Pannonia; see *Letter* 76, p. 244, for a reference to this journey.

were to attain that which we ever seek after and desire—come, I will plead my case before you as though by the rules of a lawsuit, and I will prove that far from having neglected any of my duties towards you I have never even ventured to postpone them.

It is now three years since I arrived from Pannonia,[1] with difficulty escaping safely from the dangers and troubles that you know of. When I had crossed the Chalcedonian strait and approached the city of Nicomedia, to you first as though to the god of my fathers I paid vows as the first thank-offering for my deliverance, by sending you as a token of my arrival my salutation in place of a sacred offering. The man who took charge of my letter was one of the imperial guard named Julian, the son of Bacchylus, a native of Apamea, and to him I all the more readily entrusted the letter because he asserted that he was going in your direction and that he knew you very well. Afterwards, as though from Apollo, a sacred letter came to me from you, in which you declared that you had been pleased to hear of my arrival. This was to my mind an auspicious omen and a fount of fairest hopes,—Iamblichus the wise and the letter of Iamblichus to me. Need I say how I rejoiced or assure you how deeply I was moved by your letter? For if you had received what I wrote to you with no other purpose—and it was sent to you by one of the couriers who came from where you are,—you would certainly know from what I then said how great was the pleasure that I felt on receiving it. Again, when the custodian of my children[2] was returning

[2] This phrase is perhaps metaphorical; see p. 214, note 1.

D τῶν ἐμαυτοῦ παιδίων, ἑτέρων ἦρχον πρὸς σὲ γραμμάτων, ὁμοῦ καὶ τὴν ἐπὶ τοῖς φθάνουσι χάριν ὁμολογῶν καὶ πρὸς τὸ ἑξῆς ἐν ἴσῳ παρὰ σοῦ τὴν ἀντίδοσιν αἰτῶν. μετὰ ταῦτα ἐπρέσβευσεν ὡς ἡμᾶς ὁ καλὸς Σώπατρος· ἐγὼ δὲ ὡς ἔγνων, εὐθὺς ἀναπηδήσας ᾖξα καὶ περιπλακεὶς ἐδάκρυον ὑφ' ἡδονῆς, οὐδὲν ἄλλο ἢ σὲ καὶ τὰ παρὰ σοῦ πρὸς ἡμᾶς ὀνειροπολῶν γράμματα. ὡς δὲ ἔλαβον, ἐφίλουν καὶ τοῖς ὀφθαλμοῖς προσῆ-
418 γον, καὶ ἀπρὶξ εἰχόμην, ὥσπερ δεδιὼς μὴ λάθῃ με ἀποπτὰν ἐν τῇ τῶν γραμμάτων ἀναγνώσει τὸ τῆς σῆς εἰκόνος ἴνδαλμα. καὶ δὴ καὶ ἀντέγραφον εὐθύς, οὐ πρὸς σὲ μόνον, ἀλλὰ καὶ πρὸς τὸν ἱερὸν Σώπατρον, τὸν ἐκείνου παῖδα, καθάπερ θρυπτόμενος ὅτι τὸν κοινὸν ἑταῖρον ἐκ τῆς Ἀπαμείας οἷον ἐνέχυρον τῆς ὑμετέρας ἀπουσίας ἀντειληφότες εἴημεν. ἐξ ἐκείνου τρίτην ἤδη πρὸς σὲ γεγραφώς, αὐτὸς οὐδεμίαν ἄλλην ἢ τὴν ἐν ᾗ μέμφεσθαι δοκεῖς ἐπιστολὴν ἐδεξάμην.

B Εἰ μὲν δὴ διὰ τοῦτο ἐγκαλεῖς, ἵνα τῷ τῆς αἰτίας σχήματι πλείονας ἡμῖν ἀφορμὰς τοῦ γράφειν προξενῇς, δέχομαι τὴν μέμψιν ἄσμενος πάνυ, καὶ ἐν οἷς λαμβάνω τὸ πᾶν τῆς χάριτος εἰς ἐμαυτὸν οἰκειοῦμαι· εἰ δὲ ὡς ἀληθῶς ἐλλιπόντα τι τοῦ πρὸς σὲ καθήκοντος αἰτιᾷ, τίς ἂν ἐμοῦ γένοιτ' ἂν ἀθλιώτερος[1] διὰ γραμματοφόρων ἀδικίαν ἢ ῥᾳ-

[1] Nauck, *Tragicorum Graecorum Fragmenta*, *Adespota* 280 suggests τίς ἄρ'; Schmidt τίς ἀντ'. The verse does not occur elsewhere, but cf. Sophocles, *Oedipus Tyrannus* 815 τίς τοῦδε νῦν ἔστ' ἀνδρὸς ἀθλιώτερος;

---

[1] This may be the Sopater whom Julian mentions in *Letter*

home, I began another letter to you in which I at the same time spoke to you of my gratitude for your previous favours and begged for a like return from you for the immediate future. After this the excellent Sopater[1] came on an embassy to our city. When I recognised him I at once started up and flew to him and when I had embraced him I wept for joy, dreaming of nothing else but you and a letter from you to me. And when I received it I kissed it and held it to my eyes and kept tight hold of it as though I were afraid that while I was in the act of reading your letter the phantom of your image might elude me and fly away. And, moreover, I at once wrote an answer, not to you only but also to the revered Sopater, that great man's son, telling him, as though giving myself airs, that I accepted our mutual friend from Apamea as a sort of hostage for your absence. This is the third letter that I have written to you since that time, but I have myself received no other letter from you save that in which you seem to reproach me.

Now if you are accusing me merely for the purpose of providing me with further motives for writing to you, and only pretend to reproach me, then I am very glad to receive your criticism, and in this very letter that has now come I take to myself the whole of the kindness implied. But if you really accuse me of being in any way remiss in my duty to you, "who could be more wretched than I"[2] through the wrong-doing or negligence of letter-carriers, when I, least

58 *To Libanius*, p. 207. But he is more probably the elder Sopater who was executed by Constantine.

[2] An iambic trimeter whose source is not known; see critical note.

C θυμίαν πάντων ἥκιστα ἀξίου τούτου τυγχάνειν
ὄντος;[1] καίτοι ἐγὼ μέν, κἂν μὴ πλεονάκις γράφω,
δίκαιός εἰμι συγγνώμης παρὰ σοῦ τυγχάνειν· οὐ
τῆς ἀσχολίας ἣν ἐν χερσὶν ἔχω φαίην ἄν· μὴ
γὰρ οὕτω πράξαιμι κακῶς, ὡς μὴ καὶ ἀσχολίας
ἁπάσης, καθά φησι Πίνδαρος, τὸ κατὰ σὲ κρεῖτ-
τον ἡγεῖσθαι· ἀλλ' ὅτι πρὸς ἄνδρα τηλικοῦτον,
οὗ καὶ μνησθῆναι φόβος, ὁ καὶ γράφειν κατοκνῶν
τοῦ πλέον ἢ προσήκει θαρροῦντός ἐστι σωφρονέ-
D στερος. ὥσπερ γὰρ οἱ ταῖς Ἡλίου μαρμαρυγαῖς
ἀντιβλέπειν συνεχῶς τολμῶντες, ἂν μὴ θεῖοί τινες
ὦσι καὶ τῶν ἀκτίνων αὐτοῦ καθάπερ οἱ τῶν
ἀετῶν γνήσιοι καταθαρρῶσιν, οὔτε ἃ μὴ θέμις
ὀφθῆναι θεωρεῖν ἔχουσι, καὶ ὅσῳπερ μᾶλλον
φιλονεικοῦσι, τοσούτῳ πλέον ὅτι μὴ δύνανται
τυχεῖν ἐμφαίνουσιν, οὕτω καὶ ὁ πρὸς σὲ γράφειν
τολμῶν, ὅσῳπερ ἂν ἐθέλῃ θαρρεῖν, τοσούτῳ
μᾶλλον ὅτι χρὴ δεδιέναι καθαρῶς δείκνυσι. σοί
419 γε μήν, ὦ γενναῖε, παντὸς ὡς εἰπεῖν τοῦ Ἑλ-
ληνικοῦ σωτῆρι καθεστῶτι, πρέπον ἦν ἀφθόνως
τε ἡμῖν γράφειν καὶ τὸν παρ' ἡμῖν ὄκνον ἐφ' ὅσον
ἐξῆν καταστέλλειν. ὥσπερ γὰρ ὁ Ἥλιος· ἵνα δὴ
πάλιν ἐκ τοῦ θεοῦ πρός σε τὴν εἰκόνα λάβῃ ὁ
λόγος· ὁ δ' οὖν Ἥλιος ὥσπερ, ὅταν ἀκτῖσι κα-
θαραῖς ὅλος λάμπῃ, οὐδὲν ἀποκρίνει τοῦ πρὸς
τὴν αἴγλην ἐλθόντος, ἀλλὰ τὸ οἰκεῖον ἐργάζεται,

[1] ἀξίου τούτου τυγχάνειν ὄντος Hertlein suggests; τούτου τογχάνοντος MSS., τυγχάνειν Reiske.

of all men, deserve the reproach? And yet even if I do not write oftener I may well claim indulgence from you—I do not mean because of the many affairs which I have on my hands—for may I never sink so low as not to count you more important than any business whatever, as Pindar[1] says!—but because there is more wisdom in hesitating to write more than is fitting to so great a man as yourself, whom one cannot so much as think of without awe, than in being too presumptuous. For even as those who venture to gaze steadily at the bright beams of Helios, unless indeed they be in some sort divine and like the genuine offspring of eagles[2] can brave his rays, are unable to behold what is not lawful for their eyes to see, and the more they strive for this the more do they show that they have not the power to attain it, even so, I say, he who ventures to write to you shows clearly that the more he allows himself to presume the more he ought to be afraid. For you, however, my noble friend, who have been appointed as the saviour, so to speak, of the whole Hellenic world, it would have been becoming not only to write to me without stint, but also to allay as far as you could the scruples felt by me. For as Helios—if my argument may again employ in reference to you a simile from the god,—even as Helios, I say, when he shines in full splendour with his brilliant rays rejects naught of what encounters his beams,

[1] *Isthmian Odes* 1. 1 *τὸ τεόν . . . πρᾶγμα καὶ ἀσχολίας ὑπέρτερον θήσομαι.*

[2] For this allusion to the eagle's test of its offspring see *Letter* 59, *To Maximus*; Themistius 240c; Lucian, *Icaromenippus* 14; Claudian, *On the Third Consulship of Honorius*, Preface 1-14.

B οὕτω δὲ καὶ σὲ χρῆν ἀφθόνως τῶν παρὰ σοῦ
καλῶν οἷον φωτὸς τὸ Ἑλληνικὸν ἐπαρδεύοντα μὴ
ἀποκνεῖν, εἴ τις ἢ αἰδοῦς ἢ δέους ἕνεκα τοῦ πρὸς
σὲ τὴν ἀντίδοσιν δυσωπεῖται. οὐδὲ γὰρ ὁ Ἀσ-
κληπιὸς ἐπ' ἀμοιβῆς ἐλπίδι τοὺς ἀνθρώπους
ἰᾶται, ἀλλὰ τὸ οἰκεῖον αὐτῷ φιλανθρώπευμα
πανταχοῦ πληροῖ. ὃ δὴ καὶ σὲ χρῆν ὡσπερεὶ
ψυχῶν ἐλλογίμων ἰατρὸν ὄντα ποιεῖν καὶ το τῆς
ἀρετῆς παράγγελμα διὰ πάντων σώζειν, οἷον
C ἀγαθὸν τοξότην, ὅς, κἂν μὴ τὸν ἀντίπαλον ἔχῃ,
πάντως ἐς τὸ καίριον ἀεὶ τὴν χεῖρα γυμνάζει.
ἐπεὶ μηδὲ ὁ σκοπὸς ἑκατέροις ὁ αὐτός, ἡμῖν
δὲ τῶν παρὰ σοῦ δεξιῶν τυχεῖν καὶ σοὶ τοῖς
παρ' ἡμῶν διδομένοις ἐντυχεῖν. ἀλλ' ἡμεῖς, κἂν
μυριάκις γράφωμεν, ἴσα τοῖς Ὁμηρικοῖς παισὶ
παίζομεν, οἳ παρὰ τὰς θῖνας ὅτι ἂν ἐκ πηλοῦ
D πλάσωσιν ἀφιᾶσιν κλύζεσθαι· παρὰ σοῦ δὲ καὶ
μικρὸν γράμμα παντός ἐστι γονίμου ῥεύματος
κρεῖττον, καὶ δεξαίμην ἂν ἔγωγε Ἰαμβλίχου
μᾶλλον ἐπιστολὴν μίαν ἢ τὸν ἐκ Λυδίας χρυσὸν
κεκτῆσθαι. εἰ δὲ μέλει τί σοι τῶν ἐραστῶν τῶν
σῶν· μέλει δέ, εἰ μὴ σφάλλομαι· μὴ περιίδῃς
ὥσπερ νεοττοὺς ἡμᾶς ἀεὶ τῶν παρὰ σοῦ τροφῶν
ἐν χρείᾳ τυγχάνοντας, ἀλλὰ καὶ γράφε συνεχῶς
καὶ τοῖς παρὰ σαυτοῦ καλοῖς ἑστιᾶν μὴ κατόκνει.
κἂν ἐλλίπωμεν, αὐτὸς ἑκατέρου τὴν χρείαν οἰκειοῦ,
420 καὶ ὧν δίδως καὶ ὧν ἀνθ' ἡμῶν τὸ ἴσον πρεσβεύεις.
πρέπει δὲ Ἑρμοῦ λογίου μαθητήν, εἰ δὲ βούλει

but ever performs his function, so ought you also not to shrink from bountifully pouring forth the flood of your blessings like light over the Hellenic world even when, whether from modesty, or fear of you, one is too bashful to make any return. Asclepius, again, does not heal mankind in the hope of repayment, but everywhere fulfils his own function of beneficence to mankind. This, then, you ought to do also, as though you were the physician of souls endowed with eloquence, and you ought to keep up on all occasions the preaching of virtue, like a skilled archer who, even though he have no opponent, keeps training his hand by every means in view of future need. For in truth we two have not the same ambition, since mine is to secure the wise teachings that flow from you and yours is to read letters sent by me. But as for me, though I should write ten thousand times, mine is still mere child's play, and I am like the boys in Homer who on the sea-shores model something in wet sand and then abandon it all for the sea to wash away; whereas even a short letter from you is more potent than any fertilising flood, and for my part I would rather receive one letter from Iamblichus than possess all the gold of Lydia. If, then, you care at all for your fond admirers—and you do care if I am not mistaken—do not neglect me who am like a fledgling constantly in need of sustenance from you, but write regularly, and moreover do not be reluctant to feast me on the good things that come from you. And if I prove to be remiss, do you take on yourself to provide both things, not only what you yourself give but equally what you furnish in my place. For it befits you as a pupil of Hermes, the god of eloquence, or, if you

καὶ τρόφιμον ὄντα σε, τὴν ἐκείνου ῥάβδον οὐκ ἐν τῷ καθεύδειν ποιεῖν, ἀλλ᾿ ἐν τῷ κινεῖν καὶ διεγείρειν μᾶλλον ἐθέλειν μιμεῖσθαι.

79

Τῷ αὐτῷ[1]

405 Ὀδυσσεῖ μὲν ἐξήρκει τοῦ παιδὸς τὴν ἐφ᾿ αὑτῷ
B φαντασίαν ἀναστέλλοντι λέγειν

οὔτις τοι θεός εἰμι· τί μ᾿ ἀθανάτοισιν ἐΐσκεις;

ἐγὼ δὲ οὐδ᾿ ἐν ἀνθρώποις εἶναι φαίην ἂν ὅλως, ἕως ἂν Ἰαμβλίχῳ μὴ συνῶ. ἀλλ᾿ ἐραστὴς μὲν εἶναι σὸς ὁμολογῶ, καθάπερ ἐκεῖνος τοῦ Τηλε-
C μάχου πατήρ. κἂν γὰρ ἀνάξιόν με λέγῃ τις εἶναι, οὐδὲ οὕτω τοῦ ποθεῖν ἀφαιρήσεται· ἐπεὶ καὶ ἀγαλμάτων καλῶν ἀκούω πολλοὺς ἐραστὰς γενέσθαι μὴ μόνον τοῦ δημιουργοῦ τὴν τέχνην μὴ βλάπτοντας, ἀλλὰ καὶ τῷ περὶ αὐτὰ πάθει τὴν ἔμψυχον ἡδονὴν τῷ ἔργῳ προστιθέντας. τῶν γε μὴν παλαιῶν καὶ σοφῶν ἀνδρῶν, οἷς ἡμᾶς ἐγκρίνειν ἐθέλεις παίζων, τοσοῦτον ἀπέχειν ἂν
D φαίην, ὁπόσον αὐτῷ σοι τῶν ἀνδρῶν μετεῖναι πιστεύω. καίτοι σύ γε οὐ Πίνδαρον μόνον οὐδὲ Δημόκριτον ἢ Ὀρφέα τὸν παλαιότατον, ἀλλὰ καὶ ξύμπαν ὁμοῦ τὸ Ἑλληνικόν, ὁπόσον εἰς ἄκρον φιλοσοφίας ἐλθεῖν μνημονεύεται, καθάπερ ἐν λύρᾳ ποικίλων φθόγγων ἐναρμονίῳ συστάσει πρὸς τὸ ἐντελὲς τῆς μουσικῆς κεράσας ἔχεις.
406 καὶ ὥσπερ Ἄργον τὸν φύλακα τῆς Ἰοῦς οἱ μῦθοι

[1] Hertlein 34, with title Ἰαμβλίχῳ φιλοσόφῳ.

prefer, his nursling, to desire to imitate his use of the wand, not by putting men to sleep, but by rousing and awakening them.

79

To the Same

When Odysseus was trying to remove his son's illusion about him, it was enough for him to say: "No God am I. Why then do you liken me to the immortals?"[1] But I might say that I do not exist at all among men so long as I am not with Iamblichus. Nay, I admit that I am your lover, even as Odysseus that he was the father of Telemachus. For even though someone should say that I am unworthy, not even so shall he deprive me of my longing. For I have heard that many men have fallen in love with beautiful statues[2] and far from injuring the art of the craftsman they have by their passion for them imparted to the workmanship the added delight in what lives and breathes. But as for the wise men of old among whom you are pleased to reckon me in jest, I should say that I fall as far short of them as I believe that you are to be ranked among them. And indeed you have succeeded in combining with yourself not only Pindar or Democritus or most ancient Orpheus, but also that whole genius of the Hellenes which is on record as having attained to the summit of philosophy, even as in a lyre by the harmonious combination of various notes the perfection of music is achieved. And just as the myths give Argus, Io's guardian, an encircling ring of ever-

[1] *Odyssey* 16. 187.
[2] For such cases cf. Aelian, *Varia Historia* 9. 39.

πρόνοιαν ἔχοντα τῶν Διὸς παιδικῶν ἀκοιμήτοις
πανταχόθεν ὀμμάτων βολαῖς περιφράττουσιν,
οὕτω καὶ σὲ γνήσιον ἀρετῆς φύλακα μυρίοις
παιδεύσεως ὀφθαλμοῖς ὁ λόγος φωτίζει. Πρωτέα
μὲν δὴ τὸν Αἰγύπτιόν φασι ποικίλαις μορφαῖς ἑαυ-
τὸν ἐξαλλάττειν, ὥσπερ δεδιότα μὴ λάθῃ τοῖς δε-
B ομένοις ὡς ἦν σοφὸς ἐκφήνας· ἐγὼ δὲ εἴπερ ἦν ὄντως
σοφὸς ὁ Πρωτεὺς καὶ οἷος[1] πολλὰ τῶν ὄντων
γινώσκειν, ὡς Ὅμηρος λέγει, τῆς μὲν φύσεως
αὐτὸν ἐπαινῶ, τῆς γνώμης δ' οὐκ ἄγαμαι, διότι
μὴ φιλανθρώπου τινός, ἀλλ' ἀπατεῶνος ἔργον
ἐποίει κρύπτων ἑαυτόν, ἵνα μὴ χρήσιμος ἀνθρώ-
ποις ᾖ. σὲ δέ, ὦ γενναῖε, τίς οὐκ ἂν ἀληθῶς
θαυμάσειεν, ὡς οὐδέν τι τοῦ Πρωτέως τοῦ σοφοῦ
C μείων εἶ,[2] εἰ μὴ καὶ μᾶλλον εἰς ἀρετὴν ἄκραν
τελεσθεὶς ὧν ἔχεις καλῶν οὐ φθονεῖς ἀνθρώποις,
ἀλλ' ἡλίου καθαροῦ δίκην ἀκτῖνας σοφίας ἀκραι-
φνοῦς ἐπὶ πάντας ἄγεις, οὐ μόνον παροῦσι
τὰ εἰκότα ξυνών, ἀλλὰ καὶ ἀπόντας ἐφ' ὅσον
ἔξεστι τοῖς παρὰ σαυτοῦ σεμνύνων. νικῴης δ'
ἂν οὕτω καὶ τὸν Ὀρφέα τὸν καλὸν οἷς πράττεις,
εἴγε ὁ μὲν τὴν οἰκείαν μουσικὴν εἰς τὰς τῶν
θηρίων ἀκοὰς κατανάλισκε, σὺ δ' ὥσπερ ἐπὶ
D σωτηρίᾳ τοῦ κοινοῦ τῶν ἀνθρώπων γένους τεχ-
θείς, τὴν Ἀσκληπιοῦ χεῖρα πανταχοῦ ζηλῶν,
ἅπαντα ἐπέρχῃ λογίῳ τε καὶ σωτηρίῳ νεύματι.[3]

[1] οἷός τε ? Hertlein.
[2] εἶ, εἰ μὴ καὶ *Baroccianus*; εἶ καὶ μὴ Vossianus, εἰ μὴ καὶ Hertlein.
[3] πνεύματι "breath," Martin.

wakeful eyes as he keeps watch over the darling of Zeus, so too does true report endow you, the trusted guardian of virtue, with the light of the countless eyes of culture. They say that Proteus the Egyptian used to change himself into various shapes[1] as though he feared being taken unawares and showing those who needed his aid that he was wise. But for my part, if Proteus was really wise and the sort of man to know the truth about many things, as Homer says, I applaud him for his talent, but I cannot admire his attitude of mind, since he played the part, not of one who loves mankind, but of an impostor by concealing himself in order to avoid being of service to mankind. But who, my noble friend, would not genuinely admire you, since though you are inferior in no way to wise Proteus if not even more fully initiated than he in consummate virtues, you do not begrudge mankind the blessings that you possess, but, like the bright sun, you cause the rays of your pure wisdom to shine on all men, not only by associating, as is natural, with those near you, but also as far as possible by making the absent proud through your writings. And in this way by your achievements you surpass even charming Orpheus; for he squandered on the ears of wild beasts his own peculiar musical gift, but you, as though you had been born to save the whole human race, emulate everywhere the hand of Asclepius and pervade all things with the saving power of your

[1] *Odyssey* 4. 363 foll. ; Vergil, *Georgics* 4. 388 foll.

ὥστ᾽ ἔμοιγε δοκεῖ καὶ Ὅμηρος, εἰ ἀνεβίω, πολλῷ δικαιότερον ἂν ἐπὶ σοὶ τὸ ἔπος αἰνίξασθαι τὸ

εἷς δ᾽ ἔτι που ζωὸς κατερύκεται εὐρέι κόσμῳ.

τῷ γὰρ ὄντι τοῦ παλαιοῦ κόμματος ἡμῖν οἱονεὶ σπινθήρ τις ἱερὸς ἀληθοῦς καὶ γονίμου παιδεύσεως ὑπὸ σοὶ μόνῳ ζωπυρεῖται. καὶ εἴη γε, Ζεῦ σῶτερ
407 καὶ Ἑρμῆ λόγιε, τὸ κοινὸν ἁπάσης τῆς οἰκουμένης ὄφελος, Ἰάμβλιχον τὸν καλόν, ἐπὶ μήκιστον χρόνου τηρεῖσθαι. πάντως που καὶ ἐφ᾽ Ὁμήρῳ καὶ Πλάτωνι καὶ Σωκράτει[1] καὶ εἴ τις ἄλλος ἄξιος τοῦ χοροῦ τούτου, δικαίας εὐχῆς ἐπίτευγμα τοῖς πρότερον εὐτυχηθὲν οὕτω τοὺς ἐκείνων καιροὺς ἐπὶ μεῖζον ηὔξησεν. οὐδὲν δὴ κωλύει καὶ ἐφ᾽ ἡμῶν ἄνδρα καὶ λόγῳ καὶ βίῳ τῶν
B ἀνδρῶν ἐκείνων ἀντάξιον ὑφ᾽ ὁμοίαις εὐχαῖς ἐς τὸ ἀκρότατον τοῦ γήρως ἐπ᾽ εὐδαιμονίᾳ τῶν ἀνθρώπων παραπεμφθῆναι.

80

390 Σαραπίωνι τῷ λαμπροτάτῳ[2]

B Ἄλλοι μὲν ἄλλως τὰς πανηγύρεις νομίζουσιν, ἐγὼ δὲ ἡδύ σοι γλυκείας ἑορτῆς σύνθημα τῶν ἐπι-

[1] Ἰσοκράτει Cumont, since Socrates was only seventy when he died.

[2] Hertlein 24.

---

[1] *Odyssey* 4. 498. The original verse ends with πόντῳ,

eloquence. Wherefore I think that Homer, too, if he were to return to life, would with far more justice allude to you in the verse:

"One is still alive and is detained in the wide world."[1]

For, in very truth, for those of us who are of the antique mould, a sacred spark, so to speak, of true and life-giving culture is kindled by your aid alone. And grant, O Zeus the saviour, and Hermes, god of eloquence, that this blessing which is the common property of the whole world, even the charming Iamblichus, may be preserved for the longest possible period of time! Indeed, there is no doubt that in the case of Homer and Plato and Socrates[2] and others who were worthy to be of that company, the prayers of the just were successful and did avail men of old, and thus increased and prolonged the natural term of those great men's lives. So there is no reason why in our day, also, a man who in his eloquence and virtuous life is the peer of those famous men, should not by means of similar prayers be conducted to the extreme limit of old age for the happiness of mankind.

80

To the most illustrious Sarapion[3]

People observe the public festivals in various ways. But I am sending you a hundred long-stalked, dried, homegrown figs as a sweet token of this

"on the sea"; the verse was a rhetorical commonplace and the ending is often altered to suit the context.

[2] There would be more point in the reading "Isocrates" (Cumont) since he lived to be nearly one hundred.

[3] Sarapion is otherwise unknown.

C χωρίων ἰσχάδων μακροκέντρους ἑκατὸν ἐκπέμπω,
τῷ μὲν τοῦ δώρου μεγέθει μικράν, τῷ κάλλει δὲ
ἴσως ἀρκοῦσαν ἡδονὴν μνηστεύων. Ἀριστοφάνει
μὲν οὖν δοκεῖ εἶναι πλὴν μέλιτος τῶν ἄλλων γλυ-
κύτερον τὰς ἰσχάδας, καὶ οὐδὲ τοῦτ' ἀνέχεται τῶν
ἰσχάδων εἶναι γλυκύτερον, ὡς αὐτὸς ἐπικρίνας
λέγει·[1] Ἡροδότῳ δὲ ἄρα τῷ συγγραφεῖ πρὸς ἐπί-
δειξιν ἐρημίας ἀληθοῦς ἤρκεσεν εἰπόντι "Παρ'
D οἷς οὔτε σῦκά ἐστιν οὔτε ἄλλο ἀγαθὸν οὐδέν," ὡς
ἄρ' οὔτε ἄλλου τινὸς ἐν καρποῖς ἀγαθοῦ προτέρου
τῶν σύκων ὄντος, οὔτε ἔτι πάντως ἀγαθοῦ δέον
τοῖς[1] παρ' οἷς ἂν ᾖ τὸ σῦκον. Ὅμηρος δὲ ὁ σοφὸς
τὰ μὲν ἄλλα τῶν καρπῶν εἰς μέγεθος ἢ χρόαν ἢ
κάλλος ἐπαινεῖ, μόνῳ δὲ τῷ σύκῳ τὴν τῆς γλυκύ-
τητος ἐπωνυμίαν συγχωρεῖ. καὶ τὸ μέλι χλωρὸν
391 καλεῖ, δεδιὼς μὴ λάθῃ γλυκὺ προσειπών, ὃ καὶ
πικρὸν εἶναι πολλαχοῦ συμβαίνει· τῷ σύκῳ δὲ
ἄρα μόνῳ ἀποδίδωσι τὴν οἰκείαν εὐφημίαν, ὥσπερ
τῷ νέκταρι, διότι καὶ μόνον γλυκὺ τῶν ἄλλων ἐστί.
καὶ μέλι μὲν Ἱπποκράτης φησὶ γλυκὺ μὲν εἶναι
τὴν αἴσθησιν, πικρὸν δὲ πάντως τὴν ἀνάδοσιν, καὶ
οὐκ ἀπιστῶ τῷ λόγῳ· χολῆς γὰρ αὐτὸ ποιητικὸν
εἶναι ξύμπαντες ὁμολογοῦσι καὶ τρέπειν τοὺς
χυμοὺς εἰς τοὐναντίον τῆς γεύσεως. ὃ δὴ καὶ
B μᾶλλον τῆς ἐκ φύσεως αὐτοῦ πικρότητος κατη-
γορεῖ τὴν γένεσιν· οὐ γὰρ ἂν εἰς τοῦτο μετέβαλλεν
ὃ πικρόν ἐστιν, εἰ μὴ καὶ πάντως αὐτῷ προσῆν
ἐξ ἀρχῆς τοῦτο, ἀφ' οὗ πρὸς τὸ ἕτερον μετέπιπτε.

[1] δέον τοῖς Hertlein suggests; δέοντος MSS.

[1] Quoted in Athenaeus, *Deipnosophists* 652F; *Fragg. Incert. Fab.* 7 οὐδὲν γὰρ ὄντως γλυκύτερον τῶν ἰσχάδων.

pleasant festal season. If you measure the gift by its size, the pleasure I offer you is trifling, but if measured by its beauty it will perhaps suffice. It is the opinion of Aristophanes[1] that figs are sweeter than anything else except honey, and on second thoughts he does not allow that even honey is sweeter than figs. Herodotus[2] the historian also, in order to describe a really barren desert thought it enough to say: "They have no figs or anything else that is good"; as though to say that among the fruits of the earth there is none to be ranked above figs, and that where men had figs they did not wholly lack something good. Again, the wise Homer praises other fruits for their size or colour or beauty, but to the fig alone he allows the epithet "sweet."[3] And he calls honey "yellow,"[4] for fear he should inadvertently call "sweet" what is in fact often bitter; accordingly, to the fig alone[5] he assigns this epithet for its own, just as he does to nectar, because alone of all things it is sweet. Indeed Hippocrates[6] says that honey, though it is sweet to the taste, is quite bitter to the digestion, and I can believe his statement; for all agree that it produces bile and turns the juices to the very opposite of its original flavour, which fact even more surely convicts it of being in its origin naturally bitter.[7] For it would not change to this bitterness if in the beginning this quality had not belonged to it, from which it changed to the

[2] 1. 71. [3] *Odyssey* 7. 116. [4] *Odyssey* 10. 234.

[5] Homer does however call honey "sweet" in *Odyssey* 20. 69 μέλιτι γλυκερῷ.

[6] *De internis affectionibus* 84A; Hippocrates is speaking of honey that has been cooked.

[7] *Oration* 8. 241A, Julian says that honey is made from the bitterest herbs.

σῦκον δὲ οὐκ αἰσθήσει μόνον ἡδύ, ἀλλὰ καὶ ἀναδόσει κρεῖττόν ἐστιν. οὕτω δέ ἐστιν ἀνθρώποις ὠφέλιμον, ὥστε καὶ ἀλεξιφάρμακον αὐτὸ παντὸς ὀλεθρίου φαρμάκου φησὶν Ἀριστοτέλης εἶναι, κἂν τοῖς δείπνοις οὐκ ἄλλου τινὸς ἢ τούτου χάριν τῶν ἐδεσμάτων προπαρατίθεσθαί τε καὶ ἐπιτραγηματίζεσθαι,
C καθάπερ ἀντ' ἄλλης τινὸς ἀλεξήσεως ἱερᾶς ταῖς τῶν βρωμάτων ἀδικίαις περιπτυσσόμενον. καὶ μὴν ὅτι καὶ θεοῖς τὸ σῦκον ἀνάκειται, καὶ θυσίας ἐστὶν ἁπάσης ἐμβώμιον, καὶ ὅτι παντὸς λιβανωτοῦ κρεῖττον ἐς θυμιάματος σκευασίαν ἐστίν, οὐκ ἐμὸς ἴδιος οὗτος ὁ λόγος, ἀλλ' ὅστις τὴν χρείαν αὐτοῦ ἔμαθεν, οἶδεν ὡς ἀνδρὸς σοφοῦ καὶ ἱεροφάντου λόγος ἐστί. Θεόφραστος δὲ ὁ καλὸς ἐν γεωργίας παραγγέλμασι τὰς τῶν ἑτεροφύτων
D δένδρων γενέσεις ἐκτιθεὶς καὶ ὅσα ἀλληλούχοις ἐγκεντρίσεσιν εἴκει, πάντων, οἶμαι, τῶν φυτῶν μᾶλλον ἐπαινεῖ τῆς συκῆς τὸ δένδρον ὡς ἂν ποικίλης καὶ διαφόρου γενέσεως δεκτικὸν καὶ μόνον τῶν ἄλλων εὔκολον παντοίου γένους ἐνεγκεῖν βλάστην, εἴ τις αὐτοῦ τῶν κλάδων ἐκτεμὼν ἕκαστον, εἶτα ἐκρήξας ἄλλην ἐς ἄλλο τῶν πρέμνων ἐμφυῆ
392 γονὴν ἐναρμόσειεν, ὡς ἀρκεῖν ἤδη πολλάκις αὐτοῦ καὶ ἀνθ' ὁλοκλήρου κήπου τὴν ὄψιν, οἷον ἐν λειμῶνι χαριεστάτῳ ποικίλην τινὰ καὶ πολυειδῆ τῶν καρπῶν ἀφ' ἑαυτοῦ τὴν ἀγλαΐαν ἀντιπεπομφότος. καὶ τὰ μὲν ἄλλα τῶν ἀκροδρύων ἐστὶν ὀλιγοχρόνια καὶ τὴν μονὴν οὐκ ἀνέχεται, μόνῳ δὲ τῷ σύκῳ καὶ ὑπερενιαυτίζειν ἔξεστι καὶ τῇ τοῦ μέλλοντος

[1] Aristotle, *Frag.* 105, Rose.

reverse. But the fig is not only sweet to taste but it is still better for digestion. And it is so beneficial to mankind that Aristotle[1] even says that it is an antidote for every deadly poison, and that for no other reason than this is it served before other food as a first course at meals and then at the end for dessert, as though we embraced it in preference to any other sacred means of averting the injury caused by the things we eat. Moreover, that the fig is offered to the gods also, and is set on the altar in every sacrifice, and that it is better than any frankincense for making fragrant fumes, this is a statement not made by me alone,[2] but whoever is acquainted with its use knows that it is the statement of a wise man, a hierophant. Again, the admirable Theophrastus[3] in his precepts of agriculture, when he is describing the kinds of grafted trees and what sorts admit of being grafted on one another, commends the fig tree above all other plants, if I am not mistaken, as being able to receive various and different kinds, and as the only one of them all that easily bears a growth of any other sort, if you cut out every one of its boughs and then break off and insert a different engrafted stock into each of the cleft stumps; hence to look at it is often equivalent to a complete garden, since it returns you the variegated and manifold splendours of other fruits, as happens in the loveliest orchard. And whereas the fruits of other fruit-bearing trees are short-lived and cannot last for any time, the fig alone can survive beyond the year, and is present at the birth

[2] A Julianic commonplace, cf. note on Vol. 2 *Fragment of a Letter* 299c, and above, p. 222.

[3] *Enquiry into Plants* 2. 5. 6.

καρποῦ γενέσει συνενεχθῆναι. ὥστε φησὶ καὶ Ὅμηρος ἐν Ἀλκίνου κήπῳ τοὺς καρποὺς ἀλλήλοις
B ἐπιγηράσκειν. ἐπὶ μὲν οὖν τῶν ἄλλων ἴσως ἂν μῦθος ποιητικὸς εἶναι δόξειε· μόνῳ δὲ τῷ σύκῳ πρὸς τὸ τῆς ἀληθείας ἐναργὲς ἂν συμφέροιτο, διότι καὶ μόνον τῶν ἄλλων καρπῶν ἐστὶ μονιμώτερον. τοιαύτην δὲ ἔχον, οἶμαι, τὸ σῦκον τὴν φύσιν, πολλῷ κρεῖττόν ἐστι παρ' ἡμῖν τὴν γένεσιν, ὡς εἶναι τῶν μὲν ἄλλων φυτῶν αὐτὸ τιμιώτερον, αὐτοῦ δὲ τοῦ σύκου τὸ παρ' ἡμῖν θαυμασιώτερον, καὶ νικᾶν μὲν αὐτὸ τῶν ἄλλων τὴν γένεσιν, αὖθις δ' ὑπὸ τοῦ
C παρ' ἡμῖν ἡττᾶσθαι καὶ τῇ πρὸς ἑκάτερον ἐγκρίσει πάλιν σώζεσθαι, κρατοῦντι μὲν ἐοικός, οἷς δ' αὖ κρατεῖσθαι δοκεῖ, πάλιν ἐς τὸ καθόλου νικῶντι. καὶ τοῦτο οὐκ ἀπεικότως παρ' ἡμῖν μόνοις συμβαίνει· ἔδει γάρ, οἶμαι, τὴν Διὸς πόλιν ἀληθῶς καὶ τὸν τῆς ἑῴας ἁπάσης ὀφθαλμόν· τὴν ἱερὰν καὶ μεγίστην Δαμασκὸν λέγω· τοῖς τε ἄλλοις σύμπασιν, οἷον ἱερῶν κάλλει καὶ νεῶν μεγέθει καὶ ὡρῶν εὐκρασίᾳ[1] καὶ πηγῶν ἀγλαΐᾳ, καὶ ποταμῶν πλή-
D θει καὶ γῆς εὐφορίᾳ νικῶσαν μόνην ἄρα καὶ τῷ τοιούτῳ φυτῷ πρὸς τὴν τοῦ θαύματος ὑπεροχὴν ἀρκέσαι. οὐδὲν οὖν ἀνέχεται μεταβολῆς τὸ δένδρον, οὐδὲ ὑπερβαίνει τοὺς ἐπιχωρίους ὅρους τῆς βλάστης, ἀλλ' αὐτόχθονος φυτοῦ νόμῳ τὴν ἐξ ἀποικίας γένεσιν ἀρνεῖται. καὶ χρυσὸς μέν, οἶμαι,

[1] εὐκρασίᾳ Cobet cf. *Timaeus* 24 C, εὐκαιρίᾳ Hertlein, MSS.

---

[1] *Odyssey* 7. 120.

of the fruit that is to follow it. Hence Homer[1] also says that in the garden of Alcinous the fruits "wax old on" one another. Now in the case of other fruits this might perhaps seem to be a poetic fiction, but for the fig alone it would be consistent with the plain fact, because alone of all fruits it lasts for some time. Such, I think, is the nature of the fig in general, but the kind that grows with us is much better than others; so that in proportion as the fig is more valuable than other plants, our fig is more admirable than the fig in general; and while the latter in its kind surpasses all other fruits, it is in its turn excelled by ours, and again holds its own by comparison in both respects, first in being plainly superior, and secondly, in points where it seems to be inferior it wins on the general count. And it is quite natural that this should be so in our country alone. For it was fitting, I think, that the city which in very truth belongs to Zeus and is the eye of the whole East,—I mean sacred and most mighty Damascus,—[2] which in all other respects bears the palm, for instance, for the beauty of its shrines and the size of its temples and for its exquisitely tempered climate and the splendour of its fountains, the number of its rivers and the fertility of its soil—I say it is fitting that she alone should keep up her reputation by the possession of a plant of this excellence and thus excite an excess of admiration. Accordingly our tree does not brook transplanting, nor does it overstep the natural boundaries of its growth, but as though by a law that governs the indigenous plant refuses to grow in colonies abroad. The same sorts of gold and silver are, I believe,

[2] Julian, as far as we know, never visited Damascus.

καὶ ἄργυρος ὁ αὐτὸς πολλαχοῦ φύεται, μόνη δὲ ἡ παρ' ἡμῖν χώρα τίκτει φυτὸν ἀλλαχοῦ φῦναι μὴ
393 δυνάμενον. ὥσπερ δὲ τὰ ἐξ Ἰνδῶν ἀγώγιμα καὶ οἱ Περσικοὶ σῆρες ἢ ὅσα ἐν τῇ Αἰθιόπων γῇ τίκτεται μὲν καὶ λέγεται,[1] τῷ δὲ τῆς ἐμπορίας νόμῳ πανταχοῦ διαβαίνει· οὕτω δὴ[2] καὶ τὸ παρ' ἡμῖν σῦκον, ἀλλαχοῦ τῆς γῆς οὐ γινόμενον, πανταχοῦ παρ' ἡμῶν στέλλεται, καὶ οὔτε πόλις οὔτε νῆσός ἐστιν, ἣν οὐκ ἐπέρχεται τῷ τῆς ἡδονῆς θαύματι. ἀλλὰ καὶ τράπεζαν βασιλικὴν κοσμεῖ, καὶ παντὸς
B δείπνου σεμνόν ἐστιν ἐγκαλλώπισμα, καὶ οὔτ' ἔνθρυπτον οὔτε στρεπτὸν οὔτε νεήλατον οὔτε ἄλλο καρυκείας γένος ἥδυσμα ἴσον ᾗ ἂν ἀφίκηται·[3] τοσοῦτον αὐτῷ τῶν τε ἄλλων ἐδεσμάτων καὶ δὴ καὶ τῶν ἑκασταχοῦ σύκων[4] περίεστι τοῦ θαύματος. καὶ τὰ μὲν ἄλλα τῶν σύκων ἢ ὀπωρινὴν ἔχει τὴν βρῶσιν ἢ τερσαινόμενα ἐς τὸ ταμεῖον[5] ἔρχεται, τὸ δὲ παρ' ἡμῖν μόνον ἀμφοτερίζει τῇ χρείᾳ, καὶ καλὸν μέν ἐστιν ἐπιδένδριον, πολλῷ δὲ κάλλιον, εἰ ἐς
C τὴν τερσιὰν ἔλθοι. εἰ δὲ καὶ τὴν ὥραν αὐτοῦ τὴν ἐν τοῖς δένδροις ὀφθαλμῷ λάβοις, καὶ ὅπως ἑκάστου τῶν πρέμνων ἐπιμήκεσι τοῖς κέντροις οἱονεὶ καλύκων δίκην ἀπήρτηται, ἢ ὅπως ἐν κύκλῳ περιθεῖ τῷ καρπῷ τὸ δένδρον, ἄλλας ἐπ' ἄλλαις ἐν στοίχῳ[6] περιφερεῖ πολυειδεῖς ἀγλαΐας μηχανᾶσθαι[7] φαίης ἂν αὐτὸ καθάπερ ἐν ὅρμῳ δέρης. αἱ

[1] λέγεται MSS., Bidez would retain = colliguntur, Hertlein σρέφεται.

[2] οὕτω δὲ Hertlein in error for MSS., δή, restored by Bidez.

[3] Hercher and Hertlein οὔτ' ἂν—οὐδὲν ἐς τὸ ἴσον ἀφίκοιτο; MSS οὔτ'—ἔσται ἥδυσμα ἴσον ᾗ; Bidez οὔτ'—ἥδυσμα ἴσον ᾗ (cf. Thucydides 2. 100 = "where") ἂν ἀφίκηται.

[4] After ἑκασταχοῦ Hertlein suggests σύκων.

produced in many places, but our country alone gives birth to a plant that cannot be grown anywhere else. And just like the wares of India, or Persian silks, or all that is produced and collected in the country of the Ethiopians but travels everywhere by the law of commerce, so, too, our native fig does not grow anywhere else on earth, but is exported by us to all parts, and there is no city or island to which it does not travel, because it is so much admired for its sweet flavour. Moreover it even adorns the imperial table and is the boast and ornament of every feast; and there is no cake or roll or pastry [1] or any kind of confectionery to match it as a sweetmeat wherever it comes; so far does it surpass in admirable qualities all other dainties, and moreover all figs from any other place. Again, other figs are either eaten in autumn, or are dried and go to the store-room, but the fig of our country alone can be used in both ways, and though it is good while on the tree it is far better when it has been dried. And should you see with your own eyes their beauty while they are still on the trees, and how from each one of the branches they hang by long stalks like flower-buds, so to speak, or again, how with their fruit they completely encircle the tree, then you would say that by this circular series one above another they compose a splendid and varied picture even as a neck in its necklace. Then again, the manner in

[1] An echo of Demosthenes, *On the Crown* 260 ἔνθρυπτα καὶ στρεπτοὺς καὶ νεήλατα.

---

[5] Thomas; ὅμοιον MSS.
[6] στοίχῳ MSS., Bidez; τοίχῳ *Vossianus*, Hertlein.
[7] μηχανώμενον, φαίης Hertlein, MSS.; μηχανᾶσθαι φαίης Bidez.

δὲ[1] τῶν δένδρων ἐξαιρέσεις αὐτοῦ[2] καὶ ἡ πρὸς
D χρονίαν μονὴν ἐπιτέχνησις οὐκ ἐλάττονα τῆς ἐς
τὴν χρείαν ἡδονῆς ἔχει τὴν φιλοτιμίαν· οὐ γὰρ
ὥσπερ τὰ ἄλλα τῶν σύκων ὁμοῦ καὶ κατὰ ταὐτὸν
ἔρριπται, οὐδὲ σωρηδὸν ἢ χύδην ἡλίῳ τερσαίνεται,
ἀλλὰ πρῶτον μὲν ἠρέμα τῶν δένδρων αὐτὰ ταῖς
χερσὶν ἀποδρέπουσιν, ἔπειτα ὅρπηξιν ἢ ῥάβδοις
ἀκανθώδεσι τῶν τοίχων ἀπαρτῶσιν, ἵνα λευκαί-
νηται μὲν ἡλίῳ καθαρῷ προσομιλοῦντα, μένῃ δ'
ἀνεπιβούλευτα τῶν ζῴων καὶ τῶν ὀρνιθίων, οἱονεὶ
394 τῶν κέντρων τῇ ἀλεξήσει δορυφορούμενα. καὶ
περὶ μὲν γενέσεως αὐτῶν καὶ γλυκύτητος καὶ
ὥρας καὶ ποιήσεως καὶ χρείας ταῦτά σοι παρ'
ἡμῶν ἡ ἐπιστολὴ προσπαίζει.

Ὅ γε μὴν τῶν ἑκατὸν ἀριθμὸς ὡς ἔστι τῶν
ἄλλων τιμιώτερος καὶ τὸ τέλεον ἐν αὐτῷ τῶν ἀρι-
θμῶν περιγράφων, μάθοι ἄν τις θεωρῶν τῇδε. καὶ
οὐκ ἀγνοῶ μὲν ὡς παλαιῶν καὶ σοφῶν ἀνδρῶν ὁ
λόγος, τοῦ ἀρτίου τὸν περιττὸν προκεῖσθαι, οὐδὲ
ὡς ἀρχήν φασιν αὐξήσεως εἶναι τὸ μὴ συνδυάζον·
τὸ γὰρ ὅμοιον θατέρῳ μένειν ὁποῖον καὶ τὸ ἕτερον,
B δυοῖν δὲ γενομένοιν τὸν τρίτον εἶναι τὴν περιτ-
τότητα. ἐγὼ δ' ἄν, εἰ καὶ τολμηρότερος ὁ λόγος
ἐστί, φαίην ὅμως· ἀρχῆς μὲν εἰσιν οἱ ἀριθμοὶ
πάντως ἐξηρτημένοι, καὶ τὸ προσεχὲς τῆς αὐξή-
σεως διὰ παντὸς ἂν κομίζοιντο. πολλῷ γε μὴν
οἶμαι δικαιότερον τῷ ἀρτίῳ μᾶλλον ἢ τῷ περιττῷ
τὴν τῆς αὐξήσεως αἰτίαν προσκεῖσθαι. ὁ μὲν

[1] αὐτὸ—δέρης. αἱ δὲ Bidez; αὐτῷ—δέρης τὰς Hertlein, MSS.

[2] αὐτοῦ καὶ ἡ Bidez; αὐτοῦ. καὶ ἡ Hertlein, MSS.

which they are taken from the tree and the means employed for preserving them for a long time involve quite as much outlay as the pleasure derived from their use. For they are not, like other kinds of figs, thrown together in one place, nor are they dried in the sun in heaps or promiscuously; but first they are gathered carefully by hand from the trees, then they are hung on walls by means of sticks or thorny twigs, so that they may be bleached by exposure to the direct rays of the sun while they are also safe from the attacks of animals and small birds, since the protection of the prickles furnishes them with a sort of bodyguard. So far my letter to you deals with their origin, sweetness, beauty, confection, and use, and is in lighter vein.

Now to consider the number one hundred,[1] which is more honourable than any other and contains in itself the perfection of all numbers, as one may learn from the following considerations. I am indeed well aware that there is a saying of wise men of old that an odd number is to be preferred to an even, and they declare that the source of increase is that which does not couple. For in a pair the one term being equal to the other remains of the same quality, but when there are two numbers the third produces oddness. But for my part, even though the statement is somewhat bold, I would nevertheless say this: Numbers surely depend on a generative principle, and can carry on consecutive increase through the whole series. But I hold that it is far more just to assign the cause of that increase to the even than to the odd number. For the number one

[1] He was sending one hundred figs.

C γὰρ εἷς ἀριθμὸς οὐκ ἂν εἴη περιττός, οὐκ ἔχων
ὅτου περιττὸς γένοιτο· ἡ δὲ τῆς δυάδος συζυγία
τίκτει διπλῆν τὴν περιττότητα, κἀκ τῶν δυοῖν
ἀριθμῶν ὁ τρίτος εἰκότως εἰς αὔξησιν ἔρχεται.
πάλιν τε ἐν τῇ τῆς ἑτέρας δυάδος μίξει τῆς τετρά-
δος τὴν ὑπεροχὴν λαμβάνει, καὶ ὅλως ἡ πρὸς
ἄλληλα κοινωνία τὴν ἐξ ἑκατέρου περιττότητα φαί-
νουσα εἰς τὸν τῆς δυάδος ἀριθμὸν περικλείεται.
δεδομένου δὴ τούτου, φαίην ἄν, οἶμαι, τῆς πρώτης
δεκάδος τὴν εἰς αὑτὴν περιφέρειαν ἀνακυκλούσης
D εἰς τὸν τῆς ἑκατοντάδος ἀριθμὸν τὸ ὅλον δια-
βαίνειν, ὡς τῷ μὲν ἑνὶ τὴν αὔξησιν ἂν εἰς δέκα
συντείνειν, πάλιν δ' αὖ τὴν δεκάδα δι' αὑτῆς ἀνι-
οῦσαν εἰς τὸν τῶν ἑκατὸν ἀριθμὸν συντελεῖσθαι.
κἀντεῦθεν αὖ πάλιν ἐξ ἑκατοντάδων τὸ ὅλον τῶν
ἀριθμῶν τὴν δύναμιν καρποῦσθαι, μήτε τοῦ ἑνὸς
ἠρεμοῦντος, εἰ μή τι τῆς δυάδος ἐν τῇ μίξει τὸ
περιττὸν ἀεὶ τικτούσης τε καὶ εἰς ἑαυτὴν αὖθις
ἀνακαλουμένης, ἄχρις ἂν ἑτέρᾳ πάλιν ἑκατοντάδι
τῶν ἀριθμῶν τὸ συναγόμενον κατακλείσῃ, καὶ τὸ
395 τέλεον αὐτῷ προσάπτουσα πάλιν ἐξ αὐτοῦ πρὸς
τὸ ἕτερον ἑρπύσῃ, ταῖς τῶν ἑκατοντάδων ἐπηγο-
ρίαις ἀεὶ τὸ ὅλον εἰς τὸ τῆς καταλήψεως ἄπειρον
ἀναφέρουσα. δοκεῖ δέ μοι καὶ Ὅμηρος οὐχ ἁπλῶς
οὐδὲ ἀργῶς ἐν τοῖς ἔπεσι τὴν ἑκατονταθύσανον
αἰγίδα τῷ Διὶ περιθεῖναι, ἀλλά τινι κρείττονι καὶ
ἀπορρήτῳ λόγῳ τοῦτο αἰνίττεσθαι λέγων, ὡς ἄρα

---

[1] *i.e.* 1 is now odd in relation to 2, and their combination results in 3, an odd number.

[2] *i.e.* when ten is multiplied by ten.

is not odd, when it has no number in respect to which it were odd. But its coupling with two produces twofold oddness,[1] and the number three, coming from the two, naturally proceeds as increase. Then again when we add two to two, the result is the higher stage of the number four, and, in a word, their conjunction, while making oddness clear in each of their two elements, is constituted in the number two. This being granted, I should say, of course, that when the first decad is revolving on itself in a circle,[2] the whole series progresses to the number one hundred, so that by the number one the increase amounts to ten, and the decad in turn is added each time to itself, and the total is reached in the number one hundred. And starting again from this point, with the hundreds, the whole series of numbers derive their power, by the activity of the number one, except that it is the number two[3] when combined with it that ever produces the odd and again recalls it to itself, until again it concludes with a second hundred the sum of all the numbers, and, making it complete, proceeds again from it to another and under the denomination of hundreds continually carries forward the sum to the conception of infinity. So I think that Homer too in his poems does not lightly or idly assign to Zeus the hundred-tasselled ægis,[4] but in a lofty and obscure saying he hinted at this:

[3] The writer, who probably could not have explained his cryptic language, insists on the superiority of the dyad, even and feminine, to the odd number 1, regarded as the male principle.

[4] The epithet is not used in our Homer of the ægis of Zeus, but of the ægis of Athene and the girdle of Hera.

τῷ τελεωτάτῳ θεῷ τὸν τελεώτατον ἀριθμὸν περιά-
B ψειε καὶ ᾧ μόνῳ παρὰ τοὺς ἄλλους ἂν δικαιότερον κοσμοῖτο, ἢ ὅτι τὸν ξύμπαντα κόσμον, ὃν εἰς αἰγίδος σχῆμα τῷ τῆς εἰκόνος περιφερεῖ ξυνείληφεν, οὐκ ἄλλος πως ἢ ὁ τῶν ἑκατὸν ἀριθμὸς περιγράφει, τῇ κατὰ κύκλον ἑκατοντάδι τὴν ἐς τὸ ὅλον τοῦ νοητοῦ κατανόησιν ἐφαρμόττων. ὁ δ' αὐτὸς λόγος οὗτος καὶ τὸν ἑκατοντάχειρα, τὸν Βριάρεω, καθίζει
C πάρεδρον τῷ Διί, καὶ πρὸς τὴν τοῦ πατρὸς ἁμιλλᾶσθαι συγχωρεῖ δύναμιν, οἷον ἐν τῷ τοῦ ἀριθμοῦ τελέῳ τὸ τέλεον αὐτῷ τῆς ἰσχύος ἀποδιδούς. καὶ μὴν καὶ Πίνδαρος ὁ Θηβαῖος τὴν ἀναίρεσιν τὴν Τυφωέως ἐν ἐπινικίοις κηρύττων καὶ τὸ τοῦ μεγίστου τούτου γίγαντος κράτος τῷ μεγίστῳ βασιλεῖ τῶν θεῶν περιτιθεὶς οὐχ ἑτέρωθεν αὐτῷ τῆς εὐφημίας κρατύνει τὴν ὑπερβολὴν ἢ ὅτι τὸν γίγαντα τὸν ἑκατοντακέφαλον ἑνὶ βλήματι καθελεῖν ἤρκεσεν, ὡς οὔτε τινὸς ἄλλου εἰς χεῖρα τοῦ Διὸς ἐλθεῖν
D ἀντιμάχου γίγαντος νομισθέντος ἢ ὃν ἡ μήτηρ μόνον τῶν ἄλλων ἑκατὸν κεφαλαῖς ὥπλισεν, οὔτε ἑτέρου τινὸς θεῶν ἢ μόνου Διὸς ἀξιονικοτέρου πρὸς τὴν τοῦ τοσούτου γίγαντος καθαίρεσιν ὄντος. Σιμωνίδῃ δὲ ἄρα τῷ μελικῷ πρὸς τὴν Ἀπόλλωνος εὐφημίαν ἀρκεῖ τὸν θεὸν Ἕκατον προσειπόντι καὶ καθάπερ ἀντ' ἄλλου τινὸς ἱεροῦ γνωρίσματος αὐτοῦ τὴν ἐπωνυμίαν κοσμῆσαι, διότι τὸν Πύθωνα, τὸν δράκοντα, βέλεσιν ἑκατόν, ὥς φησιν, ἐχειρώ-

that to the most perfect god he attached the most perfect number, that number by which alone beyond all the others he would most fittingly be adorned, or because the whole universe which he has comprehended in the shape of an ægis, by reason of the roundness of that image, no other number than the hundred describes, and so with the round number one hundred he harmonises the conception of the intelligible world as a whole. Again, on the same principle he makes Briareus with his hundred hands the assessor of Zeus and allows him to rival his father's might, as though he expressed the perfection of his strength by means of the perfect number. Again, Pindar[1] the Theban, when he celebrates the destruction of Typhoeus in his odes of victory, and ascribes to the most mighty ruler of the gods power over this most mighty giant, rises to the highest pitch of praise simply because with one blow he was able to lay low the hundred-headed giant, as though no other giant was held worthy to fight hand to hand with Zeus than he whom, alone of all the rest, his mother had armed with a hundred heads; and as though no other of the gods save Zeus only were worthy to win a victory by the destruction of so great a giant. Simonides[2] also, the lyric poet, thinks it enough for his praise of Apollo that he should call the god "Hekatos"[3] and adorn him with this title rather than with any other sacred symbol; for this reason, that he overcame the Python, the serpent, with a hundred

[1] Pindar, *Olympian Ode* 4. 7; *Pythian* 1. 16.
[2] Simonides, *frag.* 26, Bergk.
[3] This epithet means "Far-Darter" and is misinterpreted by the writer of this letter to mean "Hundredth."

396 σατο, καὶ μᾶλλον αὐτὸν Ἕκατον ἢ Πύθιον χαίρειν
προσαγορευόμενον, οἷον ὁλοκλήρου τινὸς ἐπωνυ-
μίας συμβόλῳ προσφωνούμενον. ἥ γε μὴν τὸν
Δία θρεψαμένη νῆσος, ἡ Κρήτη, καθάπερ τροφεῖα
τῆς Διὸς ὑποδοχῆς ἀντιλαβοῦσα τῷ τῶν ἑκατὸν
πόλεων ἀριθμῷ τετίμηται. καὶ Θήβας δὲ ἄρα τὰς
ἑκατονταπύλους οὐκ ἄλλου τινὸς ἢ τούτου χάριν
ἐπαινεῖ Ὅμηρος, διότι ταῖς πύλαις ταῖς ἑκατὸν
κάλλος ἦν θαυμαστόν. καὶ σιωπῶ θεῶν ἑκατόμ-
B βας καὶ νεὼς ἑκατονταπέδους καὶ βωμοὺς ἑκατον-
τακρήπιδας καὶ τοὺς ἑκατονταδόχους ἀνδρῶνας
καὶ τὰς ἀρούρας δὲ τὰς ἑκατονταπλέθρους καὶ ὅσα
ἄλλα θεῖά τε καὶ ἀνθρώπινα τῇ τοῦ ἀριθμοῦ τοῦδε
προσηγορίᾳ συνείληπται. ὅ γε μὲν ἀριθμὸς οὗτος
οἶδε καὶ στρατιωτικὴν ὁμοῦ καὶ εἰρηνικὴν τάξιν
κοσμῆσαι, καὶ φαιδρύνει μὲν τὴν ἑκατόντανδρον
λοχαγίαν, τιμᾷ δὲ ἥδε καὶ δικαστῶν ἐς τὸ ἴσον
ἤκουσαν ἐπωνυμίαν. καί με καὶ πλείω τούτων
C ἔχοντα λέγειν ὁ τῆς ἐπιστολῆς ἐπιστρέφει νόμος·
σὺ δὲ ἀλλὰ συγγνώμην ἔχειν τῷ λόγῳ, διότι καὶ
ταῦτα πλείω τῶν ἱκανῶν εἴρηται. καὶ εἰ μὲν ἔχει
μέτριον ἐπὶ σοὶ κριτῇ κάλλος τὸ ἐγχείρημα, πάν-
τως καὶ πρὸς τοὺς ἄλλους ἔκφορον ἔσται, τῆς
παρὰ σοῦ ψήφου τὴν μαρτυρίαν δεξάμενον· εἰ δὲ
χειρὸς ἑτέρας προσδεῖται πρὸς τὸ τοῦ σκοποῦ
συμπλήρωμα, τίς ἂν σοῦ κάλλιον εἰδείη τὴν γραφὴν
εἰς κάλλος ἀκριβώσας πρὸς τὴν τῆς θέας ἡδονὴν
D ἀπολεᾶναι;[1]

[1] ἀκριβώσας—ἀπολεᾶναι (cf. ἐπιλεαίνων vol. 1, *Oration* 3. 111 D in same sense) Hertlein suggests. Hercher ἀκριβῶσαι. deleting the last six words. MSS. ἀκριβώσαντος—ἀπολαῦσαι retained in Hertlein's text.

shafts, as he says, and the god himself took more pleasure in being addressed as "Hekatos" than as "the Pythian," as if he were thus invoked by the symbolic expression of his complete title. Then again, the island Crete which nurtured Zeus, has received as her reward, as though it were her fee for sheltering Zeus, the honour of cities to the number of one hundred. Homer[1] too praises Thebes the hundred-gated for no other reason than this that there was a marvellous beauty in her hundred gates. I say nothing of the hecatombs of the gods and temples a hundred feet long, altars with a hundred steps, rooms that hold a hundred men, fields of a hundred acres and other things divine and human which are classed together because they have this number for their epithet. It is a number, moreover, that has the power to adorn official rank both for war and peace, and while it lends brilliance to a company of a hundred soldiers it also confers distinction on the title of judges[2] when their number is one hundred. And I could say more than this, but the etiquette of letter-writing deters me. But do you be indulgent to my discourse, for what I have said already is more than enough. And if my essay has in your judgement even a mediocre elegance it shall surely go forth for others to read, after receiving the testimonial of your vote; but if it need another hand to make it fulfil its aim, who better than you should know how to polish the manuscript to the point of elegance and make it smooth so as to give pleasure to the eye?

[1] *Iliad* 9. 383; *Aeneid* 3. 106.
[2] The centumviri.

81

Βασιλείῳ[1]

Τὸ ἔμφυτόν μοι ἐκ παιδόθεν γαληνὸν καὶ φιλάνθρωπον μέχρι γε τοῦ παρόντος ἐπιδεικνύμενος, πάντας ὑπηκόους ἐκομισάμην τοὺς οἰκοῦντας τὴν ὑφ᾽ ἥλιον. ἰδοὺ γὰρ πᾶν γένος βαρβάρων μέχρις ὁρίων ὠκεανοῦ ποταμοῦ δῶρά μοι κομίζον ἧκε παρὰ ποσὶ τοῖς ἐμοῖς, ὁμοίως δὲ καὶ Σαγάδαρες οἱ παρὰ τὸν Δάνουβιν ἐκτραφέντες καὶ Γόττοι ποικιλοκαρόμορφοι,[2] οἷς οὐκ ἔστι θέα ὁμοιοειδὴς ἀνθρώποις, ἀλλὰ μορφὴ ἀγριαίνουσα. οὗτοι κατὰ τὴν ἐνεστῶσαν προκαλινδοῦνται ἴχνεσι τοῖς ἐμοῖς, ὑπισχνούμενοι ποιεῖν ἐκεῖνα, ἅπερ τῇ ἐμῇ ἁρμόζει βασιλείᾳ. οὐχὶ δὲ ἐν τούτῳ μόνον ἕλκομαι, ἀλλὰ δεῖ με σὺν πολλῷ τῷ τάχει καταλαβεῖν τὴν Περσῶν καὶ τροπώσασθαι τὸν Σάπωριν ἐκεῖνον τὸν ἀπόγονον Δαρείου γεγονότα, ἄχρις οὗ ὑπόφορος καὶ ὑποτελής μοι γένηται· ἐντεῦθεν δὲ καὶ τὴν Ἰνδῶν καὶ τὴν Σαρακηνῶν περιοικίδα ἐκπορθῆσαι, ἄχρις οὗ καὶ αὐτοὶ πάντες ἐν δευτέρᾳ τάξει βασιλείας γένωνται τῆς ἐμῆς ὑπόφοροι καὶ ὑποτελεῖς. ἀλλ᾽ αὐτὸς ἐπέκεινα τῆς τούτων δυνάμεως πεφρόνηκας, εὐλάβειαν μὲν λέγων ἐνδεδύσθαι, ἀναίδειαν δὲ προβαλλόμενος, καὶ πανταχοῦ διαφημίζων

[1] Hertlein 75. It occurs in a great number of MSS., sometimes with the reply of Basil, also apocryphal, and in Basil, *Letters* 3. p. 122. The text is very corrupt.

[2] ποικιλοκανθαρόμορφοι, "shaped like variegated beetles," Reiske, from εὐμορφοποικιλοκανθαρόμορφοι, the reading of *Palatinus* 146.

---

[1] This letter, generally recognised as spurious, is perhaps a Christian forgery, since it gives an unfavourable impression

81

To Basil[1]

Up to the present I have displayed the innately mild and humane temper that I have shown since childhood, and have brought under my sway all who dwell on the earth beneath the sun. For lo, every tribe of barbarians as far as the boundaries of the river of Ocean has come bringing gifts to lay at my feet! And likewise the Sagadares[2] who are bred on the banks of the Danube, and the Cotti with headdresses of many shapes and colours, who are not like the rest of mankind to look at, but have a fierce and wild appearance. These at the present time are grovelling in my footprints and promise to do whatever suits my majesty's pleasure. And not only am I distracted by this, but I must with all speed occupy the country of the Persians and put to flight the great Sapor, who is the descendant of Darius, until he consents to pay me tribute and taxes. Afterwards I must also sack the settlements of the Indians and Saracens, until they too shall all take second place in my Empire and consent to pay tribute and taxes. But you have in your own person displayed a pride far exceeding the power of all these, when you say that you are clothed in pious reserve, but in fact flaunt your impudence, and spread a rumour on all sides that I am not worthy

of Julian. The writer knew nothing of Julian's style and mannerisms. Julian was no boaster and avoided outlandish words. It was probably read by Sozomen, 5. 18. 7, and is of early date. Julian was in frequent correspondence with Basil, and for their friendly relations cf. *To Basil*, p. 81.

[2] This tribe cannot be identified. Julian himself always calls the Danube "Ister."

ἀνάξιόν με τῆς τῶν Ῥωμαίων βασιλείας γεγονέναι. ἢ οὐκ οἶσθα αὐτός, ὡς Κώνστα τοῦ κρατίστου γέγονα ἀπόγονος; καὶ τούτων οὕτω γνωσθέντων ἡμῖν σου ἕνεκα οὐδὲ τῆς προτέρας ἐξέστημεν διαθέσεως, ἧσπερ ἔτι νέοι ὄντες τῇ ἡλικίᾳ ἐγώ τε καὶ σὺ μετεσχήκαμεν. ἀλλὰ γαληνῷ τῷ φρονήματι θεσπίζω δέκα ἑκατοντάδας χρυσίου λιτρῶν ἐξαποσταλῆναί μοι παρὰ σοῦ ἐν τῇ παρόδῳ μου τῇ κατὰ τὴν Καίσαρος, ἔτι μου κατὰ τὴν λεωφόρον ὑπάρχοντος, σὺν πολλῷ τῷ τάχει μέλλοντός μου βαδίζειν ἐπὶ τὸν Περσικὸν πόλεμον, ἑτοίμου ὄντος μου, εἰ μὴ τοῦτο ποιήσεις, πάντα τόπον ἀνασκευάσαι τῆς Καίσαρος, καὶ τὰ πάλαι αὐτῆς ἐγηγερμένα καλλιουργήματα κατασκάψαι κατὰ τόπον, ναούς τε καὶ ἀγάλματα ἀναστῆσαι, ὥστε με πεῖσαι πάντας εἴκειν βασιλεῖ Ῥωμαίων καὶ μὴ ὑπεραίρεσθαι. τὸ οὖν ἐξονομασθὲν χρυσίον ἐξ ἀριθμοῦ ζυγῷ Καμπανῷ πρυτανίσας καὶ διαμετρήσας ἀσφαλῶς ἐξαπόστειλόν μοι δι' οἰκείου πιστοῦ σοι ὄντος, δακτυλίῳ τῷ σῷ σφραγισάμενος, ὥστε με ἐπεγνωκότι, κἂν ὀψέ ποτε, τοῦ καιροῦ τὸ ἀπαραίτητον γαληνόν σοι γενέσθαι περὶ τὰ ἐπταισμένα. ἃ γὰρ ἀνέγνων, ἔγνων καὶ κατέγνων.[1]

[1] This last sentence was probably not in the original letter but was quoted as Julian's by Sozomen 5. 18 and added to this letter in some MSS. It occurs separately in one MS., *Ambrosianus* B 4, with the title πρὸς ἐπισκόπους (Cumont, *Recherches*, p. 47).

to be Emperor of the Romans. What! Do you not yourself know that I am a descendant of the most mighty Constans? And although this your conduct has come to my knowledge I have not, as concerns you, departed from my former attitude—I mean that mutual regard which you and I had when we were young men of the same age. But with no harshness of temper I decree that you shall despatch to me one thousand pounds weight of gold, as I march by Caesarea, to be paid without my leaving the high-road, since I purpose to march with all speed to carry on the war with Persia, and I am prepared, if you do not do this, to lay waste the whole district of Caesarea,[1] to tear down on the spot those fine buildings erected long ago, and to set up instead temples and images, that so I may persuade all men to submit to the Emperor of Rome and not be inflated with conceit. Accordingly, weigh the above-mentioned gold to that amount on Campanian scales, oversee it yourself and measure it carefully and despatch it safely to me by someone of your household in whom you have confidence, and first seal it with your own seal-ring, so that, if you have recognised, late though it be, that the occasion admits of no evasion, I may deal mildly with your errors of the past. For what I read, I understood and condemned.[2]

[1] Caesarea had had three fine temples destroyed by the Christians. Julian ordered their restoration, confiscated the estates of the Church, and imposed a fine of 300 lbs. of gold, cf. Sozomen 5. 9. 7. Julian's death may have prevented the enforcement of the penalty.

[2] See below, *frag.* 14, p. 303.

82

Γάλλος καῖσαρ Ἰουλιανῷ ἀδελφῷ χαίρειν[1]

454 Ἡ γειτνίασις τῆς χώρας, λέγω δὲ τὴς Ἰωνίας,
C πλεῖστον ὅσον κέρδος εἰς ἡμᾶς ἤνεγκεν. ἀνιω-
μένους γὰρ ἡμᾶς καὶ δυσχεραίνοντας ἐπὶ ταῖς
πρώταις φήμαις παρεμυθήσατο. τί δὲ ἔστιν ὃ
λέγω, γνώσῃ. ἧκεν εἰς ἡμετέρας ἀκοὰς ἀποστῆ-
ναι μέν σε τῆς προτέρας θρησκείας τῆς ἐκ προγό-
νων παραδοθείσης, ἐπὶ δὲ τὴν μάταιον δεισιδαι-
μονίαν ἐληλακέναι, οἴστρῳ τινὶ κακῷ συμβούλῳ
εἰς τοῦτο ἐλαθέντα. καὶ τί οὐκ ἔμελλον πάσχειν
δυσχεραίνων; ὡς γὰρ[2] εἰ μέν τι τῶν ἐν σοὶ καλῶν
D διαβοώμενον γνοίην, κέρδος οἰκεῖον ἡγοῦμαι, οὕτω[3]
δέ τι τῶν δυσχερῶν, ὅπερ οὐκ οἶμαι, ἐξίσης ζημίω-
μα μᾶλλον ἐμὸν νομίζω. ἐπὶ τούτοις οὖν ἀνιώμενόν
με ἡ παρουσία τοῦ πατρὸς ἡμῶν Ἀετίου ηὔφραι-
νεν, ἀπαγγέλλοντος μὲν ἐναντία, ἡμῖν δὲ εὐκτά·
καὶ γὰρ σπουδάζειν σε ἔφη εἰς οἴκους εὐχῶν, καὶ
μὴ πόρρω τῆς μνείας τῶν ἀθλητῶν ἀνδρῶν ἀπο-
σπᾶσθαι, ὅλως δὲ ἔχεσθαι διεβεβαιοῦτο τῆς θεοσε-

[1] No number in Hertlein. First published by Vulcanius, Leyden, 1597; found only in *Palatinus* 209, *Barberinus* 132.
[2] γὰρ Hertlein would add.
[3] οὕτω δὲ Hertlein suggests; εἰ δὲ Reiske; οὐ δὲ MSS.

---

[1] Nearly all the critics reject this letter as a Christian forgery, but it is defended by Seeck, *Geschichte d. Untergangs d. Antiken Welt*, IV. 124, 440, 6. Philostorgius 3. 27. 53 Bidez, says that Gallus, Julian's half-brother, who was a Christian, frequently sent Aetius to instruct Julian in Christian doctrine in order to counteract the influences

82

Letter from Gallus Caesar to his brother Julian[1]

Gallus Caesar to his brother Julian, Greeting.

My nearness to the country, I mean to Ionia,[2] has brought me the greatest possible gain. For it gave me comfort when I was troubled and pained at the first reports that came to me. You will understand what I mean. It came to my ears that you had abandoned your former mode of worship which was handed down by our ancestors, and goaded by some evil kind of madness that incited you to this, had betaken yourself to that vain superstition. What pain should I not have suffered? For just as whenever I learn by public rumour of any noble quality in you I regard it as a personal gain, so too if I hear of anything disturbing, which, however, I do not think I shall, in the same way I consider it even more my personal loss. Therefore when I was troubled about these matters, the presence of our father Aetius[3] cheered me, for he reported the very contrary, which was what I prayed to hear. Moreover he said that you were zealous in attendance at the houses of prayer, and that you are not being drawn away from pious remembrance of the martyrs, and he affirmed that you entirely adhere to

that inclined him to paganism. If genuine it must be dated between 351, when Gallus was made Cæsar, and 354, as Gallus was put to death by Constantius in the latter year.

[2] Gallus Caesar resided at Antioch till 354 when he went to Constantinople. Julian, meanwhile, was studying at Pergamon and Ephesus. For his relations with Gallus, see Vol. 2, *To the Athenians* 273 A.

[3] For Aetius see Introduction and *Letter* 15.

455 βείας τῶν ἡμετέρων. ἐγὼ δέ σοι τοῦτ' ἂν εἴποιμι κατὰ[1] τὸ Ὁμηρικὸν Βάλλ' οὕτως, καὶ ἐπὶ τοιαύταις μνείαις εὔφραινε τοὺς ἀγαπῶντας, μεμνημένος ὡς οὐκ ἔστι τι θεοσεβείας ἀνώτερον. ἡ γὰρ εἰς ἄκρον ἀρετὴ παιδεύει τὸ μὲν ψεῦδος ὡς ἀπατηλὸν μισεῖν, τοῦ δὲ ἀληθοῦς ἔχεσθαι, ὅπερ μάλιστα ἐν τῇ περὶ τὸ θεῖον φαίνεται θρησκείᾳ. ὄχλος γὰρ πάντως φιλόνεικον καὶ ἄστατον· τὸ δὲ μόνον σὺν
B ἑνὶ[2] ὑπουργὸν ὂν βασιλεύει τοῦ παντός, οὐκ ἐκ δασμοῦ καὶ κλήρου, καθάπερ οἱ Κρόνου παῖδες, ἀλλ' αὐτοαρχὴ ὄν, καὶ κρατοῦν τῶν ἁπάντων, οὐδὲ δεξάμενον βίᾳ παρ' ἑτέρου,[3] ἀλλὰ πρὸ πάντων ὄν. τοῦτο ὄντως θεός, ὅνπερ σὺν τῷ ὀφειλομένῳ σεβάσματι προσκυνεῖν χρή. ἔρρωσο.

83

Ἰουλιανῷ Εὐστάθιος φιλόσοφος[4]

Ὡς ὤνησέ γε τὸ σύνθημα ἡμῖν μελλῆσαν· ἀντὶ γὰρ τοῦ τρέμειν καὶ δεδιέναι φερόμενον ἐπὶ τῆς δημοσίας ἀπήνης καὶ περιπίπτοντα κραιπαλῶσιν ὀρεωκόμοις καὶ ἡμιόνοις ἀκοστήσασι καθ' Ὅμηρον δι' ἀργίαν καὶ πλησμονὴν ἀνέχεσθαι κονιορτοῦ καὶ

[1] Reiske deletes κατά.

[2] Heyler suggests that οὐδενὶ ὑπουργὸν "subservient to none" would be more appropriate to Gallus, who was an Arian. In any case, Heyler's reading gives a better sense to ὑπουργόν.

[3] παρ' ἑτέρου Reiske suggests; ἕτερον MSS., Hertlein.

[4] Hertlein 72. The above is the correct title preserved in *Parisinus* 963 after the incorrect Λιβανίῳ σοφιστῇ καὶ κοιαίστωρι retained in brackets by Hertlein.

the religion of our family. So I would say to you in the words of Homer,[1] "Shoot on in this wise," and rejoice those who love you by being spoken of in such terms, remembering that nothing is higher than religion. For supreme virtue teaches us to hate a lie as treachery and to cling to the truth, which truth is most clearly made manifest in the worship of the Divine Being. For a crowd[2] is wholly contentious and unstable; but the Deity, ministering alone with but one other,[3] rules the universe, not by division or lot, like the sons of Cronos,[4] but existing from the beginning and having power over all things, not having received it from another by violence, but existing before all. This is verily God, whom we must adore with the reverence that we owe to him. Farewell!

83

Eustathius[5] the Philosopher to Julian

What an advantage it was for me that the token[6] came late! For instead of riding, in fear and trembling, in the public[7] carriage and, in encounters with drunken mule-drivers and mules made restive, as Homer[8] says, from idleness and overfeeding,

[1] *Iliad* 8. 282; Agamemnon to Teucer the archer.
[2] *i. e.* of the gods.
[3] *i.e.* God the Word; but see critical note.
[4] *i. e.* Zeus, Poseidon and Hades, whose separate realms are defined in *Iliad* 15. 187 foll.
[5] See Introduction, under Eustathius.
[6] The "tessera," whether ring, coin or document, served as a passport.
[7] The epithet *δημόσιος* is used (1) of the public carriage, (2) of the "state," or reserved, carriage. The first is meant here.
[8] *Iliad* 6. 506.

φωνῆς ἀλλοκότου καὶ ψόφου μαστίγων, βαδίζειν ἐπὶ σχολῆς περιέστη μοι δι' ὁδοῦ συνηρεφοῦς καὶ ἐπισκίου, πολλὰς μὲν κρήνας, πολλὰς δὲ ἐχούσης καταγωγὰς ἐπιτηδείους τῇ ὥρᾳ μεταξὺ τὸν κόπον διαναπαύοντι, ἵνα μοι φανείη κατάλυσις εὔπνους τε καὶ ἀμφιλαφὴς ὑπὸ πλατάνοις τισὶν ἢ κυπαρίττοις, τὸν Φαῖδρον ἔχοντι ἐν χερσὶ [1] ἢ ἕτερόν τινα τῶν Πλάτωνος λόγων. ταῦτά τοι, ὦ φίλη κεφαλή, ἀπολαύων τῆς ἐλευθέρας ὁδοιπορίας, ἄτοπον ὑπέλαβον τὸ μὴ καὶ τοῦτο κοινώσασθαί σοι καὶ ἀποσημῆναι.

[1] After χερσὶ MSS add τὸν Μυρρινούσιον which Hertlein would delete as inappropriate to the title of Plato's dialogue.

having to endure clouds of dust and a strange dialect and the cracking of whips, it was my lot to travel at leisure by a road arched over with trees and well-shaded, a road that had numerous springs and resting-places suitable to the summer season for a traveller who seeks relief from his weariness on the way; and where I always found a good place to stop, airy and shaded by plane trees or cypresses, while in my hand I held the *Phaedrus* or some other of Plato's dialogues. Now all this profit, O beloved, I gained from the freedom with which I travelled; therefore I considered that it would be unnatural not to communicate this also to you, and announce it.[1]

[1] The journey of Eustathius is probably that for which Julian gave his permission in *Letter* 44.

FRAGMENTA BREVIORA[1]

1

Τίς οὖν ἀγνοεῖ τὸν Αἰθιόπων ὑπὲρ τοῦ παρ' ἡμῖν τροφιμωτάτου σιτίου λόγον; ἁψάμενοι γὰρ τῆς μάζης θαυμάζειν ἔφασαν, ὅπως κόπρια σιτούμενοι ζῶμεν, εἴ τῳ πιστὸς ὁ Θούριος εἶναι λογοποιὸς δοκεῖ. ἰχθυοφάγων δὲ καὶ σαρκοφάγων ἀνθρώπων γένη μηδ' ὄναρ ἰδόντα τὴν παρ' ἡμῖν δίαιταν οἱ τὴν οἰκουμένην περιηγούμενοι γῆν ἱστοροῦσιν. ὧν εἴ τις παρ' ἡμῖν ζηλῶσαι τὴν δίαιταν ἐπιχειρήσει, οὐδὲν ἄμεινον διακείσεται τῶν τὸ κώνειον προσενεγκαμένων ἢ τὴν ἀκόνιτον ἢ τὸν ἐλλέβορον.[2]

2

Πρὸς τὴν Ἑρκυνίαν ὕλην ἐθεόμεν, καὶ εἶδον ἐγὼ χρῆμα ἐξαίσιον. ἰδοὺ γοῦν σοι θαρρῶν ἐγὼ ἐγγυῶμαι, μήποτε ὦφθαι τοιοῦτον μηδέν, ὅσα γε ἡμεῖς ἴσμεν, ἐν τῇ Ῥωμαίων. ἀλλ' εἴτε τὰ Θετταλικὰ Τέμπη δύσβατα νομίζει τις, εἴτε τὰς

[1] Hertlein *Fragments* 1 and 3 have been restored to their proper context in *Letter* 16, pp. 38 and 36.

[2] Hertlein *frag.* 2. Quoted by Suidas under Ἡρόδοτος and ὧν . . . ἐλλέβορον again under Ζηλῶσαι.

---

[1] Herodotus 3. 22 describes the amazement of the Ethiopians, who lived on boiled meat, at the diet of the Persians.

THE SHORTER FRAGMENTS

1

THEN who does not know the saying of the Ethiopians about the food that with us is held to be most nutritious? For when they first handled bread they said they wondered how we manage to live on a diet of dung, that is if one may believe the Thurian chronicler.[1] And those who write descriptions of the world relate that there are races of men who live on fish and flesh[2] and have never even dreamed of our kind of diet. But if anyone in our country tries to adopt their diet, he will be no better off than those who take a dose of hemlock or aconite or hellebore.

2

WE hastened to the Hercynian forest and it was a strange and monstrous thing that I beheld. At any rate I do not hesitate to engage that nothing of the sort has ever been seen in the Roman Empire, at least as far as we know. But if anyone considers Thessalian Tempe or Thermopylae or the

They said they were not surprised that men who lived on such food attained to a maximum of only eighty years. For the different temperaments and customs of different peoples cf. *Against the Galilaeans*, 143E.

[2] Cf. vol. 2, *Oration* 6. 191C for Julian's remarks on diet.

Θερμοπύλας, εἴτε τὸν μέγαν καὶ δυσλύγιον Ταῦρον, ἐλάχιστα ἴστω χαλεπότητος ἕνεκα πρὸς τὸ Ἑρκύνιον ὄντα.[1]

3

Ἰουλιανὸς Κορινθίοις

. . . πατρῴα μοι πρὸς ὑμᾶς ὑπάρχει φιλία· καὶ γὰρ ᾤκησε παρ' ὑμῖν ὁ ἐμὸς πατήρ, καὶ ἀναχθεὶς ἔνθεν,[2] ὥσπερ ἐκ Φαιάκων Ὀδυσσεύς, τῆς πολυχρονίου πλάνης ἀπηλλάγη . . . ἐνταῦθα ὁ πατὴρ ἀνεπαύσατο.[3]

4

. . . καὶ ὁ κλεινὸς[4] ἡμῖν ἔδειξε ἱεροφάντης Ἰάμβλιχος . . . ἡμεῖς δὲ Ἐμπεδοτίμῳ καὶ Πυθαγόρᾳ πιστεύοντες οἷς τε ἐκεῖθεν λαβὼν Ἡρακλείδης ὁ Ποντικὸς ἔφη.[5] . . .

[1] Hertlein 4. Quoted by Suidas under Χρῆμα.

[2] ἐνθένδε Hertlein.

[3] Hertlein 5. Quoted by Libanius, *Oration* 14, 29, 30. *For Aristophanes* (of Corinth).

[4] ἥρως Asmus adds.

[5] Hertlein 6. Quoted by Suidas from the *Kronia*, under Ἐμπεδότιμος and Ἰουλιανός. This fragment is all that survives of Julian's *Kronia* or *Saturnalia*, written in 361; see Vol. 1, *Oration* 4. 157C. We know nothing more as to its contents.

---

[1] Julian, *Oration* 2. 101 D. The Greek word is Platonic, cf. *Theaetetus* 161 D.

[2] For Julian's knowledge of the Hercynian forest, which in ancient Germany extended from the Black Forest on the north-east to the Hartz Mountains, cf. Vol. 2, *Misopogon* 359B; Ammianus, 17. 1. 8 Cum prope silvam venisset squalore tenebrarum horrendam . . . *i.e.* in his German campaign in 357; Zosimus, 3. 4. 3 ἄχρι τῶν Ἑρκυνίων δρυμῶν τοὺς φεύγοντας ὁ Καῖσαρ ἐπιδιώξας.

great and far-flung[1] Taurus to be impassable, let me tell him that for difficulty of approach they are trivial indeed compared with the Hercynian forest.[2]

3

To the Corinthians[3]

. . . My friendship with you dates from my father's[4] time. For indeed my father lived in your city, and embarking thence, like Odysseus from the land of the Phaeacians, had respite from his long-protracted wanderings[5]. . . there my father found repose.

4

. . . and the famous hierophant Iamblichus showed it to us . . . and we, since we believed the account of Empedotimus[6] and Pythagoras, as well as that of Heracleides of Pontus who derived it from them.[7] . . .

[3] This is all that remains of the manifesto sent to the Corinthians by Julian in 361, when he sought to justify his defection from Constantius.

[4] Julius Constantius was murdered by his nephew, the Emperor Constantius, in 337.

[5] Libanius says that Julian here spoke briefly about the "wicked stepmother" of Julius, the Empress Helena, mother of Constantine, see Zosimus 2. 8 and 9.

[6] For this famous Syracusan, who claimed to be immortal, see Vol. 2, 295B.

[7] Geffcken points out that Julian's statement is derived from a commentary on Plato and quotes Proclus, *On Plato's Republic* 2. 119. 18. "The human soul may learn the sacred truth about the affairs of the underworld and report them to mankind. This is shown by the account of Empedotimus, which Heracleides of Pontus relates." Then follows the vision of Empedotimus in Hades; cf. Rohde, *Psyche*, p. 385.

5

. . . μόνον εὔχεσθαι ᾔδεσαν.[1]

6

. . . ἵνα[2] μὴ ἀκονώμενοι τὴν γλῶτταν[3] ἑτοίμως πρὸς τοὺς διαλεκτικοὺς τῶν Ἑλλήνων ἀπαντῶσιν.

7

. . . τοῖς οἰκείοις γὰρ πτεροῖς κατὰ τὴν παροιμίαν βαλλόμεθα. ἐκ γὰρ τῶν ἡμετέρων συγγραμμάτων καθοπλιζόμενοι τὸν καθ' ἡμῶν ἀναδέχονται πόλεμον.[4]

8

Τὸ μὴ προϊδέσθαι τό τε δυνατὸν καὶ τὸ ἀδύνατον ἐν πράγμασι τῆς ἐσχάτης ἀπονοίας ἐστὶ σημεῖον.[5]

[1] Hertlein 7. Quoted by Zosimus 3. 3. 2 οἱ δὲ παρὰ Κωνσταντίου δοθέντες αὐτῷ . . . μόνον εὔχεσθαι, καθάπερ αὐτός πού φησιν, ᾔδεσαν, cf. Vol. 2, 277D, p. 267, Wright.

[2] Hertlein 8. Quoted by Socrates, *History of the Church* 3. 12; cf. Suidas under Μάρις. Socrates is quoting from an edict forbidding Christians to teach the classics; but in the extant edict, *Letter* 36, these words do not occur.

[3] Cf. Libanius, *Letter* 1588, *To Julian*, αὐτὴν (Sc. τὴν γλῶτταν) ἀκονῶν.

[4] Hertlein 9. Quoted by Theodoret, *History of the Church*, 3. 4. Theodoret, like Socrates *frag.* 6, quotes Julian on the Christian teachers of the classics.

[5] Hertlein 10. Quoted by Suidas under Ἀπόνοια.

---

[1] Julian said this of the soldiers who were assigned to him by Constantius when he went to Gaul in 355; cf. Libanius

5

They only knew how to pray [1]

6

. . . that they [2] may not, by sharpening their tongues,[3] be prepared to meet their Hellenic opponents in debate.

7

. . . for in the words of the proverb, we are stricken by our own arrows.[4] For from our own writings they [5] take the weapons wherewith they engage in the war against us.

8

Not to see beforehand what is possible and what impossible in practical affairs is a sign of the utmost foolishness.[6]

18. 94 ἕως αὐτῷ κατέλιπον ὁπλίτας εὔξασθαι μόνον δυναμένους, said of the soldiers who were to be left with Julian when Constantius summoned the best of the Gallic army to the East in 360.

[2] *i.e.* the Christians.

[3] *i.e.* by the study of rhetoric.

[4] *i.e.* the arrows are feathered from our plumage; cf. Aristophanes, *Birds* 808 τάδ' οὐχ ὑπ' ἄλλων ἀλλὰ τοῖς αὑτῶν πτέροις. The figure is used by Byron, Waller and Moore of a wounded eagle "Which on the shaft that made him die, espied a feather of his own." The original is Aeschylus, *Myrmidons, frag* 139.

[5] *i.e.* the Christians.

[6] This is apparently a criticism of that lack of political instinct in the Christians of which Julian speaks in his treatise *Against the Galilaeans*, fragment 5. Hence Neumann regards the above fragment as derived from a lost part of the treatise.

9

Λέγει (*sc.* ὁ Ἰουλιανὸς) οὖν ἐπιστέλλων· Σκύθαι δὲ νῦν μὲν ἀτρεμοῦσι, ἴσως δὲ οὐκ ἀτρεμήσουσιν.[1]

10

Πρὸς τριβοῦνον Εὐθυμέλην [2]

Ἡδονὴ βασιλεῖ πόλεμος.

11

Ἀνεγείρω γὰρ μετὰ πάσης προθυμίας τὸν ναὸν τοῦ ὑψίστου θεοῦ.[3]

12

Πρὸς δῆμον εὐφημήσαντα ἐν τῷ Τυχαίῳ [4]

Εἰ μὲν εἰς τὸ θέατρον λαθὼν εἰσῆλθον, εὐφημεῖτε· εἰ δὲ εἰς τὰ ἱερά, ἡσυχίαν ἄγετε, καὶ

[1] Not in Hertlein. Preserved by Eunapius, *frag.* 22, p. 226, 15, Dindorf.

[2] Not in Hertlein. It occurs in *Ambrosianus*, B 4, with other sayings of the Emperor; Cumont, *Recherches*, p. 47, thinks that they are derived from some lost historical work.

[3] Not in Hertlein. Preserved by Lydus, *De Mensibus*. See Cumont, *Recherches*, p. 17, note 1.

[4] Hertlein, *Letter* 64. First published by Muratori in *Anecdota Graeca*, Padua, 1709.

---

[1] In 360 Constantius bribed the Scythians to aid him in his campaign against the Persians (Ammianus 20. 8. 1), and in 363 Julian employed Scythian auxiliaries for the same purpose (Ammianus 23. 2. 7). It is uncertain to which of these dates the fragment refers; Eunapius quotes this remark as evidence of Julian's foresight.

9

Accordingly he says in a letter: At present the Scythians[1] are not restless, but perhaps they will become restless.

10

To Euthymeles the Tribune

A king delights in war.

11

For I am rebuilding with all zeal the temple of the Most High God.[2]

12

To the citizens who acclaimed him in the temple of Fortune[3]

When I enter the theatre unannounced,[4] acclaim me, but when I enter the temples be silent[5] and

[2] Lydus says that Julian wrote this to the Jews. The letter is lost. For Julian's design of rebuilding the Temple see *Letter* 51 and Introduction.

[3] At Constantinople there was a temple of Fortune (Τυχή) with a statue of the Goddess, cf. Socrates 3. 11. It was when Julian was sacrificing in this temple that he was denounced by the blind Bishop Maris of Chalcedon, as related by Sozomen 5. 4. But as Julian in the *Misopogon* 346B speaks twice of sacrificing at Antioch in the temple of Fortune, this admonition may have been addressed to the citizens of Antioch, late in 362 or early in 363.

[4] For Julian's rare visits to the theatre, see *Misopogon* 339C, 368C. For his love of applause, Ammianus 25. 4. 18 volgi plausibus laetus.

[5] Cf. Vol. 2. *Misopogon* 344B,C, where Julian reproves the citizens of Antioch for applauding him in the temples.

μετενέγκατε ὑμῶν τὰς εὐφημίας εἰς τοὺς θεούς· μᾶλλον δὲ οἱ θεοὶ τῶν εὐφημιῶν οὐ χρῄζουσιν.

13

Πρὸς ζωγράφον [1]

Εἰ μὲν μὴ εἶχον [2] καὶ ἐχαρίσω μοι, συγγνώμης ἦσθα ἄξιος· εἰ δὲ εἶχον μέν, οὐκ ἐχρησάμην δέ, τοὺς θεοὺς ἔφερον, μᾶλλον δὲ ὑπὸ τῶν θεῶν ἐφερόμην. σύ μοι ἀλλότριον σχῆμα πῶς ἐδίδους, ἑταῖρε; οἷόν με εἶδες, τοιοῦτον καὶ γράψον.

14

Πρὸς ἐπισκόπους [3]

ἔγνων, ἀνέγνων κατέγνων.

[1] Hertlein, *Letter* 65.
[2] εἰκὼν? Muratori.
[3] Not in Hertlein. Quoted by Sozomen 5. 18. In some MSS. it occurs at the end of *Letter* 81, *To Basil.*

---

[1] This and the following fragment, wrongly placed among the letters by Hertlein and earlier editors, are, as Cumont saw, isolated *mots historiques* probably quoted from some historical work. They may have occurred in an edict.

[2] Sozomen 5. 17. says that Julian had himself painted "on the public pictures" in juxtaposition with Zeus or Ares or Hermes in order that the people might be compelled when they saluted the Emperor to salute the gods also, and that few

transfer your acclamations to the gods; or rather the gods do not need acclamations.[1]

13

To a Painter [2]

If I did not possess it [3] and you had bestowed it on me, you would have deserved to be forgiven; but if I possessed it and did not use it, I carried the gods, or rather was carried by them. Why, my friend, did you give me a form other than my own? Paint me exactly as you saw me.

14

To the Bishops

I recognised, I read, I condemned.[4]

had the courage to refuse to conform with this established custom; cf. Gregory Nazianzen, *Oration* 4. 81.

[3] Whether because of mutilation or lack of context, the two first sentences are unintelligible; we do not know the object of the verbs or what is meant by the reference to the gods; but evidently Julian did not like his portrait.

[4] Sozomen 5. 18 says that Julian, in order to ridicule the Christian substitutes for the Greek classics, composed chiefly by Apollinaris, after Julian had forbidden Christians to teach the originals, wrote these words to the Bishops. Their answer was as follows: "You have read, but you have not understood; for, had you understood, you would not have condemned." See *Letter* 81, *To Basil*, p. 286.

EPIGRAMMATA

1

Εἰς οἶνον ἀπὸ κριθῆς

τίς πόθεν εἶς, Διόνυσε; μὰ γὰρ τὸν ἀλαθέα Βάκχον
οὔ σ' ἐπιγιγνώσκω· τὸν Διὸς οἶδα μόνον.
κεῖνος νέκταρ ὄδωδε, σὺ δὲ τράγον. ἦ ῥά σε Κελτοὶ
τῇ πενίῃ βοτρύων τεῦξαν ἀπ' ἀσταχύων.
τῷ σε χρὴ καλέειν Δημήτριον, οὐ Διόνυσον,
πυρογενῆ μᾶλλον καὶ Βρόμον, οὐ Βρόμιον.[1]

2

Εἰς τὸ ὄργανον [2]

ἀλλοίην ὁρόω δονάκων φύσιν. ἦπου ἀπ' ἄλλης
χαλκείης τάχα μᾶλλον ἀνεβλάστησαν ἀρούρης
ἄγριοι· οὐδ' ἀνέμοισιν ὑφ' ἡμετέροις [3] δονέονται,
ἀλλ' ἀπὸ ταυρείης προθορὼν σπήλυγγος ἀήτης
νέρθεν ἐϋτρήτων καλάμων ὑπὸ ῥίζαν ὁδεύει.

[1] Hertlein 1. *Palatine Anthology* 9. 365, and in several MSS.

[2] Hertlein 2; *The Greek Anthology* vol. 3, 365, Paton; it is found in *Parisinus* 690. [3] ἠερίοις Cumont.

---

[1] *i. e.* beer, which Julian met with in Gaul and Germany.

EPIGRAMS

1

On wine made from barley [1]

WHO art thou and whence, O Dionysus? By the true Bacchus I recognise thee not; I know only the son of Zeus. He smells of nectar, but you smell of goat. Truly it was in their lack of grapes that the Celts brewed thee from corn-ears. So we should call thee Demetrius,[2] not Dionysus, wheat-born [3] not fire-born, barley god not boisterous god.[4]

2

On the Organ

A STRANGE growth of reeds do I behold. Surely they sprang on a sudden from another brazen field, so wild are they. The winds that wave them are none of ours, but a blast leaps forth from a cavern of bull's hide and beneath the well-bored pipes travels to their roots. And a dignified person, with swift

[2] *i. e.* son of Demeter goddess of corn.
[3] πῡρογενῆ, not πῠρογενῆ, a play on words. See *The Greek Anthology*, Vol. 3. 368, Paton.
[4] βρόμος means "oats"; Bromius "boisterous" was an epithet of Dionysus; it is impossible to represent the play on the words.

καί τις ἀνὴρ ἀγέρωχος, ἔχων θοὰ δάκτυλα χειρός,
ἵσταται ἀμφαφόων κανόνας συμφράδμονας αὐλῶν,
οἱ δ' ἁπαλὸν σκιρτῶντες ἀποθλίβουσιν ἀοιδήν.

3

Αἴνιγμα εἰς κοντοπαίκτην[1]

ἔστιν τι δένδρον τῶν ἀνακτόρων μέσον,
οὗ ῥίζα καὶ ζῇ καὶ λαλεῖ καρποῖς ἅμα·
μιᾷ δ' ἐν ὥρᾳ καὶ φυτεύεται ξένως
καὶ καρπὸν αὔξει καὶ τρυγᾶται ῥιζόθεν.

4

εἰς τὸν παρόντα Ὁμηρικὸν στίχον ἓξ πόδας ἔχοντα ὧν οἱ τρεῖς εἰσι δάκτυλοι[2]

κούρη Ἰκαρίοιο περίφρων Πηνελόπεια
ἓξ ποσὶν ἐμβεβαυῖα τριδάκτυλος ἐξεφαάνθη.

[1] Hertlein 3. *Palatine Anthology* vol. 2. p. 769.
[2] Hertlein 4. *Anthology* 2. 659.

---

[1] A note in the MS. (*Parisinus* 690) explains that Julian composed this poem during a procession, when he was leaving the church of the Holy Apostles in Constantinople. He was

moving fingers of the hand, stands there and handles the keys that pass the word to the pipes; then the keys leap lightly, and press forth the melody.[1]

3

Riddle on a performer with a pole

There is a tree between the lords, whose root has life and talks, and the fruits likewise. And in a single hour it grows in strange fashion, and ripens its fruit, and gets its harvest at the roots.[2]

4

On the Homeric hexameter which contains six feet of which three are dactyls

"The daughter of Icarius, prudent Penelope," appears with three fingers [3] and walks on six feet.

then a mere boy, pursuing his education in Constantinople, before he was interned in Cappadocia.

[2] The performer balances on his forehead, between his temples, a pole at the end of which is a cage or bar, supporting a child or children.

[3] There is a play of words on δάκτυλος = "finger" and "dactyl," a metrical foot. In the title, "foot" and "dactyl" are metrical terms, in the riddle they are used in the original, physical sense. The hexameter quoted has three dactyls.

5

Εἰς ἱπποκένταυρον[1]

ἀνδρόθεν ἐκκέχυθ' ἵππος, ἀνέδραμε δ' ἱππόθεν ἀνήρ,
ἀνὴρ νόσφι ποδῶν, κεφαλῆς δ' ἄτερ αἰόλος ἵππος·
ἵππος ἐρεύγεται ἄνδρα, ἀνὴρ δ' ἀποπέρδεται ἵππον.

6

Ιουλιανοῦ τοῦ παραβάτου[2]

ὡς ἐθέλει τὸ φέρον σε
φέρειν, φέρου· ἢν δ' ἀπιθήσῃς,
καὶ σαυτὸν βλάψεις, καὶ τὸ
φέρον σε φέρει.

[1] Hertlein 6. Assigned to Julian by Tzetzes *Chiliades* 6. 959; *Anthology*, vol. 2, p. 659.

5

To a Hippocentaur

A HORSE has been poured from a man's mould, a man springs up from a horse. The man has no feet, the swift moving horse has no head. The horse belches forth as a man, the man breaks wind as a horse.

6

By Julian the Apostate

EVEN as Fate the Sweeper wills to sweep thee on, be thou swept. But if thou rebel, thou wilt but harm thyself, and Fate still sweeps thee on.[1]

[1] Perhaps there is a similar meaning in the phrase ὑπὸ τῶν θεῶν ἐφερόμην in the puzzling *frag.* 13, p. 303.

---

[2] Not in Hertlein. First ascribed to Julian, from *Baroccianus* 133, by Cumont, *Revue de Philologie*, 1892. Also ascribed to St. Basil; cf. a similar epigram in *Palatine Anthology* 10. 73, ascribed to Palladas.

AGAINST THE GALILAEANS

INTRODUCTION

Julian, like Epictetus, always calls the Christians Galilaeans[1] because he wishes to emphasise that this was a local creed, "the creed of fishermen," and perhaps to remind his readers that "out of Galilee ariseth no prophet";[2] with the same intention he calls Christ "the Nazarene."[3] His chief aim in the treatise was to show that there is no evidence in the Old Testament for the idea of Christianity, so that the Christians have no right to regard their teaching as a development of Judaism. His attitude throughout is that of a philosopher who rejects the claims of one small sect to have set up a universal religion. He speaks with respect of the God of the Hebrews, admires the Jewish discipline, their sacrifices and their prohibition of certain foods, plays off the Jews against the Christians, and reproaches the latter for having abandoned the Mosaic law; but he contrasts the jealous, exclusive "particular" (μερικός) Hebraic God with the universal Hellenic gods who do not confine their attentions to a small and unimportant portion of the world. Throughout Julian's works

[1] Cf. Gregory Nazianzen, *First Invective Against Julian* 76 (115), Γαλιλαίους ἀντὶ Χριστιανῶν ὀνομάσας καὶ καλεῖσθαι νομοθετήσας· This was ignored by Neumann in his reconstruction of the work, which he entitled Κατὰ Χριστιανῶν. Cf. Socrates 3. 12.

[2] *John* 7. 52.

[3] In the fragmentary *Letter* 55, *To Photinus*, p. 189.

there are scattered references, nearly always disdainful, to the Galilaeans, but his formal attack on their creed and on the inconsistencies of the Scriptures, which he had promised in *Letter* 55, *To Photinus,* the heretic, was not given to the general public, for whom he says he intends it, till he had left Antioch on his march to Persia in the early spring of 363. He probably compiled it at Antioch in the preceding winter.[1] Perhaps it was never completed, for at the time Julian had many things on his mind. It was written in three Books, but the fragments preserved are almost entirely from Book I. In the fifth century Cyril of Alexandria regarded the treatise as peculiarly dangerous, and said that it had shaken many believers. He undertook to refute it in a polemic of which about half survives, and from the quotations of Julian in Cyril's work Neumann has skilfully reconstructed considerable portions of the treatise. Cyril had rearranged Julian's hurriedly written polemic, in order to avoid repetitions and to bring similar subjects together. Moreover, he says that he omitted invectives against Christ and such matter as might contaminate the minds of Christians. We have seen that a similar mutilation of the letters occurred for similar reasons.

Julian's arguments against the Christian doctrine do not greatly differ from those used in the second century by Celsus, and by Porphyry in the third; but

[1] Libanius, in his *Monody on Julian,* says that at Antioch there were composed by the Emperor βιβλίων συγγραφαὶ βοηθούντων θεοῖς; in the *Epitaph on Julian,* that the attack on Christian doctrines was composed in the long nights of winter, *i. e.* 362–363, at Antioch, where he spent the winter with Julian.

his tone is more like that of Celsus, for he and Celsus were alike in being embittered opponents of the Christian religion, which Porphyry was not. Those engaged in this sort of controversy use the same weapons over and over again; Origen refutes Celsus, Cyril refutes Julian, in much the same terms. Both sides have had the education of sophists, possess the learning of their time, borrow freely from Plato, attack the rules or lack of rules of diet of the opponents' party, point out the inconsistencies in the rival creed, and ignore the weaknesses of their own.[1]

For his task Julian had been well equipped by his Christian teachers when he was interned at Macellum in Cappadocia, and he here repays them for the enforced studies of his boyhood, when his naturally pagan soul rebelled against the Christian ritual in which he had to take part. In spite of his insistence on the inconsistency of the Christians in setting up a Trinity in place of the monotheism of Moses and the prophets, he feels the need of some figure in his own pantheon to balance that of Christ the Saviour, and uses, both in this treatise and in *Oration* 4, about Asclepius or Dionysus or Heracles almost the language of the Christians about Christ, setting these pagan figures up one after another as manifestations of the divine beneficence in making a link between the gods and mankind.

Though Julian borrowed from Porphyry's lost polemic in fifteen Books,[2] he does not discuss

[1] Geffcken, *Zwei Griechische Apologeten*, p. 259, speaks of a Chinese polemic against Christianity, composed according to the regular conventions of this type.

[2] On Julian's debt to Porphyry, and his lack of sympathy with Porphyry's attitude to religion, see Harnack, *Porphyrius*, Berlin, 1916; Bidez, *Vie de Porphyre*, Gand, 1913.

questions of the chronology and authorship of the Scriptures as Porphyry is known to have done. Libanius, always a blind admirer of Julian, says[1] that in this treatise the Emperor made the doctrines of the Christians look ridiculous, and that he was "wiser than the Tyrian old man," that is, Porphyry. But apparently the Christians of the next two centuries did not agree with Cyril as to the peculiarly dangerous character of Julian's invective. At any rate, the Council of Ephesus, in a decree dated 431, sentenced Porphyry's books to be burned, but did not mention Julian's; and again in a law of Theodosius II. in 448, Julian was ignored while Porphyry was condemned. When in 529 Justinian decreed that anti-Christian books were to be burned, Porphyry alone was named, though probably Julian was meant to be included. Not long after Julian's death his fellow-student at Athens, Gregory Nazianzen, wrote a long invective against him, in which he attacked the treatise *Against the Galilaeans* without making a formal refutation of Julian's arguments. Others in the fifth century, such as Theodorus of Mopsuestia and Philip Sideta, wrote refutations which are lost. But it was reserved for Cyril, Bishop of Alexandria, writing between 429 and 441, to compose a long and formal refutation of Julian's treatise; the latter seems to have been no longer in circulation, or was at least neglected, and Neumann thinks that the bishop was urged to write his polemic by his dislike of the heretical views of other and earlier antagonists of Julian, especially Theodorus of Mopsuestia. This refutation, which was dedicated to the Emperor Theodosius II, was in at least twenty

[1] *Oration* 18. 178.

Books. But for Cyril's quotations we should have a very vague idea of Julian's treatise, and as it is we are compelled to see it through the eyes of a hostile apologist. Cyril's own comments, and his summaries of portions of the treatise have been omitted from the following translation,[1] but the substance of the summaries has been given in the footnotes. The marginal numbers in the Greek text correspond with the pages of Spanheim's (1696) edition of Cyril's polemic *Pro Christiana Religione*, from which Neumann extracted and strung together Cyril's quotations of Julian. There is, therefore, an occasional lack of connection in Julian's arguments, taken apart from their context in Cyril's treatise.

[1] For a full discussion of the work of Cyril and the other Christian apologists who attempted to refute Julian, and for an explanation of Neumann's method of reconstruction, the reader is referred to the Latin *Prolegomena* to Neumann's Edition of Julian's polemic.

The numerous passages or expressions in this treatise that can be paralleled in Julian's other works have been collected by Asmus in his Concordance, *Julian's Galiläerschrift*, 1904.

ΙΟΥΛΙΑΝΟΥ ΑΥΤΟΚΡΑΤΟΡΟΣ ΚΑΤΑ ΓΑΛΙΛΑΙΩΝ ΛΟΓΟΣ Α[1]

39 A Καλῶς ἔχειν ἔμοιγε φαίνεται τὰς αἰτίας ἐκθέσ-
θαι πᾶσιν ἀνθρώποις, ὑφ' ὧν ἐπείσθην ὅτι τῶν
Γαλιλαίων ἡ σκευωρία πλάσμα ἐστὶν ἀνθρώπων
39 B ὑπὸ κακουργίας συντεθέν. ἔχουσα μὲν οὐδὲν θεῖον,
ἀποχρησαμένη δὲ τῷ φιλομύθῳ καὶ παιδαριώδει
καὶ ἀνοήτῳ τῆς ψυχῆς μορίῳ, τὴν τερατολογίαν
εἰς πίστιν ἤγαγεν ἀληθείας.

41 E Μέλλων δὲ ὑπὲρ τῶν πρώτων λεγομένων
δογμάτων ἁπάντων ποιεῖσθαι τὸν λόγον, ἐκεῖνο
βούλομαι πρῶτον εἰπεῖν, ὅτι χρὴ τοὺς ἐντυγχά-
νοντας, εἴπερ ἀντιλέγειν ἐθέλοιεν, ὥσπερ ἐν δικα-
στηρίῳ μηδὲν ἔξωθεν πολυπραγμονεῖν μηδέ, τὸ
λεγόμενον, ἀντικατηγορεῖν, ἕως ἂν ὑπὲρ τῶν παρ'
42 A αὐτοῖς[2] ἀπολογήσωνται. ἄμεινον μὲν γὰρ οὕτω,
καὶ σαφέστερον ἰδίαν μὲν ἐνστήσασθαι πραγμα-
τείαν, ὅταν τι τῶν παρ' ἡμῖν εὐθύνειν θέλωσιν, ἐν
οἷς δὲ πρὸς τὰς παρ' ἡμῶν εὐθύνας ἀπολογοῦνται,
μηδὲν ἀντικατηγορεῖν.

42 E Μικρὸν δὲ ἀναλαβεῖν ἄξιον, ὅθεν ἡμῖν ἥκει καὶ
ὅπως ἔννοια θεοῦ τὸ πρῶτον, εἶτα παραθεῖναι τὰ
παρὰ τοῖς Ἕλλησι καὶ παρὰ τοῖς Ἑβραίοις ὑπὲρ

[1] The marginal numbers in Neumann's text represent the paging of the edition of Cyril by Spanheim, 1696, as rearranged

AGAINST THE GALILAEANS

Book I

It is, I think, expedient to set forth to all mankind the reasons by which I was convinced that the fabrication of the Galilaeans is a fiction of men composed by wickedness. Though it has in it nothing divine, by making full use of that part of the soul which loves fable and is childish and foolish, it has induced men to believe that the monstrous tale is truth. Now since I intend to treat of all their first dogmas, as they call them, I wish to say in the first place that if my readers desire to try to refute me they must proceed as if they were in a court of law and not drag in irrelevant matter, or, as the saying is, bring counter-charges until they have defended their own views. For thus it will be better and clearer if, when they wish to censure any views of mine, they undertake that as a separate task, but when they are defending themselves against my censure, they bring no counter-charges.

It is worth while to recall in a few words whence and how we first arrived at a conception of God; next to compare what is said about the divine among the Hellenes and Hebrews; and finally

---

by Neumann. In the Introduction to his edition he defends his rearrangement of the text of Aubert 1638, given by Spanheim.

[2] τῶν παρ' αὐτοῖς Neumann; MS. τῶν πρώτων Gollwitzer would retain, taking ὑπὲρ τῶν πρώτων = πρὸς τὰ πρῶτα.

43 A τοῦ θείου λεγόμενα, καὶ μετὰ τοῦτο ἐπανερέσθαι τοὺς οὔτε Ἕλληνας οὔτε Ἰουδαίους, ἀλλὰ τῆς Γαλιλαίων ὄντας αἱρέσεως, ἀνθ' ὅτου πρὸ τῶν ἡμετέρων εἵλοντο τὰ παρ' ἐκείνοις, καὶ ἐπὶ τούτῳ, τί δή ποτε μηδ' ἐκείνοις ἐμμένουσιν, ἀλλὰ κἀκείνων ἀποστάντες ἰδίαν ὁδὸν ἐτράποντο. ὁμολογήσαντες μὲν οὐδὲν τῶν καλῶν οὐδὲ τῶν σπουδαίων οὔτε τῶν παρ' ἡμῖν τοῖς Ἕλλησιν οὔτε τῶν παρὰ τοῖς ἀπὸ Μωυσέως Ἑβραίοις,[1] ἀπ' ἀμφοῖν δὲ τὰς παραπεπηγυίας τούτοις τοῖς ἔθνεσιν ὥσπερ τινὰς
43 B Κῆρας δρεπόμενοι, τὴν ἀθεότητα μὲν ἐκ τῆς Ἰουδαϊκῆς ῥᾳδιουργίας, φαῦλον δὲ καὶ ἐπισεσυρμένον βίον ἐκ τῆς παρ' ἡμῖν ῥᾳθυμίας καὶ χυδαιότητος, τοῦτο τὴν ἀρίστην θεοσέβειαν ἠθέλησαν ὀνομάζεσθαι.

52 B Ὅτι δὲ οὐ διδακτόν, ἀλλὰ φύσει τὸ εἰδέναι θεὸν τοῖς ἀνθρώποις ὑπάρχει, τεκμήριον ἡμῖν ἔστω πρῶτον ἡ κοινὴ πάντων ἀνθρώπων ἰδίᾳ καὶ δημοσίᾳ καὶ κατ' ἄνδρα καὶ ἔθνη περὶ τὸ θεῖον προθυμία. ἅπαντες γὰρ ἀδιδάκτως θεῖόν τι πεπιστεύκαμεν, ὑπὲρ οὗ τὸ μὲν ἀκριβὲς οὔτε πᾶσι ῥᾴδιον γινώσκειν οὔτε τοῖς ἐγνωκόσιν εἰπεῖν εἰς πάντας δυνατόν . . . ταύτῃ δὴ τῇ κοινῇ πάντων ἀνθρώπων ἐννοίᾳ πρόσεστι καὶ ἄλλη. πάντες γὰρ οὐρανῷ
52 C καὶ τοῖς ἐν αὐτῷ φαινομένοις θεοῖς οὕτω δή τι φυσικῶς προσηρτήμεθα, ὡς καὶ εἴ τις ἄλλον ὑπέλαβε παρ' αὐτοὺς τὸν θεόν, οἰκητήριον αὐτῷ πάντως τὸν οὐρανὸν ἀπένειμεν, οὐκ ἀποστήσας αὐτὸν τῆς γῆς, ἀλλ' οἷον ὡς εἰς τιμιώτερον τοῦ

[1] Klimek would delete Ἑβραίοις as a gloss.

---

[1] Some words are lost.

to enquire of those who are neither Hellenes nor Jews, but belong to the sect of the Galilaeans, why they preferred the belief of the Jews to ours; and what, further, can be the reason why they do not even adhere to the Jewish beliefs but have abandoned them also and followed a way of their own. For they have not accepted a single admirable or important doctrine of those that are held either by us Hellenes or by the Hebrews who derived them from Moses; but from both religions they have gathered what has been engrafted like powers of evil, as it were, on these nations—atheism from the Jewish levity, and a sordid and slovenly way of living from our indolence and vulgarity; and they desire that this should be called the noblest worship of the gods.

Now that the human race possesses its knowledge of God by nature and not from teaching is proved to us first of all by the universal yearning for the divine that is in all men whether private persons or communities, whether considered as individuals or as races. For all of us, without being taught, have attained to a belief in some sort of divinity, though it is not easy for all men to know the precise truth about it, nor is it possible for those who do know it to tell it to all men. . . .[1] Surely, besides this conception which is common to all men, there is another also. I mean that we are all by nature so closely dependent on the heavens and the gods that are visible therein, that even if any man conceives of another god besides these, he in every case assigns to him the heavens as his dwelling-place; not that he thereby separates him from the earth, but he so to speak establishes the King of

παντὸς ἐκεῖνο τὸν βασιλέα καθίσας τῶν ὅλων ἐφορᾶν ἐκεῖθεν ὑπολαμβάνων τὰ τῇδε.

69 B Τί δεῖ μοι[1] καλεῖν Ἕλληνας καὶ Ἑβραίους ἐνταῦθα μάρτυρας; οὐδείς ἐστιν, ὃς οὐκ ἀνατείνει μὲν εἰς οὐρανὸν τὰς χεῖρας εὐχόμενος, ὀμνύων δὲ θεὸν ἤτοι θεούς, ἔννοιαν ὅλως τοῦ θείου λαμβάνων, ἐκεῖσε φέρεται. καὶ τοῦτο οὐκ ἀπεικότως ἔπαθον. ὁρῶντες γὰρ οὔτε πληθυνόμενον[2] οὔτε ἐλαττούμενόν τι τῶν περὶ τὸν οὐρανὸν οὔτε τρεπόμενον οὔτε πάθος ὑπομένον τι τῶν ἀτάκτων, ἀλλ' ἐναρμόνιον μὲν αὐτοῦ τὴν κίνησιν, ἐμμελῆ δὲ τὴν τάξιν,
69 C ὡρισμένους δὲ φωτισμοὺς σελήνης, ἡλίου δὲ ἀνατολὰς καὶ δύσεις ὡρισμένας ἐν ὡρισμένοις ἀεὶ καιροῖς, εἰκότως θεὸν καὶ θεοῦ θρόνον ὑπέλαβον. τὸ γὰρ τοιοῦτον, ἅτε μηδεμιᾷ προσθήκῃ πληθυνόμενον μηδὲ ἐλαττούμενον ἀφαιρέσει, τῆς τε κατ' ἀλλοίωσιν καὶ τροπὴν ἐκτὸς ἱστάμενον μεταβολῆς πάσης καθαρεύει φθορᾶς καὶ γενέσεως, ἀθάνατον δὲ ὂν φύσει καὶ ἀνώλεθρον παντοίας ἐστὶ καθαρὸν κηλῖδος· ἀΐδιον δὲ καὶ ἀεικίνητον, ὡς ὁρῶμεν, ἤτοι
69 D παρὰ ψυχῆς κρείττονος καὶ θειοτέρας ἐνοικούσης αὐτῷ, ὥσπερ, οἶμαι, τὰ ἡμέτερα σώματα παρὰ τῆς ἐν ἡμῖν ψυχῆς, φέρεται κύκλῳ περὶ τὸν μέγαν δημιουργόν, ἢ πρὸς αὐτοῦ τοῦ θεοῦ τὴν κίνησιν παραδεξάμενον τὸν ἄπειρον ἐξελίττει κύκλον ἀπαύστῳ καὶ αἰωνίῳ φορᾷ.

[1] Gollwitzer deletes μοι.
[2] οὔτε πληθυνόμενον Klimek adds, cf. 69 C.

---

[1] Cf. *Oration* 6. 183c, Vol. 2.

the All in the heavens[1] as in the most honourable place of all, and conceives of him as overseeing from there the affairs of this world.

What need have I to summon Hellenes and Hebrews as witnesses of this? There exists no man who does not stretch out his hands towards the heavens when he prays; and whether he swears by one god or several, if he has any notion at all of the divine, he turns heavenward. And it was very natural that men should feel thus. For since they observed that in what concerns the heavenly bodies there is no increase or diminution or mutability, and that they do not suffer any unregulated influence, but their movement is harmonious and their arrangement in concert; and that the illuminations of the moon are regulated, and that the risings and settings of the sun are regularly defined, and always at regularly defined seasons, they naturally conceived that the heaven is a god and the throne of a god.[2] For a being of that sort, since it is not subject to increase by addition, or to diminution by subtraction, and is stationed beyond all change due to alteration and mutability, is free from decay and generation, and inasmuch as it is immortal by nature and indestructible, it is pure from every sort of stain. Eternal and ever in movement, as we see, it travels in a circuit about the great Creator, whether it be impelled by a nobler and more divine soul that dwells therein, just as, I mean, our bodies are by the soul in us, or having received its motion from God Himself, it wheels in its boundless circuit, in an unceasing and eternal career.

[2] Cyril 70A ridicules Julian for confusing here a god with a throne; but καὶ can be interpreted "or."

44 A Οὐκοῦν Ἕλληνες μὲν τοὺς μύθους ἔπλασαν ὑπὲρ
τῶν θεῶν ἀπίστους καὶ τερατώδεις. καταπιεῖν
44 B γὰρ ἔφασαν τὸν Κρόνον τοὺς παῖδας[1] εἶτ' αὖθις
ἐμέσαι. καὶ γάμους ἤδη παρανόμους· μητρὶ γὰρ
ὁ Ζεὺς ἐμίχθη καὶ παιδοποιησάμενος ἐξ αὐτῆς
ἔγημε μὲν αὐτὸς τὴν αὑτοῦ θυγατέρα, μᾶλλον δὲ
οὐδὲ ἔγημεν, ἀλλὰ μιχθεὶς ἁπλῶς ἄλλῳ παραδέ-
δωκεν[2] αὐτήν. εἶτα οἱ Διονύσου σπαραγμοὶ καὶ
μελῶν κολλήσεις. τοιαῦτα οἱ μῦθοι τῶν Ἑλλήνων
75 A φασίν. τούτοις παράβαλλε τὴν Ἰουδαϊκὴν διδασ-
καλίαν, καὶ τὸν φυτευόμενον ὑπὸ τοῦ θεοῦ παρά-
δεισον καὶ τὸν ὑπ' αὐτοῦ πλαττόμενον Ἀδάμ, εἶτα
τὴν γινομένην αὐτῷ γυναῖκα. λέγει γὰρ ὁ θεός
"Οὐ καλὸν εἶναι τὸν ἄνθρωπον μόνον· ποιήσωμεν
αὐτῷ βοηθὸν κατ' αὐτόν," πρὸς οὐδὲν μὲν αὐτῷ
τῶν ὅλων βοηθήσασαν, ἐξαπατήσασαν δὲ καὶ
γενομένην παραίτιον αὐτῷ τε ἐκείνῳ καὶ ἑαυτῇ
75 B τοῦ πεσεῖν ἔξω τῆς τοῦ παραδείσου τρυφῆς.
Ταῦτα γάρ ἐστι μυθώδη παντελῶς. ἐπεὶ πῶς
εὔλογον ἀγνοεῖν τὸν θεόν, ὅτι τὸ γινόμενον ὑπ'
αὐτοῦ πρὸς βοήθειαν οὐ πρὸς καλοῦ μᾶλλον, ἀλλὰ
86 A πρὸς κακοῦ τῷ λαβόντι γενήσεται; τὸν γὰρ ὄφιν
τὸν διαλεγόμενον πρὸς τὴν Εὔαν ποδαπῇ τινι
χρῆσθαι φήσομεν διαλέκτῳ; ἆρα ἀνθρωπείᾳ; καὶ
τί διαφέρει τῶν παρὰ τοῖς Ἕλλησι πεπλασμένων
89 A μύθων τὰ τοιαῦτα; τὸ δὲ καὶ τὸν θεὸν ἀπαγορεύειν
τὴν διάγνωσιν καλοῦ τε καὶ φαύλου τοῖς ὑπ'
αὐτοῦ πλασθεῖσιν ἀνθρώποις ἆρ' οὐχ ὑπερβολὴν

[1] Before εἶτ' Neumann adds καί, but this is not necessary.
[2] παρέδωκεν Klimek.

---

[1] Persephone. [2] Hades.

Now it is true that the Hellenes invented their myths about the gods, incredible and monstrous stories. For they said that Kronos swallowed his children and then vomited them forth; and they even told of lawless unions, how Zeus had intercourse with his mother, and after having a child by her, married his own daughter,[1] or rather did not even marry her, but simply had intercourse with her and then handed her over to another.[2] Then too there is the legend that Dionysus was rent asunder and his limbs joined together again. This is the sort of thing described in the myths of the Hellenes. Compare with them the Jewish doctrine, how the garden was planted by God and Adam was fashioned by Him, and next, for Adam, woman came to be. For God said, "It is not good that the man should be alone. Let us make him an help meet like him."[3] Yet so far was she from helping him at all that she deceived him, and was in part the cause of his and her own fall from their life of ease in the garden.

This is wholly fabulous. For is it probable that God did not know that the being he was creating as a help meet would prove to be not so much a blessing as a misfortune to him who received her? Again, what sort of language are we to say that the serpent used when he talked with Eve? Was it the language of human beings? And in what do such legends as these differ from the myths that were invented by the Hellenes? Moreover, is it not excessively strange that God should deny to the human beings whom he had fashioned the power to distinguish between good

[3] *Genesis* 2. 18.

ἀτοπίας ἔχει; τί γὰρ ἂν ἠλιθιώτερον γένοιτο τοῦ
μὴ δυναμένου διαγινώσκειν καλὸν καὶ πονηρόν;
δῆλον γάρ, ὅτι τὰ μὲν οὐ φεύξεται, λέγω δὲ τὰ
κακά, τὰ δὲ οὐ μεταδιώξει, λέγω δὲ τὰ καλά.
κεφάλαιον δέ, φρονήσεως ἀπηγόρευσεν ὁ θεὸς
ἀνθρώπῳ γεύσασθαι, ἧς οὐδὲν ἂν εἴη τιμιώτερον
89 B ἀνθρώπῳ.[1] ὅτι γὰρ ἡ τοῦ καλοῦ καὶ τοῦ χείρονος
διάγνωσις οἰκεῖόν ἐστιν ἔργον φρονήσεως, πρόδηλόν
93 D ἐστί που καὶ τοῖς ἀνοήτοις· ὥστε τὸν ὄφιν εὐερ-
γέτην μᾶλλον, ἀλλ' οὐχὶ λυμεῶνα τῆς ἀνθρωπίνης
93 E γενέσεως εἶναι. ἐπὶ τούτοις ὁ θεὸς δεῖ λέγεσθαι[2]
βάσκανος. ἐπειδὴ γὰρ εἶδε μετασχόντα τῆς φρο-
νήσεως τὸν ἄνθρωπον, ἵνα μή, φησί, γεύσηται τοῦ
ξύλου τῆς ζωῆς, ἐξέβαλεν αὐτὸν τοῦ παραδείσου
διαρρήδην εἰπών· "Ἰδού, Ἀδὰμ γέγονεν ὡς εἷς ἐξ
ἡμῶν τοῦ γινώσκειν καλὸν καὶ πονηρόν. καὶ νῦν
μήποτε ἐκτείνῃ τὴν χεῖρα καὶ λάβῃ ἀπὸ τοῦ ξύλου
τῆς ζωῆς καὶ φάγῃ καὶ ζήσεται εἰς τὸν αἰῶνα."
94 A τούτων τοίνυν ἕκαστον εἰ μὴ μῦθος ἔχων θεωρίαν
ἀπόρρητον εἴη, ὅπερ ἐγὼ νενόμικα, πολλῆς γέ-
μουσιν οἱ λόγοι περὶ τοῦ θεοῦ βλασφημίας. τὸ
γὰρ ἀγνοῆσαι μέν, ὡς ἡ γινομένη βοηθὸς αἰτία
τοῦ πτώματος ἔσται καὶ τὸ ἀπαγορεῦσαι καλοῦ
καὶ πονηροῦ γνῶσιν,[3] ὃ μόνον ἔοικε συνέχειν τὸν
νοῦν τὸν ἀνθρώπινον, καὶ πρόσετι τὸ ζηλοτυπῆσαι,

[1] αὐτῷ Neumann, ἀνθρώπῳ MSS.; Klimek would delete ἀνθρώπῳ; Gollwitzer rightly retains as characteristic Julianic tautology.

[2] δεῖ λέγεσθαι Neumann; λέγοιτ' ἂν Klimek; λέγεται MSS.; Gollwitzer deletes ἐπί.

[3] Gollwitzer adds λαβεῖν; Asmus ἀναλαβεῖν, *cf.* Vol. 2, 265A.

[1] *Genesis* 3. 22.

and evil? What could be more foolish than a being unable to distinguish good from bad? For it is evident that he would not avoid the latter, I mean things evil, nor would he strive after the former, I mean things good. And, in short, God refused to let man taste of wisdom, than which there could be nothing of more value for man. For that the power to distinguish between good and less good is the property of wisdom is evident surely even to the witless; so that the serpent was a benefactor rather than a destroyer of the human race. Furthermore, their God must be called envious. For when he saw that man had attained to a share of wisdom, that he might not, God said, taste of the tree of life, he cast him out of the garden, saying in so many words, "Behold, Adam has become as one of us, because he knows good from bad; and now let him not put forth his hand and take also of the tree of life and eat and thus live forever."[1] Accordingly, unless every one of these legends is a myth that involves some secret interpretation, as I indeed believe,[2] they are filled with many blasphemous sayings about God. For in the first place to be ignorant that she who was created as a help meet would be the cause of the fall; secondly to refuse the knowledge of good and bad, which knowledge alone seems to give coherence to the mind of man; and lastly to be jealous lest man should take of the

[2] For Julian's belief that myths need allegorical interpretation cf. *Oration* 5. 169–170, Vol. 1, p. 475, note; see also *Caesars* 306C, *Oration* 7. 206C, 220, for myths as emblematic of the truth. This is the regular method of Neo-Platonic writers, such as Sallustius, in dealing with the unpleasant or incongruous elements in Greek mythology.

μὴ τοῦ ξύλου τῆς ζωῆς μεταλαβὼν ἄνθρωπος ἀθάνατος ἐκ θνητοῦ γένηται, φθονεροῦ καὶ βασκάνου λίαν ἐστίν.

96 C Ὑπὲρ δὲ ὧν ἐκεῖνοί τε ἀληθῶς δοξάζουσιν ἡμῖν τε ἐξ ἀρχῆς οἱ πατέρες παρέδοσαν, ὁ μὲν ἡμέτερος ἔχει λόγος ὡδὶ [1] τὸν προσεχῆ τοῦ κόσμου τούτου δημιουργόν. . . . ὑπὲρ γὰρ θεῶν[2] τῶν ἀνωτέρω τούτου Μωυσῆς μὲν εἴρηκεν οὐδὲν ὅλως, ὅς γε οὐδὲ ὑπὲρ
96 D τῆς τῶν ἀγγέλων ἐτόλμησέ τι φύσεως· ἀλλ' ὅτι μὲν λειτουργοῦσι τῷ θεῷ πολλαχῶς καὶ πολλάκις εἶπεν, εἴτε δὲ γεγονότες, εἴτε ἀγένητοι, εἴτε ὑπ' ἄλλου μὲν γεγονότες, ἄλλῳ δὲ λειτουργεῖν τεταγμένοι, εἴτε ἄλλως πως, οὐδαμόθεν διώρισται. περὶ δὲ οὐρανοῦ καὶ γῆς καὶ τῶν ἐν αὐτῇ τίνα τρόπον διεκοσμήθη διέξεισι. καὶ τὰ μέν φησι κελεῦσαι τὸν θεὸν γενέσθαι, ὥσπερ φῶς καὶ στερέωμα, τὰ δὲ ποιῆσαι, ὥσπερ οὐρανὸν καὶ γῆν,
96 E ἥλιόν τε καὶ σελήνην, τὰ δὲ ὄντα, κρυπτόμενα δὲ τέως,[3] διακρῖναι, καθάπερ ὕδωρ, οἶμαι, καὶ τὴν ξηράν. πρὸς τούτοις δὲ οὐδὲ περὶ γενέσεως ἢ περὶ ποιήσεως τοῦ πνεύματος εἰπεῖν ἐτόλμησεν, ἀλλὰ μόνον "Καὶ πνεῦμα θεοῦ ἐπεφέρετο ἐπάνω τοῦ ὕδατος"· πότερον δὲ ἀγένητόν ἐστιν ἢ γέγονεν, οὐδὲν διασαφεῖ.

49 A Ἐνταῦθα παραβάλωμεν, εἰ βούλεσθε, τὴν Πλάτωνος φωνήν. τί τοίνυν οὗτος ὑπὲρ τοῦ δημιουργοῦ λέγει καὶ τίνας περιτίθησιν αὐτῷ

[1] ὡδὶ Asmus restores from MSS.; οὐδὲ Neumann.
[2] Asmus deletes as superfluous θεῶν added by Neumann.
[3] δέ, τέως Neumann; δὲ τέως, Asmus.

---

[1] The pagan theory is missing and also part of the Jewish, according to Asmus.

tree of life and from mortal become immortal,—this is to be grudging and envious overmuch.

Next to consider the views that are correctly held by the Jews, and also those that our fathers handed down to us from the beginning. Our account has in it the immediate creator of this universe, as the following shows. . . .[1] Moses indeed has said nothing whatsoever about the gods who are superior to this creator, nay, he has not even ventured to say anything about the nature of the angels. But that they serve God he has asserted in many ways and often; but whether they were generated or ungenerated, or whether they were generated by one god and appointed to serve another, or in some other way, he has nowhere said definitely. But he describes fully in what manner the heavens and the earth and all that therein is were set in order. In part, he says, God ordered them to be, such as light and the firmament, and in part, he says, God made them, such as the heavens and the earth, the sun and moon, and that all things which already existed but were hidden away for the time being, he separated, such as water, I mean, and dry land. But apart from these he did not venture to say a word about the generation or the making of the Spirit, but only this, "And the Spirit of God moved upon the face of the waters." But whether that spirit was ungenerated or had been generated he does not make at all clear.

Now, if you please, we will compare the utterance of Plato.[2] Observe then what he says about the creator, and what words he makes him speak

[2] In his *Letter to a Priest* 292, Vol. 2, Julian contrasts the Platonic account of the Creation with the Mosaic.

φωνὰς ἐν τῇ κοσμογενείᾳ σκόπησον, ἵνα τὴν
Πλάτωνος καὶ Μωυσέως κοσμογένειαν ἀντιπαρα-
βάλωμεν ἀλλήλαις. οὕτω γὰρ ἂν φανείη, τίς ὁ
κρείττων καὶ τίς ἄξιος τοῦ θεοῦ μᾶλλον, ἆρ᾽ ὁ τοῖς
εἰδώλοις λελατρευκὼς Πλάτων ἢ περὶ οὗ φησιν ἡ
49 B γραφή, ὅτι στόμα κατὰ στόμα ὁ θεὸς ἐλάλησεν
αὐτῷ. "Ἐν ἀρχῇ ἐποίησεν ὁ θεὸς τὸν οὐρανὸν καὶ
τὴν γῆν. ἡ δὲ γῆ ἦν ἀόρατος καὶ ἀκατασκεύαστος,
καὶ σκότος ἐπάνω τῆς ἀβύσσου, καὶ πνεῦμα θεοῦ
ἐπεφέρετο ἐπάνω τοῦ ὕδατος. καὶ εἶπεν ὁ θεός
Γενηθήτω φῶς, καὶ ἐγένετο φῶς. καὶ εἶδεν ὁ
θεὸς τὸ φῶς, ὅτι καλόν. καὶ διεχώρισεν ὁ θεὸς
ἀνὰ μέσον τοῦ φωτὸς καὶ ἀνὰ μέσον τοῦ σκότους.
καὶ ἐκάλεσεν ὁ θεὸς τὸ φῶς ἡμέραν καὶ τὸ σκότος
ἐκάλεσε νύκτα. καὶ ἐγένετο ἑσπέρα καὶ ἐγένετο
πρωί, ἡμέρα μία. καὶ εἶπεν ὁ θεός· Γενηθήτω
49 C στερέωμα ἐν μέσῳ τοῦ ὕδατος. καὶ ἐκάλεσεν ὁ
θεὸς τὸ στερέωμα οὐρανόν. καὶ εἶπεν ὁ θεός·
Συναχθήτω τὸ ὕδωρ τὸ ὑποκάτω τοῦ οὐρανοῦ εἰς
συναγωγὴν μίαν καὶ ὀφθήτω ἡ ξηρά. καὶ ἐγένετο
οὕτως. καὶ εἶπεν ὁ θεός· Βλαστησάτω ἡ γῆ βο-
τάνην χόρτου καὶ ξύλον κάρπιμον. καὶ εἶπεν ὁ
θεός· Γενηθήτωσαν φωστῆρες ἐν τῷ στερεώματι
τοῦ οὐρανοῦ, ἵνα ὦσιν εἰς φαῦσιν ἐπὶ τῆς γῆς.
καὶ ἔθετο αὐτοὺς ὁ θεὸς ἐν τῷ στερεώματι τοῦ
49 D οὐρανοῦ, ὥστε ἄρχειν τῆς ἡμέρας καὶ τῆς νυκτός."

Ἐν δὴ τούτοις Μωυσῆς οὔτε τὴν ἄβυσσον πε-
ποιῆσθαί φησιν ὑπὸ τοῦ θεοῦ οὔτε τὸ σκότος
οὔτε τὸ ὕδωρ· καίτοι χρῆν δήπουθεν εἰπόντα περὶ

at the time of the generation of the universe, in order that we may compare Plato's account of that generation with that of Moses. For in this way it will appear who was the nobler and who was more worthy of intercourse with God, Plato who paid homage to images, or he of whom the Scripture says that God spake with him mouth to mouth.[1] "In the beginning God created the heaven and the earth. And the earth was invisible and without form, and darkness was upon the face of the deep. And the spirit of God moved upon the face of the waters. And God said, Let there be light; and there was light. And God saw the light that it was good; and God divided the light from the darkness. And God called the light Day, and the darkness he called Night. And the evening and the morning were the first day. And God said, Let there be a firmament in the midst of the waters. And God called the firmament Heaven. And God said, Let the waters under the heaven be gathered together unto one place, and let the dry land appear; and it was so. And God said, Let the earth bring forth grass for fodder, and the fruit tree yielding fruit. And God said, Let there be lights in the firmament of the heaven that they may be for a light upon the earth. And God set them in the firmament of the heaven to rule over the day and over the night."[2]

In all this, you observe, Moses does not say that the deep was created by God, or the darkness or the waters. And yet, after saying concerning light

[1] *Numbers* 12. 8: "With him will I speak mouth to mouth."

[2] *Genesis* 1–17, with certain omissions.

τοῦ φωτός, ὅτι προστάξαντος θεοῦ γέγονεν, εἰπεῖν ἔτι καὶ περὶ τῆς νυκτὸς καὶ περὶ τῆς ἀβύσσου καὶ περὶ τοῦ ὕδατος. ὁ δὲ οὐδὲν εἶπεν ὡς περὶ οὐ[1] γεγονότων ὅλως, καίτοι πολλάκις ἐπιμνησθεὶς αὐτῶν. πρὸς τούτοις οὔτε τῆς τῶν ἀγγέλων μέμνηται γενέσεως ἢ ποιήσεως οὐδ' ὅντινα τρόπον
49 E παρήχθησαν, ἀλλὰ τῶν περὶ τὸν οὐρανὸν μόνον καὶ περὶ τὴν γῆν σωμάτων,[2] ὡς εἶναι τὸν θεὸν κατὰ τὸν Μωυσέα ἀσωμάτων μὲν οὐδενὸς ποιητήν, ὕλης δὲ ὑποκειμένης κοσμήτορα. τὸ γὰρ "Ἡ δὲ γῆ ἦν ἀόρατος καὶ ἀκατασκεύαστος" οὐδὲν ἕτερόν ἐστιν ἢ τὴν μὲν ὑγρὰν καὶ ξηρὰν οὐσίαν ὕλην ποιοῦντος, κοσμήτορα δὲ αὐτῆς τὸν θεὸν εἰσάγοντος.

57 B Ὅ γε μὴν Πλάτων ἄκουε περὶ τοῦ κόσμου τί
57 C φησιν. "Ὁ δὴ πᾶς οὐρανὸς ἢ κόσμος—ἢ καὶ ἄλλο, ὅ τί ποτε ὀνομαζόμενος μάλιστα ἂν δέχοιτο, τοῦτο ἡμῖν ὠνομάσθω—πότερον ἦν ἀεί, γενέσεως ἀρχὴν ἔχων οὐδεμίαν, ἢ γέγονεν, ἀπ' ἀρχῆς τινος ἀρξάμενος; γέγονεν· ὁρατὸς γὰρ ἅπτος τέ ἐστι καὶ σῶμα ἔχων. πάντα δὲ τὰ τοιαῦτα αἰσθητά, τὰ δὲ αἰσθητά, δόξῃ περιληπτὰ μετὰ αἰσθήσεως, γιγνόμενα καὶ γεννητὰ ἐφάνη . . . οὕτως οὖν κατὰ τὸν λόγον τὸν εἰκότα δεῖ λέγειν τόνδε τὸν κόσμον ζῷον ἔμψυχον ἔννουν τε τῇ ἀληθείᾳ διὰ τὴν τοῦ
57 D θεοῦ γενέσθαι πρόνοιαν."
57 E Ἓν δὲ ἑνὶ παραβάλωμεν μόνον· τίνα καὶ ποδα-

[1] Klimek ὡς περὶ οὐ; Neumann ὡς περί.

[2] Neumann σκηνωμάτων from *Marcianus* 123; σωμάτων Wright from *Marcianus* 122.

---

[1] *Timaeus* 28B, C.

that God ordered it to be, and it was, surely he ought to have gone on to speak of night also, and the deep and the waters. But of them he says not a word to imply that they were not already existing at all, though he often mentions them. Furthermore, he does not mention the birth or creation of the angels or in what manner they were brought into being, but deals only with the heavenly and earthly bodies. It follows that, according to Moses, God is the creator of nothing that is incorporeal, but is only the disposer of matter that already existed. For the words, "And the earth was invisible and without form" can only mean that he regards the wet and dry substance as the original matter and that he introduces God as the disposer of this matter.

Now on the other hand hear what Plato says about the universe: "Now the whole heaven or the universe,—or whatever other name would be most acceptable to it, so let it be named by us,—did it exist eternally, having no beginning of generation, or has it come into being starting from some beginning? It has come into being. For it can be seen and handled and has a body; and all such things are the objects of sensation, and such objects of sensation, being apprehensible by opinion with the aid of sensation are things that came into being, as we saw, and have been generated. . . .[1] It follows, therefore, according to the reasonable theory, that we ought to affirm that this universe came into being as a living creature possessing soul and intelligence in very truth, both by the providence of God."[2]

Let us but compare them, point by point. What

[2] *Timaeus* 30B; cf. Julian, *Oration* 5. 170D.

πὴν ποιεῖται δημηγορίαν ὁ θεὸς ὁ παρὰ Μωυσῇ καὶ ποδαπὴν ὁ παρὰ Πλάτωνι;

58 A "Καὶ εἶπεν ὁ θεός· Ποιήσωμεν ἄνθρωπον κατ' εἰκόνα ἡμετέραν καὶ καθ' ὁμοίωσιν. καὶ ἀρχέτωσαν τῶν ἰχθύων τῆς θαλάσσης καὶ τῶν πετεινῶν τοῦ οὐρανοῦ καὶ τῶν κτηνῶν καὶ πάσης τῆς γῆς καὶ πάντων τῶν ἑρπετῶν τῶν ἑρπόντων ἐπὶ τῆς γῆς. καὶ ἐποίησεν ὁ θεὸς τὸν ἄνθρωπον, κατ' εἰκόνα θεοῦ ἐποίησεν αὐτόν· ἄρσεν καὶ θῆλυ ἐποίησεν αὐτοὺς λέγων· Αὐξάνεσθε καὶ πληθύνεσθε καὶ πληρώσατε τὴν γῆν καὶ κατακυριεύσατε αὐ-
58 B τῆς. καὶ ἀρχέτωσαν τῶν ἰχθύων τῆς θαλάσσης καὶ τῶν πετεινῶν τοῦ οὐρανοῦ καὶ πάντων τῶν κτηνῶν καὶ πάσης τῆς γῆς."

Ἄκουε δὴ οὖν καὶ τῆς Πλατωνικῆς δημηγορίας, ἣν τῷ τῶν ὅλων περιτίθησι δημιουργῷ.

"Θεοὶ θεῶν, ὧν ἐγὼ δημιουργὸς πατήρ τε ἔργων ἄλυτα ἔσται ἐμοῦ γε ἐθέλοντος. τὸ μὲν δὴ δεθὲν πᾶν λυτόν, τό γε μὴν καλῶς ἁρμοσθὲν καὶ ἔχον εὖ λύειν ἐθέλειν κακοῦ. διὸ ἐπείπερ γεγένησθε, οὐκ ἀθάνατοι μέν ἐστε οὐδὲ ἄλυτοι τὸ πάμπαν, οὔτι γε μὴν λυθήσεσθε οὐδὲ τεύξεσθε θανάτου μοίρας,
58 C τῆς ἐμῆς βουλήσεως μείζονος ἔτι δεσμοῦ καὶ κυριωτέρου λαχόντες ἐκείνων, οἷς ὅτε ἐγίνεσθε ξυνεδεῖσθε. νῦν οὖν ὃ λέγω πρὸς ὑμᾶς ἐνδεικνύμενος μάθετε. θνητὰ ἔτι γένη λοιπὰ τρία ἀγέννητα, τούτων δὲ μὴ γενομένων οὐρανὸς ἀτελὴς ἔσται. τὰ γὰρ πάντα ἐν αὐτῷ γένη ζῴων οὐχ ἕξει· ὑπ' ἐμοῦ δὲ ταῦτα γενόμενα καὶ βίου μετα-

[1] *Genesis* 26. 27. 28.

and what sort of speech does the god make in the account of Moses, and what the god in the account of Plato?

"And God said, Let us make man in our image, and our likeness; and let them have dominion over the fish of the sea, and over the fowl of the air, and over the cattle, and over all the earth, and over every creeping thing that creepeth upon the earth. So God created man, in the image of God created he him; male and female created he them, and said, Be fruitful and multiply and replenish the earth, and subdue it; and have dominion over the fish of the sea, and over the fowl of the air, and over all the cattle and over all the earth."[1]

Now, I say, hear also the speech which Plato puts in the mouth of the Artificer of the All.

"Gods of Gods! Those works whose artificer and father I am will abide indissoluble, so long as it is my will. Lo, all that hath been fastened may be loosed, yet to will to loose that which is harmonious and in good case were the act of an evil being. Wherefore, since ye have come into being, ye are not immortal or indissoluble altogether, nevertheless ye shall by no means be loosed or meet with the doom of death, since ye have found in my will a bond more mighty and more potent than those wherewith ye were bound when ye came into being. Now therefore hearken to the saying which I proclaim unto you: Three kinds of mortal beings still remain unborn, and unless these have birth the heaven will be incomplete. For it will not have within itself all the kinds of living things. Yet if these should come into being and receive a share of life at

σχόντα θεοῖς ἰσάζοιτο ἄν. ἵν᾽ οὖν θνητά τε ᾖ τό τε πᾶν τόδε ὄντως ἅπαν ᾖ, τρέπεσθε κατὰ φύσιν ὑμεῖς ἐπὶ τὴν τῶν ζῴων δημιουργίαν, μιμούμενοι
58 D τὴν ἐμὴν δύναμιν περὶ τὴν ὑμετέραν γένεσιν. καὶ καθ᾽ ὅσον μὲν αὐτῶν ἀθανάτοις ὁμώνυμον εἶναι προσήκει, θεῖον λεγόμενον ἡγεμονοῦν τε ἐν αὐτοῖς τῶν ἀεὶ δίκῃ καὶ ὑμῖν ἐθελόντων ἕπεσθαι, σπείρας καὶ ὑπαρξάμενος ἐγὼ παραδώσω. τὸ δὲ λοιπὸν ὑμεῖς, ἀθανάτῳ θνητὸν προσυφαίνοντες ἀπεργάζεσθε ζῷα καὶ γεννᾶτε τροφήν τε διδόντες αὐξάνετε καὶ φθίνοντα πάλιν δέχεσθε."

65 A Ἀλλ᾽ ἆρα μὴ τοῦτο ὄναρ ἐστὶν ἐννοήσοντες
65 B αὐτὸ μαθέτε. θεοὺς ὀνομάζει Πλάτων τοὺς ἐμφανεῖς, ἥλιον καὶ σελήνην, ἄστρα καὶ οὐρανόν, ἀλλ᾽ οὗτοι τῶν ἀφανῶν εἰσιν εἰκόνες· ὁ φαινόμενος τοῖς ὀφθαλμοῖς ἡμῶν ἥλιος τοῦ νοητοῦ καὶ μὴ φαινομένου, καὶ πάλιν ἡ φαινομένη τοῖς ὀφθαλμοῖς ἡμῶν σελήνη καὶ τῶν ἄστρων ἕκαστον εἰκόνες εἰσὶ τῶν νοητῶν. ἐκείνους οὖν τοὺς νοητοὺς καὶ
65 C ἀφανεῖς θεοὺς ἐνυπάρχοντας καὶ συνυπάρχοντας καὶ ἐξ αὐτοῦ τοῦ δημιουργοῦ γεννηθέντας καὶ προελθόντας ὁ Πλάτων οἶδεν. εἰκότως οὖν φησιν ὁ δημιουργὸς ὁ παρ᾽ αὐτῷ "θεοί," πρὸς τοὺς ἀφανεῖς λέγων, "θεῶν," τῶν ἐμφανῶν δηλονότι. κοινὸς δὲ ἀμφοτέρων δημιουργὸς οὗτός ἐστιν ὁ τεχνησάμενος οὐρανὸν καὶ γῆν καὶ θάλασσαν καὶ

---

[1] *Timaeus* 41A,B,C. Julian may have been quoting from memory, as there are omissions and slight variations from our text of the *Timaeus*.

[2] Cf. Julian, Vol. 1, *Oration* 4. 149A, 156D.

[3] Julian's *Fourth Oration*, Vol. 1. is an exposition of this theory held by the late Neo-Platonists; in the present treatise he does not, as in the *Fourth* and *Fifth Orations*,

my hands they would become equal to gods. Therefore in order that they may be mortal, and that this All may be All in very truth, turn ye according to your nature to the contriving of living things, imitating my power even as I showed it in generating you. And such part of them as is fitted to receive the same name as the immortals, which is called divine and the power in them that governs all who are willing ever to follow justice and you, this part I, having sowed it and originated the same, will deliver to you. For the rest, do you, weaving the mortal with the immortal, contrive living beings and bring them to birth; then by giving them sustenance increase them, and when they perish receive them back again."[1]

But since ye are about to consider whether this is only a dream, do ye learn the meaning thereof. Plato gives the name gods to those that are visible, the sun and moon, the stars and the heavens, but these are only the likenesses of the invisible gods. The sun which is visible to our eyes is the likeness of the intelligible and invisible sun,[2] and again the moon which is visible to our eyes and every one of the stars are likenesses of the intelligible.[3] Accordingly Plato knows of those intelligible and invisible gods which are immanent in and coexist with the creator himself and were begotten and proceeded from him. Naturally, therefore, the creator in Plato's account says "gods" when he is addressing the invisible beings, and "of gods," meaning by this, evidently, the visible gods. And the common creator of both these is he who fashioned the heavens and

distinguish the intelligible (νοητοί) gods from the intellectual (νοεροί).

ἄστρα καὶ γεννήσας ἐν τοῖς νοητοῖς τὰ τούτων ἀρχέτυπα.

Σκόπει οὖν,[1] ὅτι καὶ τὰ ἐπὶ τούτοις καλῶς. "Λείπει" γάρ φησι "τρία θνητὰ γένη," δηλονότι τὸ τῶν ἀνθρώπων καὶ τὸ τῶν ζῴων καὶ τὸ τῶν φυτῶν· τούτων γὰρ ἕκαστον ἰδίοις ὥρισται λόγοις. "Εἰ μὲν οὖν" φησι "καὶ τούτων ἕκαστον ὑπ' ἐμοῦ
65 D γένοιτο, παντάπασιν ἀναγκαῖον ἀθάνατον αὐτὸ γενέσθαι." καὶ γὰρ τοῖς νοητοῖς θεοῖς οὐδὲν ἄλλο τῆς ἀθανασίας αἴτιον καὶ τῷ φαινομένῳ κόσμῳ ἢ τὸ ὑπὸ τοῦ δημιουργοῦ γενέσθαι. ὅτι οὖν φησιν "Ὁπόσον ἐστὶν ἀθάνατον, ἀναγκαῖόν ἐστι τούτοις παρὰ τοῦ δημιουργοῦ δεδόσθαι," τοῦτο δέ ἐστιν ἡ λογικὴ ψυχή. "Τὸ δὲ λοιπὸν" φησιν "ὑμεῖς
65 E ἀθανάτῳ θνητὸν προσυφαίνετε." δῆλον οὖν ὅτι παραλαβόντες οἱ δημιουργικοὶ[2] θεοὶ παρὰ τοῦ σφῶν πατρὸς τὴν δημιουργικὴν δύναμιν, ἀπεγέννησαν ἐπὶ τῆς γῆς τὰ θνητὰ τῶν ζῴων. εἰ γὰρ μηδὲν ἔμελλε διαφέρειν οὐρανὸς ἀνθρώπου καὶ ναὶ μὰ Δία θηρίου καὶ τελευταῖον αὐτῶν τῶν ἑρπετῶν καὶ τῶν ἐν τῇ θαλάσσῃ νηχομένων ἰχθυδίων, ἔδει τὸν δημιουργὸν ἕνα καὶ τὸν αὐτὸν εἶναι πάντων. εἰ δὲ πολὺ τὸ μέσον ἐστὶν ἀθανάτων καὶ
66 A θνητῶν, οὐδεμιᾷ προσθήκῃ μεῖζον οὐδὲ ἀφαιρέσει μειούμενον οὐδὲ μιγνύμενον πρὸς τὰ θνητὰ καὶ ἐπίκηρα[3] αἴτιον εἶναι προσήκει τούτων μὲν ἄλλους, ἑτέρων δὲ ἑτέρους.

Οὐκοῦν ἐπειδήπερ οὐδὲ περὶ τοῦ προσεχοῦς τοῦ

[1] οὖν ἔτι Klimek suggests.
[2] δημιουργικοὶ Asmus; δημιουργοὶ Neumann.
[3] Asmus adds οὐδὲ μιγνύμενον retains πρὸς—ἐπίκηρα; Neu-

the earth and the sea and the stars, and begat in the intelligible world the archetypes of these.

Observe then that what follows is well said also. "For," he says, "there remain three kinds of mortal things," meaning, evidently, human beings, animals and plants; for each one of these has been defined by its own peculiar definition. "Now," he goes on to say, "if each one of these also should come to exist by me, it would of necessity become immortal." And indeed, in the case of the intelligible gods and the visible universe, no other cause for their immortality exists than that they came into existence by the act of the creator. When, therefore, he says, "Such part of them as is immortal must needs be given to these by the creator," he means the reasoning soul. "For the rest," he says, "do ye weave mortal with immortal." It is therefore clear that the creative gods received from their father their creative power and so begat on earth all living things that are mortal. For if there were to be no difference between the heavens and mankind and animals too, by Zeus, and all the way down to the very tribe of creeping things and the little fish that swim in the sea, then there would have had to be one and the same creator for them all. But if there is a great gulf fixed between immortals and mortals, and this cannot become greater by addition or less by subtraction, nor can it be mixed with what is mortal and subject to fate, it follows that one set of gods were the creative cause of mortals, and another of immortals.

Accordingly, since Moses, as it seems, has failed

mann deletes *πρὸς—ἐπίκηρα*; Gollwitzer *μειούμενον ὥσπερ τὰ θνητὰ καὶ ἐπίκηρα.*

κόσμου τούτου δημιουργοῦ πάντα διειλεγμένος Μωυσῆς φαίνεται, τήν τε Ἑβραίων καὶ τὴν τῶν
99 E ἡμετέρων πατέρων δόξαν ὑπὲρ ἐθνῶν τούτων ἀντιπαραθῶμεν ἀλλήλαις.

Ὁ Μωυσῆς φησι τὸν τοῦ κόσμου δημιουργὸν ἐκλέξασθαι τὸ τῶν Ἑβραίων ἔθνος καὶ προσέχειν ἐκείνῳ μόνῳ καὶ ἐκείνου φροντίσαι καὶ δίδωσιν αὐτῷ τὴν ἐπιμέλειαν αὐτοῦ μόνου. τῶν δὲ ἄλλων ἐθνῶν, ὅπως ἢ ὑφ' οἷστισι διοικοῦνται θεοῖς, οὐδ' ἡντινοῦν μνείαν πεποίηται· πλὴν εἰ μή τις ἐκεῖνα συγχωρήσειεν, ὅτι τὸν ἥλιον αὐτοῖς καὶ τὴν σελήνην ἀπένειμεν. ἀλλ' ὑπὲρ μὲν τούτων καὶ μικρὸν
100 A ὕστερον. πλὴν ὅτι τοῦ Ἰσραὴλ αὐτὸν μόνου θεὸν καὶ τῆς Ἰουδαίας καὶ τούτους ἐκλεκτούς φησιν αὐτός τε καὶ οἱ μετ' ἐκεῖνον προφῆται καὶ Ἰησοῦς ὁ Ναζωραῖος ἐπιδείξω, ἀλλὰ καὶ τὸν πάντας πανταχοῦ τοὺς πώποτε γόητας καὶ ἀπατεῶνας ὑπερβαλλόμενον Παῦλον. ἀκούετε δὲ τῶν λέξεων αὐτῶν, καὶ πρῶτον μὲν τῶν Μωυσέως· "Σὺ δὲ ἐρεῖς τῷ Φαραῷ· υἱὸς πρωτότοκός μου Ἰσραήλ. εἶπον δέ· ἐξαπόστειλον τὸν λαόν μου, ἵνα μοι
100 B λατρεύσῃ. σὺ δὲ οὐκ ἐβούλου ἐξαποστεῖλαι αὐτόν." καὶ μικρὸν ὕστερον· "Καὶ λέγουσιν αὐτῷ· ὁ θεὸς τῶν Ἑβραίων προσκέκληται ἡμᾶς. πορευσόμεθα οὖν εἰς τὴν ἔρημον ὁδὸν ἡμερῶν τριῶν, ὅπως θύσωμεν κυρίῳ τῷ θεῷ ἡμῶν." καὶ μετ' ὀλίγα πάλιν ὁμοίως· "Κύριος ὁ θεὸς τῶν Ἑβραίων ἐξαπέσταλκέ με πρὸς σὲ λέγων· ἐξαπό-

also to give a complete account of the immediate creator of this universe, let us go on and set one against another the opinion of the Hebrews and that of our fathers about these nations.

Moses says that the creator of the universe chose out the Hebrew nation, that to that nation alone did he pay heed and cared for it, and he gives him charge of it alone. But how and by what sort of gods the other nations are governed he has said not a word,—unless indeed one should concede that he did assign to them the sun and moon.[1] However of this I shall speak a little later. Now I will only point out that Moses himself and the prophets who came after him and Jesus the Nazarene, yes and Paul also, who surpassed all the magicians and charlatans of every place and every time, assert that he is the God of Israel alone and of Judaea, and that the Jews are his chosen people. Listen to their own words, and first to the words of Moses: "And thou shalt say unto Pharaoh, Israel is my son, my firstborn. And I have said to thee, Let my people go that they may serve me. But thou didst refuse to let them go."[2] And a little later, "And they say unto him, The God of the Hebrews hath summoned us; we will go therefore three days' journey into the desert, that we may sacrifice unto the Lord our God."[3] And soon he speaks again in the same way, "The Lord the God of the Hebrews hath sent

[1] *Deuteronomy* 4. 19: "And lest . . . when thou seest the sun and the moon and the stars, even all the host of heaven, thou be drawn away and worship them, and serve them, which the Lord thy God hath divided unto all the peoples under the whole heaven."

[2] *Exodus* 4. 22. [3] *Exodus* 4. 23.

στειλον τὸν λαόν μου, ἵνα λατρεύσωσιν ἐν τῇ ἐρήμῳ."

106 A 'Αλλ' ὅτι μὲν 'Ιουδαίων μόνων ἐμέλησε τῷ
106 B θεῷ τὸ ἐξ ἀρχῆς καὶ κλῆρος αὐτοῦ γέγονεν οὗτος ἐξαίρετος, οὐ Μωυσῆς μόνον καὶ 'Ιησοῦς, ἀλλὰ καὶ Παῦλος εἰρηκὼς φαίνεται· καίτοι τοῦτο ἄξιον θαυμάσαι περὶ τοῦ Παύλου. πρὸς γὰρ τύχας, ὥσπερ χρῶτα οἱ πολύποδες πρὸς τὰς πέτρας, ἀλλάττει τὰ περὶ θεοῦ δόγματα, ποτὲ μὲν 'Ιουδαίους μόνον τὴν τοῦ θεοῦ κληρονομίαν εἶναι διατεινόμενος, πάλιν δὲ τοὺς Ἕλληνας ἀναπείθων αὐτῷ προστίθεσθαι, λέγων· "Μὴ 'Ιουδαίων ὁ θεὸς μόνον, ἀλλὰ καὶ ἐθνῶν· ναὶ καὶ ἐθνῶν." δίκαιον
106 C οὖν ἐρέσθαι τὸν Παῦλον, εἰ μὴ τῶν 'Ιουδαίων ἦν ὁ θεὸς μόνον, ἀλλὰ καὶ τῶν ἐθνῶν, τοῦ χάριν πολὺ μὲν εἰς τοὺς 'Ιουδαίους ἔπεμπε τὸ προφητικὸν χάρισμα καὶ τὸν Μωυσέα καὶ τὸ χρῖσμα καὶ τοὺς προφήτας καὶ τὸν νόμον καὶ τὰ παράδοξα καὶ τὰ τεράστια τῶν μύθων; ἀκούεις γὰρ αὐτῶν βοώντων· "Ἄρτον ἀγγέλων ἔφαγεν ἄνθρωπος." ἐπὶ τέλους δὲ καὶ τὸν 'Ιησοῦν ἔπεμψεν ἐκείνοις, ἡμῖν δὲ οὐ προφήτην, οὐ χρῖσμα, οὐ διδάσκαλον, οὐ κήρυκα περὶ τῆς μελλούσης ὀψέ ποτε γοῦν ἔσεσ-
106 D θαι καὶ εἰς ἡμᾶς ἀπ' αὐτοῦ φιλανθρωπίας. ἀλλὰ καὶ περιεῖδεν ἐτῶν μυριάδας, εἰ δὲ ὑμεῖς βούλεσθε, χιλιάδας ἐν ἀγνωσίᾳ τοιαύτῃ τοῖς εἰδώλοις, ὥς φατε, λατρεύοντας τοὺς ἀπὸ ἀνίσχοντος ἡλίου μέχρι δυομένου καὶ τοὺς ἀπὸ τῶν ἄρκτων ἄχρι μεσημβρίας ἔξω καὶ μικροῦ γένους οὐδὲ πρὸ δισ-

me unto thee, saying, Let my people go that they may serve me in the wilderness."[1]

But that from the beginning God cared only for the Jews and that He chose them out as his portion, has been clearly asserted not only by Moses and Jesus but by Paul as well; though in Paul's case this is strange. For according to circumstances he keeps changing his views about God, as the polypus changes its colours to match the rocks,[2] and now he insists that the Jews alone are God's portion, and then again, when he is trying to persuade the Hellenes to take sides with him, he says: "Do not think that he is the God of Jews only, but also of Gentiles: yea of Gentiles also."[3] Therefore it is fair to ask of Paul why God, if he was not the God of the Jews only but also of the Gentiles, sent the blessed gift of prophecy to the Jews in abundance and gave them Moses and the oil of anointing, and the prophets and the law and the incredible and monstrous elements in their myths? For you hear them crying aloud: "Man did eat angels' food."[4] And finally God sent unto them Jesus also, but unto us no prophet, no oil of anointing, no teacher, no herald to announce his love for man which should one day, though late, reach even unto us also. Nay he even looked on for myriads, or if you prefer, for thousands of years, while men in extreme ignorance served idols, as you call them, from where the sun rises to where he sets, yes and from North to South, save only that

[1] *Exodus* 5. 3: the sayings of Jesus and the prophets, which Julian said he would quote, are missing.

[2] For this proverb, derived from Theognis, cf. *Misopogon* 349D, Vol. 2.

[3] *Romans* 3. 29; *Galatians* 3. 28.

[4] *Psalms* 78. 25.

χιλίων ὅλων ἐτῶν ἐν[1] ἑνὶ μέρει συνοικισθέντος τῆς Παλαιστίνης. εἰ γὰρ πάντων ἡμῶν ἐστι θεὸς καὶ πάντων δημιουργὸς ὁμοίως, τί περιεῖδεν
100 C ἡμᾶς; προσήκει τοίνυν τὸν τῶν Ἑβραίων θεὸν οὐχὶ δὴ παντὸς κόσμου γενεσιουργὸν ὑπάρχειν οἴεσθαι καὶ κατεξουσιάζειν τῶν ὅλων, συνεστάλθαι δέ, ὡς ἔφην, καὶ πεπερασμένην ἔχοντα τὴν
106 ἀρχὴν ἀναμὶξ τοῖς ἄλλοις νοεῖσθαι θεοῖς. ἔτι
D, E προσέξομεν ὑμῖν, ὅτι τὸν τῶν ὅλων θεὸν ἄχρι ψιλῆς γοῦν ἐννοίας ὑμεῖς ἢ τῆς ὑμετέρας τις ἐφαντάσθη ῥίζης; οὐ μερικὰ πάντα ταῦτά ἐστι; θεὸς ζηλωτής· ζηλοῖ γὰρ διὰ τί καὶ ἁμαρτίας ἐκδικῶν πατέρων ἐπὶ τέκνα;[1]

115 D Ἀλλὰ δὴ σκοπεῖτε πρὸς ταῦτα πάλιν τὰ παρ' ἡμῶν. οἱ γὰρ ἡμέτεροι τὸν δημιουργόν φασιν ἁπάντων μὲν εἶναι κοινὸν πατέρα καὶ βασιλέα, νενεμῆσθαι δὲ ὑπ' αὐτοῦ τὰ λοιπὰ τῶν ἐθνῶν ἐθνάρχαις καὶ πολιούχοις θεοῖς, ὧν ἕκαστος ἐπιτροπεύει τὴν ἑαυτοῦ λῆξιν οἰκείως ἑαυτῷ. ἐπειδὴ
115 E γὰρ ἐν μὲν τῷ πατρὶ πάντα τέλεια καὶ ἓν πάντα, ἐν δὲ τοῖς μεριστοῖς ἄλλη παρ' ἄλλῳ κρατεῖ δύναμις, Ἄρης μὲν ἐπιτροπεύει τὰ πολεμικὰ τῶν ἐθνῶν, Ἀθηνᾶ δὲ τὰ μετὰ φρονήσεως πολεμικά, Ἑρμῆς δὲ τὰ συνετώτερα μᾶλλον ἢ τολμηρότερα, καὶ καθ' ἑκάστην οὐσίαν τῶν οἰκείων θεῶν ἕπεται καὶ τὰ ἐπιτροπευόμενα παρὰ σφῶν ἔθνη. εἰ μὲν οὖν οὐ μαρτυρεῖ τοῖς ἡμετέροις λόγοις ἡ πεῖρα, πλάσμα μὲν ἔστω τὰ παρ' ἡμῶν καὶ πιθανότης

[1] ἐν Klimek supplies.

---

[1] *Exodus* 20. 5.

little tribe which less than two thousand years before had settled in one part of Palestine. For if he is the God of all of us alike, and the creator of all, why did he neglect us? Wherefore it is natural to think that the God of the Hebrews was not the begetter of the whole universe with lordship over the whole, but rather, as I said before, that he is confined within limits, and that since his empire has bounds we must conceive of him as only one of the crowd of other gods. Then are we to pay further heed to you because you or one of your stock imagined the God of the universe, though in any case you attained only to a bare conception of Him? Is not all this partiality? God, you say, is a jealous God. But why is he so jealous, even avenging the sins of the fathers on the children?[1]

But now consider our teaching in comparison with this of yours. Our writers say that the creator is the common father and king of all things, but that the other functions have been assigned by him to national gods of the peoples and gods that protect the cities; every one of whom administers his own department in accordance with his own nature. For since in the father all things are complete and all things are one, while in the separate deities one quality or another predominates, therefore Ares rules over the warlike nations, Athene over those that are wise as well as warlike, Hermes over those that are more shrewd than adventurous; and in short the nations over which the gods preside follow each the essential character of their proper god. Now if experience does not bear witness to the truth of our teachings, let us grant that our traditions are a figment and a misplaced

116 A ἄκαιρος, τὰ παρ' ὑμῖν δὲ ἐπαινείσθω· εἰ δὲ πᾶν
τοὐναντίον οἷς μὲν ἡμεῖς λέγομεν, ἐξ αἰῶνος ἡ
πεῖρα μαρτυρεῖ, τοῖς ὑμετέροις δὲ λόγοις οὐδὲν
οὐδαμοῦ φαίνεται σύμφωνον, τί τοσαύτης τῆς
φιλονεικίας ἀντέχεσθε;

Λεγέσθω γάρ μοι, τίς αἰτία τοῦ Κελτοὺς μὲν
εἶναι καὶ Γερμανοὺς θρασεῖς, Ἕλληνας δὲ καὶ
Ῥωμαίους ὡς ἐπίπαν πολιτικοὺς καὶ φιλανθρώ-
πους μετὰ τοῦ στερροῦ τε καὶ πολεμικοῦ, συνε-
τωτέρους δὲ καὶ τεχνικωτέρους Αἰγυπτίους,
ἀπολέμους δὲ καὶ τρυφηλοὺς Σύρους μετὰ τοῦ
συνετοῦ καὶ θερμοῦ καὶ κούφου καὶ εὐμαθοῦς.
116 B ταύτης γὰρ τῆς ἐν τοῖς ἔθνεσι διαφορᾶς εἰ μὲν
οὐδεμίαν τις αἰτίαν συνορῴη, μᾶλλον δὲ αὐτά
φησι καὶ ἐκ τοῦ αὐτομάτου συμπεσεῖν, πῶς ἔτι
προνοίᾳ διοικεῖσθαι τὸν κόσμον οἴεται; εἰ δὲ
τούτων αἰτίας εἶναί τις τίθεται, λεγέτω μοι πρὸς
131 B αὐτοῦ τοῦ δημιουργοῦ καὶ διδασκέτω. τοὺς μὲν
γὰρ νόμους εὔδηλον, ὡς ἡ τῶν ἀνθρώπων ἔθετο
φύσις οἰκείους ἑαυτῇ, πολιτικοὺς μὲν καὶ φιλαν-
131 C θρώπους, οἷς ἐπὶ πλεῖστον ἐντέθραπτο τὸ φιλάν-
θρωπον, ἀγρίους δὲ καὶ ἀπανθρώπους, οἷς ἐναντία
φύσις ὑπῆν καὶ ἐνυπῆρχε τῶν ἠθῶν. οἱ γὰρ
νομοθέται μικρὰ ταῖς φύσεσι καὶ ταῖς ἐπιτηδειό-
τησι διὰ τῆς ἀγωγῆς προσέθεσαν. οὔκουν Ἀνά-
χαρσιν οἱ Σκύθαι βακχεύοντα παρεδέξαντο· οὐδὲ

---

[1] In *Misopogon* 359B Julian speaks of the fierceness of the Celts compared with the Romans.

[2] A Scythian prince who travelled in search of knowledge and was counted by some among the seven sages. On his return to Thrace he is said to have been killed while celebrating the rites of Cybele, which were new to the Scythians; Herodotus 4. 76, tells the tale to illustrate the

attempt to çonvince, and then we ought to approve the doctrines held by you. If, however, quite the contrary is true, and from the remotest past experience bears witness to our account and in no case does anything appear to harmonise with your teachings, why do you persist in maintaining a pretension so enormous?

Come, tell me why it is that the Celts and the Germans are fierce,[1] while the Hellenes and Romans are, generally speaking, inclined to political life and humane, though at the same time unyielding and warlike? Why the Egyptians are more intelligent and more given to crafts, and the Syrians unwarlike and effeminate, but at the same time intelligent, hot-tempered, vain and quick to learn? For if there is anyone who does not discern a reason for these differences among the nations, but rather declares that all this so befell spontaneously, how, I ask, can he still believe that the universe is administered by a providence? But if there is any man who maintains that there are reasons for these differences, let him tell me them, in the name of the creator himself, and instruct me. As for men's laws, it is evident that men have established them to correspond with their own natural dispositions; that is to say, constitutional and humane laws were established by those in whom a humane disposition had been fostered above all else, savage and inhuman laws by those in whom there lurked and was inherent the contrary disposition. For lawgivers have succeeded in adding but little by their discipline to the natural characters and aptitudes of men. Accordingly the Scythians would not receive Anacharsis[2] among them when he

Scythian hatred of foreign, and especially of Greek, customs; cf. Lucian, *Anacharsis*.

τῶν Ἑσπερίων ἐθνῶν εὕροις ἄν τινας εὐκόλως πλὴν ὀλίγων σφόδρα ἐπὶ τὸ φιλοσοφεῖν ἢ γεωμετρεῖν ἤ τι τῶν τοιούτων ηὐτρεπισμένους, καίτοι κρατούσης ἐπὶ τοσοῦτον ἤδη τῆς Ῥωμαίων ἡγεμονίας. ἀλλ' ἀπολαύουσι μόνον τῆς διαλέξεως καὶ
131 D τῆς ῥητορείας οἱ λίαν εὐφυεῖς, ἄλλου δὲ οὐδενὸς μεταλαμβάνουσι μαθήματος. οὕτως ἴσχυρον ἔοικεν ἡ φύσις εἶναι. τίς οὖν ἡ διαφορὰ τῶν ἐθνῶν ἐν τοῖς ἤθεσι καὶ τοῖς νόμοις;

134 D Ὁ μὲν γὰρ Μωυσῆς αἰτίαν ἀποδέδωκε κομιδῇ μυθώδη τῆς περὶ τὰς διαλέκτους ἀνομοιότητος. ἔφη γὰρ τοὺς υἱοὺς τῶν ἀνθρώπων συνελθόντας
134 E πόλιν ἐθέλειν οἰκοδομεῖν καὶ πύργον ἐν αὐτῇ μέγαν, φάναι δὲ τὸν θεόν, ὅτι χρὴ κατελθεῖν καὶ τὰς διαλέκτους αὐτῶν συγχέαι. καὶ ὅπως μή τίς με νομίσῃ ταῦτα συκοφαντεῖν, καὶ ἐκ τῶν Μωυσέως ἀναγνωσόμεθα τὰ ἐφεξῆς. "Καὶ εἶπον· δεῦτε, οἰκοδομήσωμεν ἑαυτοῖς πόλιν καὶ πύργον, οὗ ἔσται ἡ κεφαλὴ ἕως τοῦ οὐρανοῦ, καὶ ποιήσωμεν ἑαυτοῖς ὄνομα πρὸ τοῦ διασπαρῆναι ἐπὶ προσώπου πάσης τῆς γῆς. καὶ κατέβη κύριος ἰδεῖν τὴν πόλιν καὶ τὸν πύργον, ὃν ᾠκοδόμησαν οἱ υἱοὶ τῶν ἀνθρώπων. καὶ εἶπε κύριος· ἰδού, γένος ἓν καὶ
135 A χεῖλος ἓν πάντων, καὶ τοῦτο ἤρξαντο ποιῆσαι καὶ νῦν οὐκ ἐκλείψει ἀπ' αὐτῶν πάντα, ὅσα ἂν ἐπίθωνται ποιεῖν. δεῦτε, καταβάντες ἐκεῖ συγχέωμεν αὐτῶν τὴν γλῶσσαν, ἵνα μὴ ἀκούωσιν ἕκαστος τῆς φωνῆς τοῦ πλησίον. καὶ διέσπειρεν αὐτοὺς κύριος ὁ θεὸς ἐπὶ πρόσωπον πάσης τῆς γῆς καὶ ἐπαύσαντο οἰκοδομοῦντες τὴν πόλιν καὶ τὸν πύργον." εἶτα τούτοις ἀξιοῦτε πιστεύειν

was inspired by a religious frenzy, and with very few exceptions you will not find that any men of the Western nations[1] have any great inclination for philosophy or geometry or studies of that sort, although the Roman Empire has now so long been paramount. But those who are unusually talented delight only in debate and the art of rhetoric, and do not adopt any other study; so strong, it seems, is the force of nature. Whence then come these differences of character and laws among the nations?

Now of the dissimilarity of language Moses has given a wholly fabulous explanation. For he said that the sons of men came together intending to build a city, and a great tower therein, but that God said that he must go down and confound their languages. And that no one may think I am falsely accusing him of this, I will read from the book of Moses what follows: "And they said, Go to, let us build us a city and a tower, whose top may reach unto heaven; and let us make us a name, before we be scattered abroad upon the face of the whole earth. And the Lord came down to see the city and the tower, which the children of men had builded. And the Lord said, Behold, the people is one, and they have all one language; and this they have begun to do; and now nothing will be withholden from them which they purpose to do. Go to, let us go down, and there confound their language, that no man may understand the speech of his neighbour. So the Lord God scattered them abroad upon the face of all the earth: and they left off to build the city and the tower."[2] And then you demand that we should

[1] He means the Gauls and Iberians, since the Germans at that time were distinguished only in warfare.

[2] *Genesis* 11. 4–8.

ἡμᾶς, ἀπιστεῖτε δὲ ὑμεῖς τοῖς ὑφ' Ὁμήρου λεγομένοις ὑπὲρ τῶν Ἀλωαδῶν, ὡς ἄρα τρία ἐπ'
135 B ἀλλήλοις ὄρη θεῖναι διενοοῦντο, "ἵν' οὐρανὸς ἀμβατὸς εἴη." φημὶ μὲν γὰρ ἐγὼ καὶ τοῦτο παραπλησίως ἐκείνῳ μυθῶδες εἶναι. ὑμεῖς δέ, ἀποδεχόμενοι τὸ πρότερον, ἀνθ' ὅτου πρὸς θεῶν ἀποδοκιμάζετε τὸν Ὁμήρου μῦθον; ἐκεῖνο γὰρ οἶμαι δεῖν σιωπᾶν πρὸς ἄνδρας ἀμαθεῖς, ὅτι κἂν μιᾷ φωνῇ καὶ γλώσσῃ πάντες οἱ κατὰ πᾶσαν τὴν οἰκουμένην ἄνθρωποι χρήσωνται, πύργοι οἰκοδομεῖν οὐ δυνήσονται πρὸς τὸν οὐρανὸν ἀφικνούμενον,[1] κἂν ἐκπλινθεύσωσι τὴν γῆν πᾶσαν·
135 C ἀπείρων γὰρ δεήσει πλίνθων ἰσομεγεθῶν τῇ γῇ ξυμπάσῃ τῶν δυνησομένων ἄχρι τῶν σελήνης ἐφικέσθαι κύκλων. ὑποκείσθω γὰρ πάντας μὲν ἀνθρώπους συνεληλυθέναι γλώσσῃ καὶ φωνῇ μιᾷ κεχρημένους, πᾶσαν δὲ ἐκπλινθεῦσαι τὴν γῆν καὶ ἐκλατομῆσαι, πότε ἂν μέχρις οὐρανοῦ φθάσειεν, εἰ καὶ λεπτότερον ἁρπεδόνος ἐκμηρυομένων αὐτῶν ἐκταθείη; τοῦτον οὖν οὕτω φανερὸν ὄντα τὸν μῦθον ἀληθῆ νενομικότες καὶ περὶ τοῦ θεοῦ δοξάζοντες, ὅτι πεφόβηται τῶν ἀνθρώπων τὴν μιαι-
135 D φονίαν τούτου τε χάριν καταπεφοίτηκεν αὐτῶν συγχέαι τὰς διαλέκτους, ἔτι τολμᾶτε θεοῦ γνῶσιν αὐχεῖν;

137 E Ἐπάνειμι δὲ αὖθις πρὸς ἐκεῖνο, τὰς μὲν γὰρ διαλέκτους ὅπως ὁ θεὸς συνέχεεν. εἴρηκεν ὁ Μωυσῆς τὴν μὲν αἰτίαν, ὅτι φοβηθεὶς μή τι κατ' αὐτοῦ πράξωσι προσβατὸν ἑαυτοῖς τὸν οὐρανὸν
138 A κατεργασάμενοι, ὁμόγλωττοι ὄντες καὶ ὁμόφρονες

[1] ἐφικνούμενον Klimek.

believe this account, while you yourselves disbelieve Homer's narrative of the Aloadae, namely that they planned to set three mountains one on another, "that so the heavens might be scaled."[1] For my part I say that this tale is almost as fabulous as the other. But if you accept the former, why in the name of the gods do you discredit Homer's fable? For I suppose that to men so ignorant as you I must say nothing about the fact that, even if all men throughout the inhabited world ever employ one speech and one language, they will not be able to build a tower that will reach to the heavens, even though they should turn the whole earth into bricks. For such a tower will need countless bricks each one as large as the whole earth, if they are to succeed in reaching to the orbit of the moon. For let us assume that all mankind met together, employing but one language and speech, and that they made the whole earth into bricks and hewed out stones, when would it reach as high as the heavens, even though they spun it out and stretched it till it was finer than a thread? Then do you, who believe that this so obvious fable is true, and moreover think that God was afraid of the brutal violence of men, and for this reason came down to earth to confound their languages, do you, I say, still venture to boast of your knowledge of God?

But I will go back again to the question how God confounded their languages. The reason why he did so Moses has declared: namely, that God was afraid that if they should have one language and were of one mind, they would first construct for themselves a path to the heavens and then do some

[1] *Odyssey* 11. 316.

ἀλλήλοις· τὸ δὲ πρᾶγμα ὅπως ἐποίησεν οὐδαμῶς, ἀλλὰ μόνον, ὅτι κατελθὼν ἐξ οὐρανοῦ—μὴ δυνάμενος ἄνωθεν αὐτὸ ποιεῖν, ὡς ἔοικεν, εἰ μὴ κατῆλθεν ἐπὶ τῆς γῆς. ὑπὲρ δὲ τῆς κατὰ τὰ ἤθη καὶ τὰ νόμιμα διαφορᾶς οὔτε Μωυσῆς οὔτε ἄλλος ἀπεσάφησέ τις. καίτοι τῷ παντὶ μείζων ἐστὶν ἡ περὶ τὰ νόμιμα καὶ τὰ πολιτικὰ τῶν ἐθνῶν ἐν τοῖς ἀνθρώποις τῆς περὶ τὰς διαλέκτους διαφορᾶς. τίς
138 B γὰρ Ἑλλήνων ἀδελφῇ, τίς δὲ θυγατρί, τίς δὲ μητρί φησι δεῖν μίγνυσθαι; τοῦτο δὲ ἀγαθὸν ἐν Πέρσαις κρίνεται. τί με χρὴ καθ' ἕκαστον ἐπιέναι, τὸ φιλελεύθερόν τε καί ἀνυπότακτον Γερμανῶν ἐπεξιόντα, τὸ χειρόηθες καὶ τιθασὸν Σύρων καὶ Περσῶν καὶ Πάρθων καὶ πάντων ἁπλῶς τῶν πρὸς ἕω καὶ πρὸς μεσημβρίαν βαρβάρων καὶ ὅσα καὶ τὰς βασιλείας ἀγαπᾷ κεκτημένα δεσποτικωτέρας; εἰ μὲν οὖν ἄνευ προνοίας μείζονος καὶ θειοτέρας ταῦτα συνηνέχθη τὰ μείζω καὶ τιμιώτερα, τί
138 C μάτην περιεργαζόμεθα καὶ θεραπεύομεν τὸν μηδὲν προνοοῦντα; ᾧ γὰρ οὔτε βίων οὔτε ἠθῶν οὔτε τρόπων οὔτε εὐνομίας οὔτε πολιτικῆς ἐμέλησε καταστάσεως, ἆρ' ἔτι προσήκει μεταποιεῖσθαι τῆς παρ' ἡμῶν τιμῆς; οὐδαμῶς. ὁρᾶτε, εἰς ὅσην ὑμῖν[1] ἀτοπίαν ὁ λόγος ἔρχεται. τῶν γὰρ ἀγαθῶν ὅσα περὶ τὸν ἀνθρώπινον θεωρεῖται βίον, ἡγεῖται μὲν τὰ τῆς ψυχῆς, ἕπεται δὲ τὰ τοῦ σώματος. εἰ τοίνυν τῶν ψυχικῶν ἡμῶν ἀγαθῶν κατωλιγώρησεν, οὐδὲ τῆς φυσικῆς ἡμῶν κατασκευῆς προ-

[1] ὑμῖν Klimek; ὑμῶν Neumann.

mischief against him. But how he carried this out Moses does not say at all, but only that he first came down from heaven,—because he could not, as it seems, do it from on high, without coming down to earth. But with respect to the existing differences in characters and customs, neither Moses nor anyone else has enlightened us. And yet among mankind the difference between the customs and the political constitutions of the nations is in every way greater than the difference in their language. What Hellene, for instance, ever tells us that a man ought to marry his sister or his daughter or his mother? Yet in Persia this is accounted virtuous. But why need I go over their several characteristics, or describe the love of liberty and lack of discipline of the Germans, the docility and tameness of the Syrians, the Persians, the Parthians, and in short of all the barbarians in the East and the South, and of all nations who possess and are contented with a somewhat despotic form of government? Now if these differences that are greater and more important came about without the aid of a greater and more divine providence, why do we vainly trouble ourselves about and worship one who takes no thought for us? For is it fitting that he who cared nothing for our lives, our characters, our manners, our good government, our political constitution, should still claim to receive honour at our hands? Certainly not. You see to what an absurdity your doctrine comes. For of all the blessings that we behold in the life of man, those that relate to the soul come first, and those that relate to the body are secondary. If, therefore, he paid no heed to our spiritual blessings, neither took thought for our physical conditions, and moreover,

138 D νοησάμενος, οὔτε ἡμῖν ἔπεμψε διδασκάλους ἢ
νομοθέτας ὥσπερ τοῖς Ἑβραίοις κατὰ τὸν Μωυσέα
καὶ τοὺς ἐπ' ἐκείνῳ προφήτας, ὑπὲρ τίνος ἕξομεν
αὐτῷ καλῶς εὐχαριστεῖν;
141 C Ἀλλ' ὁρᾶτε, μή ποτε καὶ ἡμῖν ἔδωκεν ὁ θεὸς
οὓς ὑμεῖς ἠγνοήκατε θεούς τε καὶ προστάτας
ἀγαθούς, οὐδὲν ἐλάττονας τοῦ παρὰ τοῖς Ἑβραίοις
ἐξ ἀρχῆς τιμωμένου τῆς Ἰουδαίας, ἧσπερ ἐκεῖνος
προνοεῖν ἔλαχε μόνης, ὥσπερ ὁ Μωυσῆς ἔφη καὶ
141 D οἱ μετ' ἐκεῖνον ἄχρις ἡμῶν. εἰ δὲ ὁ προσεχὴς
εἴη τοῦ κόσμου δημιουργὸς ὁ παρὰ τοῖς Ἑβραίοις
τιμώμενος, ἔτι καὶ βέλτιον ὑπὲρ αὐτοῦ διενοήθη-
μεν ἡμεῖς ἀγαθά τε ἡμῖν ἔδωκεν ἐκείνων μείζονα
τά τε περὶ ψυχὴν καὶ τὰ ἐκτός, ὑπὲρ ὧν ἐροῦμεν
ὀλίγου ὕστερον, ἔστειλέ τε καὶ ἐφ' ἡμᾶς νομοθέτας
οὐδὲν Μωυσέως χείρονας, εἰ μὴ τοὺς πολλοὺς
μακρῷ κρείττονας.
143 A Ὅπερ οὖν ἐλέγομεν, εἰ μὴ καθ' ἕκαστον ἔθνος
ἐθνάρχης τις θεὸς ἐπιτροπεύων ἄγγελός τε ὑπ'
143 B αὐτῷ καὶ δαίμων καὶ ἥρως[1] καὶ ψυχῶν ἰδιάζον
γένος ὑπηρετικὸν καὶ ὑπουργικὸν τοῖς κρείττοσιν
ἔθετο τὴν ἐν τοῖς νόμοις καὶ τοῖς ἤθεσι διαφορό-
τητα, δεικνύσθω, παρ' ἄλλου πῶς γέγονε ταῦτα.
καὶ γὰρ οὐδὲ ἀπόχρη λέγειν· "Εἶπεν ὁ θεὸς καὶ
ἐγένετο." ὁμολογεῖν γὰρ χρὴ τοῖς ἐπιτάγμασι
τοῦ θεοῦ τῶν γινομένων τὰς φύσεις. ὃ δὲ λέγω,
σαφέστερον ἐρῶ. ἐκέλευσεν ὁ θεὸς ἄνω φέρεσθαι

[1] Asmus adds καὶ ἥρως from *Oration*, 4. 145C ἀγγέλοις, δαίμοσιν, ἥρωσι, ψυχαῖς τε μερισταῖς.

did not send to us teachers or lawgivers as he did for the Hebrews, such as Moses and the prophets who followed him, for what shall we properly feel gratitude to him?

But consider whether God has not given to us also gods[1] and kindly guardians of whom you have no knowledge, gods in no way inferior to him who from the beginning has been held in honour among the Hebrews of Judaea, the only land that he chose to take thought for, as Moses declared and those who came after him, down to our own time. But even if he who is honoured among the Hebrews really was the immediate creator of the universe, our beliefs about him are higher than theirs, and he has bestowed on us greater blessings than on them, with respect both to the soul and to externals. Of these, however, I shall speak a little later. Moreover, he sent to us also lawgivers not inferior to Moses, if indeed many of them were not far superior.

Therefore, as I said, unless for every nation separately some presiding national god (and under him an angel,[2] a demon, a hero, and a peculiar order of spirits which obey and work for the higher powers) established the differences in our laws and characters, you must demonstrate to me how these differences arose by some other agency. Moreover, it is not sufficient to say, "God spake and it was so." For the natures of things that are created ought to harmonise with the commands of God. I will say more clearly what I mean. Did God ordain that fire should mount upwards by chance and earth

[1] Cf. *Oration* 4, 140A, Vol. 1, on the creative gods.

[2] Cf. *Oration* 4. 141B, note, and 145C, note; Plato, *Laws* 713D.

τὸ πῦρ, εἰ τύχοι, κάτω δὲ τὴν γῆν; οὐχ ἵνα τὸ πρόσταγμα γένηται τοῦ θεοῦ, τὸ μὲν ἐχρῆν εἶναι κοῦφον, τὸ δὲ βρίθειν; οὕτω καὶ ἐπὶ τῶν ἑτέρων
143 C ὁμοίως . . . τὸν αὐτὸν τρόπον καὶ ἐπὶ τῶν θείων. αἴτιον δέ, ὅτι τὸ μὲν τῶν ἀνθρώπων ἐπίκηρόν ἐστι καὶ φθαρτὸν γένος. εἰκότως οὖν αὐτοῦ φθαρτὰ καὶ τὰ ἔργα καὶ μεταβλητὰ καὶ παντοδαπῶς τρεπόμενα· τοῦ θεοῦ δὲ ὑπάρχοντος ἀϊδίου, καὶ τὰ προστάγματα τοιαῦτ' εἶναι προσήκει. τοιαῦτα δὲ ὄντα ἤτοι φύσεις εἰσὶ τῶν ὄντων ἢ τῇ φύσει τῶν ὄντων ὁμολογούμενα. πῶς γὰρ ἂν ἡ φύσις τῷ προστάγματι μάχοιτο τοῦ θεοῦ; πῶς
143 D δ' ἂν ἔξω πίπτοι τῆς ὁμολογίας; οὐκοῦν εἰ καὶ προσέταξεν ὥσπερ τὰς γλώσσας συγχυθῆναι καὶ μὴ συμφωνεῖν ἀλλήλαις, οὕτω δὲ καὶ τὰ πολιτικὰ τῶν ἐθνῶν, οὐκ ἐπιτάγματι δὲ μόνον ἐποίησε τοιαῦτα καὶ πεφυκέναι, οὐδὲ ἡμᾶς πρὸς ταύτην κατεσκεύασε τὴν διαφωνίαν. ἐχρῆν γὰρ πρῶτον διαφόρους ὑπεῖναι φύσεις τοῖς ἐν τοῖς ἔθνεσι διαφόρως ἐσομένοις. ὁρᾶται γοῦν τοῦτο, καὶ τοῖς σώμασιν εἴ τις ἀπίδοι Γερμανοὶ καὶ Σκύθαι
143 E Λιβύων καὶ Αἰθιόπων ὁπόσον διαφέρουσιν. ἆρα καὶ τοῦτό ἐστι ψιλὸν ἐπίταγμα, καὶ οὐδὲν ὁ ἀὴρ οὐδὲ ἡ χώρα τῷ πῶς ἔχειν πρὸς τὸ χρῶμα θεοῖς συμπράττει;

146 A Ἔτι δὲ καὶ ὁ Μωυσῆς ἐπεκάλυπτε τὸ τοιοῦτον
146 B εἰδὼς οὐδὲ τὴν τῶν διαλέκτων σύγχυσιν ἀνατέ-

[1] A few words are lost.

sink down? Was it not necessary, in order that the ordinance of God should be fulfilled, for the former to be light and the latter to weigh heavy? And in the case of other things also this is equally true. . . .[1] Likewise with respect to things divine. But the reason is that the race of men is doomed to death and perishable. Therefore men's works also are naturally perishable and mutable and subject to every kind of alteration. But since God is eternal, it follows that of such sort are his ordinances also. And since they are such, they are either the natures of things or are accordant with the nature of things. For how could nature be at variance with the ordinance of God? How could it fall out of harmony therewith? Therefore, if he did ordain that even as our languages are confounded and do not harmonise with one another, so too should it be with the political constitutions of the nations, then it was not by a special, isolated decree that he gave these contitutions their essential characteristics, or framed us also to match this lack of agreement.[2] For different natures must first have existed in all those things that among the nations were to be differentiated. This at any rate is seen if one observes how very different in their bodies are the Germans and Scythians from the Libyans and Ethiopians. Can this also be due to a bare decree, and does not the climate or the country have a joint influence with the gods in determining what sort of complexion they have?

Furthermore, Moses also consciously drew a veil over this sort of enquiry, and did not assign the

[2] *i.e.* if there were to be differences of speech and political constitution, they must have been adapted to pre-existing differences of nature in human beings.

θεικε τῷ θεῷ μόνῳ. φησὶ γὰρ αὐτὸν οὐ μόνον κατελθεῖν οὐ μὴν οὐδὲ ἕνα συγκατελθεῖν αὐτῷ, πλείονας δέ, καὶ τούτους οἵτινές εἰσιν οὐκ εἶπεν· εὔδηλον δέ, ὅτι παραπλησίους αὐτῷ τοὺς συγκατιόντας ὑπελάμβανεν. εἰ τοίνυν πρὸς τὴν σύγχυσιν τῶν διαλέκτων οὐχ ὁ κύριος μόνος, ἀλλὰ καὶ οἱ σὺν αὐτῷ κατέρχονται, πρόδηλον, ὅτι καὶ πρὸς τὴν σύγχυσιν τῶν ἠθῶν οὐχ ὁ κύριος μόνος, ἀλλὰ καὶ οἱ σὺν αὐτῷ τὰς διαλέκτους συγχέοντες εἰκότως ἂν ὑπολαμβάνοιντο ταύτης εἶναι τῆς διαστάσεως αἴτιοι.

148 B Τί οὖν, οὐκ ἐν μακροῖς εἰπεῖν βουλόμενος, τοσαῦτα ἐπεξῆλθον; ὡς, εἰ μὲν ὁ προσεχὴς εἴη τοῦ κόσμου δημιουργὸς ὁ ὑπὸ τοῦ Μωυσέως κηρυττόμενος, ἡμεῖς ὑπὲρ αὐτοῦ βελτίους ἔχομεν δόξας οἱ κοινὸν μὲν ἐκεῖνον ὑπολαμβάνοντες ἁπάντων δεσπότην, ἐθνάρχας δὲ ἄλλους, οἳ τυγχάνουσι μὲν ὑπ᾿ ἐκεῖνον, εἰσὶ δὲ ὥσπερ ὕπαρχοι βασιλέως, ἕκαστος τὴν ἑαυτοῦ διαφερόντως ἐπαν-
148 C ορθούμενος φροντίδα· καὶ οὐ καθίσταμεν αὐτὸν οὐδὲ ἀντιμερίτην τῶν ὑπ᾿ αὐτὸν θεῶν καθισταμένων. εἰ δὲ μερικόν τινα τιμήσας ἐκεῖνος ἀντιτίθησιν αὐτῷ τὴν τοῦ παντὸς ἡγεμονίαν, ἄμεινον τὸν τῶν ὅλων θεὸν ἡμῖν πειθομένους ἐπιγνῶναι μετὰ τοῦ μηδὲ ἐκεῖνον ἀγνοῆσαι, ἢ τὸν τοῦ ἐλαχίστου μέρους εἰληχότα τὴν ἡγεμονίαν ἀντὶ τοῦ πάντων τιμᾶν δημιουργοῦ.

152 B Ὁ νόμος ἐστὶν ὁ τοῦ Μωυσέως θαυμαστός, ἡ

[1] *Genesis* 11. 7. "Go to, let us go down, and there confound their language." . . . The word "us" has been variously interpreted.

confusion of dialects to God alone. For he says[1] that God did not descend alone, but that there descended with him not one but several, and he did not say who these were. But it is evident that he assumed that the beings who descended with God resembled him. If, therefore, it was not the Lord alone but his associates with him who descended for the purpose of confounding the dialects, it is very evident that for the confusion of men's characters, also, not the Lord alone but also those who together with him confounded the dialects would reasonably be considered responsible for this division.

Now why have I discussed this matter at such length, though it was my intention to speak briefly? For this reason: If the immediate creator of the universe be he who is proclaimed by Moses, then we hold nobler beliefs concerning him, inasmuch as we consider him to be the master of all things in general, but that there are besides national gods who are subordinate to him and are like viceroys of a king, each administering separately his own province; and, moreover, we do not make him the sectional rival of the gods whose station is subordinate to his. But if Moses first pays honour to a sectional god, and then makes the lordship of the whole universe contrast with his power, then it is better to believe as we do, and to recognise the God of the All, though not without apprehending also the God of Moses; this is better, I say, than to honour one who has been assigned the lordship over a very small portion, instead of the creator of all things.

That is a surprising law of Moses, I mean the

δεκάλογος ἐκείνη· "Οὐ κλέψεις, οὐ φονεύσεις, οὐ ψευδομαρτυρήσεις." γεγράφθω δὲ αὐτοῖς τοῖς[1]
152 C ῥήμασιν ἑκάστη τῶν ἐντολῶν, ἃς ὑπ' αὐτοῦ φησι γεγράφθαι τοῦ θεοῦ.

"'Εγὼ εἰμι κύριος ὁ θεός σου, ὃς ἐξήγαγέ σε ἐκ γῆς Αἰγύπτου." δευτέρα μετὰ τοῦτο· "Οὐκ ἔσονταί σοι θεοὶ ἕτεροι πλὴν ἐμοῦ. οὐ ποιήσεις σεαυτῷ εἴδωλον." καὶ τὴν αἰτίαν προστίθησιν· "'Εγὼ γάρ εἰμι κύριος ὁ θεός σου, θεὸς ζηλωτής, ἀποδιδοὺς πατέρων ἁμαρτίας ἐπὶ τέκνα ἕως τρίτης γενεᾶς." "Οὐ λήψῃ τὸ ὄνομα κυρίου τοῦ θεοῦ σου ἐπὶ ματαίῳ." "Μνήσθητι τὴν ἡμέραν τῶν σαββάτων." "Τίμα σου τὸν πατέρα καὶ τὴν μητέρα." "Οὐ μοιχεύσεις." "Οὐ φονεύσεις." "Οὐ
152 D κλέψεις." "Οὐ ψευδομαρτυρήσεις." "Οὐκ ἐπιθυμήσεις τὰ τοῦ πλησίον σου."

Ποῖον ἔθνος ἐστί, πρὸς τῶν θεῶν, ἔξω τοῦ "Οὐ προσκυνήσεις θεοῖς ἑτέροις" καὶ τοῦ "Μνήσθητι τῆς ἡμέρας τῶν σαββάτων," ὃ μὴ τὰς ἄλλας οἴεται χρῆναι φυλάττειν ἐντολάς, ὡς καὶ τιμωρίας κεῖσθαι τοῖς παραβαίνουσιν, ἐνιαχοῦ μὲν σφοδροτέρας, ἐνιαχοῦ δὲ παραπλησίας ταῖς παρὰ Μωυσέως νομοθετείσαις, ἔστι δὲ ὅπου καὶ φιλανθρωποτέρας;

155 C 'Αλλὰ τὸ "Οὐ προσκυνήσεις θεοῖς ἑτέροις"—ὃ δὴ μετὰ μεγάλης περὶ τὸν θεόν φησι διαβολῆς. "Θεὸς γὰρ ζηλωτής" φησι· καὶ ἐν ἄλλοις πάλιν·
155 D "'Ο θεὸς ἡμῶν πῦρ καταναλίσκον." εἶτα ἄνθρωπος ζηλωτὴς καὶ βάσκανος ἄξιος εἶναί σοι φαίνεται

[1] τοῖς Klimek adds.

[1] *Exodus* 20. 2–3. [2] *Exodus* 20. 4. [3] *Exodus* 20. 13–17.

famous decalogue! "Thou shalt not steal." "Thou shalt not kill." "Thou shalt not bear false witness." But let me write out word for word every one of the commandments which he says were written by God himself.

"I am the Lord thy God, which have brought thee out of the land of Egypt."[1] Then follows the second: "Thou shalt have no other gods but me." "Thou shalt not make unto thee any graven image."[2] And then he adds the reason: "For I the Lord thy God am a jealous God, visiting the iniquity of the fathers upon the children unto the third generation." "Thou shalt not take the name of the Lord thy God in vain." "Remember the sabbath day." "Honour thy father and thy mother." "Thou shalt not commit adultery." "Thou shalt not kill." "Thou shalt not steal." "Thou shalt not bear false witness." "Thou shalt not covet anything that is thy neighbour's."[3]

Now except for the command "Thou shalt not worship other gods," and "Remember the sabbath day," what nation is there, I ask in the name of the gods, which does not think that it ought to keep the other commandments? So much so that penalties have been ordained against those who transgress them, sometimes more severe, and sometimes similar to those enacted by Moses, though they are sometimes more humane.

But as for the commandment "Thou shalt not worship other gods," to this surely he adds a terrible libel upon God. "For I am a jealous God," he says, and in another place again, "Our God is a consuming fire."[4] Then if a man is jealous and envious you think him blameworthy, whereas if God

[4] *Deuteronomy* 4. 24; *Hebrews* 12. 29.

μέμψεως, ἐκθειάζεις δέ, εἰ ζηλότυπος ὁ θεὸς λέγεται; καίτοι πῶς εὔλογον οὕτω φανερὸν πρᾶγμα τοῦ θεοῦ καταψεύδεσθαι; καὶ γὰρ εἰ ζηλότυπος, ἄκοντος αὐτοῦ πάντες οἱ θεοὶ προσκυνοῦνται καὶ πάντα τὰ λοιπὰ τῶν ἐθνῶν τοὺς θεοὺς προσκυνεῖ. εἶτα πῶς οὐκ ἀνέστειλεν αὐτὸς ζηλῶν οὕτω καὶ μὴ βουλόμενος προσκυνεῖσθαι τοὺς ἄλλους, ἀλλὰ μόνον ἑαυτόν; ἆρ' οὖν οὐχ οἷός τε ἦν ἢ οὐδὲ τὴν
155 E ἀρχὴν ἠβουλήθη κωλῦσαι μὴ προσκυνεῖσθαι καὶ τοὺς ἄλλους θεούς; ἀλλὰ τὸ μὲν πρῶτον ἀσεβές, τὸ δὴ λέγειν ὡς οὐκ ἠδύνατο· τὸ δεύτερον δὲ τοῖς ἡμετέροις ἔργοις ὁμολογεῖ. ἄφετε τοῦτον τὸν λῆρον καὶ μὴ τηλικαύτην ἐφ' ὑμᾶς αὐτοὺς ἕλκετε
159 E βλασφημίαν. εἰ γὰρ οὐδένα θέλει προσκυνεῖσθαι, τοῦ χάριν αὐτοῦ τὸν νόθον υἱὸν τοῦτον προσκυνεῖτε καὶ ὃν ἐκεῖνος ἴδιον οὔτε ἐνόμισεν οὔθ' ἡγήσατο πώποτε. καὶ δείξω γε τοῦτο ῥᾳδίως. ὑμεῖς δέ, οὐκ οἶδ' ὅθεν, ὑπόβλητον αὐτῷ προστίθετε . . . .[1]

160 D Οὐδαμοῦ χαλεπαίνων ὁ θεὸς φαίνεται οὐδὲ ἀγανακτῶν οὐδὲ ὀργιζόμενος οὐδὲ ὀμνύων οὐδ' ἐπ' ἀμφότερα ταχέως ῥέπων οὐδὲ στρεπτός,[1] ὡς ὁ Μωυσῆς φησιν ἐπὶ τοῦ Φινεές. εἴ τις ὑμῶν ἀνέγνω τοὺς ἀριθμούς, οἶδεν ὃ λέγω. ἐπειδὴ γὰρ Φινεὲς τὸν τελεσθέντα τῷ Βεελφεγὼρ μετὰ τῆς ἀναπεισάσης αὐτὸν γυναικὸς αὐτοχειρίᾳ λαβὼν ἀπέκτεινεν αἰσχρῷ καὶ ὀδυνηροτάτῳ τραύματι, διὰ τῆς μή-

[1] Neumann suggests οὐδὲ στρεπτὸς or οὐδὲ μεταβλητὸς to represent *neque mutabilis esse*, the translation of one MS., *Oecolampadius*.

---

[1] According to Cyril's summary, Julian next reproaches the Christians for having forsaken the Greek doctrines about God.

is called jealous you think it a divine quality? And yet how is it reasonable to speak falsely of God in a matter that is so evident? For if he is indeed jealous, then against his will are all other gods worshipped, and against his will do all the remaining nations worship their gods. Then how is it that he did not himself restrain them, if he is so jealous and does not wish that the others should be worshipped, but only himself? Can it be that he was not able to do so, or did he not wish even from the beginning to prevent the other gods also from being worshipped? However, the first explanation is impious, to say, I mean, that he was unable; and the second is in accordance with what we do ourselves. Lay aside this nonsense and do not draw down on yourselves such terrible blasphemy. For if it is God's will that none other should be worshipped, why do you worship this spurious son of his whom he has never yet recognised or considered as his own? This I shall easily prove. You, however, I know not why, foist on him a counterfeit son. . . .[1]

Nowhere[2] is God shown as angry, or resentful, or wroth, or taking an oath, or inclining first to this side, then suddenly to that, or as turned from his purpose, as Moses tells us happened in the case of Phinehas. If any of you has read the *Book of Numbers* he knows what I mean. For when Phinehas had seized with his own hand and slain the man who had dedicated himself to Baal-peor, and with him the woman who had persuaded him, striking her with a shameful and most painful wound through

[2] *i. e.* in the Greek accounts of the gods; probably Julian refers to Plato and a phrase to this effect may have dropped out at the beginning of the sentence.

160 E τρας, φησί, παίσας τὴν γυναῖκα, πεποίηται λέγων
ὁ θεός· “Φινεὲς υἱὸς Ἐλεάζαρ υἱοῦ Ἀαρὼν
τοῦ ἱερέως κατέπαυσε τὸν θυμόν μου ἀπὸ υἱῶν
Ἰσραὴλ ἐν τῷ ζηλῶσαί μου τὸν ζῆλον ἐν αὐτοῖς.
καὶ οὐκ ἐξανήλωσα τοὺς υἱοὺς Ἰσραὴλ ἐν τῷ
ζήλῳ μου.” τί κουφότερον τῆς αἰτίας, δι' ἣν θεὸς
ὀργισθεὶς οὐκ ἀληθῶς ὑπὸ τοῦ γράψαντος ταῦτα
161 A πεποίηται; τί δὲ ἀλογώτερον, εἰ δέκα ἢ πεντε-
καίδεκα, κείσθω δὲ καὶ ἑκατόν, οὐ γὰρ δὴ χιλίους
ἐροῦσι—θῶμεν δὲ ἡμεῖς καὶ τοσούτους τολμή-
σαντάς τι τῶν ὑπὸ τοῦ θεοῦ τεταγμένων νόμων
παραβῆναι· ἑξακοσίας ἐχρῆν διὰ τοὺς ἅπαξ
χιλίους ἀναλωθῆναι χιλιάδας.; ὡς ἔμοιγε κρεῖττον
εἶναι τῷ παντὶ φαίνεται χιλίοις ἀνδράσι βελτί-
στοις ἕνα συνδιασῶσαι πονηρὸν ἢ συνδιαφθεῖραι
τοὺς χιλίους ἑνί. . . .

Εἰ γὰρ καὶ ἑνὸς ἡρώων καὶ οὐκ ἐπισήμου
δαίμονος δύσοιστος ἡ ὀργὴ χώραις τε καὶ πόλεσιν
ὁλοκλήροις, τίς ἂν ὑπέστη τοσούτου θεοῦ δαίμοσιν
168 B ἢ ἀγγέλοις ἢ καὶ ἀνθρώποις ἐπιμηνίσαντος; ἄξιόν
γέ ἐστι παραβαλεῖν αὐτὸν τῇ Λυκούργου πραότητι
168 C καὶ τῇ Σόλωνος ἀνεξικακίᾳ ἢ τῇ Ῥωμαίων πρὸς
171 D τοὺς ἠδικηκότας ἐπιεικείᾳ καὶ χρηστότητι. πόσῳ
δὲ δὴ τὰ παρ' ἡμῖν τῶν παρ' αὐτοῖς κρείττονα,
καὶ ἐκ τῶνδε σκοπεῖτε. μιμεῖσθαι κελεύουσιν
ἡμᾶς οἱ φιλόσοφοι κατὰ δύναμιν τοὺς θεούς, εἶναι
δὲ ταύτην τὴν μίμησιν ἐν θεωρίᾳ τῶν ὄντων. ὅτι
171 E δὲ τοῦτο δίχα πάθους ἐστὶ καὶ ἐν ἀπαθείᾳ κεῖται,

---

[1] *Numbers* 25. 11.

[2] According to Cyril, Julian then argued that the Creator ought not to have given way so often to violent anger against, and even wished to destroy, the whole Jewish people.

the belly, as Moses tells us, then God is made to say: "Phinehas, the son of Eleazar, the son of Aaron the priest, hath turned my wrath away from the children of Israel, in that he was jealous with my jealousy among them; and I consumed not the children of Israel in my jealousy."[1] What could be more trivial than the reason for which God was falsely represented as angry by the writer of this passage? What could be more irrational, even if ten or fifteen persons, or even, let us suppose, a hundred, for they certainly will not say that there were a thousand,—however, let us assume that even as many persons as that ventured to transgress some one of the laws laid down by God; was it right that on account of this one thousand, six hundred thousand should be utterly destroyed? For my part I think it would be better in every way to preserve one bad man along with a thousand virtuous men than to destroy the thousand together with that one. . . .[2]

For if the anger of even one hero or unimportant demon is hard to bear for whole countries and cities, who could have endured the wrath of so mighty a God, whether it were directed against demons or angels or mankind? It is worth while to compare his behaviour with the mildness of Lycurgus and the forbearance of Solon, or the kindness and benevolence of the Romans towards transgressors. But observe also from what follows how far superior are our teachings to theirs. The philosophers bid us imitate the gods so far as we can, and they teach us that this imitation consists in the contemplation of realities. And that this sort of study is remote from passion and is indeed based on freedom from passion,

πρόδηλόν ἐστί που, κἂν ἐγὼ μὴ λέγω· καθ' ὅσον ἄρα ἐν ἀπαθείᾳ γινόμεθα, τεταγμένοι περὶ τῶν ὄντων τὴν[1] θεωρίαν, κατὰ τοσοῦτον ἐξομοιούμεθα τῷ θεῷ. τίς δὲ ἡ παρ' Ἑβραίοις ὑμνουμένη τοῦ θεοῦ μίμησις; ὀργὴ καὶ θυμὸς καὶ ζῆλος ἄγριος. "Φινεὲς" γάρ φησι "κατέπαυσε τὸν θυμόν μου ἀπὸ υἱῶν Ἰσραὴλ ἐν τῷ ζηλῶσαι τὸν ζῆλόν μοῦ ἐν αὐτοῖς." εὑρὼν γὰρ ὁ θεὸς τὸν συναγανακτοῦντα καὶ συναλγοῦντα ἀφεὶς τὴν ἀγανάκτησιν
172 A φαίνεται. ταῦτα καὶ τὰ τοιαῦτα περὶ θεοῦ ἕτερα πεποίηται λέγων ὁ Μωυσῆς οὐκ ὀλιγαχοῦ τῆς γραφῆς.

176 AB Ὅτι δὲ οὐχ Ἑβραίων μόνον ἐμέλησε τῷ θεῷ, πάντων δὲ ἐθνῶν κηδόμενος ἔδωκεν ἐκείνοις μὲν οὐδὲν σπουδαῖον ἢ μέγα, ἡμῖν δὲ μακρῷ κρείττονα καὶ διαφέροντα, σκοπεῖτε λοιπὸν τὸ ἐντεῦθεν. ἔχουσι μὲν εἰπεῖν καὶ Αἰγύπτιοι, παρ' ἑαυτοῖς ἀπαριθμούμενοι σοφῶν οὐκ ὀλίγων ὀνόματα, πολλοὺς ἐσχηκέναι τοὺς ἀπὸ τῆς Ἑρμοῦ διαδοχῆς, Ἑρμοῦ δέ φημι τοῦ τρίτου ἐπιφοιτήσαντος τῇ Αἰγύπτῳ, Χαλδαῖοι δὲ καὶ Ἀσσύριοι τοὺς ἀπ' Ὠάννου καὶ Βήλου, μυρίους δὲ Ἕλληνες τοὺς ἀπὸ
176 C Χείρωνος. ἐκ τούτου γὰρ πάντες ἐγένοντο τελεστικοὶ φύσει καὶ θεολογικοί, καθὸ δὴ δοκοῦσι μόνον Ἑβραῖοι τὰ ἑαυτῶν ἀποσεμνύνειν . . . . .

[1] τὴν Klimek adds.

---

[1] A reference to Hermes Trismegistus, "thrice greatest Hermes," whom the Greeks identified with the Egyptian god Thoth. The Neo-Platonists ascribed certain mystic writings to this legendary being and regarded him as a sage.

[2] A Babylonian fish-god described by Berosus in his *History of Babylonia*. He was supposed to have taught the Chaldaeans the arts of civilisation and has some analogy with the serpent of *Genesis*.

is, I suppose, evident, even without my saying it. In proportion then as we, having been assigned to the contemplation of realities, attain to freedom from passion, in so far do we become like God. But what sort of imitation of God is praised among the Hebrews? Anger and wrath and fierce jealousy. For God says: "Phinehas hath turned away my wrath from the children of Israel, in that he was jealous with my jealousy among them." For God, on finding one who shared his resentment and his grief, thereupon, as it appears, laid aside his resentment. These words and others like them about God Moses is frequently made to utter in the Scripture.

Furthermore observe from what follows that God did not take thought for the Hebrews alone, but though he cared for all nations, he bestowed on the Hebrews nothing considerable or of great value, whereas on us he bestowed gifts far higher and surpassing theirs. For instance the Egyptians, as they reckon up the names of not a few wise men among themselves, can boast that they possess many successors of Hermes, I mean of Hermes who in his third manifestation visited Egypt;[1] while the Chaldaeans and Assyrians can boast of the successors of Oannes[2] and Belos;[3] the Hellenes can boast of countless successors of Cheiron.[4] For thenceforth all Hellenes were born with an aptitude for the mysteries and theologians, in the very way, you observe, which the Hebrews claim as their own peculiar boast. . . .[5]

[3] This is the Greek version of the Assyrian *bil*, "lord" or "god," the Baal of the Bible.

[4] The Centaur who taught Achilles.

[5] According to Cyril's summary, Julian then ridicules David and Samson and says that they were not really brave warriors, but far inferior to the Hellenes and Egyptians, and their dominion was very limited.

178 A Ἀλλ᾽ ἀρχὴν ἔδωκεν ὑμῖν ἐπιστήμης ἢ μάθημα
φιλόσοφον; καὶ ποῖον; ἡ μὲν γὰρ περὶ τὰ φαι-
178 B νόμενα θεωρία παρὰ τοῖς Ἕλλησιν ἐτελειώθη, τῶν
πρώτων τηρήσεων παρὰ τοῖς βαρβάροις ἐν Βαβυ-
λῶνι γενομένων· ἡ δὲ περὶ τὴν γεωμετρίαν ἀπὸ
τῆς γεωδαισίας τῆς ἐν Αἰγύπτῳ τὴν ἀρχὴν λα-
βοῦσα πρὸς τοσοῦτον μέγεθος ηὐξήθη· τὸ δὲ
περὶ τοὺς ἀριθμοὺς ἀπὸ τῶν Φοινίκων ἐμπόρων
ἀρξάμενον τέως εἰς ἐπιστήμης παρὰ τοῖς Ἕλλησι
κατέστη πρόσχημα. ταῦτα[1] δὴ τρία μετὰ[2] τῆς
συναρίθμου[3] μουσικῆς Ἕλληνες εἰς ἓν συνῆψαν,
ἀστρονομίαν γεωμετρίᾳ προσυφήναντες, ἀμφοῖν
δὲ προσαρμόσαντες τοὺς ἀριθμοὺς καὶ τὸ ἐν τού-
τοις ἐναρμόνιον κατανοήσαντες. ἐντεῦθεν ἔθεντο
τῇ παρὰ σφίσι μουσικῇ τοὺς ὅρους, εὑρόντες τῶν
ἁρμονικῶν λόγων πρὸς τὴν αἴσθησιν τῆς ἀκοῆς
ἄπταιστον ὁμολογίαν ἢ ὅτι τούτου μάλιστα ἐγγύς.
184 B Πότερον οὖν χρή με κατ᾽ ἄνδρα ὀνομάζειν ἢ
κατ᾽ ἐπιτηδεύματα; ἢ τοὺς ἀνθρώπους, οἷον Πλά-
τωνα, Σωκράτην, Ἀριστείδην, Κίμωνα, Θαλῆν,
Λυκοῦργον, Ἀγησίλαον, Ἀρχίδαμον—ἢ μᾶλλον
τὸ τῶν φιλοσόφων γένος, τὸ τῶν στρατηγῶν, τὸ
τῶν δημιουργῶν, τὸ τῶν νομοθετῶν; εὑρεθήσονται
γὰρ οἱ μοχθηρότατοι καὶ βδελυρώτατοι τῶν στρα-
184 C τηγῶν ἐπιεικέστερον χρησάμενοι τοῖς ἠδικηκόσι τὰ
μέγιστα ἢ Μωυσῆς τοῖς οὐδὲν ἐξημαρτηκόσιν.
190 C τίνα οὖν ὑμῖν ἀπαγγείλω βασιλείαν; πότερα τὴν
Περσέως ἢ τὴν Αἰακοῦ ἢ Μίνω τοῦ Κρητός, ὃς
ἐκάθηρε μὲν λῃστευομένην τὴν θάλασσαν, ἐκβα-

[1] ταῦτα Klimek, τὰ Neumann.
[2] Klimek defends μετά, Neumann suggests μαθήματα.
[3] For συμαωίθμου corrupt, Neumann suggests εὐρύθμου.

But has God granted to you to originate any science or any philosophical study? Why, what is it? For the theory of the heavenly bodies was perfected among the Hellenes, after the first observations had been made among the barbarians in Babylon.[1] And the study of geometry took its rise in the measurement of the land in Egypt, and from this grew to its present importance. Arithmetic began with the Phoenician merchants, and among the Hellenes in course of time acquired the aspect of a regular science. These three the Hellenes combined with music into one science, for they connected astronomy with geometry and adapted arithmetic to both, and perceived the principle of harmony in it. Hence they laid down the rules for their music, since they had discovered for the laws of harmony with reference to the sense of hearing an agreement that was infallible, or something very near to it.[2]

Need I tell over their names man by man, or under their professions? I mean, either the individual men, as for instance Plato, Socrates, Aristeides, Cimon, Thales, Lycurgus, Agesilaus, Archidamus,—or should I rather speak of the class of philosophers, of generals, of artificers, of lawgivers? For it will be found that even the most wicked and most brutal of the generals behaved more mildly to the greatest offenders than Moses did to those who had done no wrong. And now of what monarchy shall I report to you? Shall it be that of Perseus, or Aeacus, or Minos of Crete, who purified the sea

[1] Cf. *Oration* 4. 156c, the Hellenes perfected the astronomy of the Chaldaeans and Egyptians.

[2] They had discovered the laws of musical intervals.

λῶν καὶ ἐξελάσας τοὺς βαρβάρους ἄχρι Συρίας
καὶ Σικελίας, ἐφ' ἑκάτερα προβὰς τοῖς τῆς ἀρχῆς
ὁρίοις, οὐ μόνων δὲ τῶν νήσων, ἀλλὰ καὶ τῶν
παραλίων ἐκράτει; καὶ διελόμενος πρὸς τὸν ἀδελ-
φὸν Ῥαδάμανθυν, οὔτι τὴν γῆν, ἀλλὰ τὴν ἐπιμέ-
λειαν τῶν ἀνθρώπων, αὐτὸς μὲν ἐτίθει παρὰ τοῦ
Διὸς λαμβάνων τοὺς νόμους, ἐκείνῳ δὲ τὸ δικαστι-
κὸν ἠφίει μέρος ἀναπληροῦν . . . .
193 C Ἀλλ' ἐπειδὴ κτισθεῖσαν αὐτὴν πολλοὶ μὲν
περιέστησαν πόλεμοι, πάντων δὲ ἐκράτει καὶ
κατηγωνίζετο καί, παρ' αὐτὰ μᾶλλον αὐξανομένη
τὰ δεινά, τῆς ἀσφαλείας ἐδεῖτο μείζονος, αὖθις
ὁ Ζεὺς τὸν φιλοσοφώτατον αὐτῇ Νουμᾶν ἐφί-
στησιν. οὗτος ἦν ὁ καλὸς καὶ ἀγαθὸς ὁ
193 D Νουμᾶς, ἄλσεσιν ἐρήμοις ἐνδιατρίβων καὶ συνὼν
ἀεὶ τοῖς θεοῖς κατὰ τὰς ἀκραιφνεῖς αὐτοῦ
νοήσεις. . . . . οὗτος τοὺς πλείστους τῶν ἱερα-
194 B τικῶν κατέστησε νόμους. ταῦτα μὲν οὖν ἐκ
κατοχῆς καὶ ἐπιπνοίας θείας ἔκ τε τῶν τῆς Σιβύλ-
λης καὶ τῶν ἄλλων, οἳ δὴ γεγόνασι κατ' ἐκεῖνον
τὸν χρόνον κατὰ τὴν πάτριον φωνὴν χρησμολόγοι,
φαίνεται δοὺς ὁ Ζεὺς τῇ πόλει. τὴν δὲ ἐξ ἀέρος
πεσοῦσαν ἀσπίδα καὶ τὴν ἐν τῷ λόφῳ κεφαλὴν
194 C φανεῖσαν, ὅθεν, οἶμαι, καὶ τοὔνομα προσέλαβεν ἡ

---

[1] According to Cyril, Julian then related stories about Minos, and the myth of Dardanus, the account of the flight of Aeneas, his emigration to Italy and the founding of Rome. [2] *i. e.* Rome.

[3] Numa Pompilius, a legendary king who is supposed to have succeeded Romulus; various portents manifested the favour of the gods towards Numa. Cf. Julian, *Oration* 4. 155A, note, Vol. 1.

[4] A few words are missing.

of pirates, and expelled and drove out the barbarians as far as Syria and Sicily, advancing in both directions the frontiers of his realm, and ruled not only over the islands but also over the dwellers along the coasts? And dividing with his brother Rhadamanthus, not indeed the earth, but the care of mankind, he himself laid down the laws as he received them from Zeus, but left to Rhadamanthus to fill the part of judge. . . .[1]

But when after her [2] foundation many wars encompassed her, she won and prevailed in them all; and since she ever increased in size in proportion to her very dangers and needed greater security, then Zeus set over her the great philosopher Numa.[3] This then was the excellent and upright Numa who dwelt in deserted groves and ever communed with the gods in the pure thoughts of his own heart. . . .[4] It was he who established most of the laws concerning temple worship. Now these blessings, derived from a divine possession and inspiration which proceeded both from the Sibyl and others who at that time uttered oracles in their native tongue, were manifestly bestowed on the city by Zeus. And the shield which fell from the clouds [5] and the head which appeared on the hill,[6] from which, I suppose,

[5] A small shield, *ancile*, on whose preservation the power of Rome was supposed to depend, was said to have fallen from the sky in Numa's reign. Livy 1. 20 refers to it in the plural, caelestia arma quae ancilia appellantur; cf. also *Aeneid* 8. 664, lapsa ancilia coelo.

[6] When the foundations were dug for the temple of Jupiter a human head, caput, was found; this was regarded as an omen, and hence the Capitoline Hill received its name; cf. Livy 1. 55. For Julian's belief in such traditions cf. *Oration* 5. Vol. 1, 161B on the legend of Claudia and the image of Cybele.

τοῦ μεγάλου Διὸς ἕδρα, πότερον ἐν τοῖς πρώτοις ἢ τοῖς δευτέροις ἀριθμήσωμεν τῶν δώρων; εἶτα, ὦ δυστυχεῖς ἄνθρωποι, σωζομένου τοῦ παρ᾽ ἡμῖν ὅπλου διοπετοῦς, ὃ κατέπεμψεν ὁ μέγας Ζεὺς ἤτοι πατὴρ Ἄρης, ἐνέχυρον διδοὺς οὐ λόγον, ἔργον δέ, ὅτι τῆς πόλεως ἡμῶν εἰς τὸ διηνεκὲς προασπίσει, προσκυνεῖν ἀφέντες καὶ σέβεσθαι, τὸ τοῦ σταυροῦ προσκυνεῖτε ξύλον, εἰκόνας αὐτοῦ σκιαγραφοῦντες ἐν
194 D τῷ μετώπῳ καὶ πρὸ τῶν οἰκημάτων ἐγγράφοντες.

Ἆρα ἀξίως ἄν τις τοὺς συνετωτέρους ὑμῶν μισήσειεν ἢ τοὺς ἀφρονεστέρους ἐλεήσειεν, οἳ κατακολουθοῦντες ὑμῖν, εἰς τοσοῦτον ἦλθον ὀλέθρου, ὥστε τοὺς αἰωνίους ἀφέντες θεοὺς ἐπὶ τὸν Ἰου-
197 C δαίων μεταβῆναι νεκρόν; . . . παρίημι γὰρ τὰ τῆς μητρὸς τῶν θεῶν μυστήρια καὶ ζηλῶ τὸν Μάριον.
198 B . . . τὸ γὰρ ἐκ θεῶν εἰς ἀνθρώπους ἀφικνούνενον
C πνεῦμα σπανιάκις μὲν καὶ ἐν ὀλίγοις γίνεται καὶ οὔτε πάντα ἄνδρα τούτου μετασχεῖν ῥᾴδιον οὔτε ἐν παντὶ καιρῷ. ταύτῃ τοι καὶ τὸ παρ᾽ Ἑβραίοις προφητικὸν πνεῦμα ἐπέλιπεν, οὐκοῦν οὐδὲ παρ᾽ Αἰγυπτίοις εἰς τοῦτο σώζεται. φαίνεται δὲ καὶ τὰ αὐτοφυῆ χρηστήρια σιγῆσαι ταῖς τῶν χρόνων εἴκοντα περιόδοις. ὃ δὴ φιλάνθρωπος ἡμῶν δεσπότης καὶ πατὴρ Ζεὺς ἐννοήσας, ὡς ἂν μὴ παντάπασι τῆς πρὸς τοὺς θεοὺς ἀποστερηθῶμεν κοινωνίας, δέδωκεν ἡμῖν διὰ τῶν ἱερῶν τεχνῶν
198 D ἐπίσκεψιν, ὑφ᾽ ἧς πρὸς τὰς χρείας ἕξομεν τὴν ἀποχρῶσαν βοήθειαν.

[1] Here Cyril retorts that Julian admired what others condemn, *e.g.* the cruel and superstitious Marius, who, said he, was given to the Romans by the gods. The worship of Cybele was another gift from heaven to Rome. Julian then referred to various kinds of divination.

the seat of mighty Zeus received its name, are we to reckon these among the very highest or among secondary gifts? And yet, ye misguided men, though there is preserved among us that weapon which flew down from heaven, which mighty Zeus or father Ares sent down to give us a warrant, not in word but in deed, that he will forever hold his shield before our city, you have ceased to adore and reverence it, but you adore the wood of the cross and draw its likeness on your foreheads and engrave it on your housefronts.

Would not any man be justified in detesting the more intelligent among you, or pitying the more foolish, who, by following you, have sunk to such depths of ruin that they have abandoned the everliving gods and have gone over to the corpse of the Jew.[1] . . . For I say nothing about the Mysteries of the Mother of the Gods, and I admire Marius. . . . For the spirit that comes to men from the gods is present but seldom and in few, and it is not easy for every man to share in it or at every time. Thus it is that the prophetic spirit has ceased among the Hebrews also, nor is it maintained among the Egyptians, either, down to the present. And we see that the indigenous oracles[2] of Greece have also fallen silent and yielded to the course of time. Then lo, our gracious lord and father Zeus took thought of this, and that we might not be wholly deprived of communion with the gods has granted us through the sacred arts[3] a means of enquiry by which we may obtain the aid that suffices for our needs.

[2] Julian is thinking of the oracle of Delphi which he had in vain endeavoured to restore.

[3] *i. e.* of divination by entrails and other omens.

200 A Ἔλαθέ με μικροῦ τὸ μέγιστον τῶν Ἡλίου καὶ Διὸς δώρων. εἰκότως δὲ αὐτὸ ἐφύλαξα ἐν[1] τῷ τέλει. καὶ γὰρ οὐκ ἴδιόν ἐστιν ἡμῶν μόνον, ἀλλ', οἶμαι, κοινὸν πρὸς Ἕλληνας, τοὺς ἡμετέρους συγγενεῖς. ὁ γάρ τοι Ζεὺς ἐν μὲν τοῖς νοητοῖς ἐξ ἑαυτοῦ τὸν Ἀσκληπιὸν ἐγέννησεν, εἰς δὲ τὴν γῆν διὰ τῆς Ἡλίου γονίμου ζωῆς ἐξέφηνεν. οὗτος ἐπὶ γῆς ἐξ οὐρανοῦ ποιησάμενος τὴν πρόοδον, ἑνοειδῶς μὲν ἐν ἀνθρώπου μορφῇ περὶ τὴν Ἐπίδαυρον
200 B ἀνεφάνη, πληθυνόμενος δὲ ἐντεῦθεν ταῖς προόδοις ἐπὶ πᾶσαν ὤρεξε τὴν γῆν τὴν σωτήριον ἑαυτοῦ δεξιάν. ἦλθεν εἰς Πέργαμον, εἰς Ἰωνίαν, εἰς Τάραντα μετὰ ταῦθ', ὕστερον ἦλθεν εἰς τὴν Ῥώμην. ᾤχετο δὲ εἰς Κῶ, ἐνθένδε εἰς Αἰγάς. εἶτα πανταχοῦ γῆς ἐστι καὶ θαλάσσης. οὐ καθ' ἕκαστον ἡμῶν ἐπιφοιτᾷ, καὶ ὅμως ἐπανορθοῦται ψυχὰς πλημμελῶς διακειμένας καὶ τὰ σώματα ἀσθενῶς ἔχοντα.

201 E Τί δὲ τοιοῦτον ἑαυτοῖς Ἑβραῖοι καυχῶνται παρὰ τοῦ θεοῦ δεδόσθαι, πρὸς οὓς ὑμεῖς ἀφ' ἡμῶν αὐτομολήσαντες πείθεσθε; εἰ τοῖς ἐκείνων γοῦν προσείχετε λόγοις, οὐκ ἂν παντάπασιν ἐπεπράγειτε δυστυχῶς, ἀλλὰ χεῖρον μὲν ἢ πρότερον, ὁπότε σὺν ἡμῖν ἦτε, οἰστὰ δὲ ὅμως ἐπεπόνθειτε ἂν καὶ φορητά. ἕνα γὰρ ἀντὶ πολλῶν θεὸν[2] ἐσέβεσθε ἂν οὐκ ἄνθρωπον, μᾶλλον δὲ πολλοὺς ἀν-
202 A θρώπους δυστυχεῖς. καὶ νόμῳ σκληρῷ μὲν καὶ τραχεῖ καὶ πολὺ τὸ ἄγριον ἔχοντι καὶ βάρβαρον ἀντὶ τῶν παρ' ἡμῖν ἐπιεικῶν καὶ φιλανθρώπων

[1] Klimek would omit ἐν.
[2] θεὸν Klimek; θεῶν MSS., Neumann.

I had almost forgotten the greatest of the gifts of Helios and Zeus. But naturally I kept it for the last. And indeed it is not peculiar to us Romans only, but we share it, I think, with the Hellenes our kinsmen. I mean to say that Zeus engendered Asclepius from himself among the intelligible gods,[1] and through the life of generative Helios he revealed him to the earth. Asclepius, having made his visitation to earth from the sky, appeared at Epidaurus singly, in the shape of a man; but afterwards he multiplied himself, and by his visitations stretched out over the whole earth his saving right hand. He came to Pergamon, to Ionia, to Tarentum afterwards; and later he came to Rome. And he travelled to Cos and thence to Aegae. Next he is present everywhere on land and sea. He visits no one of us separately, and yet he raises up souls that are sinful and bodies that are sick.

But what great gift of this sort do the Hebrews boast of as bestowed on them by God, the Hebrews who have persuaded you to desert to them? If you had at any rate paid heed to their teachings, you would not have fared altogether ill, and though worse than you did before, when you were with us, still your condition would have been bearable and supportable. For you would be worshipping one god instead of many, not a man, or rather many wretched men.[2] And though you would be following a law that is harsh and stern and contains much that is savage and barbarous, instead of our mild and humane laws,

[1] See Vol. 1, Introduction to *Oration* 4, p. 349; and for Asclepius, *Oration* 4. 144B, where Julian, as here, opposes Asclepius to Christ; and 153B for Asclepius the saviour.

[2] The martyrs.

χρώμενοι τὰ μὲν ἄλλα χείρονες ἂν ἦτε, ἁγνότεροι
δὲ καὶ καθαρώτεροι τὰς ἁγιστείας. νῦν δὲ ὑμῖν
συμβέβηκεν ὥσπερ ταῖς βδέλλαις τὸ χείριστον
ἕλκειν αἷμα ἐκεῖθεν, ἀφεῖναι δὲ τὸ καθαρώτερον.
191 D ὁ δὲ Ἰησοῦς ἀναπείσας τὸ χείριστον τῶν παρ'
191 E ὑμῖν, ὀλίγους πρὸς τοῖς τριακοσίοις ἐνιαυτοῖς
ὀνομάζεται, ἐργασάμενος παρ' ὃν ἔζη χρόνον οὐδὲν
ἀκοῆς ἄξιον, εἰ μή τις οἴεται τοὺς κυλλοὺς καὶ
τυφλοὺς ἰάσασθαι καὶ δαιμονῶντας ἐξορκίζειν ἐν
Βηθσαιδᾷ καὶ ἐν Βηθανίᾳ ταῖς κώμαις τῶν μεγί-
205 E στων ἔργων εἶναι. ἁγνείας μὲν οὐδὲ γὰρ εἰ πεποίη-
ται μνήμην ἐπίστασθε· ζηλοῦτε δὲ Ἰουδαίων τοὺς
θυμοὺς καὶ τὴν πικρίαν, ἀνατρέποντες ἱερὰ καὶ
206 A βωμοὺς καὶ ἀπεσφάξατε οὐχ ἡμῶν μόνον τοὺς
τοῖς πατρῴοις [1] ἐμμένοντας, ἀλλὰ καὶ τῶν ἐξ ἴσης
ὑμῶν πεπλανημένων αἱρετικοὺς τοὺς μὴ τὸν αὐτὸν
τρόπον ὑμῶν τὸν νεκρὸν θρηνοῦντας. ἀλλὰ ταῦτα
ὑμέτερα μᾶλλόν ἐστιν· οὐδαμοῦ γὰρ οὔτε Ἰησοῦς
αὐτὰ παραδέδωκε κελεύων ὑμῖν οὔτε Παῦλος.
αἴτιον δέ, ὅτι μηδὲ ἤλπισαν εἰς τοῦτο ἀφίξεσθαί
ποτε δυνάμεως ὑμᾶς· ἠγάπων γάρ, εἰ θεραπαίνας
ἐξαπατήσουσι καὶ δούλους καὶ διὰ τούτων τὰς
γυναῖκας ἄνδρας τε, οἵους Κορνήλιος καὶ Σέργιος.
206 B ὧν εἷς ἐὰν φανῇ τῶν τηνικαῦτα γνωριζομένων
ἐπιμνηθεὶς—ἐπὶ Τιβερίου γὰρ ἤτοι Κλαυδίου
ταῦτα ἐγίνετο—, περὶ πάντων ὅτι ψεύδομαι
νομίζετε.

[1] πατρίοις Asmus, but Julian uses both forms.

---

[1] Cf. *Misopogon* 361B, Vol. 2.

[2] For the massacres of heretics by the Christians cf. Julian's letter *To the Citizens of Bostra*, p. 129.

[3] Jesus Christ; cf. above, 194D.

and would in other respects be inferior to us, yet you would be more holy and purer than now in your forms of worship. But now it has come to pass that like leeches you have sucked the worst blood from that source and left the purer. Yet Jesus, who won over the least worthy of you, has been known by name for but little more than three hundred years: and during his lifetime he accomplished nothing worth hearing of, unless anyone thinks that to heal crooked and blind men and to exorcise those who were possessed by evil demons in the villages of Bethsaida and Bethany can be classed as a mighty achievement. As for purity of life you do not know whether he so much as mentioned it; but you emulate the rages and the bitterness of the Jews, overturning temples and altars,[1] and you slaughtered not only those of us who remained true to the teachings of their fathers, but also men who were as much astray as yourselves, heretics,[2] because they did not wail over the corpse[3] in the same fashion as yourselves. But these are rather your own doings; for nowhere did either Jesus or Paul hand down to you such commands. The reason for this is that they never even hoped that you would one day attain to such power as you have; for they were content if they could delude maidservants and slaves, and through them the women, and men like Cornelius[4] and Sergius.[5] But if you can show me that one of these men is mentioned by the well-known writers of that time,—these events happened in the reign of Tiberius or Claudius,—then you may consider that I speak falsely about all matters.

[4] *Acts* 10, the story of Cornelius the centurion.
[5] *Acts* 13. 6–12; Sergius was the proconsul.

209 D Ἀλλὰ τοῦτο μὲν οὐκ οἶδ' ὅθεν ὥσπερ ἐπιπνεόμε-
νος ἐφθεγξάμην, ὅθεν δὲ ἐξέβην, ὅτι "Πρὸς τοὺς Ἰου-
δαίους ηὐτομολήσατε, τί τοῖς ἡμετέροις ἀχαριστή-
σαντες θεοῖς;" ἆρ' ὅτι βασιλεύειν ἔδοσαν οἱ θεοὶ
τῇ Ῥώμῃ, τοῖς Ἰουδαίοις ὀλίγον μὲν χρόνον ἐλευ-
θέρους εἶναι, δουλεῦσαι δὲ ἀεὶ καὶ παροικῆσαι;
σκόπει τὸν Ἀβραάμ· οὐχὶ πάροικος ἦν ἐν ἀλλο-
209 E τρίᾳ; τὸν Ἰακώβ· οὐ πρότερον μὲν Σύροις, ἑξῆς
δὲ ἐπὶ τούτοις Παλαιστινοῖς, ἐν γήρᾳ δὲ Αἰγυπ-
τίοις ἐδούλευσεν; οὐκ ἐξ οἴκου δουλείας ἐξαγα-
γεῖν αὐτοὺς ὁ Μωυσῆς φησιν ἐξ Αἰγύπτου ἐν
βραχίονι ὑψηλῷ; κατοικήσαντες δὲ τὴν Παλαι-
στίνην, οὐ πυκνότερον ἤμειψαν τὰς τύχας ἢ τὸ
χρῶμά φασιν οἱ τεθεαμένοι τὸν χαμαιλέοντα, νῦν
μὲν ὑπακούοντες τοῖς κριταῖς, νῦν δὲ τοῖς ἀλλο-
φύλοις δουλεύοντες; ἐπειδὴ δὲ ἐβασιλεύθησαν—
ἀφείσθω δὲ νῦν ὅπως· οὔτε γὰρ ὁ θεὸς ἑκὼν αὐτοῖς
τὸ βασιλεύεσθαι συνεχώρησεν, ὡς ἡ γραφή φησιν,
210 A ἀλλὰ βιασθεὶς ὑπ' αὐτῶν καὶ προδιαστειλάμενος,
ὅτι ἄρα φαύλως βασιλευθήσονται. πλὴν ἀλλ'
ᾤκησαν γοῦν τὴν ἑαυτῶν καὶ ἐγεώργησαν ὀλίγα
πρὸς τοῖς τριακοσίοις ἔτεσιν. ἐξ ἐκείνου πρῶτον
Ἀσσυρίοις, εἶτα Μήδοις, ὕστερον Πέρσαις ἐδού-
213 A λευσαν, εἶτα νῦν ἡμῖν αὐτοῖς. καὶ ὁ παρ' ὑμῖν
κηρυττόμενος Ἰησοῦς εἷς ἦν τῶν Καίσαρος ὑπη-
κόων. εἰ δὲ ἀπιστεῖτε, μικρὸν ὕστερον ἀποδείξω·
μᾶλλον δὲ ἤδη λεγέσθω. φατὲ μέντοι μετὰ τοῦ
πατρὸς αὐτὸν ἀπογράψασθαι καὶ τῆς μητρὸς ἐπὶ
Κυρηνίου.

---

[1] See above 201E. [2] *Exodus* 6. 6.
[3] *Judges* 2. 16.

But I know not whence I was as it were inspired to utter these remarks. However, to return to the point at which I digressed,[1] when I asked, "Why were you so ungrateful to our gods as to desert them for the Jews?" Was it because the gods granted the sovereign power to Rome, permitting the Jews to be free for a short time only, and then forever to be enslaved and aliens? Look at Abraham: was he not an alien in a strange land? And Jacob: was he not a slave, first in Syria, then after that in Palestine, and in his old age in Egypt? Does not Moses say that he led them forth from the house of bondage out of Egypt "with a stretched out arm"?[2] And after their sojourn in Palestine did they not change their fortunes more frequently than observers say the chameleon changes its colour, now subject to the judges,[3] now enslaved to foreign races? And when they began to be governed by kings,—but let me for the present postpone asking how they were governed: for as the Scripture tells us,[4] God did not willingly allow them to have kings, but only when constrained by them, and after protesting to them beforehand that they would thus be governed ill,—still they did at any rate inhabit their own country and tilled it for a little over three hundred years. After that they were enslaved first to the Assyrians, then to the Medes, later to the Persians, and now at last to ourselves. Even Jesus, who was proclaimed among you, was one of Caesar's subjects. And if you do not believe me I will prove it a little later, or rather let me simply assert it now. However, you admit that with his father and mother he registered his name in the governorship of Cyrenius.[5]

[4] 1 *Samuel* 8. [5] *Luke* 2. 2.

213 B 'Αλλὰ γενόμενος ἄνθρωπος[1] τίνων ἀγαθῶν αἴτιος κατέστη τοῖς ἑαυτοῦ συγγενέσιν; οὐ γὰρ ἠθέλησαν, φασίν, ὑπακοῦσαι τοῦ 'Ιησοῦ. τί δέ; ὁ σκληροκάρδιος καὶ λιθοτράχηλος ἐκεῖνος λαὸς πῶς ὑπήκουσε τοῦ Μωυσέως· 'Ιησοῦς δέ, ὁ τοῖς πνεύμασιν ἐπιτάττων καὶ βαδίζων ἐπὶ τῆς θαλάσσης καὶ τὰ δαιμόνια ἐξελαύνων, ὡς δὲ ὑμεῖς λέγετε, τὸν οὐρανὸν καὶ τὴν γῆν ἀπεργασάμενος—οὐ γὰρ δὴ ταῦτα τετόλμηκέ τις εἰπεῖν περὶ αὐτοῦ τῶν
213 C μαθητῶν, εἰ μὴ μόνος 'Ιωάννης οὐδὲ αὐτὸς σαφῶς οὐδὲ τρανῶς· ἀλλ' εἰρηκέναι γε συγκεχωρήσθω—οὐκ ἠδύνατο τὰς προαιρέσεις ἐπὶ σωτηρίᾳ τῶν ἑαυτοῦ φίλων καὶ συγγενῶν μεταστῆσαι;

218 A Ταῦτα μὲν οὖν καὶ μικρὸν ὕστερον, ὅταν ἰδίᾳ περὶ τῆς τῶν εὐαγγελίων τερατουργίας καὶ σκευωρίας ἐξετάζειν ἀρξώμεθα. νυνὶ δὲ ἀποκρίνεσθέ μοι πρὸς ἐκεῖνο. πότερον ἄμεινον τὸ διηνεκῶς μὲν
218 B ἐλεύθερον εἶναι, ἐν δισχιλίοις δὲ ὅλοις ἐνιαυτοῖς ἄρξαι τὸ πλεῖον γῆς καὶ θαλάσσης, ἢ τὸ δουλεύειν καὶ πρὸς ἐπίταγμα ζῆν ἀλλότριον; οὐδεὶς οὕτως ἐστὶν ἀναίσχυντος, ὡς ἑλέσθαι μᾶλλον τὸ δεύτερον. ἀλλὰ τὸ πολέμῳ κρατεῖν οἰήσεταί τις τοῦ κρατεῖσθαι χεῖρον; οὕτω τίς ἐστιν ἀναίσθητος; εἰ δὲ ταῦτα ἀληθῆ φαμεν, ἕνα μοι κατὰ 'Αλέξανδρον δείξατε στρατηγόν, ἕνα κατὰ Καίσαρα παρὰ τοῖς 'Εβραίοις. οὐ γὰρ δὴ παρ' ὑμῖν. καίτοι, μὰ τοὺς θεούς, εὖ οἶδ' ὅτι περιυβρίζω τοὺς ἄνδρας, ἐμνη-
218 C μόνευσα δὲ αὐτῶν ὡς γνωρίμων. οἱ γὰρ δὴ τούτων ἐλάττους ὑπὸ τῶν πολλῶν ἀγνοοῦνται, ὧν ἕκαστος

[1] ἄνθρωπος Neumann would add.

---

[1] *Ezekiel* 3. 7.

But when he became man what benefits did he confer on his own kinsfolk? Nay, the Galilaeans answer, they refused to hearken unto Jesus. What? How was it then that this hardhearted[1] and stubborn-necked people hearkened unto Moses; but Jesus, who commanded the spirits[2] and walked on the sea, and drove out demons, and as you yourselves assert made the heavens and the earth,—for no one of his disciples ventured to say this concerning him, save only John, and he did not say it clearly or distinctly; still let us at any rate admit that he said it—could not this Jesus change the dispositions of his own friends and kinsfolk to the end that he might save them?

However, I will consider this again a little later when I begin to examine particularly into the miracle-working and the fabrication of the gospels. But now answer me this. Is it better to be free continuously and during two thousand whole years to rule over the greater part of the earth and the sea, or to be enslaved and to live in obedience to the will of others? No man is so lacking in self-respect as to choose the latter by preference. Again, will anyone think that victory in war is less desirable than defeat? Who is so stupid? But if this that I assert is the truth, point out to me among the Hebrews a single general like Alexander or Caesar! You have no such man. And indeed, by the gods, I am well aware that I am insulting these heroes by the question, but I mentioned them because they are well known. For the generals who are inferior to them are unknown to the multitude, and yet every one of them deserves

[2] *Mark* 1. 27.

πάντων ὁμοῦ τῶν παρ' Ἑβραίοις γεγονότων ἐστὶ θαυμαστότερος.

221 E Ἀλλ' ὁ τῆς πολιτείας θεσμὸς καὶ τύπος τῶν δικαστηρίων, ἡ δὲ περὶ τὰς πόλεις οἰκονομία καὶ τῶν νόμων[1] τὸ κάλλος, ἡ δὲ ἐν τοῖς μαθήμασιν ἐπίδοσις, ἡ δὲ ἐν ταῖς ἐλευθερίοις τέχναις ἄσκησις
222 A οὐχ Ἑβραίων μὲν ἦν ἀθλία καὶ βαρβαρική; καίτοι βούλεται ὁ μοχθηρὸς Εὐσέβιος εἶναί τινα καὶ παρ' αὐτοῖς ἑξάμετρα, καὶ φιλοτιμεῖται λογικὴν εἶναι πραγματείαν παρὰ τοῖς Ἑβραίοις, ἧς τοὔνομα ἀκήκοε παρὰ τοῖς Ἕλλησι. ποῖον ἰατρικῆς εἶδος ἀνεφάνη παρὰ τοῖς Ἑβραίοις, ὥσπερ ἐν Ἕλλησι τῆς Ἱπποκράτους καί τινων ἄλλων μετ'
224 C ἐκεῖνον αἱρέσεων; ὁ σοφώτατος Σολομῶν παρόμοιός ἐστι τῷ παρ' Ἕλλησι Φωκυλίδῃ ἢ Θεόγνιδι ἢ Ἰσοκράτει; πόθεν; εἰ γοῦν παραβάλοις τὰς Ἰσοκράτους παραινέσεις ταῖς ἐκείνου παροιμίαις,
224 D εὕροις ἄν, εὖ οἶδα, τὸν τοῦ Θεοδώρου κρείττονα τοῦ σοφωτάτου βασιλέως. ἀλλ' ἐκεῖνος, φασί, καὶ περὶ θεουργίαν ἤσκητο. τί οὖν; οὐχὶ καὶ ὁ Σολομῶν οὗτος τοῖς ἡμετέροις ἐλάτρευσε θεοῖς, ὑπὸ τῆς γυναικός, ὥς λέγουσιν, ἐξαπατηθείς; ὢ μέγεθος ἀρετῆς. ὢ σοφίας πλοῦτος. οὐ περιγέγονεν ἡδονῆς, καὶ γυναικὸς λόγοι τοῦτον παρήγαγον. εἴπερ οὖν ὑπὸ γυναικὸς ἠπατήθη, τοῦτον σοφὸν μὴ λέγετε. εἰ δὲ πεπιστεύκατε σοφόν, μή τοι παρὰ γυναικὸς αὐτὸν ἐξηπατῆσθαι νομίζετε,

[1] After καὶ a lacuna; Gollwitzer, followed by Asmus, suggests τῶν νόμων; Neumann τῶν πολιτῶν.

---

[1] Eusebius, *Praeparatio Evangelica* 11. 5. 5 says that Moses and David wrote in "the heroic metre."

more admiration than all the generals put together whom the Jews have had.

Further, as regards the constitution of the state and the fashion of the law-courts, the administration of cities and the excellence of the laws, progress in learning and the cultivation of the liberal arts, were not all these things in a miserable and barbarous state among the Hebrews? And yet the wretched Eusebius[1] will have it that poems in hexameters are to be found even among them, and sets up a claim that the study of logic exists among the Hebrews, since he has heard among the Hellenes the word they use for logic. What kind of healing art has ever appeared among the Hebrews, like that of Hippocrates among the Hellenes, and of certain other schools that came after him? Is their "wisest" man Solomon at all comparable with Phocylides or Theognis or Isocrates among the Hellenes? Certainly not. At least, if one were to compare the exhortations of Isocrates with Solomon's proverbs, you would, I am very sure, find that the son of Theodorus is superior to their "wisest" king. "But," they answer, "Solomon was also proficient in the secret cult of God." What then? Did not this Solomon serve our gods also, deluded by his wife, as they assert?[2] What great virtue! What wealth of wisdom! He could not rise superior to pleasure, and the arguments of a woman led him astray! Then if he was deluded by a woman, do not call this man wise. But if you are convinced that he was wise, do not believe that he was deluded by a woman, but that, trusting to his

[2] 1 *Kings* 11. 4: "His wives turned away his heart after other gods." Julian may allude to Pharaoh's daughter, see 1 *Kings*, 3. 1.

224 E κρίσει δὲ οἰκείᾳ καὶ συνέσει καὶ τῇ παρὰ τοῦ φανέντος αὐτῷ θεοῦ διδασκαλίᾳ πειθόμενον λελατρευκέναι καὶ τοῖς ἄλλοις θεοῖς. φθόνος γὰρ καὶ ζῆλος οὐδὲ ἄχρι τῶν ἀρίστων ἀνθρώπων ἀφικνεῖται, τοσοῦτον ἄπεστιν ἀγγέλων καὶ θεῶν. ὑμεῖς δὲ ἄρα περὶ τὰ μέρη τῶν δυνάμεων στρέφεσθε, ἃ δὴ δαιμόνιά τις εἰπὼν οὐκ ἐξαμαρτάνει. τὸ γὰρ φιλότιμον ἐνταῦθα καὶ κενόδοξον, ἐν δὲ τοῖς θεοῖς οὐδὲν ὑπάρχει καὶ τοιοῦτον.

229 C Τοῦ χάριν ὑμεῖς τῶν παρ' Ἕλλησι παρεσθίετε μαθημάτων, εἴπερ αὐτάρκης ὑμῖν ἐστιν ἡ τῶν ὑμετέρων γραφῶν ἀνάγνωσις; καίτοι κρεῖττον ἐκείνων εἴργειν τοὺς ἀνθρώπους ἢ τῆς τῶν ἱεροθύτων ἐδωδῆς. ἐκ μὲν γὰρ ἐκείνης, καθὰ καὶ ὁ Παῦλος λέγει, βλάπτεται μὲν οὐδὲν ὁ προσφερόμενος, ἡ δὲ συνείδησις τοῦ βλέποντος ἀδελφοῦ σκανδαλισθείη ἂν καθ' ὑμᾶς, ὦ σοφώτατοι καὶ ὑπερήφανοι.[1] διὰ δὲ τῶν μαθημάτων τούτων ἀπέ-
229 D στη τῆς ἀθεότητος πᾶν ὅτι περ παρ' ὑμῖν ἡ φύσις ἤνεγκε γενναῖον. ὅτῳ οὖν ὑπῆρξεν εὐφυΐας κἂν μικρὸν μόριον, τούτῳ τάχιστα συνέβη τῆς παρ' ὑμῖν ἀθεότητος ἀποστῆναι. βέλτιον οὖν εἴργειν μαθημάτων, οὐχ ἱερείων τοὺς ἀνθρώπους. ἀλλ' ἴστε καὶ ὑμεῖς, ὡς ἐμοὶ φαίνεται, τὸ διάφορον εἰς σύνεσιν τῶν παρ' ὑμῖν γραφῶν πρὸς τὰς ἡμετέρας,[2] καὶ ὡς ἐκ τῶν παρ' ὑμῖν οὐδεὶς ἂν γένοιτο γενναῖος ἀνήρ, μᾶλλον δὲ οὐδὲ ἐπιεικής, ἐκ δὲ τῶν παρ' ἡμῖν αὐτὸς αὑτοῦ πᾶς ἂν γένοιτο καλλίων, εἰ καὶ
229 E παντάπασιν ἀφυής τις εἴη. φύσεως δὲ ἔχων εὖ

[1] After σοφώτατοι lacuna, for which Neumann suggests καὶ ὑπεοήφανοι.

[2] After ἡμετέρας Neumann suggests κακόν, unnecessary.

own judgement and intelligence and the teaching that he received from the God who had been revealed to him, he served the other gods also. For envy and jealousy do not come even near the most virtuous men, much more are they remote from angels and gods. But you concern yourselves with incomplete and partial powers,[1] which if anyone call daemonic he does not err. For in them are pride and vanity, but in the gods there is nothing of the sort.

If the reading of your own scriptures is sufficient for you, why do you nibble at the learning of the Hellenes? And yet it were better to keep men away from that learning than from the eating of sacrificial meat. For by that, as even Paul says,[2] he who eats thereof is not harmed, but the conscience of the brother who sees him might be offended according to you, O most wise and arrogant men! But this learning of ours has caused every noble being that nature has produced among you to abandon impiety. Accordingly everyone who possessed even a small fraction of innate virtue has speedily abandoned your impiety. It were therefore better for you to keep men from learning rather than from sacrificial meats. But you yourselves know, it seems to me, the very different effect on the intelligence of your writings as compared with ours; and that from studying yours no man could attain to excellence or even to ordinary goodness, whereas from studying ours every man would become better than before, even though he were altogether without natural fitness. But when a man is naturally well endowed, and

[1] Julian seems to refer to the saints

[2] 1 *Corinthians* 8. 7–13.

καὶ τὰς ἐκ τούτων προσλαχὼν παιδείας ἀτεχνῶς γίνεται τῶν θεῶν τοῖς ἀνθρώποις δῶρον, ἤτοι φῶς ἀνάψας ἐπιστήμης ἢ πολιτείας γένος ὑφηγησάμενος[1] ἢ πολεμίους πολλοὺς τρεψάμενος ἢ καὶ πολλὴν μὲν γῆν, πολλὴν δὲ ἐπελθὼν θάλασσαν καὶ τούτῳ φανεὶς ἡρωικός. . . .

229 E Τεκμήριον δὲ τοῦτο σαφές· ἐκ πάντων ὑμῶν ἐπιλεξάμενοι παιδία ταῖς γραφαῖς ἐμμελετῆσαι
230 A παρασκευάσατε. κἂν φανῇ τῶν ἀνδραπόδων εἰς ἄνδρας[2] τελέσαντα σπουδαιότερα, ληρεῖν ἐμὲ καὶ μελαγχολᾶν νομίζετε. εἶτα οὕτως ἐστὲ δυστυχεῖς καὶ ἀνόητοι, ὥστε νομίζειν θείους μὲν ἐκείνους τοὺς λόγους, ὑφ᾽ ὧν οὐδεὶς ἂν γένοιτο φρονιμώτερος οὐδὲ ἀνδρειότερος οὐδ᾽ ἑαυτοῦ κρείττων· ὑφ᾽ ὧν δὲ ἔνεστιν ἀνδρείαν, φρόνησιν, δικαιοσύνην προσλαβεῖν, τούτους ἀποδίδοτε τῷ σατανᾷ καὶ τοῖς τῷ σατανᾷ λατρεύουσιν.

235 B Ἰᾶται Ἀσκληπιὸς ἡμῶν τὰ σώματα, παιδεύουσιν ἡμῶν αἱ Μοῦσαι σὺν Ἀσκληπιῷ καὶ Ἀπόλλωνι καὶ Ἑρμῇ λογίῳ τὰς ψυχάς, Ἄρης[3] δὲ καὶ Ἐνυὼ τὰ πρὸς τὸν πόλεμον συναγωνίζεται, τὰ δὲ εἰς τέχνας Ἥφαιστος ἀποκληροῖ καὶ διανέμει,
235 C ταῦτα δὲ πάντα Ἀθηνᾶ μετὰ τοῦ Διὸς παρθένος ἀμήτωρ πρυτανεύει. σκοπεῖτε οὖν, εἰ μὴ καθ᾽ ἕκαστον τούτων ὑμῶν ἐσμεν κρείττους, λέγω δὲ τὰ περὶ τὰς τέχνας καὶ σοφίαν καὶ σύνεσιν· εἴτε γὰρ τὰς πρὸς τὴν χρείαν σκοπήσειας, εἴτε τὰς τοῦ καλοῦ χάριν μιμητικάς, οἷον ἀγαλματοποιητικήν,

[1] For lacuna after γένος Neumann suggests ὑφηγησάμενος.
[2] ἄνδρας Asmus, cf. *Misopogon* 356C. ; ἄνδρα Neumann.
[3] Ἄρει Neumann because verb in singular, but no change is necessary.

moreover receives the education of our literature, he becomes actually a gift of the gods to mankind, either by kindling the light of knowledge, or by founding some kind of political constitution, or by routing numbers of his country's foes, or even by travelling far over the earth and far by sea, and thus proving himself a man of heroic mould. . . .[1]

Now this would be a clear proof: Choose out children from among you all and train and educate them in your scriptures, and if when they come to manhood they prove to have nobler qualities than slaves, then you may believe that I am talking nonsense and am suffering from spleen. Yet you are so misguided and foolish that you regard those chronicles of yours as divinely inspired, though by their help no man could ever become wiser or braver or better than he was before; while, on the other hand, writings by whose aid men can acquire courage, wisdom and justice, these you ascribe to Satan and to those who serve Satan!

Asclepius heals our bodies, and the Muses with the aid of Asclepius and Apollo and Hermes, the god of eloquence, train our souls; Ares fights for us in war and Enyo also; Hephaistus apportions and administers the crafts, and Athene the Motherless Maiden with the aid of Zeus presides over them all. Consider therefore whether we are not superior to you in every single one of these things, I mean in the arts and in wisdom and intelligence; and this is true, whether you consider the useful arts or the imitative arts whose end is beauty, such as the statuary's art,

[1] Some words are missing. The summary of Cyril shows that Julian next attacked the Old Testament and ridiculed it because it is written in Hebrew.

γραφικήν, ἢ οἰκονομικήν, ἰατρικὴν τὴν ἐξ Ἀσκληπιοῦ, οὗ πανταχοῦ γῆς ἐστι χρηστήρια, ἃ δίδωσιν ἡμῖν ὁ θεὸς μεταλαγχάνειν διηνεκῶς. ἐμὲ γοῦν ἰάσατο πολλάκις Ἀσκληπιὸς κάμνοντα ὑπαγορεύ-
235 D σας φάρμακα· καὶ τούτων μάρτυς ἐστὶ Ζεύς. εἰ τοίνυν οὐ[1] προσνείμαντες ἑαυτοὺς τῷ τῆς ἀποστασίας πνεύματι τὰ περὶ ψυχὴν ἄμεινον ἔχομεν καὶ περὶ σῶμα καὶ τὰ ἐκτός, τίνος ἕνεκεν ἀφέντες ταῦτα ἐπ᾽ ἐκεῖνα βαδίζετε;

238 A Ἀνθ᾽ ὅτου δὲ μηδὲ τοῖς Ἑβραϊκοῖς λόγοις ἐμ-
238 B μένετε μήτε ἀγαπᾶτε τὸν νόμον, ὃν δέδωκεν ὁ θεὸς ἐκείνοις, ἀπολιπόντες δὲ τὰ πάτρια καὶ δόντες ἑαυτοὺς οἷς ἐκήρυξαν οἱ προφῆται, πλέον ἐκείνων ἢ τῶν παρ᾽ ἡμῖν ἀπέστητε; τὸ γὰρ ἀληθὲς εἴ τις ὑπὲρ ὑμῶν ἐθέλοι σκοπεῖν, εὑρήσει τὴν ὑμετέραν ἀσέβειαν ἔκ τε τῆς Ἰουδαϊκῆς τόλμης καὶ τῆς παρὰ τοῖς ἔθνεσιν ἀδιαφορίας καὶ χυδαιότητος συγκειμένην. ἐξ ἀμφοῖν γὰρ οὔτι τὸ κάλλιστον, ἀλλὰ τὸ χεῖρον ἑλκύσαντες παρυφὴν κακῶν εἰργά-
238 C σασθε. τοῖς μὲν γὰρ Ἑβραίοις ἀκριβῆ τὰ περὶ θρησκείαν ἐστὶ νόμιμα καὶ τὰ σεβάσματα καὶ φυλάγματα μυρία καὶ δεόμενα βίου καὶ προαιρέσεως ἱερατικῆς. ἀπαγορεύσαντος δὲ τοῦ νομοθέτου τὸ πᾶσι μὴ δουλεύειν τοῖς θεοῖς, ἑνὶ δὲ μόνον, οὗ "μερίς ἐστιν Ἰακὼβ καὶ σχοίνισμα κληρονομίας Ἰσραήλ," οὐ τοῦτο δὲ μόνον εἰπόντος, ἀλλὰ γάρ, οἶμαι, καὶ προσθέντος "Οὐ κακολογήσεις

[1] οὐ Klimek; οἱ Neumann, who regards προσνείμαντες—πνεύματι as a quotation from a Christian polemic against the Pagans.

painting, or household management, and the art of healing derived from Asclepius whose oracles are found everywhere on earth, and the god grants to us a share in them perpetually. At any rate, when I have been sick, Asclepius has often cured me by prescribing remedies; and of this Zeus is witness. Therefore, if we who have not given ourselves over to the spirit of apostasy, fare better than you in soul and body and external affairs, why do you abandon these teachings of ours and go over to those others?

And why is it that you do not abide even by the traditions of the Hebrews or accept the law which God has given to them? Nay, you have forsaken their teaching even more than ours, abandoning the religion of your forefathers and giving yourselves over to the predictions of the prophets? For if any man should wish to examine into the truth concerning you, he will find that your impiety is compounded of the rashness of the Jews and the indifference and vulgarity of the Gentiles.[1] For from both sides you have drawn what is by no means their best but their inferior teaching, and so have made for yourselves a border[2] of wickedness. For the Hebrews have precise laws concerning religious worship, and countless sacred things and observances which demand the priestly life and profession. But though their lawgiver forbade them to serve all the gods save only that one, whose "portion is Jacob, and Israel an allotment of his inheritance";[3] though he did not say this only, but methinks added also "Thou shalt not revile the

[1] Cf. 43B.

[2] παρυφή, Latin *clavus*, is the woven border of a garment.

[3] Cf. *Deuteronomy* 32. 9.

θεούς," ἡ τῶν ἐπιγινομένων βδελυρία τε καὶ τόλμα, βουλομένη πᾶσαν εὐλάβειαν ἐξελεῖν τοῦ πλήθους, ἀκολουθεῖν ἐνόμισε τῷ μὴ θεραπεύειν τὸ βλασφη-
238 D μεῖν, ὃ δὴ καὶ ὑμεῖς ἐντεῦθεν εἱλκύσατε μόνον· ὡς τῶν γε ἄλλων οὐθὲν ὑμῖν τέ ἐστι κἀκείνοις παραπλήσιον. ἀπὸ μὲν οὖν τῆς Ἑβραίων καινοτομίας τὸ βλασφημεῖν τοὺς παρ' ἡμῖν τιμωμένους θεοὺς ἡρπάσατε. ἀπὸ δὲ τῆς παρ' ἡμῖν θρησκείας τὸ μὲν εὐσεβές τε ὁμοῦ πρὸς ἅπασαν τὴν κρείττονα φύσιν καὶ τῶν πατρίων ἀγαπητικὸν ἀπολελοίπατε, μόνον δ' ἐκτήσασθε τὸ πάντα ἐσθίειν ὡς λάχανα χόρτου. καὶ εἰ χρὴ τἀληθὲς εἰπεῖν, ἐπιτεῖναι τὴν παρ' ἡμῖν ἐφιλοτιμήθητε χυδαιότητα·[1]
238 E τοῦτο δέ, οἶμαι, καὶ μαλ' εἰκότως, συμβαίνει πᾶσιν ἔθνεσιν· καὶ βίοις ἀνθρώπων εὐτελῶν,[2] καπήλων, τελωνῶν, ὀρχηστῶν, ἑταιροτρόφων καὶ ἁρμόττειν ᾠήθητε τὰ παρ' ὑμῖν.

245 A Ὅτι δὲ οὐχ οἱ νῦν, ἀλλὰ καὶ οἱ ἐξ ἀρχῆς, οἱ πρῶτοι παραδεξάμενοι τὸν λόγον παρὰ τοῦ Παύ-
245 B λου τοιοῦτοί τινες γεγόνασιν, εὔδηλον ἐξ ὧν αὐτὸς ὁ Παῦλος μαρτυρεῖ πρὸς αὐτοὺς γράφων. οὐ γὰρ ἦν οὕτως ἀναίσχυντος, οἶμαι, ὡς μὴ συνειδὼς αὐτοῖς ὀνείδη τοσαῦτα πρὸς αὐτοὺς ἐκείνους ὑπὲρ αὐτῶν γράφειν, ἐξ ὧν, εἰ καὶ ἐπαίνους ἔγραψε τοσούτους αὐτῶν, εἰ καὶ ἀληθεῖς ἐτύγχανον, ἐρυθριᾶν

[1] χυδαιότητα·—καὶ Klimek; χυδαιότητα, καὶ <γὰρ> Neumann, failing to see the parenthesis.

[2] Asmus; ἑτέρων MSS, Neumann; Asmus πᾶσι γὰρ τοῖς ἔθεσιν καὶ—εὐτελῶν—ᾠήθητε χρῆναι: "For you thought you must adapt your ways to all the customs and lives of worthless men."

[1] *Exodus* 22. 28.

gods";[1] yet the shamelessness and audacity of later generations, desiring to root out all reverence from the mass of the people, has thought that blasphemy accompanies the neglect of worship. This, in fact, is the only thing that you have drawn from this source; for in all other respects you and the Jews have nothing in common. Nay, it is from the new-fangled teaching of the Hebrews that you have seized upon this blasphemy of the gods who are honoured among us; but the reverence for every higher nature, characteristic of our religious worship, combined with the love of the traditions of our forefathers, you have cast off, and have acquired only the habit of eating all things, "even as the green herb."[2] But to tell the truth, you have taken pride in outdoing our vulgarity, (this, I think, is a thing that happens to all nations, and very naturally) and you thought that you must adapt your ways to the lives of the baser sort, shopkeepers,[3] tax-gatherers, dancers and libertines.

But that not only the Galilaeans of our day but also those of the earliest time, those who were the first to receive the teaching from Paul, were men of this sort, is evident from the testimony of Paul himself in a letter addressed to them. For unless he actually knew that they had committed all these disgraceful acts, he was not, I think, so impudent as to write to those men themselves concerning their conduct, in language for which, even though in the same letter he included as many eulogies of them, he ought to have blushed, yes, even if those

[2] Cf. 314C and *Oration* 6. 192D, Vol. 2, where he quotes with a sneer "these words of the Galilaeans," from *Genesis* 9. 3.

[3] Cf. *Letter* 36 for Julian's reproach against the Christian rhetoricians that they behave like hucksters.

ἦν, εἰ δὲ ψευδεῖς καὶ πεπλασμένοι, καταδύεσθαι φεύγοντα τὸ μετὰ θωπείας λάγνου καὶ ἀνελευθέρου κολακείας ἐντυγχάνειν δοκεῖν. ἃ δὲ γράφει
245 C περὶ τῶν ἀκροασαμένων αὐτοῦ Παῦλος πρὸς αὐτοὺς ἐκείνους, ἐστὶ ταῦτα· "Μὴ πλανᾶσθε· οὔτε εἰδωλολάτραι, οὔτε μοιχοί, οὔτε μαλακοί, οὔτε ἀρσενοκοῖται, οὔτε κλέπται, οὔτε πλεονέκται, οὐ μέθυσοι, οὐ λοίδοροι, οὐχ ἅρπαγες βασιλείαν θεοῦ κληρονομήσουσι. καὶ ταῦτα οὐκ ἀγνοεῖτε, ἀδελφοί, ὅτι καὶ ὑμεῖς τοιοῦτοι ἦτε. ἀλλ' ἀπελούσασθε, ἀλλ' ἡγιάσθητε ἐν τῷ ὀνόματι Ἰησοῦ Χριστοῦ."[1] ὁρᾷς, ὅτι καὶ τούτους γενέσθαι φησὶ τοιούτους, ἁγιασθῆναι δὲ καὶ ἀπολούσασθαι, ῥύπτειν ἱκανοῦ καὶ διακαθαίρειν ὕδατος εὐπορή-
245 D σαντος, ὃ μέχρι ψυχῆς εἰσδύσεται; καὶ τοῦ μὲν λεπροῦ τὴν λέπραν οὐκ ἀφαιρεῖται τὸ βάπτισμα, οὐδὲ λειχῆνας οὐδὲ ἀλφοὺς οὔτε ἀκροχορδῶνας οὐδὲ ποδάγραν οὐδὲ δυσεντερίαν, οὐχ ὕδερον, οὐ παρωνυχίαν, οὐ μικρόν, οὐ μέγα τῶν τοῦ σώματος ἁμαρτημάτων, μοιχείας δὲ καὶ ἁρπαγὰς καὶ πάσας ἁπλῶς τῆς ψυχῆς παρανομίας ἐξελεῖ; . . . .[2]

253 A Ἐπειδὴ δὲ πρὸς μὲν τοὺς νυνὶ Ἰουδαίους διαφέρεσθαί φασιν, εἶναι δὲ ἀκριβῶς Ἰσραηλῖται
253 B κατὰ τοὺς προφήτας αὐτῶν, καὶ τῷ Μωυσῇ μάλιστα πείθεσθαι καὶ τοῖς ἀπ' ἐκείνου περὶ τὴν Ἰουδαίαν ἐπιγενομένοις προφήταις, ἴδωμεν, κατὰ τί μάλιστα ὁμολογοῦσιν αὐτοῖς. ἀρκτέον δὲ ἡμῖν ἀπὸ τῶν Μωυσέως, ὃν δὴ καὶ αὐτόν φασι προκη-

---

[1] 1 *Corinthians* 6. 9–11.

[2] In Cyril's summary, Julian next compares the Christian converts with slaves who run away from their masters in the

eulogies were deserved, while if they were false and fabricated, then he ought to have sunk into the ground to escape seeming to behave with wanton flattery and slavish adulation. But the following are the very words that Paul wrote concerning those who had heard his teaching, and were addressed to the men themselves: "Be not deceived: neither idolaters, nor adulterers, nor effeminate, nor abusers of themselves with men, nor thieves, nor covetous, nor drunkards, nor revilers, nor extortioners, shall inherit the kingdom of God. And of this ye are not ignorant, brethren, that such were you also; but ye washed yourselves, but ye were sanctified in the name of Jesus Christ."[1] Do you see that he says that these men too had been of such sort, but that they "had been sanctified" and "had been washed," water being able to cleanse and winning power to purify when it shall go down into the soul? And baptism does not take away his leprosy from the leper, or scabs, or pimples, or warts, or gout, or dysentery, or dropsy, or a whitlow, in fact no disorder of the body, great or small, then shall it do away with adultery and theft and in short all the transgressions of the soul? . . .[2]

Now since the Galilaeans say that, though they are different from the Jews, they are still, precisely speaking, Israelites in accordance with their prophets, and that they obey Moses above all and the prophets who in Judaea succeeded him, let us see in what respect they chiefly agree with those prophets. And let us begin with the teaching of Moses, who himself also, as they claim, foretold the birth of

belief that, even if they do not succeed in escaping, their state will be no worse than before.

ρύξαι τὴν ἐσομένην Ἰησοῦ γέννησιν. ὁ τοίνυν
Μωυσῆς οὐχ ἅπαξ οὐδὲ δὶς οὐδὲ τρίς, ἀλλὰ
πλειστάκις ἕνα θεὸν μόνον ἀξιοῖ τιμᾶν, ὃν δὴ
καὶ ἐπὶ πᾶσιν ὀνομάζει, θεὸν δὲ ἕτερον οὐδαμοῦ·
253 C *ἀγγέλους δὲ ὀνομάζει καὶ κυρίους καὶ μέντοι καὶ*
θεοὺς πλείονας, ἐξαίρετον δὲ τὸν πρῶτον, ἄλλον
δὲ οὐχ ὑπείληφε δεύτερον οὔτε ὅμοιον οὔτε ἀνό-
μοιον, καθάπερ ὑμεῖς ἐπεξείργασθε. εἰ δέ ἐστί
που παρ' ὑμῖν ὑπὲρ τούτων μία Μωυσέως ῥῆσις,
ταύτην ἐστὲ δίκαιοι προφέρειν. τὸ γὰρ "Προ-
φήτην ὑμῖν ἀναστήσει κύριος ὁ θεὸς ἡμῶν ἐκ τῶν
ἀδελφῶν ὑμῶν ὡς ἐμέ· αὐτοῦ ἀκούσεσθε" μάλιστα
μὲν οὖν οὐκ εἴρηται περὶ τοῦ γεννηθέντος ἐκ
Μαρίας. εἰ δέ τις ὑμῶν ἕνεκα συγχωρήσειεν,
253 D *ἑαυτῷ φησιν αὐτὸν ὅμοιον γενήσεσθαι καὶ οὐ τῷ*
θεῷ, προφήτην ὥσπερ ἑαυτὸν καὶ ἐξ ἀνθρώπων,
ἀλλ' οὐκ ἐκ θεοῦ. καὶ τὸ "Οὐκ ἐκλείψει ἄρχων
ἐξ Ἰούδα οὐδὲ ἡγούμενος ἐκ τῶν μηρῶν αὐτοῦ"
μάλιστα μὲν οὐκ εἴρηται περὶ τούτου, ἀλλὰ περὶ
τῆς τοῦ Δαβὶδ βασιλείας, ἣ δὴ κατέληξεν εἰς
Σεδεκίαν τὸν βασιλέα. καὶ δὴ ἡ γραφὴ διπλῶς
πως ἔχει "ἕως ἔλθῃ τὰ ἀποκείμενα αὐτῷ," παρα-
πεποιήκατε δὲ ὑμεῖς "ἕως ἔλθῃ ᾧ ἀπόκειται."
253 E *ὅτι δὲ τούτων οὐδὲν τῷ Ἰησοῦ προσήκει, πρό-*
δηλον· οὐδὲ γάρ ἐστιν ἐξ Ἰούδα. πῶς γὰρ ὁ καθ'
ὑμᾶς οὐκ ἐξ Ἰωσήφ, ἀλλ' ἐξ ἁγίου πνεύματος
γεγονώς; τὸν Ἰωσὴφ γὰρ γενεαλογοῦντες εἰς
τὸν Ἰούδαν ἀναφέρετε καὶ οὐδὲ τοῦτο ἐδυνήθητε

---

[1] *Acts* 3. 22; *Deuteronomy* 18. 18. *Genesis* 49. 10.

[3] Or "whose it is"; Julian follows the Septuagint. The version "until Shiloh come" was not then current; cf. Skinner, *Genesis*, p. 522. It is still debated whether these

Jesus that was to be. Moses, then, not once or twice or thrice but very many times says that men ought to honour one God only, and in fact names him the Highest; but that they ought to honour any other god he nowhere says. He speaks of angels and lords and moreover of several gods, but from these he chooses out the first and does not assume any god as second, either like or unlike him, such as you have invented. And if among you perchance you possess a single utterance of Moses with respect to this, you are bound to produce it. For the words "A prophet shall the Lord your God raise up unto you of your brethren, like unto me; to him shall ye hearken,"[1] were certainly not said of the son of Mary. And even though, to please you, one should concede that they were said of him, Moses says that the prophet will be like him and not like God, a prophet like himself and born of men, not of a god. And the words "The sceptre shall not depart from Judah, nor a leader from his loins,"[2] were most certainly not said of the son of Mary, but of the royal house of David, which, you observe, came to an end with King Zedekiah. And certainly the Scripture can be interpreted in two ways when it says "until there comes what is reserved for him"; but you have wrongly interpreted it "until he comes for whom it is reserved."[3] But it is very clear that not one of these sayings relates to Jesus; for he is not even from Judah. How could he be when according to you he was not born of Joseph but of the Holy Spirit? For though in your genealogies you trace Joseph back to Judah, you could not invent

words refer to the Davidic kingdom or to a future Messiah, and there is no universally accepted rendering of the Hebrew original.

πλάσαι καλῶς. ἐλέγχονται γὰρ Ματθαῖος καὶ Λουκᾶς περὶ τῆς γενεαλογίας αὐτοῦ διαφωνοῦντες
261 E πρὸς ἀλλήλους. ἀλλὰ περὶ μὲν τούτου μέλλοντες ἐν τῷ δευτέρῳ συγγράμματι τὸ ἀληθὲς ἀκριβῶς ἐξετάζειν, ὑπερτιθέμεθα. συγκεχωρήσθω δὲ καὶ ἄρχων ἐξ Ἰούδα, οὐ "θεὸς ἐκ θεοῦ" κατὰ τὰ παρ' ὑμῶν λεγόμενα οὐδὲ "Τὰ πάντα δι' αὐτοῦ ἐγένετο καὶ χωρὶς αὐτοῦ ἐγένετο οὐδὲ ἕν." ἀλλ' εἴρηται καὶ ἐν τοῖς ἀριθμοῖς· "Ἀνατελεῖ ἄστρον ἐξ Ἰακὼβ καὶ ἄνθρωπος ἐξ Ἰσραήλ."[1] τοῦθ' ὅτι τῷ Δαβὶδ προσήκει καὶ τοῖς ἀπ' ἐκείνου, πρόδηλόν ἐστί που· τοῦ γὰρ Ἰεσσαὶ παῖς ἦν ὁ Δαβίδ.

Εἴπερ οὖν ἐκ τούτων ἐπιχειρεῖτε συμβιβάζειν, ἐπιδείξατε μίαν ἐκεῖθεν ἑλκύσαντες ῥῆσιν, ὅποι πολλὰς πάνυ ἐγώ. ὅτι δὲ θεὸν τὸν ἕνα τὸν τοῦ Ἰσραὴλ νενόμικεν, ἐν τῷ Δευτερονομίῳ φησίν· "Ὥστε εἰδέναι σε, ὅτι κύριος ὁ θεός σου, οὗτος θεὸς εἷς ἐστι, καὶ οὐκ ἔστιν ἄλλος πλὴν αὐτοῦ."
262 B καὶ ἔτι πρὸς τούτῳ· "Καὶ ἐπιστραφήσῃ τῇ διανοίᾳ σου, ὅτι κύριος ὁ θεός σου οὗτος θεὸς ἐν τῷ οὐρανῷ ἄνω καὶ ἐπὶ τῆς γῆς κάτω καὶ οὐκ ἔστι πλὴν αὐτοῦ." καὶ πάλιν· "Ἄκουε, Ἰσραήλ, κύριος ὁ θεὸς ἡμῶν κύριος εἷς ἐστι." καὶ πάλιν· "Ἴδετε, ὅτι ἐγώ εἰμι καὶ οὐκ ἔστι θεὸς πλὴν ἐμοῦ." ταῦτα μὲν οὖν ὁ Μωυσῆς ἕνα διατεινόμενος μόνον εἶναι θεόν. ἀλλ' οὗτοι τυχὸν ἐροῦσιν· οὐδὲ ἡμεῖς δύο λέγομεν οὐδὲ τρεῖς. ἐγὼ δὲ λέγοντας μὲν αὐτοὺς καὶ τοῦτο δείξω, μαρτυ-

[1] Neumann in view of the next two sentences would read Ἰεσσαί, "Jesse."

---

[1] Cf. *Matthew* 1. 1–17 with *Luke* 3. 23–38.

even this plausibly. For Matthew and Luke are refuted by the fact that they disagree concerning his genealogy.[1] However, as I intend to examine closely into the truth of this matter in my Second Book, I leave it till then.[2] But granted that he really is "a sceptre from Judah," then he is not "God born of God," as you are in the habit of saying, nor is it true that "All things were made by him; and without him was not any thing made."[3] But, say you, we are told in the *Book of Numbers* also: "There shall arise a star out of Jacob, and a man out of Israel."[4] It is certainly clear that this relates to David and to his descendants; for David was a son of Jesse.

If therefore you try to prove anything from these writings, show me a single saying that you have drawn from that source whence I have drawn very many. But that Moses believed in one God, the God of Israel, he says in *Deuteronomy*: "So that thou mightest know that the Lord thy God he is one God; and there is none else beside him."[5] And moreover he says besides, "And lay it to thine heart that this the Lord thy God is God in the heaven above and upon the earth beneath, and there is none else."[6] And again, "Hear, O Israel: the Lord our God is one Lord."[7] And again, "See that I am and there is no God save me."[8] These then are the words of Moses when he insists that there is only one God. But perhaps the Galilaeans will reply: "But we do not assert that there are two gods or three." But I will show that they do assert this

[2] Cyril's reply to this part of Julian's Second Book is lost, so that the Emperor's more detailed discussion cannot be reconstructed. [3] *John* 1. 3. [4] *Numbers* 24. 17.
[5] *Deuteronomy* 4. 35. [6] *Deuteronomy* 4. 39.
[7] *Deuteronomy* 6. 4. [8] *Deuteronomy* 32. 39.

ρόμενος Ἰωάννην λέγοντα· "Ἐν ἀρχῇ ἦν ὁ λόγος
262 C καὶ ὁ λόγος ἦν πρὸς τὸν θεὸν καὶ θεὸς ἦν ὁ λόγος."
ὁρᾷς, ὅτι πρὸς τὸν θεὸν εἶναι λέγεται; εἴτε ὁ ἐκ Μαρίας γεννηθεὶς εἴτε ἄλλος τίς ἐστιν—ἵν' ὁμοῦ καὶ πρὸς Φωτεινὸν ἀποκρίνωμαι—, διαφέρει τοῦτο νῦν οὐδέν· ἀφίημι δῆτα τὴν μάχην ὑμῖν. ὅτι μέντοι φησὶ "πρὸς θεὸν" καὶ "ἐν ἀρχῇ," τοῦτο ἀπόχρη μαρτύρασθαι. πῶς οὖν ὁμολογεῖ τ αὖτα τοῖς Μωυσέως;

Ἀλλὰ τοῖς Ἠσαΐου, φασίν, ὁμολογεῖ. λέγει γὰρ Ἠσαΐας· "Ἰδοὺ ἡ παρθένος ἐν γαστρὶ ἕξει καὶ τέξεται υἱόν." ἔστω δὴ καὶ τοῦτο λεγόμενον
262 D ὑπὲρ θεοῦ, καίτοι μηδαμῶς εἰρημένον· οὐ γὰρ ἦν παρθένος ἡ γεγαμημένη καὶ πρὶν ἀποκυῆσαι συγκατακλιθεῖσα τῷ γήμαντι· δεδόσθω δὲ λέγεσθαι περὶ ταύτης—μή τι θεόν φησιν ἐκ τῆς παρθένου τεχθήσεσθαι; θεοτόκον δὲ ὑμεῖς οὐ παύεσθε Μαρίαν καλοῦντες, εἰ μή πού φησι τὸν ἐκ τῆς παρθένου γεννώμενον "υἱὸν θεοῦ μονογενῆ" καὶ "πρωτότοκον πάσης κτίσεως";[1] ἀλλὰ τὸ λεγόμενον ὑπὸ Ἰωάννου "Πάντα δι' αὐτοῦ ἐγένετο καὶ χωρὶς αὐτοῦ ἐγένετο οὐδὲ ἕν" ἔχει τις ἐν ταῖς
262 E προφητικαῖς δεῖξαι φωναῖς; ἃ δὲ ἡμεῖς δείκνυμεν, ἐξ αὐτῶν ἐκείνων ἑξῆς ἀκούετε· "Κύριε, ὁ θεὸς ἡμῶν, κτῆσαι ἡμᾶς, ἐκτὸς σοῦ ἄλλον οὐκ οἴδαμεν"· πεποίηται δὲ παρ' αὐτῶν καὶ Ἑζεκίας ὁ βασιλεὺς

[1] κτίσεως; Neumann, κτίσεως. MSS.

---

[1] *John* 1. 1.

[2] The heretical bishop Photinus of Sirmium was tried under Constantius before the synod at Milan in 351 for denying the divinity of Christ; see Julian's letter to him, p. 187.

also, and I call John to witness, who says: "In the beginning was the Word, and the Word was with God and the Word was God."[1] You see that the Word is said to be with God? Now whether this is he who was born of Mary or someone else,—that I may answer Photinus[2] at the same time,—this now makes no difference; indeed I leave the dispute to you; but it is enough to bring forward the evidence that he says "with God," and "in the beginning." How then does this agree with the teachings of Moses?

"But," say the Galilaeans, "it agrees with the teachings of Isaiah. For Isaiah says, 'Behold the virgin shall conceive and bear a son.' "[3] Now granted that this is said about a god, though it is by no means so stated; for a married woman who before her conception had lain with her husband was no virgin,—but let us admit that it is said about her,—does Isaiah anywhere say that a god will be born of the virgin? But why do you not cease to call Mary the mother of God, if Isaiah nowhere says that he that is born of the virgin is the "only begotten Son of God"[4] and "the firstborn of all creation"?[5] But as for the saying of John, "All things were made by him; and without him was not any thing made that was made,"[6] can anyone point this out among the utterances of the prophets? But now listen to the sayings that I point out to you from those same prophets, one after another. "O Lord our God, make us thine; we know none other beside thee."[7] And Hezekiah the king has been represented by

[3] *Isaiah* 7. 14. [4] *John* 1. 18.
[5] *Colossians* 1. 15. [6] *John* 1. 3.
[7] A paraphrase of *Isaiah* 26. 13.

εὐχόμενος· "Κύριε, ὁ θεὸς Ἰσραήλ, ὁ καθήμενος ἐπὶ τῶν Χερουβίμ, σὺ εἶ ὁ θεὸς μόνος." μή τι
276 E τῷ δευτέρῳ καταλείπει χώραν; ἀλλ' εἰ θεὸς ἐκ θεοῦ καθ' ὑμᾶς ὁ λόγος ἐστὶ καὶ τῆς οὐσίας ἐξέφυ τοῦ πατρός, θεοτόκον ὑμεῖς ἀνθ' ὅτου τὴν παρθένον εἶναί φατε; πῶς γὰρ ἂν τέκοι θεὸν ἄνθρωπος οὖσα καθ' ὑμᾶς; καὶ πρός γε τούτῳ λέγοντος ἐναργῶς θεοῦ "Ἐγώ εἰμι καὶ οὐκ ἔστι πάρεξ ἐμοῦ
277 A σώζων," ὑμεῖς σωτῆρα τὸν ἐξ αὐτῆς εἰπεῖν τετολμήκατε;

290 B Ὅτι δὲ Μωυσῆς ὀνομάζει θεοὺς τοὺς ἀγγέλους, ἐκ τῶν ἐκείνου λόγων ἀκούσατε· "Ἰδόντες δὲ οἱ
290 C υἱοὶ τοῦ θεοῦ τὰς θυγατέρας τῶν ἀνθρώπων ὅτι καλαί εἰσιν, ἔλαβον ἑαυτοῖς γυναῖκας ἀπὸ πασῶν ὧν ἐξελέξαντο." καὶ μικρὸν ὑποβάς· "Καὶ μετ' ἐκεῖνο ὡς ἂν εἰσεπορεύοντο οἱ υἱοὶ τοῦ θεοῦ πρὸς τὰς θυγατέρας τῶν ἀνθρώπων, καὶ ἐγεννῶσαν ἑαυτοῖς· ἐκεῖνοι ἦσαν οἱ γίγαντες οἱ ἀπ' αἰῶνος οἱ ὀνομαστοί." ὅτι τοίνυν τοὺς ἀγγέλους φησίν, εὔδηλόν ἐστι καὶ ἔξωθεν οὐ προσπαρακείμενον,[1] ἀλλὰ καὶ δῆλον ἐκ τοῦ φάναι, οὐκ ἀνθρώπους, ἀλλὰ γίγαντας γεγονέναι παρ' ἐκείνων. δῆλον γάρ, ὡς, εἴπερ ἀνθρώπους ἐνόμιζεν αὐτῶν εἶναι
290 D τοὺς πατέρας, ἀλλὰ μὴ κρείττονος καὶ ἰσχυροτέρας τινὸς φύσεως, οὐκ ἂν ἀπ' αὐτῶν εἶπε γεννηθῆναι τοὺς γίγαντας· ἐκ γὰρ θνητοῦ καὶ ἀθανάτου μίξεως ἀποφήνασθαί μοι δοκεῖ τὸ τῶν γιγάντων ὑποστῆναι γένος. ὁ δὴ πολλοὺς υἱοὺς ὀνομάζων θεοῦ καὶ τούτους οὐκ ἀνθρώπους, ἀγγέλους δέ, τὸν μονογενῆ λόγον θεὸν ἢ υἱὸν θεοῦ ἢ

[1] After προσπαρακείμενον Klimek adds μόνον.

them as praying as follows: "O Lord God of Israel, that sittest upon the Cherubim, thou art God, even thou alone."[1] Does he leave any place for the second god? But if, as you believe, the Word is God born of God and proceeded from the substance of the Father, why do you say that the virgin is the mother of God? For how could she bear a god since she is, according to you, a human being? And moreover, when God declares plainly "I am he, and there is none that can deliver beside me,"[2] do you dare to call her son Saviour?

And that Moses calls the angels gods you may hear from his own words, "The sons of God saw the daughters of men that they were fair; and they took them wives of all which they chose."[3] And a little further on: "And also after that, when the sons of God came in unto the daughters of men, and they bare children to them, the same became the giants which were of old, the men of renown."[4] Now that he means the angels is evident, and this has not been foisted on him from without, but it is clear also from his saying that not men but giants were born from them. For it is clear that if he had thought that men and not beings of some higher and more powerful nature were their fathers, he would not have said that the giants were their offspring. For it seems to me that he declared that the race of giants arose from the mixture of mortal and immortal. Again, when Moses speaks of many sons of God and calls them not men but angels, would he not then have revealed to mankind, if he had known thereof, God

[1] *Isaiah* 37. 16.
[2] Apparently a paraphrase of *Deuteronomy* 32. 39.
[3] *Genesis* 6. 2. [4] *Genesis* 6. 4.

ὅπως ἂν αὐτὸν καλῆτε,[1] εἴπερ ἐγίνωσκεν, οὐκ ἂν
290 E εἰς ἀνθρώπους ἐμήνυσεν; ὅτι δὲ οὐ μέγα τοῦτο ἐνόμιζεν, ὑπὲρ τοῦ Ἰσραὴλ φησιν· "υἱὸς πρωτότοκός μου Ἰσραήλ"; τί οὐχὶ καὶ περὶ τοῦ Ἰησοῦ ταῦτ' ἔφη Μωυσῆς; ἕνα καὶ μόνον ἐδίδασκε θεόν, υἱοὺς δὲ αὐτοῦ πολλοὺς τοὺς κατανειμαμένους τὰ ἔθνη. πρωτότοκον δὲ υἱὸν θεοῦ[2] ἢ θεὸν λόγον ἤ τι τῶν ὑφ' ὑμῶν ὕστερον ψευδῶς συντεθέντων οὔτε ᾔδει κατ' ἀρχὴν οὔτε ἐδίδασκε φανερῶς. αὐτοῦ τε Μωυσέως καὶ τῶν ἄλλων ἐπηκούσατε
291 A προφητῶν. ὁ οὖν Μωυσῆς πολλὰ τοιαῦτα καὶ πολλαχοῦ λέγει· "Κύριον τὸν θεόν σου φοβηθήσῃ καὶ αὐτῷ μόνῳ λατρεύσεις." πῶς οὖν ὁ Ἰησοῦς ἐν τοῖς εὐαγγελίοις παραδέδοται προστάττων "Πορευθέντες μαθητεύσατε πάντα τὰ ἔθνη, βαπτίζοντες αὐτοὺς εἰς τὸ ὄνομα τοῦ πατρὸς καὶ τοῦ υἱοῦ καὶ τοῦ ἁγίου πνεύματος," εἴπερ μὴ[3] καὶ αὐτῷ λατρεύειν ἔμελλον; ἀκόλουθα δὲ τούτοις καὶ ὑμεῖς διανοούμενοι μετὰ τοῦ πατρὸς θεολογεῖτε τὸν υἱόν . . .

Ὑπὲρ δὲ ἀποτροπαίων ἐπάκουσον πάλιν ὅσα λέγει· "Καὶ λήψεται δύο τράγους ἐξ αἰγῶν περὶ ἁμαρτίας καὶ κριὸν ἕνα εἰς ὁλο-
299 B καύτωμα. καὶ προσάξει ὁ Ἀαρὼν τὸν μόσχον τὸν περὶ τῆς ἁμαρτίας τὸν περὶ ἑαυτοῦ καὶ

[1] καλῆτε Klimek; καλεῖτε Neumann.
[2] θεοῦ Neumann adds.
[3] Neumann εἴπερ καὶ αὐτῷ, referring αὐτῷ to Moses; Gollwitzer adds μὴ to improve sense; αὐτῷ refers to Jesus.

---

[1] *Exodus* 4. 22. [2] *Deuteronomy* 6. 13.
[3] *Matthew* 28. 19.

the "only begotten Word," or a son of God or however you call him? But is it because he did not think this of great importance that he says concerning Israel, "Israel is my firstborn son?"[1] Why did not Moses say this about Jesus also? He taught that there was only one God, but that he had many sons who divided the nations among themselves. But the Word as firstborn son of God or as a God, or any of those fictions which have been invented by you later, he neither knew at all nor taught openly thereof. You have now heard Moses himself and the other prophets. Moses, therefore, utters many sayings to the following effect and in many places: "Thou shalt fear the Lord thy God and him only shalt thou serve."[2] How then has it been handed down in the Gospels that Jesus commanded: "Go ye therefore and teach all nations, baptising them in the name of the Father, and of the Son, and of the Holy Ghost,"[3] if they were not intended to serve him also? And your beliefs also are in harmony with these commands, when along with the Father you pay divine honours to the son. . . .[4]

And now observe again how much Moses says about the deities that avert evil: "And he shall take two he-goats of the goats for a sin-offering, and one ram for a burnt offering. And Aaron shall bring also his bullock of the sin-offering, which is for him-

[4] According to Cyril's summary, Julian says that the Hellenes, unlike the Christians, observe the same laws and customs as the Jews, except that they worship more than one god and practise soothsaying. Circumcision is approved by the temple priests of Egypt, the Chaldaeans and Saracens. All alike offer the various sorts of sacrifice, including those for atonement and purification. Moses sacrificed to the abominable deities who avert evil, the *di averrunci*.

ἐξιλάσεται περὶ αὐτοῦ καὶ τοῦ οἴκου αὐτοῦ. καὶ λήψεται τοὺς δύο τράγους καὶ στήσει αὐτοὺς ἔναντι κυρίου παρὰ τὴν θύραν τῆς σκηνῆς τοῦ μαρτυρίου. καὶ ἐπιθήσει Ἀαρὼν ἐπὶ τοὺς δύο τράγους κλῆρον ἕνα τῷ κυρίῳ καὶ κλῆρον ἕνα τῷ ἀποπομπαίῳ," ὥστε ἐκπέμψαι αὐτόν, φησίν, ἀποπομπήν, καὶ[1] ἀφεῖναι αὐτὸν εἰς τὴν ἔρημον. ὁ μὲν οὖν τῷ ἀποπομπαίῳ πεμπόμενος οὕτως ἐκπέμπεται. τὸν δέ γε ἕτερον τράγον φησί· "Καὶ
299 C σφάξει τὸν τράγον τὸν περὶ τῆς ἁμαρτίας τοῦ λαοῦ ἔναντι κυρίου, καὶ εἰσοίσει τοῦ αἵματος αὐτοῦ ἐσώτερον τοῦ καταπετάσματος, καὶ ῥανεῖ τὸ αἷμα ἐπὶ τὴν βάσιν τοῦ θυσιαστηρίου, καὶ ἐξιλάσεται ἐπὶ τῶν ἁγίων ἀπὸ τῶν ἀκαθαρσιῶν τῶν υἱῶν Ἰσραὴλ καὶ ἀπὸ τῶν ἀδικημάτων αὐτῶν
305 B περὶ πασῶν τῶν ἁμαρτιῶν αὐτῶν." ὡς μὲν οὖν τοὺς τῶν θυσιῶν ἠπίστατο τρόπους Μωυσῆς, εὔδηλόν ἐστί που διὰ τῶν ῥηθέντων. ὅτι δὲ οὐχ ὡς ὑμεῖς ἀκάθαρτα ἐνόμισεν αὐτά, πάλιν ἐκ τῶν ἐκείνου ῥημάτων ἐπακούσατε· "Ἡ δὲ ψυχή, ἥτις ἐὰν φάγῃ ἀπὸ τῶν κρεῶν τῆς θυσίας τοῦ σωτηρίου, ὅ ἐστι κυρίου, καὶ ἡ ἀκαθαρσία αὐτοῦ ἐπ' αὐτῷ, ἀπολεῖται ἡ ψυχὴ ἐκείνη ἐκ τοῦ λαοῦ αὐτῆς." αὐτὸς οὕτως εὐλαβὴς ὁ Μωυσῆς περὶ τὴν τῶν ἱερῶν ἐδωδήν.

305 D Προσήκει δὴ λοιπὸν ἀναμνησθῆναι τῶν ἔμπροσθεν, ὧν ἕνεκεν ἐρρήθη καὶ ταῦτα. διὰ τί γὰρ ἀποστάντες ἡμῶν οὐχὶ τὸν τῶν Ἰουδαίων ἀγαπᾶτε νόμον οὐδὲ ἐμμένετε τοῖς ὑπ' ἐκείνου λεγομένοις; ἐρεῖ πάντως τις ὀξὺ βλέπων· οὐδὲ

[1] καὶ Neumann adds.

self, and make an atonement for himself and for his house. And he shall take the two goats and present them before the Lord at the door of the tabernacle of the covenant. And Aaron shall cast lots upon the two goats; one lot for the Lord and the other lot for the scape-goat"[1] so as to send him forth, says Moses, as a scape-goat, and let him loose into the wilderness. Thus then is sent forth the goat that is sent for a scape-goat. And of the second goat Moses says: "Then shall he kill the goat of the sin-offering that is for the people before the Lord, and bring his blood within the vail, and shall sprinkle the blood upon the altar-step,[2] and shall make an atonement for the holy place, because of the uncleanness of the children of Israel and because of their transgressions in all their sins."[3] Accordingly it is evident from what has been said, that Moses knew the various methods of sacrifice. And to show that he did not think them impure as you do, listen again to his own words. "But the soul that eateth of the flesh of the sacrifice of peace-offerings that pertain unto the Lord, having his uncleanness upon him, even that soul shall be cut off from his people."[4] So cautious is Moses himself with regard to the eating of the flesh of sacrifice.

But now I had better remind you of what I said earlier,[5] since on account of that I have said this also. Why is it, I repeat, that after deserting us you do not accept the law of the Jews or abide by the sayings of Moses? No doubt some sharp-sighted

[1] A paraphrase of *Leviticus* 16. 5–8.
[2] "Mercy-seat" is the usual version.
[3] *Leviticus* 16. 15. [4] *Leviticus* 7. 20. [5] Cf. 43A.

γὰρ Ἰουδαῖοι θύουσιν. ἀλλ' ἔγωγε ἀμβλυώττοντα δεινῶς αὐτὸν ἀπελέγξω, πρῶτον μέν, ὅτι μηδὲ τῶν ἄλλων τι τῶν παρὰ τοῖς Ἰουδαίοις νενομισμένων ἐστὶ καὶ ὑμῖν ἐν φυλακῇ· δεύτερον δέ, ὅτι θύουσι μὲν ἐν ἀδράκτοις[1] Ἰουδαῖοι καὶ νῦν ἔτι
306 A πάντα ἐσθίουσιν ἱερὰ καὶ κατεύχονται πρὸ τοῦ θῦσαι καὶ τὸν δεξιὸν ὦμον διδόασιν ἀπαρχὰς τοῖς ἱερεῦσιν, ἀπεστερημένοι δὲ τοῦ ναοῦ, ἤ, ὡς αὐτοῖς ἔθος λέγειν, τοῦ ἁγιάσματος, ἀπαρχὰς τῷ θεῷ τῶν ἱερείων εἴργονται προσφέρειν. ὑμεῖς δὲ οἱ τὴν καινὴν θυσίαν εὑρόντες, οὐδὲν δεόμενοι τῆς Ἱερουσαλήμ, ἀντὶ τίνος οὐ θύετε; καίτοι τοῦτο
306 B μὲν ἐγὼ πρὸς ὑμᾶς ἐκ περιουσίας εἶπον, ἐπεί μοι τὴν ἀρχὴν ἐρρέθη βουλομένῳ δεῖξαι τοῖς ἔθνεσιν ὁμολογοῦντας Ἰουδαίους ἔξω τοῦ νομίζειν ἕνα θεὸν μόνον. ἐκεῖνο γὰρ αὐτῶν μὲν ἴδιον, ἡμῶν δὲ ἀλλότριον, ἐπεὶ τά γε ἄλλα κοινά πως ἡμῖν ἐστι, ναοί, τεμένη, θυσιαστήρια, ἁγνεῖαι, φυλάγματά τινα, περὶ ὧν ἢ τὸ παράπαν οὐδαμῶς ἢ μικρὰ διαφερόμεθα πρὸς ἀλλήλους . . .

314 C Ἀνθ' ὅτου περὶ τὴν δίαιταν οὐχὶ τοῖς Ἰουδαίοις ὁμοίως ἐστὲ καθαροί, πάντα δὲ ἐσθίειν ὡς λάχανα χόρτου δεῖν φατε Πέτρῳ πιστεύσαντες, ὅτι, φασίν, εἶπεν ἐκεῖνος· "Ἃ ὁ θεὸς ἐκαθάρισε, σὺ μὴ κοίνου"; τί τούτου τεκμήριον, ὅτι πάλαι μὲν

[1] Cf. Hesychius *s.v.* ἄδρακτον· ἴδιον. Not in L. and S. The Latin version *Oecolampadius* translates *in propriis*.

---

[1] Sozomen 5. 22, Socrates 3. 20 and Theodoret 3. 15 relate that Julian summoned the leading Jews and exhorted them to resume their sacrifices. Their reply that they could lawfully sacrifice only in the Temple led him to order its restoration.

person will answer, "The Jews too do not sacrifice." But I will convict him of being terribly dull-sighted, for in the first place I reply that neither do you also observe any one of the other customs observed by the Jews; and, secondly, that the Jews do sacrifice in their own houses, and even to this day everything that they eat is consecrated; and they pray before sacrificing, and give the right shoulder to the priests as the firstfruits; but since they have been deprived of their temple, or, as they are accustomed to call it, their holy place, they are prevented from offering the firstfruits of the sacrifice to God.[1] But why do you not sacrifice, since you have invented your new kind of sacrifice and do not need Jerusalem at all? And yet it was superfluous to ask you this question, since I said the same thing at the beginning, when I wished to show that the Jews agree with the Gentiles, except that they believe in only one God. That is indeed peculiar to them and strange to us; since all the rest we have in a manner in common with them—temples, sanctuaries, altars, purifications, and certain precepts. For as to these we differ from one another either not at all or in trivial matters. . . .[2]

Why in your diet are you not as pure as the Jews, and why do you say that we ought to eat everything "even as the green herb,"[3] putting your faith in Peter, because, as the Galilaeans say, he declared, "What God hath cleansed, that make not thou common"?[4] What proof is there of this, that of old

[2] According to Cyril, Julian then says that the Christians in worshipping not one or many gods, but three, have strayed from both Jewish and Hellenic teaching.

[3] Cf. 238D, note. [4] *Acts* 10. 15.

314 D ἅττα[1] ἐνόμιζεν ὁ θεὸς μιαρά, νυνὶ δὲ καθαρὰ πεποίηκεν αὐτά; Μωυσῆς μὲν γὰρ ἐπὶ τῶν τετραπόδων ἐπισημαινόμενος πᾶν τὸ διχηλοῦν, φησίν, ὁπλὴν καὶ ἀναμαρυκίζον μαρυκισμὸν καθαρὸν εἶναι, τὸ δὲ μὴ τοιοῦτον ἀκάθαρτον εἶναι. εἰ μὲν οὖν ὁ χοῖρος ἀπὸ τῆς φαντασίας Πέτρου νῦν προσέλαβε τὸ μαρυκᾶσθαι, πεισθῶμεν αὐτῷ· τεράστιον γὰρ ὡς ἀληθῶς, εἰ μετὰ τὴν φαντασίαν Πέτρου προσέλαβεν αὐτό. εἰ δὲ ἐκεῖνος ἐψεύσατο ταύτην ἑωρακέναι, ἵν' εἴπω καθ' ὑμᾶς, τὴν ἀποκά-
314 E λυψιν ἐπὶ τοῦ βυρσοδεψίου, τί ἐπὶ τηλικούτων οὕτω ταχέως πιστεύσομεν; τί γὰρ ὁ Μωυσῆς ὑμῖν ἐπέταξε τῶν χαλεπῶν, εἰ ἀπηγόρευσεν ἐσθίειν πρὸς τοῖς ὑείοις τά τε πτηνὰ καὶ τὰ θαλάττια, ἀποφηνάμενος ὑπὸ τοῦ θεοῦ καὶ ταῦτα πρὸς ἐκείνοις ἐκβεβλῆσθαι καὶ ἀκάθαρτα πεφηνέναι;

319 D Ἀλλὰ τί ταῦτα ἐγὼ μακρολογῶ λεγόμενα παρ' αὐτῶν, ἐξὸν ἰδεῖν, εἴ τινα ἰσχὺν ἔχει; λέγουσι γὰρ τὸν θεὸν ἐπὶ τῷ προτέρῳ νόμῳ θεῖναι τὸν δεύτερον. ἐκεῖνον μὲν γὰρ γενέσθαι πρὸς καιρὸν περιγεγραμμένον χρόνοις ὡρισμένοις, ὕστερον δὲ τοῦτον ἀναφανῆναι διὰ τὸ τὸν Μωυσέως χρόνῳ τε καὶ τόπῳ περιγεγράφθαι. τοῦτο ὅτι ψευδῶς λέγουσιν, ἀποδείξω σαφῶς, ἐκ μὲν τῶν Μωυσέως οὐ δέκα μόνας, ἀλλὰ μυρίας παρεχόμενος μαρ-
319 E τυρίας, ὅπου τὸν νόμον αἰώνιόν φησιν. ἀκούετε δὲ νῦν ἀπὸ τῆς ἐξόδου. "Καὶ ἔσται ἡ ἡμέρα αὕτη ὑμῖν μνημόσυνον, καὶ ἑορτάσατε αὐτὴν

[1] ἅττα Klimek; αὐτὰ Neumann.

God held certain things abominable, but now has made them pure? For Moses, when he is laying down the law concerning four-footed things, says that whatsoever parteth the hoof and is cloven-footed and cheweth the cud[1] is pure, but that which is not of this sort is impure. Now if, after the vision of Peter, the pig has now taken to chewing the cud, then let us obey Peter; for it is in very truth a miracle if, after the vision of Peter, it has taken to that habit. But if he spoke falsely when he said that he saw this revelation,—to use your own way of speaking,—in the house of the tanner, why are we so ready to believe him in such important matters? Was it so hard a thing that Moses enjoined on you when, besides the flesh of swine, he forbade you to eat winged things and things that dwell in the sea, and declared to you that besides the flesh of swine these also had been cast out by God and shown to be impure?

But why do I discuss at length these teachings of theirs,[2] when we may easily see whether they have any force? For they assert that God, after the earlier law, appointed the second. For, say they, the former arose with a view to a certain occasion and was circumscribed by definite periods of time, but this later law was revealed because the law of Moses was circumscribed by time and place. That they say this falsely I will clearly show by quoting from the books of Moses not merely ten but ten thousand passages as evidence, where he says that the law is for all time. Now listen to a passage from *Exodus*: "And this day shall be unto you for a memorial; and ye shall keep it a feast to the Lord

[1] *Leviticus* 11. 3. [2] *i. e.* of the Galilaeans.

ἑορτὴν κυρίῳ εἰς τὰς γενεὰς ὑμῶν. νόμιμον
αἰώνιον ἑορτάσατε αὐτήν. ἀπὸ δὲ τῆς ἡμέρας
τῆς πρώτης ἀφανιεῖτε ζύμην ἐκ τῶν οἰκιῶν
ὑμῶν." . . .[1] πολλῶν ἔτι τοιούτων παραλελειμ-
μένων, ἀφ' ὧν τὸν νόμον τοῦ Μωυσέως αἰώνιον
ἐγὼ μὲν εἰπεῖν διὰ τὸ πλῆθος παρῃτησάμην·
ὑμεῖς δὲ ἐπιδείξατε, ποῦ τὸ παρὰ τοῦ Παύλου
μετὰ τοῦτο τολμηθὲν εἴρηται, ὅτι δὴ "τέλος
νόμου Χριστός." ποῦ τοῖς Ἑβραίοις ὁ θεὸς
320 B ἐπηγγείλατο νόμον ἕτερον παρὰ τὸν κείμενον;
οὐκ ἔστιν οὐδαμοῦ, οὐδὲ τοῦ κειμένου διόρθωσις.[2]
ἄκουε γὰρ τοῦ Μωυσέως πάλιν· "Οὐ προσθήσετε
ἐπὶ τὸ ῥῆμα, ὃ ἐγὼ ἐντέλλομαι ὑμῖν, καὶ οὐκ
ἀφελεῖτε ἀπ' αὐτοῦ. φυλάξασθε τὰς ἐντολὰς
κυρίου τοῦ θεοῦ ὑμῶν, ὅσα ἐγὼ ἐντέλλομαι ὑμῖν
σήμερον" καὶ "Ἐπικατάρατος πᾶς ὃς οὐκ ἐμμένει
πᾶσιν." ὑμεῖς δὲ τὸ μὲν ἀφελεῖν καὶ προσθεῖναι
τοῖς γεγραμμένοις ἐν τῷ νόμῳ μικρὸν ἐνομίσατε,
τὸ δὲ παραβῆναι τελείως αὐτὸν ἀνδρειότερον τῷ
320 C παντὶ καὶ μεγαλοψυχότερον, οὐ πρὸς ἀλήθειαν,
ἀλλ' εἰς τὸ πᾶσι πιθανὸν βλέποντες . . .

[1] Lacuna. Before πολλῶν Neumann would insert, in order to connect, ἱκανὰς δὲ δοκῶ μοι χρήσεις ἤδη παρατεθεῖσθαι, "But I think I have now cited enough passages."

[2] διόρθωσις Klimek; διόρθωσιν MSS., Neumann, with a verb, *e.g.* "promises," understood.

---

[1] *Exodus* 12. 14–15; Julian went on to quote several similar passages from the Old Testament, but these are missing. [2] *Romans* 10. 4.

[3] "The gods, not being ignorant of their future intentions, do not have to correct their errors," says Julian, *Oration* 5. 170A. [4] *Deuteronomy* 4. 2.

throughout your generations; ye shall keep it a feast by an ordinance forever; the first day shall ye put away leaven out of your houses." . . .[1] Many passages to the same effect are still left, but on account of their number I refrain from citing them to prove that the law of Moses was to last for all time. But do you point out to me where there is any statement by Moses of what was later on rashly uttered by Paul, I mean that "Christ is the end of the law."[2] Where does God announce to the Hebrews a second law besides that which was established? Nowhere does it occur, not even a revision of the established law.[3] For listen again to the words of Moses: "Ye shall not add unto the word which I command you, neither shall ye diminish aught from it. Keep the commandments of the Lord your God which I command you this day."[4] And "Cursed be every man who does not abide by them all."[5] But you have thought it a slight thing to diminish and to add to the things which were written in the law; and to transgress it completely you have thought to be in every way more manly and more high-spirited, because you do not look to the truth but to that which will persuade all men. . . .[6]

[5] *Deuteronomy* 27, 26, "Cursed be he that confirmeth not all the words of this law to do them." Cf. *Galatians* 3. 10.

[6] According to Cyril, Julian next discussed the letter of the Apostles to the Christian converts, and, quoting *Acts* 15. 28, 29, which forbid the eating of meats offered to idols and things strangled, says that this does not mean that the Holy Ghost willed that the Mosaic law should be disregarded. He ridicules Peter and calls him a hypocrite, convicted by Paul of living now according to Greek, now Hebrew, customs.

327 A Οὕτω δέ ἐστε δυστυχεῖς, ὥστε οὐδὲ τοῖς ὑπὸ τῶν ἀποστόλων ὑμῖν παραδεδομένοις ἐμμενενήκατε· καὶ ταῦτα δὲ ἐπὶ τὸ χεῖρον καὶ δυσσεβέστερον ὑπὸ τῶν ἐπιγινομένων ἐξειργάσθη. τὸν γοῦν Ἰησοῦν οὔτε Παῦλος ἐτόλμησεν εἰπεῖν θεὸν οὔτε Ματθαῖος οὔτε Λουκᾶς οὔτε Μάρκος. ἀλλ'
327 B ὁ χρηστὸς Ἰωάννης, αἰσθόμενος ἤδη πολὺ πλῆθος ἑαλωκὸς ἐν πολλαῖς τῶν Ἑλληνίδων καὶ Ἰταλιωτίδων πόλεων ὑπὸ ταύτης τῆς νόσου, ἀκούων δέ, οἶμαι, καὶ τὰ μνήματα Πέτρου καὶ Παύλου λάθρᾳ μέν, ἀκούων δὲ ὅμως αὐτὰ θεραπευόμενα πρῶτος ἐτόλμησεν εἰπεῖν. μικρὰ δὲ εἰπὼν περὶ Ἰωάννου τοῦ βαπτιστοῦ, πάλιν ἐπανάγων ἐπὶ τὸν ὑπ' αὐτοῦ κηρυττόμενον λόγον "Καὶ ὁ λόγος" φησὶ "σάρξ ἐγένετο καὶ ἐσκήνωσεν ἐν ἡμῖν," τὸ δὲ ὅπως οὐ λέγει αἰσχυνόμενος. οὐδαμοῦ δὲ αὐτὸν
327 C οὔτε Ἰησοῦν οὔτε Χριστόν, ἄχρις οὗ θεὸν καὶ λόγον ἀποκαλεῖ, κλέπτων δὲ ὥσπερ ἠρέμα καὶ λάθρᾳ τὰς ἀκοὰς ἡμῶν, Ἰωάννην φησὶ τὸν βαπτιστὴν ὑπὲρ Χριστοῦ Ἰησοῦ ταύτην ἐκθέσθαι τὴν μαρτυρίαν, ὅτι ἄρ' οὗτός ἐστιν, ὃν χρὴ πεπιστευ-
333 B κέναι θεὸν εἶναι λόγον. ἀλλ' ὅτι μὲν τοῦτο περὶ Ἰησοῦ Χριστοῦ φησιν Ἰωάννης, οὐδὲ αὐτὸς ἀντιλέγω. καίτοι δοκεῖ τισι τῶν δυσσεβῶν ἄλλον
333 C μὲν Ἰησοῦν εἶναι Χριστόν, ἄλλον δὲ τὸν ὑπὸ Ἰωάννου κηρυττόμενον λόγον. οὐ μὴν οὕτως ἔχει. ὃν γὰρ αὐτὸς εἶναί φησι θεὸν λόγον, τοῦτον ὑπὸ Ἰωάννου φησὶν ἐπιγνωσθῆναι τοῦ βαπτιστοῦ Χριστὸν Ἰησοῦν ὄντα. σκοπεῖτε οὖν, ὅπως εὐλαβῶς, ἠρέμα καὶ λεληθότως ἐπεισάγει

But you are so misguided that you have not even remained faithful to the teachings that were handed down to you by the apostles. And these also have been altered, so as to be worse and more impious, by those who came after. At any rate neither Paul nor Matthew nor Luke nor Mark ventured to call Jesus God. But the worthy John, since he perceived that a great number of people in many of the towns of Greece and Italy had already been infected by this disease,[1] and because he heard, I suppose, that even the tombs of Peter and Paul were being worshipped —secretly, it is true, but still he did hear this,—he, I say, was the first to venture to call Jesus God. And after he had spoken briefly about John the Baptist he referred again to the Word which he was proclaiming, and said, "And the Word was made flesh, and dwelt among us."[2] But how, he does not say, because he was ashamed. Nowhere, however, does he call him either Jesus or Christ, so long as he calls him God and the Word, but as it were insensibly and secretly he steals away our ears, and says that John the Baptist bore this witness on behalf of Jesus Christ, that in very truth he it is whom we must believe to be God the Word. But that John says this concerning Jesus Christ I for my part do not deny. And yet certain of the impious think that Jesus Christ is quite distinct from the Word that was proclaimed by John. That however is not the case. For he whom John himself calls God the Word, this is he who, says he, was recognised by John the Baptist to be Jesus Christ. Observe accordingly how cautiously, how quietly and in-

[1] For Christianity a disease cf. *Oration* 7. 229D, and *Letter* 58 *To Libanius* 401C.

[2] *John* 1. 14.

τῷ δράματι τὸν κολοφῶνα τῆς ἀσεβείας οὕτω τέ ἐστι πανοῦργος καὶ ἀπατεών, ὥστε αὖθις ἀναδύεται προστιθείς· "Θεὸν οὐδεὶς ἑώρακε πώποτε· ὁ μονογενὴς υἱός, ὁ ὢν ἐν τοῖς κόλποις τοῦ πατρός,
333 D ἐκεῖνος ἐξηγήσατο." πότερον οὖν οὗτός ἐστιν ὁ θεὸς λόγος σάρξ γενόμενος, ὁ μονογενὴς υἱός, ὁ ὢν ἐν τοῖς κόλποις τοῦ πατρός; καὶ εἰ μὲν αὐτός, ὅνπερ οἶμαι, ἐθεάσασθε δήπουθεν καὶ ὑμεῖς θεόν. "ἐσκήνωσε" γὰρ "ἐν ὑμῖν καὶ ἐθεάσασθε τὴν δόξαν αὐτοῦ." τί οὖν ἐπιλέγεις, ὅτι θεὸν οὐδεὶς ἑώρακε πώποτε; ἐθεάσασθε γὰρ ὑμεῖς εἰ καὶ μὴ τὸν πατέρα θεόν, ἀλλὰ τὸν θεὸν λόγον. εἰ δὲ ἄλλος ἐστὶν ὁ μονογενὴς υἱός, ἕτερος δὲ ὁ θεὸς λόγος, ὡς ἐγώ τινων ἀκήκοα τῆς ὑμετέρας αἱρέσεως, ἔοικεν οὐδὲ ὁ Ἰωάννης αὐτὸ τολμᾶν ἔτι.

335 B Ἀλλὰ τοῦτο μὲν τὸ κακὸν ἔλαβε παρὰ Ἰωάννου τὴν ἀρχήν· ὅσα δὲ ὑμεῖς ἐξῆς προσευρήκατε, πολλοὺς ἐπεισάγοντες τῷ πάλαι νεκρῷ τοὺς προσφάτους νεκρούς, τίς ἂν πρὸς ἀξίαν βδελύξαιτο; πάντα
335 C ἐπληρώσατε τάφων καὶ μνημάτων, καίτοι οὐκ εἴρηται παρ' ὑμῖν οὐδαμοῦ τοῖς τάφοις προσκαλινδεῖσθαι καὶ περιέπειν αὐτούς. εἰς τοῦτο δὲ προεληλύθατε μοχθηρίας, ὥστε οἴεσθαι δεῖν ὑπὲρ τούτου μηδὲ τῶν γε Ἰησοῦ τοῦ Ναζωραίου ῥημά-

---

[1] *John* 1. 18. [2] *John* 1. 19.

[3] Yet in *Letter* 47. 434c, Julian reproaches the Alexandrians with worshipping as God the Word "one whom neither you nor your fathers have ever seen, even Jesus."

[4] *i.e.* that Jesus was God.

[5] For the collection of the "bones and skulls of criminals," and the apotheosis of the martyrs as it struck a contemporary pagan, see Eunapius, *Lives* p. 424 (Loeb edition). Julian, in

sensibly he introduces into the drama the crowning word of his impiety; and he is so rascally and deceitful that he rears his head once more to add, "No man hath seen God at any time; the only begotten Son which is in the bosom of the Father, he hath declared him."[1] Then is this only begotten Son which is in the bosom of the Father the God who is the Word and became flesh? And if, as I think, it is indeed he, you also have certainly beheld God. For "He dwelt among you, and ye beheld his glory."[2] Why then do you add to this that "No man hath seen God at any time"? For ye have indeed seen, if not God the Father, still God who is the Word.[3] But if the only begotten Son is one person and the God who is the Word another, as I have heard from certain of your sect, then it appears that not even John made that rash statement.[4]

However this evil doctrine did originate with John; but who could detest as they deserve all those doctrines that you have invented as a sequel, while you keep adding many corpses newly dead to the corpse of long ago?[5] You have filled the whole world with tombs and sepulchres, and yet in your scriptures it is nowhere said that you must grovel among tombs[6] and pay them honour. But you have gone so far in iniquity that you think you need not listen even to the words of Jesus of Nazareth on this

Letter 22. 429D, commends the Christian care of graves; here he ridicules the veneration of the relics of the martyrs, which was peculiarly Christian and offensive to pagans.

[6] For this phrase, derived from Plato, *Phaedo* 81D, cf. *Misopogon* 344A. Eunapius, *Lives* p. 424 προσεκαλινδοῦντο τοῖς μνήμασι, of the Christian worship at the graves of the martyrs.

των ἀκούειν. ἀκούετε οὖν, ἅ φησιν ἐκεῖνος περὶ τῶν μνημάτων· "Οὐαὶ ὑμῖν, γραμματεῖς καὶ Φαρισαῖοι ὑποκριταί, ὅτι παρομοιάζετε τάφοις κεκονιαμένοις· ἔξωθεν ὁ τάφος φαίνεται ὡραῖος, ἔσωθεν δὲ γέμει ὀστέων νεκρῶν καὶ πάσης ἀκαθαρσίας."
335 D εἰ τοίνυν ἀκαθαρσίας Ἰησοῦς ἔφη πλήρεις εἶναι τοὺς τάφους, πῶς ὑμεῖς ἐπ' αὐτῶν ἐπικαλεῖσθε τὸν θεόν; . . .

339 E Τούτων οὖν οὕτως ἐχόντων, ὑμεῖς ὑπὲρ τίνος προσκαλινδεῖσθε τοῖς μνήμασι; ἀκοῦσαι βούλεσθε τὴν αἰτίαν; οὐκ ἐγὼ φαίην ἄν, ἀλλ' Ἡσαΐας ὁ προφήτης. "Ἐν τοῖς μνήμασι καὶ ἐν τοῖς σπηλαί-
340 A οις κοιμῶνται δι' ἐνύπνια." σκοπεῖτε οὖν, ὅπως παλαιὸν ἦν τοῦτο τοῖς Ἰουδαίοις τῆς μαγγανείας τὸ ἔργον, ἐγκαθεύδειν τοῖς μνήμασιν ἐνυπνίων χάριν. ὃ δὴ καὶ τοὺς ἀποστόλους ὑμῶν εἰκός ἐστι μετὰ τὴν τοῦ διδασκάλου τελευτὴν ἐπιτηδεύσαντας ὑμῖν τε ἐξ ἀρχῆς παραδοῦναι τοῖς πρώτοις πεπιστευκόσι, καὶ τεχνικώτερον ὑμῶν αὐτοὺς μαγγανεῦσαι, τοῖς δὲ μεθ' ἑαυτοὺς ἀποδεῖξαι δημοσίᾳ τῆς μαγγανείας ταύτης καὶ βδελυρίας τὰ ἐργαστήρια.

343 C Ὑμεῖς δέ, ἃ μὲν ὁ θεὸς ἐξ ἀρχῆς ἐβδελύξατο καὶ διὰ Μωυσέως καὶ τῶν προφητῶν, ἐπιτηδεύετε, προσάγειν δὲ ἱερεῖα βωμῷ καὶ θύειν παρῃτήσασθε. πῦρ γάρ, φασίν, οὐ κάτεισιν, ὥσπερ ἐπὶ Μωυσέως
343 D τὰς θυσίας ἀναλίσκον. ἅπαξ τοῦτο ἐπὶ Μωυσέως

---

[1] *Matthew* 23. 27.

[2] According to Cyril, Julian quoted *Matthew* 8. 21, 22: "Let the dead bury their dead," to prove that Christ had no respect for graves.

matter. Listen then to what he says about sepulchres: "Woe unto you, scribes and Pharisees, hypocrites! for ye are like unto whited sepulchres; outward the tomb appears beautiful, but within it is full of dead men's bones, and of all uncleanness."[1] If, then, Jesus said that sepulchres are full of uncleanness, how can you invoke God at them? . . .[2]

Therefore, since this is so, why do you grovel among tombs? Do you wish to hear the reason? It is not I who will tell you, but the prophet Isaiah: "They lodge among tombs and in caves for the sake of dream visions."[3] You observe, then, how ancient among the Jews was this work of witchcraft, namely, sleeping among tombs for the sake of dream visions. And indeed it is likely that your apostles, after their teacher's death, practised this and handed it down to you from the beginning, I mean to those who first adopted your faith, and that they themselves performed their spells more skilfully than you do, and displayed openly to those who came after them the places in which they performed this witchcraft and abomination.

But you, though you practise that which God from the first abhorred, as he showed through Moses and the prophets, have refused nevertheless to offer victims at the altar, and to sacrifice. "Yes," say the Galilaeans, "because fire will not descend to consume the sacrifices as in the case of Moses." Only once, I answer, did this happen in the case of

[3] In part from *Isaiah* 65. 4; the literal meaning of the Hebrew is "that sit in graves and pass the night in secret places," a reference to incubation for the sake of dream oracles, a Hellenic custom. Julian professes to believe that this practice, which Isaiah abhorred, was kept up by the Christians.

ἐγένετο καὶ ἐπὶ Ἡλίου τοῦ Θεσβίτου πάλιν μετὰ πολλοὺς χρόνους. ἐπεί, ὅτι γε πῦρ ἐπείσακτον αὐτὸς ὁ Μωυσῆς εἰσφέρειν οἴεται χρῆναι καὶ Ἀβραὰμ ὁ πατριάρχης ἔτι πρὸ τούτου, δηλώσω διὰ βραχέων . . .

346 E Καὶ οὐ τοῦτο μόνον, ἀλλὰ καὶ τῶν υἱῶν Ἀδὰμ ἀπαρχὰς τῷ θεῷ διδόντων, "Ἐπεῖδεν ὁ θεὸς"
347 A φησὶν "ἐπὶ Ἄβελ καὶ ἐπὶ τοῖς δώροις αὐτοῦ. ἐπὶ δὲ Κάιν καὶ ἐπὶ ταῖς θυσίαις αὐτοῦ οὐ προσέσχε. καὶ ἐλύπησε τὸν Κάιν λίαν, καὶ συνέπεσε τὸ πρόσωπον αὐτοῦ. καὶ εἶπε κύριος ὁ θεὸς τῷ Κάιν· Ἵνα τί περίλυπος ἐγένου, καὶ ἵνα τί συνέπεσε τὸ πρόσωπόν σου; οὐκ ἐὰν ὀρθῶς προσενέγκῃς, ὀρθῶς δὲ μὴ διέλῃς, ἥμαρτες;" ἀκοῦσαι οὖν ἐπιποθεῖτε, τίνες ἦσαν αὐτῶν αἱ προσφοραί; "Καὶ ἐγένετο μεθ' ἡμέρας, ἀνήνεγκε Κάιν ἀπὸ τῶν καρπῶν τῆς γῆς θυσίαν τῷ κυρίῳ. καὶ Ἄβελ
347 B ἤνεγκε καὶ αὐτὸς ἀπὸ τῶν πρωτοτόκων τῶν προβάτων καὶ ἀπὸ τῶν στεάτων αὐτῶν." ναί, φασίν, οὐ τὴν θυσίαν, ἀλλὰ τὴν διαίρεσιν ἐμέμψατο πρὸς Κάιν εἰπών· "Οὐκ ἐὰν ὀρθῶς προσενέγκῃς, ὀρθῶς δὲ μὴ διέλῃς, ἥμαρτες;" τοῦτο ἔφη τις πρὸς ἐμὲ τῶν πάνυ σοφῶν ἐπισκόπων· ὁ δὲ ἠπάτα μὲν ἑαυτὸν πρῶτον, εἶτα καὶ τοὺς ἄλλους. ἡ γὰρ διαίρεσις μεμπτὴ κατὰ τίνα τρόπον ἦν, ἀπαιτούμενος, οὐκ εἶχεν ὅπως διεξέλθῃ, οὐδὲ ὅπως πρὸς ἐμὲ ψυχρολογήσῃ.[1] βλέπων δὲ αὐτὸν ἐξαπορού-

[1] ψυχρολογήσῃ Klimek; ψυχρολογήσειε Neumann.

[1] *Leviticus* 9. 24. [2] 1 *Kings* 18. 38.

[3] Cyril says that Julian told the story of the interrupted sacrifice of Isaac by Abraham from *Genesis* 22.

Moses;[1] and again after many years in the case of Elijah the Tishbite.[2] For I will prove in a few words that Moses himself thought that it was necessary to bring fire from outside for the sacrifice, and even before him, Abraham the patriarch as well. . . [3]

And this is not the only instance, but when the sons of Adam also offered firstfruits to God, the Scripture says, "And the Lord had respect unto Abel and to his offerings; but unto Cain and to his offerings he had not respect. And Cain was very wroth, and his countenance fell. And the Lord God said unto Cain, Why art thou wroth? and why is thy countenance fallen? Is it not so—if thou offerest rightly, but dost not cut in pieces rightly, thou hast sinned?"[4] Do you then desire to hear also what were their offerings? "And at the end of days it came to pass that Cain brought of the fruits of the ground an offering unto the Lord. And Abel, he also brought of the firstlings of his flock and of the fat thereof."[5] You see, say the Galilaeans, it was not the sacrifice but the division thereof that God disapproved when he said to Cain, "If thou offerest rightly, but dost not cut in pieces rightly, hast thou not sinned?" This is what one of your most learned bishops[6] told me. But in the first place he was deceiving himself and then other men also. For when I asked him in what way the division was blameworthy he did not know how to get out of it, or how to make me even a frigid explanation. And when I saw that he was greatly

[4] *Genesis* 4. 4–7. The Hebrew text of the last sentence is corrupt, and its meaning is disputed. Skinner, *Genesis*, p. 106, calls the Septuagint version, followed by Julian, fantastic.

[5] *Genesis* 4. 3–4.

[6] This was, perhaps, Aetius, for whom see p. 289.

347 C μενον, "Αὐτὸ τοῦτο," εἶπον "ὃ σὺ λέγεις, ὁ θεὸς ὀρθῶς ἐμέμψατο. τὸ μὲν γὰρ τῆς προθυμίας ἴσον ἦν ἀπ' ἀμφοτέρων, ὅτι δῶρα ὑπέλαβον χρῆναι καὶ θυσίας ἀναφέρειν ἀμφότεροι τῷ θεῷ. περὶ δὲ τὴν διαίρεσιν ὁ μὲν ἔτυχεν, ὁ δὲ ἥμαρτε τοῦ σκοποῦ. πῶς καὶ τίνα τρόπον; ἐπειδὴ γὰρ τῶν ἐπὶ γῆς ὄντων τὰ μέν ἐστιν ἔμψυχα, τὰ δὲ ἄψυχα, τιμιώτερα δὲ τῶν ἀψύχων ἐστὶ τὰ ἔμψυχα τῷ ζῶντι καὶ ζωῆς αἰτίῳ θεῷ, καθὸ καὶ ζωῆς μετείληφε καὶ ψυχῆς οἰκειοτέρας [1]—διὰ τοῦτο τῷ τελείαν προσάγοντι θυσίαν ὁ θεὸς ἐπηυφράνθη."

351 A Νυνὶ δὲ ἐπαναληπτέον ἐστί μοι πρὸς αὐτούς· διὰ τί γὰρ οὐχὶ περιτέμνεσθε; "Παῦλος," φασίν, "εἶπε περιτομὴν καρδίας, ἀλλ' οὐχὶ τῆς σαρκὸς δεδόσθαι πιστεύσαντι [2] τῷ Ἀβραάμ. οὐ μὴν ἔτι τὰ κατὰ σάρκα ἔφη, καὶ δεῖ πιστεῦσαι τοῖς ὑπ' αὐτοῦ καὶ Πέτρου κηρυττομένοις λόγοις οὐκ ἀσεβέσιν." ἄκουε δὲ πάλιν, ὅτι τὴν κατὰ σάρκα περιτομὴν εἰς διαθήκην ὁ θεὸς λέγεται δοῦναι καὶ
351 B εἰς σημεῖον τῷ Ἀβραάμ· "Καὶ αὕτη ἡ διαθήκη, ἣν διατηρήσεις ἀνὰ μέσον ἐμοῦ καὶ σοῦ [3] καὶ ἀνὰ μέσον τοῦ σπέρματός σου εἰς τὰς γενεὰς ὑμῶν. καὶ περιτμηθήσεσθε τὴν σάρκα τῆς ἀκροβυστίας ὑμῶν, καὶ ἔσται ἐν σημείῳ διαθήκης ἀνὰ μέσον ἐμοῦ καὶ σοῦ καὶ ἀνὰ μέσον ἐμοῦ καὶ τοῦ σπέρματός σου." . . . ὅτε τοίνυν, ὅτι προσήκει τηρεῖν

[1] οἰκειοτέρας Asmus; οἰκειότερα Neumann.
[2] πιστεύσαντι Neumann suggests; καὶ τοῦτο εἶναι MSS.
[3] σοῦ Wright; ὑμῶν Neumann.

---

[1] An allusion to *Romans* 4. 11–12 and 2. 29.

embarrassed, I said, "God rightly disapproved the thing you speak of. For the zeal of the two men was equal, in that they both thought that they ought to offer up gifts and sacrifices to God. But in the matter of their division one of them hit the mark and the other fell short of it. How, and in what manner? Why, since of things on the earth some have life and others are lifeless, and those that have life are more precious than those that are lifeless to the living God who is also the cause of life, inasmuch as they also have a share of life and have a soul more akin to his—for this reason God was more graciously inclined to him who offered a perfect sacrifice."

Now I must take up this other point and ask them, Why, pray, do you not practise circumcision? "Paul," they answer, "said that circumcision of the heart but not of the flesh was granted unto Abraham because he believed.[1] Nay it was not now of the flesh that he spoke, and we ought to believe the pious words that were proclaimed by him and by Peter." On the other hand hear again that God is said to have given circumcision of the flesh to Abraham for a covenant and a sign: "This is my covenant which ye shall keep, between me and thee and thy seed after thee in their generations. Ye shall circumcise the flesh of your foreskin, and it shall be in token of a covenant betwixt me and thee and betwixt me and thy seed." . . .[2] Therefore when He[3] has undoubtedly taught that it is proper

[2] A paraphrase of *Genesis* 17. 10–11; according to Cyril, Julian quoted *Matthew* 5. 17, 19, to prove that Christ did not come to destroy the law.

[3] *i. e.* Christ.

τὸν νόμον, ἀναμφισβητήτως προστέταχε καὶ τοῖς
μίαν παραβαίνουσιν ἐντολὴν ἐπήρτησε δίκας,
ὑμεῖς, οἱ συλλήβδην ἁπάσας παραβεβηκότες,
ὁποῖον εὑρήσετε τῆς ἀπολογίας τὸν τρόπον; ἢ
γὰρ ψευδοεπήσει ὁ Ἰησοῦς, ἤγουν ὑμεῖς πάντη
351 D καὶ πάντως οὐ νομοφύλακες. "Ἡ περιτομὴ ἔσται
354 A περὶ τὴν σάρκα σου," ὁ Μωσῆς φησι. παρα-
κούσαντες τούτου "Τὰς καρδίας" φασὶ "περι-
τεμνόμεθα." πάνυ γε· οὐδεὶς γὰρ παρ' ὑμῖν
κακοῦργος, οὐδεὶς μοχθηρός· οὕτω περιτέμνεσθε
τὰς καρδίας. "Τηρεῖν ἄζυμα καὶ ποιεῖν τὸ πάσχα
οὐ δυνάμεθα" φασίν· "ὑπὲρ ἡμῶν γὰρ ἅπαξ
ἐτύθη Χριστός." καλῶς· εἶτα ἐκώλυσεν ἐσθίειν
ἄζυμα; καίτοι, μὰ τοὺς θεούς, εἷς εἰμι τῶν
354 B ἐκτρεπομένων συνεορτάζειν Ἰουδαίοις, ἀεὶ δὲ προσ-
κυνῶν τὸν θεὸν Ἀβραὰμ καὶ Ἰσαὰκ καὶ Ἰακώβ,
οἳ ὄντες αὐτοὶ Χαλδαῖοι, γένους ἱεροῦ καὶ θεουρ-
γικοῦ, τὴν μὲν περιτομὴν ἔμαθον Αἰγυπτίοις
ἐπιξενωθέντες, ἐσεβάσθησαν δὲ θεόν, ὃς ἐμοὶ καὶ
τοῖς αὐτόν, ὥσπερ Ἀβραὰμ ἔσεβε, σεβομένοις
εὐμενὴς ἦν, μέγας τε ὢν πάνυ καὶ δυνατός, ὑμῖν
δὲ οὐδὲν προσήκων. οὐδὲ γὰρ τὸν Ἀβραὰμ
μιμεῖσθε, βωμούς τε ἐγείροντες αὐτῷ καὶ οἰκοδο-
354 C μοῦντες θυσιαστήρια καὶ θεραπεύοντες ὥσπερ
356 C ἐκεῖνος ταῖς ἱερουργίαις. ἔθυε μὲν γὰρ Ἀβραάμ,
ὥσπερ καὶ ἡμεῖς, ἀεὶ καὶ συνεχῶς. ἐχρῆτο δὲ
μαντικῇ τῇ τῶν διαττόντων ἄστρων· Ἑλληνικὸν
ἴσως καὶ τοῦτο. οἰωνίζετο δὲ μειζόνως. ἀλλὰ

---

[1] Cf. *Genesis* 17. 13.

[2] This is a sneer rather than an argument.

[3] Cf. *Letter* 20, *To Theodorus*, 454A, where Julian says that the Jewish god "is worshipped by us under other names."

to observe the law, and threatened with punishment those who transgress one commandment, what manner of defending yourselves will you devise, you who have transgressed them all without exception? For either Jesus will be found to speak falsely, or rather you will be found in all respects and in every way to have failed to preserve the law. "The circumcision shall be of thy flesh," says Moses.[1] But the Galilaeans do not heed him, and they say: "We circumcise our hearts." By all means. For there is among you no evildoer, no sinner; so thoroughly do you circumcise your hearts.[2] They say: "We cannot observe the rule of unleavened bread or keep the Passover; for on our behalf Christ was sacrificed once and for all." Very well! Then did he forbid you to eat unleavened bread? And yet, I call the gods to witness, I am one of those who avoid keeping their festivals with the Jews; but nevertheless I revere always the God of Abraham, Isaac and Jacob;[3] who being themselves Chaldaeans, of a sacred race, skilled in theurgy, had learned the practice of circumcision while they sojourned as strangers with the Egyptians. And they revered a God who was ever gracious to me and to those who worshipped him as Abraham did, for he is a very great and powerful God, but he has nothing to do with you. For you do not imitate Abraham by erecting altars to him, or building altars of sacrifice and worshipping him as Abraham did, with sacrificial offerings. For Abraham used to sacrifice even as we Hellenes do, always and continually. And he used the method of divination from shooting stars. Probably this also is an Hellenic custom. But for higher things he augured from the flight of birds.

καὶ τὸν ἐπίτροπον τῆς οἰκίας εἶχε συμβολικόν.
356 D εἰ δὲ ἀπιστεῖ τις ὑμῶν, αὐτὰ δείξει[1] σαφῶς τὰ ὑπὲρ τούτων εἰρημένα Μωυσῇ· "μετὰ δὲ τὰ ῥήματα ταῦτα ἐγενήθη κυρίου λόγος πρὸς Ἀβραὰμ λέγων ἐν ὁράματι τῆς νυκτός· μὴ φοβοῦ, Ἀβραάμ, ἐγὼ ὑπερασπίζω σου. ὁ μισθός σου πολὺς ἔσται σφόδρα. λέγει δὲ Ἀβραάμ· δέσποτα, τί μοι δώσεις; ἐγὼ δὲ ἀπολύομαι ἄτεκνος, ὁ δὲ υἱὸς Μασὲκ τῆς οἰκογενοῦς μου[2] κληρονομήσει με. καὶ εὐθὺς φωνὴ τοῦ θεοῦ ἐγένετο πρὸς αὐτὸν λέγοντος· οὐ κληρονομήσει σε οὗτος, ἀλλ' ὃς ἐξελεύσεται
356 E ἐκ σοῦ, οὗτος κληρονομήσει σε. ἐξήγαγε δὲ αὐτὸν καὶ εἶπεν αὐτῷ· ἀνάβλεψον εἰς τὸν οὐρανὸν καὶ ἀρίθμησον τοὺς ἀστέρας, εἰ δυνήσῃ ἐξαριθμῆσαι αὐτούς. καὶ εἶπεν· οὕτως ἔσται τὸ σπέρμα σου. καὶ ἐπίστευσεν Ἀβραὰμ τῷ θεῷ καὶ ἐλογίσθη αὐτῷ εἰς δικαιοσύνην."

Εἴπατε ἐνταῦθα μοι τοῦ χάριν ἐξήγαγεν αὐτὸν καὶ τοὺς ἀστέρας ἐδείκνυεν ὁ χρηματίζων ἄγγελος ἢ θεός; οὐ γὰρ ἐγίνωσκεν ἔνδον ὤν, ὅσον τι τὸ
357 A πλῆθός ἐστι τῶν νύκτωρ ἀεὶ φαινομένων καὶ μαρμαρυσσόντων ἀστέρων; ἀλλ', οἶμαι, δεῖξαι τοὺς διᾴττοντας αὐτῷ βουλόμενος, ἵνα τῶν ῥημάτων ἐναργῆ πίστιν παράσχηται τὴν πάντα κραίνουσαν καὶ ἐπικυροῦσαν οὐρανοῦ ψῆφον.
358 C ὅπως δὲ μή τις ὑπολάβῃ βίαιον εἶναι τὴν τοιαύ-

[1] δείξει Klimek; δείξω Neumann.

[2] οὗτος Δαμασκὸς Ἐλιέζερ which follow now in the Septuagint are omitted by Julian, who seems to have quoted this passage from memory.

And he possessed also a steward of his house who set signs for himself.[1] And if one of you doubts this, the very words which were uttered by Moses concerning it will show him clearly: "After these sayings the word of the Lord came unto Abraham in a vision of the night, saying, Fear not, Abraham: I am thy shield. Thy reward shall be exceeding great. And Abraham said, Lord God what wilt thou give me? For I go childless, and the son of Masek the slave woman will be my heir. And straightway the word of the Lord came unto him saying, This man shall not be thine heir: but he that shall come forth from thee shall be thine heir. And he brought him forth and said unto him, Look now toward heaven, and tell the stars, if thou be able to number them: and he said unto him, So shall thy seed be. And Abraham believed in the Lord: and it was counted to him for righteousness."[2]

Tell me now why he who dealt with him, whether angel or God, brought him forth and showed him the stars? For while still within the house did he not know how great is the multitude of the stars that at night are always visible and shining? But I think it was because he wished to show him the shooting stars, so that as a visible pledge of his words he might offer to Abraham the decision of the heavens that fulfills and sanctions all things. And lest any man should think that such an interpre-

[1] *Genesis* 24. 2, 10, 43, foll. This was Eleazar. Maimonides the Jewish jurist, writing in the twelfth century, says, "One who sets signs for himself . . . like Eleazar the servant of Abraham," with reference to *Genesis* 24. 14. The epithet *συμβολικὸς* is probably a translation of the Hebrew. I am indebted for this note to Professor Margoliouth.

[2] Partly paraphrased from *Genesis* 15. 1–6.

την ἐξήγησιν, ἐφεξῆς ὅσα πρόσκειται παραθεὶς αὐτῷ πιστώσομαι. γέγραπται γὰρ ἑξῆς· "Εἶπε δὲ πρὸς αὐτόν· ἐγώ εἰμι ὁ θεὸς ὁ ἐξαγαγών σε ἐκ χώρας Χαλδαίων, ὥστε δοῦναί σοι τὴν γῆν ταύτην κληρονομῆσαι αὐτήν. εἶπε δέ· δέσποτα κύριε,
358 D κατὰ τί γνώσομαι, ὅτι κληρονομήσω αὐτήν; εἶπε δὲ αὐτῷ· λάβε μοι δάμαλιν τριετίζουσαν καὶ αἶγα τριετίζουσαν καὶ κριὸν τριετίζοντα καὶ τρυγόνα καὶ περιστεράν. ἔλαβε δὲ αὐτῷ πάντα ταῦτα καὶ διεῖλεν αὐτὰ μέσα· καὶ ἔθηκεν αὐτὰ ἀντιπρόσωπα ἀλλήλοις· τὰ δὲ ὄρνεα οὐ διεῖλε. κατέβη δὲ ὄρνεα ἐπὶ τὰ διχοτομήματα καὶ συνεκάθισεν αὐτοῖς Ἀβραάμ.

Τὴν τοῦ φανέντος ἀγγέλου πρόρρησιν ἤτοι θεοῦ διὰ τῆς οἰωνιστικῆς ὁρᾶτε κρατυνομένην, οὐχ, ὥσπερ παρ' ὑμῖν, ἐκ παρέργου, μετὰ θυσιῶν
358 E δὲ τῆς μαντείας ἐπιτελουμένης; φησὶ δέ, ὅτι τῇ τῶν οἰωνῶν ἐπιπτήσει βεβαίαν ἔδειξε τὴν ἐπαγγελίαν. ἀποδέχεται δὲ τὴν πίστιν Ἀβραὰμ προσεπάγων, ὅτι ἀληθείας ἄνευ πίστις ἠλιθιότης ἔοικέ τις εἶναι καὶ ἐμβροντησία. τὴν δὲ ἀλήθειαν οὐκ ἔνεστιν ἰδεῖν ἐκ ψιλοῦ ῥήματος, ἀλλὰ χρή τι καὶ παρακολουθῆσαι τοῖς λόγοις ἐναργὲς σημεῖον, ὃ πιστώσεται γενόμενον τὴν εἰς τὸ μέλλον πεποιημένην προαγόρευσιν. . . .

351 D Πρόφασις ὑμῖν τῆς ἔν γε τούτῳ ῥᾳστώνης περιλέλειπται μία, τὸ μὴ ἐξεῖναι θύειν ἔξω γεγονόσι
324 τῶν Ἱεροσολύμων, καίτοι Ἡλίου τεθυκότος ἐν τῷ
C, D Καρμηλίῳ, καὶ οὐκ ἔν γε τῇ ἁγίᾳ πόλει.

---

[1] Cyril says that Julian then asserted that he himself had been instructed by omens from birds that he would sit on the throne.

tation is forced, I will convince him by adding what comes next to the above passage. For it is written next: "And he said unto him, I am the Lord that brought thee out of the land of the Chaldees, to give thee this land to inherit it. And he said, Lord God, whereby shall I know that I shall inherit it? And he said unto him, Take me an heifer of three years old, and a she-goat of three years old, and a ram of three years old, and a turtle-dove and a pigeon. And he took unto him all these, and divided them in the midst, and laid each piece one against another; but the birds divided he not. And the fowls came down upon the divided carcases, and Abraham sat down among them."

You see how the announcement of the angel or god who had appeared was strengthened by means of the augury from birds, and how the prophecy was completed, not at haphazard as happens with you, but with the accompaniment of sacrifices? Moreover he says that by the flocking together of the birds he showed that his message was true. And Abraham accepted the pledge, and moreover declared that a pledge that lacked truth seemed to be mere folly and imbecility. But it is not possible to behold the truth from speech alone, but some clear sign must follow on what has been said, a sign that by its appearance shall guarantee the prophecy that has been made concerning the future. . . .[1]

However, for your indolence in this matter there remains for you one single excuse, namely, that you are not permitted to sacrifice if you are outside Jerusalem, though for that matter Elijah sacrificed on Mount Carmel, and not in the holy city.[2]

[2] 1 *Kings* 18. 19.

FRAGMENTA[1]

1

τοιαῦτα πολλάκις ἐγίνετο καὶ γίνεται, καὶ πῶς ταῦτα συντελείας σημεῖα;[2]

2

Μωυσῆς ἡμέρας τεσσαράκοντα νηστεύσας ἔλαβε τὸν νόμον, Ἡλίας δὲ τοσαύτας νηστεύσας θείων αὐτοψιῶν ἔτυχεν. Ἰησοῦς δὲ τί μετὰ τοσαύτην νηστείαν ἔλαβεν;[3]

3

καὶ πῶς εἰς τὸ πτερύγιον τοῦ ἱεροῦ τὸν Ἰησοῦν ἀνήγαγεν ὄντα ἐν τῇ ἐρήμῳ;[4]

[1] Only the fragments which preserve the actual words of Julian are here given; several of Neumann's are therefore omitted.

[2] Neumann *frag.* 3; from Julian, Book 2, derived from Cyril, Book 12. Quoted by Theodorus, bishop of Mopsuestia, in his Commentary on the New Testament. Neumann thinks that Theodorus probably wrote a refutation of Julian at Antioch about 378 A.D.

FRAGMENTS

1

Such things[1] have often happened and still happen, and how can these be signs of the end of the world?[2]

2

Moses after fasting forty days received the law,[3] and Elijah, after fasting for the same period, was granted to see God face to face.[4] But what did Jesus receive, after a fast of the same length?[5]

3

And how could he lead Jesus to the pinnacle of the Temple when Jesus was in the wilderness?[6]

[1] *i.e.* wars, famines, etc.
[2] Cf. *Matthew* 24. 3–14.
[3] *Exodus* 31. 18.
[4] 1 *Kings* 19. 9.
[5] *Matthew* 4. 2, foll.
[6] *Matthew* 4. 5.

---

[3] Neumann *frag.* 4; from the same source as 1.
[4] Neumann *frag.* 6. From the same source as 1 and 2.

4

Ἀλλὰ καὶ τοιαῦτα προσεύχεται ὁ Ἰησοῦς, οἷα ἄνθρωπος ἄθλιος συμφορὰν φέρειν εὐκόλως οὐ δυνάμενος, καὶ ὑπ᾽ ἀγγέλου θεὸς ὢν ἐνισχύεται. τίς δὲ καὶ ἀνήγγειλέ σοι, Λουκᾶ, περὶ τοῦ ἀγγέλου, εἰ καὶ γέγονε τοῦτο; οὐδὲ οἱ τότε παρόντες εὐχομένῳ κατιδεῖν οἷοί τε ἦσαν· ἐκοιμῶντο γάρ. διὸ καὶ ἀπὸ τῆς προσευχῆς ἐλθὼν εὗρεν αὐτοὺς κοιμωμένους ἀπὸ τῆς λύπης καὶ εἶπε· "Τί καθεύδετε; ἀναστάντες προσεύχεσθε" καὶ τὰ ἑξῆς· εἶτα· "Καὶ ἔτι αὐτοῦ τοῦτο λαλοῦντος, ἰδοὺ ὄχλος πολὺς καὶ Ἰούδας." διὸ οὐδὲ ἔγραψεν Ἰωάννης, οὐδὲ γὰρ εἶδε.[1]

5

Ἀκούσατε καλοῦ καὶ πολιτικοῦ παραγγέλματος· "Πωλήσατε τὰ ὑπάρχοντα καὶ δότε πτωχοῖς· ποιήσατε ἑαυτοῖς βαλάντια μὴ παλαιούμενα." ταύτης τίς εἰπεῖν ἔχει πολιτικωτέραν τῆς ἐντολῆς; εἰ γὰρ πάντες σοι πεισθεῖεν, τίς ὁ ὠνησόμενος; ἐπαινεῖ τίς ταύτην τὴν διδασκαλίαν, ἧς κρατυνθείσης οὐ πόλις, οὐκ ἔθνος, οὐκ οἰκία μία συστήσεται; πῶς γὰρ πραθέντων ἁπάντων οἶκος ἔντιμος εἶναι δύναταί τις ἢ οἰκία; τὸ δέ, ὅτι πάντων ὁμοῦ τῶν ἐν τῇ πόλει πιπρασκομένων, οὐκ ἂν εὑρεθεῖεν οἱ ἀγοράζοντες, φανερόν ἐστι καὶ σιωπώμενον.[2]

[1] Neumann *frag*. 7. From the same source as 3.

[2] Neumann, *frag*. 12. From Cyril, Book 18, quoted by Photius.

4

Furthermore, Jesus prays in such language as would be used by a pitiful wretch who cannot bear misfortune with serenity, and though he is a god is reassured by an angel. And who told you, Luke, the story of the angel, if indeed this ever happened? For those who were there when he prayed could not see the angel; for they were asleep. Therefore when Jesus came from his prayer he found them fallen asleep from their grief and he said: "Why do ye sleep? Arise and pray," and so forth. And then, "And while he was yet speaking, behold a multitude and Judas."[1] That is why John did not write about the angel, for neither did he see it.

5

Listen to a fine statesmanlike piece of advice: "Sell that ye have and give to the poor; provide yourselves with bags which wax not old."[2] Can anyone quote a more statesmanlike ordinance than this? For if all men were to obey you who would there be to buy? Can anyone praise this teaching when, if it be carried out, no city, no nation, not a single family will hold together? For, if everything has been sold, how can any house or family be of any value? Moreover the fact that if everything in the city were being sold at once there would be no one to trade is obvious, without being mentioned.

[1] *Luke* 22. 42–47.
[2] *Luke* 12. 33.

6

Πῶς ἦρε τὴν ἁμαρτίαν ὁ τοῦ θεοῦ λόγος αἴτιος πολλοῖς μὲν πατροκτονίας, πολλοῖς δὲ παιδοκτονίας γενόμενος, ἀναγκαζομένων τῶν ἀνθρώπων ἢ τοῖς πατρίοις βοηθεῖν καὶ τῆς ἐξ αἰῶνος αὐτοῖς εὐσεβείας παραδεδομένης ἀντέχεσθαι ἢ τὴν καινοτομίαν ταύτην προσίεσθαι; διὰ τί γὰρ οὐχὶ καὶ Μωυσῆς, ὃς ἀναιρέτης ἐλθὼν τῆς ἁμαρτίας πλειστηριάσας ταύτην κατείληπται;[1]

7

Quod de Israel scriptum est, Matthaeus evangelista ad Christum transtulit, ut simplicitati eorum qui de gentibus crediderant illuderet.[2]

[1] Not in Neumann; reconstructed by him from the polemical writings of Archbishop Arethas of Caesarea who wrote in refutation of Julian in the tenth century. First published by Cumont, *Recherches sur la tradition manuscrite de l'empereur Julien*, Brussels, 1898. Neumann's reconstruction is in *Theologische Litteraturzeitung*, 10. 1899.

[2] Neumann *frag.* 15. Preserved by the fifth century writer Hieronymus in his *Latin Commentary on Hosea* 3. 11.

---

[1] Julian is criticising St. John's Gospel, as he criticised its prologue in *Against the Galilaeans*, Book 1. He attacks *John* 1. 29; cf. *John* 1. 3. 5.

6

How did the Word of God take away sin,[1] when it caused many to commit the sin of killing their fathers, and many their children?[2] And mankind are compelled either to uphold their ancestral customs and to cling to the pious tradition that they have inherited from the ages[3] or to accept this innovation. Is not this true of Moses also, who came to take away sin, but has been detected increasing the number of sins?[4]

7

The words that were written concerning Israel[5] Matthew the Evangelist transferred to Christ,[6] that he might mock the simplicity of those of the Gentiles who believed.

[2] *Matthew* 10. 21. "And the brother shall deliver up the brother to death, and the father the child; and the children rise up against their parents, and cause them to be put to death."

[3] He means that in this case too their sins have not been taken away by the Word, since they remain heathens.

[4] In *Leviticus* 16. Aaron is to make atonement for the sins of Israel, but the severe Mosaic law increased the opportunities for transgression.

[5] *Hosea* 11. 1. "When Israel was a child, then I loved him and called my son out of Egypt."

[6] *Matthew* 2. 15. "That it might be fulfilled which was spoken of the Lord by the prophet, saying, 'Out of Egypt have I called my son.'"

TABLE OF NUMBERS

Hertlein.		Wright.	Bidez-Cumont.
LETTERS 1.[1]		—	—
2.	To Prohaeresius	14	31
3.	To Libanius	52	96
4.	To Aristoxenus	35	78
5.	To Theodora	33	85
6.	To Ecdicius	46	112
7.	To Atarbius[2]	37	83
8.	To George	67	188
9.	To Ecdicius	23	107
10.	To the Alexandrians	21	60
11.	To the Byzacians[3]	39	54
12.	To Basil	26	32
13.	To Count Julian	9	28
14.	To Libanius	53	97
15.	To Maximus	12	190
16.	To Maximus	59	191
17.	To Oribasius	4	14
18.	To Eugenius	60	193
19.	To Hecebolius	63	194
20.	To Eustochius	54	41
21.	To Callixeine	42	81
22	To Leontius	11	152
23.	To Hermogenes	13	33
24.	To Sarapion	80	180
25.	To the Jews	51	204
25 b.	Concerning Physicians	31	75 b
26.	To the Alexandrians	24	110

[1] Hertlein 1 is by the sophist Procopius of Gaza and is not reprinted here.
[2] Hertlein, *To Artabius.*
[3] Hertlein, *To the Byzantines.*

TABLE OF NUMBERS

	Hertlein.	Wright.	Bidez-Cumont.
LETTERS 27.	To Libanius . . .	58	98
28.	To Gregory . . .	71	196
29.	To Alypius . . .	6	9
30.	To Alypius . . .	7	10
31.	To Aetius . . .	15	46
32.	To Lucian . . .	64	197
33.	To Dositheus . .	68	200
34.	To Iamblichus . .	79	187
35.	For the Argives . .	28	198
36	To Porphyrius . .	38	106
37.	To Himerius [1] . .	69	201
38.	To Maximus . . .	8	26
39.	To Eustathius . .	44	35
40.	To Iamblichus . .	78	184
41.	To Iamblichus . .	74	186
42.	On Christian Teachers [2]	36	61 c
43.	To Hecebolius . .	40	115
44.	To Priscus . . .	5	11
45.	To Zeno . . .	17	58
46.	To Evagrius . . .	25	4
47.	To the Thracians . .	27	73
48.	To Plutarch [3] . .	72	153
49.	To Arsacius . . .	22	84 a
50.	To Ecdicius . . .	45	108
51.	To the Alexandrians .	47	111
52.	To the Bostrenians .	41	114
53.	To Iamblichus . .	75	185
54.	To George . . .	66	189
55.	To Eumenius and Pharianus	3	8
56.	To Ecdicius . . .	49	109
57	To Elpidius . . .	65	195
58.	To the Alexandrians .	48	59
59.	To Nilus-Dionysius [4] .	50	82
60.	To Iamblichus . .	77	183

[1] Hertlein, *To Amerius.*
[2] Hertlein no title.
[3] Hertlein, *To Zeno.*
[4] Hertlein, *To Dionysius.*

TABLE OF NUMBERS

Hertlein.		Wright.	Bidez-Cumont.
Letters 61.	To Iamblichus	76	181
62.	To an Official [1]	18	88
63.	To Theodorus	20	89 a
64.	To the People	*fr.* 12	176
65.	To a Painter	*fr.* 13	177
66.	To Arsaces	57	202
67.	To Sopater [2]	61	182
68.	To Philip	30	40
69.	To Eutherius	10	29
70.	To Diogenes	70	199
71.	To Priscus	1	13
72.	[To Julian] [3]	83	36
73.	To Eucleides	62	192
74.	To Libanius	53	97
75.	To Basil	81	205
76.	To Eustathius	43	34
77.	Concerning Funerals [4]	56	136 b
78.	To a Priest [5]	19	79
79.	To Photinus [6]	55	90

Papadopoulos-Kerameus.		Wright.	Bidez-Cumont.
Letters 1.*	To Count Julian	29	80
2.*	To Theodora	32	86
3.*	To Theodorus	16	30
4.*	To Priscus	2	12
5.*	To Maximinus	73	19
6.*	To Theodora?	34	87

[1] Hertlein no title.
[2] Hertlein, *To Sosipater.*
[3] By Eustathius. Hertlein, *To Libanius.*
[4] Hertlein no title.
[5] Hertlein no title.
[6] Hertlein no title.

TABLE OF NUMBERS

Hertlein.	Wright.	Bidez-Cumont.
FRAGMENTS 1	p. 38	30
2	1	155
3	p. 36	30
4	2	25 b
5	3	20
6	4	161
7	5	25 a
8	6	61 d
9	7	61 d
10	8	165 a
—	9	94
—	10	178
—	11	134
LETTER 64	12	176
LETTER 65	13	177
—	14	157

Hertlein.	Wright.	Bidez-Cumont.
EPIGRAMS 1	1	168
2	2	166
3	3	172
4	4	169
5	5	174
—	6	170

INDEX

INDEX

INDEX

INDEX

INDEX

INDEX

INDEX

INDEX

INDEX

INDEX